UNSUNG HEROES & HEROINES
of Australia

UNSUNG HEROES & HEROINES
of Australia
EDITED BY SUZY BALDWIN

Australia 1788-1988

Greenhouse Publications

First published in 1988 by
Greenhouse Publications Pty Ltd
122–126 Ormond Road
Elwood Victoria 3184 Australia

© The Australian Bicentennial Authority 1988

Designed by Pam Brewster and Dorothy Woodgate
Typeset in 10½/11½ Bodoni by Trade Graphics Melbourne
Printed in Australia by Globe Press

National Library of Australia
Cataloguing-in-publication data:

Unsung Heroes and Heroines of Australia.
Includes Index.
ISBN 0 86436 159 9.
1. Australia — Biography. I. Baldwin, Suzy.
920'.094

All rights reserved. No part of this publication may be
reproduced, stored in a retrieval system, or transmitted
in any form or by any means, electronic, mechanical,
photocopying, recording or otherwise, without prior
written permission of the copyright owners.

This publication has been funded by The Australian
Bicentennial Authority to celebrate Australia's
Bicentenary in 1988.

Preface

Late in 1986, the Australian Bicentennial Authority invited us to form an assessment panel for the *200 Unsung Heroes and Heroines* programme. This became better known as the *200 Greatest Stories Never Told*, a title coined by John Singleton.

A national advertising campaign was set up to involve Australians in all walks of life, getting them talking, comparing notes, and submitting stories of heroic people they knew or knew about. The 4020 stories submitted by the people of Australia demonstrate the success of that campaign.

The assessment panel's task, when first explained, seemed challenging but straightforward enough. We were to read all the stories and select the best two hundred for publication in a commemorative book. Some aspects of the assessment, however, proved tantalising and at times frustrating.

What was heroism, and how would we identify its presence in an individual or an action? What was meant by unsung? Was someone whose deeds were well known in one state, but not elsewhere, an unsung hero or heroine? Did a military decoration or a civilian award mean that the recipient could still be called unsung?

The panel was concerned about these issues. From the outset, we agreed not to be too rigid on the definition of heroism, or on the notion of being Unsung. Such an exercise had not been attempted before, either in Australia or elsewhere, so we had to develop our own criteria through regular discussion.

We recognised that stories of oustanding people would often have improved in the telling. So part of the challenge was to identify those stories which were not only impressive and inspiring, but also factual. In this we were assisted by the dedicated and professional work of a small team of researchers. Some six hundred of the four thousand and twenty stories were progressively identified as a long short list and handed to the research team. With the benefit of the researchers' reports, the panel was then able to reduce the list to the two hundred reproduced in this book.

We accepted that, even after careful research, some of the chosen stories might retain an element of myth or embellishment. Nevertheless we believe that all the stories finally selected fulfil the spirit of the concept.

We did not attempt to select the stories according to occupation, gender, geographical distribution or state of origin. The final selection reflects the pattern of groups and eras in the stories submitted.

The most exciting and inspiring aspect of this whole exercise has been that we have been able to participate in the gathering and recording of a unique set of documents of Australian social history. the stories in this book, and the others which have not been reproduced here, are truly a people's history of Australia.

The panel is pleased that the 3820 stories not included in this book will not be lost to the future. The National Library of Australia has accepted them for permanent preservation in the Library's Australian collections. There they will be available for researchers to read about that great band of people whose lives have been shown to us.

The stories in this book reveal the soul of Australia. We are grateful for the opportunity the project has given us to help Australians speak to one another about oustanding men and women who have done noble deeds and endured great hardship with fortitude and often with great humour. We believe that their stories will inspire and encourage Australians to face courageously the challenges of our time.

Brian Sweeney, CMG (Chairman)
Quentin Bryce
Frank Dunn
John Hartigan
Sir Richard Kingsland
Dr William Oats
Justine Saunders
Sophia Turkiewicz

Contents

Contributors	18
Researchers	18
Acknowledgements	19
Introduction	21

1 EXILE 1788–1847

Pemulwuy
'A riotous and troublesome savage' — 26
Esther Abrahams
Jewish convict becomes First Lady — 27
Mary Wade
Child convict becomes founding mother — 29
Thomas Laycock Junior
Tasmania's unknown explorer — 30
William Chamberlain
Shanghaied at eight — 31
Joseph Wharton
Convict's courageous stand — 33
Emanuel Solomon
South Australia's founding father — 34
Andrew Bent
Father of Tasmanian printing — 35
Edward Smith Hall
'The great mocker' — 37
Cecilia Cosgrove
Embattled survivor — 39
Peter Oldham
Emancipist whaler and shipper — 41
Alured Tasker Faunce
'Man of iron' — 42

Joseph Grimaldi
Grimaldi the Scourger 43
Richard Elsworthy Pym
Intrepid sailor and explorer 44
Robert McCulloch
Policeman of principle 46

2   OPPORTUNITY 1848–1883

William Tipple Smith
Discoverer of the first payable gold 50
Esther Anne Ballantyne
'How to laugh' 52
Charles Ledger
Adventures in the Andes with alpacas 54
Lowe Kong Meng
Champion of racial tolerance 57
Karl Deuffel
Migrant child's epic trek 58
Adelaide Eliza Ironside
Painter and patriot 59
Andrew Cleary
The bushrangers' foe 61
David Carson
Pastoral and mining entrepreneur 63
Beattie Traill
'The Grace Darling of Tasmania' 65
John Parry
King Island's rescuer 66
Frederick Charles Bonfield Fairey
Seafaring evangelist 67
John Brown Gribble
'The Blackfellow's Friend' 69
Tommaso Enrico Fiaschi
Renaissance man 71
Jesse Dowsett
The man who fought with a legend 73
David Lindsay
Champion of the North 76

3 PROGRESS 1884–1914

Pattie Lewis Fotheringhame
Journalist and pioneer photo-engraver — 82

Ellen Flanagan
Woman with a mission — 85

Marie Kirk
'For God, home and humanity' — 86

Jean Beadle
Sweatshop worker, labor leader — 88

Dora Robertson Armitage
Mother of the modern business girl — 89

Maybanke Susannah Anderson
Womanly and fearless feminist — 93

Emma Miller
'Grand old woman of Queensland labor' — 96

Phoebe Farrar
'No one could keep Phoebe down' — 97

Arthur Albert Devlin
Lone fighter against anthrax — 99

Tullie Cornthwaite Wollaston
'Stunned by glory' — 100

Simon Engelhardt Jörgensen
A life-saving invention — 102

Agnes Hyland O'Brien
'The greatest horsewoman in the world' — 105

Gertrude Abbott
'One of God's hidden saints' — 107

William and Claudie Lakeland
The Lakelands of the Rockies — 109

Annie Berry
Intrepid Irishwoman — 110

Thomas Whitmore
Across Australia for gold — 111

Edward M. Collick
Coolgardie's muscular Christian — 112

Harry Kneebone
Crusading newspaperman — 113

Margaret May 'Mabel' Cole
Girl of ten in a 'man's country' — 115

Susannah Katherina Schardt
'Being blind, she chose to help others'   118
Arnold Wienholt
Australian patriot, African adventurer   119
James Smith
'I did not know...what we were doing'   121
John Degotardi
Plague photographer   122
Catherine Anne Bennett
Survived Governor brothers' attack   124
Arthur John Shepherd
Bywong boy supports family and town   125
Evelyn Gough
Lively newspaperwoman and feminist   126
Lucy Ann Ward
Maternity home for outback women   130
Neville Gilbert McWilliam
'Out of darkness'   131
Annie 'Topsy' Hansen
Woman of the outback   132
Cecil Palmer Jessop
Brought water to the outback   134
William Morris
Teacher with a vision   135
Leslie James F. Thomson
Australian Antarctic adventurer   136

4   WORLD WAR I 1914–1918

Claire Trestrail
'There is so much to do'   140
Mary Ann Benallack
'Little adventures' in World War I   143
George Pinnock Merz
Australia's first wartime air casualty   144
Herbert W. R. Latrobe
Latrobe and his donkey   146
Alice Maxwell Chisholm
'Mother Chisholm'   147

Douglas Grant
Aboriginal soldier   148
Maurice Vincent Buckley
VC winner's change of identity   150
Eleanor Jacob
Australian Women's Service Corps   151
Charles Henry Hilder
Mysterious message in a bottle   153
Henry John Smith
Forgotten hero of Dunsterforce   155

5   UNEASY PEACE 1918–1939

Amy Wilkinson
'The life of a woman who loves work'   160
Rose Harris
'The Rose of Clermont'   162
Charles Robert Dadds
Unorthodox missionary   163
R. Graham Carey
Pioneer civil aviator   164
Amram Lewis
Miners' advocate   165
John Borland Brown
Sacrifice at Bellbird coalmine   166
Olivia Marquis Ferguson
Kindly mother of a dozen   167
Angelo and Irene Palmos
Marriage of cultures   169
Sister Vianney Byrne
Angel of Charity   172
Turo Downes
Ambassador of Hardy's Bay   174
Charles Frederick Maynard
Vision of justice for Aborigines   174
Friedrich Wilhelm Albrecht
Ingkata innura — the lame pastor   177
Mary Magdelene Bowers
Queanbeyan's earthy Nightingale   180

C.E.A. 'Mick' Cook
'Guiding hand' of Territory medicine   182

Clyde Cornwall Fenton
Australia's first flying doctor   185

Ruth Heathcock
Pitjiri — the snake that will not sink   190

Alyandabu
'If you were white...'   192

Lucy Bryce
Blood transfusion pioneer   193

George Downton
Self-help for the unemployed   194

Irene Dorling
One woman's survival   195

H. E. 'Harry' Ding
Mail along the Birdsville Track   197

Fred Teague
Outback driver   200

Percy Clyde Statton
Fearless firefighter   201

Muriel Constance North
City woman drover   202

John Riddock Rymill
Polar explorer   206

Majorie Dobson Silver
The Far West's flying sister   209

Edmund Albert 'Ted' Colson
Man of the desert   211

Joe Binstead
Aircrash survivor   213

Doreen Flavel
'The Promise and the Challenge'   215

William Ashley Beet
Doctor of Beaudesert   216

William John McBride
The miner's mate   217

Aileen Grice
'The Lord will provide'   217

6 WORLD WAR II 1939–1946

Berek Lewcowicz
Survival of the boy from Bedzyn — 222

Rose Golding
'Rambling Rose' — 225

Ruby Boye-Jones
Courageous coastwatcher — 227

John Margrave Lerew
'We who are about to die salute you' — 230

Frederick Getty Higgs
'To Higgs. Good show... Lerew' — 234

Father Edward Harris
'Greater love hath no man than this' — 235

Clive Roberts Bernard
'Come on my lot, we'll beat it' — 236

Father John Corbett Glover
Flying priest — 238

Arthur J. Bryant
Salvage at the bombing of Darwin — 240

Archibald 'Snowy' Halls
Dutiful telegraphist — 242

Charlie One Lampungmeiua
Tiwi coastwatcher — 244

Colin Fleming Brien
He survived his own execution — 245

Marjorie Jean Lyon
Lion by name and by nature — 247

Joyce Tweddell
Forgotten prisoners of war — 251

Alfredo Jose Dos Santos
'The Great Rebel' — 254

Ronald Taylor
Went down with his ship — 255

Frank Smallhorn
'Never a dull moment' — 257

Geoffrey Hampden Vernon
Doctor of the Kokoda Trail — 261

Edward Peachey
Escapee extraordinaire — 263

Bernard Hazelden Quin
Doctor to the Nauruans   264
Keith W. Mathieson
Padre in war and peace   265
Bruce Hunt and Roy Mills
Doctors on the Burma Railway   267
John Joseph Murphy
Courage rewarded with injustice   270
Owen Price
'An officer and a gentleman'   274
Alan Douglas Bouch
Ali Baba and his forty thieves   275
Conrad 'Connie' Larsen
Saves RAAF Rathmines   277
Reg
The unknown soldier   278
Tom Hall
Lest we forget   279

7   RECOVERY 1946–1968

Harold Cochrane
Penicillin pioneer   284
Pearlie Watling
Shale miner and musician   286
Albert Freund Zinnbauer
'Alien' pastor   288
Ned and Tabitha Tscharke
Medical missionaries of Karkar   289
John Cade
'Mending the mind'   291
Elizabeth Rogers
'From the dust of ignominy...'   292
Arnold Cook
Stubborn visionary   296
Lloyd Stuchbery
'Happiness is helping'   298
Leopold Siegellak
'An anonymous righteous man'   299

Luigi Resciniti
The newcomers' friend — 302

Marianne Mills
'Sister Pav' — 303

Isabel McCorkindale
Far-sighted social reformer — 305

Marjorie Stapleton
Emergency wage dropper — 306

Maryanne 'May' McLelland
Plucky postmistress — 309

Malcolm Maloney — Jakamarra
Prodigal son — 309

Joyce Wilding
Compassionate mother to all — 311

Doris Taylor
Meals on Wheels founder — 312

Mother Giovanni Ackman
Founding spirit of Mt Olivet Hospital — 313

Alice Briggs
Fierce fighter for justice — 316

Eric James Stewart
Latter-day adventurer — 318

Sheila Stubbs
Jill of all trades — 320

Ronald Alfred Phillips
Founder of the MS Society — 323

Christopher F. A. Cummins
First flying surgeon — 324

Frank R. Woodwell
A mission of justice — 325

Donald Norman Farquhar
Triumph over prejudice — 327

James Edward Smith
Professional rescuer — 328

Colin Edward Johnston
Determined to teach — 329

Hazel McKellar
Recording her people's history — 330

Michel 'Mickey' Beaton
True friend of the Aborigines — 331

Albert Edwin 'Totty' Young
Newcastle's life saver — 332
Anne Boyd
Mountain nurse — 334
Brother Andrew
Missionary Brother of Charity — 336
Lex Banning
'Poetry is not the wine but the cognac' — 337

8 SURVIVAL 1968–1988

John Fraser
Vietnam. Killed in action — 342
James Gurriwiwi
The littlest hero — 343
Ruth Frances Bishop
Research saves the children — 345
Winsome Mahoney
Triumph of day-to-day courage — 347
Terry Wu
Daring rescue by Cambodian refugee — 348
Casey Antarctic Expeditioners, 1979
Man against Nature — 350
Jeannie Auld
Bush nurse — 351
Edward 'Teddy' Burgess
Unexpected artist — 353
Clare Stevenson
Commonsense carer — 354
David Henshaw
Open home, open heart — 356
Luke Cuni
Man of peace — 358
George and Maude Tongerie
Saviours of Oodnadatta — 359
Malen Rumbelow
'Last of his tribe' — 360
Terry Hill and Cliff Hills
Casual act of courage — 361

Mt Macedon Volunteer Fire Brigade
Anonymous heroes — 362
Betty DeBono
Working class heroine — 363
Richard Willis
Champion of Youth Hostels — 365
Douglas Fong
Courage in Chinatown — 366
Sister Patrice Kennedy
River-bank dwellers' friend — 367
Judith Louise Collins
Fostercare for foster parents — 368
Peter Treseder
Runner in the wilderness — 370
Elizabeth Johnson
Salvation for the young — 371
Lily Jubilee Slattery
Normanton's 'mother' — 373
Mert and Nell Thomas
A couple of survivors — 375
Tim Rakuwurlma
A man of his people — 379
Margaret Oats
Angel of Collingwood — 381
Rosemary Taylor
Behind the lines — 384

Index of Unsung Heroes and Heroines — 391

General Index — 393

Australian Bicentennial Authority Project Team

Director: Des Walsh
Project Officers: Laura McLeod
Peter Wright

Contributors

Suzy Baldwin
Tim Bowden
Robert Carter
Debby Cramer
Jennifer Dabbs
Louise Egerton
Judith Elen
Suzanne Falkiner
Rodrick Faulkner
Susan Hamilton
Lois Hunter
Anthea Hyslop
Jacqueline Kent
Katie Lawley
Andrea Jane Loder
Angelo Loukakis
Niall Lucy
Terri McCormack
Billy Marshall-Stoneking
David Millar
Drusilla Modjeska
Rosemary Neill
Cathy Peake
Sue Phillips
Jill Poulton
Elizabeth Riddell
Jan Roberts
Lynette R. Silver
Russell Smith
Lucinda Strauss
Sophia Turkiewicz
Linda Whitford
Pam Young

Researchers

Research Co-ordinator: Suzy Baldwin
Chief researcher: Terri McCormack
Joseph Brewster
Fiona Chisholm
Louise Scahill

Acknowledgements

This book owes its existence to all those who sent in their stories of Australia's unsung heroes and heroines. We thank them all.

To those whose nominations have been included in this book, to those who have allowed their stories to be told, and to their families and friends, we are deeply indebted for their unfailing generosity in providing us with their own research material and family details, and for their cheerful response to our often frantic calls for further information. We are particularly grateful to them for lending us precious family photographs and documents.

So many people other than nominators and nominees have helped with the stories in this book that it is impossible to thank them all. At the risk of offending those who have been omitted, we would like to thank: John Armitage, Richard Appleton, Dr John Becherbaise, Lyall Booth, Beryl Bowick, Peter and Angela Buchanan, Helene Burns, Tom Cole, Hazel Collins, Jim Comerford, Enid Cook, Mrs Ding, Gwen Dundon, Ted Evans, Dr Marcus Faunce, Bonnie Fenton (for permission to quote and reproduce a photograph from *Flying Doctor*), Mr Gould, Millicent Harry, David Huggonson, Ron Hutchinson, Catherine Kenny, Rabbi John Levi, Bill McLarty, Robin McIntyre, Moya Midena, Kerry Murphy, Peter and Vince O'Reilly, Mrs J. M. Pike, Bob Piper, Sir John Proud, Carmel Quinlan, Eleanor Rymill (for permission to quote from John Rymill's *Southern Lights*), Dr Kevin Smith, Isador Solomon, Peter Thomas, Ann Voysey, Gwen Watsford, and John Young.

Thanks are also due to the staff and members of the following institutions and organisations who so willingly provided documentary or pictorial material: Archives Office of New South Wales, Art Gallery of New South Wales, Australian Jewish Historical Society, Australian War Memorial, J. S. Battye Library of West Australian History, Beaudesert Historical Society, the Brisbane *Telegraph*, Burns Philp Pty Ltd, Dixson Library (State Library of NSW), Federated Miscellaneous Workers Union of Australia, Fryer Memorial Library (University of Queensland), Guide Dog Association of New South Wales, Latrobe Library (State Library of Victoria), Mount Olivet Hospital, National Art Gallery of Victoria, National Council of Women (NSW), National Council of Women (Vic), National Library of Australia, John Oxley Library (Queensland State Library), Queensland Women's Historical Association, RAAF Historical Section, Red Cross Blood Bank of Victoria, St Margaret's Hospital Archives, St Vincent's Hospital, Sisters of Charity, Social History Museum (Deakin University), Sydney Hospital Archives, Victorian State Gallery, Woodside Petroleum, and the Zonta Club of Rockhampton.

Although every effort has been made to contact families, there were some whom we failed to find, including the copyright holder of Amy Wilkinson's memoir. We invite him or her to contact us.

I am also personally indebted to the contributors, who met impossible deadlines with good humour and cared enough to agonise about doing justice to a life in a small space. I am especially grateful to Terri for her commitment to this project from the early days and for her courage in taking on the index, to Billy for his ability to pull rabbits out of the hat with apparent ease, and to Susan for her wise counsel.

Finally, I thank my sons, Ben and Joshua, who lived through this with me and, in the dog days, made me laugh. My part in this is for them.

Suzy Baldwin

Introduction

This is perhaps the most democratic Australian history yet written. It is not only of and for the people, but by the people. When Australians were asked who they considered to be the country's unsung heroes and heroines, these are the people they — we — chose. Both the content and the form of this book have been determined by many people — the 4020 who wrote and telephoned from all over the country, the 4020 whom they nominated, and hundreds of others who added their comments to the stories. Those included here speak for all of them: they have made it a genuine people's history.

This collection makes no claim to be comprehensive or to give a general overview of Australian history. On the contrary, it gives a very personal and idiosyncratic view of the 200 years since the arrival of the Europeans by telling the stories of some of the people who have lived during that time. The view that biography is history is as old as Plutarch, but the people whose fragmentary biographies are collected here are not the 'great men' whose lives and deeds have long been considered the proper subject of history. These stories belong to those usually excluded from conventional Australian histories — women, children, Aborigines, immigrants other than Anglo-Celts, 'ordinary' people. In the telling of their stories we see how extraordinary so many of these ordinary people prove themselves to be.

The first advertisements inviting nominations for this project appeared in December 1986, the last in May 1987. Through national press, television and radio; local and ethnic newspapers, and letters to special interest groups, minority organisations and isolated communities in remote parts of the country, the Bicentennial Authority attempted to reach as many people as possible.

People were asked to write between 250 and 500 words or to send a tape. Translation was offered for those who did not speak English. Later, there was a national toll-free phone-in. Neither literacy nor English was, therefore, a prerequisite for participation.

Nonetheless, most people chose to write. The submissions varied from chapters of unpublished manuscripts to two or three painfully written sentences. For a number of people it had clearly been a great effort to express themselves on paper. Some submissions — particularly the many family histories — were accompanied by detailed and often copious research; others were reminiscences with barely a hard fact in sight. But each of the 4020 had a story to tell.

Each submission was read by two members of the panel and the research co-ordinator. A researcher then interviewed each of those whose nominations had been selected for the shortlist, together with any living nominees, their families, friends, and anyone else who could help fill out the details of the story. Library research was done where necessary and a detailed research report written. The purpose of this stage of research was, first, to determine whether this was a tall tale or true and, second, to locate and gather additional material that would add flesh to the bones of the hero or heroine and provide a starting point for writing the final stories. As it turned out, very few were tall tales and we gathered some remarkable oral and written material.

The final selection of the heroes and heroines proceeded by a combination of debate and gut reaction. Some nominations were immediately agreed upon, others were discussed and argued about at length. Some were passionately defended and equally passionately opposed. Not all decisions were unanimous. Many of those left out could equally well have been included. When the selection panel had chosen the final 200, the project left the ABA and went to the publisher.

The shape of the book was determined by the lives of the people whose stories it tells. Although factual detail was necessary, alone it was not sufficient: this was not to be a dictionary of biography or a collection of encyclopaedia entries. These were true *stories* and, although it was impracticable to publish them in their submitted form, I wanted the published version to retain the sense of individual drama of so many of the submissions and interviews and for the reader to hear, wherever possible, the voice of the person whose story this was. It seemed to me more important to use the limited space available to capture a glimpse of the spirit of these men and women and reveal something of the nature of their experience than to give all the facts from cradle to grave. Some, it must be confessed, remained enigmas on all counts.

The stories are arranged chronologically. Read this way, the diversity of individual experience at any one period becomes apparent and the stories provide an interesting perspective on the 'great events' which structure traditional Australian histories. Some of these events — the wars in particular — touched everyone alive at the time, a fact reflected in the large number of war stories in the collection. Federation, on the other hand, is referred to in only one story, and then it is not central but one of a number of elements in the fight for women's rights.

The stories in this collection are not always comforting. It cannot be said that they endorse an uncritical view of either the past or the future. While all provide considerable grounds for admiration of individuals, few offer any cause for national self-congratulation. This is particularly true of the stories in the last section, which covers the years from 1968 to the present. Many of these stories are about welfare workers — those who help others to survive. While we are indebted to their achievements, it is sobering to contemplate the conditions that make such work necessary in an affluent society in 1988.

Yet, as these stories show, contemplation is not, in itself, enough. Whether through isolated acts of great bravery or through a different kind of courage that endures in circumstances that seem determined to break the heart and the spirit, most of these lives demonstrate Rosemary Taylor's belief that, even in the darkest days, 'We must continue to create the world; we *can* change things.' We are all responsible for history.

Sydney
July 1988

1
Exile
1788–1847

At first they were all exiles. Whether convicts, their families, or their keepers, they had been banished, as one wrote bitterly, 'to suffer hardship in a foreign clime'.

All of these early stories tell of confrontation — with the law, with those in power, and with the land. Some survived with gusto — Solomon, the most rebellious of the convicts, became a spectacular success — while others fought to survive against a harsh climate, a forbidding landscape and a system riddled with abuses and injustice.

It took courage to challenge the system, but one convict, Wharton, gave evidence for another against the powerful NSW Corps and Bent, an emancipist champion of a free press, challenged the autocratic power of colonial governors. Free settlers continued these acts of resistance.

Out of the struggle for survival in this place of exile, these people and thousands like them made a life. Out of the gaol without bars, they made a colony and a home. But in doing so, they dispossessed those whose home this had been for thousands of years. For the original inhabitants, home was to become a place of exile.

Pemulwuy
c1756–1802
'A riotous and troublesome savage'
Written by: Terri McCormack
Nominated by: John Snodgrass

When the ships of the First Fleet sailed into Port Jackson on 26 January 1788, they entered the territory of a large Sydney-based tribe of Aborigines, the now-vanished Eora. No-one knows whether Pemulwuy, a member of the Eora, witnessed their arrival or not but it soon became clear that, unlike Aranbanoo, Bennelong and Colbee, who were intrigued by the white man's civilisation, Pemulwuy intuitively recognised the threat to his people from the strange newcomers.

Born about 1756, Pemulwuy was from the Bidjigal subgroup, traditional hunters in the Botany Bay region. He was already known as a leader among his countrymen when, in December 1790, he speared a convict gamekeeper, John McIntyre, at close range near Cook's River. Although McIntyre was detested by both whites and blacks, fellow members of his hunting expedition attested that this attack was entirely unprovoked. Pemulwuy, now wanted for murder, was described as a young man with a caste in his left eye and newly shaven, an indication of contact with the white settlement.

Despite Governor Phillip's efforts to abide by his own instructions to avoid bloodshed, wanton spearing could not be tolerated and the superiority of the white men had to be demonstrated. A massive punitive expedition consisting of two captains, fifty men and three days'

Previous page. A view of Sydney Cove, New South Wales. Edward Dayes c. 1802. Fourteen years after the arrival of the First Fleet, the penal colony has begun to shape itself into a permanent settlement. However the harmonious co-existence of the Aboriginal and European inhabitants suggested by this drawing was more ideal than real. Mitchell Library provisions was instructed to collect the heads of six natives — hatchets and bags were provided — or to bring in six captives, of whom two would be hanged as an example of the consequences if they did not 'continue peaceable and quiet'. The humane Captain Watkin Tench was the reluctant leader of this 'terrific procession' which, in two marches to the head of Botany Bay, failed to sight a single Aborigine.

Far from remaining 'peaceable and quiet', Pemulwuy became the leader of attacks on farms north of Parramatta. With a hundred followers, he pursued a party of armed settlers to the outskirts of the town. According to David Collins's *Account of the English Colony in NSW* (1798), when the settlers entered Parramatta, they 'were followed by a large body of natives, headed by Pemulwuy, a riotous and troublesome savage'. Defiantly threatening the farmers, he hurled a spear at a soldier. A battle between spears and muskets ensued until five natives were killed and Pemulwuy had received seven buckshot in his head and body. Secured in irons in hospital, he managed to escape, much to the consternation of the authorities and the satisfaction of his fellows who regarded him as a 'clever man' immune to European fire-arms.

By 1802, the natives of the Sydney and Hawkesbury area 'continued as domesticated as ever' but the depredations against Parramatta and Toongabbee settlers persisted, led by Pemulwuy, 'known to be the principal in all these and former barbarities'. With London's approval an order was issued for his capture 'dead or alive'. In October 1802, Pemulwuy and a companion were captured by two settlers who, 'not having the means of securing the persons', shot them. Pemulwuy's head was sent to England but his spirit of rebellion lived on in his son Tedbury who was not taken prisoner until 1805.

Until recently obliterated from published Australian history, although his name appears frequently in unpublished records, Pemulwuy is now, in hindsight, seen as a courageous resistance fighter against a threat which, as he foresaw, overwhelmed the way of life of his people. Even Governor King, constrained as he was by the values of his time, recognised Pemulwuy as 'a brave and independent character' and 'an active daring leader'.

Young Aboriginal boy, probably a member of Pemulwuy's Eora tribe. Sketch by Juan Ravenet, artist with the Spanish Scientific Expedition under Malaspina which visited Sydney Cove in 1793. Dixson Galleries, State Library of New South Wales

Esther Abrahams
c1771–1846

Jewish convict becomes First Lady
Written by: Judith Elen
Nominated by: Donald K. W. Perry

On 30th August, 1786, when she was fifteen, Esther Abrahams was charged with stealing twenty-four yards of black lace from a shop. Although the evidence against her was circumstantial and three witnesses gave her a 'very good character', she was found guilty and sentenced to seven years transportation. Confined in Newgate Prison, the young milliner 'pleaded her belly' petitioning the Home Secretary for 'Royal

Mercy' because she was pregnant. Sixteen months later, the decision came down against her. By this time, Esther was already in Australia.

She arrived with the First fleet, a prisoner on the infamous *Lady Penrhyn*. On the voyage, she was taken up by the handsome young George Johnston — First Lieutenant of Marines; future head of the NSW Corps, Aide-de-Camp to Governors Philip and Hunter. Until his death thirty-five years later, Esther, who became known as Mrs Esther Julian, lived as Johnston's wife and bore him seven children.

In 1808, Johnston led the troops that deposed Govenor Bligh and for six months acted as Lieutenant-Governor, with Esther as the colony's unofficial 'First Lady'. Johnston was finally cashiered over the mutiny but was allowed to retain his extensive land grants. After an absence of four years, he returned to New South Wales, continued his career as an influential landowner and became a trusted friend of Governor Macquarie. While he was away, Esther administered his estates, standing up with great courage to those who tried to take advantage of Johnston's absence. Records show that she was a successful farmer and in 1809 received a grant of 570 acres of her own.

Johnston finally married Esther in 1814, but her gender, her convict origins and her long de facto status — as well, perhaps, as her Jewishness — made it impossible for her to maintain a secure social position in her own right. Approaching sixty when her husband died in 1823, Esther inherited the 2460 acre estate of Annandale. Her son, David, had been left property of his own, but the other son, the wilful Robert who was to inherit Annandale after Esther's death, became increasingly unpleasant and, eventually, violent. In March, 1829, in an attempt to wrest her property from her, he issued a writ against his mother and proceeded to have her declared insane.

An old Jewish emancipee, Jacob Isaacs, was Esther's only witness. A neighbour, he testified that 'she had accumulated her property by hard struggling, that it was not the red jacket [Johnston] who got the money'. And, although he 'knows she takes a glass, so do we all, the higher classes as well as the lower', she was still capable of minding her own affairs or those of 'any other person'. Unfortunately, his sincere evidence was discredited by the jury because of his 'comical manner' of speaking.

Esther's counsel pointed out that 'her exertions and judgement during many years past had succeeded in accumulating an extensive property' and this 'was certainly no proof of insanity'. Even the prosecution's medical witness said only that 'she is a woman of rather eccentric habits, hasty in temper and has an abrupt mode of expressing herself'. And while he had seen her 'driving most furiously through the streets', he admitted that 'a woman doing such acts as these might, nevertheless, be very capable of managing her house and farming concerns'.

However, at the end as at the beginning of her life, Esther was powerless to prevent legal injustice. Despite noting her 'lucid intervals' and that Robert 'was not heir at law' to her property, the judge declared her 'incapable of managing her own affairs'. Removed to David's estate on the George's River, Esther spent the last fifteen years of her life as historian George Bergman has described her — bereft of 'everything she had fought for and of everyone she had loved'.

George Johnston's name is well known. But this woman, put to rest by his side in the elaborate Greenway-designed family vault on 'her' estate, was simply 'Esther, his relict'.

Only known portrait of Esther Abrahams, wife of Lieutenant-Governor George Johnston. c.1811. Painting by Richard Reed. Courtesy R. Simon

Mary Wade
1778–1859

Child convict becomes founding mother
Written by: Judith Elen
Nominated by: Rowena Brooker; Marjorie Morrow

Mary Wade is one of our many founding mothers. Sentenced to death at the age of ten, she survived into her eighties to become a respected member of a new society.

At ten, Mary Wade spent her days sweeping the streets of London as a means of begging 'to get two or three halfpence'. She was one of the large family of a single mother living in poverty. With another child who described herself in court as 'going on fourteen', Mary 'took a frock, a tippet, and a cap off a little girl, in the Treasury' and pawned the frock for eighteen pence. After being 'turned in' by another child of the neighbourhood, the children were arrested and brought before the court.

In his summing up at their trial at the Old Bailey, the Lord Chief Baron condemned Mary's mother and her bringing up of the child. 'I am afraid,' he said, 'you are as much in fault as she is, by not taking proper care of her, and keeping her at home, and making her industrious; letting her run about the streets was the sure way to lead her to the place where she is now.' Continuing his draconian judgement, he addressed the jury: 'the very circumstance of such a child [referring to the eight-year-old victim] falling into the hands of two strangers, young as they are, standing over her and stripping her, does seem to me to be equivalent to holding a pistol to the breast of a grown person; therefore, I cannot state it to be anything less than robbery; the consequence of that is, that they must answer it with their lives.' The 'gentlemen of the jury' agreed and sentenced the two girls to be 'hanged by the neck until dead'.

Daily expecting execution, Mary spent the following ninety-three days imprisoned in the notorious Newgate Prison, described by Daniel Defoe in his novel, *Moll Flanders*, fifty years earlier: 'the hellish noise, the roaring, swearing, and clamour, the stench and nastiness, and all the dreadful afflicting things that I saw there joined to make the place seem an emblem of hell itself, and a kind of an entrance into it.' Mary's sentence was finally commuted to transportation for life and she was removed to the transport ship *Lady Juliana* of the Second Fleet.

Not yet twelve when she arrived in Australia, Mary Wade had voyaged for eleven months in circumstances where it was usual for officers and seamen to choose a 'mistress' from the convict women on board. Once in the colony, most female convicts were assigned to free men, ostensibly as house servants. If Mary Wade was assigned in this way, her master cannot be found in the records. Neither is there a record of the father of her first two children, one born to Mary on Norfolk Island before her fifteenth birthday, and the second, two years after.

Taken from Norfolk Island to Sydney, Mary lived in a tent by the Tank Stream she had a third child to an emancipated Irish transportee, Teague Harrigan, who joined a whaling and sealing expedition three years later.

By 1809 Mary was living with her husband Jonathan Brooker near the Hawkesbury, where she raised her growing family — eventually twenty-one children, seven of whom lived to raise families of their own. Leaving this flood-prone area, Mary and Jon, by now emancipees, established a farm at Airds in Campbelltown, New South Wales. By 1822 Jonathan was a landholder with nineteen acres cleared, ten acres of wheat, and half an acre of garden and orchard. But in the following year bushfires destroyed the dwelling, crops, garden, and Jonathan's carpentry tools — his tools of trade. The family was destitute. By 1828, however, when Jon was sixty-eight and Mary in her fifties, they had fifty acres cleared and twelve acres cultivated in the Illawarra where Mary continued to live for twenty-six years after Jon's death.

From inauspicious beginnings, Mary Wade became the matriarch of one of our largest pioneering families. When she died in 1859, a period in which few women were honoured with a public obituary, the *Illawarra Mercury* described Mary as a 'venerable lady...highly esteemed as well as being widely known and respectably connected'. Her funeral service was the first to be held in St. Paul's Church of England, Fairy Meadow, for which her son had donated the land.

One of Mary's two surviving great, great grand-daughters, Marjorie Morrow, decided to research and document her family history. With the benefit of what must also have been her ancestor's energy and determination, she publicised her research and called a family 'muster'. A family committee was formed and the Mary Wade Historical Association established. With unexpected profits from sales of the published history, *From Mary Wade to Us*, the Association has established a Scholarship for Australian History at the University of Wollongong.

In its violent beginnings, suffered injustices and struggles towards survival, Mary Wade's life parallels the history of the country since European settlement. Her story provides a model of hope for future equality and justice.

Thomas Laycock Junior
c1786–1823
Tasmania's unknown explorer
Written by: Terri McCormack
Nominated by: Kenneth G. Laycock

Thomas Laycock was only nine when he joined the New South Wales Corps in 1795, eventually becoming one of its tallest officers. He inherited his stature, name, and military background from his father who had served with the Horse Grenadier Guards before arriving in Sydney in 1791 with his family to become quartermaster with the New South Wales Corps.

Thomas Junior was promoted to Lieutenant in 1802 and arrived in the struggling northern Tasmania settlement of Port Dalrymple (later Launceston) in 1806. Aged twenty-one, he was assigned to penetrate the unknown hinterland to seek assistance from Hobart Town. Departing on foot on 3 February 1807 with four men and three weeks' provisions, he crossed the mountainous interior in nine days and returned in six days, unfortunately without relief from the equally famine-stricken southern colony. Laycock's Journal (6 Feb 1807) describes the terrain; 'The best proof of the difficulty of our passage is that it took me more than five hours to go the three miles.' On the way, however, he discovered fine grazing land and limestone deposits as well as the Lake River and the large circular Laycock's Lake, later renamed Wood's Lake. His reward was a cow from the government herd at Port Dalrymple.

On his return to Sydney, Laycock participated in the arrest of Governor Bligh in January 1808, an accidental injury making him the only casualty of this affray. With Governor Macquarie's arrival in 1810, he returned to England with the disbanded New South Wales Corps, accompanied by his wife, Isabella, whom he had married in June 1809.

Laycock gained his captaincy with the 98th Regiment in the American War. The family returned to Sydney as settlers in 1817 and, after Isabella's death, he married Mary Connell and had two more children. He became a landowner and hotelier and died at his Bringelly Estate on 7 November 1823.

Lieutenant Laycock's Tasmanian expedition is largely unrecognised. In the words of his great-great-grandson: 'His lake was taken from him by the renaming, so he is probably the only early explorer who has nothing named after him — and the cow has long since died!'

Captain Thomas Laycock of the 98th Regiment with which he served in North America from 1811. Courtesy K. Laycock

William Chamberlain
1804–1880
Shanghaied at eight
Written by: Terri McCormack
Nominated by: Leon D'Aulnais

On 7 October 1811, William Chamberlain, barely eight years old, disappeared without a trace. Enticed on board the South Sea whaler *Frederick* by a young crew member, William remained a captive as the ship slipped away from Sydney, bound for sperm whale fishing at the Ile de France, now Mauritius. Shanghaied, young William was not to see his parents — Sydney bricklayer James and his wife Elizabeth — again until he reappeared in Sydney on board the convict transport *Morley* in April 1817.

His experiences in the interim are the stuff of boyhood fantasies. By September 1812, the *Frederick* had reached St Helena Island off the west coast of Africa after a successful whaling trip which had yielded 1100 barrels of sperm oil. With the *Argo* and the *Admiral*

*Above. Capt William Chamberlain, whose career began when he was kidnapped at 8
Below. 'Boats attacking a sperm whale'; a scene familiar to William Chamberlain.
W.J. Huggins, 1834.
Mitchell Library*

Berkeley, she was homeward bound when fears of French attack were realised and she was seized by the privateer *Sans Souci*. Several of the crew of thirty were killed, including the mate and the master. The whaler was destroyed and Chamberlain and the surviving crew were held prisoner on the *Sans Souci* for nine days until she in turn was captured by the Royal Naval frigate *Andromeche*.

The lad was discovered among the prisoners and, being wounded during the transfer to the naval ship, was placed under the care of Surgeon Daniel Quarrier who described his condition as 'destitute and forlorn', a state which 'naturally excited the feeling of compassion and humanity'. William remained on the *Andromeche* until she was paid off at Portsmouth in July 1814, thereby becoming one of the first and certainly the youngest of the 'currency lads' to join the Royal Navy.

'Finding that the poor boy was again to be thrown upon the wide world without friends', Dr Quarrier undertook responsibility for his education at a school in Musselborough in Scotland. By January 1816, Chamberlain was back at sea with Dr Quarrier, then Surgeon on HMS *Leander*, and on 27 August he witnessed the historic bombardment of Algiers which ended the slavery of Christians in this Ottoman territory.

By November 1816, the thirteen-year-old was suffering from hip joint disease and was 'rendered unfit for His Majesty's Service.' Dr Quarrier arranged for his passage home, provided him with clothing and wrote to Earl Bathurst and Governor Macquarie requesting, 'all the Assistance and Protection in your power on his arrival at Port Jackson'.

Young Chamberlain was obviously well able to look after himself and, soon after his reunion with his parents, joined the *Jupiter* under Captain Bunster to serve his apprenticeship in the sealing trade off Tasmania. Before long, he returned to the business he had learnt so

early in life and commanded three whalers before commencing whaling on his own account at Maria Island. With his ships *Joanna* and *Marie Laure*, he became one of Australia's most successful and respected sperm whaling captains.

When he died in Tasmania on 9 February 1880, William Chamberlain left a widow, several daughters, and three sons who carried on his whaling business. According to the *Tasmanian Times*, he was universally respected as 'a plain, genuine, unobtrusive seaman who had worked himself by his own earnest exertions to a position of competence and independence.' He could also be seen as a man of courage and determination who, rather than being intimidated by his extraordinary boyhood adventures, took full advantage of these experiences to become successful in later life.

Joseph Wharton
1778–1853
Convict's courageous stand
Written by: Terri McCormack
Nominated by: Douglas A. Boag

In the litigious penal colony of New South Wales, many convicts appeared in court, usually as victims of the system. Few were brave, or foolhardy, enough to appear voluntarily as witnesses against a military officer as Joseph Wharton did.

The case heard in the Court of Criminal Justice on 30 April 1817 was a most unusual one. The convict architect Francis Greenway charged Edward Sanderson, Esquire, Captain of the 46th Regiment of Foot, with assault and battery. This notorious case originated with an angry letter from the quarrelsome Greenway protesting at Sanderson's transfer of some of his work — the decoration of Freemasons' aprons — to the artist John Lewin. Regretting the impropriety of this action, Greenway sent a further letter of apology. When he was called to Sanderson's quarters on the morning of 20 December 1816, he expected his apology to be accepted but, instead, was allegedly met with blows from the enraged Captain. None of the officers, soldiers, or workmen in the busy Barracks yard could recall the event, except Joseph Wharton.

In his evidence, Wharton stated that Greenway 'is no particular acquaintance of mine' but he undoubtedly knew the man. Born in Oxford in 1778, Wharton was a carpenter who received seven years' transportation in 1813 for the theft of his master's tools. He arrived in Sydney in July 1814 on the *General Hewitt* after an horrendous voyage during which thirty-four of the 300 convicts perished from dysentery. A fellow survivor was Francis Greenway, an architect sentenced in 1812 to fourteen years for forgery. The two men's skills were welcome in Sydney Town and by 1817 Wharton was Overseer of Carpenters working under Greenway's supervision on the construction of a new roof at the George Street Barracks where the assault took place.

As well as the Judge Advocate, the court consisted of Sanderson's fellow officers who objected to the case and continually disrupted proceedings. The only clear evidence came from Joseph Wharton: 'I saw Captain Sanderson strike him [Greenway] six or seven times with the whip violently — I heard him call Mr Greenway a damned rascal and a swindler.' He persisted with his account despite prolonged and hostile cross-examination: 'Captain Sanderson was beating him all the way till he got off the steps.' Both Greenway and Wharton maintained that there were officers and soldiers in the yard beneath the Barrack steps and several carpenters working by the pump. All, apart from Wharton, suffered loss of memory over the incident.

Most reluctantly, the court was obliged to accept the evidence of, to quote the Judge Advocate, 'the honest and clearsighted carpenter, Mr Wharton'. Sanderson received a token £10 fine. Before the crowded court room, however, the officers compelled the Judge Advocate to express the court's opinion that 'as an officer and a gentleman, Captain Sanderson's behaviour was perfectly justifiable'. Contemporaries saw the case as a display of military justice 'as well as the degradation a British Judge was obliged to undergo'.

After his courageous and unlikely stand for British justice, Wharton, unlike Greenway, returned to obscurity. If he suffered retribution from the military clique, it is unrecorded. His Petition for Pardon was successful in January 1818. As Government Carpenter, he erected a palisade in Macquarie Place in 1819 and a fence around the military garden in 1820. That same year he married and subsequently had two sons. By 1825, he was a Kissing Point landholder. His death was recorded at Albury on 24 August 1853.

Emanuel Solomon
c1802–1873
South Australia's founding father
Written by: Judith Elen
Nominated by: Jill & Murray Brown

In 1817 Emanuel Solomon and his brother Vaiben were convicted at the Durham Assizes of stealing clothing. Emanuel was sixteen and his brother fifteen. Sons of 'Moshe the Pencil Maker', they were among the 15 000 Jews living in London at the turn of the century — three-quarters of England's Jewish population at the time. Not of the few Jewish elite, the Solomon brothers were among London's desperately poor. Sentenced to seven years' transportation to Van Diemen's Land they had little to hope for but not much to lose.

Fifty-four years later in Adelaide, Emanuel Solomon gave a Grand Banquet for the colony's thirty-fifth anniversary. He invited 520 of Adelaide's 'old colonists', ensuring that 'the bone and sinew as well as the brain of the infant settlement were thoroughly represented'. Emanuel's magnificent final gesture only two years before his death was a public celebration of his success.

As a transportee Emanuel was a rebel. He continually escaped, was repeatedly recaptured and in 1821 was sent to Newcastle for three years' labour in irons.

Within five years of receiving their Certificates of Freedom in 1824, the brothers Solomon were operating a thriving auctioneering business in King Street, Sydney. They gradually acquired property and Emanuel began to establish his civic reputation, giving generously to charity and becoming a prominent figure in Sydney's early Jewish community.

In 1838 Emanuel moved to Adelaide. In this newly-established colony Jews enjoyed full civil and political rights, far in advance of Britain and other Australian colonies.

Then 37, Emanuel established his auctioneering business while rapidly developing one of the colony's biggest shipping trades between Sydney and Adelaide and investing in mining and exploration during South Australia's mid-century copper mining boom. While certainly serving his own interest, Emanuel's willingness to speculate also stimulated the fledgling colony's economy. Indeed, his business letter book virtually charts the development of the South Australian economy from 1840–46.

From the very earliest days of his success, Emanuel fed money back into his society. He was instrumental in founding the Adelaide Hebrew Philanthropic Society to help distressed families, he built Adelaide's first theatre, and made generous gifts of land and money to all denominations, prompting a speaker at his 1871 banquet to claim that Emanuel 'had a stone in every church and chapel in the city of Adelaide'.

The faith and respect of his peers is evident in a petition requesting Emanuel to accept nomination for the first election of South Australia's Legislative Council in 1857. He was not successful, but six years later was elected to the House of Assembly and later entered the Legislative Council, where 'on many occasions [he] advocated important reforms particularly in the interests of the working classes.'

South Australia prided itself on its freedom from the 'taint' of the convict and any public reference to the circumstances of Emanuel's arrival was carefully avoided. Yet Emanuel Solomon was one of several convict emancipists who were among South Australia's most respected pioneers. An 1843 newspaper commented : 'Perhaps to no one private individual is South Australia so much indebted as to Mr Emanuel Solomon'.

Emanuel Solomon, the rebellious convict who became one of Adelaide's most important early religious, civic and business leaders. Courtesy D. Smith

Andrew Bent
1790–1851
Father of Tasmanian printing
Written by: Terri McCormack
Nominated by: Mrs. J. Zmak

On the streets of Sydney in 1844 a pathetic tract appeared entitled 'An Appeal to the Sympathies and Benevolence of the Australasian Public for Relief for Mr Andrew Bent and his large family now in a state of Utter Destitution'. This was the same Andrew Bent who had established the first viable newspaper in Tasmania and whose determination to maintain a free press in a turbulent penal society cost him his livelihood.

An apprentice printer in London, Andrew Bent was twenty-two years old when he was transported for life for theft. On his arrival at Hobart in February 1812, his skills were immediately utilised. In 1816, the year of his conditional pardon and his marriage to Mary Kirk, he was appointed Government Printer and began the *Hobart Town Gazette and Southern Reporter*. Early copies of this newspaper which first appeared on 11 May 1816 are now collector's items, not only for their rarity but also for their technical ingenuity and craftsmanship. Using a small hand-press and making his own ink, Bent produced a regular two-page paper from an inadequate supply of old assorted type. As well as carrying advertisements, the newpaper reflected growing optimism in the colony's future as a free society.

By 1824, Bent was a prosperous and respected citizen who had availed himself of the opportunities available to skilled emancipists. With his limited equipment, he had produced Tasmania's first book in 1818, an account of the bushranger Michael Howe, as well as the *Van Diemen's Land Pocket Almanack* in 1824.

In May 1824, however, the relaxed rule of Governor Sorell was replaced by that of George Arthur, a stern authoritarian determined to enforce discipline in the penal establishment. When articles highly critical of his administration appeared in the *Hobart Gazette*, Arthur attempted, unsuccessfully, to claim the paper as Government property and curb its contents. Supported by a clique whose privileges were threatened by Arthur's restrictive rule, the editor Evan Henry Thomas and a vituperative corrrespondent Robert Lathrop Murray intensified their attacks until Bent, as proprietor and publisher, was charged with libel in July 1825. Continuing dissension brought further libel trials with Bent being heavily fined and imprisoned twice, his wife producing the newspaper in the interim.

Bent was sacked as Government Printer and the title of his paper confiscated. From June to August 1825, he published the *Colonial*

One of the earliest issues of the Hobart Town Gazette, *skilfully produced by emancipist Andrew Bent, who died destitute because of his belief in a free press. Mitchell Library*

Times and Tasmanian Advertiser using the *Gazette's* numbering system. A persistent advocate of a free press, Bent refused to apply for a licence under the Licensing Act of 1827. In 1828, he began another short-lived paper *The Colonial Advocate and Tasmanian Monthly Review* and later revived the *Colonial Times* before selling it as a going concern to Henry Melville. In yet another libel trial in 1830, he was referred to as 'this Nimrod of printers, this Franklin of the Southern Hemisphere.'

In 1839, Bent, and his family of ten children, now heavily indebted, moved to Sydney where he established *Bent's News and New South Wales Advertiser* which was soon sold and renamed the *Australasian Chronicle*. His attempts to become a hotelier and cedar-getter at the Macleay river were unsuccessful and by 1844 he was impoverished. He died in the Sydney Benevolent Asylum on 26 August 1851.

The courage required by the ex-convict Andrew Bent to fight for private ownership and free expression of the press in an authoritarian society is evident when one considers Governor Arthur's assertion that 'the government decidedly objects to persons in his position holding any responsible office'.

Edward Smith Hall
1786–1860
'The great mocker'
Written by: Elizabeth Riddell
Nominated by: Meryl & Trevor Finch

Whatever colonial society knew about Edward Smith Hall, what made him really memorable was the occasion in July 1820 when, dressed in his frock coat and top hat, he led his six daughters in their Sunday best up the aisle to the front pew in St James's Church. And found it padlocked against his entry.

While the already assembled congregation held its breath, Mr Hall broke the lock and entered the pew, ushering his girls before him, then knelt to pray. It was the first move in the game between Hall and Archdeacon Scott, the highest Anglican in Sydney.

Next Sunday when Hall arrived at the church he found his pew decked over and two parish bailiffs standing beside the entrance. Mr Hall climbed over the obstacle, ignoring the constables, and lifted his daughters over, one by one. Next Sunday the pew was barred more effectively, so Mr Hall and his daughters sat on the altar steps.

The cause of the confrontation was the denunciation of Scott as 'a wine merchant in gaiters' and looter of the public purse in Hall's paper, the *Monitor*. A series of actions for trespass and defamation followed. At the same time Governor Darling, a supporter of Scott, was on a campaign of revenge against Hall for accusations made by the *Monitor* against *him*. As it happened, however, St James's Church was not in the charge of the Anglican ministry. It belonged to King George IV, oddly enough, so Scott had no authority to bar Hall from occupying the pew which he had leased. After a long series of court

Edward Smith Hall, radical reformer and newspaper proprietor, locked horns with Governor Darling. Portrait by Gladstone Eyre, Mitchell Library

cases, Hall was awarded £25 damages while Archdeacon Scott packed his bags and, in high dudgeon, retreated to England.

Hall was born unto trouble as the sparks fly upward. From a Lincolnshire banking family, he arrived in Sydney with his first wife Charlotte (he married three times and had eleven children) and all the right introductions, commending him for his religious and social interests and persuasive manners. Lachlan Macquarie was the Governor, and Hall was granted up to 2000 acres (800 hectares) in Surry Hills (the part that is now Moore Park), Bringelly and Bathurst Lakes.

From his arrival, Hall tried to set the colony (in which, he wrote to his father, he was very disappointed) on the right path. He helped found what is now the Benevolent Society and when Macquarie started his bank Hall became its first secretary and cashier, at £200 a year. A condition was that he had to live in the bank, a tiny cottage, too small for a family, at Macquarie Place. His family lived at Surry Hills and he could not see them often. When the bank directors refused to allow Hall's assistant to sleep at the bank instead, Hall left and took up farming. But agriculture was not his line. Macquarie, who quite liked him, reported that he was a 'useless and discontented free gentleman settler' who was not industrious and wanted his land cleared and a house built for him for nothing. Nevertheless, Macquarie appointed Hall coroner, and made him a member of the Court of Civil Jurisdiction in 1813, 1814 and 1816.

Permanently back in Sydney — there is an extraordinary story that Hall left the Bathurst property in the hands of his nine-year-old son, who did quite well at it — Hall and a man named Arthur Hill launched a newspaper, the *Monitor*, that was to set the colony on its ears. Its motto was: 'Nothing extenuate, nor set down aught in malice' and in its first issue Hall promised to 'preserve freedom from personal invective, to use the language of sense and moderation and to campaign for the law of the land'. He stuck with the motto, but not always with the promise.

Hall believed in a free press, trial by jury, representative government, the rights of the (white) native-born and protection for convicts against oppressive regulations and brutal punishments. He abjured the native-born settlers not to be a 'poor grovelling race' and to 'stand up to Governor Darling and his hirelings'. Manning Clark in his history calls him 'the great mocker', and it was this mockery of pretension, and of what he saw as Darling's support of corrupt army officers and the 'exclusives' who ran the colony from the Legislative Council, that brought down on him the Governor's wrath. About the least abusive adjective Darling had for Hall was 'apostate missionary'. Darling sued time and again for defamation, as did his cronies, with the result that Hall, who defended himself in these cases, was finally sent to jail in 1829 for a term of three years, some of which he served. The warden let him wear his own clothes, and he edited the *Monitor* from his cell.

Hall was in fact the epitome of what we think of as the crusading editor, and as editors after him have found, it is a lonely business and often leaves the crusader lacking friends and money. A firebrand who was at the same time a genial friend, Hall wrote to the Colonial Office charging Darling with fourteen 'offences against mankind'. When Darling was recalled by the Colonial Office in 1831 Hall claimed victory, and Darling blamed Hall for the disgrace. The Colonial Office, however, denied that it was in the least influenced by 'any observations contained in an intemperate newspaper'. What may have been the last straw was the wide publicity given to the cases of two soldiers of the 57th Regiment of Foot, Joseph Sudds and Patrick Thompson. They were punished for theft by having to parade before their fellow soldiers wearing spiked iron collars linked by chains to their ankles. Darling had ordered a blacksmith to make the collars and had checked them himself at Government House. Sudds died five days after the parade, still wearing the collar, and Thompson became severely ill. 'The Governor,' wrote Hall in the *Monitor*, 'has power surpassed only by that of the Great Mogul, the Tsar of Muscovy and the Emperor of China.'

After Darling's recall, Hall calmed down. He sold the *Monitor* and entered the public service, in which he stayed until he died, aged seventy-four, in 1860.

Everything Hall had wanted for the colony eventually came to pass, but his role in events was largely forgotten. Sir Henry Parkes, however, remembered Hall briefly in 1891 when he proposed a toast to 'the memory of the early friends of Australian freedom': 'Edward Smith Hall was a man of singularly pure and heroic disposition...who, in an inauspicious period, tried to preserve the public spirit and awaken a love of liberty.'

Cecilia Cosgrove
1787–1858
Embattled survivor
Written by: Suzanne Falkiner
Nominated by: Brian J. Johnston

One of the most enduring images of Australian literature is that of the woman battling alone in the bush, the settler's wife who through tragedy or necessity is left without male protection. In mainstream recorded history, these women — women like Cecilia Cosgrove — usually pass unnoted.

She was born Cecilia Tracey, the daughter of a farmer in County Galway, Ireland. In 1823, aged thirty-six, she came to Australia as a free passenger on the *Woodman*, a ship carrying female convicts. Her husband, David Cosgrove, also the son of a Galway farmer, had been transported the year before for burglary.

The story behind Cecilia's arrival was distinctly odd: she had been instrumental in the detention and arrest of a politically-motivated murderer, Edward Loughan, and because of subsequent threats on her life, the Irish government decided to send her and her son Michael after her husband to New South Wales. Patrick, the eldest son, aged eight, had accompanied his father on the convict ship.

On arrival, Cecilia petitioned the Governor of New South Wales to assign her husband to her as a servant, and the family settled as tenant farmers at Abbotsbury farm near Prospect, not far from

Parramatta. Three other children — John, David and Sarah — were born here, but David died within a few years. Patrick, who had been held in the Sydney Male Orphan Institution, rejoined the family but he too died in 1825.

In about 1829 the family followed a stream of settlers over the steep passes of the Blue Mountains along the route discovered by Blaxland, Lawson and Wentworth sixteen years earlier. The Cosgroves travelled by bullock dray, bringing some cattle and other livestock and with Cecilia carrying her one-year-old baby, Sarah, in her arms. They settled in the wild country around the Abercrombie River, south of Oberon, where Cecilia, now in her early forties, gave birth to Patrick II in 1830.

Now, history repeated itself. In 1830 David Cosgrove gave evidence against two notorious cattle stealers who were later executed at Campbelltown. The family, again fearing for their safety, moved south to the Laggan district, near Crookwell, only returning to the Abercrombie River a few years later.

Misfortune struck again in 1837 when Michael, now twenty-one, was convicted of horse-stealing and transported to Tasmania for life. Soon after, the family was forced to move off the land on which they had been squatting when it was bought by someone else, Cecilia having bid for it but lost. Now the Cosgroves moved to the Little River, Porter's Retreat, near Oberon. This time, when the 1160 acre property became available for sale, Cecilia was successful in her bid.

Just five months later her husband David, still a prisoner of the Crown and an assigned servant, was taken away by the police for unwittingly harbouring a bushranger, in the person of their farm worker. The police impounded the family's cattle and horses. These were later released back to Cecilia on payment of a fine, but were nearly starving. One died and twenty more were lost on the trip home. Sentenced to twelve months in irons doing roadwork at Bathurst, David did not return to his family until several years later. In one short period, Cecilia, with three children under fourteen, had lost her husband, eldest living son, and only farm labourer. At this time, there were scarcely more than a dozen white women living in the entire Goulburn district.

In October 1838 Cecilia petitioned the Governor, pleading her husband's innocence. Unsuccessful, she petitioned twice more, in November 1839 and March 1840, but her husband, sentence expired, remained in Government Service. In the meantime, she and her children faced a bleak and lonely time on the large farm, facing cold winters and uncertain economic conditions.

David Cosgrove finally gained a ticket of leave in 1841, but this good fortune was followed by the loss of the Little River property in 1844 when one Charles Marshall, who had bought the property in his name on Cecilia's behalf, went bankrupt and failed to pay off the mortgage. It was not until 1847 that David received a conditional pardon and Michael returned home a free man from Tasmania: in the same year another son, John, twenty-three, was jailed in Sydney for horse-stealing. There is a suggestion that some of these brushes with the law were a result of malicious prosecution by the Macarthur family who were rival bidders for their land.

After thirty-five years of exhausting struggle to keep her family together, Cecilia died aged seventy-one at her son's property, Mount Mary, near

Porter's Retreat in 1858. David died at eighty-seven in 1871, also at Mount Mary. The couple had forty grandchildren in the district. Perhaps it should have been noted on Cecilia Cosgrove's tombstone that her maiden name, Tracey, from the Gaelic and established in Galway in the twelfth century, means 'embattled'.

Peter Oldham
1812–1894
Emancipist whaler and shipper
Written by: Terri McCormack
Nominated by: John A. Leckey

When Captain Peter Oldham died in Hobart on 4 September 1894, aged eighty-two, the *Mercury* obituary paid tribute to the popularity, nerve and courage of this man who had spent most of his life in the coasting and whaling trades.

As a pioneer of the Huon district, he demonstrated 'the true spirit of self help characteristic of early settlers' by diving for crayfish to sustain his party. From his sawmilling business he made 'an ample fortune' which was substantially reduced by his inability 'to believe a man lacks principle until he discovered it for himself'.

Oldham became a successful whaler, shipowner and master who 'tempered his discipline by a kind and genial bearing towards all who served under him'. Salvaging sunken ships was his favourite occupation. When his large trading ketch *Seabird* ran ashore off New Zealand in 1865, he refloated her after 'great exertion'. He showed even greater fortitude during the salvage of the *Priscilla* near Huon Island in 1880. Rather than jeopardize the difficult operation when his fingers became caught in the lifting gear, Captain Oldham said 'never mind, heave away' and later had two fingers amputated.

Known as an ardent monarchist, Oldham vigorously supported Imperial ties in correspondence to colonial and British newspapers both in his own name and under the pseudonym 'John Ploughman'. He was twice married and had six children, two of whom remained at an English school after he revisited his birthplace in 1853.

Captain Oldham was renowned for 'his accurate memory of the early history of the colony.' One indelible date would have been 26 March 1831 when he arrived in Hobart as a convict on the *Red Rover*. At the Warwick Assizes in July 1830, he had been sentenced to seven years' transportation for stealing fowls, his second offence of this nature.

Oldham received his ticket-of-leave in July 1837 and in January 1853 was elected as a 'People's Candidate' in the first Hobart elections, ironically as a supporter of continued transportation. At this time, his background was described as 'obscure' and so it remained throughout his life. Only in hindsight can we appreciate the courage and determination which enabled a former chicken thief to overcome the stigma of his conviction to become a successful entrepreneur and respected Tasmanian citizen.

Captain Peter Oldham in his late forties, his former career as a chicken thief behind him. Portrait by ex-convict artist Thomas Bock, courtesy R. Cuthbert

Alured Tasker Faunce
1808–1856
'Man of Iron'
Written by: Terri McCormack
Nominated by: Elizabeth Y. Stephens

In the penal colony of New South Wales in the 1830s, the power structure was decidedly weighted in favour of the entrenched clique of landowners who used their magisterial powers to manipulate the lives of their convict assignees. Placing his reputation and livelihood in jeopardy, a young police magistrate made a bold stand for a more equitable system of justice.

Alured Tasker Faunce was born in 1808, the son of a distinguished military family of French Huguenot descent. At sixteen, he joined the 4th or King's Own Regiment and, with his brother Thomas, arrived in Sydney with the Regiment in August 1832. He retired as captain in October 1836 to become Police Magistrate at Brisbane Water, then a notorious area for cattle stealing, escaped convicts, and sly grog selling.

The young magistrate brought a style of military efficiency and meticulousness to his job which was not appreciated by the local landholders, many of whom had enhanced their positions by the misuse of their honorary magisterial duties. He incurred further antagonism by gaining a reputation for leniency towards convict offenders.

During a court hearing on 14 November 1836, Faunce took the unprecedented step of ordering his startled fellow magistrate, Henry Donnison, to stand down from the Bench to face a charge of cattle theft. Also implicated in this case involving ownership of a cow named Blindberry were two other prominent landowners, John Moore, also a magistrate, and Willoughby Bean. In what was seen by many as an act of unwarranted tyranny, Faunce ordered Donnison's house to be searched and the accused conveyed to Sydney for trial in irons, thus earning himself the sobriquet 'Ironman Faunce'. At the trial, Donnison and his colleagues were found not guilty and Faunce was subsequently fined £1500 for wrongful arrest.

Captain Faunce's youthful zeal had catapulted him into the midst of an unedifying wrangle for political power between Governor Richard Bourke and the vested interests of the squattocracy. In its unceasing efforts to discredit Bourke and his police magistracy, the *Sydney Gazette* seized on the 'Blindberry case' to run a series of vicious editorials accusing Faunce of 'tyrannical oppression' and 'summary and autocratic justice'. When Governor Bourke, on the eve of his departure, suggested that Faunce's court costs might be defrayed by the colonial Government, the *Gazette* reached new heights of vituperation, denigrating the 'man of iron' as a mental imbecile who was 'unfit to be entrusted with the guidance of anything of more value than an old stock-horse'. Even after Faunce's transfer to Queanbeyan in November 1837 and Governor Gipps' arrival, the press attacks continued until Faunce was

Police Magistrate Captain Alured Tasker Faunce, 1835, before his involvement in the notorious 'Blindberry Cow' case. Portrait by Richard Reed, courtesy M. de L. Faunce

forced to sue the editor, George Cavenagh, for defamation of character.

Prior accusations of inefficiency were more than vindicated during Captain Faunce's magistracy at Queanbeyan, although his humane treatment of convicts remained unorthodox. As the first Police Magistrate in this lawless region, he pursued bushrangers on horseback, often risking his own life, and conducted court hearings in extremely primitive conditions. His reputation grew with the town itself and its citizens came to respect his concern for impartial justice. An 1840 testimonial congratulated him on his 'urbane and gentlemanly conduct on the Bench' and assured him of the 'respect and sincere feelings' of the prominent signatories.

In January 1835, Faunce had married Elizabeth, daughter of Lieutenant-Colonel John MacKenzie of the 4th Regiment. Their six sons and three daughters were reared on Faunce's estate near Limestone Plains, several of them later becoming prominent citizens of the region. A lover of cricket, Captain Faunce died on 26 April 1856 while playing for the Queanbeyan and Ginninderra Club he had founded.

In hindsight, Captain Faunce's determined, even foolhardy, actions in dispensing equal justice for all in a society deeply divided between convict and free can be seen as those of a humane and extremely courageous man.

Joseph Grimaldi
1815–?
Grimaldi the Scourger
Written by: Russell Smith
Nominated by: Russell Smith

We all know of Batman, of Fawkner, of Bourke
   And of others who history hold dear
But who of us wandering 'round Melbourne today
   Know Grimaldi the Scourger was here...?

Well, he was. Convict Joey Grimaldi was the 'Scourge of Port Phillip' from September 1838 to August 1839.

He was born in Paris in 1815 and as a youth worked in the theatre. His slightly older namesake and probable relative, Joseph Grimaldi, was the most famous of all British clowns. In June 1834, Joey was working in Ireland. He robbed his boss, was caught, and fourteen months later found himself in New South Wales wearing a convict uniform.

About mid-1837 he accompanied his then master to the infant settlement at Port Phillip. A year later he was re-assigned, as a watchman. 'Special Constable Grimaldi' joined other serving convicts to make up the bulk of the thirteen-man Port Phillip Police.

Then came a terrible day for watchman Grimaldi. He was nominated for the position of scourger. He could not refuse, unless he wanted to be flogged himself.

Happier days followed. On 6 July 1839 Joey made application, as was necessary for a convict, to marry sixteen-year-old Eliza Herd and earlier that same week he had been recommended for his ticket of leave. But the love-struck Joey then made another mistake. Tired of waiting for his marriage application to be processed, he told the Rev Grylls that he was a free man and therefore no approval was necessary. The young couple were duly wed.

It took the authorities only a few weeks to learn of the illegal marriage. The bridegroom was promptly whisked away and placed in prison. Weeks dragged into months and the Melbourne Police Magistrate could not get a clear ruling from Sydney on what to do with this dreadful criminal. Eventually he was attached to a road gang, digging ditches, grubbing trees, breaking rocks and occasionally managing a secret night-time visit to Eliza.

On 17 December 1839, Joey was working on a road in the centre of Melbourne when a great explosion rocked the town. The Collins Street gunsmith shop of John Blanch blew sky high when a large stockholding of gunpowder ignited. Blanch, his wife, and two others died in the explosion.

The sole hero of the day was Joey Grimaldi. He alone ventured into the wreckage of the building, risking his life several times to rescue the injured who were trapped under burning rubble.

Many leading citizens of Melbourne quickly raised a petition pointing out Joey's act of great heroism and requesting that he be freeed immediately. The official reaction? Nothing. Joey Grimaldi kept working on the streets of Melbourne until 12 February 1840, when he was brought before the Melbourne Bench to answer for his 'extreem ill conduct' in deceiving the Rev Grylls. He was found guilty of perjury and sentenced to twelve months in the iron gang back at Woolloomoolloo, in Sydney.

Seven months later, Eliza gave birth to a daughter. The baby was christened Mary Jane Grimaldi, but it is doubtful if Joey ever knew about his child.

The unfortunate Joey lost both his freedom and his wife. By the time he was finally granted his ticket of leave at Newcastle on 4 April 1843, Eliza had had a second child to another Melbourne-based convict, James Hunter. She married Hunter in 1849.

Richard Elsworthy Pym
1820–1880

Intrepid sailor and explorer
Written by: Billy Marshall-Stoneking
Nominated by: Richard Elsworthy Pym

In 1878, the Italian explorer D'Albertis sailed nearly 1000 kilometres up the Fly River in New Guinea, igniting landmines and petroleum bombs to ward off hostile natives. He could have been excused for thinking he was the first European to lay eyes on this wild and exotic country — there was certainly no evidence of previous visits. But if D'Albertis thought he was going where no white man had gone before, he was wrong.

In 1842, the HMS *Fly* and *HMS Bramble* were sent to Australia. Under the command of Captain Blackwood, the expedition had orders to survey and chart the Great Barrier Reef and the Torres Strait. At the front, leading the flotilla into uncharted seas, sailed the pinnace *Midge*, skippered by Richard Pym, RN, a man who liked a challenge.

During the long journey to the Antipodes, the two ships weathered numerous storms and rescued survivors from three shipwrecks, putting them all safely ashore at Port Essington in Northern Australia. While surveying the northern coast of Australia, Pym and his crew made several isolated survey landings only to be attacked by bands of Aboriginal warriors intent on defending their territory from the strange, ghost-like figures who stepped ashore.

But Pym's greatest challenge lay to the north on the island of New Guinea. Curious as to the nature and extent of that land mass, Captain Blackwood ordered Pym to sail the *Midge* close to the shoreline and investigate. While doing so, Pym discovered the mouth of what he christened the Fly River after Blackwood's ship. With the HMS *Fly* and HMS *Bramble* anchored at the mouth of the Fly River, Pym sailed the *Midge* up the river for closer investigation.

The mighty Fly, more than eighty kilometres wide at its mouth, was as tantalising as it was treacherous. Pym sought to discover the full extent of the river.

As the *Midge* navigated its way upstream through lowland swamps, mangroves and rain forest, Pym was awe-struck by the magnitude of what he saw. He was convinced that the Fly was one of the world's greatest watercourses but he would never have the chance to explore the river fully. Time and a lack of provisions were against him.

With only a small portion of the 1000 kilometres of navigable waters explored, Pym and his crew were nearly overtaken by catastrophe. Suddenly, the jungle grew very still. Then the air around the *Midge* exploded with shouts and, suddenly, Pym's ship was attacked by several war canoes of local tribesmen. After a desperate struggle in which Pym ordered his men to 'open fire', the *Midge* beat a hasty retreat back down the river.

Meanwhile, at the river's mouth, a huge tropical storm had forced Blackwood to seek safety, and he had sailed out of the area to avoid being wrecked. By the time Blackwood returned to the mouth of the Fly, Pym had come and gone. Thinking he had been abandoned, and fearful of another attack, Pym had already headed for the Australian coast.

Pym and his crew completed the 1000 kilometre journey across the Torres Strait and all arrived at Port Essington, safe, but on the verge of starvation. Pym then had to weather another crisis.

When Blackwood finally returned to Australia, he was furious to find Pym already there. He ordered court martial proceedings and, after being reprimanded, Pym was transferred to Admiral Cochrane's squadron to fight pirates in the South China Sea.

Pym may never have returned to Australia but for being seriously wounded during a confrontation with pirates off Borneo. After a lengthy recovery, he was posted to command the royal yacht *Victoria and Albert* but, because of his leg wound, was relieved of that command and

Staff commander R. E. Pym, RN, discoverer of New Guinea's Fly River, survived pirates in Borneo to live out his life plagued by bureaucratic inefficiency in Brisbane. Courtesy R.E. Pym

re-posted as customs officer and harbourmaster at Bowen, Queensland.

In Australia, he married and lived in relative obscurity in a slab hut. After a life of extraordinary excitement, the greatest challenges of his later years were 'the inefficient bureaucracy in Brisbane, as well as that of the Admiralty'.

Robert McCulloch

?

Policeman of principle
Written by: Terri McCormack
Nominated by: Michael F. Joseph

On 29 March 1847, Thomas Donelly gained notoriety by being the first white man to be hanged in South Australia for the murder of an Aborigine. This followed a period of serious conflict between white settlers and natives in the State's south-east and was intended to demonstrate the justice of British law to the Aborigines and reduce white atrocities.

Less well-known is the man who pursued and captured Donelly, Corporal Robert McCulloch. A Scottish-born immigrant, McCulloch had joined the South Australian Police Force in 1840 and was promoted to Corporal in 1845. He accompanied Inspector Gordon on a tour of the troublesome south-east and in January 1846 was appointed to the newly-established Mount Gambier Police Station.

On 1 September 1846, at Mr Davenport's station near Rivoli Bay, an Aborigine known as Kingberrie or Billy interfered in a quarrel

'Blacks on the way to Adelaide in Custody' depicts the usual outcome of conflict between Aborigines and Europeans in SA in the 1840s and 50s. McCulloch's capture of Donelly challenged the inequity of the justice system. Painting by 'E.S.', 1850, Mitchell Library

among the white farm workers and was shot by Donelly, who fled with a native boy. News of the murder reached Mount Gambier Police Station on 3 September but McCulloch, who was on routine stock-stealing patrol, remained unaware of the event until located by Constable Joseph Guy with a warrant on 7 September. McCulloch had actually spent a silent night sharing a room with the wanted man at Mr Hunter's property and had sighted him several times on neighbouring stations in the intervening days.

On the morning of 7 September, McCulloch set off in pursuit, crossing the Glenelg River at McPherson's station. For the next three days, he struggled through country which he described in court as being almost impassable where there was the constant danger of losing his horse at night. On the Port Fairy road, 'without the bounds of the Colony', he surprised Donelly coming towards him. His evidence belied the drama of the event: 'I was alone, dismounted, took the pistol from his belt and handcuffed him, then read the warrant to him. He told me that the pistol was loaded...'

Refused assistance by a local magistrate, McCulloch was obliged to retrace his journey through the thick bushland, this time with a dangerous prisoner in tow who had nothing to lose. One wonders what communication there was between these unlikely companions as they traversed the rough country for the next five days and nights, reaching Mount Gambier on 17 September after a journey of 186 kilometres. McCulloch's condition after his arduous pursuit is evident from the Police journal entry of 18 September: 'Cpl.McCulloch unfit for duty through illness'.

On 12 December, McCulloch assisted Surgeon Matthew Moorhouse with the exhumation of the victim's body and, amidst the putrified flesh, identified the bullet which had been fired from the pistol he had taken from Donelly. The evidence was conclusive and, in his summary on 17 March 1847, the judge emphasised that the colour of the murdered man's skin was unimportant in law and in the eyes of heaven.

McCulloch was promoted to Sergeant and in March 1849 became Sergeant Major, now Senior Sergeant. When he resigned in 1851, he was commended for showing 'great courage and determination in bringing to justice many desperate characters'. A constable now stationed at Mount Gambier who discovered this intriguing story admits: 'I do not think too many of our fellow officers (myself included) would be too thrilled about tackling a job the way McCulloch had to'.

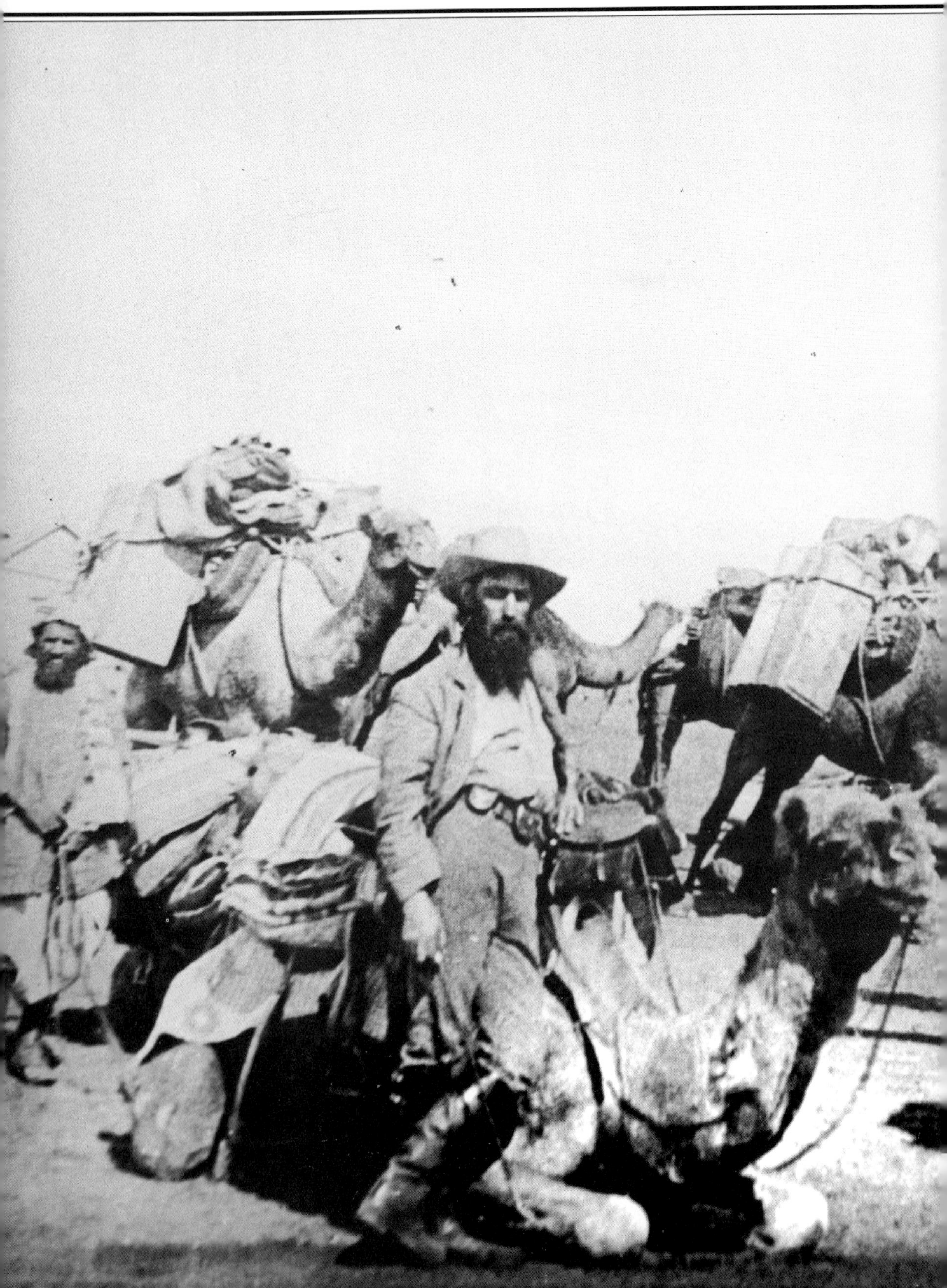

2
Opportunity
1848–1883

By 1847, transportation to the eastern colonies had ceased. With the discovery of gold, the land that had seemed so strange and inhospitable now looked like a land of promise.

The long boom was marked by exploration and expansion — Carson opening up pastures in Queensland, Lindsay taking his camels across the desert into the far north — and a great wave of immigration. But the promise was not always fulfilled. Gold discoverer Tipple Smith died libelled and broken; the extraordinary entrepreneur, Ledger, and his llamas were treated most shabbily.

Now, too, the Chinese shared the racial hostility previously reserved for those who were black. While a wealthy Chinese mandarin in Little Bourke Street fought for the rights of Chinese miners, the Rev Gribble in the outback kept up a passionate battle against the dark side of pastoral expansion — the inhumane exploitation of the Aborigines.

Bushrangers like Ned Kelly, whose capture appears here, also saw this as a land of opportunity. As their careers demonstrate, one man's opportunity was frequently another's downfall.

William Tipple Smith
1803–1852
Discoverer of first payable gold
Written by: Lynette Ramsay Silver
Nominated by: Lynette Ramsay Silver

Mineralogist William Tipple Smith, eldest son of a lapidary, was born in the Suffolk town of Aldeburgh in 1803. After emigrating to Australia in 1835, he opened a mineralogy and jewellery business in Sydney's George Street North. In September 1847, Smith read a newspaper article reporting predictions by the eminent English geologist, Sir Roderick Murchison, that gold would probably be found on the western slopes of the Blue Mountains. Small isolated finds had been reported since 1823, but nothing of any commercial value had been discovered. Smith, although physically handicapped by the loss of his right hand, immediately left for the area, exploring it extensively and eventually finding, near Bathurst, gold in sufficient quantities to prove Murchison's theories correct.

In February 1848 he wrote to Murchison informing him of the discoveries and enclosing gold samples as evidence. Smith then undertook another long, lonely journey consolidating his earlier finds in the rugged hills near Lewis Ponds Creek and the Turon, finding silver and copper in the process. From Yorkey's Corner, he obtained nuggets as large as three and a half ounces.

In New South Wales at this time all mineral rights belonged to those who held title to the land, while in England they remained with the Crown. In 1846 the New South Wales government had attempted

Previous page. The Elder Scientific Exploring Expedition led by David Lindsay (second from left), about to start out from Warrina in 1891 to explore the centre of Australia. Lindsay's was the first expedition to cross the Great Victoria Desert on camels. Mitchell Library

to gain control of all precious metals but the land owners, many of whom were members of the Executive Council, blocked the move. Smith was uncertain as to where he stood, and requested that Murchison discuss the matter with the Secretary of State, Earl Grey. Murchison immediately informed Grey of Smith's discoveries, urging the government to encourage organised gold exploration, clarify the mining laws and secure mineral rights for the Crown, suggestions which Grey chose to ignore.

While awaiting advice from England, Smith embarked upon another mining enterprise. With his brother Thomas and two businessmen, he pioneered the iron industry by building a blast furnace in the wilderness at Mittagong, south of Sydney. Named the Fitzroy Iron Works, the mine was up and running in the space of three months, its superior quality iron attracting wide acclaim. Meanwhile, there was no reply from Murchison as he was away on a geological expedition.

In January 1849, when the first reports of the Californian gold rush began to lure emigrants away from Australia, Smith told the Colonial Secretary, Edward Deas Thomson, of his discoveries. He offered to reveal the location of the gold field in return for £500 for his 'considerable expense and trouble'. Thomson was impressed by both the gold and the news and promised to inform Governor Fitzroy. Smith entrusted Thomson with a splendid three and a half ounce specimen, with which the Colonial Secretary proceeded to tour the countryside in an abortive effort to detect secretly where it had been found. The Governor was eventually informed of Smith's discovery, but apart from passing on the news to Earl Grey, he took no action.

Six months passed. In June 1849 Smith's patience wore out and he wrote to Thomson requesting an answer to his proposition. The answer was that everything must be left 'to the consideration of the government'. By the time Murchison's letter arrived, indignantly informing him of Grey's lack of interest, Smith had suffered a crippling stroke, which paralysed his good left side. Initially the paralysis was mild enough to allow him to return to his gold field in April 1850, but his condition worsened, resulting in a loss of speech for some time and forcing him to leave the iron mine and return to Sydney.

In May 1851 Smith was horrified to hear the claims of E.H. Hargraves who announced that he had discovered a gold field. He had, in fact, found only five tiny specks, so small that they could barely be seen. Hargraves' partners, Tom and Lister, were the ones to hit the jackpot. Using inside information that gold had previously been found at Yorkey's Corner, they had, in a few short hours, found six ounces of alluvial granular gold. Four ounces were sold to Hargraves who converted them into a magnificent 'faked' nugget which was used to engineer a massive gold rush at the exact locations discovered by Smith years before. Aghast that Hargraves had proclaimed himself gold discoverer, Smith, using a scribe, wrote to the government. Although he named further gold localities in his letter, his pleas for recognition were disregarded. Hargraves had pulled off a brilliant coup and presented the government with a *fait accompli*.

When Smith's claims arrived, backed by Murchison who had also lodged the gold samples in London's Geological Museum, the Governor faced a dilemma. Because of its previous apathy, the government had not secured any rights to minerals (thereby losing millions of pounds in revenue), had a gold rush on its hands which it was hard put to control and had been forced to publicly recognise Hargraves. In the name of political expediency, Fitzroy immediately set up a train of events which portrayed Smith as a trickster trying to pass off Californian gold and refusing to disclose the location of his supposed gold field when asked to do so. These totally untrue allegations became the official version of events and were transmitted as such to London. Meanwhile Hargraves, after declaring all partnerships null and void, consolidated his position as the sole discoverer of gold, reaping ultimately £12 381 reward plus a lifetime annuity of £250.

In an effort to obtain justice, Smith, now in increasingly ill health, solicited help from Murchison to present an appeal and to intercede on his behalf with Earl Grey. Murchison immediately came to Smith's aid, but it was a lost cause. The new Secretary of State, Sir John Pakington, sent for the dispatches which branded Smith a fraud. Confronted with totally conflicting evidence and realising that his government was vulnerable as it too had failed to act upon Smith's earlier information, Pakington took the easy way out by declaring it was a matter for the local government.

A brief, cold letter from the Colonial Secretary, reprimanding Smith for using an 'indirect channel of communication', informed him that the appeal had been an utter failure. Within four days, on 3 December 1852, Smith was dead, leaving a wife and seven children. He died a broken man, the tragic victim of political expediency.

Smith had hidden copies of his correspondence in a safe place, while the government filed its copies away so that they could not be found. It was not until the discovery of the documents that the real story of William Tipple Smith was uncovered, 134 years after his death.

Smith lies in a mean, unmarked grave in Rookwood Cemetery. With the truth now exposed, this remarkable pioneer, the father of Australia's iron industry and the first discoverer of payable gold, has attained his rightful place in the annals of Australian mineral history.

Esther Anne Ballantyne c.1910. Her story reminds us that Victorian portraits often disguise the intrepid spirit and lively humour of our pioneer women

Esther Anne Ballantyne
1833–1916
'How to laugh'
Written by: Suzy Baldwin & Frank O'Neill
Nominated by: Frank Willestra O'Neill

Esther Anne Ballantyne is one of Australia's many pioneer women whose lives are not recorded in letters or diaries. However, she has left behind a wonderful scrapbook — an old leather-bound ledger that was originally the 1866–67 account book for one of the properties that her husband owned in partnership with the Henty brothers. Over the top of pages of copperplate handwriting listing stock and stores (on 26 November 1866, these included 138 tins of sardines and thirty-nine pairs of 'mole trousers') and 'Rations sold to Shearers' ('505 lbs flour @ 4d, 21 sheep @ 10/-, 1 bar soap 4/-'), Esther has stuck a collection of recipes, knitting patterns, cures for croup and arthritis, cartoons, puzzles, poems, Pear's soap cards, newspaper cuttings, photographs of friends, drawings by her gifted daughter Ivy and letters from her grandchildren. Among these last is one claiming, in a very young child's careful hand, 'I am getting better' on which Esther has written the poignant note 'I received this letter by post the day my darling died 18th June 1902.'

Despite such losses, Esther's collection displays a quirky sense of humour and a taste for the exotic. She is clearly an opponent of dullness and pomposity and many of the clippings reveal her delight in the eccentricities of human behaviour. Others give a personal immediacy to historical events. Beside a newsclipping of 20 August 1905, commemorating the 45th anniversary of the departure of Burke and Wills, Esther has written 'We were living at Borodomaran Station near Mansfield at the time they started off'.

The collection tells us a great deal about the person who made it, but it is the memory of her grandson, Frank Willestra O'Neill, that breathes real life into Esther. Now ninety, Mr O'Neill was in his teens when his grandmother died in 1916 and vividly recalls both Esther and her stories of her early life. Through him, we hear once again the lively voice — and the laughter — of a woman born over 150 years ago.

'On a wintry Bristol day at the beginning of the year 1849, fifteen-year-old Esther Anne Haines hugged her friends for the last time and joined her family in the carriage bound for Plymouth and the ship that would take them 12 000 miles away from all that was familiar. It was, Esther later said, "a daunting experience". But Esther, lively, witty and wise, was never to be daunted by anything for long.

'On reaching Plymouth, the Haines family boarded the *Sir George Seymour* whose log describes them as 'emigrants with agricultural experience'. On 14 May 1849, after a voyage of 126 days, they arrived at Point Henry, Geelong, Victoria.

'Prior to their arrival, five brothers called Henty and one Scot, William Ballantyne, had brought sheep to Portland in Victoria. They now extended to Geelong where William wooed and won the heart of Esther. They married in 1851 when Esther was seventeen and set off by bullock wagon with their sheep to take up land. They pushed on to a part now known as Tocumwal, New South Wales, where they struck camp. And so began the pioneering of a sheep station...

'As the dawn came up on the first day at their camp site, Esther spied a crow on the branch of a nearby tree. But on looking around further she noticed that from behind every gum tree two eyes were peering her way. Being outnumbered, her heart was playing a tattoo but she noticed that the old crow was still there. "Ballantyne, pass me the gun" (She always called her husband Ballantyne). She thought that if she could pip that crow, she would greatly impress those watching eyes so, when her heart was at nadir, she fired and Lo! down came the crow. Then from behind every bush leapt a black man waving and laughing "and from then on they would do anything I asked of them. We of course gave them food, blankets, tobacco and so on."

'Esther's book contains many items on "How to cure," "How to make" and "How to laugh". She practised all of these.
How to cure...
'During her first three years there, Esther never saw another white

From Esther's scrapbook: a 1905 letter from her grandson, Frank O'Neill, who now, at 90, tells his grandmother's story

From Esther's scrapbook: a cartoon to which she has added her own quirky touch, with old ledger entries just visible underneath

woman. She learned the Aborigines' language and was doctor, nurse, bookkeeper, carpenter and referee. Long before the Flying Doctor, messages were sent and received in forked sticks and to Esther came many in need. Oh yes, William was there, but he was a true gentleman. He never took off his collar and tie (except, presumably, to sleep). How to make...

'Apart from the bad language that often came from the kitchen caused by the monkey that spent a lot of time on a ledge over the kitchen door and used to swipe the cook's tall white hat whenever he passed, the cook, who was Chinese, was a very good cook. His great achievement was his yeast pastry whose secret he refused to reveal. Esther decided to spy. One fine early morning she saw the cook with a large dish of pastry. Furtively looking over his shoulder, he made his way to his quarters. When the coast was clear, Esther had a peep and this met her eye: a warm blanket ridged like a sheet of corrugated iron and nestling in every groove, a pastry, gently rising as it puffed away. How to laugh...

'She told me of a time when they were expecting visitors from Sydney by coach. Esther collected the Aborigines and requested them, when the coach arrived, to cover themselves in front. Oh yes, they would certainly do that. When Cobb and Co came to a halt, there they were, all lined up, holding kerosene tins in front of themselves.

'Later Esther and William owned a sheep station in Benalla, Victoria, and on one of their trips by coach from New South Wales the driver was suddenly taken ill and it was "Everybody out". But Esther had other views. "Give me the reins", and she climbed up to the driver's box seat and so away went another successful trip by Cobb and Co.

'Esther was the anvil of the forge and they came to her to have their troubles hammered into shape.

William seems to have been a bright lad
But
To you Esther, I dips my lid
God Bless.'

Charles Ledger
1818–1905

Adventures in the Andes with alpacas
Written by: Terri McCormack
Nominated by: C. Matters; George Pavlu

In November 1858, the citizens of Sydney were treated to the spectacle of hundreds of llamas and alpacas grazing in the Domain. An apparently grotesque combination of long-necked camel and woolly sheep, they were a bizarre sight behind which lay a story of high adventure linking Australia's history with that of the wild Andes country of South America and one of the most remarkable men ever to visit our shores.

Charles Ledger, born in London in 1818, was one of that breed of nineteenth-century entrepreneurs who sought profit, renown and innovative enterprises in unlikely places. By 1842, he was established in Tacna, Peru, as an exporter of *cinchona* (quinine tree) bark, copper, alpaca wool and vicuna skins. In 1852, his advice was sought by the British Consul on the feasibility of exporting alpacas to New South Wales. Ledger had long been aware of the wool-producing potential of these valuable animals. Despite stringent restrictions on their export by the Peruvian Government and continual obstruction from his Indian workers, he had built up a herd of 600 at his estate on the Peruvian-Bolivian frontier in the hope of a change of policy or a revolution.

Having been discreetly assured of the support of Her Majesty's Government for his extraordinary enterprise, Ledger visited New South Wales and found the Monaro district suited to their husbandry. Governor Fitzroy was enthusiastic: 'If you succeed in introducing 100 alpacas only into the Colony, we will treat you with the same liberality as the McArthurs...you shall have a grant of 10,000 acres.'

Returning to South America in May 1853, Ledger re-joined his flock and shepherds who had already begun their epic trek from Peru through Bolivia and the Argentine to the Chilean coast. In their five-year journey, the expedition traversed some of the world's highest and most inhospitable regions where attacks by vicuna-hunting bandits were a constant threat as was death through starvation or exposure. In August 1855, Ledger managed to foil an attempt by a Bolivian military force to arrest him and his property. He received assistance to drive his flock across the Argentine and arrived at Copiapo in Chile in April 1858.

'Only those acquainted with the country and its habitants can form any idea of the difficulty and dangers I had to surmount', said Ledger after his arrival in Australia, but some appreciation of the terrors and beauties of the lands through which the expedition passed can be gained from a sketchbook now in Sydney's Mitchell Library. The naïve charm and humour of these coloured sketches, drawn by the unknown artist Santiago Savage, do not disguise the hardship and perils encountered during this remarkable journey.

In Valparaiso, Ledger incurred debts of £6000 for freight, fodder, salaries and insurance before embarking with 336 animals and thirteen shepherds, in August 1858. The mountain-bred animals suffered greatly from seasickness, But on 28 November, 275 animals — one hundred and eighty-four alpacas, eleven llamas, seventy-four crossbreds and six vicunas — were landed at Sydney.

From their spectacular lodgings at the Domain, the flock was moved to the Saphienbury estate near Liverpool. Alpaca meat received favourable receptions at fashionable dinners and Ledger was awarded with medals from scientific societies and the 1862 London Exhibition for his efforts. By this time, however, his hopes of being generously reimbursed by the Government had been dashed and he was obliged to accept a Government offer of £1500 for the flock with the proviso that he remained as Superintendent on an annual salary of £500 with which to maintain his remaining six men.

When the Acclimatisation Society of Victoria expressed interest, Ledger immediately began organising further exports of alpacas and vicunas 'of superior breed'. In the prevailing climate of inter-colonial rivalry, this was interpreted as a breach of faith by the then Minister of Lands, John Robertson, and Ledger's battle with entrenched and short-sighted

The medal presented to Charles Ledger by the Societé Imperiale d'Acclimatisation in 1860, one side featuring an alpaca in recognition of his feat in bringing over 200 of this species of llama to Australia. Mitchell Library

bureaucracy culminated in his suspension from office in August 1862 after a heated interview with the Minister.

His appeal to the Governor, Sir John Young, for recompense for his efforts was rejected because of lack of any record of promises given by the British Consul in Peru, necessarily verbal, and by Governor Fitzroy, since deceased. Having failed in his attempt to sue the New South Wales Government, Ledger returned to his estranged family in Peru in August 1864 'unable to support the expense and delay and abandoning all hope of ever obtaining justice'.

The remaining animals failed to be sold at auction and were given away to farmers and zoos. The failure of the enterprise was attributed to the low rate of increase and coarse hair of the animals but the powerful merino lobby may also have played a part. In 1920 the Lands Department acknowledged: 'Mr Ledger always affirmed that if the Government had carried out his suggestions and taken the flock to the Monaro district in the first place, a different end would have resulted.'

On his return to Peru, Ledger was, as he anticipated, met with extreme hostility and a price was reputedly put on his head. Undaunted, he became engaged in another far more successful and beneficial project. Circumventing Peruvian and Bolivian export regulations yet again, he smuggled out seeds of the *cinchona* tree which were bought by the Dutch Government and successfully cultivated in Java. Later known as *Cinchona Calisya Ledgerianna*, these trees provided an inexpensive source of quinine. By 1900, Java supplied two-thirds of the world's supply of this life-saving drug. However, for his part in supplying Ledger with the original seeds, his servant Manuel was starved to death by the Bolivian authorities.

After living in the US, Argentine and Uruguay, Ledger was back in New South Wales by 1895. Although, in 1897, the Dutch Government recognised his services to humanity by granting him an annuity of £100 a year, when Ledger died at Leichhardt in Sydney on 19 May 1905, his estate was valued at only £2.

Charles Ledger 'giving orders to scouts' on his five-year expedition through the Andes gathering llamas and alpacas to bring to Australia. From a collection of watercolour sketches of Ledger's Andes expedition, 1853–8, by otherwise unknown artist Santiago Savage. Mitchell Library

A man of vision and indomitable perseverance, Charles Ledger was both an entrepreneur and a public benefactor to whom peril and vicissitude were small obstacles. Well might the New South Wales graziers have felt threatened by his supreme confidence in the fine quality wool he expected to produce from his strange animals: 'If my views are carried out or I live long enough to carry them out New South Wales will be celebrated as the only country producing this "non plus ultra" in wool. — I spare no trouble or expense and I can only hope that parties of enterprise in New South Wales will supply the means to enable me to realise my fond hope and expectations.'

Lowe Kong Meng
1831–1888
Champion of racial tolerance
Written by: Terri McCormack
Nominated by: Lesley Van de Velde

In the mid-1850s, when reactions to the increasing Chinese presence on the Victorian goldfields were turning from unease to outraged intolerance of these 'pagan idolators', Lowe Kong Meng was an enigma. A cultured gentleman who was fluent in English, French and Cantonese, he was held in high esteem by both Chinese immigrant miners and the Melbourne business establishment.

The son of a wealthy Cantonese merchant family, Lowe Kong Meng was born in 1831 in the British colony of Penang. He received an excellent education and traded extensively with Mauritius, Calcutta, and Singapore before visiting Melbourne as supercargo on his own ship in 1853. Aware of mercantile opportunities generated by the gold rushes, he returned a year later to set up an import business in Little Bourke Street. He extended his fleet of ships, procuring bêche-de-mer in Torres Strait, trading with Hong Kong, and attempting, unsuccessfully, to establish a trade link with the newly-established settlement at Darwin. His several mining interests included the rich Kong Meng mine at Majorca.

With another influential compatriot, Louis Ah Mouy, he was a foundation member of the Commercial Bank of Australia in 1866, becoming one of its largest shareholders. He co-founded the Hop Wah Sugar Company in Cairns, had company branches throughout Australia and New Zealand, and held large tracts of prime Melbourne land devoted to vegetables and tobacco. By the time of his death in 1888, he was recognised as one of Melbourne's wealthiest men.

In 1860, Lowe Kong Meng married Mary Ann Prussia and fathered twelve children. Highly regarded as a gentleman of 'exceedingly generous disposition who gave liberally to churches and public charities, without respect to creed or denomination', he was an honoured guest at Melbourne social events and was elected by the Government as Commissioner for the Melbourne Exhibitions of 1880 and 1888.

Despite his elite position, Lowe Kong Meng was far from unaware

Lowe Kong Meng, cultured Chinese gentleman, Mandarin of the Blue Button Order, successful businessman and champion of Chinese immigrant workers. From T.W.H. Leavitt's Australian Representative Men *(Melb. 1887)*

of the plight of his fellow countrymen. As leader of the See Yap and Gee Hing societies, he assisted impoverished lonely Chinese and sought to minimise racial tension by instructing newcomers in the law and acceptable ways of behaviour. He appeared before the Select Committee on Chinese Immigration in 1856 and was a vocal opponent to the discriminatory mining tax imposed on Chinese goldseekers in addition to the ten shilling 'head tax' demanded on entry. The combined Chinese societies, with Lowe Kong Meng leading the Melbourne campaign, resisted this obnoxious tax in a sustained show of strength.

Although the majority of Chinese returned to China after their year's bondage on the gold fields, many remained as the rushes subsided, to become station hands, market gardeners and cabinetmakers. Their alien customs and appearance and the perceived threat to local employment reinforced racial prejudice which culminated in the 1880s with vitriolic cartoons of the Chinese as physical and moral lepers. Insisting that his countrymen needed only 'to be properly understood and discreetly dealt with', Lowe Kong Meng was the co-author of a pamphlet 'The Chinese Question in Australia' in 1879. In an attempt to counter one of the common accusations, he conferred with his Sydney counterpart Quong Tart on ways to curb the opium trade.

As a successful businessman and leader of several Chinese societies, Lowe Kong Meng held tremendous influence over the Victorian Chinese. For his work as unofficial consul, the Emperor of China elevated him to the prestigious rank of Mandarin of the Blue Button Order in 1863, reputedly the first expatriate Chinese to be awarded this honour. He played a prominent part during the visit of the Chinese Commissioners in 1887 and only his death prevented his appointment as the first official Chinese Consul General.

As one who always wore Chinese dress but had the manners of an Englishman, Lowe Kong Meng was a man of two cultures who was respected by all for his humanity, culture, and generosity. At a time of extreme racial intolerance preceding the introduction of the White Australia Policy, he sought mutual understanding. In this year of the centenary of his death, the words in one of his many letters to Government are particularly potent: 'Australia will look back with regret and shame on many of the injustices meted out to my countrymen.'

Karl Deuffel
1843–1933
Migrant child's epic trek
Written by: Louise Egerton
Nominated by: Joe Egan; Merleen M. Freeman

Eleven-year-old Karl Deuffel left Germany in November 1854 with his parents aboard the *Merbz*, the first recorded ship to carry German immigrants to Australia. Karl, his parents and his younger brother and sister were among 267 migrants destined for Nundah, the first free settlement in northern New South Wales. Most of the passengers were friends and relatives from the Tauber Valley, recruited as labour for the new colony. Many wealthy squatters on the Darling Downs were losing their traditional labour to the gold fields and were in need of agricultural workers. The villagers had agreed to work for two years on the squatters' land to pay for their passage.

The sea voyage was a nightmare. Food and water were rationed and the medical supplies inadequate. Before long, typhus and measles had taken hold on the ship. By March 1855, when it docked in Moreton Bay, forty-six people, including Karl's mother, had died and had been tipped unceremoniously overboard.

The Deuffels arrived in Nundah griefstruck and unable to speak English, with Karl's father seriously ill. He was taken to Brisbane's convict hospital and died shortly after.

Karl, now twelve years old, was suddenly head of the household. Left to care for eight-year-old Andreas and three-year-old Amy, he decided to honour his father's bond and hope that the squatters would accept his labour in place of his father's. However, Tieryboo station, to which his father had been allocated, lay 350 kilometres west of Nundah, across the Great Divide.

There were almost no white settlements along the way, an uneasy Aboriginal population in the bush and a host of natural hazards. But Karl had no money so there was no alternative but to walk the entire distance with his little brother and sister. Miraculously, the three children arrived safely at Tieryboo. The boys were taken on as shepherds but what became of little Amy remains a mystery.

Karl continued to work on at Tieryboo after his two year contract. When the station was finally broken up Karl had saved enough money to buy one of the blocks of land. He married a German girl, bought his own team of bullocks and became a carrier on a regular run between Roma and Ipswich.

When Karl's wife died, he was left to raise five daughters and one son, which he did with skill and devotion.

Karl died in 1933, aged ninety. He never re-married and rarely spoke of his childhood but before he died he told his daughter how he and the other two small children had walked through the bush to reach Tieryboo.

Karl Deuffel, who, at twelve, walked 350 kilometres with his younger brother and sister to fulfil his dead father's bond

Adelaide Eliza Ironside
1831–1867
Painter and patriot
Written by: Jill Poulton
Nominated by: Jill Poulton

Adelaide Ironside was born into a socially mobile society. Her father, James Ironside, was a commercial gentleman. Her mother, Martha, a linguist, was the daughter of John Redman, probably a First Fleet marine and a woman, who was transported to the colony for forgery. Because of her father's drinking Adelaide's parents separated while she was still a toddler, and her mother devoted the rest of her life to caring for her delicate but very gifted daughter.

Adelaide was fortunate enough to gain the best classical education a colonial girl could obtain. She studied languages and sciences until, perhaps for her health, her mother took her to live on the secluded North Shore. Here, amid gum trees and solitude, Adelaide developed her love of the romantic and the supernatural. A psychic by nature, she was later to paint visions seen in a crystal ball.

Working prolifically in pencil, crayon and water colour, Adelaide had by her early twenties produced many delicate and exquisitely detailed portraits and pictures of flowers. Her forty-three 'Australian Wild Flowers' won her *mentions honorables* in 1855 when displayed at the Paris International Exhibition alongside the works of established male artists. At that time, even in Europe, women were not allowed into the prestigious male academies to sketch the nude from life and learn the figure drawing necessary in works of 'High Art'. They usually contented themselves with painting flora and fauna. Adelaide Ironside, however, a true romantic, was influenced by the emotive paintings of the English Pre-Raphaelites and was determined to compete in the male 'High Art' stakes.

One of the most influential people in Adelaide's early life was her pastor, Dr John Dunmore Lang, the radical Presbyterian minister, writer and politician, from whom she gained her strong Protestant and republican views. With Dr Lang's encouragement, Adelaide, just twenty-three years old, set off with her mother in 1855 to tread the classic ground of Italy.

On her arrival in Rome, Adelaide, a fluent speaker of Italian, set to work in her studio, despite a shortage of money, sketching portraits for a living. At the same time she continued studying for up to eighteen hours a day. She also spent a summer at Perugia in central Italy, learning fresco-painting from a learned old artist-monk, as she hoped to fresco the walls of Sydney University and Parliament House on her return home.

Visiting Australians came to pay their respect and Bertie, Prince of Wales, visited her studio and bought a painting for five hundred pounds. William Charles Wentworth, who commissioned Adelaide to draw his two daughters, paid a similar amount.

Adelaide was kind and generous. She was admired by artists and courtiers in Rome, and a monk, Padre Serafino, fell completely in love with her. Even John Ruskin, the illustrious art critic, fell under her spell. Although a Protestant, she received a private audience with Pope Pius IX, who gave her a silver medal for her contribution to art.

The highlight of Adelaide's career came when she went to London to display her four oil paintings, 'The Marriage in Cana', 'The Pilgrim of Art' (a self-portrait of the artist and her mother), 'St Catherine' and 'St Agnes' at the 1862 International Exhibition. These works were highly commended and negotiations were begun, but never completed, for the acquisition of 'The Marriage in Cana' (now hanging in St Paul's College at Sydney University) by the citizens of Sydney. The broken promises of men in authority to arrange such a purchase greatly saddened the young artist's heart.

On her return to Rome, she was elected a member of the elite Academy of the Quirites and despite her failing health, painted her last major

A crayon sketch thought to be one of Adelaide Ironside's idealised self-portraits. Considerably plainer than this image allows, Adelaide was otherwise gifted and brilliant company. The dashing Dan Deniehy, whom she loved, remained her friend but married a prettier face. Adelaide remained single. Mitchell Library

work, 'The Adoration of the Magi,' which she took to England for the Dublin International Exhibition in 1865. In London, she became a friend and pupil of the eminent John Ruskin. Though patronising in his criticism of her work, he acknowledged her great talent and they developed a curious father-daughter relationship.

Meanwhile, in Sydney, Lang had tried unsuccessfully to persuade Parliament to give Adelaide a study-grant. He also endeavoured to raise funds for the colony's purchase of 'The Marriage in Cana', but few were interested in the artist they had all but forgotten. Back in Rome, Adelaide sank into a decline and died of tuberculosis — and perhaps a broken heart — still unrecognised by all but a handful of her countryfolk.

Small and frail, with deeply-penetrating eyes, Adelaide was probably more homely than her idealised self-portraits reveal. In her youth in Sydney, perhaps through Lang's Australian League, Adelaide met and fell in love with the dashing Dan Deniehy, a superb orator, literary critic and politician. Though his ardour changed to a deep friendship after he married a beauty, he maintained an unbroken correspondence with Adelaide until his death, shortly before hers.

Adelaide, like Deniehy, had been a member of Sydney's intellectual circle which met regularly at the lawyer Stenhouse's home at Balmain. She also wrote fiery, patriotic poems some of which were published in the republican *People's Advocate*. In Rome, Garibaldi was her republican hero. Since she saw him as the saviour of Italy she painted Garibaldi as both the bridegroom and Christ in her 'Marriage in Cana'.

Adelaide was like a hothouse flower, unique and exotic. She was Australia's first professional woman artist, but no Ironside paintings hang today in any major galleries and few remember her. Yet she was a woman ahead of her times. Her contributions include not only her works of art, but also her courageous determination to achieve professional recognition in a male-dominated field, and in a country which at that time showed little appreciation of the fine arts.

Andrew Cleary
1839–1917
The bushrangers' foe
Written by: Terri McCormack
Nominated by: Rosalie E. McNeill

Born in Tipperary in 1839, Andrew Cleary arrived in Sydney in 1859 with his young wife Honorah O'Connor. He joined the Metropolitan Police, a far less efficient force than the semi-military Royal Irish Constabulary in which he had previously served. In 1861, Cleary was one of seventy metropolitan police sent, together with military and naval detachments, to quell anti-Chinese riots on the Lambing Flat goldfields. He later recalled their disquieting reception: 'The diggers gathered in front of us and gave three cheers for the military, three more for the Jack Tars, and boo'hoos and hoots for the police. It

Andrew Cleary, an 'old bushman', some years after his capture of bushranger Captain Starlight whom Clearly declared to be 'the best company I ever travelled with'

hurt us a bit, as we were sore-footed and had been standing in our position for some hours.' The police were unable to prevent atrocities against the Chinese and were withdrawn to Yass.

After working with the gold escort on the Lachlan diggings, Cleary was transferred to the mounted police and, in July 1862, sent to Coonamble. 'And then,' he told an *Evening News* reporter in 1912, 'my bushranging career commenced'.

In April 1863, he received word that magistrate Robert Lowe had shot one of two highwaymen on the Mudgee road. The other fled along the flooded Namoi River with Cleary in pursuit. 'Near Walgett,' said Cleary, 'I got within twenty-four hours of him, but my horse knocked up and I had to get a remount from Bungle Gully.' He caught up with him after a day and a half and brought him back through Coonamble and Dubbo to Mudgee gaol to await trial with several other bushrangers.

On race day in Mudgee, everyone went to the big event, including the gaoler who left his warders in charge. The imprisoned bushrangers seized the warders' revolvers and escaped, led by Tom Dillon whom Cleary described as 'a daring highway robber'. Learning that Dillon had been sighted on a fine stolen racehorse, Cleary set off with a black tracker. After a casual drink at Hall's public house, forty kilometres from Coonamble, Dillon swam the Castlereagh River with his stolen revolver in his mouth. Determined to get man, horse, and revolver, Cleary gave his assistant 'a stiff nip of whisky to give him extra pluck to swim the river'. He surprised the bushranger leaning against a station fence and disarmed him, only to find his ammunition too saturated for use. On being handcuffed, the enraged Dillon smashed the irons against the fence but was eventually brought back to Mudgee to receive a sentence of fourteen years.

Cleary was promoted to Sergeant and transferred to Bourke. In April 1866, he and two colleagues captured Sullivan, Clarke and Donnelly in Gordon's Hotel where, in dirty tattered clothes after the pursuit, they were themselves mistaken for bushrangers. Cleary was gratified by the capture of this trio who, among other outrages, had assaulted an elderly woman. A heatstroke attack in 1867 led to Cleary's transfer to the Jindera Mountains to search for the notorious Clarke brothers. His part in their capture in April 1867 is unrecorded and by February 1868 he was back in Bourke with the rank of Senior Sergeant.

As Cleary said, 'The men we had to deal with in those days were wild enough for anything.' Police efforts were constantly hampered by lack of cooperation from the bush populace who admired — or feared — the adventurous highwaymen, and by contemptuous criticism from politicians decrying the loss of gold consignments and squatters' property.

In October 1868, Cleary and Thomas Roberts were summoned to William Shearer's public house on the Warrego River where Senior Constable McCabe had been wounded by Captain Starlight after a pursuit from Queensland. Starlight, also injured, escaped with the assistance of his partner Charles Rutherford. McCabe, like Cleary, a former member of the Irish Constabulary, died twenty-one days later.

Receiving information on 20 December, Cleary, Constable Johns and several black trackers followed Starlight to John Smith's station in the Gundabooka Mountains near Cobar. When fired on, the bushranger fell from his horse, dropped his pouch of ammunition, and fled up a mountain. Johns and Smith guarded the horses and waterholes while Cleary and the trackers scoured the rocky ledges for twenty-four hours. It was early on Christmas morning when the keen-sighted Mulga blacks excitedly discovered a footprint. Starlight was soon located in a deep cave. Cautiously lowering himself down, Cleary found a parched almost naked man shouting for water. 'Apart from arresting him,' he said, 'I was thankful for having saved him from the torments of thirst, starvation, and the ants.'

While escorting Starlight back to Bourke in leg-irons, Cleary found him 'the best company I ever travelled with'. Indeed, Cleary visited him in Darlinghurst gaol in later years as did the Chaplain, Father James Garvey, who secured his release in April 1884. Cleary knew Starlight as William Henry Pearson. This charming imposter died in Perth in 1909 as Major Patrick Pelly, VC, one of his many pseudonyms. He had accidentally swallowed the hair dye used to disguise himself as a distinguished employee of the Perth Geological Department.

Andrew Cleary remained at Bourke until 1872 but years of heavy bush work led to ill health which forced him to retire on 20 December 1882. His wife had accompanied him on all his postings and had borne ten children, only one of whom had survived. By 1912, Cleary was living as a bachelor in a Redfern boarding house. Described as a tall, big-boned Irishman with a genial nature, he told a reporter 'an old bushman can always manage for himself'. On his wall was an illuminated address from the grateful citizens of Bourke, his only recognition for the capture of Starlight. This now hangs proudly in the home of his great grand-daughter. Stirring bushranging tales only remind her of the courage and dedication of men like Andrew Cleary.

David Carson
1843–1931

Pastoral and mining entrepreneur
Written by: Terri McCormack
Nominated by: Janet Evans

David Carson was born in Melbourne in July 1843, one year after his Scottish-born parents arrived in this struggling village on the Yarra River. His early memories, recorded in letters and diaries, vividly recall the hardships of daily life in the Port Phillip settlement, the excitement of the gold rushes, the fear of bushrangers, and such natural hazards as the bushfire which claimed the lives of two brothers and a sister. His father established a successful boot and shoe business and sent his son to Scotch College to be educated.

In 1859, John Carson and a group of fellow Scotsmen secured long leases on land in north Australia which had been described in the explorer Ludwig Leichhardt's journal. With the separation of Queensland from New South Wales, regulations were introduced for compulsory stocking of leased land. In 1863, young David was sent north

David Carson, Melbourne businessman, geologist, botanist, pioneer of remote regions of Queensland and accomplished diarist

to join William Kirk and James Sutherland on the land they held in partnership with his father at Suttor Creek, inland from Mackay, then the most northerly property in Australia.

Soon after his arrival by ship at Rockhampton, Carson became inured to the discomfort of prolonged travel on horseback on the twelve-day trek with a large party of men and horses to Suttor Creek. Some months were spent stocking the station with sheep, planting gardens, building stockyards and quarters, shearing, and gathering information about land and hostile Aboriginal tribes further out.

In November 1863, Carson and a party of men set off with 7000 sheep, fifty horses, four bullock teams, and provisions for the unknown Barcoo country. After crossing the flooded Belyando River by improvised bridge, the party spelled the sheep at one of the few dry spots with good green feed. At sunrise on 24 December, 'the camp presented a shocking sight with about 200 sheep dead and about that number poorly'. Carson, who had inherited an interest in botany from his father, suspected that the cause was a small weed with a blue flower. Samples were sent to Dr Mueller at Melbourne's Botanical Gardens who classified it as the deadly *Gastolobium grandiflora*. Carson's party and a parallel group led by a Mr Ranken, lost some 10 000 sheep, but many more were saved by early identification of this bush.

With the remaining sheep, Carson's party pushed on through the flooded country, losing more stock through drowning or poisoning. One shepherd was killed by the ever-present Aborigines who 'were very clever in following and watching you without giving any indication of their presence until a favourable opportunity arose'. When the party was flooded in for weeks, Carson returned alone to the bullock drays 160 kilometres behind for medicine to treat malaria and ague which were debilitating the men. 'With the black fires keeping me company, I skirted the flooded country...I saw on a clifftop...a number of blacks. They were painted and they stood up and yelled and shook spears and nullas...They were the same tribe who had killed Mr Ranken's man recently.' To everyone's astonishment, Carson got through to the drays without being attacked and returned with supplies.

On 10 March 1864, Carson reached Walker Creek and he and James Sutherland pegged out the boundary of Mt Walker Station, being the first settlers to bring sheep to the Flinders country. In later years, Marathon, Keira and Clutha were added to the holdings.

Carson's diaries detail the hazards, disasters, and triumphs involved in pioneering this remote corner of North Queensland but, more importantly, they reveal the enquiring mind of a man intrigued by every aspect of his strange environment. His fascination not only with flora and fauna but also with fossil remains prompted him to send a collection of geological samples to Melbourne. At a Royal Society meeting on 19 August 1865, Professor Frederick McCoy credited Carson with the discovery of a cretaceous rock system in Australia. Carson remained on the Flinders properties as settlement expanded to the north and west until commercial panic and unprecedented floods necessitated the sale of the stations and his return to Melbourne in 1870.

Carson married Annie Baker in 1876, fathered seven children, and attempted to settle down as manager of his father's shoe emporium. He participated in Melbourne's public life, taking an interest in the National Museum which housed his collections of marine and geological specimens, but his attraction to the vast outback was undiminished. As a director of the Victorian Squatting Company in 1886, he engaged Surveyor Charles A. Burrows to explore a lease for him in the Kimberleys where both a river and an escarpment were named after him.

Mines and minerals were Carson's first love and, during the 1880s, he travelled throughout Queensland and Central Australia searching for specimens and opening up mining ventures. At his Lake Eyre mine, his experiences with Aborigines differed markedly from those of his early Queensland years: 'They were splendid workmen and well worth the 20 shillings and tucker which was their rate of pay.' In 1905, he made a nostalgic return trip to North Queensland and was amazed to find his old properties stocked with 200 000 sheep and equipped with artesian wells. In 1907, he was again involved in mining, having taken out a licence on a tin mine at Helensvale, near Cooktown.

Back in Melbourne once more, Carson found himself heavily indebted from his many ventures but with his spirit for new enterprises undaunted. He was enthusiastic about a ploughing system which would revolutionise farming methods, later patented by another. 'At seventy-six years of age I suppose it was rather too late for me to pursue it too much but I would like to be a part of the progress.'

David Carson died at his Elsternwick home on 30 November 1931. He left sons who inherited his faith in Australia's future and a written account of his long and fruitful life which well illustrates the courage and spirit of so many of our pioneers.

Beattie Traill
1841–1924
'The Grace Darling of Tasmania'
Written by: Cathy Peake
Nominated by: Jean Dixon

A winter storm 'of unusual severity' had been raging for several days on 26 June 1863, when a ship entering Tasmania's Tamar River signalled that it required the services of a pilot. A boarding boat containing the head pilot and four others set out, successfully off-loaded the pilot, and then was capsized returning to shore, pitching the four men into the water some 180 metres from land.

Three of them, after struggling for well over an hour, managed to get ashore, but the fourth — apparently nearly unconscious and barely visible — seemed to be tossing about on the foam-covered waves. Beattie Traill's mother asked her if she could swim out and assist him. An expert swimmer, Beattie did not hesitate, though the agitated lighthouse keeper shouted that the rescue would never succeed, and another man refused to help her tie a long rope around her waist, declaring that to do so would mean her death.

Once the rope was tied, she plunged into the waves fully dressed and buoyed up by a new crinoline. Her rescue was retold in the Launceston *Telegraph* on the fifty-ninth anniversary of the event:

'Swimming strongly she lost sight of the man, but suddenly discovered his body being dashed against a rock. Hastening to the spot she had the greatest difficulty in attaching the rope to the drowning man, but she succeeded, and after a grim struggle with waves reached the shore with the man in tow. He was still alive, but had nearly succumbed...'

Only one hoop of Beattie's crinoline remained when she emerged from the sea and she had lost the rest of her clothing. However, she emerged a heroine.

John Parry
1842–1887
King Island's heroic rescuer
Written by: Billy Marshall-Stoneking
Nominated by: Cynthia Vivian

Second Officer John Parry was worried. The ship *Netherby*, driven before storms for the past two weeks, was now entering the most treacherous phase of its long journey. Anyone who had sailed these waters knew the reputation of Bass Strait. It was a reputation that was well deserved. Parry could think of at least seven ships that had gone down here, all victims of the perils of Cape Otway and King Island. The narrow strait had tested the best sea captains, and found many of them wanting.

Unfortunately, Parry's fears were well founded. On the evening of 14 July 1866, the *Netherby* struck a reef off the west coast of King Island. Parry knew at once that she was irrevocably stranded, and set about preparing the passengers to abandon ship.

Collecting whatever provisions they could manage, the 451 emigrants and crew huddled on deck and gazed at the ravaged lifeboats. Only one lifeboat remained intact.

By some means left unrecorded by history, a lifeline was taken ashore and secured there. Then the one remaining lifeboat was pulled back and forth along this line until all passengers and crew were ferried to safety.

Once ashore, however, Parry soon realised they were not out of danger. Although provisions had been brought from the *Netherby*, these would not be adequate to feed so many; and it might be months before another ship passed this way and rescued them. Parry, showing remarkable courage and presence of mind, realised that there was only one alternative — to trek back along the coast to the lighthouse at Cape Wickham and raise the alarm.

On 18 July, the lighthouse keeper at Cape Wickham recorded: '...the Second Officer and six passengers arrived from the wreck of the *Netherby* and reported that she was stranded...with 451 souls on board, all saved.'

Parry and the others, with little rest or food, had taken four days to reach the lighthouse, a journey of nearly fifty kilometres. But even here salvation eluded them. Their hopes for rescue were shattered when they learned that the telegraph at the lighthouse was out of action.

But this was not the worst of it.

Six months' worth of rations had been delivered to the lighthouse several weeks earlier, but the quantity of supplies had been calculated on the basis of providing sustenance for four men, not 451 men, women and children. Unless Parry could find some other way of getting word to the outside world, starvation on a massive scale seemed inevitable. Parry contemplated his options, then, with three others, commandeered the lighthouse's whaleboat and set off for the mainland.

Even in the summer months, such a journey was difficult, but in the middle of winter, in an open boat, Parry and the others were inviting catastrophe. Still, it was their only chance. Battling high winds and freezing temperatures, Parry kept a steady course to the north. His single-mindedness did not allow room for contemplating failure, and his mates took heart from his courage.

Thirty-two hours later, after a miracle run, Parry stepped ashore. Without stopping to rest, he made his way to a nearby sheep station and broke the news of the *Netherby's* fate. Next day, he rode a horse into Geelong where he telegraphed Melbourne. Taking a train into the city, Parry joined the newly-formed rescue party. Two ships set sail on the 29 July and collected the survivors at King Island.

But even after he was assured of the passengers' safety, Parry's job was still not over. Knowing that the amount of money paid by the captain to the crew would depend on how much the captain received from the salvagers, Parry stayed behind to guard the *Netherby* from looters and pirates, a task which he carried out faithfully until his makeshift shack was destroyed by fire under suspicious circumstances.

When the news of the rescue operation and Parry's unflinching efforts made the Melbourne press, it was suggested that Parry be given a gold medal. But there was not enough money in the Rescue Committee's fund for this. Instead, a certificate from the shipping line thanking Parry for his services was the only recognition he received. Today, even on King Island, there are few who remember either his name or his deeds.

John Parry, the ship's officer whose determination and resourcefulness saved the lives of 450 shipwrecked survivors from the Netherby

Frederick Charles B. Fairey
1844–1924

Seafaring evangelist
Written by: Terri McCormack
Nominated by: Glenn Moore; Ross K. Turvey

On a dark night in February 1879, a bearded cleric stepped ashore at Hobart Town and informed incredulous onlookers that he had just spent a month negotiating his twelve-foot (3.7 metre) wooden canoe around Tasmania's eastern coast from his parish at Forth on the north-west coast.

Those who knew Rev Fairey would not have been surprised. Born in Brighton, England, in 1844, he had spent many adventurous years in the merchant navy and South America before migrating in 1876

Rev Frederick Charles Bonfield Fairey with his 'ministerial assistant', the Evangelist, *the canoe in which he took the Word to isolated settlements*

Rev Bonfield Fairey, who conducted a mission with a difference

to Australia. By 1878, he had married an Australian girl and was an ordained Congregational minister at St Kilda in Melbourne.

Marooned ashore, Fairey came up with an ingenious idea for combining his love of the sea and his mission to spread the Gospel. He ordered a seagoing 'Rob Roy' canoe. Invented in Scotland, this versatile vessel carried a stove, buoyancy tanks, waterproof apron, double-bladed paddle, linen lugsail, and a foot-operated rudder. How Fairey's parishioners and clerical colleagues reacted to this apparition is unrecorded but the tiny craft responded well to its sea trials to Geelong and back through treacherous Port Phillip Heads. With the name *Evangelist* painted in blue letters on the varnished bow, the sleek little thirty-six kilogram canoe was ready to help spread God's word to the isolated inhabitants of coastal and river settlements.

When Reverend Fairey and his family were transferred to the River Forth parish in Tasmania, the *Evangelist* accompanied them, lodging in the spare room while the minister did most of his work on horseback. When called to Launceston on business, he seized the opportunity to make the arduous trip by canoe, sleeping overnight on offshore islands.

The voyage to Hobart during his annual holidays in 1879 enabled him to make ministerial visits to outlying settlements while testing the stamina and endurance of himself and his canoe. Sailing or paddling for twenty sleepless hours at a time, he was in constant danger of being dashed onto the rocky coast and on one occasion suffered a temporary setback when he capsized, losing his mast, compass, field glasses and boots. His appearance was invariably greeted with amazement and delight by such isolated villages as that at Seymour where farmers' wives walked through a stormy night to attend their first service in two years. Further on in his journey, heavy seas off Blackman Bay forced him to spend an exhausting night battling the elements offshore. When he finally found a landing place on Forestier Peninsula and dragged himself on shore, he had to haul his canoe and gear overland to the settlement where, uncharacteristically, he rested for two days before completing the final leg of his epic trip to the Derwent.

Reverend Fairey and the *Evangelist* spent many years ministering to up-river settlements in Queensland, South Australia, New Zealand and New South Wales. One of his trips took him 240 kilometres down the Murray River. In 1881, he was honoured by being invited to demonstrate the finer points of his canoe to visiting royalty aboard HMS *Baccante*. One can imagine his grief when his 'ministerial assistant' burned to the waterline in North Adelaide in September 1888.

A father of eight, Reverend Fred C.B. Fairey died at Tempe, New South Wales, in 1924. He was an evangelist whose mission extended far beyond the four walls of a church and whose vision of Heaven must surely have included some challenging form of water transport.

John Brown Gribble
1847–1893
'The Blackfellow's Friend'
Written by: Niall Lucy
Nominated by: Fr Greg Davies; Lorna J. Harris

Recent years have seen the beginnings of an attempt to raise the white community's awareness of the disastrous effects of European settlement on the country's original inhabitants. However, the devastation of Aboriginal tribal culture and the inhumane treatment of the Aborigines were not previously allowed to go entirely unopposed. There were, in the past, a handful of Europeans who, like the Reverend 'Benjamin' John Brown Gribble, were appalled at 'the terrible wrongs to which [these people] have been subjected' and risked their livelihoods and their lives to act against this oppression.

John Brown Gribble, the only son of Cornish parents, was born in 1847 and migrated to Australia with his family the following year. The Gribbles settled in Sydney at first, until Benjamin Snr rushed to Ballarat in Victoria in the 'Roaring Fifties' with his son, four daughters and his wife, Mary, in search of gold. John Brown was sent to work by day as a pit-boy down the mines, and studied hard at night to gain an education. At the age of twenty, after the family had moved to Geelong, he married Mary Ann Elizabeth Bulmer with whom he had four sons and five daughters.

In 1876 John Brown Gribble was admitted to the ministry of the United Free Methodist Church. He later joined the Congregational Union of Victoria and became the first resident missionary appointed to Jerilderie in the Riverina district. There, Gribble demonstrated the courage apparent throughout his life when he challenged Ned Kelly, one of whose gang had just relieved Gribble of his watch at gun point. Kelly returned the watch.

Here John Brown's work took him to outlying stations where he came into contact with remnants of Aboriginal tribes, 'in a condition most shocking to contemplate.' Resolving that something must be done to alleviate their 'wretchedness and woe,' he set out in 1879 with his

Reverend J. B. Gribble, founder of Warangesda home and school for Aborigines, fought all his life to improve the lot of Australia's original inhabitants

wife and children and £6 15s to found Warangesda ('Camp of Mercy') on the Murrumbidgee river at Darlington Point, New South Wales.

In spite of local opposition, Warangesda flourished. Cottages, store rooms, a schoolhouse, and a church were built in quick succession with the support of his family and the Aborigines, and 'in the course of two years quite a township sprang up in the lonely bush'. The school was a particular success, was recognised by the Department of Public Instruction and raised to the level of a public school, 'thereby securing to our institution all the facilities and benefits enjoyed by every white boy in the colony.'

Gribble was ordained by the Anglican Bishop Thomas of Goulburn in 1883 and was invited by Bishop Parry of Perth the following year to work among Aborigines in the Gascoyne River district of north-west Western Australia. Because of ill health, Gribble was advised by doctors first to take a sea voyage to England, where he embarked on a lecture tour to raise funds for the Gascoyne venture and published *Black But Comely*.

While he was still at Warangesda, Gribble's ministry was attacked in the Letters Page of the *Sydney Morning Herald* in 1882. A signatory purporting to be an Aborigine, but who was most likely a white troublemaker from the mission district, submitted a litany of complaints against the Reverend in a ludicrous parody of pidgin English. As comic as this letter was, it was a foreboding of far more threatening and malicious opposition to come.

Within three months of arriving in the Gascoyne region of Western Australia in 1885 to establish the new mission of Galilee, John Brown discovered that 'the whole district was confederate against me'. Local pastoralists had convened a public meeting, at which 'my person and work were thoroughly denounced, and a petition praying for my immediate withdrawal was prepared and signed'. A placard bearing the slogan 'DOWN WITH GRIBBLE AND HIS SUPPORTERS' was posted in the nearby township of Carnarvon, and a further petition was hawked about from house to house and sent to Bishop Parry. Gribble, who had never before encountered such organised hostility, quicky wrote to the *Inquirer* newspaper in Perth expressing his dismay and exposing the conspiracy against him. 'The majority of the settlers of the Gascoyne,' he maintained, '...want to be a law unto themselves.'

The pastoralists were protecting a system of slavery practised almost universally on station properties throughout the north-west interior and exposed by Gribble in his 1887 book, *Dark Deeds in a Sunny Land*.

Everywhere he went, Gribble was shocked by the rampant violence and abuse shown to Aborigines across the Gascoyne. Because enforced black labour was a cornerstone of prosperity in the region, hundreds of tribal Aborigines were 'run down and captured and taken to the stations' where they were made to sign papers they could not read enslaving them as bondservants to the pastoralists. Any who tried to escape were recaptured, 'taken to the Junction Police Station and there chained up for a few weeks'. The practice of distributing black women among white station hands was widespread and several pastoralists themselves were known to keep Aboriginal women as concubines against their will.

Nor could the Aborigines look to the police and the courts for justice. The police themselves often were guilty of violence towards blacks, especially to women, and the courts seldom upheld charges against the powerful pastoralists and their men and even less frequently inflicted harsh penalties on the few who *were* found guilty.

Gribble's humanitarian efforts were resisted throughout Western Australia. His own life was threatened many times, and the fear of reprisal from the station owners kept the number of Aborigines at the mission to a mere handful. In 1887, Gribble was forced to flee the colony when he lost a libel suit brought against him by the pastoralists and returned to New South Wales where his family had remained. In 1905, Government investigations vindicated Gribble's claims, but John Brown's body had been mouldering in the grave for twelve years when the enquiry officially cleared his name.

For a time Gribble was engaged in parish work in the Goulbourn diocese, until his attention was drawn to the country around Bellender Ker Mountains in North Queensland. Taking leave of absence from his parish, Gribble journeyed to Cairns at his own expense and obtained from the Government a land reserve on which he would found the Yarrabah Mission. He raised funds on a lecture tour of eastern Australia and returned on 12 June 1892, accompanied only by a white labourer, a South Sea Islander, and an Aboriginal boy. Within three months they had cleared a path for a road and had started work on several buildings when Gribble was brought down with malaria and taken to Prince Alfred Hospital in Sydney. He died a short time later at his home in Marrickville at the age of forty-five. He was succeeded at Yarrabah by his eldest son, the Reverend Ernest Gribble, who continued his father's passionate advocacy.

The younger Gribble continued to speak out, publishing in the 1930s two books about his father's work and the continuing 'deplorable condition' of the black community.' The older Gribble lies buried in Waverley Cemetery with these words on his grave:

> In Loving Memory of John Brown Gribble
> Founder of Warangesda
> The Blackfellow's Friend 3.6.1893.

Tommaso Enrico Fiaschi
1853–1927
Renaissance man
Written by: Andrea Jane Loder
Nominated by: Renata Salteri

Few nineteenth-century Italians migrated to Australia. When twenty-one-year-old Tommaso Enrico Fiaschi arrived in north Queensland from Florence in 1875, only about a thousand of his fellow countrymen had settled in the Australian colonies. Most of those who had preceded him were agricultural labourers; others had come during the gold rushes. Tommaso Fiaschi, however, was one of a small group of Italian professionals who built successful careers here in the arts and sciences between 1850 and 1900, and who passed on aspects of their nation's rich artistic and intellectual heritage to Anglo-Australians.

The son of a professor of mathematics and an Englishwoman who had tutored the children of a Florentine prince, Tommaso Fiaschi studied medicine and surgery at the universities of Florence and Pisa. His first job in Australia was as a doctor on the Palmer River gold fields where he won some small fame for his innovative treatment of malaria. After eighteen months in this frontier environment he moved south to the more civilised surroundings of Sydney and a position as house surgeon at St Vincent's Hospital, run by the Sisters of Charity.

The tall, handsome young doctor soon married, but to the horror of his employers his bride was one of the hospital nuns, Irish-born Catherine Anne Reynolds. In the furore that followed, the couple escaped to Florence where Tommaso continued his medical studies and Catherine gave birth to the first of their five children. 'As you can understand,' he wrote later, 'I had to take my wife away and marry her. I couldn't very well ask permission!'

On returning to Australia in 1879 they settled just outside Sydney in the quiet country town of Windsor, on the Hawkesbury River. There, in addition to setting up a medical practice, Dr Fiaschi established a vineyard, 'Tizzana' — named after a region outside Florence — which is still in operation today. He began with a little over two hectares and as demand grew, increased his plantings to a little over twenty. In 1891 the *Windsor and Richmond Gazette* reported that 'Dr Fiaschi was convinced that the taste for colonial wine only needed cultivation...his aim was to place upon the market the perfect article, both in colour and flavour.' Tommaso Fiaschi remained active in the wine industry for the rest of his life, setting up cellars in Sydney, another vineyard at Mudgee, and acting as a president of the New South Wales Wine Producers' Association.

In 1883 Dr Fiaschi took his family back to Sydney. Soon after, he began a long affiliation with Sydney Hospital as an honorary surgeon, which included pioneering work in Listerian and bone surgery, hydatid disease and goitre treatment. This was interspersed by a notable career as an army medical officer, beginning in 1891 when he was appointed an honorary surgeon-captain in the New South Wales Lancers.

Dr Fiaschi served overseas in three wars, with the armies of both his adopted country and his native land. In 1896 he was in Abyssinia, treating Italian prisoners of war, and was subsequently decorated for valour by the Italian Government. In 1899 he went to the Boer War with the Australian forces, and was awarded the Distinguished Service Order for conspicuous bravery and devotion to duty — on one occasion while searching the trenches for wounded he captured a troupe of Boer soldiers. Although he was sixty-one when World War I broke out, he took command of an Australian field hospital in Greece and later worked for the Italian Red Cross at the Austrian front, accompanied by his second wife, Amy Curtis, a nurse he had married after Catherine's death in 1912. Back in Australia in 1917 he joined the Australian Army Medical Corps Reserve as a colonel, and by his retirement had risen to the rank of Honorary Brigadier-General.

Dr Fiaschi's military habits became part of his personality, making him somewhat eccentric in civilian life. So stringent was his ward discipline at Sydney Hospital that he would have the house doctor and nurses stand to attention when he entered the room, and, permitting no unnecessary conversation, he did his rounds with a quick step and keen searching eyes that let no detail escape his attention. In spite of his strictness and legendary outbursts of bad temper, he was nevertheless greatly loved by his patients and colleagues for his compassion, sense of humour, and dedication to his profession.

In 1926 he celebrated fifty years of professional life and community service at a dinner organised by the Dante Alighieri Society, established for the promotion of Italian literature and language in the late nineteenth century by an Italian homesick for his culture in a foreign land. Tommaso Fiaschi had founded the first Australian branch in Sydney in 1895. The Society had gone into suspension the following year, however, when Fiaschi went off to the wars. It was eventually re-inaugurated by him in May 1925.

The dinner that the Society gave to honour its founder was attended by representatives of the diverse sections of Australian society with which he had been involved. In reply to speeches referring to him as a pioneer in many fields, Dr Fiaschi exclaimed that he was overjoyed to hear himself described as such, for there was no one on earth he admired more than the Australian pioneer.

The man described by one of his colleagues as 'a fine surgeon, great citizen, soldier and patriot', died the following year at the age of seventy-three — 'regretted by all, respected and beloved' — from broncho-pneumonia contracted after sleeping outdoors at his Mudgee vineyard. He is remembered, along with his son Piero who was also a surgeon and a military medical officer, by the 'Il Porcellino' statue outside Sydney Hospital, donated in 1968 by his daughter Clarissa, the Marchesa Torrigiani, as 'a link of friendship between Italy and Australia'. It is a replica of a fountain that has stood in Tommaso Fiaschi's birthplace of Florence since the Renaissance.

Dr Tommaso Fiaschi, surgeon, soldier, vintner and founder of the Dante Alighieri Society in Australia. Sydney Hospital Archives

Jesse Dowsett
1843–1931

The man who fought with a legend
Written by: Billy Marshall-Stoneking
Nominated by: Maurie Albert

Sunday 27 June 1880, dawned cold and grey in Benalla, Victoria — the usual mid-winter morning. Jesse Dowsett, a guard with the Victorian Railways, did not give it a second thought. Today was his day off and he planned to enjoy it. Others could worry about the weather.

Jesse stoked the wood in the stove and had just poured himself a cup of tea when there was a knock on the door. Putting the kettle down, he went to answer it. A young boy, wide-eyed, faced him in the doorway, 'The station master wants to see you straightway.' Dowsett thanked him and closed the door.

To disturb a man on his one day off, it had to be important. Gulping down some tea, Dowsett threw on his coat and left.

'There's been some trouble,' the station master began. 'The Kelly gang killed a bloke over in the Wombat Ranges and the police are sending a special train up from Melbourne. I want you to hold yourself in readiness to assist them.'

Dowsett nodded. No-one had to tell him about the Kelly Gang. They had been terrorising eastern Victoria for the past two and a half years. The police particularly were keen to catch them since the Kellys had killed four of their own at Stringybark Creek two years earlier.

Dowsett frowned as he thought about the legend that had grown up around the band of bushrangers. Some people reckoned that Ned Kelly — the leader of the gang — was a latter-day Robin Hood. A group of labourers down at the hotel had even described him as a revolutionary, a good man who fought for the rights of the working man. All Dowsett knew was that any job involving a clash with the Kelly Gang was bound to be dangerous, and he wished they'd chosen some other place for their confrontation with the police. With the Special due in at one or two the following morning, Dowsett went home to get some sleep.

Early on the 28 June, Dowsett was woken and told that the Special had arrived from Melbourne. According to the police, the Kelly Gang had been reported 'fighting over at Glenrowan'. Dowsett grabbed his revolver — 'a splendid breech loader supplied to me by the Department' he explained in the detailed report he was to make of this day's events — and jumped onto the engine next to Driver Coleman.

Unknown to the police on the train, the gang had torn up the line just beyond Glenrowan station in an attempt to wreck the train. And their plan might have succeeded if it had not been for the courage of the local schoolmaster, Curnow, who stood beside the tracks with a lighted candle held behind a red scarf. Dowsett, spotting the light and seeing the man, ordered the driver to stop.

'What's going on?' Dowsett called out. 'The Kellys!' Curnow replied. 'They're in Glenrowan. They're holding the townspeople in the hotel.' Curnow then told Dowsett about the broken line, ready to tip the train over as soon as it nosed past the station. Dowsett conferred with the driver and the police. They would go on, taking care to stop short of the break. The train started up again.

Slowly, almost tentatively, the train pulled into the station at Glenrowan. The place was like a ghost town. Silently but swiftly, the troopers and black trackers took up their positions around the hotel. Then Dowsett heard something that made his heart stop.

'My attention was attracted by...some dreadful screams from a woman proceeding from the hotel. I went up in the bush a bit and then crawled on my knees to within about 40 yards of the [hotel] when I could see a woman with a baby in arms crying not to shoot her child...'

Dowsett called softly to the woman, urging her to come toward him. Just then, the police at the front opened fire, and Mrs Reardon, holding her child close to her, ran for Dowsett. Satisfied that she was unharmed, Dowsett accompanied her to the station where he placed her in the care of two other women, then returned to the fracas which had now moved from the hotel to the surrounding bush.

'I heard the thud of a bullet on the tree next to me. Looking back,

Jesse Dowsett, railway guard and forgotten hero of Glenrowan, in later life with his sister Mrs Priscilla Turner

Opportunity 75

'I saw what seemed a tremendous big black fellow with something like a blanket on him...'

It was 6.45 am, and the early morning light mixed with smoke and fog was eerie, other-worldly. Dowsett squinted at the large figure as it shambled slowly towards him. He called out to a constable, 'Who is that?' but there was no reply.

The figure continued to advance through the haze towards Dowsett. Then Dowsett noticed that he was carrying a revolver in one hand. 'All at once he opened fire on us, and then we knew it was one of "them" Someone yelled out, "Scatter boys", and everybody went for cover. I fired a few shots at him, but he stopped in a clump of saplings about fifty yards from us. I wanted to get closer [so] I worked along the ground in the scrub till I got to a fallen tree about thirty yards from him. [Then] I emptied my revolver at him...But he kept coming, and a harsh voice called out, "You can't shoot me...go on, try, you bloody dogs!"'

Dowsett had never seen anything like this before in his life. 'I gave him four shots for the centre of his body, and hearing, in fact, almost seeing, them jump off his body, I felt very queer. I said to myself, this must be the Devil himself.'

Suddenly, Dowsett and the others realised that they were faced with a man clad in armour. The bullets were bouncing right off and as they ricocheted in all directions, they produced weird, ringing, bell-like noises that filled the air.

Coming around behind the armour-clad figure, Dowsett started calling out, demanding that he surrender. 'Never while I have a shot left,' a gruff voice yelled back. Then Dowsett aimed his revolver directly

*Glenrowan railway station on the morning of 28 June 1880. Apparently oblivious to danger, a curious crowd gathered to watch the capture of the Kellys. Those with their backs to the camera are peering into the station master's office at the wounded Ned, just captured by police and Jesse Dowsett. The rest of the gang are still inside Jones' Hotel (on the left), which police are about to burn to the ground, killing Steve Hart, Dan Kelly and Joe Byrne.
Photograph by Wadeley, Copyright Collection, State Library of Victoria*

at the man's head, not more than five metres away, and fired. 'How do you like that old man?' Dowsett called out.

The armoured man turned laboriously and fired back. 'How do *you* like it?' he replied. Then he pointed his revolver at Dowsett a second time, and was just about to fire when a volley of gunfire brought him down. Dowsett had acted as decoy to allow Sergeant Steele to come close enough to shoot the man in his legs, the only unprotected parts of his body.

Dowsett and the police immediately converged on the man, and Dowsett wrenched the revolver out of his hand. Then Steele pulled the head gear off and the mouths of the troopers dropped open. It was Ned Kelly himself.

Superintendent Sadlier, appearing before the Kelly Reward Board, remarked that Dowsett... 'armed with a pistol only...behaved with great pluck'. For his services, Jesse was awarded the sum of £135 13s 9p — his share of the reward — and was promoted by the railways to passenger guard with a raise in pay amounting to one shilling extra a day.

Dowsett was transferred to Queenscliff after he was threatened by Kelly sympathisers, but he kept Ned's revolver until his death in 1931. During his lifetime, Jesse Dowsett was known as the man who helped capture Ned Kelly but after his death, his role faded from memory. As Ned would have said, 'Such is life.'

David Lindsay
1856–1922
Champion of the North
Written by: Billy Marshall-Stoneking
Nominated by: George A. Champion

The people of the Rembarunga tribe had known for several days that the white men were in their country. One evening, just on sunset, a large group of men from the tribe tracked the white men to their camp and, to test the fearlessness of these interlopers, if not to scare them away, began shouting and shaking their spears, giving every indication that they were preparing to attack. But the white outsiders remained calm. Their leader had taught them this if nothing else.

Then, suddenly, the Rembarunga men were startled by a jolt of sound, not unlike thunder during the rainy season. The sky exploded and light streaked through the trees high over their heads. The Rembarunga men scattered.

There was no-one to tell them about 'fireworks', and yet this was precisely the cause of the commotion. It was David Lindsay's way of keeping the natives at bay — rockets in Arnhem Land in 1883.

Numerous tales have been told of men and women who have been captured by the spirit of Australia's vast Northern Territory. Something about the place casts a spell, they say, so that once you have been there you can never completely free yourself of it. Even those who leave find themselves returning over and over again as if the place fulfilled some need nothing else could satisfy.

David Lindsay, explorer and surveyor, was one of the first white men to fall under the magic of the Territory. Born in Goolwa, South Australia, on 20 June 1856, he grew up around Aboriginal people, and at a very early age learned about the Australian bush and the bush skills that had helped the Aborigines survive and transform even the harshest country into a home.

At the age of fifteen, Lindsay left school and worked for a short time as a chemist's assistant before joining the office staff of a mining agent in Adelaide. A bright boy, always eager and fascinated by new challenges, he was rewarded with an apprenticeship, and in 1873, joined the Survey Department of the South Australian Government as a cadet surveyor. In 1878, he was posted to the Northern Territory as a surveyor third class.

Lindsay was amazed by what he found. Here was a virtual Garden of Eden, a landscape as various as it was huge. From the wetlands of the far north to the grasslands and gibber plains in the south, the country seemed full of promise — a wilderness which, with hard work, could be transformed into one of Australia's greatest assets.

Then, in 1883, came a major turning point. Lindsay was appointed to head an expedition into some of the most remote and wild country in Northern Australia. From July to November, Lindsay's party traversed Arnhem Land in the far north of the Northern Territory, a feat never before accomplished by a white man; and though they were confronted and even attacked by several groups of Aborigines, not one man was lost.

Lindsay put his success down to the fact that he understood 'the ways of the natives'. 'One must trust,' he later commented, 'to the moral effect of an outward show of calmness, coolness and determination. I have at times turned a mob of howling demons thirsting for our blood into friends who have led us later to water and brought us food.'

Back in Adelaide, Lindsay spent a brief period working for the Water Conservation Department of South Australia, but the lure of the Territory proved too strong, and by 1885 he had outfitted the Great Central Exploring Expedition at his own expense and, together with six men and twelve camels, headed north again, this time to explore the unknown country along the Northern Territory-Queensland border, all the way to the Gulf of Carpenteria.

While on this expedition, Lindsay made extensive property surveys in the Barkly Tablelands, traced the Finke River to its mouth and sought information concerning the fate of the explorer, Ludwig Leichhardt, who had disappeared in the Gulf region in 1848. An attempt to cross the Simpson Desert proved unsuccessful because of inadequate supplies of water.

Lindsay's plans for further expeditions were abruptly curtailed with the collapse of the Commonwealth Bank of South Australia in 1886, resulting in the complete loss of his savings. But even financial hardship could not keep him from the land he had grown to love.

In 1887, he carried out mineral surveying work for an English syndicate, and reported on the gold-bearing potential of several mines near Port Darwin. In the following year he surveyed and planned the township of Alice Springs. Finally, he returned to South Australia, travelling on horseback, accompanied only by an Aboriginal boy. The journey

David Lindsay, FRGS, explorer, surveyor, and one of the first white men to fall under the spell of the Northern Territory. On his favourite desert transport, the camel. Coolgardie, 1894. Mitchell Library

of 2200 kilometres lasted five weeks, and took Lindsay and his young companion through some of the driest and most inhospitable country in Australia.

Back in Adelaide, Lindsay was made a Fellow of the Royal Geographical Society of London, then worked for a time as a sharebroker. But there was little to compare with the adventures he had known in the bush and he found himself, once again, growing restless. 'In the desert,' he wrote, 'what a man is counts for but little; what he can do, for much.'

Lindsay longed to return to the Territory, but had no idea when this might be possible. Then, in 1891, he was appointed to lead the Elder Scientific Exploring Expedition to explore the interior of Central Australia, a task which he welcomed with great enthusiasm. It was on this expedition that he discovered a great extension of the artesian

David Lindsay with Aboriginal child in the Great Victorian Desert, September 1891, when he was leader of the Elder Scientific Exploring Expedition. Lindsay was proud of never having harmed an Aborigine

basin, extending 1100 kilometres across the country. In addition, he reported 'possibly auriferous' — gold-bearing — country around Coolgardie, Western Australia, an observation which would soon be proven correct. By the time he had finished his work, he had travelled thousands of kilometres through unmapped country, crossing the Great Victorian Desert — the first time this had ever been done using camels.

Lindsay was an adventurer and an astute observer, but he also possessed a natural ingenuity. He recalled: 'My beard grew so long that it became very useful. Frequently when the mosquitoes were excessively troublesome, I was accustomed to fasten it over the face like a veil to keep them off.' His long beard had other uses as well. As a filter, for example. With it doubled over his mouth, he found he could 'drink more freely from water full of animalculae'.

Certainly, Lindsay never tired of extolling the virtues of the Northern Territory, and was always seeking ways of interesting Australians in its marvellous possibilities. In 1910, believing that the Commonwealth would expedite the establishment of a rail link between Darwin and Adelaide, he appeared before the Bar of the Federal Houses of Parliament where he advised a joint sitting that the Commonwealth should take over the administration of the Northern Territory from the South Australian government. A year later, as Lindsay had hoped, power was transferred from Adelaide to Canberra.

For Lindsay, 'the great problem awaiting early solution for North Australia — the empty North — [was], can it be settled by white races, or must it be left empty?' To Lindsay, a product of his time, those were the only two choices.

But Lindsay, for all his racial bias and unquestioned belief in white supremacy, was not a man who sought confrontation with, or destruction of, the Aborigines. 'He put the lives of his men and animals first, but always boasted that he never harmed or killed an Aborigine.'

Lindsay died in Darwin on 17 December 1922, while trying to purchase land for the development of a cotton industry. He was buried in the Old Gardens Road Cemetery in Darwin, but his gravestone was destroyed in the Japanese attack on Darwin in 1942. It was as if the spell of the Territory had worked its final magic and absorbed him into its vast landscape for ever.

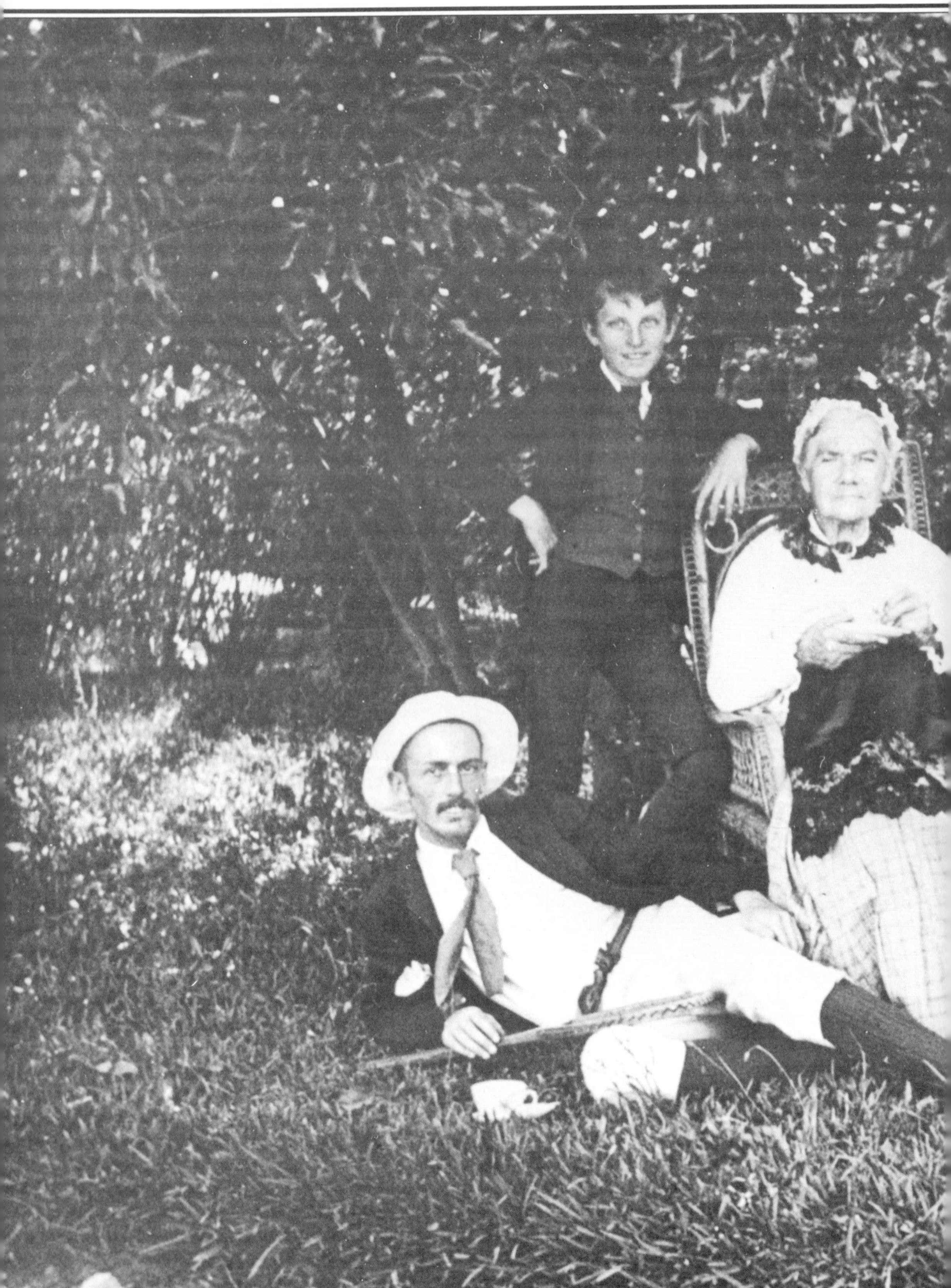

3
Progress
1884–1914

The *Bulletin* warned its readers against them: 'Beware women with a mission!'. But, despite its powerful and lasting influence, the *Bulletin* and its readers could not stop the women who fought for social reform, the rights of women and children, and female suffrage.

They were city women, product of the urbanisation that characterised the second half of the nineteenth century, and which brought with it the usual companions of industrial progress — slums, disease, exploitation and despair. Like their sisters in the outback, these women were courageous and resilient. Apparently so unalike, Emma the sweatshop worker, Maybanke the teacher, and Dora, trained to be a gentleman's wife, had much in common — they turned the necessity of supporting a family into a career and a passionate commitment to social justice.

These stories offer several perspectives on progress. For Topsy Hansen, as for the country itself, progress was, in part, ironic — a progression towards irretrievable loss. But, by the outbreak of World War I, largely through the efforts of these forgotten women, the nation that these colonies had become was acclaimed as 'the social laboratory of the world'.

Pattie Lewis Fotheringhame
1852–1955

Journalist and pioneer photo-engraver
Written by: Suzy Baldwin
Nominated by: Joan Fotheringhame

Previous page. Maybanke Wolstenholme Anderson (centre right, behind table), writer, reformer and leader of the fight for women's suffrage, with (from left) her brilliant son Harry, youngest son Ted, mother Mrs Bessie Selfe, and Maude Fox, fiancée of Arthur (far right), Maybanke's son who was drowned in 1895. Sydney, c. 1890. Mitchell Library

One of the most interesting products of the women's movement of the nineteen sixties and seventies has been the reassessment of the traditional myths of Australian history. While the all-male and one horse pantheon of Australian gods is now generally acknowledged to be only a partial emblem of the spirit and history of the country, writing the missing women back into history has proved to be more difficult. Many of their achievements and contributions have been misappropriated or devalued, a large number have sunk without trace and others remain tantalisingly anonymous.

The *Bulletin*, a major influence in both the formation and dissemination of the traditional concept of 'the true Australian', has written its own history accordingly. But, although there is no mention of her in histories of Australia's most famous journal, there *was* a woman on the early *Bulletin*. Her name was Pattie Fotheringhame, formerly Lewis, and she was the *Bulletin's* — and probably Sydney's — first woman journalist.

Pattie was teaching music and writing for the *Mail* when her brother-in-law, W. H. Traill, proprietor and editor of the *Bulletin* from 1881–86, persuaded her to come over to his paper, where she wrote the social and music pages for seven years, both anonymously and under the pen-name 'Mab'.

On 19 May 1883, Traill launched the famous New Series *Bulletin* with its pink cover. The feature accorded most fanfare was 'NUMEROUS UNIQUE ILLUSTRATIONS' by American cartoonist Livingston 'Hop' Hopkins, hired by Traill on his recent trip to the United States at a lavish annual salary of £1000. These illustrations were reproduced by a brand-new process — photo-engraving. Still in its pioneering stages in America, photo-engraving was to revolutionise magazine printing. The *Bulletin* introduced the process to Australia through the pioneering work of Pattie Fotheringhame, who had single-handedly taught herself the technique by trial and almost fatal error.

The new process, in which the image was transferred photographically to a zinc plate and then etched, solved all the problems of the old wood-engraving process — the image could be enlarged or reduced, fine detail was retained and the artist did not have to draw in reverse. In cartoonist Les Tanner's words, 'It was to magazine illustration what moveable type was to the Gutenberg Bible.' It was, in short, the breakthrough that made possible the famous *Bulletin* tradition of black and white art.

Traill, Archibald and Haynes, the *Bulletin's* three proprietors, had first seen an illustration printed by this new process in an overseas magazine in 1880. They determined to discover how it was done but, after many attempts, they and their printers had to admit defeat. Traill set off for America, looking not only for an artist, but for someone who would bring to the *Bulletin* the secrets of this new process. However, the process was so new that he could find no photo-engraver ready to come to Australia, so Traill tried to pick up what information he could in a desperate, jackdaw sort of way.

The proprietor of a photo-engraving establishment showed Traill around and gave him the few books that had been written on the subject. This proprietor later commented drily to a friend: 'Our friend, the Editor of the *Bulletin*, little knows the difficulties he is about to tackle if he thinks he is going to make a success of the process with merely a glance at the works and a few books to put him wise.' Pattie, the one who actually tackled the difficulties, commented: 'This man never spoke a truer word.'

In two wittily acerbic articles, which she waited to publish until 1929 when all 'the dear men' involved were dead, Pattie describes how she was inveigled into taking on the herculean task.

'The dear men' turned to Pattie when they realised that 'It had cost so much money to journey to America...that the secret could hardly be given away to a strange man.' As no man who was not a stranger wanted to touch it, Pattie was their last resort, although 'Archibald hadn't the slightest faith in the scheme, for at the time his opinion of women's work was not worth much.'

But Pattie didn't want the job either. 'I was expected to master the difficulties in three months' time, ready for the new *Bulletin*, and considering that I did not even know how to take a photograph — nor had I any ambition to know — it was a very tall order. Naturally I refused — and then the band began to play.'

One can almost hear the violins. However, the emotional blackmail employed by the *Bulletin* triumvurate was effective if crude. '"Would I see them ruined rather than undertake a job which was dead easy — so easy that a child could do it? Surely I could not be so heartless!"'

Pattie Fotheringhame, older and wiser than in the days when she worked for the Bulletin *and reluctantly became Australia's first photo-engraver. Mitchell Library*

Well, what was a girl to do?...The end was I was talked over...[but] I only half realised what a stupendous task I had undertaken, and surely only men who were desperate would have asked me to do so. It was almost inhuman.'

Traill handed Pattie his notes, which were useless; the books which were limited; an ordinary camera, lens, and printing press — quite the wrong kind for process work — and left her to get on with it, using the back verandah of her house as gallery and darkroom. 'Not only had I absolutely no knowledge of photography, but I was expected to make shift with most ridiculously faulty appliances.'

Despite all this, Pattie succeeded. 'Never shall I forget the first cartoon I succeeded in transferring to a sheet of zinc. It was one of Hop's pictures, but although the members of the firm were jubilant when they saw my first effort, Hop was by no means enthusiastic. He pointed out that a line in the drawing was missing.'

The firm was equally jubilant when a young man turned up at the *Bulletin* office one day and claimed that he knew all about process work. They hired him on the spot for £6 a week, three times the salary they were paying Pattie. Dispensing with the niceties owing to both family connection and common courtesy, Traill and company sent the young man around to Pattie 'with a note saying he would relieve me of the whole business if I would hand over to him camera, press etc. This seemed almost too good to be true.'

It was. After two days, the young man confessed the obvious — he knew absolutely nothing about it. 'I often wondered afterwards why he professed a knowledge of the process, but probably he thought that it could not be a difficult matter, as a girl was attempting it.'

The *Bulletin* trio, naturally, were in a great panic and 'wired me to resume work'. But Pattie, rightly feeling that they had behaved abominably, refused. 'Even a worm will turn, and although I had been in seventh heaven at the idea of following my own bent once more, I felt sore that, when relieving me, the firm had not seen fit to give me one word of thanks for what I had done in order to help them, so I declined to be made use of any further.'

Once again, Traill, Archibald and Haynes shamelessly manipulated Pattie. Her resolve held 'until one said it would be ruination if I forsook them. I weakened then, as it meant that some of my connections would suffer.' The trio were so elated that they offered Pattie the same £6 a week that they had been prepared to pay the imposter. Pattie retorted that 'it was not the smallness of the remuneration...but the lack of appreciation of all I had given up in my life just to help them that made me feel sore'. There is no record of whether she kept the salary but when they sent her a cheque for £50 the next day 'as a small appreciation' of her work, she promptly sent it back.

It had cost Pattie dearly to take up this work for the *Bulletin*. A keen musician, she had been forced to give up her music pupils and then, 'so much time had to be given up studying the business that for the first year I gave up all my usual enjoyments — balls, concerts, theatres...All for the magnificent sum of £2 per week.'

But it nearly cost Pattie more than this. Her health and life were also endangered as the process required the use of a number of poisonous chemicals, about which she knew nothing. Often 'quite stupefied' by ether fumes, Pattie constantly handled the most deadly chemical of all, cyanide. 'One day, I...inhaled the poisonous fumes to such an extent that I was nearly going to a place where there is no process work. I found anxious people pouring hot black coffee down my throat...and was told I was found unconscious in the dark room.'

Against these formidable odds, the new *Bulletin* duly appeared, full of illustrations reproduced by Pattie's process. Then it occurred to the trio that 'I might marry or die, and then what were they to do?' They sent to America for help and eventually hired Charles Shugg, a trained process operator.

With some glee, Pattie describes Shugg's first sight of the *Bulletin's* process room: 'Never shall I forget his look of horror when he beheld the tools with which I was working. He thought too much of his reputation to attempt to use them, so he waited the few weeks until the arrival of a lens and a press he had fortunately secured before leaving America...he has told me many times since that he marvelled how I got any results at all with such appliances.'

Pattie continued her journalistic career for most of her long life, as well as raising two children — often alone while her husband, a master mariner, was at sea. After many years at the *Bulletin*, she published *Splashes* weekly, a women's magazine which ran from 1899 to 1917, and Australia's first children's magazines — *Young Australia*, which she bought from Louisa Lawson, and *Junior Australians*, which she published and edited for over thirty years. Pattie also edited the *Sphere*, a monthly paper for women, and wrote for many other different publications. In 1955, when she was 103, Pattie was described as 'the eyes and ears of four generations of Australian women'.

Lyall Booth, then Head of the Photo-Engraving Department at Sydney Technical College, learned about Pattie's pioneering process work and interviewed her not long before her death. 'Even at 103, it was apparent that she had always been interested in anything that was new and a challenge.' Mr Booth believes it is impossible to praise Pattie too highly. 'By proving the feasibility of the process, she speeded up the use of photo-engraving in Australia by many years. Pattie Fotheringhame's achievement was the equivalent of climbing Everest.'

Ellen Flanagan
1859–1936

Woman with a mission
Written by: Judith Elen
Nominated by: Shirley Robson

Ellen Flanagan is described by a great grand-daughter as 'a woman born before her time'. In a period when women were not given the choice between a 'private' or a 'public' life, Ellen Flanagan made the choice for herself. A woman was supposed to be 'naturally maternal'; Ellen left her husband and children, choosing to work for the cause in which she believed. While her great granddaughter remembers her as a 'very formidable...tough person who never showed...a great deal of affection', she also describes her as a woman 'of vision and passion'.

Born Ellen Mary Harper Jones, she came to Sydney with her mother after the death of her father when she was seven. Educated at St Mary's Cathedral School, she became a teacher and 'was very radical in her views...determined to get reform for women'. She met and married her first husband in her seventeenth year; nearly twenty years later she was to embark on a second unsuccessful marriage.

Like many Irish-Australian Catholics, Ellen joined the newly-formed Labor League. Absorbed by politics, she found her society's conception of marriage and motherhood unbearably oppressive. A wife had no time to think her own thoughts, she believed, let alone develop and better herself; she had no money to spend, nor had she a complete right to her own children.

Ellen wanted justice and equality and she campaigned amongst women, doorknocking and public speaking. For her pains — and her passionately held beliefs — she suffered public ridicule. She was pilloried by the *Bulletin* which warned men to be on their guard against 'women with a mission' and, like other women who dared to speak in public, she was charged with 'unladylike behaviour'. Nevertheless, she and 'her girls' addressed the Sunday afternoon crowds in Sydney's Domain where she was subjected to the boos and jeers, tomatoes and rotten eggs, that the men chose as expressions of their disapproval.

Her great grand-daughter regrets that Ellen did not live to see equal pay and anti-discrimination legislation. The formidable Ellen, she is sure, 'would have danced in the streets of Sydney'.

Ellen Flanagan, 'a woman born before her time'

Marie Kirk
1855–1928
'For God, home and humanity'
Written by: Anthea Hyslop
Nominated by: Betty Finch

To the late twentieth century mind, temperance and progressive radical politics might seem odd bedmates. However, to many late nineteenth century women like Marie Kirk, feminism and total abstinence were inextricably bound together.

Marie Kirk was born Maria Elizabeth Sutton, on 9 December 1855 in London. Reared as a Quaker, she worked as a missionary in London's slums, and there saw enough of drink's depredations to make her an advocate of total abstinence. In 1878, Marie married Frank Kirk, an ironmonger's assistant, and later bore him a daughter, Lilian. Then, in her late twenties, she joined the British Women's Temperance Association, which, in 1886, she represented at an international convention in Canada. There Marie Kirk encountered the source of its inspiration: the Woman's Christian Temperance Union, to which she would devote the rest of her life.

Founded in the United States in 1874 by Frances Willard, the WCTU had emerged from a larger evangelical temperance movement, which because of the impact of alcoholism on families, attracted widespread female support. Since women were not only physically but legally and economically at the mercy of drunken husbands, the WCTU in 1876 began advocating women's suffrage as a further means for securing 'Home Protection'.

In 1886 Marie Kirk emigrated to Melbourne with her family, settling in suburban Camberwell, where Frank Kirk worked as a bootmaker. That same year brought a widow from West Virginia, with first-hand experience of the American WCTU. 'What can I do to help stem the tide of iniquity?' asked Mary M. Love, when she saw Melbourne's numerous hotels and breweries. Marie Kirk answered it in November 1887, when, with the aid of a Congregational clergyman, she organised a conference of delegates from all over the colony to found the Woman's Christian Temperance Union of Victoria.

With Mrs Love as its first president and Mrs Kirk soon appointed secretary, the new Union flourished, attracting many members into a network that rapidly spread throughout city and countryside. Like their leaders, most of these women were aged between twenty-five and fifty, married to men who were invariably self-employed — many in trade, some in the professions — and, in their devout Christianity, sometimes evangelical Anglicans but usually nonconformists. The WCTU was non-sectarian, but the Catholic Church preferred to encourage its own total abstinence societies.

As general secretary for twenty-six years, Marie Kirk wrought a powerful influence within the WCTU. Through its journal, *The White Ribbon Signal*, of which she was first editor, she exhorted her fellows to support many reforms, including women's suffrage, and inspired them all with her own spiritual fervour. Mrs Kirk, as she was always known, was inexhaustibly active: establishing new branches, raising funds, running the Victorian headquarters, organising annual conventions, and helping with a club for working girls. For many years she presided over the Union's local Melbourne branch; in 1891 she became secretary of a new Australasian WCTU; and in 1897 she represented Victoria at international temperance conventions in Britain and North America. Mrs Kirk also served as WCTU delegate to other organisations, helping to found both the Victorian Women's Franchise League (1894) and the National Council of Women of Victora (1902). The first cause of the WCTU was temperance and Marie Kirk sought the vote 'for the protection, of the Home, and for Purity'. But she also organised the huge Women's Petition of 1891, with its 30 000 signatures, which argued the case for the vote in terms of justice alone.

If the WCTU's feminism had a markedly moral tone, it also stressed the rights and worth of women as men's equals. In 1893, the Union agitated successfully to secure the age of consent at sixteen rather than twelve years. It stoutly opposed any double standard, whether that which hounded female prostitutes but not their clients, or that which denied women equal pay. Marie Kirk was active in all these efforts, and led the campaign to appoint police matrons for female prisoners. In 1902 she and Evelyn Gough arranged an investigation by the new National Council of Women, which exposed sordid prison conditions. Evelyn Gough, founding secretary of the National Council of Women, concluded, in the detailed report on the prisons that she wrote for

Marie Kirk, founder of the WCTU in Victoria, opposed the Demon Drink, supported votes for women and worked tirelessly for social reform. Town & Country Journal, 31 March 1894. La Trobe Library, State Library of Victoria

the *Sphere*: 'The lowest human being calling herself woman has the right to the services of her own sex'. After many more representations, Victoria's first police matrons were finally appointed in 1909.

With its devotion to family interests, the WCTU reinforced woman's traditional roles of wife and mother. However, this was in keeping with the progessivism of the early twentieth century, which sought to strengthen the nation through child welfare. From 1900, the WCTU advocated juvenile courts on the American model, to protect children from what Marie Kirk called the 'hardening influences' of the public court-room. When children's courts were introduced in 1906, she and her colleagues ensured the provision of special judges and a probation system. The WCTU also supported the establishment of playgrounds and kindergartens in crowded inner suburbs, helping to found the Free Kindergarten Union of Victora (1909), and opening one of its own in Richmond. In 1917, this kindergarten was named in honour of Marie Kirk, who had been the moving spirit in its development.

In 1913, failing health forced Marie Kirk to retire from her post of general secretary, although she remained an active member of the WCTU several years longer. When Parkinson's disease put an end to her work, she could look back with pride to the temperance campaign of 1906, which brought the liquor trade tighter control, and to that of the war years, which led to six o'clock closing of bars. In 1908, too, Victorian women had won the vote at last; and to all these measures her Union had substantially contributed. Marie Kirk gave all her energies to temperance and to the welfare of women and children. When she died 14 January 1928, her friends set this epitaph upon her tombstone: 'Her works do follow her'.

Jean Beadle
1868–1942

Sweatshop worker, labor leader
Written by: Judith Elen
Nominated by: Beverley J. Wilson

At the time of her death, a newspaper article noted Jean Beadle's 'gentleness and charm of manner', 'her keen sense of justice and her great desire to do good'. Jean Beadle was not, however, the archetypal Victorian 'lady' that this suggests. She was a working-class woman committed to working for the reforms urgently needed by working women and their children.

In a public address half a century earlier, Jean Beadle had defended her political activism against the accusation that it was 'unladylike.' 'I could not resist from saying — well, if it is ladylike to recline on soft cushions with interesting books, attend amusements, wear fine clothes etc all purchased by the sweat and brains, nay out of the very life of sweated labour and to be content with such conditions, then I had no desire to be ladylike.'

The hardships of Jean Beadle's own life informed her later campaigns. The daughter of a miner, forced to leave school early to keep house for her widowed father, her story echoes that of many young nineteenth century women. She gained first-hand knowledge of 'sweated labour' in the clothing trade in Melbourne. She married at twenty-one and within six weeks of her marriage, her husband was out on strike. The strike was to persist for six months in the bitter depression years of the 1880s. During this period, and when he was later boycotted by employers, Jean supported her husband and became actively involved in the union movement.

Wherever she lived, Jean worked for other working women and their families. She initiated or was prominent in Labor women's organisations in Melbourne, Fremantle, the Eastern Goldfields and Perth. She organised a women's relief committee for striking miners. On the creation of the Labor Women's Central Executive in 1927 she became vice-president and was later appointed to the State Executive of the Labor Party. In 1931 she was a candidate for Senate pre-selection.

One of the first female magistrates, Jean worked with women and children in the court and prison system. She was vice-president of the Workers' Education Association and, during the Depression, relief worker and youth adviser. She agitated for an urgently needed maternity hospital in Perth and subsequently served on its Advisory Board.

For Jean, issues of social justice for women and men were interwoven — the needs of working women supporting families equalled those of men; men's working conditions were vitally linked with the wellbeing of their families. She worked tirelessly to improve the lot of women in the home as well as outside, fighting for unionisation of women in industry; for equal pay; and for maternity allowances and child endowment to be paid directly to mothers.

Jean lacked formal education, but she was an avid reader, skilled writer, a fluent and convincing speaker, and could organise and 'chair a meeting brilliantly'. When she died, Prime Minister Curtin wrote of the strength and inspiration of 'this truly great Australian woman'.

Some English leaders of the women's movement are household names; less familiar are the names of Australian women like Jean Beadle who paved the way for later generations, improving the social conditions of men and women alike.

Jean Beadle, who fought to improve the lot of working women. 1929. J. S. Battye Library of West Australian History

Dora Robertson Armitage
1858–1946
Mother of the modern business girl
Written by: Suzy Baldwin
Nominated by: Marcia R. Gall

In May 1888, Dora Armitage opened the doors of Sydney's first typing school. Accompanied by three of her four young children, Dora had arrived the previous September from England where she had offered one of the first typing services in London and had, in 1886, opened the first typewriting office in Birmingham.

As founding secretary of the New South Wales National Council of Women, Dora Armitage (seated, far left) was delegate to the International Council of Women in London, 1899, where she spoke on two of her favourite topics — women's civil and legal disabilities, and agriculture as a career for women

Armed with this experience and a Caligraph typewriter, Dora approached the businessmen of Sydney for copying work. It was, she wrote later, 'rather uphill': the men were courteous but 'very conservative' and she had to overcome a double prejudice. Not only was she a woman — probably the first woman to enter most Sydney offices on business — but she was asking them to try a technology so new that most of her prospective clients either had no idea what it was or regarded it with deep suspicion: 'My dear Madam, we have done without typewriting all these years, and think we can do without it longer.'

But Dora was, from the very beginning, a survivor. Born in 1858 amongst American Indians in the backwoods of Michigan, Dora's first four years were spent in a lumber settlement where her father, a young Scot with no particular prospects and a taste for adventure, supervised the felling of huge trees and hoped to make his fortune.

When the American Civil War forced the family to leave their adopted home in 1862, Dora's father exchanged one kind of colonial adventure for another, joined the Chartered Mercantile Bank and set off with his wife and three children to open a branch in Galle in Ceylon.

When Dora was eight, her mother took her back to England to be educated. Dora spent the next nine years in Bath receiving a lady's education — private schools, governesses, lessons in the socially desirable accomplishments of painting, music, singing, riding and dancing. When, in 1876, she boarded a P&O liner for Colombo, Dora was superbly trained to be a charming young lady and a gentleman's wife.

The gentleman who won Dora was Charles Armitage, a partner in one of Ceylon's oldest and most respected firms. The family was wealthy and Charles was regarded as 'a good match' but the following years were to prove that Charles was no match for Dora at all.

The next four years were filled with travel, parties, dances and elephant-hunting safaris with visiting royalty. But by the end of 1881, blight had struck the coffee crop and the family company was in serious trouble. By May 1882, the firm had collapsed and the golden world of the Armitages was shattered. 'I was only twenty-four years of age, the mother of four young children, and my husband a ruined man.' Dora's hair had begun to turn white with worry.

Dora had to leave her husband behind, return to England with her children and live with her bullying mother-in-law in the country. It was 'a bitterly cold and bleak place...and lonely'. Dora, miserable and frozen, resolved to find some way of supporting herself and her children so that she need no longer be dependent on old Mrs Armitage.

Escaping to London, Dora was taken in by her grandaunt, Mrs Traill. 'Being a very strict Presbyterian' Aunt Traill was 'quite horrified' at Dora's original idea of going on the stage. But Mrs Traill's scruples did not extend to all things modern. As an alternative to a life of imagined harlotry, she bought Dora what was, in the early 1880s, a very new-fangled machine — a Hall typewriter.

Dora took a house in London, sold her jewellery to pay the bills, and began typing at home for friends. At the same time, she successfully coached Jack, her eldest, for the entry exam to Christ's Hospital, most famous of the Bluecoat schools for boys with brains but no money. By the time Dora opened her office in Birmingham, she had not seen her husband for five years. After Ceylon he had come to Australia but the business that had sent him had failed 'so he was left stranded once more'. The family — probably hoping that Dora would rescue Charles, which indeed she did — paid Dora's passage so, in July 1887, she sailed for Sydney.

Marrying Dora seems to have been the most successful thing that Charles Armitage managed to do. Certainly, his career as a breadwinner was less than glorious. Dora arrived in Australia to discover that Charles was not earning enough to support them. She immediately bought her Caligraph typewriter and launched herself on her pioneering business career.

Fortunately the women of Sydney took a different view from their men on the question of typewriting. Dora had an introduction to a Lady Fairfax who was a member of the Committee preparing Sydney's first Exhibition of Women's Industries. With her support, Dora began her typing classes.

The Exhibition opened on 1 October 1888, with Dora's pupils and their writing machines prominently featured. On the same day, with money lent by Lady Fairfax and soon repaid, Dora opened the Ladies' Typewriting Association in Victoria Arcade. In these offices Dora combined her typing school with Sydney's first women's copying service.

In November 1888, Dora sent the first of her pupils to an employer. When Miss Muriel Edwards joined the staff of the Water Board, the modern Sydney 'business girl' was born. Before long, Dora's pupils were in all the best offices in the city and several had entered the public service, passing at the top of fiercely competitive examinations.

Dora always insisted that typing was a profession 'well suited to educated women'. In fact, education was the essential prerequisite for the job. Not only must a typist have 'a thoroughly sound English education,' but 'for a copying office, a knowledge of French, Latin and even

Dora Elizabeth Robertson Armitage Cooke, c.1900, supported her family by opening Sydney's first typing school. She maintained that the ideal typist needed a knowledge of the classics, 'a perfect temper and a cast iron nerve'

of Heathen mythology will not come amiss'. Given that, 'there is certainly no other business that a woman could undertake where she would have a better chance of earning her livelihood in a comparatively short time, provided that she studies hard during that time'. This new profession was congenial, reasonably paid — well trained typists were earning twenty-five to thirty shillings a week — and it allowed women to be independent. It was a definite improvement on the barely-disguised slavery of governess or companion that many still regarded as the only suitable professions for educated, 'respectable' girls.

Dora was concerned that *every* woman — whether well educated or not — should be able to earn a decent livelihood with dignity. When, in June 1896, the National Council of Women of NSW was formed at a public meeting in the Sydney Town Hall, Dora, who became founding secretary, gave the keynote address. After acknowledging the assistance she had received from other women in launching her profession, she suggested that the primary task of the National Council should be to draw to public attention: 'The crying evils...to be remedied amongst our sister workers...the Factory girls, the Tailoresses, the shop assistants...in order that the law may step in and make their condition better.'

Through the National Council, Dora lobbied energetically for improved domestic education for girls and the establishment of an agricultural college for women. Both would provide women with healthy alternatives to the factory for earning a living.

In her 1898 speech to the Minister for Public Instruction, Dora explains this primary concern: 'In my work amongst the women of NSW, I am constantly brought face to face with the fact that for those left with families to provide for there are practically no openings.' Dora, whose own business career was the result of being suddenly faced with a family to support and no training for the task, spoke with the passion of personal experience.

Charles died at the beginning of 1897. Two years later, Dora was one of two delegates from the NSW National Council of Women to attend the International Conference of Women in London. She presented two papers on favourite topics: one on women, education and agriculture, and the other on laws relating to women.

Travelling back to Australia, Dora was seated at the Captain's table. By the end of the voyage, she was engaged to the widowed and impressively-named Captain Walter White Wingrove Cooke. Dora married Captain Cooke in 1902, sold her business interests and returned to England where she continued to work for women's suffrage and social reform. On each of her regular trips back to Sydney to visit her four older children, she was entertained by the businesswomen of Sydney in recognition of her pioneering work for business girls. Always immensely proud to speak as 'a Woman Worker and representative of my profession — the Typists of this city,' Dora told a friend that it was always a thrill to see Sydney's modern business girls pouring out of ferries and stations on their way to work and to know that her young women had been the first.

Dora died in 1946 at the age of eighty-seven. She used to say that the ideal typist needed, in addition to everything else, 'a perfect temper and a cast iron nerve'. Dora would probably never have claimed to have the perfect temper but she certainly had nerve.

Maybanke Susannah Anderson
1845–1927
Womanly and fearless feminist
Written by: Jan Roberts
Nominated by: Jan Roberts

When Mrs Maybanke Anderson died at St Germain en Laye near Paris on Good Friday 1927, Sydney newspapers and university and kindergarten journals all carried the sad news. There was widespread surprise too, as if the eighty-two-year-old woman had no right to die on foreign soil. Terms like 'one of Australia's noble and notable women' and 'in this woman Deity would seem to have surpassed Itself' were used to describe one who is now virtually unknown, who has slipped out of the human memory process called 'History'. Who was Maybanke Anderson, this now unsung, forgotten Australian heroine?

Maybanke was born in 1845 in a quiet English village, Kingston-on-Thames, to Bessie and Henry Selfe, plumber and inventor. When she was ten years old her family decided to emigrate to Sydney.

The Selfes settled in the Rocks area of Sydney, in Mary Reiby's historic house, so Maybanke grew up in that lively, picturesque world of sailing ships and windmills where extremes of wealth and poverty existed side by side. Maybanke became a teacher, and in 1967 at nearby St Philip's, Church Hill, she married a Maitland timber-merchant Edmund Kay Wolstenholme. After their first child, Harry, was born in Maitland, the young Wolstenholmes returned to Sydney to live in Balmain.

Over the next eleven years of their married life together six more babies were born, but only Harry and his brothers Arthur and Edmund reached adulthood, the others dying of TB-related diseases in what was then a fairly typical infant mortality rate. The marriage was very unhappy for years, and in 1885 Edmund deserted the family. To support herself and the three boys, Maybanke ran first a boarding house, then, until 1899, a successful private girls' school, Maybanke College, at Dulwich Hill. Gradually life improved.

It is no coincidence that Maybanke's most active decade, the 1890s, was a landmark period in Australian history; the long boom had ended in a terrible depression, and in Sydney the slums and squalor were breeding grounds for vice and disease. Soon Maybanke Wolstenholme joined a group of like-minded and extremely able women and men who worked together to turn Australia from a collection of backwater colonies to a nation that was being hailed as a 'social laboratory of the world' at the outbreak of the World War I. With Rose Scott, Louisa Lawson, the Windeyer family and others, she began the struggle, first for Womanhood Suffrage, then for other important legal, political and educational reforms.

Maybanke became a famous 'platform woman', and made many fiery public speeches which were widely reported in the newspapers of the day; in 1891 for example: 'There was a great deal about training

Maybanke Susannah Anderson, feminist reformer, believed that social problems must be discussed honestly, 'without cant or humbug' and did so, both in her newspaper, the Woman's Voice, *and on the platform. Photographed in 1899, probably at the time of her second marriage. Mitchell Library*

for motherhood, but what puzzled her was that they never heard anything about training for fatherhood (laughter). If they were to improve their family life they would have to improve their fatherhood (applause).'

From the Women's Literary Society — the first group of Sydney women to meet in the evenings — Maybanke helped found the Womanhood Suffrage League of New South Wales in 1891. She was its first Vice President, and in 1893 its second President and continued in that position until 1897, resigning when she believed the politicians' promises that the vote for women was imminent in New South Wales.

Maybanke's stamina was prodigious. To select one year of the decade at random — 1893 — in addition to leadership of her school and the suffrage struggle, her activities were as follows: foundation Vice President of Sydney University Women's Society (later Sydney University Settlement); member of the Council of the Teachers' Association of New South Wales; founder and Secretary-Treasurer of the Australasian Home Reading Union, and Vice President of the International Women's Union. In the same year she also became a Theosophist and obtained a divorce under Sir Alfred Stephen's radical Divorce Extension and Amendment Act of 1892. Maybanke joined a very small group of early divorcees, but the social stigma appears not to have daunted her.

The next year Maybanke started her own paper *The Woman's Voice* to spread her reforming ideas still wider: its motto was very much an expression of her life-long ideals:

Democratic but not revolutionary
Womanly but not weak
Fearless without effrontery
Liberal without licence.

In 1895 Maybanke helped found the Kindergarten Union of New South Wales, beginning an enormous commitment to the youngest and most vulnerable in human society. But her great joy in this was shattered when her second son Arthur, aged twenty-four, was drowned in the *Catterthun* shipping disaster off Seal Rocks. *The Woman's Voice* ceased publication, but gradually Maybanke recovered. She helped open the

Masthead of first issue of Maybanke's fortnightly feminist paper, The Woman's Voice. *'Our object is to encourage thought, the great lever of humanity.' Mitchell Library*

The Woman's Voice

EDITOR: **M. S. WOLSTENHOLME,** "Maybanke," Dulwich Hill.

DEMOCRATIC BUT NOT REVOLUTIONARY.
WOMANLY BUT NOT WEAK.
FEARLESS WITHOUT EFFRONTERY.
LIBERAL WITHOUT LICENSE.

SYDNEY AGENT: **E. B. ROBSON** Woman's Guild, Sydney Arcade.

VOL. I.—No. 1.   THURSDAY, AUGUST 9, 1894.   TWO PENCE.

BUSINESS NOTICE.

ANY Person desirous of becoming a subscriber to the WOMAN'S VOICE is requested to send name and address to Miss E. B. Robson, Sydney Agent, No. 3 Sydney Arcade. Subscription, 4s. per annum, in advance; postage to neighboring colonies, 2s. 2d. extra. Subscriptions may be sent in postage stamps, postal note, or P.O. order.

E. B. ROBSON,

will be one with the welfare of the race, one with the welfare of humanity; and the journals of that bright day will meet the united demands of a higher and purer life. But that time is not yet. Before the dawn of the harvest home there must be the ploughing of the fallow field of mind, the sowing of many a seed of love and truth. Women must wake up to wider knowledge of themselves, their work, and their responsibilities; and the women who can see the need of

first Free Kindergarten, in Charles Street, Woolloomooloo in 1896, and others followed, all in inner-city slum areas where Maybanke felt the need was greatest.

Towards the end of the nineteenth century Federation was looming. Maybanke saw the debates and conventions — where women were not included — as a venue to pressure the fathers of the constitution to give women the vote federally, thereby shaming stubborn New South Wales and other colonial politicians into following suit. A timely petition, the forming of the Women's Federal League of New South Wales, and her tactics paid off. In 1902 Australian women were the first in the world to win the right to vote and stand for the national parliament, and New South Wales politicians did 'follow the leader' and grant women the right to vote in state elections.

In 1899, when she was fifty-four, Maybanke married Scottish-born Francis Anderson, Professor of Philosophy at Sydney University and a bachelor thirteen years her junior. Together they achieved a great deal of educational reform in New South Wales — the State education system, teacher training, kindergartens and adult education with the Workers' Educational Association (WEA) all felt the influence of Maybanke and Francis Anderson.

On their honeymoon overseas Maybanke commenced work as a journalist, and until her death wrote regularly as 'Lois' in the *Sydney Morning Herald*. On their second trip in 1908 she returned with new ideas and started the Playgrounds Association which eventually gave inner-city children safe recreational parks instead of only the dangerous streets. Her persistent theme was 'Formation, not Reformation' — love and look after the young, and gaols and reformatories will not be necessary.

Maybanke College, Dulwich Hill. When Edmund Wolstenholme deserted his family in 1885, Maybanke supported her three boys first by taking in boarders, then by opening this successful private school for girls. Mitchell Library

Maybanke worked and lobbied to help the welfare of women and children wherever she saw the need. In 1916, when she was seventy-one, the WEA published her influential pamphlet, *The Root of the Matter; Social and Economic Aspects of the Sex Problem*. This dealt in a practical and compassionate manner with the problems of wartime venereal diseases which were causing untold suffering to many women, especially mothers and their babies.

Maybanke's writings and undertakings continued throughout her long life: among other works, she wrote a chapter on 'Women in Australia' in Atkinson's *Australia: Economic and Political Studies;* a popular, helpful booklet on care of the very young called 'Motherlore'; and local histories of Pittwater and Hunters' Hill, as well as leading a rich and full family life with her children and grandchildren.

In an interview when she was eighty Maybanke Anderson summed up her personal creed: 'Religion is doing what you can for the welfare of humanity and developing your own spiritual life.' When she died, her daughter-in-law published a tribute to her. Its conclusion is most apt for this forgotten Australian heroine: 'The world is poorer for the loss of her, but it is a better place because she lived in it.'

Emma Miller
1839–1917
'Grand old woman of Queensland labor'
Written by: Pam Young
Nominated by: Pam Young

When, in 1906, the women of western Queensland heard that Emma Miller, president of the Woman's Equal Franchise Association and foundation member of the Labor Party, was to tour their centres, they were not sure what to expect. Picturing her as a prominent, forceful person with strong convictions, they were amazed when a tiny, frail, elderly woman stepped from the train.

Born in England's Derbyshire in 1839, Emma, the eldest of four children, became a rebel against the existing social order through the influence of her Chartist father, a Unitarian cord wainer, Daniel Holmes. In 1857 Emma eloped with Jabez Silcock and had four children. Widowed and remarried, she migrated to Brisbane in 1879 with her second husband, William Calderwood, a stonemason, hoping that the sunshine would cure his T.B. It did not and William died in 1880. As social services were non-existent, Emma provided for her family by working as a 'gentlemen's white shirtmaker', sewing twelve hours a day for six days a week. Concerned at the unprotected conditions of shop assistants, domestics and factory workers, Emma became involved in the Early Closing Association and the formation of the first women's trade union in 1890, and in 1891 gave evidence at the Royal Commission into Shops, Factories and Workshops, exposing the sweat-shop owners who callously exploited women outworkers.

Emma Miller believed that the social and economic burdens placed on women retarded the whole human race and that the winning of the vote would be a first step in advancing their position. From its foundation in 1894 until the vote was granted to Queensland women in 1905, she was the volatile President of the womens' Equal Franchise Association.

After 1903, she became President of the Women Workers Political Organisation, formed to educate women in the use of their vote, and in 1908 she and Kate Dwyer of New South Wales were the first women delegates to attend a Commonwealth Labor Conference. During the 1912 general strike for the rights of trade unionists, the fiery Emma was an inspiring force. She became a legendary figure during 'Black Friday' (2 February) when over 15 000 people gathered in Brisbane city streets to protest at the ban on strike processions. Ignoring police with bayonets drawn, Emma courageously led an equally brave group of women to Parliament House in an unsuccessful bid to see the Premier. On their return to the city centre they were encircled by baton-swinging police. Bruised and outraged at the unwarranted brutal attack on them the women brandished their umbrellas and drew their hatpins. Emma's found its way into Police Commissioner Cahill's horse. The horse reared, throwing Cahill who was left with a permanent limp.

Anti-militarist from an early age and still following the Chartist creed — 'The world is my country; to do good is my religion' — Emma vigorously opposed World War I and conscription. She believed that those who make the quarrel should be the only ones to fight. Emma loved elections and thrived on campaigning. She was always in great demand as a speaker although she did not have a natural gift of eloquence. Her appeal was her sincerity: she spoke from the heart and from her life's experiences.

When Emma Miller died on 22 January 1917, seventy-eight and 'still fighting', she had had three husbands and four children and had outlived them all but one son (her third husband, Andrew Miller, died on 1897). In recognition of her pioneering work as the champion of the people's causes, a publicly-funded marble bust of Emma was installed at the Brisbane Trades Hall. On the day of her funeral, the flag at the Brisbane Trades Hall flew at half mast and this woman — the grand old woman of Queensland labor — was mourned throughout the nation.

Emma Miller, rebel, courageous feminist and champion of the people's causes

Phoebe Farrar
1868–1960

'No one could keep Phoebe down'
Written by: Phyllis Uren
Nominated by: Phyllis Uren

'A young girl Phoebe Wright, my Grandmother, born at Fish River in 1868 fourteen years old in 1882, accompanied the Farrar family by boat to Normanton. They then changed to wagons, Phoebe driving one of them 1000 kilometres to the Limmen River corner of the Gulf of Carpentaria. Many months on the road — flies mosquitoes,

Phoebe Farrar, Northern Territory pioneer, at home on horseback

swamps, heat, were some of the discomforts, also worrying about attacks by Aborigines. Phoebe had to help with cooking, washing, as well as drive the wagon. At the station she was to go mustering cattle, roping, throwing cattle, branding and castrating. She was as good as any man.

'Phoebe married Robert the eldest son of John and MaryAnn Farrar. They had five children and her mother-in-law was her only help. She then moved to Hodgson Downs, where she was known as the "Bush Mother". Phoebe never turned anyone away that came for help — all were welcomed. Phoebe and MaryAnn were often left alone at the homestead with the children. Many nights they would have their rifles poked through the wooden slats of the walls firing at the Aborigines who were attacking them. The children when older took up arms as well.

'Phoebe had to run the station when Robert was away getting supplies. Phoebe did all her own housework, as well as muster cattle, cook during the night, baking bread and corn beef. Some beef was salted, thrown on the roofs to dry, packed in saddle bags, then they would cut a thin slice off with their knives and eat. Meals were dry bread, beef and rice. Phoebe had her own quart pot; light a fire, put water in pot, put in the fire, when the water boils throw in tea leaves, sugar, drink when cool enough, cut off thin slice of corn beef, hunk of bread. That was a meal, one hour, and they were on the road again. It certainly was a hard life.

'Phoebe with her children and MaryAnn met Mrs Aeneas Gunn on their way to Darwin — Phoebe was Mrs Bob — it was their first visit to Darwin or anywhere else. Mrs Gunn was the first white woman, apart from MaryAnn, that Phoebe had seen since 1882.

'In 1925 Robert and Phoebe bought land at Brocks Creek. Phoebe and Half Caste Fred and a dog drove the cattle from Hodgson Downs to Brocks Creek. She had inspected the land for a homestead, picked a small rise with a spring at the bottom and called it Ban Ban Springs Station.

'Around 1935 when she was sixty-seven Phoebe and husband Robert and Half Caste Fred, went down to the cattle yard to do the drafting of the cattle. Some had to be branded, one had to be put into another yard to be killed for beef for the homestead. Fred had the fire going, and the branding irons were in the fire heating.

'Everything had been going well, they had nearly sorted out all the cattle, when two bulls got fighting, Robert and Fred started to hit them with sticks, trying to separate them, they eventually succeeded, one charged for the gate which Phoebe was holding open, she tried to close the gate, but the bull crashed through felling the gate onto Phoebe, then the bull fell onto her too.

'Robert and Fred came running, the bull had got to its feet, groggy and bleeding. After removing the gate, and examining Phoebe, they found she could not move her leg and was in need of medical attention.

'They made a rough stretcher to carry her up to the homestead. Robert quickly got onto the Medical Air Service by two way radio, who said they would do everything they could to send a plane. Dr Fenton took the message, he was on another call but would attend the Farrar's call as soon as possible. They waited two days before the plane arrived, Dr Fenton on arriving explaining that he had crashed the first plane, and had to wait for a replacement.

'On arriving at the Darwin Hospital Phoebe was operated on immediately. She had a broken hip. The Doctor told Phoebe she would never walk again. She said, "We'll see". A year later Phoebe and Robert came down to Darwin, stayed at their son, Henry's home. Phoebe walked into the surgery at the clinic, saw the Doctor and said to him, "Here's the cripple". The Doctor was amazed. He said, "You are a marvel, how did you do it?" She replied, "By sheer hard work and plenty of guts".

'Phoebe continued to ride her horse Irish. She had to have a box on the ground, to help her mount the horse, otherwise she was as good as new.

'Phoebe died aged ninety-two in Darwin Hospital. My Mum said Phoebe could fold a buffalo hide like other people could fold a piece of paper.'

Arthur Albert Devlin
1844–1912
Lone fighter against anthrax
Written by: Lois Hunter
Nominated by: Stanley L. Devlin

In the last decades of the nineteenth century, Arthur Albert Devlin saved the lives of millions of livestock animals and the livelihoods of hundreds of settlers. But while he had the respect of the great French scientist Louis Pasteur, Arthur Devlin received no reward and little recognition at home. On the contrary, his efforts brought him financial ruin.

Born in 1844 into a life of considerable wealth by colonial standards, Arthur was the third son of the eight children of James Devlin, a pioneer settler, and schoolmaster's daughter Susannah Hughes. In the year that Arthur Devlin was born, his father was building Ryde House, Australia's finest example of Georgian architecture, and was the first settler to go down the Murrumbidgee, where he chose the best land for three fine runs. These were inherited by his sons and, by the 1880s these three Devlin brothers' stations in the Riverina — Ualah (Arthur), Ganmain (Matthew) and Deepwater (William) — were carrying 220 000 sheep, 5 000 cattle and 500 horses. By now Arthur was a prosperous farmer and landowner and the father of seven children.

Then — catastrophe. In 1885, 42 000 sheep, 500 cattle and sixty horses died on the Devlin properties. The mystery killer was known as 'Cumberland' after the area in which it first started. The disease appeared on property after property with disastrous results.

Arthur Devlin applied himself to solving the enormous problem almost single-handed. He ordered veterinary science books from England and from his research became convinced that 'Cumberland' was anthrax. Learning that Pasteur had developed an anthrax vaccine, Devlin wrote to him in Paris. Pasteur was willing to help but told Devlin that it was useless to ship the vaccine to Australia as it would be ineffective after the long voyage.

Arthur A. Devlin, whose years of dedication to Australia's primary industry have been largely unrecognized

Devlin then sought the assistance of the New South Wales government but to no avail. He finally persuaded Pasteur to send a team to Australia to confirm that 'cumberland' was indeed anthrax and to develop an effective vaccine against it. Their tests confirmed Devlin's belief. By now he had such debts that he lost Ualah Station but he continued his fight.

In 1889, after being approached by stockowners who were being ruined by anthrax, Devlin tried again. He asked the New South Wales government to pay £1000 to cover the costs of bringing out a Pasteur team to set up a laboratory to make the vaccine. But the government again refused help, saying that it considered the matter one for the stockowners themselves — an extraordinary response considering the importance of the beef and wool industries to the economy.

After many appeals from Devlin, Pasteur finally wrote to say that a syndicate in Paris would advance the money required to set up a laboratory to manufacture and distribute the vaccine in Australia provided a fee of two pence per head for sheep and four pence per head for cattle and horses was paid to the syndicate for three years. This first vaccine had to be administered twice with not less than fourteen days and not more than thirty days between each injection. Devlin accepted the offer and for the next eight and a half years, he and his four sons travelled the state, vaccinating three and a quarter million sheep and more than 50 000 horses.

In 1893, as a tribute to his work, Pasteur sent notes and records of the discovery of the anthrax vaccine, acknowledging Devlin as a world authority on the disease. Devlin then suggested to Pasteur's representative in Australia that efforts should be made to produce a single vaccine but Pasteur resisted, believing that a single shot would be less effective. Later another stockholder, J.A. Gunn, and a scientist, John McGarvie Smith, who worked with the Pasteur men, developed the single vaccine.

In 1897 Arthur Devlin retired and became stock inspector for the districts of Grafton, Tweed, Lismore and Casino while his sons continued to vaccinate with the Pasteur vaccine. His death in 1912 when he was sixty-eight went almost unrecorded.

Tullie C. Wollaston
1863–1931

'Stunned by glory'
Written by: Niall Lucy
Nominated by: G. Rowe; D. Walker; D. Wollaston

Born of pioneering stock on the wild west coast of South Australia, Tullie Cornthwaite Wollaston was a man of unbridled energy who never did anything by halves. At school in St Peters College, Adelaide, he excelled both in the classroom and on the sportsfield but, unexpectedly, he at first chose a mundane career in the Government Survey Department as a draughtsman.

His imagination was soon captured, however, by something far more luminous than office work. In 1888, Tullie left behind his young wife and six-week-old daughter (the first of their nine children) and set out from Maree in South Australia with a business partner, David Morton Tweedie, for the opal deposits 1100 kilometres away in western Queensland's Kyabra Hills.

They travelled by camel for seven weeks in the hottest summer then recorded. But the gruelling discomfort of the journey fell away when Tullie saw his first top-grade opal. There, in the heat and dust of the Queensland outback, he was, he wrote later, 'stunned by glory.'

In those days, opals were a little-valued gemstone on the world market. They had been mined in Hungary since Roman times, but most European opals are dull and lack the flashing fire of the stones that so dazzled Tullie at Kyabra Hills. He paid the miners a fair price for them and returned to Adelaide, soon afterwards embarking for England in the hope that London jewellers too would be stunned at their first sight of the brilliant opals from Australia.

Instead, the jewellers were inclined to believe that Tullie's stones were fake. He eventually found a buyer who agreed to market them, but by the time he returned to Australia, Tweedie had perished of thirst in the outback and the syndicate they had formed was running into strife for passing dud cheques in Tullie's absence.

Undaunted, Tullie was on hand to buy up all the opals when a deposit was discovered at White Cliffs, New South Wales, in 1889. He formed a new syndicate with another associate and the miners themselves, set up a company in London to market the stones, paying three-quarters of the value of an opal to the miner who found it.

In 1903, the first black opals were discovered in Queensland, and Tullie's enthusiasm for the unique gems was met with renewed scepticism on the part of London jewellers. But the trade soon learned to accept the new stones and they captivated the public, quickly becoming the most popular and most valuable of all opals. Black opals were later found in greater quantity at another Australian field, Lightning Ridge, which was opened up with the help of Tullie and his syndicate.

Although opals were his first love, Tullie also took a keen interest in Tasmanian emeralds and invested (unsuccessfully, as it transpired) in a pearling venture on the north-west coast of Western Australia. He also made a notable contribution to the fossil history of the Pleistocene era by discovering the opalised skeleton of a dinosaur that now bears his name.

Tullie was a daring businessman, but it was by no means his only accomplishment. He was known in his lifetime as the author of three books, the most popular being *Opal: The Gem of the Never Never* (1924), an account of his hazardous camel trek to Kyabra Hills and his subsequent adventures in Australia's opal industry.

But Tullie's greatest passion was the glorious garden he created at Raywood in Adelaide's Mount Lofty Ranges. Extending over eighty hectares, it included all that was rare and beautiful in native flora and selected plants from overseas. From among other rare seedlings, Tullie propagated the imposing claret ash which was later given the scientific name of *Fraxinus Oxycarpa 'Raywoodii'* after his resplendent garden, which now belongs to the Education Department of South Australia.

When Tullie died in 1931, he had only one regret. Following an

Above. Tullie Cornthwaite Wollaston, (standing) with his father George Gledstanes

Below. The older Tullie Wollaston, writer, naturelover, gemmologist and father of Australia's opal industry

exhibition at Queen's Hall in Parliament House of his magnificent private collection of opals, Tullie had generously offered the collection to the National Museum in Canberra at virtually cost price. A newspaper of the time reported that 'most of the members appeared strongly in favour of the proposal,' yet the Federal Government eventually declined the offer. Sadly, the collection was broken up and lost forever.

But the vision of Tullie Cornthwaite Wollaston, father of the Australian opal industry, will abide always in the living splendour of Raywood.

Simon Engelhardt Jörgensen
1848–c.1926
A life-saving invention
Written by: Suzy Baldwin
Nominated by: Jane Jörgensen

In August, 1890, hundreds of people crowded onto the Adelaide wharves to cheer two Norwegian seamen and their unique little boat at the end of a remarkable voyage begun eleven months earlier at London's West India Docks. As master and co-owner of the SS *Ragna*, Captain Simon Engelhardt Jörgensen had made frequent voyages to Australia and had married in Melbourne in 1886. However, this time Jörgensen had not come in the handsome *Ragna* but in a curious-looking little vessel called the *Storm King*. She was 9 metres long, 2.7 metres wide and 1.4 metres deep and she was made of three ships' watertanks bolted together.

Appalled by the terrible loss of life in a recent series of shipwrecks which had proved existing lifeboats to be inadequate in every way, Jörgensen had invented a lifeboat which was unsinkable, self-righting, self-launching and protective of passengers. Warned by experts that his boat would sink as soon as she hit the water, Jörgensen had sailed her from England to Australia, via the Cape, to prove that she was seaworthy in the most dangerous of seas. It was acclaimed at the time as 'the most extraordinary feat of seamanship ever recorded' and Jörgensen and his crew of one, Johannes Nielsen, were hailed around the world as modern Vikings, their journey the very stuff of the great Northern legends.

The idea for the *Storm King* was born in the middle of a hurricane as Jörgensen was rounding Cape Horn in the *Ragna*. Amidst 'blinding snow and hail squalls', Jörgenson considered the impossibility of saving his crew should the ship hit an iceberg. Noticing an empty, capped kerosene tin pass the ship, Jörgensen was struck by its buoyancy: 'That caused me to fancy myself floating in such a sea in one of the 400 gallon water tanks we had on deck. All I would require was two bottoms in the tank for ballast to keep the tank always upright; in subdividing the ballast space I could have plenty of fresh water and still keep the tank's stability, for as one of the divisions emptied, it could be refilled with sea water. I felt positively sure that people would be perfectly safe in such a tank. They would have shelter, the provisions would be protected, there would be plenty of fresh water and, best of all, they could be made to float off a sinking ship.'

Like many revolutionary ideas, it was brilliantly simple. It also overcame all the major failings of the lifeboats then in use.

Had it not cost thousands of lives every year, the existing system could have been accurately described as a farce. For a start, ships carried only enough lifeboats to hold half the people on board. On ocean-going liners, this meant that only 500 of the 1000 passengers and crew had even a theoretical chance of survival. However, in the end, this scarcely mattered as the boats were virtually useless in the conditions that made them necessary. Most of them were never launched, as the suddenness of most disasters left no time for boats to be untied from their davits. Of the boats that reached the water, most either capsized or were swamped by heavy seas. If all this were somehow overcome, the prospect for survivors in open boats was equally grim. They usually died from exposure which claimed its victims faster than the alternatives of starvation or thirst.

Jörgensen's *Storm King* system solved all these problems. It was, he continually emphasised, developed 'to save all on board'. Simply by being a decked boat, it could carry fifty percent more people than an open boat, with survivors taking turns at sheltering within. Sufficient provisions for at least three weeks could be permanently stowed inside and fresh water was an integral part of the design.

While most boats would be complete, sections could also be custom made to fit spaces on deck. The three sections of the *Storm King* could be bolted together in five or six minutes but if there were no time to join them, each section alone was also a perfect life-saving device, with the same advantages, except navigation, as the complete boat.

The boats would rest in chocks on deck, held firm against the normal motion of the ship but lifted up from below by the water as soon as a ship should sink. Even if a boat were sucked under, it must always rise again like a corked empty bottle.

'The brave little Storm King' *on display in the Adelaide baths with her inventor-captain and crew after her voyage from London, August 1890*

Captain Simon Jörgensen (left) and his crew of one, Johannes Nielsen, on their arrival in Adelaide, August 1890

Jörgensen had models and plans made and began to look for a backer but no-one was prepared to convert concern into hard cash. Undaunted, Jörgensen decided to finance the building of the prototype himself. He resigned his command of the *Ragna*, sold his half share in her to his brother, and took his wife, small daughter and £660 to London to take out patents and give concrete form to his idea.

As no nautical engineer would risk becoming involved in the design of the boat, Jörgensen designed the whole thing — 'her joints, her fittings, everything' — himself and had her built to his specifications. When the boat was almost finished, the British Board of Trade dealt him a blow that would have stopped a less determined visionary in his tracks. 'The Board of Trade surveyors told me that they considered that the fastenings holding the sections together were not strong enough and predicted that the first heavy sea I came out for, the sections would break from each other and down we would go.'

Jörgensen called in a second surveyor. When this opinion agreed with his own, Jörgensen decided to ignore the Board of Trade but judiciously refrained from telling his wife and family of their prediction. He even, 'to my shame', omitted to mention it to Nielsen.

So, at 3.00am on 12 September 1889, the *Storm King* slowly manoeuvred her way into the Thames after 'the saddest parting I have ever been out for'.

Throughout the voyage, Jörgensen kept a diary and a ship's log in both Norwegian and English. He writes with delighted pride of the continuing sturdiness of his little boat, with affection of Nielsen's sailing and cooking skills (whipping up dumplings and pancakes on the kerosene stove) and with great good humour of his own domestic shortcomings.

He also writes honestly of his fears, as in the moving entry for 16 September 1889: '8 p.m. Saw Lizard light...the last light we would see on the English coast. None did know better than I what it meant to cross the Bay of Biscay at this time of year, having so often been out for those terrible gales and seas one so often meets with there. ...it was yet time to turn back. Should the Board of Trade experts be right after all, then it would mean certain death to continue the voyage. If on the other hand I returned, it meant utter ruin for myself, and what was worse still, I would have lost my self respect. For how could I ever hold my head up again? I had said I would do it and when it came to the point, I dared not. But what about my dear wife and children, and my responsibilities to them? Ruin and disgrace on the one hand. Fortune or death on the other. I chose the last. May none have that agony I had there, looking at Lizard light, beacon of safety, and sailing away from it.'

The real test came for the *Storm King* when, as Jörgensen had feared, she hit a furious storm in the Bay of Biscay just before midnight on 23 September. 'This storm will decide the fate of my tank boat and means death or life for Nielsen and me.'

The little boat not only held together, but ran before the storm for most of a day, weathering mountainous seas with great ease. Jörgensen and Nielsen were overjoyed. 'We in our exultation gave three cheers for the *Storm King*. There was not a prouder man that day in Europe than I...Nielsen was, if possible, as proud of the boat as myself. In his exuberance, he patted her on the side, saying in his hearty way "Well done, old girl." It was the grandest sailing I was ever out for.'

After surviving many storms, sharks, three cyclones, and a collision with a sleeping whale, the final triumph came when the voyage was almost at an end. On a wild night between Albany and Adelaide, something struck the *Storm King* with such force that she turned completely upside down. But after a few moments, the boat did exactly what Jörgensen had always claimed she would do — turned herself right side up again, 'shook her feathers like a duck' and continued on her way. Jörgensen thought it must have been a tidal wave, but they had been run down by a large steamer whose captain, convinced that rescue in such seas was impossible, had reported them dead.

Jörgensen's wonderful lifeboat was exhibited in the Adelaide Baths then at the Waxworks in Melbourne. Jörgensen received hundreds of letters of congratulation but his attempts to have his system accepted as standard lifesaving equipment met with one rejection after another. He returned to England in 1891 with the boat, but the Board of Trade continued to obstruct him. As Jörgensen remarked, 'Had it been some new invention for killing people — a gun or torpedo — governments would have paid the inventor large sums and taken over the same for use in the service.'

Eventually Jörgensen gave his boat to a Norwegian life-saving society and returned to Melbourne, where he became commodore-captain of the Melbourne Steamship Company's fleet and, later, harbourmaster at Geraldton (WA). Captain Jörgensen's son, Justus, went on to establish Victoria's famous artists' community, Montsalvat, the realisation of a different, but no less controversial, vision. Justus is the Jörgensen now remembered, the *Storm King* having long since crumbled back into Scandinavian earth and her inventor-captain's great heroic voyage long forgotten by all but family.

In 1912, the world was horrified when the *Titanic* hit an iceberg and sank. 1500 people died, many hundreds of them from exposure in open lifeboats. 'If their lifeboats had been modelled on the *Storm King*,' said Jörgensen sadly, 'none of them need have perished.'

Agnes Hyland O'Brien
1878–1939

'The greatest horsewoman in the world'
Written by: Debby Cramer
Nominated by: Eileen F. Venning

'Miss Agnes Hyland has knocked 'em silly at the circus,' wrote an unnamed critic at the turn of the century. 'She is what Shakespeare would have called a bonzer.'

Agnes Emily Roberts was born on 28 December 1878 at Millrey station, near Charters Towers, Queensland, where her father, John Thomas Roberts, was the station manager. A skilled horseman and trick rider, he taught Agnes to work with horses while she was very young. At the age of twelve, she accompanied her father on horseback on a 1300 kilometre trek from Charters Towers to the gold rush at Normanton.

But Roberts's skills as a prospector were only mediocre and he and his wife had four children to support. He discovered however, that the gold fields people, starved of entertainment, enjoyed watching him — and Agnes — train and ride horses. These skills proved to be more rewarding than looking for gold.

Roberts changed the family's name to Hyland and when the children — eventually twelve of them — were old enough, they became riders, acrobats, clowns, tumblers, trapeze and wire-walking artists. Each child also played an instrument, so the circus had its own band. Their mother, Elizabeth, was the tailor and cook, while her husband, now the 'Professor', was the ringmaster and leader of the circus.

The Hyland Circus was noted for its equestrian acts and tall, dark Agnes was the star lady rider of the company. 'Miss Agnes Hyland and her Educated Ponies' were praised in newspapers from Kiama to Geraldton and from Cairns to Mount Lyell. Her performances included the four-horse hurricane act; the Mexican act; the Olympians act where she stood barebacked on a cantering pony and carried her little brother standing on her shoulders; and another act in which she rode two horses bareback while driving two more and in the meantime put her sister Rosie through a series of acrobatics. The Melbourne *Herald* of 20 April 1895 reported that 'Miss Hyland is probably the finest horsewoman seen inside an Australian arena'.

The tricks presented by the 'educated ponies' also brought great applause. The reporter from the Gundagai *Independent* thought it 'well worth the admission money' just to see the pony Sovereign, who played euchre with members of the audience, sniffed out hidden handkerchiefs and after untying the ropes around his own legs, would 'free' his fellow pony 'prisoners' in the ring.

In 1911, King George V's coronation year, Agnes was selected to join the 'Wild Australia Troupe', which represented Australia at the Festival of Empire in London. When she was not performing to capacity audiences at the Crystal Palace, she was in demand as a horse trainer for the British aristocracy. Her 'Humane Hyland System' of horse breaking received much publicity. Explaining that 'the whole secret is to get hold of a horse's heart' and that 'everything must be done by kindness', Agnes produced spectacular results.

After the Festival of Empire, Agnes toured the United States as a horse trainer and performer with the Hagenbeck and Wallace Circus and then Germany with the Schumann Circus, where she performed before Kaiser Wilhelm II. The excitement of touring the world was marred, however, because she missed Frank O'Brien, a horse trainer and breeder she had met in Western Australia around 1906.

Agnes returned to Australia in 1913 and the following year married Frank who had waited for eight years. They shared a love and understanding of horses, which Agnes regarded as saner than people. At an interview in Fremantle she declared that 'if a man had the same temperament as a horse, there would be less divorces in the world.'

The life of Agnes O'Brien was dramatically different from that of Agnes Hyland. While no one would claim that travelling the backblocks of Australia by horse and dray, setting up the tent, rehearsing, performing, tearing down the tent, loading up and travelling on to the next community was life on easy street, there were, nonetheless, moments when the glamour and magic of the circus bestowed rich rewards. But by the time Agnes married Frank, the heyday of the travelling circus was waning and by the early 1920s Hyland's Circus had broken up.

The O'Briens settled on a small dairy farm at Yarloop, near Bunbury, Western Australia and soon had three daughters. Despite their hard work, the farm failed. Frank worked camel teams on the gold fields but when he died of pneumonia in 1922, Agnes found herself widowed at the age of forty-four with three young girls to support.

About 1926 Agnes became the licensee of the wayside inn at Tuckanarra, north of Cue, in Western Australia. At that time Tuckanarra was just a pub and a mine shaft on the barren Murchison gold fields, over 650 kilometres north of Perth. Almost single-handedly Agnes ran the hotel, the attached general store and the unofficial post office.

When they weren't at school, the girls helped. Mary Cocking, Agnes's eldest daughter, remembers: 'Mum's motto was "Get up early and get on with the chores."' The day started at 5.00 a.m. and rarely finished before midnight. Monday, without fail, was washing day. Tom Cocking recalls spending the night at Mrs O'Brien's hotel: 'She woke me up at 5.30 on the Monday morning — the copper was boiling and she wanted my sheets!'

Respectability was important to Agnes, whether in Berlin or the Australian bush. 'If you spit on the floor at home you can spit on the floor here', said a sign above the bar. The prospectors respected her and valued her kindness. She never turned away anyone in need and often backed a struggling prospector by extending credit for food and supplies, even though there were times when a prospector would strike gold and not repay his debt.

By 1937 running the operation at Tuckanarra had become too much and Agnes moved to Reedy, a small mining community twenty-two kilometres east of Tuckanarra. Here she ran the general store she had built several years before. She died on 6 June 1939 and was buried at Cue. Few now have heard of Agnes Hyland O'Brien, yet in her way she made the world a better place — from London to Berlin to Tuckanarra.

Agnes Hyland, star performer of Hyland's Vice Regal Circus and expert horse trainer. With her 'educated ponies' she performed before King and Kaiser before ending up in a pub in Tuckanarra. J. S. Battye Library of West Australian History

Gertrude Abbott
1846–1934

'One of God's hidden saints'
Written by: Elizabeth Riddell
Nominated by: Sister M. Dympna McFadden

On a winter night in 1893, as rain beat against the windows, Gertrude Abbott heard a knock at the door of her little terrace house in Sydney's Surry Hills. She opened it to a policeman holding by the arm a pale-faced girl. 'Madam,' he said, 'can you please help this girl? I don't know what to do.'

Gertrude had only fourpence in her purse, and her grocery cupboard was empty. But she had a bed. She put the girl into it, the policeman left, and an hour later the baby was born.

It was not long before other girls, married and unmarried, but all in need of help, came to the Surry Hills house. Between them, the pathetic girl and the policeman and Gertrude Abbott had started what was to become St Margaret's Hospital for Women, the third biggest obstetric hospital in the biggest city in the Commonwealth.

Gertrude Abbott was christened Mary Jane O'Brien in Sydney in 1846. Her father, a schoolteacher, had moved from New South Wales to Dry Creek South Australia and taken up farming. In 1868, when Mary Jane entered Sister Mary McKillop's congregation at Penola, she became Sister Ignatius. She and another young nun, influenced (according to the *Australian Dictionary of Biography*) by Father Julian Tenison Woods, claimed to have seen visions. There was a small scandal when the other nun was found to have faked 'manifestations'. Although blameless, Sister Ignatius left the McKillop congregation in July 1872, only two months after she had made her final vows, and returned to Sydney. No longer able to use her religious name, and for some reason not wishing to revert to Mary O'Brien, she became Gertrude Abbott. She leased a terrace house in Surry Hills and gathered about her a group of pious women. They lived by dressmaking, and adopted the rule of a contemplative congregation. Gertrude hoped that the Catholic church would give her group the status of a religious order.

At St Margaret's Maternity Home in the first year she took in nine married and twenty-three unmarried patients and trained three nurses in midwifery with the help of another great friend, a certificated nurse Magdalen Foley, who took a degree in pharmacy in order to be able to dispense medicines. Regarded as a quasi-religious community, the women gradually acquired status in the church as their service to Sydney citizens was recognised. The hospital was run on donations.

In 1904 the hospital began to treat diseases of women. After it overflowed its four adjacent terrace houses, Gertrude leased and eventually bought a two hectare block near Taylor Square in Darlinghurst.

Her great friend and mentor, Father Tenison Woods, had died in her care in 1889, leaving her his estate, the sum of £609. Then her other great friend, Magdalen Foley, died in 1926. Despite the enormous growth of the busy hospital, Gertrude felt alone, and gradually withdrew as matron and manager. Forty years after that fateful rainy night she died, aged eighty-eight.

'She was a little Queen Victoria-shaped woman,' a friend and admirer wrote, 'with a golden heart, and her name should be written large in the annals of truly Christian workers.' She said of her girls, 'On the first occasion I regarded the patient with the deepest sympathy. If she returned a second time I expressed great disappointment, lectured and advised her. A third time, I kept her with me and mothered her not allowing her to return to danger that was too great.'

In the year that she died the hospital recorded 760 patients treated, 619 births registered and no maternal deaths. In a gesture that says much about Gertrude's character, and perhaps about longings still unfulfilled in spite of the work done, she passed her hospital into the hands of the Sisters of St Joseph whose order she had left unhappily sixty-two years before.

Matron Gertrude Abbott whose care of unmarried mothers and their babies became St Margaret's Hospital for Women. St Margaret's Hospital Archives

William & Claudie Lakeland
1844–1920; 1889–1963
The Lakelands of the Rockies
Written by: Terri McCormack
Nominated by: April Y. Firns

In 1920, Herb Thompson of Silver Plains station on Cape York Peninsula made the grisly discovery of human remains scattered by dingoes and wild pigs. They were those of William Lakeland who had been missing for some months It was a lonely but fitting end for the seventy-three-year-old prospector who had spent most of his life exploring the wild Peninsula country.

Born in Sydney's Rushcutters' Bay in 1844, Lakeland was one of thousands who joined the Palmer River goldrush in 1873. Unlike so many others who sought a quick fortune, he was a dedicated prospector whose searches for mineral deposits opened up previously unknown and inaccessible parts of the rugged North Queensland wilderness. In 1874, he and Robert Sefton found traces of gold at Batavia River and Sefton Creek, and tin at Pascoe Creek. With Christie Palmerston, another colourful identity, he gained eighty ounces of gold from the Palmer diggings in the following year.

In 1876, Lakeland rejoined Sefton on a prospecting trip to the Coen through virtually impenetrable country known for its hostile native tribes. At dawn one morning, Lakeland's tent was attacked and he was speared in his arm and shoulder. Two natives were killed and one wounded before being driven off by gunfire. The time-honoured panacea, rum, was used as external disinfectant and internal anaesthetic while the spears were hacked off with a white-hot knife. Typically, Lakeland was up and about in a few hours. A minor gold rush from Cooktown and the Palmer followed the track made by this party to the Coen.

Lakeland's knowledge of the north was sought by the surveyor J.T. Embley on his 1884 exploratory expedition. Always seeking new horizons, Lakeland discovered the rich Iron Range deposit, wolfram at Lloyd's Bay, was among the first at the Batavia River rush, and found alluvial gold on the Rocky River.

For a brief period, Lakeland owned Pioneer Downs and was a joint partner in a Cooktown brewery but was unable to resist the lure of prospecting. Esther Culton must have known this when she married him. Not long after the birth of Claudie Ethel May in December 1889, the family travelled out past the Coen River to his find at Rocky River.

Most of the diggers left the area when the alluvial gold ran out but Lakeland remained to work the reefs. He built a small crushing plant on the Leo River, using native labour and lawyer-vines to haul the battery over the Chester Ranges from Port Stewart, and a small pinewood house in the midst of the jungle at Rocky Scrub. Here in

'Billy' Lakeland, explorer, prospector, and colourful character of Cape York Peninsula. 'The bush is his shroud'

Claudie Lakeland, renowned throughout the North as a splendid bushwoman and unbeatable shot, at eighteen wearing her first dress. Her father Billy named a river and a goldfield after her

the wilderness, often alone, Esther Lakeland coped with poisonous snakes, hostile natives, and her husband's absences on prospecting trips while she raised three children. Intrepid, and an excellent horsewoman, Esther used to take her own string of horses on the two-day trek to Coen for supplies and was one of the few women to have ridden through the treacherous overhanging rocks known as Hell's Gates.

With such parents, it was not surprising that Claudie soon developed into an independent, capable person. The Claudie River, one of several rivers discovered by Lakeland, was named after her and she had acquired her own name from one of her father's successful racehorses. Eight years older than her only surviving brother, she grew up at Rocky Scrub with only Aboriginal children for company. She soon became her father's 'right-hand man', helping him with the battery work from the age of seven and absorbing her parents' knowledge of bushlore.

Raised in dangerous country, Claudie early became a crack shot with a rifle. Reports of her shooting prowess spread to Coen where, collecting supplies one day, she was challenged to prove her skill by the local police sergeant. In a bizarre version of a 'High Noon' encounter, the townsfolk watched in awe as the discomfited officer was forced to concede defeat to the blue-eyed thirteen-year-old with the long fair hair.

At the age of sixteen, 'C.L.' the tomboy was introduced to such civilised niceties as frocks when her mother took her to Mossman to be formally educated. At nineteen, she married Percival Hodges in Townsville, moved with him to Sydney and had five children.

The Lakelands were forced to leave their Rocky Scrub retreat when water flooded the mine. Esther went south to Cooktown while her husband cut sandalwood at Lloyd Bay, found reefs at Nesbit, and continued prospecting until his unexplained death near the entrance to Rocky Scrub. Esther Lakeland died in Cooktown in 1949 aged eighty-one, Claudie died in 1963 and her brother Leo in 1966.

Near the junction of Attack Creek and the Hull River where Lakeland's bones were found, the people of Coen erected a marble tombstone, hauled by horsedrawn sled to his burial site. The inscription, written by his beloved Claudie who understood her father so well, included the words: 'Gold lured to Death and yet he would have had it so.'

Annie Berry
1866–1942
Intrepid Irishwoman
Written by: Cathy Peake
Nominated by: C. J. Weir

When the Western Australian Centenary celebrations were held in 1929, Annie Berry was justifiably annoyed that she was not acknowledged as the first woman in Kalgoorlie.

Born in Ireland in 1866, Annie Berry's journey to the Australian gold fields was long and almost unbelievably arduous. Separated from her two brothers with whom she was to emigrate to America, she boarded the wrong ship in Ireland and subsequently arrived in Australia unescorted. At the wharf, she met John Weir, a Scot and a saddler with a business in Brisbane.

They married and eventually settled between Gigealpa and Innaminka after travelling the outback selling and repairing harness, frequently taking their payment in livestock. Annie bore four children, and at first it looked as though their station would prosper. However, a severe drought set in, and in about 1892 the Weirs decided to return to Brisbane, taking all their livestock with them.

Unfortunately, they reached the Birdsville crossing just as the drought broke and the Diamantina River came down in flood, Weir was forced to swim his horses back to the south riverbank where his family had been stranded. Hit by a floating log, his ribs were fractured and he died of pneumonia several days later.

Realising that it might be months before she could cross the river, Annie Berry harnessed up the teams, packed the children into a wagon and herself into a sulky and, with a baby on her knee, drove from Birdsville to Adelaide where the livestock was sold.

It was in Adelaide that Annie heard of the Kalgoorlie gold strike. She bought eight heavy horses and four horse drays, loaded two with food and two with roofing iron, and sailed for Albany.

Annie Berry then made her way to Kalgoorlie where she set up an eating house and remarried. Her second husband, Carl Cosh was a Russian who produced one of the first salt water condensers for the Kalgoorlie and Coolgardie gold fields. Resourceful as Cosh undoubtably was, however, he had a long way to go to match his wife, the redoubtable Annie.

Thomas Whitmore
1832–1916

Across Australia for gold
Written by: Terri McCormack
Nominated by: Pamela H. Buchanan

In 1904, a *Gympie Times* reporter, interviewing seventy-two year old Thomas Whitmore at his Pie Creek farm, remarked that few would recognise the pluck and determination hidden beneath his unassuming exterior. It was these qualities, plus common sense and superb bushmanship, that enabled him to make his epic trek in 1893.

Thomas Whitmore was born in Leicestershire and migrated to Queensland with his wife, Jane Daykin, in 1866. He was one of the earliest miners on the Gympie goldfields in 1868, also running a carrying business from Maryborough. From 1882, he was a timber-getter at Pie Creek but, like so many other old miners, was excited by news of the Western Australian gold discoveries in the 1890s. In March 1893, he left Gympie with a horse team, two bullock teams, his young sons Tom, known as Dick, and Charlie, and the knowledge that Western

Australia was in the direction of the setting sun.

At Charleville, drought held him up for nine months and Charlie returned to help his mother with the farm. Thomas and Dick crossed the South Australian border south of Birdsville, delivering supplies to workers on the rabbit-roof fence, and crossed the many flooded channels of Coopers Creek without unyoking the teams. From the Overland Telegraph Line, they crossed barren country to Paddykillan where one bullock team was sold for £60. Here they were confronted with a 400 kilometre 'camel pad' of desert with sandhills 'as steep as the roof of any house'. At the sixty-two mile well, they lost the horses and while Dick searched in vain for them, his father subsisted for nine days on salt water and plums.

Minus dray and harness, the pair reached Fowler's Bay on the South Australian coast where Whitmore was outraged at being charged duty on the bullocks he had sold. At Nellarbor Plains station, they belatedly acquired water tanks and 'bidding goodby to Nellarbor and possibly the world' covered 190 kilometres of waterless desert to Eucla in five days. 'I had cause to know that I was passing into another colony as I was again mulcted of £22 as duty on the cattle, horses, etc.' At Kenney and McGills station, Whitmore was persuaded to exchange the bullocks for a horse team, only to discover later he could have doubled the price.

When the horses strayed 130 kilometres on, young Dick tracked them for six weeks while his distraught father sheltered from sandstorms beneath the dray. In later life, the old man wept as he recalled his relief when he was reunited with his son in that vast uninhabited country. The boy was temporarily blinded by sandblight and Whitmore himself lost the sight of one eye.

After two years on the road, the Whitmores reached Kurnalpie gold field with two horses and a dray. They soon left this small alluvial field for the new rush at Pendennie where water was scarce, rations expensive, and Whitmore 'never saw so much poverty in my life'. Disillusioned, he left his son and caught a steamer from Fremantle to Queensland, taking just six weeks. In that laconic style so typical of the Australian bushman, his final comment on his remarkable journey was '... and very glad I am to get back to Queensland'.

Edward M. Collick
1868–1959
Coolgardie's muscular Christian
Written by: David Millar
Nominated by: Jo Donnellan

When Edward Collick, a young English curate, saw an advertisement for 'a clergyman to minister to new people arriving at Coolgardie — mostly men', he volunteered, and arrived in Perth in 1894. Whilst no intellectual, and without a university degree, Collick had physical robustness, social confidence and an uncomplicated faith upon which he could rely in the toughest of circumstances.

His English parochial experience had been in Hoxton, a London slum full of louts and pickpockets where Collick had won a reputation for being something of a boxer who was not ashamed to mix it in the ring with some of his more physical young parishioners. Administering square cuts and left jabs to his local Boy's Club, along with 'London doorstops' — thick slices of bread and dripping or jam — was as good a preparation as any for his future work in the tough, male community of the Australian gold fields.

His new parish was a challenge from the very start. After erecting his tent Collick was off to help deal with a plague of typhoid that was sweeping the goldfields. He learned very quickly to cope with the raw conditions, such as burying a friend, a typhoid victim, in a coffin hurriedly made out of a packing case with its stencilled instruction still visible on the side: 'Stow away from boilers. This side up.'

Impressed by his work, the miners decided to give him a holiday when the ravages of typhoid had debilitated him seriously and a purse of £250 was subscribed to send him to Melbourne. His flock was dismayed to find him later, somewhat shamefaced and still on the gold fields, with the money gone to widows, orphans and sick Aborigines.

Collick worked hard amongst the local Aborigines. He organised meals when drought and dispossession from their land brought some of the local communities close to starvation, and his Christmas dinners, where local white parishioners waited on the Aboriginal diners, followed by Aboriginal dances and competitions on the local sports' ground, were famous for decades. For years afterwards, every minister on the fields was known to many Aborigines as 'a Mister Collick'.

Collick worked on the gold fields for nearly forty years, broken only by chaplaincy work with the army during the Boer War and World War I. When he left this, for his second and last parish in Western Australia, that of St John's, Fremantle, his farewell service was packed and expressions of regret, gratitude and affection poured in.

Canon Collick remained rector of St John's for almost a quarter of a century. He eventually retired but felt bored and frustrated after sixty-five active working years. He died in 1951 at the grand age of ninety-one.

Harry Kneebone
1876–1933

Crusading newspaperman
Written by: Sue Phillips
Nominated by: Joan Tiver

There is a Cornish saying, 'Those who cannot schemey must louster'(those who cannot use their brains must perform manual labour). With this firmly in mind, Cornish migrant to South Australia Elizabeth Kneebone, a woman of little education and much determination, resolved that her son Harry would not 'louster' in the Kadina

Top. Harry Kneebone, aged 24, Editor of the Coolgardie Miner, *Western Australia*

Below. Senator Harry Kneebone leaving for Canberra in 1930

copper mines as his father, unable even to sign his name, was forced to do.

Harry Kneebone was born in 1876 in Kadina and attended the local school until a leg fracture, poorly set by a drunken doctor, confined him to bed and traction for twelve months. During his long days of convalescence, his mother, set on 'improving' her twelve-year-old son, plied him with books borrowed from the local libraries. The novels of Charles Dickens, champion of the poor and oppressed, had such a powerful effect on the boy that the seeds of his later obsession with improving the lot of the working class were well and truly sown.

When Harry was finally allowed out of bed, albeit with one leg permanently shortened, he had a brief taste of the miner's life: standing at the side of other boys and girls of his age, he worked as a 'picky boy', separating the ore from the trash, while his understanding of the ruthlessness of the economic system under which he laboured deepened. Meanwhile, his mother wasted no time organising more promising employment for her boy, and at the age of thirteen he became a printer's apprentice on the *Kadina and Wallaroo Times*.

Then, towards the end of his apprenticeship, came news of the fabulous riches to be had for the picking on the Coolgardie gold fields. 'Setting up news items about gold being found in the West made typesetting for the uncertain payment of sixpence per 1,000 more drab than ever,' reported the *Journalist*, 'and Harry Kneebone dropped his stick and rule.'

It was decided that Harry and his father should go to Coolgardie, and that when they struck it rich Mrs Kneebone and Harry's sisters would join them. Not only did they fail to strike it rich, but Mrs Kneebone's arrival, prompted by improved conditions on the gold fields, put an end to Harry's mining career permanently: several newspapers had started production and she urged Harry to return to his old field. Beginning as a compositor on the *Coolgardie Miner*, he was only twenty-three when he was appointed its printer and publisher in 1899.

For the next ten years, Harry Kneebone immersed himself in the working life of Coolgardie. He was a foundation member of the Goldfields Typographical Society, a teacher of stenography at the Technical College, president of the Australian Workers' Association, a local councillor, and in 1908 became secretary of the goldfields' branch of the ALP. Despite the conservatism of the owners of the *Coolgardie Miner*, Harry Kneebone was appointed managing editor in 1906 and was given free rein to promote the causes of the workers on the gold fields.

The paper, which had previously been on its last legs, flourished under his energetic rule. Eventually however, 'tiring of his Atlas act', Harry Kneebone moved his family back to Adelaide where in 1909 he was appointed sub-editor and later editor of the struggling Labor newspaper, the Daily Herald. 'Many a time,' says one of Harry's five children, Frank, 'frantic efforts had to be made to find the necessary finance to purchase newsprint on which to print the future issues, and on many occasions the employees had to wait for their pay...I know that my father more often than not was not paid.'

In 1912 Harry was appointed press officer to the Australian High Commissioner in London, Sir George Reid. At the outbreak of war he 'filled in his spare time between working all day at the High Commissioner's office and all night at the Press Bureau', as his daughter Joan Tiver relates, by joining the United Arts Rifles, a home defence unit, and founding the Anzac Buffet which supplied free meals and entertainment to wounded Australian soldiers in London. What he saw and heard in his capacity of war correspondent of the cannon-fodder mentality of the war chiefs outraged him, confirming his ardent pacifism, disapproval of conscription and distaste for censorship, and in 1916, aged nearly forty, he decided he had had enough, and accepted the *Daily Herald's* invitation to return to Adelaide as managing editor.

He returned to confront the conscription crisis that was splitting the country, and indeed his own colleagues, into two opposing camps. 'What Would Jesus Do?' was the title of one of his anti-conscription articles but, unacceptable to the censors, it never saw the light of day, reports Joan Tiver.

With the exception of a brief period as a Member of State Parliament in 1924, Harry Kneebone remained a journalist at the same time holding numerous executive and advisory positions in the labour movement until 1931 when he was elected to the Senate. His tenure, at the height of the Depression, was also destined to be brief, for the Labor government was thrown out of office by the end of that year. But in the few months allowed him he vehemently articulated the articles of his Labor faith — articles which more than fifty years later look tame but which then earned him the name of 'Red Harry': conciliation before arbitration; the setting up of a central reserve bank controlled by the nation; support for the unemployed who, 'when they demand consideration, are termed Communists' (*Hansard*, 5 August 1931); opposition to press monoplies.

Jobless, the *Daily Herald* no longer in existence and with a large family to support, Harry Kneebone had no option but to seek employment from the very press barons whose monopolies he had consistently opposed. Hardly surprisingly, his overtures were met with stony indifference.

Two years later, after trying to establish a radical newspaper, the *Labor Advocate*, Harry Kneebone was dead at the age of fifty-two. Tributes poured in from his Labor colleagues.

'He was a man of such integrity,' says Joan Tiver, 'Although it meant poverty, he remained steadfast to the end. Our mother stood by him always, embittered only by people who betrayed him. People *should* know there are politicians with such strong principles. He was a Christian in the true sense of the word.'

Margaret May 'Mabel' Cole
1883–1964
Girl of ten in a 'man's country'
Written by: Suzy Baldwin
Nominated by: Alfred Watts

In 1895, Joe and Deborah Bridge sold what little property they had in Normanton on the Gulf, packed their remaining possessions and three young children — one a new baby — into a horse-drawn covered wagon and, droving their cattle, horses and goats ahead of them, set off on a 3000 kilometre trek across the top of the continent.

They were headed for Halls Creek in the far north-west of Western Australia, staking everything they had on the cattle country just then opening up in the Kimberley region.

Following his exploratory expedition in 1879, Alexander Forrest had predicted that the pastures around the Ord River would become 'a cattleman's paradise'. The famous pioneering Duracks, inspired by Forrest's report of vast plains and great rivers surrounded by spectacular mountain ranges, made their own expedition to inspect the west country then, some ten years before the Bridges drove out of Normanton, overlanded their cattle from Coopers Creek into the Kimberleys. Following water, they travelled around the Gulf of Carpentaria, then from river to river until they reached the Ord. The trek took two and a half years and half their stock perished along the way. But the Durack stockmen were loyal and their resources enormous. They were left with enough surviving cattle to found the great Kimberley stations.

The Bridges' expedition is an altogether different story. Joe Bridge was a tough bushman, used to long, dry stages, rough country and unfriendly Aborigines. He had worked as a teamster between Normanton and Cloncurry for many years, but those 500 rough kilometres were at least familiar, unlike the vast interior which was then largely unexplored and uncharted, always perilously short of water, and peopled by Aborigines whose attitude was unpredictable. Joe was undaunted by this prospect — this was his one opportunity to acquire a decent slice of land — but his hired men were not so intrepid. After leaving Cloncurry, they took one long look at the country ahead, turned tail and fled, leaving Joe to handle the stock, and the family's covered wagon without a driver.

Fortunately, the new wagon driver was made of stronger stuff. Born and raised in Normanton, the Bridges' eldest daughter had spent her life around cattle and horses. Climbing into the driver's seat, she now took charge of the four-in-hand and its load. Margaret May — always known as Mabel, her father's nickname for her — drove the outfit for almost a year through country that was beyond the endurance of most grown men. When she first took the reins on this great overland trek, Mabel Bridge was ten years old.

Mabel also became the protector of her mother and her younger brother and sister. Her mother, a young Irish immigrant, was plucky enough to embark on this adventure with her husband but she drew the line at handling a gun. So each morning, while Joe was away from camp mustering the horses, the rest of the family would climb into the wagon and Mabel would sit guard with the shotgun. Relief came when the sound of the Condamine bells told them that Joe had returned safely.

Mrs Aila Cole, another remarkable outback woman who became Mabel's daughter-in-law many years later, maintains: 'The blacks in that part of the country never attacked white women and children then. They would kill the men along the tracks, but that was because the men used to take their women.'

Bridges took the more direct but more dangerous route pioneered by the extraordinary Nat 'Bluey' Buchanan in the 1880s. They struck out across the Barkly Tableland to Newcastle Waters on the Overland Telegraph Line in the middle of the Northern Territory, and from there travelled along the Murranji Track. 'Drovers knew that they tackled [this route] at their peril,' wrote Mary Durack. Some died, some lost all their stock, but those who got through 'go down among the legends of the land.' One of earliest to get through was the ten-year-old Mabel Bridge, but, curiously, she and her father are missing from the written legends.

The route taken by the Bridges brought them into contact with tribal Aborigines who had never before seen a European. Mabel, in conversation years later with Michael Terry, fellow bushman and explorer, recalls their meeting: 'They were so taken up with seeing white children...that they followed us for days. They camped near us at night and came over just to look at the white baby.' As she had from her earliest days in Normanton, Mabel counted the Aborigines as her friends for the rest of her life.

After twelve months of hard tucker (salted meat) and harder travel, the Bridges reached Halls Creek. Joe was so short of cash that he had to sell practically everything he had but he had come 3000 kilometres to find land and he was not going to give up now. He explored carefully until he found the land he wanted. Almost halfway between Halls Creek and Wyndham, Joe Bridge staked his claim to what is now 709 000 hectares and named it Mabel Downs after his remarkable daughter.

The isolation that prompted Michael Durack to insist that this was fine country for men and cattle, but no place for white women and children, bred its own distinctive group of independent and unusual women. ('It's the isolation that's the hardest to take,' says Aila Cole. 'That, and the hard tucker. But I'd go back tomorrow if I could.') Mabel had no schooling of any kind, but taught herself to read and write. And she made herself an outfit — complete with hat — from blue dungaree cloth which she wore always with Cossack-style boots. Mabel regarded this as 'a badge of the pioneer' and wore only this style of clothing until, in 1909, at the age of twenty-five, she married Tom Cole.

Tom Cole was another true pioneer, one of Australia's famous stockmen. In 1911, he became the first man to bring cattle through the Canning Stock Route, a 1500 kilometre stretch of the Great Sandy Desert, running south from Halls Creek to the railroad at Wiluna, north of Perth. Blazed only a year or two earlier by A.W. Canning, Surveyor-General of Western Australia, it was the toughest stock route of them all. Two other men preceded Cole down the Canning. He followed a few days later with 500 cattle given to him and Mabel by her father as a wedding present. At one of the fifty-one wells, he found the bodies of his friends, speared by Aborigines. He buried the two men and rode on, arriving safely in Wiluna with his cattle in good condition. While Tom was driving their stock through the most arid land on the continent, Mabel was giving birth to Tom Jr, the first of her eight children.

The fierce independence that made her refuse to be left temporarily behind with friends in Normanton in 1895 (presumably to her parents' subsequent relief) never diminished. During World War II, Mabel was living in Wyndham when the town was bombed by Japanese planes. The Army ordered the immediate evacuation of all women and children to Perth but Mabel refused to leave her husband. By then fifty-seven, she eluded the authorities by leaping onto a horse and riding eighty kilometres across rough country to Ivanhoe, one of the Durack's stations. Aila Cole laughs as she says of her mother-in-law, 'She was very determined: there was no stopping her.'

After Tom Cole died in 1943, Mabel went to live in Alice Springs but spent much of the rest of her life travelling between the families of her four sons and four daughters. 'She could never stay put,' recalls Aila. 'She was always on the move, and always happy. She had her mother's wonderful Irish sense of humour.'

Mabel Cole died in 1964, aged seventy-nine, at Alice Springs and is buried in the tiny cemetery at the foot of the MacDonnell Ranges. She was, as the Alice Springs newspaper said at the time, 'a real woman of the Outback...one of the most remarkable women of Northern Australia.'

Susannah Katherina Schardt
1872–1934
'Being blind, she chose to help others'
Written by: Lois Hunter
Nominated by: Rex Lawrence Cross

In 1872, Susannah Katherina Schardt was born blind. Her parents were German emigrees who had arrived in New South Wales for the 1850s Lambing Flat gold rush, struck it lucky and bought property at Queanbeyan, near Canberra. Blindness, they determined, should not preclude an education so, when she was eight, they despatched Susannah to the Blind School in Sydney. The child missed 'the cattle and their bells; talking to the shearers' and her parents. An earnest and religous girl, she did, however, find a friend in the 'true Christian' headmaster and, with some precocity, an early sense of her own destiny. 'I always had an ambition in life to leave the world better because I lived in it,' she records in her memoir.

What she should *do* to effect any improvement became a little clearer when, becoming ill at school, she was sent to hospital where, on visiting days, 'every other patient had a visitor and I had none...It made me realise what it felt like to be alone and ill in the city.'

In the 1890s, Susannah, then in her twenties, was reunited with her family who had moved to Sydney. She was much occupied as a hospital visitor, and it was on visiting day at Camperdown Hospital, talking to a man whose legs had been amputated, that the young Miss Schardt found to her disbelief that incurable patients were being discharged from New South Wales hospitals with nowhere to go. Queensland and Victoria had refuges for the incurably ill but NSW offered them nothing but a bed in the asylum.

What the State of New South Wales did not provide, blind faith, Susannah Schardt and twenty-one shillings a week did — and her first patient, the amputee, was housed in a room in Riley Street, East Sydney. Then came a cottage for sixteen in Cleveland Street, Redfern. What the founder and her dedicated group of friends could not pay for, they somehow managed to obtain on time payment.

Miss Schardt had 'the audacity' to name it 'The Commonwealth Home for Destitute Invalids'. 'We had to have something big about it, even if it was only the name.' The first patient was, of course, 'the poor man without legs'. Contributions from people with 'big hearts and small pockets' kept them going. Susannah Katherina took courage and 'addressed' anyone who would listen.

By 1906, needing more space, money and help because she was finding more 'incurables', she formed a committee and asked Sir George Reid to be its President. He accepted and, producing £5 'for an afternoon tea', announced that he would bring the Governor of New South Wales, Sir Harry Rawson, to the home for a visit. This official recognition was timely for the Home was under threat — a Council notice to quit had been served because the Redfern house was 'inadequate for the purpose for which it was being used'.

Susannah borrowed a large marquee which was erected in the yard where the washing usually hung, and a piano from Palings. Such a good effort, it seemed, moved Sir Harry for he called a meeting at Sydney Town Hall where Sir Henry Moses offered Weemala, his house at Ryde with seventeen hectares of land, for £7000, towards which he donated £3500. Sir George Reid proved to be a passionate advocate and the meeting netted several thousand pounds. One year later, in 1907, Weemala, housing sixty-five patients, opened as the New South Wales Homes for Incurables. Renamed Royal Ryde Homes in 1954, it is now the Royal Ryde Rehabilitation Hospital.

After this success, Miss Schardt went lecturing throughout New South Wales and raised the staggering sum of £30 000. With her companion, Beatrice Ricketts, her travelling had taken her from Queensland to the Victorian border, visiting every town and village.

Susannah Schardt died, aged sixty-two, in 1934 in the home she had founded thirty-four years earlier. She had wanted to leave the world better because she had lived in it. And so she did.

Arnold Wienholt
1877–1940
Australian patriot, African adventurer
Written by: Niall Lucy
Nominated by: Cyril George Grabs

Arnold Wienholt, soldier, patriot, statesman, author and adventurer, was born in 1877 at Goomburra Station, his family's property on Queensland's Darling Downs. The son of an affluent Welsh grazier, Wienholt was educated at Eton, where Winston Churchill was among his classmates, then took over the management of a family-owned station, Jondaryan. At the outbreak of the Boer War in 1899, Wienholt equipped a company of Light Horse at his own expense and enlisted in the 4th Queensland Imperial Bushmen Contingent with whom he served until the end of the war in 1902, winning the Queen's

Captain Arnold Wienholt, DSO, MC & Bars, MLA, MMR fought for his beliefs in Australian parliaments and the wilds of Africa. Fryer Memorial Library, University of Queensland

Medal with Clasps for bravery under fire.

Interested in politics from an early age (his father had been MLA for Western Downs and Darling Downs from 1870-75), Wienholt was elected in 1909 to the Queensland Legislative Assembly for the constituency of Fassibern but resigned in 1913 to contest the Federal seat of Wide Bay, held by the then Prime Minister, Andrew Fisher. Although he was defeated, Wienholt's tally of 12 543 votes to the PM's 15 702 was considered an outstanding result.

'To become Prime Minister is one man's ambition; another would win the Derby or the Melbourne Cup,' Wienholt wrote in *The Story of a Lion Hunt* (1922), the first of his four books. 'For my own part I have always thought that to shoot a lion was something quite worth doing.' Following the setback to his Federal political aspirations in 1913, Wienholt decided to fulfil his long-held ambition of going on safari to the 'Dark Continent'. But his first experience as a big game hunter nearly cost him his life: Wienholt all but lost the use of his right hand when he was mauled by a wounded lion. He was hospitalised in Angola when the Great War broke out in 1914.

After returning briefly to Australia for medical treatment, Wienholt accepted the leadership of a group of British Special Intelligence Service Scouts in Salisbury, Rhodesia, who undertook a succession of dangerous intelligence missions throughout Angola and German South-West Africa. One such mission resulted in the capture of a large German force heading east across the continent and earned the praise of a Major Gordon who wrote in a communique to headquarters: 'They are a splendid body of men and with such a leader, capable of performing even the impossible.' Wienholt himself was later captured by the Germans but escaped after six months and returned to the front at Dar es Salaam, where he continued fighting until the Armistice was signed in November 1918. He received a Distinguished Service Order and Military Cross with Bar for his 'continuous gallant conduct and endurance under most trying circumstances', and arrived in Melbourne almost a year later as a national hero.

In April 1919, following his return to Queensland, Wienholt married Enid Frances Sydney-Jones, daughter of a wealthy Rockhampton family, and in that same year became the Federal Country Party Member for Moreton, a seat he retained until 1922. Wienholt was an eloquent champion of unfashionable causes. In his maiden speech to Parliament he attacked the cruelty and injustice suffered by German settlers in the Darling Downs district — branded 'Hun' and interned during the Great War, they had been disenfranchised when the war was over. It was a measure of Wienholt's sincerity as a politician that he donated his parliamentary salary to charity.

Declining to seek re-endorsement at the end of his first term, Wienholt spent much of the 1920s on safari in Africa. When he once again settled back in Queensland with his wife and daughter, he declared he had seen enough of the hypocrisy of party politics and announced his candidature an an independent for his old constituency of Fassibern in the coming State election. In 1930, at the age of fifty-three he took his seat for the second time in the Queensland House, representing his electorate with dignity and vigour until the end of 1934.

Ever the adventurer, Wienholt set off for Africa once again in 1935, this time to Abyssinia to offer his services to Emperor Haile Selassie in the Ethiopian fight against Mussolini's Fascist invaders.

A short time before the Italians captured the Ethiopian capital of Addis Ababa in 1936, Wienholt returned to Australia where he wrote and lectured in condemnation of Mussolini's massacre of defenceless villagers. In 1939, his old school friend, Winston Churchill, appointed him to a secret mission to restore the exiled Emperor Selassie to the Ethiopian throne. Mission 101, as it was called, proved to be a success, but only at the expense of Arnold Wienholt's life.

The exact circumstances of his death remain a mystery, though it is likely that Wienholt was killed on the 10 September 1940, when his party of three Sudanese and several Ethiopians was ambushed at camp near the town of Mutabi. One report says that the Australian was last seen stumbling towards the bush with a bullet wound in his side, deserted by the rest of his party. He must have died shortly afterwards, but his body was never recovered and no trace of his belongings, besides a brown leather boot at the campsite, was ever found.

For his services to the Emperor, a tablet was erected in Wienholt's honour in the Coptic Church of Addis Ababa. For his gallant service as soldier and statesman to the country of his birth, a commemorative cairn was posted outside the Fassibern Memorial Park in 1951. The monument is dedicated to the district's pioneers and to Captain Arnold Wienholt, 'A Distinguished Australian.'

James Smith
1873–1951
'I did not know... what we were doing'
Written by: Niall Lucy
Nominated by: Pamela T. Wilson

On the 18 May 1900, Private 203 James Smith of the First Queensland Imperial Bushmen sailed out of Brisbane on the good ship *Manchester* for active duty at the front line in South Africa. The son of a Scottish miner who emigrated to Queensland in the 1860s, Smith disembarked at Capetown in June and within days was thrown into the fray against the Boer forces led by General De Wet. For the next fourteen months, James Smith kept a personal diary 'more as a pastime and an assistance in letter-writing'. Enlivened with his own poems and sketches, this diary is now regarded as the most honest and comprehensive eyewitness account of the Boer War written by any Australian. It is not only one man's story of fear and deprivation but a narrative which speaks for all Australians who fought on the Empire's behalf in a strange land.

'I did not know where we were or what we were doing,' Private Smith recorded in one of his earliest entries, 'and I could not find anyone else who could tell me.'

But it was the climate rather than the lack of information which made combat conditions so unbearable. On the afternoon of 25 July a violent thunderstorm shattered the skies over Balmoral, 'and whew

Private James Smith of the First Queensland Imperial Bushmen whose illustrated Boer War diary tells of the experiences of the ordinary soldier

— wasn't it cold!,' Smith noted in his diary. 'No fires and consequently no tea. Two men and one officer...died during the night from exposure, and there were no less than five hundred bullocks, mules, and horses dead when morning broke.'

A few days later, Smith was among the 5000 cavalrymen who rode triumphantly into the vanquished capital of Pretoria and were presented to the British commander, Lord Roberts, 'who sat on a coal black charger in front of the Parliament House of the former Republic and returned the salute of his dusty and travel-stained minions.' The city itself impressed the young Queenslander with its splendid buildings and monuments.

Despite enjoying his few days spent in admiration of Pretoria's architecture, Smith's overwhelming experience of the war was less edifying. Under constant threat of enemy attack, he was exhausted from trekking through the bush veldt a distance of twenty-five to sixty-five kilometres a day in pursuit of De Wet's troops. Poor rations and little sleep only compounded the misery.

Perhaps the most endearing feature of Smith's diary is that his detailed account of the war is mediated through a troubled conscience. His entry of 7 November 1900, is a typical example: 'The column is destroying all houses belonging to the enemy as we go. This wholesale destruction is a matter that should be very carefully dealt with. Justifiable it may be in some cases but not in all. What will be the fruits of it remain to be seen, but it will be many years before the bitterness engendered thereby will be forgotten, and many an unsuspecting settler who takes to farming in this country after the war will have to pay for it with his life.'

Upon returning to Australia in 1901, James Smith married his late brother's widow and worked for many years as a reporter for the *Queensland Times*. His soldier's journal, however, remains his most valuable piece of writing. An important historical document, the diary of James Smith is not only a journal of military facts and figures but also a revealing insight into the thoughts and feelings of the average Australian enlisted man who took part in the Boer War. In its passages of bewilderment, compassion and understanding of the enemy's point of view, it also bears witness to the sentiments of many soldiers in any war.

John Degotardi
1860–1937
Plague photographer
Written by: Terri McCormack
Nominated by: Joan D. Parsons

John Degotardi, Public Works photographer 1874–1920

Born in Sydney in 1860, John Degotardi was named after his father, an Austrian-born immigrant who was one of Australia's photography and printing pioneers.

John Degotardi junior was employed as a photographer by the New South Wales Public Works Department from 1874 to 1920. He took

Demolition in progress in Wexford Street, a now-vanished part of inner Sydney during Sydney's outbreak of bubonic plague in 1900. Slum-dwellers watch as their rat-infested homes are destroyed. Photograph by John Degotardi, Mitchell Library

Against the background of a prosperous city's skyline, an impoverished family is captured by Degotardi's camera beside its Oxford Street hovel, Paddington, 1900. Mitchell Library

innumerable photographs of the State's public buildings but his most significant work was achieved during quarantine operations in Sydney following the outbreak of bubonic plague in January 1900. Under the direction of architect George McCredie, his task was to photograph buildings destined for demolition in order to avert future litigation.

Degotardi far exceeded his bureaucratic brief by providing future historians with invaluable evidence of the appalling conditions in which inner-city residents were living at a time when it was more acceptable to emphasise Australia's prosperity in the pre-Federation euphoria. The people and buildings he portrayed were only too evidently unprepared for being photographed. Working in close proximity to an epidemic which claimed 103 lives, he was himself in constant danger. His granddaughter recalls his wife's fears that he would fall victim to the plague during his photographic assignments.

Because of the risks taken by Degotardi in the course of his duty, we now have a unique and unromanticised record of an aspect of Sydney's physical and social history which vanished with the plague. His father predicted that photography would be 'the truest and most lasting monument of the combined powers of man, art and nature'. His son's work more than justified that expectation.

Catherine Anne Bennett
1845–1919
Survived Governor brothers' attack
Written by: Katie Lawley
Nominated by: Anne Margaret O'Neill

Catherine Anne Bennett, (seated) with her granddaughter Catherine Egan

On 24 July 1900 Catherine Anne Bennett, local nurse and midwife at Merriwa in the Upper Hunter Region of New South Wales, was at the outlying homestead of the O'Brien family awaiting the birth of Mrs O'Brien's second child. There was growing fear in the region at the time as there had recently been shootings and violent murders at other stations in the area. Attempts to capture the two men responsible, Jimmy and Joe Governor, were constantly thwarted by their ability to disappear into the bush leaving no tracks or clues.

Catherine and Mrs O'Brien were alone in the kitchen when the door opened and the Governors burst into the room. When Catherine asked what they wanted, Jimmy Governor replied 'I'll show you what I want', lifted his rifle and shot her three times, leaving her prostrate body on the floor. Thinking she was dead, the brothers turned on the pregnant Mrs O'Brien and her fifteen-month-old son and murdered them both.

Hearing them leave, Catherine crawled through the kitchen window, mounted her horse and rode off to find Mr O'Brien. After delivering the grisly news, she collapsed from shock and loss of blood. The neighbours found her some hours later in a critical condition lying off the track, amongst fallen timber where she had crawled in dread of the murderers returning. Five hundred police and civilians searched daily for the men who were now outlawed and could be shot on sight. Some months later, this law was put into effect when, on the 31 October, Joe Governor was shot and Jimmy captured. In the film *Chant of Jimmy Blacksmith*, which recounts the story of the Governor brothers,

Catherine's part is played by Ruth Cracknell.

The real Catherine recovered from her ordeal, although scarred on the back, chest and leg. Something of a local hero, she continued to carry out her duties as district nurse and midwife until her death, nineteen years later.

Arthur John Shepherd
1887-1964

Bywong boy supports family and town
Written by: Niall Lucy
Nominated by: Norman J. Moore

Arthur fell into a fitful sleep, waking as the night's blackness began to fade in the eastern sky. He was cold and stiff, but his mind was gradually forming a plan to recoup the family's income from the lost gold reef — lost forever, it seemed, when it disappeared into a dig the previous afternoon. Before the cave-in, that little dolley vein at Bywong, near present-day Canberra, had yielded its golden treasure without interruption. But by cutting and splitting a few fence posts ('Maybe Mr. Millyn would help out?) he might be able to shore up the mine shaft and trace that vein.

Barely thirteen years of age, Arthur John Shepherd had taken charge of his nine brothers and sisters (Archie, the eldest, was only sixteen: not a leader, but always there for the heavy work) since his mother's death a few months before. Their drunken father spent most of his time in the pub at Collector, trying to forget that voyage on the HMS *Harbrow* out of England to the Promised Land in 1883 — and his wife. Always pregnant, always another mouth to feed. And God, that awful screaming as she died!

'Bad that, Mother dyin' with the food poisonin',' young Arthur thought to himself as he climbed out of bed at dawn. 'Bloody awful screamin' 'fore she went.'

Helped by their neighbour, Donald Millyn, the two Shepherd boys soon cleared out enough debris for Arthur to begin searching for the lost vein. It was hard and dangerous work, but within a short time his labours were producing an ounce of gold a day. The quartz was broken up and dollied in a crude stamp mill which Archie turned with a crank, reading cowboy stories aloud to himself.

Eventually, Arthur's gold production increased to such an extent that he was able to support at least half of Bywong's 300 inhabitants, a factor which told in the Shepherd family's favour when a charge of neglect was brought against the ten children. Complimenting Arthur on his initiative and maturity, the magistrate was quick to dismiss the case.

It was during the great drought of 1905 that Arthur's community spirit showed to its best advantage, helping to save the population of Bywong from despair. Under the supervision of this resourceful boy the townsfolk repaired and improved the local dam site and cleared their wells. They survived the drought by carefully conserving their precious water supplies, and rejoiced in great numbers at the Shepherds' place when the rains finally came. Florrie, the eldest Shepherd girl, provided soup and damper while her sister, Rose, led the town in a stirring rendition of 'Abide With Me'. The sound of many voices rolled across the bushland to fade against the lonely hills.

There was only one man in Bywong who begrudged the revellers their delight — Old Nicholas, a mean-spirited prospector who had lost his right hand in a mining accident years before and now sported a fearsome metal hook in its place. He had for some time been envious of Arthur's success, and planned a hundred ways to kill him. One night, shortly after the drought broke, the old scoundrel lay in wait at the entrance to Arthur's mine, leaping out with murderous intent when the lad appeared. The evil hook swung high, then plunged towards the boy's neck. In an instant, Arthur jumped back, dislodging the cover of the mine shaft and causing his assailant to fall headlong to his death in the murky water below. The whole town agreed the old man had met his just deserts and Arthur lived to be seventy-eight.

Evelyn Gough
1854–1931
Lively newspaperwoman and feminist
Written by: Billy Marshall-Stoneking
Nominated by: Beatrice Bewley

Evelyn Gough gazed around the nine-by-nine foot cell, then made a few notes in her writing pad. She was appalled by what she had seen and experienced over the past few days and she wanted to be able to remember all of it, in as much detail as possible.

As part of a subcommittee appointed by the newly-founded National Council of Women of Victoria (NCWV), Evelyn Gough had been visiting gaols in and around the centre of Melbourne for several months of 1902 and 1903, trying to ascertain the nature of gaol conditions for female prisoners, many of whom were prostitutes. It was her belief that women were being shown less respect and consideration than male prisoners, but Evelyn was not the sort of person whose curiosity could be satisfied by calling in and observing the cells at arm's length, or speaking briefly to a few, select inmates. She had to know, at first hand, as much as she could about the hardships women faced in prison; so she had asked, and had been given, permission to spend a few nights in one of the cells.

A successful writer/journalist, and a woman who had always had access to the so-called finer things in life, Gough had no way of predicting what it would be like. The conditions, she discovered, were practically inhuman. 'The wooden floor served as a receptacle for vomit and excreta...four and sometimes five prisoners are locked in 9 x 9 foot cells...sober women were locked up with drunken ones...'

But what appalled her the most was the fact that the dignity of women prisoners in Melbourne gaols was all but ignored. 'The lowest human being calling herself a woman,' Gough wrote in her report, 'has the right to the services of her own sex.' But in the gaols in Russell and Little Bourke Streets, no consideration had been given to employing female matrons. 'Men arrested girls from fifteen years of age to aged women; men took them in charge, men attended to them during the night; men liberated them in the morning; [and] accompanied them to court...'

The reporting of such conditions in frank and vivid prose, especially by a woman, did much to embarrass the government of the day and there is little doubt that Gough's writings and outspoken criticism caused it to review its policies with the result that matrons were finally employed on a fulltime basis.

From the time she was a little girl in Auckland, New Zealand, Evelyn Gough had displayed an independent nature and a temperament that was as caring as it was cheeky — in short, she was extremely self-possessed, and was not afraid to speak her mind when it came to a matter of principle, particularly if it had anything to do with the improvement of women in society.

But the struggle for full equality under the law was still only a dream at the turn of the century, the merest of possibilities, and no-one knew that better than Evelyn Gough. The question was: how could one best advertise the fact that women were every bit as capable and skilled as men?

Evelyn had always had a flair for writing, and for years had contributed to various magazines and journals, so it was natural for her to use the written word in her campaign for justice and equality. In 1899, together with Miss C.H. Thomson, Evelyn purchased *The Sun — A Journal for the Home and Society*, a publication begun by Louisa Lawson, mother of Henry. The newspaper, according to the new editors, aimed at giving its readers — mainly women — 'a high-class and interesting family journal' that would cover such diverse areas as literature, business, sport, politics and art. In Gough's view, women were equally as intelligent and enquiring as men, and the more they knew about every facet of the world and society, the better off everyone would be.

Evelyn herself was a frequent contributor to the newspaper. Often writing under pseudonyms, such as 'Buzz' and 'Whang', her topics were as varied as they were unusual. From an article about her visit to an opium den (she did not partake), to a colourful and vivid description of Melbourne Cup Day, Gough's writing reflects a lively wit and a remarkable eye for detail.

In 1900, Gough published a series of articles that addressed themselves to the matter of the inequality of pay for women compared with men, and for some time this became one of her chief concerns. 'Women,' she wrote in 1900, 'must demand equal reward for equal labour. And [man] must concede equal remuneration to her for the same quality of work that she performs with himself.' This, in Evelyn Gough's view, was the only solution to the sex-labour problem.

Through a series of detailed tables and explanations she put up a very strong case against pay inequities in the postal and teaching professions, as well as in the Insane and Penal Departments.

Her arguments, however, were not without a certain characteristically acute sense of humour. Noting that female postal workers were paid less for the same work, Evelyn wrote, '...if the public were logical

Evelyn Anna Walker Rigg in 1873, before her marriage to Thomas Bunbury Gough

Evelyn Gough, journalist, newspaper proprietor, and woman of spirit, in her prime with unidentified companions. Although she lived her private life very differently from WCTU's Marie Kirk, Evelyn worked with her for factory and prison reform and equal rights for women

it would insist, taking Government values for work done, that letters despatched by women and telegrams sent by them should go at reduced rates. If the Public Service profits by the labour of women so enormously, it ought certainly to take the public who supports it into partnership.'

Evelyn Gough's tireless work on behalf of Australia's women helped produce many much-needed reforms, and it was through the National Council of Women of Victoria, of which Gough was a founding member, that some of her most important work was done, including factory reforms that served to transform conditions for ship and factory workers throughout Australia. Together with other like-minded and public spirited women, Gough campaigned vigorously for the establishment of an epileptic colony and a programme for the proper inspection of boarded-out children.

Children were extremely important to Evelyn, and her own six children were always loved and provided for emotionally, in spite of the fact that their mother led an active life.

When Evelyn was asked by the NCWV to be their representative at an international conference in Canada in 1909, she accepted the task, and in the six months that she was away wrote volumes of letters to her children, many of which have been preserved by the family. Apart from being testaments to her love and devotion, they reflect in a very informal and often amusing way the naturalness and strength of this remarkable intelligent, independent and spirited woman.

In a letter to her daughter 'Bee', written en route to Canada onboard the RMS *Makura*, she confessed that 'the millionaire has not yet appeared, but an old dear Dr Anderson...is most entertaining and clever. He followed me round and horrified [some of the ladies] by sitting down beside me at dinner last night. He has come to each meal since. I saw great looks...when I went out on deck after dinner and got into a quiet corner, he found me and stayed beside me all evening. Great were the sneers and jeers of the Council ladies. I go on my way unheeding, for a man like this is not met every day.'

In all of her affairs, Gough demonstrated a high degree of independence and self-reliance that, in its time, must have raised many eyebrows. But it never worried her. She was never one to use or be impressed by snobbery, and she could not abide pretence of any sort. 'We have [onboard ship],' she wrote in another letter, 'a Lady Fitzgerald who refuses to speak to the common herd. She is an old, grey-haired frump with a humorous face something like Lena Mac. She asked Mrs Staunton (?) to introduce me to her yesterday. She felt she could speak to me as I was one of *the* Goughs!'

Publicly, Evelyn had always taken a stand against what she felt were the injustices of society, but she was never completely alone in this. Many women of her time shared similar views, so it would be somewhat misleading to see her as the exception.

But she was exceptional in many ways, particularly in her private life. Evelyn Gough did not conform to the social norms prescribed by so-called respectable society. The real love of her life was not her husband but a man named Tom whom she mentions in her 1892 diary.

It is alleged that she actually 'moved her husband's bed out of her room', and lived, at least part of the time, with Tom. The diary also suggests that she continued to maintain a relationship with both men, and that when Tom was taken sick with pneumonia, Bunbury — or, 'Bun' as Evelyn affectionately referred to her husband — even visited him in the hospital. Her diary entry for 19 May 1892 gives some indication of the feelings she had for Tom. 'Today,' she wrote, 'I lost my best and truest friend. At 7.30 a.m. I knew what I had to endure. O! The long sorrowful day and at five my dear one was with God.'

Evelyn herself would live to the age of seventy-seven, old enough to see her children married and have children of their own. One of her grandchildren, Pegg, once wrote to her asking how she might become a writer like her grandmother. Even in 1928, female journalists were not common, but then Evelyn Gough had spent her entire life convincing women and men that women could do anything they put their minds to. Her advice to her grand-daughter reflects the confidence and common sense that she carried with her all her life.

'Write simply,' she advised her grand-daughter, 'write sincerely, write naturally and just as if you were talking to a dear chum, tell that chum — whether him or her — all that appealed to you, amused you, all that startled you; write its strangeness, all that was in contrast to your usual everyday experiences.'

And, by way of indicating her belief in young Pegg's abilities, she finished the letter by encouraging her to write a book saying: 'Now then dear, make a start. I will do the editing as a joyous pleasure.'

A peaceful interlude for Evelyn Gough towards the end of her long and fruitful life

Lucy Ann Ward
1856–1935

Maternity home for outback women
Written by: Judith Elen
Nominated by: Gisela Ervin-Ward

Lucy Ann Ward was born in 1856 to parents only six years out of England. At the time of her marriage at twenty-two, she was a milliner operating a shop in North Adelaide. She left her city life, travelling by horse and buggy with her new husband and 'all their worldly possessions', to settle at Willochra, 400 kilometres away near the Flinders Ranges; they cleared the land, sowed, fenced and built, but times were hard and they took extra work wherever they could.

Lucy's first daughter, Lucy Evelyn, was born at Willochra in 1880. There was no doctor present and she was probably assisted by her mother-in-law. 'Little Addie', born two years later, died of meningitis in her third year; a baby niece, adopted after the death of its mother in childbirth, died of diptheria at the age of five. At the time of this second loss, Lucy Ann was thirty-three. She was to have no more children of her own, but later adopted two more babies — the child of a young Adelaide girl whom Lucy had taken into her home and another baby niece whose mother had died at her birth.

When relatives in Hawker decided to leave the district, Lucy and Henry bought their home — the long, low house that was to become refuge for hundreds of outback women.

Lucy Ann Ward was not a trained nurse but with practical knowledge acquired through her own experience and in the homes of other women settlers, she began to take in women far from help of any other kind. With the difficulties of travel, women from outlying areas often needed to stay for several weeks, and when they came they brought with them the other young children they were unable to leave at home. Since ability to pay was never a criterion, finances were not easy. Lucy Ann cleaned, cooked carted water for the continual washing and mangling, and added to the stores with milk and hand-churned butter from her own dairy.

The demand rapidly became greater than the house could accommodate, so Henry build additional rooms and in 1909 The Gables was registered as a Lying-in-Home under the *State Children Act* (1895).

When a severe influenza epidemic struck in 1910, Lucy had tents erected to accommodate the many local people and itinerant railway workers who fell ill. Lucy's grand-daughter, Olive Bischoff, remembers hearing 'an old resident of the area talking about her grandmother moving from tent to tent at night, with a kerosene lantern, tending the sick'.

In 1928, three years after the opening of the Hawker Hospital, Lucy Ann, then seventy-two, recorded her last patient. Over thirty years she had helped deliver between 400 and 500 babies.

Lucy Ann Ward at 'The Gables', the Lying-in Home she ran for 30 years at Hawker, SA

Like her qualifications, Lucy Ann's recognition was not official but grew through the homes of the hundreds of women to whom she brought comfort and help where there was previously none. A hand-embroidered tablecloth — one of Lucy Ann's treasured belongings — bears the name or initials of each of the women she cared for over the years. The embroidered names record an important chapter in the 'unwritten' history of women.

Neville Gilbert McWilliam
1883–1960
'Out of darkness'
Written by: Lois Hunter
Nominated by: Virginia M. Skipworth

In 1906, Neville Gilbert McWilliam became Australia's first blind barrister. McWilliam, the bursary boy, by seventeen was enrolled at Sydney University; by twenty had acquired an Arts Degree with Honours in Philosophy and by twenty-four, despite the absence of law books in Braille, had gained his LLB and been admitted to the Bar. Yet Neville McWilliam was not the Faculty swot but: 'Mac, the good all-round man. He could row, play the piano and typewrite, he could sing, play cards and chess.'

The all-round-man's accomplishments, both social and academic, were not, however, all his own work but had been cultivated since he was six by his four sisters and a remarkable mother. Rosina McWilliam and her businessman husband, John, had left their comfortable Christchurch, New Zealand, home in 1889 to live in Sydney because it offered better facilities for their six-year-old son who had been blind since he was three. On the North Shore, the child had a tutor who taught him the French system of Braille and he was enrolled by the time he was eight, not at a School for the Blind, but at St Leonard's Public School in Blue Street, North Sydney, chosen so 'he should not be pampered or kept from ordinary contacts for fear of injury'.

As soon as her son had some grasp of 'the French System', Rosina found a Braille edition of the Old Testament and *The Merchant of Venice* and 'in pain that I would become a street mendicant, I became a fluent reader', McWilliam writes in a memoir.

Though he was urged on to learn Braille quickly by fear of becoming a blind beggar, once the system was mastered he set off on a search for Braille editions of books he wanted to read. The school choir netted him a Braille psalter and hymnbook. The discovery of Euclid may not have thrilled many small boys but the complete book of theorems in Braille was for Neville McWilliam a find and, at eleven, a Braille Latin grammar inspired him 'to go in for the law'.

An outstanding headmaster took a special interest in his remarkable pupil with the retentive memory and the blind scholar was dux of St Leonard's School three times in his last three years. Nonetheless, the University Entrance Matriculation Examination was initially refused

Neville Gilbert McWilliam, Australia's first blind barrister

Neville McWilliam as 'an impossible novelty'. When he did sit it he was not allowed to use his Braille geometry book 'but had to construct the figures from little hoops and wires used by my sisters in fancy work'. But hoops and all, he was through and by seventeen University life began.

His Arts Degree years, financed by his bursary, were happy. He sang baritone in the choir at Christ's Church, North Sydney, he belonged to the Sydney University Dramatic Society and he coached in French and Latin. But the Law Faculty gave no bursaries. His parents supplied most of the money 'by dint of great sacrifice', while the absence of standard law books in Braille was overcome by a mother and four sisters who read him tomes while he took notes in Braille.

There was faith in him at home but at the Faculty his professor in Law redressed the balance. Each term he would announce that he did not think McWilliam would pass. Each term proved him wrong. Even his student's remarkable feat of transcribing the Institutes of Justinian into the Braille system from Latin (which work was to become a major reference book) failed to impress him. The obtaining of the law degree much to the old professor's surprise, elicited only a warning to McWilliam that 'he would never make a living out of law on account of the natural prejudice against a man who could not see witnesses'.

And prejudice *did* keep Neville McWilliam almost starving for years. Useful advice to a fellow barrister, W.A. Holman, who was stuck on a case changed his luck, however, and when the Government changed and Labour came to power, Holman became Attorney General. By 1914 McWilliam had achieved success as a barrister. A happy marriage to Agnes Watt and the birth of a son and daughter followed. By the 1930s McWilliam had become Chairman of the New South Wales Conciliation and Arbitration Commission and co-author with Richard Boyt of a definitive book on Arbitration Law in New South Wales.

When Neville McWilliam died at seventy-two, in 1960, it was remarked that 'Performing a remarkable feat in the Supreme Court ... he led a woman client who is almost deaf through fairly lengthy and difficult evidence, eliciting one by one a set of facts with a rapidity and particularity as if human infirmity were not a factor...' His life, both personal and professional, argued that it was not an insurmountable one.

Annie 'Topsy' Hansen
1907–

Woman of the outback
Written by: Marian K. Dent
Nominated by: Marian K. Dent

She was found under a coolibah tree in 1907, two or three hours after she was born. Her Aboriginal mother, a member of the Biltara tribe, was lying dead beside her. There were no nursing mothers at Glenormiston, a large North Queensland cattle station extending hundreds of kilometres into the sandhills of the Simpson Desert and

Toko Ranges, so the tiny baby was suckled by a dingo.

Her father, a hard-drinking Scottish boundary rider, gave her only her name — Annie Daley. Quickly named 'Topsy' by the white people who took charge of her, when she was nine months old the Biltara claimed her as their own, when, during the 'wet', Old Mary swam the flooded Georgina River and snatched the baby. Before the flooding subsided, the tribe and Topsy had vanished into the sandhills of the border country.

'My father gave me my white name.' Topsy says, 'but it was the tribe that reared me.' The next seven years, when the Biltara had no contact with white settlers, were, Topsy remembers, always happy. Now, four decades later, the beliefs, customs and values that she learned in her childhood with the tribe still dominate Topsy's life.

But Topsy's happiness was not to last. At the age of seven, on walkabout in the channel country, Topsy was taken to Roxborough station by members of her tribe searching for food. The station owner stole Topsy back.

For the couple who took her there, the consequences were terrible — enraged elders had them speared to death. For Topsy, handed from one station to another as a domestic servant, it was the beginning of the most miserable period of her life. 'I still had the wildness of the tribe in me,' she says. 'I didn't want to stay with the white people — I wanted to go back to the tribe so I used to run away every chance I got. Oh, I was beaten all right and every time the manager's wife used to leave the station, I would be locked in the pantry and fed like a bird until she returned.'

At ten, given to yet another cattle station, Topsy escaped more than sixty kilometres down the Georgina River until she found an Aboriginal camp. Discovered and recaptured once more, she was passed on to Lake Nash station.

Here, Topsy finally admitted defeat and accepted the inevitable. She learned to cook and clean, but she was also cared for by the Suttons, the Scottish couple who managed the property. 'Mrs Sutton was nice,' says Topsy. 'She used to let me go out with all the gins and down to the camp. That way I was happy. She was one of those old women who was good to the children. She would coax them, teach them, give them lollies and make them clothes.'

Mrs Sutton was to have a great influence on Topsy's life. A kindly woman whose own five-year-old daughter had died, Mrs Sutton was genuinely devoted to her unruly charges and handled them with tact, patience and wisdom. She recognised the importance of Aboriginal life to Topsy and encouraged her to go walkabout with the tribe. Mrs Sutton could not save the Aborigines from the white man's world but she did much to protect them until they had learned its ways.

Topsy stayed at Lake Nash station, slowly becoming less involved in tribal life. When the Suttons left in the early 1920s, Topsy left too and for a number of years worked on many of the big cattle stations in the district. Just before World War II, the many Chinese and Japanese who worked as domestic servants were interned and their places were taken by Aborigines. Once again Topsy went on walkabouts and there were corroborees being danced at the camps near the big homesteads, but real tribal life as she had known it as a child had disappeared forever.

At a bush race meeting Topsy caught up with an old acquaintance,

Topsy Hansen, woman of two cultures and one of the last links with a vanished era of Australia's past

Jack Hansen. 'Jack Hansen and me — we was kids together,' Topsy explains. 'Then he used to go into Boulia races, so my old stepfather came to me and said, "Well now, instead of you walkin' around and going here and there, you get married now." So I did.'

Jack and Topsy had a lot in common. Jack's mother was black and his father a German working at Glenormiston.' His father's way of dealing with his mother's people was simple — he shot them. 'The tribe blamed Jack's mother for the killings so they speared her to death and Jack was brought up by the tribe at Glenormiston.'

A resourceful bushman, and a gifted horseman and cattleman, Jack was known as 'Snapshot' for his skill with a rifle. Like most outback pioneers, both Jack and Topsy could turn their hands to any job. They spent the first few months of married life droving, then returned to Glenormiston where Jack became head stockman (and remained so for twenty-eight years) and Topsy was cook. Topsy recalls, 'If I wasn't in the house, I was helping to butcher a "killer" or working in the camp — boundary riding or droving. When the manager was out at the mustering camp, I looked after the station too.'

Of Topsy's four children, only two survived. 'Because Jack and I couldn't read or write, we made sure our girls had a good education. We saved our wages and sent them away to boarding school and they did well too.'

Still a lively, handsome and energetic woman at eighty-one, despite her fading eyesight, Topsy remains fiercely independent and proudly Aboriginal. She now lives with her daughter Isabel just outside Brisbane, and visits Mt Isa three or four times a year. But Topsy hates city life and her heart remains in the ochre red ranges and channel country of Queensland's north-west.

Although she welcomes the opportunities available to her children and grandchildren, Topsy, one of the last of her tribe, grieves for the tribal life now vanished forever. 'Out there,' she laments, 'lies my home country. Out there is where the tribe used to roam. That's where we had our corroborees and where our campfires used to burn. On rock faces and in caves are paintings and carvings that white men have never seen. In that country lie the bones of my people. I would like to go back just once more.'

Cecil Palmer Jessop
1874–1965
Brought water to the outback
Written by: Katie Lawley
Nominated by: Glenne Harvey

Cecil Palmer Jessop was a self-taught mechanical engineer whose windmill system brought water to the Queensland outback.

Manually skilful, Jessop had an extremely inventive and curious mind, and a 'passion for nuts and bolts' that started in early childhood and carried through to his death at ninety-one. Given only the briefest of formal educations from age six to eleven, his farming parents were at a loss to understand his fascination with mechanics, which started with steam, at the age of five. 'Mostly self-taught, he would read everything he could acquire about steam engines', says his grand-daughter. 'He would walk miles to see any variation or improvement in design.'

Growing up, the young Jessop saw the hundreds of hours of backbreaking manual labour involved in a farmer's life. Teaching himself draughting, moulding and casting, his aim became 'to develop special machines to speed up production that would benefit the man on the land'. To this end, he established a family company 'Nile Engineering', which supplied draughting and manufacturing machines, sawmilling and irrigation equipment and 'much more' to the rural sector.

Of all the machinery Jessop designed, his major accomplishment was a series of windmills, achieving the apparently impossible task of supplying water to the Queensland outback. The most celebrated of these are the geared and self-oiling Southern Cross windmills. With little or no maintenance needed, they are still in use. A well-known symbol of the outback, the windmills are a constant reminder of Jessop's outstanding contributions to mechanical engineering in Australia.

Cecil Palmer Jessop, standing on one of the windmills he designed, an invention which brought water to parched regions of outback Queensland

William Morris

?

Teacher with a vision
Written by: Billy Marshall-Stoneking
Nominated by: Dorothy Michell

William Morris had watched the population of Mathoura, in New South Wales dwindle, and he had watched as the number of pupils attending his school had fallen as well. As the timber workers moved farther afield, taking their young children with them into areas where there were no schools or teachers at all, Morris became so concerned about what would happen to the youngsters he had been teaching, that, in 1913, he wrote to the New South Wales Education Department.

A few months earlier, Morris had written a paper on correspondence education in which he suggested that 'this work be a continuation of lessons already taken in schools but which were discontinued for reasons of parental movement or the closing of the school.' Morris insisted that this system had worked with adults and that it would work just as easily and effectively with bush children.

Mr Smith, Inspector of Continuation Schools, was interested in Morris's ideas and suggested that he promote the course of instruction himself, taking a limited number of children and following an elementary programme of the three Rs. After an article by Morris in the Inverell *Argus*, he had so many applications for correspondence education that he ended up with more pupils than he could manage.

On 15 August 1914, Morris wrote to Inspector Smith providing him with the names of his pupils, samples of their work and their results. Smith was extremely impressed.

But Morris already had his own school to run and the load became too much. Convinced that a full-time staff was needed to meet the ever-growing demand for correspondence schooling, Morris suggested that the Education Department take on the responsibility.

In April 1916, the department appointed a Mr Carter as Principal in Charge of Correspondence Schools, his office being a table in the Building Branch of the Department of Education, Sydney.

Over the next few years, the system grew and then in 1924, hearing of the successes of the New South Wales experiment, a woman in Victoria applied for correspondence lessons for her children and the Victorian Correspondence School was formed.

From the doorway of his little school on the edge of the bush, William Morris had dreamed of a time when distance and isolation would not be barriers to learning, and, in his own lifetime, saw the realisation of that dream.

Leslie James F. Thomson
1886–1946

Australian Antarctic adventurer
Written by: Billy Marshall-Stoneking
Nominated by: Malcolm P. Thomson

Leslie James Felix Thomson, master mariner, who served in two world wars and volunteered for Shackleton's Antarctic Expedition of 1914–16

Why do men climb mountains which have never been climbed before? Why do they venture into unmapped deserts and jungles, and risk their lives in the far reaches of space? Perhaps it is this unquenchable curiosity, this need to push back the barriers of ignorance and increase their knowledge of the world that distinguishes human beings from other animals.

In his quest for information and insights, however, man has not always progressed in a straight line. More often than not, it has been three steps forward and two steps back.

This is particularly true of man's exploration of the world's polar regions and perhaps his greatest challenge has been Antarctica. For in the search to discover the secrets of this great polar land mass, every explorer has had to deal with the same, relentless enemy — the cruel and persistent ice. 'It is not so strange, therefore, that most polar explorers have regarded ice as the only thing to be conquered.'

The polar explorer, Ernest Shackleton, was well aware of this when he advertised for men in the London *Times* in 1915. He made no attempt at all to gloss over the difficulties and treacherous circumstances that awaited anyone who ventured to the Antarctic.

'Men Wanted for Hazardous Journey,' the advertisement read. 'Small wages, bitter cold, long months of complete darkness, constant danger, safe return doubtful. Honour and recognition in case of success.'

Leslie Thomson was already an experienced merchant seaman when one of Shackleton's ships, the *Aurora*, dropped anchor in Hobart, Tasmania, in 1915. Although he had no polar experience, when he discovered the ship's ultimate destination he wasted no time in signing on. By that evening he was on his way to Cape Evans in the Ross Sea as Second Officer.

In January 1916, Captain McIntosh, the *Aurora's* captain, and several other men were put ashore. The plan, as outlined by Shackleton, was that 'the *Aurora* should wait at Glacier Tongue, nine or ten miles from Discovery hut, and serve as a main base with a small party at Cape Evans hut to carry out scientific work'. Unfortunately, nature was against them.

Writing in his diary on 6 May 1915, Thomson recorded: 'At 9:35 pm or thereabouts I had just been turned in when the after moorings began to strain and the decks to groan and then I knew the ice had again started to go out of North Bay C. Evans.' The bad weather caused the ship to be blown clear, and by the evening of the following day, it was encased in pack ice. With the ship stranded in the ice and Captain McIntosh on shore, Stenhouse took on the responsibilities of ship's captain and Thomson became First Officer.

The *Aurora* remained stuck in the ice for over a year during which time the crew suffered privation and extreme hardships. During the twelve months of their 'imprisonment', Thomson kept a faithful account of the daily challenges and anxieties that he and the others faced and his observations and descriptions reveal an inner calmness that most certainly was invaluable in maintaining a relatively high degree of morale among his men.

'There are,' he wrote on 26 July, 'a couple of signs amongst some of the party that they are developing nerves. Just imagine anybody going to sea with such luxuries as nerves, as if they are any use to anybody down in these Latitudes...'

Throughout it all, he maintained a sense of humour writing, of a row brought on by his 'Republicanism', 'anything for a change'.

Finally, in February 1917, the *Aurora* — badly damaged from its ordeal — limped out of the ice and sailed for New Zealand to report on what had transpired and to organise a relief party to be despatched to the Ross Sea.

Thomson was later awarded a silver Polar Medal by the King, and then promptly forgotten by history. But there is little doubt that his selfless efforts were largely responsible for the fact that the *Aurora* and her crew survived the rigours of the ice.

HMS Aurora, *which was trapped in pack ice for over a year during the Shackleton Antarctic Expedition*

Leslie Thomson (second from right) with fellow crew members of the Aurora *on which he served as first officer*

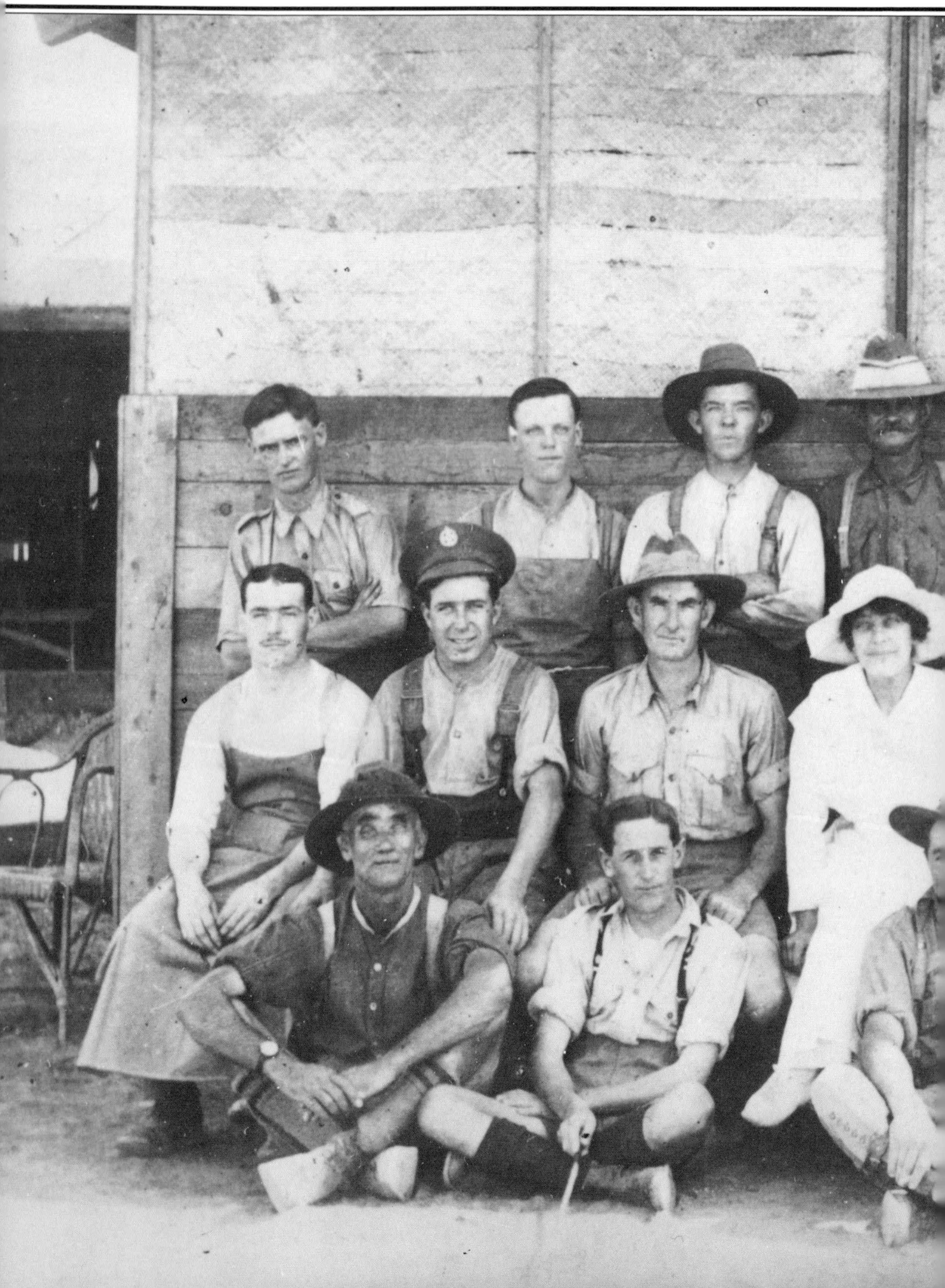

4

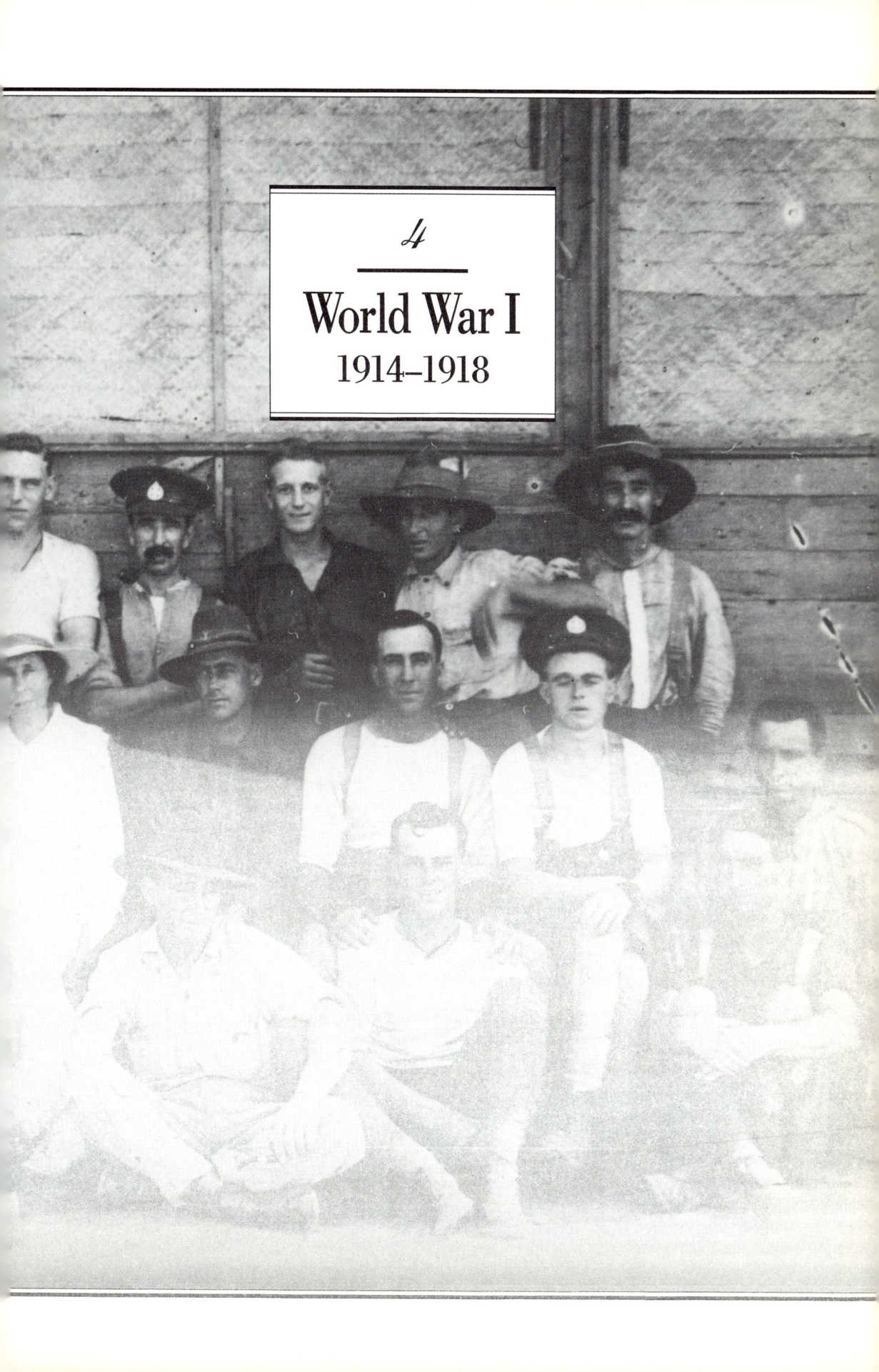

World War I
1914–1918

When the century began, Australians were fighting at the Boer War. To Sergeant James Smith it was bewildering. 'I did not know...what we were doing,' he wrote in his diary.

Smith's bewilderment was shared by thousands of enlisted men in World War I. 'We were intensely patriotic', recalls Mert Thomas who enlisted, like so many others in this war and the next, at the age of seventeen. 'But nobody told us anything.' Mert found himself on the Somme at the Battle of Fromelles where 5500 Australians, ordered 'to go over the top', were killed in just one night. 'They simply mowed us down.'

There is no Anzac here, but there are two stories of those who made their lives more bearable — Latrobe, who carried the Gallipoli wounded on his donkey, and Alice Chisholm, who went to take care of her own son and stayed to become 'Mother' to the sons of thousands of other women.

One of the shocks of this war was the devastating effects of new technology. But while the new technology of war was all too efficient at destroying lives, the infant technology of flight, as the story of George Pinnock Merz sadly reveals, was not yet adequate to save them.

Claire Trestrail
1889–1960
'There is so much to do'
Written by: Sue Phillips
Nominated by: Mary Nilsson

In World War I some 3000 Australian nurses served abroad in England, France, Italy, Egypt, Palestine, the Persian Gulf, Burma, India, Vladivostok, Abyssinia and on hospital ships and transports. This figure does not include those nurses who, travelling overseas when war broke out, enlisted in London. Just how many joined up in this way is not known precisely, but two of their number were Sister Claire Trestrail from South Australia and Matron Mary Benallack from Victoria, both of whom enlisted in 1914 with the 'QAs' - Queen Alexandra's Imperial Military Nursing Service Reserve.

Claire Trestrail, born in 1889, was one of Australia's earliest nursing graduates. At the age of twenty-five she set out to see the world and arrived in London in 1914 as war was declared. Claire was among the handful of Australian nurses to volunteer for service in those early days. She joined Queen Alexandra's Imperial Military Nursing Service Reserve and was despatched almost immediately to Belgium. In a letter written to her sister in 1914, and published in an Adelaide newspaper, Claire Trestrail describes those days of bombardment in Antwerp:

'We left London on Sunday (September 20), and arrived in Antwerp on Tuesday morning...We were met by the British Consul and members of the Red Cross, and taken in motors and carriages to the convent,

Previous page. Dame Alice Chisholm (centre right), her staff and some of her 'boys' outside 'Mother Chisholm's Canteen', Kantara, Egypt, during World War I

which was our home for three weeks. Opposite...was the hospital.

'On Monday (September 28) the siege of the city began, and the patients came in by the score. We had to put some on camp beds and some on straw mattresses on the floor. The wounds were awful. Some of the men had been lying for hours in the dirt and cold until the blood was dry on them, and they were hungry and exhausted. All day and all night for 10 days the guns continued to roar, until we became so used to them that we could even joke about them, and listen, first for the Huns' growl, and then the Belgians' answer...They shelled the reservoir and left us without water for 10 days...

'On Wednesday, October 7, at midnight, the bombardment of the city began. There was the report of the gun, a long weird scream resembling the scream of some wounded animal, and then the crash. We flew to the hospital in various stages of dress and undress, and carried the patients on stretchers, screens, even on our backs to the dark, damp little cellars below. In 25 minutes the 130 were in safety. All the girls were "true blue," and so were the patients...You quite understand that we were all women — 29 of us, doctors, nurses, and orderlies.

'In the morning all those who could walk went to the station, and we managed to get an ambulance to take six of the worst to another hospital which had safe and clean cellars. We also got a British motor lorry to take 16 patients, three nurses, one doctor, and an interpreter, to Ostend. But there was no one to take us, and so the hours crept on, and the shells continued to yell and scream all around us. The fires broke out in place after place, and night began to fall. We felt pretty blue. At last someone saw three London buses full of ammunition, rushing along the street and asked them to take us with them. "Yes, if you are quick," they said. In we bundled, bag and baggage, tore on through the burning street, over boughs of fallen trees, broken telegraph wires, and tons of broken glass, to the bridge of boats. Once over, and we were out of those piercing shells. The burning city behind us and the burning oil tanks ahead. It was a scene that we will remember to the end of our lives. The buses were under orders, and could do no more for us, so we left our luggage and set out to walk to a station 20 miles away. But fortune favoured us again, and we met a Belgian General, who put us in Red Cross motors, and sent us in charge of two officers to St Gilles. There we had coffee at a convent and slept, for a few hours, on the floor with the refugees.

'At four o'clock we went on the transport train with the retreating English troops bound for Ostend. The journey took 13 hours, and I think the distance is about 60 miles. We ate with the soldiers, ration biscuits and sardines. We were all equally glad to be out of Antwerp, and also all equally, dirty, tired, and hungry. That night we slept on the floor for the third night in a hotel in Ostend, and left next day for England. We are going, we hope, to France now, there is so much to do. I know you will wish us to do our best.'

'There is so much to do' became the refrain of this woman's war. Back in France she served in L'Infirmerie Major L'Auxiliare, the Paris military hospital where, in primitive, unhygienic conditions, she and her embattled colleagues worked around the clock to treat the horrific wounds caused by the new weapons of the Great War — machine guns, shrapnel, land mines, mortars and bombs, tanks and flamethrowers. Trench feet, trench fever, shell shock — this was human suffering on a scale without precedent. But out of the mayhem, the mud and the misery Sister Trestrail helped bring order, solace and, where possible, healing to the endless procession of casualties.

Eventually Claire Trestrail and her colleagues were repatriated to England and, as her daughter Claire Birmingham recounts 'having been torpedoed in the English Channel, they were paraded before a fearsome English matron who reprimanded them for their dishevelled appearance and granted them 5/- compensation to replace their uniforms'. For her work, Claire Trestrail was awarded the 1914 Star, a medal which few Australians were eligible to receive for service in that pre-Gallipoli year.

After the Armistice Claire Trestrail studied at the Remedial and Massage School of Guy's Hospital, where she developed the skills that she would later use with polio victims. Back in Australia, she married and had three children. When her marriage failed, she single-handedly and with typical determination and dedication reared her children who all remember her 'with much love'. Volunteering once again for service in World War II and undeterred, though bitterly disappointed, by her rejection on the grounds of age ('It'll take me a long time to laugh this one off, but laugh I will, in the end'), she worked for the Red Cross and Voluntary Aid Detachments as a matron, her two daughters serving alongside her.

Claire Trestrail died in 1960, shortly before the blossoming of the century's second great wave of feminism. For more than fifty years, however, she had lived by one of its central tenets — the belief that women should be 'brave, strong and self-reliant'.

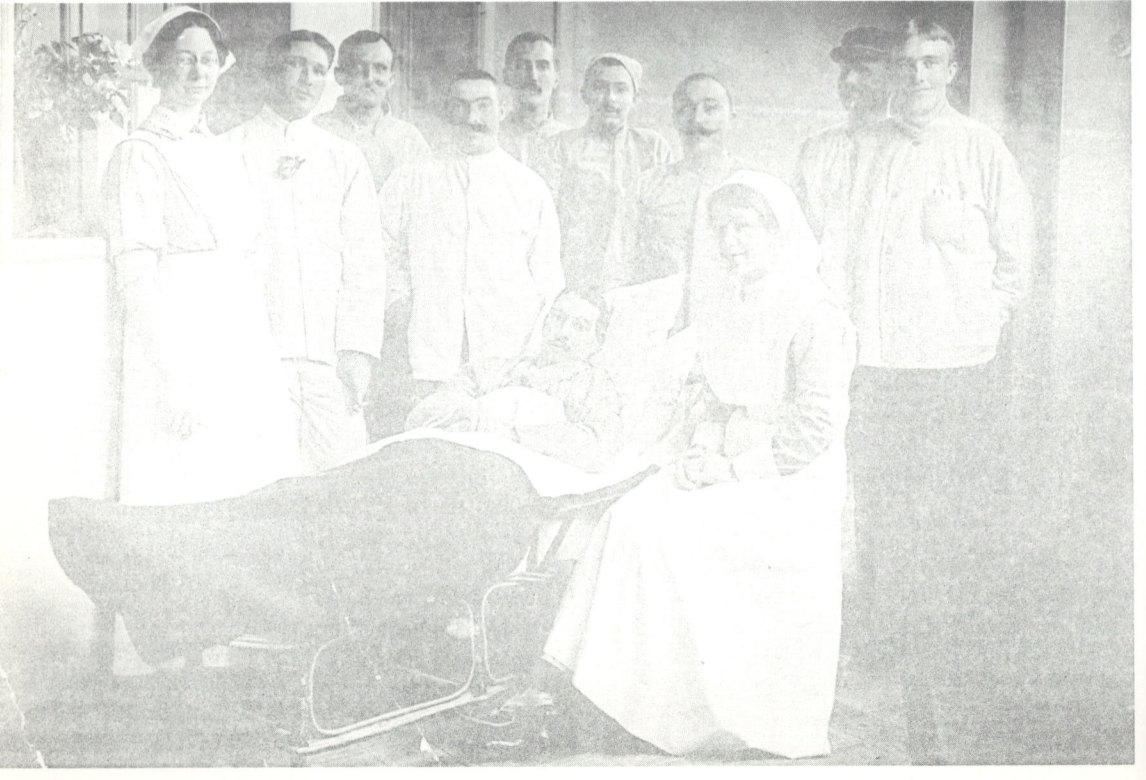

A postcard sent by Claire Trestrail from her Paris military hospital showing herself (right), her auxiliary and patients. 'You can see by their faces that they are nice and that they are brave and suffered'

Mary Ann Benallack
c1875–1937

'Little adventures' in World War I
Written by: Jacqueline Kent
Nominated by: Ida M. Trompf

Until her late thirties, Mary Benallack seemed destined for the comfortable, unspectacular life of an Australian rural nurse. Born in Colac, Victoria, in about 1875, the youngest child of prosperous parents, she trained at the local hospital and at nearby Maryborough, where she gained her matron's certificate.

In 1914, Mary set off alone on a world cruise. No sooner had she reached London than she learned that Britain had declared war on Germany. Determined to join the Australian Nursing Corps, she found that she could not return to Australia because of wartime shipping conditions, so she enlisted in the Queen Alexandra Imperial Military Nursing Service Reserve. On 14 November, as part of a contingent of volunteer Army nurses, she was sent to the battlefields of northern France and Belgium.

Nothing she had seen in the Victorian bush could possibly have prepared Mary Benallack for the horror of life behind the British lines. In the stench and mud of an improvised field hospital, she had to help amputate smashed and gangrenous limbs and try to ease the last moments of shockingly-wounded young men. Often very close to the pounding of German guns in Ypres, Reims and Wimereux, she risked her life almost every day. Soldiers were sometimes considered lucky to survive one month in the trenches: Mary Benallack survived as a nurse for almost three years.

Yet Mary wrote very little about these experiences to friends and family at home. In 1917, she published an article in the London *Weekly News* that makes her part in the war sound almost genteel. She refers to 'my own little adventures in that grim area of titanic combat...called the Western Front' and adds, 'For nearly three years I have had the honour of tending the sick, the wounded, and the dying.' The real story of Mary Benallack, however, is one of great courage.

In July 1917, Mary was one of four nurses aboard a barge that had been converted into a hospital, proceeding along a canal 'somewhere in France' for the purpose of bringing back wounded men from the front. Her barge arrived in a small town 'and over the next two hours over a score of monster shells landed in and about the town'.

Suddenly a shell burst in a potato field no more than twelve metres from the barge. 'We were hurled off the hatch and thrown violently to the deck...my recollection of what took place within the next few seconds is of the vaguest description [but] I was completely buried beneath the debris created by the bursting of the shell.' Suffering severe shell shock, her face covered with cuts and bruises, Mary Benallack was taken to a field hospital.

Matron Mary Benallack, one of the first Australian nurses to serve on the French front

From there, she was sent back to England to convalesce. After crossing the Channel, she was transferred to a troop train. Because her head was swathed in bandages, she was mistakenly taken into a compartment full of wounded soldiers. 'They glanced in my direction and one of them smiled and said, "Well, old fellow, and how are you getting along? That's a fine bunch of linen they've tied round your cranium". Merciful goodness! The bold warriors regarded me as being of the male gender. This was a serious matter indeed!'

Mary Benallack returned to Australia shortly afterwards. In 1918 and 1919, during the worldwide epidemic of influenza that claimed the lives of almost 12 000 Australians, she set up and ran an emergency hospital at the Colac showgrounds. She subsequently became matron of Derrinook Private Hospital, Colac.

Mary Benallack's practical, no-nonsense heroism was recognised by the award of several service medals. On any list of Australians who served in World War I, she commands an honoured place.

George Pinnock Merz
1891–1915
Australia's first wartime air casualty
Written by: Niall Lucy
Nominated by: Julia McClelland Nicholls

At the outbreak of war in 1914 the technology of flight had barely got off the ground. Compared with craft developed by the end of the war, the flimsy aircraft which took to the skies in the early days of attrition were as dodos to eagles: the fledgling Caudrons, Farmans, and Bristol Box-Kites were capable of a maximum speed of around only ninety-five kilometres per hour and a pilot who could fly to a height of 900 metres in ten minutes was thought to have performed with distinction. The early machines carried no guns, were mounted with no greater than an eighty horse-power engine, and were forever at the mercy of any unfavourable breeze — often being blown backwards by a strong head-wind. To fly them took the right stuff.

In spite, or because, of the danger and difficulties involved, flying captured the imagination of many young men. It certainly took hold of George Pinnock Merz, a recent honours graduate in medicine from Melbourne University and an officer of the Melbourne University Rifles, who enrolled with three others in the first Australian course in war-flight instruction at Point Cook, near Melbourne, on the 17 August 1914. The course lasted three months and all four candidates qualified as pilots, with Merz topping the class.

But if Merz was among the first to win a commission with the Australian Flying Corps (the nascent RAAF), he was also the first Australian pilot ever to be killed in action.

The history of Australia's military air service began with an expedition called 'Half-Flight' up the Tigris valley towards Baghdad in Mesopotamia (latter-day Iraq) in 1915. Merz and three other Australian

Lieutenant George Merz, seated on bucket, doctor and top graduate of Australia's first war-flight instruction course, with fellow members of the Australian Flying Corps' 'Half Flight' in Mesopotamia, 1915

pilots — supported by a ground consort of aircraft mechanics, artillery and motor-transport units, and AIF infantrymen — were attached to the Australian 'Expeditionary Force D' which had been sent to swell the ranks of the British and Indian brigades against the massed Turkish troops who were threatening to take control of the region. The airmen were engaged on dangerous reconnaissance missions, resulting in several decisive victories to the Allies.

Because of the fierce heat (offical logs record an average temperature of 40°C in the shade from June to September) and the constant dust storms, the air-cooled aircraft engines were often stressed to the point of breakdown. As hostile Arabs roamed the whole country beyond the Allied trenches, the fear of engine failure posed a serious threat: to be forced to land among the nomadic tribes of Mesopotamia, far from ground support, was perhaps the gravest risk the airmen faced.

Apart from the toll on machinery, the sweltering climate led to many cases of sunstroke and respiratory complaints among the Expeditionary troops, and the mosquito-ridden swamps along the banks of the Tigris produced outbreaks of malaria and other tropical diseases. When he was not flying reconnaissance patrols, Merz was kept busy at an understaffed and ill-equipped hospital in Nasiriyeh, about eighty kilometres from the main base at Basra.

Although he could not have known it at the time, George Pinnock Merz tended his last patient on the night of 29 July 1915. The following dawn he set off in his Caudron with Lieutenant W.W.A. Burn, a New Zealand airman, to return to the base at Basra. It was the last their

Merz aloft in his flimsy aircraft

comrades ever saw of them.

According to the reports of two Arab eye-witnesses, engine failure forced Merz and Burn to land in the desert about 30 kilometres from a refilling station at Abu Salibiq. Armed only with revolvers, the airmen could not have been in greater peril. Within minutes, a band of Arabs, heavily armed with high-calibre rifles, appeared over the dunes. In their desperate flight towards the safety of the fuel depot, the men ran a distance of eight kilometres, killing one and wounding five other Arabs, before one of the pilots — nobody knows which — was badly wounded. The other stood beside his comrade until both were shot and hacked to death by the nomads.

No trace of the missing airmen was ever found. A punitive expedition accompanied by Captain T.W. White, who had graduated with Merz in the original class of four at Point Cook, though unable to apprehend any of the principal culprits, burnt the houses of a sheikh by way of reprisal. The plane, smashed and splintered, was discovered on special reconnaissance a few days later.

'But wherever on the limitless desert their graves may be,' White subsequently wrote in his book, *Guests of the Unspeakable*, 'the spot needs no monument and is hallowed by their heroism.'

Not long after Merz and Burn's death, improvements were made in flight technology which led, by the end of the War, to planes capable of speeds in excess of 240 kilometres per hour and able to climb to 3000 metres in five minutes. They were armed with machine-guns, fitted with engines of greater horse power, and less susceptible to the ravages of heat and dust. However, the good fellowship and precious flight experience of Merz and Burn were lost forever to their comrades-in-arms. 'In the rush mess hut at Basra,' Captain White lamented, 'we missed them sadly.'

Herbert W. R. Latrobe
1893–1947
Latrobe and his donkey
Written by: David Millar
Nominated by: Rosemarie & Charles Mathews

The story of Simpson and his donkey is indelibly written in the Australian legend of the Anzacs at Gallipoli. Private John 'Simpson' Kirkpatrick, ferrying wounded soldiers down the ravines of Gallipoli to the Beach Casualty Clearing Station, despite murderous fire from the surrounding Turks, seems to many to symbolise the mateship of the Australian soldiers during the Dardanelles Campaign.

Without detracting from that story, there is another which deserves to be more widely known. One of the young Australians who landed at Gallipoli was twenty-one-year-old Herbert 'Bert' Latrobe, the son of a gold battery worker near Dungog, NSW. Volunteering for the army, he found himself as a stretcher bearer on the *Euripides*, steaming for the Dardanelles as a member of the First Field Ambulance.

Early in the campaign, the army had imported donkeys with Greek drivers as water carriers, but it had not been a success. The Greeks had been sent away and the donkeys turned loose to feed, somewhat precariously, up in the hills. When on 25 April 1915, an offensive was launched against the Turks, these donkeys once again became useful. Young Bert Latrobe, faced with the problem of carrying wounded over difficult terrain, acquired one of these animals and was soon regularly turning up at the Regimental Aid Post with his donkey to pick up the wounded for the tortuous scramble down the ravine to the beach. For nearly four months, in appallingly dangerous conditions, Latrobe worked his donkey drop until an exploding shell tore his stomach open. Invalided out on 14 August to the nearby island of Heliopolis, Latrobe was soon transferred to an Egyptian hospital before being honourably discharged from the army.

Simpson was shot dead on 19 May 1915, after only a month ferrying out the injured. Latrobe went on to become a detective in NSW, remembered by crime watchers for his solving of the famous 'pyjama girl' case and the Forbes murder. He died prematurely at the age of fifty-four as the result of the wounds received at Gallipoli, where he and Simpson, with their donkeys, had saved so many lives.

Bert Latrobe of the First Field Ambulance carrying the wounded on his donkey. Gallipoli, 1915

Alice Maxwell Chisholm
1856–1954
'Mother Chisholm'
Written by: Elizabeth Riddell
Nominated by: Janet Maxwell Champion

The woman who thousands upon thousands of battle-weary Australian, New Zealand and British soldiers knew as 'Mother' Chisholm was slim, brown-eyed, pale-olive skinned, dressed from neck to ankle in starched white, a wide-brimmed hat on her greying hair. This was Alice Chisholm, later Dame Alice (only the second Australian Dame after Nellie Melba), the Canteen Lady of World War I. She was sixty, a widow with four grown-up children, the youngest of whom, Bertram, was a Light Horseman. When he was wounded at the Gallipoli landing and lying gravely ill in hospital, Alice Chisholm took a berth on a steamer and fetched up in Cairo to look after him.

Having seen to Bertram's need, Mrs Chisholm was confronted with another. She saw that soldiers needed some link with home, a place where they could get a meal when they came in from the front. In the face of enormous obstruction from the 'authorities' she chose Heliopolis, a Cairo suburb, for her first canteen. She acquired a tent, a table, some basic food supplies, using £30 of her own money and £30 advanced by the Australian Comforts Fund. After Heliopolis came Port Said, Rafa, Kantara (now El Qantara) Sinai, Jerusalem.

Alice Chisholm did not see herself in the role of the Angel of the Tea Urn. She recruited Australians, New Zealanders and English women to supervise the canteens with mainly Egyptian staff. Her job was

Dame Alice Chisholm, DBE, who went to Egypt to comfort her son and stayed to set up six canteens for the men of the First AIF. Cairo, c.1916

to keep the service going: to out-guess the civilian and military blimps who wanted to remove her or constrict the work; to beg, borrow and steal equipment, assisted by some resourceful operators among her 'boys'; to sort out the logistics of supplies and transport; and to cope with emergencies. Once at Kantara she rounded up 50 000 eggs (small eggs, she commented) for troops unexpectedly straight out of the front lines. Another time she put together a meal for 1000 men in twenty minutes. At one of the canteens she and her staff were on their feet for three successive nights. She even made a profit — £22 063 at Kantara in under two years — an extraordinary feat when a cup of tea cost only a penny. The money was ploughed back into the canteens and military charities such as St Dunstan's Institute for the Blind.

Kantara was the star canteen and always called 'Mother Chisholm's'. It had dormitories, dining rooms, showers, hot fresh bread, and butter kept on ice. And it had Alice Chisholm. She made it a point to be there, to be seen, to keep in touch. Mrs Chisholm, her work done, returned to Sydney in 1919. She had been awarded an OBE in 1918 and in 1920 was invested with the order of a Dame of the British Empire by the Prince of Wales. In 1926 Bertram, who was an architect, built her a handsome house in the bush at West Pennant Hills, northwest of Sydney. Alice Chisholm died aged ninety-seven in 1954. Four former Light Horsemen were pallbearers when she was buried in the Chisholm family vault at Kippilaw near Goulburn.

Mrs Chisholm set up her first canteen because she saw it as a necessity. She believed that women were good at such practical things. Her grand-daughter, Janet Maxwell Champion, who has written an unpublished memoir of Mrs Chisholm, remembers her as 'gentle, resolute and humorous'.

Douglas Grant
1885–1951
Aboriginal soldier
Written by: Niall Lucy
Nominated by: Anonymous

It is a remarkable fact that 300 to 400 Aborigines, mainly from New South Wales and Queensland, saw active service with the AIF in World War I. Remarkable, because an amendment to the Defence Act in 1909 made domestic military training compulsory for all men except those 'not substantially of European origin or descent'. Black Australians were thus officially prohibited from enlisting.

Unofficially, however, it was easier for Aborigines to join up after the heavy casualties suffered by Australian troops at the Dardanelles and the Somme and the defeat of the conscription referendum in 1917, although it was not uniform across the States. In Western Australia especially, the Defence Act was rigidly enforced throughout the War.

One of the few black Australians to enlist before 1917 was also one of only a handful of 'full-blood' Aborigines to serve with the AIF in World War I. His name was Douglas Grant, Private 6020 of the 13th Battalion, and the story of his failure to win acceptance in Australian society after the War is typical of the way in which many Aboriginal and part-Aboriginal 'diggers' were received back into civilian life. In other ways, however, his story is unique.

'Poppin Jerri,' as Grant is said to have been known by his own people, may have come from the Bandjin tribe in North Queensland. He was orphaned at about the age of two when his parents were killed in a violent skirmish with troopers in the Queensland bush. But for the chance intervention of Robert Grant, a Scottish naturalist, and his wife, who were collecting specimens in the area for the Australian Museum in Sydney, the child would certainly have suffered the same fate. Seeing that a black trooper was about to dash the infant's brains out on a tree, Grant levelled his rifle and ordered him to 'Drap the boy!'. He dropped the child and fled, and the Grants took the boy back to the family home in Lithgow to be raised as their own.

By all accounts, Douglas led an outwardly full and happy life as a youth in Sydney society. He received the same schooling as the Grants' other children and later trained as a draughtsman, being in some demand as a calligrapher as he was able to write a fine hand in copperplate. In 1897, at the age of twelve, he won first prize in the Queen's Diamond Jubilee Exhibition for a drawing of Queen Victoria, but in spite of the promise he must have shown as a talented sketch artist there is no record of Douglas ever pursuing art as a career.

Douglas Grant was thirty when he enlisted in Sydney in 1915, having been rejected six months before. We can only speculate on his motives for joining up.

Despite the claim by one of his foster father's colleagues at the Australian Museum that Douglas's social background made him 'nothing more or less than the normal European', Douglas Grant did not enjoy the same opportunites as the other young men of Sydney. Certainly his marriage prospects were severely limited and so too were his chances of gaining permanent employment, as opposed to piecemeal work as a calligrapher. He might have been raised as a white boy, but he could never escape the social inequity of being black.

When Douglas Grant sailed out of Circular Quay in 1916 to fight in Europe, his own people were strangers to him and his adopted society would never treat him as one of its own. Like the other black recruits, he must have seen the War as a means of 'proving' his equality. Ironically, however, he was captured at Bullencourt soon after his arrival and interned as a prisoner in Berlin, where he was repeatedly reminded of his difference from the other POWs by the German medical staff who subjected him to such indignities as measuring his skull for brain size.

After returning to Australia, Grant worked for a while in Lithgow and built up a bank account of some £600. Then he went on a two-month holiday to Tasmania and came back without a penny to his name. He was already a heavy drinker when the Depression took its toll on him, and he had long ago been made aware that his colour would always prevent him from getting permanent work.

It is a measure of Douglas Grant's courage that he undertook perhaps the bravest act of his life at a time of greatest despair. In 1931 he published an article in the Sunday edition of Sydney's *Daily Telegraph*, in which he spoke out on behalf of the social injustices and suffering of his race. It is a powerful example of his public identification with the heritage from which he had been dispossessed at the age of two, and clearly shows that his loyalty lay with the Aboriginal people of Australia rather than with the white society in which he was raised.

Pleading for Government intervention in the appalling plight of his race, Grant refers to the shooting of thirty-one Aborigines in Central Australia in 1928. The massacre is remembered by the Walbiri tribe today as 'the killing times', when a policeman called Murray slaughtered their people and chained many more to trees. But violence was not the only form of oppression suffered by blacks: they were also prevented by the Constitution from voting in elections, and were among the few minorities to be denied the old age and maternity pensions. It was not until as recently as 1975 that Aborigines were made full citizens with equal rights.

Although he was born a 'full-blood' Aborigine, it is not hard to believe that Douglas was writing of his own experience when he called for special consideration of the 'half or quarter caste', who, 'like Hagar's son Ishmael, has become a wanderer, an outcast on the face of the earth'. It is certainly as an outcast that Douglas lived the rest of his life in Sydney until his death in 1951, the same year in which the racist amendment to the Defence Act was finally repealed (even though a further 5000 Aborigines had served in World War II).

Douglas Grant must have died a sad and lonely man. An old family friend recalls that he last saw Douglas on Anzac Day in the early 1940s, standing alone under a tree in Sydney's Domain as the veterans marched by. 'I don't belong any more,' Douglas said when asked why he was not marching. 'I've lived long enough to see that I don't belong anywhere; they don't want me.'

In his final years, Douglas Grant ran errands for a mental hospital in Callan Park in return for meals and accommodation. But he will be remembered most for his article in the *Daily Telegraph*. Bold and outspoken, it is one of the first published accounts by an Aborigine of the history of his people's degradation since 1788.

'When the rightful owners of this land ... call for justice,' Douglas Grant wrote, 'they are answered with the lash or the gun.' It is time that they were answered with compassion.

Maurice Vincent Buckley
1891–1921
VC winner's change of identity
Written by: Niall Lucy
Nominated by: James F. Yeomans

For reasons of their own, a number of Australians enlisted for service in the Great War under aliases. It is unlikely that one of these men foresaw that his deception would be revealed by his winning the Victoria Cross.

A motor trimmer by trade, Maurice Vincent Buckley was born at

Upper Hawthorn, Victoria, in 1891 and enlisted under his correct name with the 13th Light Horse Regiment in 1914. He was discharged upon returning to Australia a year later from action overseas, but re-enlisted under his mother's name of 'Sexton' on 16 May 1916, also adopting a dead brother's name of 'Gerald'.

Under his new alias, Buckley again went overseas (this time with the 13th Battalion), and was awarded the Distinguished Conduct Medal for 'conspicuous gallantry and devotion to duty' during the big offensive in August 1918, in the Morcourt area. The following month, Sergeant 'Gerald Sexton' and his battalion were engaged in the Allied advance on the Hindenburg Line, capturing several enemy outposts near the village of Le Verguier to the north-west of St Quentin. Firing his Lewis gun from the hip, Buckley took two of these outposts on his own.

As the fog and artillery smoke cleared around the village, a field gun and mortar nests were spotted on the bank directly ahead of Buckley's section. Dashing across the flat, the Sergeant shot the gun crews and opened fire on the enemy dugouts, from which thirty Germans emerged to be taken prisoner. Single-handedly 'Sexton' had captured the headquarters of the Line Battalion of the German 58th Regiment.

His citation for the Victoria Cross was published in the *London Gazette* just five weeks after the Armistice. It was awarded for 'great feats of bravery and endurance without faltering or for a moment taking cover'. But Buckley had indeed taken cover, of course, under the alias of 'Gerald Sexton', and the gazetting of his award under this false name forced him to reveal his true identity shortly afterwards. This resulted in a further notice in the *Gazette* on the 8 August 1919, which established that the Victoria Cross had in fact been awarded to Maurice Vincent Buckley, 'the correct Christian and surname of this NCO which he has been permitted to resume'.

Sergeant M. V. Buckley, alias Gerald Sexton, who was forced to reveal his real name when he won the Victoria Cross

Eleanor Jacob
1891–1949
Australian Women's Service Corps
Written by: Terri McCormack
Nominated by: Eleanor W. Benson

'As the men won't, I will' was Eleanor Jacob's rallying cry in the Sydney *Sun* of 2 November 1916 as she sought recruits for an Australian Women's Battalion to help 'beat the Huns'.

Born in Maitland in 1891, Eleanor and her two younger brothers were left fatherless at an early age and all later became school teachers. Eleanor graduated from Sydney University with a Bachelor of Arts and was an accomplished pianist. By the time of the Great War, she was also a vocal advocate of votes for women and other contentious feminist issues.

Eleanor's call to arms brought an overwhelming response from women who 'thought of more than writing cheering letters and knitting comfortable garments for our soldiers'. Forming themselves into the

Australian Women's Service Corps (AWSC) with country and interstate branches, they offered the services of 700 women to the Defence Department. Their objective was to undertake 'Active Service duties now performed by men who would thus be released for the fighting line'. In a barrage of letters to the Minister of Defence and the Prime Minister, founding President Eleanor Jacob gave assurances that the Corps had no desire to usurp men's work but were capable of doing 'women's work' in field kitchens, hospitals, laundries, offices, and as drivers.

The offical response was unenthusiastic, due no doubt to the women's insistence on enlistment on the same basis as men. Undaunted by this 'Spirit of Red Tapeism', and insisting that it was only a matter of time before the services of women must be accepted, Eleanor trained her girls for the front. Only childless women between twenty-one and forty-five were accepted. Fitness and practicality were developed with classes in physical culture, marching, stretcher drill, swimming, home nursing, French and cooking. Regular meetings were held in the Returned Soldiers' Association rooms and in February 1917 the informative *AWSC Despatch* appeared. But offers of trained women to reinforce English women of the Army Auxiliary Corps in France were rejected by both the Governor-General and Lloyd George.

Eleanor Jacob, founder of the Australian Women's Service Corps, in 1915 when she was twenty-five. An accomplished pianist and advocate of female equality, she fought for women to be allowed to do more for the war effort than write 'cheering letters' and knit socks

Denied active service, the AWSC used their abilities and energies to 'shame the men' by assisting the Voluntary Workers Association physically to clear forty-five-acre blocks of land at the French's Forest Soldiers' Settlement. They participated in recruiting marches and a range of voluntary war work. Their marching prowess was demonstrated at the second Anzac Day celebration in 1917 when a spectator called them 'Australia's Last Hope'. In June 1917, they were the first women to march in Sydney's Military Tattoo. With offical badges and smart uniforms of dark skirts and hats and 'the daintiest of white blouses', they were led by Miss Jacob who, remarked a colleague, was 'in her glory with a few field-marshals and the like'.

While working tirelessly for the war effort at home, the AWSC continued their pressure for service abroad. In November 1917, they conveyed a unanimous resolution to Prime Minister Hughes requesting the conscription of women. Despite 'coping with situations before which their grandmothers would have swooned gracefully away', their services were not used. It was not until August 1941, eight years before her death, that the Australian Women's Army Service was formed to perform the duties so vigorously advocated by Eleanor Jacob twenty-five years earlier.

Charles Henry Hilder
1879–1961

Mysterious message in a bottle
Written by: Terri McCormack
Nominated by: Beverley Lewis

On the afternoon of 27 July 1917, the Burns Philp coastal steamer SS *Matunga* left Sydney's Darling Harbour on a routine voyage to Rabaul, the former capital of German New Britain, with a cargo of prime Westport coal. Her passengers included military officers and coconut planters who, with their wives, were returning from leave. One of the firemen was the thirty-eight-year old Londoner Charles Hilder who regretted leaving his English wife and five-month-old daughter in lonely isolation in suburban Balmain. As she farewelled him, Lily Hilder anticipated his return in less than a month but it was to be more than a year and a half before she saw her merchant seaman again.

Her nightmare began when the *Matunga* failed to reach Rabaul on 7 August, the date of arrival previously indicated by two wireless messages. From 15 August, alarming headlines appeared in Australian newspapers — 'FEARED LOSS OF S. MATUNGA' — 'NO TRACE OF THE MATUNGA' — 'GRAVE ANXIETY' — STILL NO NEWS'. Lists of passengers and crew were published and theories accounting for the disappearance included internal explosions and seismic disturbances. Questions of government assistance arose when Burns Philp ceased payment to its missing crewmen whose dependants, like Lily Hilder, were forced to take menial jobs in order to survive.

Charles Hilder, merchant seaman, who risked his life to alert the world to the presence of the German raider Wolf *in Australian waters*

Not until late February 1918 did cable news reach Australia that the *Matunga* was one of eight vessels captured by the German raider *Wolf* during a fifteen-month cruise harassing and destroying Allied shipping. Passengers arriving in Europe told of 'barbarity on the *Wolf*' during their seven months' incarceration. Although the fate of the *Matunga* remained unclear, small weekly payments were made to relatives when it was learned that the crew had become POWs in Germany.

Charles Hilder had in fact made courageous and desperate attempts to alert the world to the *Matunga's* fate soon after its capture on 6 August 1917. According to Captain Alex Donaldson's later account, the Germans were quickly alerted to the numerous messages being dropped overboard from the captured *Matunga* and confiscated all tins, bottles and boxes. Despite this, and the threat of savage retaliation if detected, Hilder despatched a note dated 14 August, just before the crew and much-needed coal were transferred to the *Wolf* from the *Matunga*, which was then scuttled. A year later, on 2 August 1918, a bottle containing his carefully hand-written note washed up on Maiana Island in the Gilbert Group. It contained details of the capture of the *Matunga* and other missing Allied ships, the extent of the *Wolf's* armaments, the existence of a hydroplane assisting the raider, and the presence of 150 prisoners on board. The brief reference 'Get all wireless news' explained the raider's success.

At first thought to be a hoax, the message eventually reached the Department of Navy via the local Burns Philp representative. The fact that the bottle was carried so far east when the general set of currents in those latitudes was westerly created great interest. At last the facts surrounding the *Matunga's* disappearance became known with one newspaper proclaiming 'MYSTERIOUS MESSAGE FROM THE DEEP'. It was presumably some relief to Hilder's wife to receive, even a year late, the message: 'Good luck and best love from husband to baby and yourself'. The well-travelled note concluded: 'See that my wife does not want. Goodbye for a time. This will be the last bottle as we are going to leave Matunga and go on to the raider.'

Having survived imprisonment on the *Wolf* and in Germany, Hilder returned to Sydney on the *Barambah* on 25 February 1919. His wife died in November 1987 but his daughter can still recall the excitement of wearing a new dress to greet this stranger. With him, Hilder brought another letter which he had carried around his neck with his seaman's book throughout his ordeal. Fearing he might not survive, his thoughts were with his wife and child. 'I often wonder,' he wrote, 'how you have managed out there all alone.'

Hilder received the British War Medal and Mercantile Marine Medal as well as the official welcome-home acknowledgement from King George V. He received no recognition for his efforts to convey information regarding the *Wolf's* activities and capabilities in his water-borne message. He resumed work with Burns Philp and, after a period of unemployment during the 1930s, worked for the Sydney Harbour Trust. During World War II he worked on the Captain Cook dock in Sydney. He died, aged eighty-two, in 1961.

In February 1920, the Resident Commissioner of the Gilbert and Ellice Islands sent him the original message thrown overboard in 1917. Although now badly worn, this remains a treasured family memento of one man's courage under extraordinary circumstances.

Henry John Smith
1890–1971

Forgotten hero of Dunsterforce
Written by: Niall Lucy
Nominated by: Donald M. Smith

In January 1918, the Allies made a desperate plea for officers willing to undertake 'a hazardous enterprise, requiring initiative, resource, and courage'. Following the success of the Bolshevik Revolution in October of the preceding year, the Russian Army had withdrawn from the Trans-Caucasian Front, leaving the civilian populations of Georgia, Armenia, and Assyria vulnerable to wholesale massacre by the Turks. The Allied forces, seriously depleted by the heavy casualites of the previous four years, were already stretched to the limit in other parts of Europe. The Trans-Caucasians had somehow to be mobilised to form a resistance force.

Many answered the call for volunteers. On 14 January a hand-picked group of twenty Australian officers was joined for its initial briefing in the Tower of London by fifty-six officers from the British, Canadian, New Zealand, and South African Armed Forces. A subsequent request called for volunteers from among the enlisted ranks. A week later, twenty AIF NCOs arrived in London to complete the Australian quota for the mission that was to be known officially as 'Dunsterforce' after its commander-in-chief, Major-General Dunsterville.

Only the most outstanding volunteers were chosen for the mission. Typical of the military records of the AIF detachment was that of Sergeant Henry John Smith, a miner from Queenstown in Tasmania who had enlisted with the 40th Battalion in July 1916, and had been decorated in France with the Military Medal and Bar for rescuing wounded comrades under fire. Like the other NCOs, however, Smith was unaware of the purpose of the mission until intensive training began with the arrival of Dunsterforce in Baghdad on 28th March.

Three months later, the Tasmanian sergeant was one of the 'Baku Expedition', under the command of Captain Stan Savige of the 24th Battalion, AIF. Its purpose was to organise the Assyrian and Armenian rebels into a unified revolt against the Turks. Armed with twelve Lewis machine guns and 100 000 rounds of ammunition, the party set out on the morning of 19 July — officers on horseback and NCOs on mules — to make contact with the rebel leader, Agha Petros, at the town of Sain Kala in the northern highlands of Persia.

Shortly after reaching the rendezvous on the evening of 3 August, Savige's party was treated to a magnificent spectacle as column after column of Assyrian cavalry rode into camp in full regalia, the most resplendent of all, Agha Petros himself, at their head. The following morning a messenger brought shocking news: the city of Urmiah had fallen to the Turks and 80 000 civilian refugees were marching southward on the open road for the Allied camp at Bijah, their rear

Sergeant H. J. Smith who volunteered for Dunsterforce and almost perished on the Baku Expedition

The non-commissioned officers of Dunsterforce on the banks of the Tigris River in 1917–18. (Henry Smith in front row, 10th from left.) Their CO, Major-General Dunsterville, said 'I am prouder of my command [of them] than of any other command I have ever held'

unprotected from attack by Turkish soldiers and Kurdish tribesmen. Leaving the Assyrian cavalry to defend the main body of refugees, Savige formed a patrol of two officers and six enlisted men, including Sergeant Smith, and rode out with a week's rations and three Lewis guns to protect the tail.

Cheered as they passed through the motley procession of civilians and their flocks which stretched for twenty-four kilometres, the Dunsterforce men arrived at the tail to find a token rearguard of twenty-four armed refugees and an American missionary and his wife. Relocating the Americans to a safer position in the column, the Australian captain pushed northwards with the armed civilians and his own party of eight to intercept the enemy. Ten kilometres ahead they came on the deserted village of Karawaran, where they agreed to lie in ambush for the Turks. At first sight of the 500 Turks and Kurds who came to loot the village, however, all but two of the refugees fled in terror — taking most of the ammunition with them.

The terrible battle which followed lasted until late the following afternoon. Chosen for their prowess under fire, the Dunsterforce men, who at least held the advantage of surprise over the enemy, knew that they could rely on each other to withstand the odds against them. Savige and Smith, defending the crucial right flank from which the village could be cut off, sprang the surprise by opening their Lewis guns on the looters as they were dismounting at the edge of town. Immediately, the Turks were panicked into headlong retreat, rendering themselves easy targets to the rest of the Dunsterforce brigade and the two refugees. But the Turks and the brilliant Kurdish horsemen soon regrouped, combining in a barrage of attacks on the village until their numbers were depleted to fewer than 250 men. Preferring to avoid any further risk of casualties, the looting party withdrew and left the Dunsterforce men to claim one of the war's most remarkable victories at the cost of only one of their own lives — an abiding testament to their combat skills and courage.

Their stock of ammunition almost spent, Captain Savige and his patrol returned for fresh supplies to Sain Kala where they received orders from General Dunsterville to reform the original party and carry on their defence of the refugee column's rearguard. In the weeks that followed, the Australian captain led his gallant little band in countless skirmishes with the enemy, often in the absence of any support from Agha Petros and his cavalry. But the greatest source of anxiety to the Dunsterforce brigade was the conduct of thousands of armed men in the refugee column: though unwilling to engage with the Turks and Kurds, they were adept at butchering the defenceless people of the Persian villages en route to Bijah, and seemed not to be satisfied until they had plundered homes and burnt crops into the bargain.

Across desolate enemy territory, the Dunsterforce brigade continued to protect the refugee column until its safe arrival in Bijah at the end of August. No more than 5000 of the 80 000 refugees had been lost and most of these to factors beyond the control of Savige's party, such as malnutrition and disease. But the toll on the Australian party was high: all were critically fatigued and several had died from cholera, dysentery, and malaria. Many more were seriously ill with these diseases, but they were given one last assignment.

Within two days of escorting the refugee column to Bijah, Savige's men were sent to Baku in support of General Dunsterville's efforts to hold the seaport against a Turkish seige. But this phase of the mission proved to be a disconcerting failure, mainly due to the lack of cooperation by the Armenian inhabitants who were too afraid to fight against the Turks. Dunsterville withdrew and the mission was abandoned.

Nevertheless, the overall purpose of the mission — to protect the civilian population and quiet the marauding Turks and wild Kurdish tribesmen — had been achieved. In this, the role of the NCOs was vital. Though less celebrated by historians than the conspicuous part played by the Allied officers, the contribution of enlisted men like Henry John Smith was invaluable to the success of the mission and ultimately to the outcome of the war. The Tasmanian sergeant, who was one of those to come down with cholera and who almost died as a result, received a second Military Cross for his services to Dunsterforce. In an official report of the operation, Captain Savige paid him a special tribute: 'Smith remained true to duty until he collapsed under the most frightful conditions imaginable, and for his valour and determination...was awarded a decoration.'

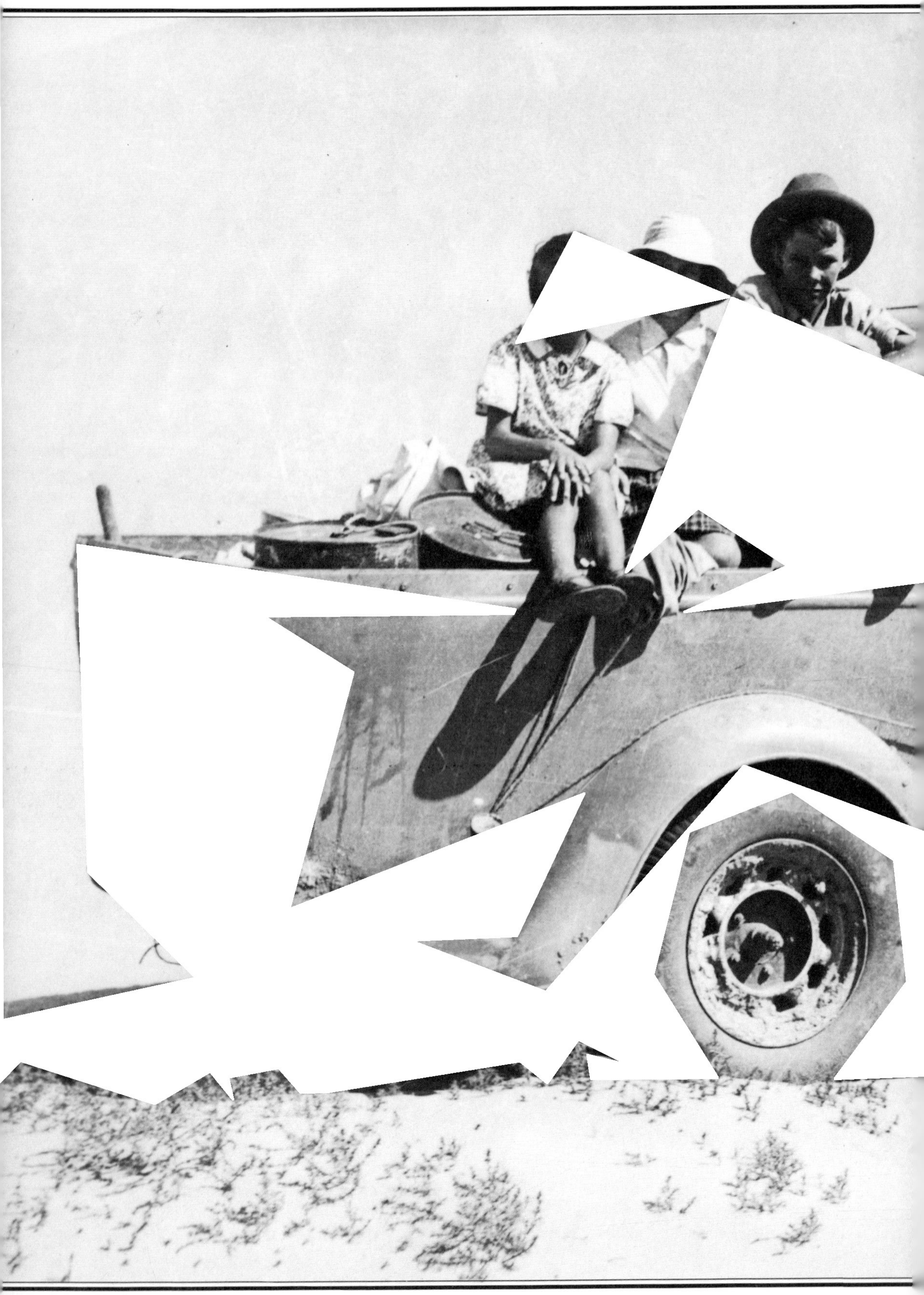

5
Uneasy Peace
1918–1939

There was little that was easy about this peace for most of those whose stories are told here. Little, either, that was peaceful. For most, particularly during the Depression, peace meant the absence only of world war. At home, war continued on many fronts, especially against the old, entrenched enemies — poverty, disease, and racial prejudice.

In the outback, illness combined with distance and isolation was one of the deadliest enemies. While bush nurses Sister Vianney, Mary Bowers, Ruth Heathcock and Marjorie Silver provided remarkable nursing and inexhaustible care, doctors Clyde Fenton and Mick Cook fought government apathy and intransigence to provide medical care for all the inhabitants of the Northern Territory.

Official opposition was also one of the chief enemies of Frederick Maynard and Pastor Friedrich Albrecht, each of whom fought for radical changes in the perception and treatment of Aborigines. Although they won a number of battles, their war, like that of Irene Dorling and Amy Wilkinson to keep a roof over their heads and their children alive, was to continue long after this uneasy peace.

Amy Wilkinson
1894–1983

'The life of a woman who loves work'
Written by: Amy Wilkinson in 1947
Nominated by: Elizabeth Chapman

'When I was twenty in the year 1915, on the 15 April I married a man named Albert Wilkinson. He was a boilermaker at Mort Dock, Balmain. For two years I lived the life of leisure. In 1917 the trouble came. There was a strike which put my husband out of work. After four months strike there was no place left for him so he went to the country — a place called Moree. I stayed behind with a baby of a year old. I went to work as a chef and for four years I stayed; then my husband wanted me to go to him to the outback of New South Wales by the Queensland border — a place called Mungindi. That is where my life began. I went to him with the one ambition that some day I would have a home of my own.

'We had some hard times. We were road contractors. I worked alongside my husband like a man. They were long hours. The first year I was there we had a drought and things were very bad for us. It was in 1920 — the worst drought I ever saw. The animals were dying all around us. We could not buy meat and only got bread once a week and we never saw butter for weeks. Jam and dripping and vegetables were a thing of the past. We had to go eight miles for water which used to take me nearly a day as I had to carry all the water up the bank of the Boomie River. In 1921 I had another son and while I was in hospital the drought broke and the road was very bad.

Previous page. Children of one of Harry Ding's intrepid Birdsville transport drivers. Their father was one of the handful of men who took mail and supplies through the 'dead heart' of the continent in the 1930s

It rained for three weeks and when I came out of hospital I had to go home by dray and as the road was so bad I had to walk seventeen miles which took two days as our horses were very poor with the shortage of food.

'After three weeks back on the road again, the river all full, our horse got on an island with water all round so, as my husband could not swim, we were in a fix as the food was running short. I wanted to swim across to get them. My husband would not let me in case I got swept away so he cut a tree down but it did not go across so I swam the rest. It was nineteen miles to the nearest township which could only be reached by saddle horse in the wet.

'Times got better after that and we were back on the road again on a big job. I used to pick and shovel, drive the scoop and grader, help to plough and my little baby slept in a dress basket under a tree. As time went on we seemed to be getting a few more horses together and I was toiling away as happy as a lark still thinking that some day I would have a lovely home somewhere. Flies and ants — they were my worst trouble. Snakes never troubled me. I was never frightened. Sometimes I was left for a fortnight on the side of the road when my husband went in to get stores. I always had plenty of work to do as my husband was a very hard man. He did not believe in idleness and, as I love work myself, and still do to this day, when my work was over in the daytime I crocheted all night — yards of lace by a lantern.

'We never stayed in one place long and I never saw many people as on the road only a few swaggies or a black fellow there used to come and ask for some food but was no trouble. We used to have some terrible dust storms. As times went on we got on better and my husband had a man to help him but I was always wanted. When I did the cooking for the day in a camp oven, I would have to go out and cut the limbs of the trees, and it was one of these days that a station owner saw me. I was expecting my second daughter. He told his mother and I was not let on the road again for some time. But how I loved those days even if my husband was hard. The love for that man was still there and my children I adored. They were my life — I just lived for them.

'Time went on and my eldest son had to go to school so we shifted into Mungindi into a tin shed with no windows and only one door. Money did not mean anything to me on the roads but when I went into town I wanted some and my husband would not allow me any so we quarrelled. He said I could go to the store but I had five children. I had things I had to buy for them that I could not get at the store. I also had my second son nearly blind with pollen blight. He was not allowed at school because of his eyes.

'Life was very hard for me then. All my hopes of a home were gone. Sometimes I never saw my husband for months. Things never went right. My eldest son was shot and had his left hand nearly blown off and a hole in his side. He was six months in the Mungindi hospital. For the want of money I went to work. I was still living in the tin shed. It had no tank. I had to cart my water from the river by a horse and cart in a small tank. To earn money for myself I cleaned the school, the Post Office and the New South Wales Bank. It was not much money but to me it was a lot. I earned enough to buy a cow and calf and after fours years of toil I had five cows milking. And then the Depression came. My husband was out of work for eleven months. All my cows and calves were sold except one and then my luck was out — I broke the main tendon of my leg and for two years I was on crutches waiting to get to Sydney for an operation. In due course I got there and when I came home I was not wanted, so I left Mungindi and came to Melbourne and took my three girls with me. I found out then I was expecting another baby. I went back to work at the Shepparton cannery until a fortnight before he was born.

'I had my baby, another boy. I struggled on, still fighting for this home for my family. I came to Melbourne as my eldest girl was ready to work and was only in Melbourne a fortnight when my baby got scalded with hot tea. He was six months in the Alfred Hospital.

'I worked hard and with the help of the good folk I worked for I never looked back. I reared my family but I still have not that home of my own.

'When I thought times was changing my eldest son came to Melbourne to be near me. He could not get work because he was over twenty-one. I sent him to the youth employment school. He learned to be a chef. When he left the school to start out for himself, war broke out and he was taken away.

'I still struggle on, still hoping. One by one my girls started work and now they are all married, except my little boy who is working to help get his mother a home. With his help I am still trusting in God to have this Wilkinson Lodge.'

Amy got her house. First, there was a brief second marriage, then more hard work. But, in the early fifties, probably through the intervention of one of the many people for whom she worked and who thought so well of her, Amy was given a substantial loan. She built the house at Ringwood herself, with the help of her youngest son. She even managed to pay off the loan and, almost blind, lived out her last years with her dog in her own home. Amy died in 1983. She was in her eighty-ninth year. She did not think her life at all remarkable.

Rose Harris
1885–1977

'The Rose of Clermont'
Written by: Cathy Peake
Nominated by: Roslyn Haylock

During the flash floods in Clermont, Central Queensland, in December 1916, Rose Harris and her father saved five men from death when a three metre wall of water tore through the town taking with it public buildings and dwellings and drowning sixty-two people.

The Harris Saddlery — a strong, two-storey building — was damaged but remained intact as did most of their stock, Rose and her father having moved the saddles and other property to the top floor. In a moment of inspiration Rose also snatched up a bundle of halters, knotting these into a lifeline which could be cast out into the flood waters.

One of the five men saved by this contraption was an Aborigine who, the story goes, spent the following night in hospital wearing Rose's best nightdress. Sadly, a sixth young man was not saved — he let go of the halters when he realised that it was Rose at the other end and that he had lost all his clothes. He was never seen again.

Born in 1885 in Clermont, Rose Harris followed her father's example and was apprenticed as a saddler — a profession she was to pursue for sixty-nine years until osteo-arthritis forced her to retire at the age of eighty. One of the few, and perhaps the only, professional women saddlers in Queensland, Rose made something of a speciality of lining saddles, and was well known in the district for her skills with leather.

She never married, but was a stalwart of the Clermont community, teaching girls to swim in the local creek, playing the piano in the local, otherwise all-male band, and serving as an organist in the Clermont Church of England for forty years. She also painted — mostly horses — and, after she had retired, her collections of these and other memorabilia, such as ribbons won in riding competitions and early photographs, were to prove invaluable to the production of the Clermont Centenary Book in 1962.

Rose Harris died in Rockhampton in 1977 at the age of ninety-two. At her own request she was buried in Clermont where her heroism in the floods of 1916 is still remembered and celebrated.

Rose Harris, heroine of the Clermont floods and expert saddler, in 1923

Charles Robert Dadds
1891–1968
Unorthodox missionary
Written by: Niall Lucy
Nominated by: Dean W. Dadds

Charles Robert Dadds was a man of boundless drive and initiative. Educated at the McGill Primary and Wellington Road Public Schools in Adelaide, he worked as a tram conductor, motor mechanic, and bottle-topper to finance his Methodist ministerial studies at Prince Alfred College in Brighton, South Australia. But, although devoted to his vocation, Charlie Dadds had no time for the obstructive pettiness of institutions. The year before his ordination in 1918, he married Clare Stevens in defiance of his Church's wish that he should wait until after he was ordained. The marriage and the means by which he financed his studies were both characteristic of Charlie Dadds.

On the 6 June in the year of his ordination, Charlie and Clare, with their new born son, Lincoln, sailed from Sydney for the exotic wilds of Fiji, arriving at Suva a few weeks later with no more than seven shillings to their name. Thus began a forbidding three years for Charlie as a missionary among the Fijian islanders.

Clare became seriously ill and was forced to return with Lincoln to their home in South Australia. Although lonely, Charlie attended to his missionary duties with spiritual and practical vigour. This, and

Reverend Charlie Dadds, missionary, inventor, community worker, practical visionary and sportsman. Yorke Peninsular, South Australia, c.1964

his willingness to lend a hand with such chores as vehicle maintenance and boat repairs, won him great favour in the parish.

Having temporarily recovered from her bout of nervous exhaustion and a failing heart condition, Clare returned to Fiji with Lincoln in November 1919. A year and a half later, however, the delicacy of Clare's health forced the Dadds to give up their tropical paradise and settle back in South Australia. They left expressing great concern for the fate of the Fijian people whose way of life, they believed, was under threat from foreign commercial interests.

For the next forty years, Charlie's pastoral community work kept the family on the move as he spread his humane teaching of the gospel from rural to city parishes across the State. Charlie's faith continued to be as evident in practice as in his preaching. He lobbied local councils for better schools and safer roads, and was always among the first to pitch in during a crisis.

Central to Charlie's belief that his ministry should play a vital role in the community life of his parish were his keen sporting interests and he remained an active sportsman until his retirement in the 1960s. His death in 1968 was mourned by all who treasured his practical Christianity, his compassion and his humour.

R. Graham Carey
1874–1959

Pioneer civil aviator
Written by: Billy Marshall-Stoneking
Nominated by: Bertha G. Harvey

R. Graham Carey, Adelaide, 1917. In 1957, he re-enacted his inaugural air mail run from Adelaide to Gawler, delivering a mail bag to the same person who had received it forty years before

The seventy-year-old woman peered over the edge of the fusilage at the farm buildings several hundred metres below her. 'Gracious me, they look just like toys!' she exclaimed.

It was the 1920s. Australians were getting their first view of the world from the perspective of an aeroplane and most of them were enjoying the experience very much. R. Graham Carey, the man at the controls of the bi-plane, made sure of it.

Throughout the 1920s Carey, who was 'mad on flying', and convinced that the aeroplane would revolutionise human life, had made a career of introducing the idea of aviation to people right around southeastern Australia. 'It is the small initial flight,' he remarked, 'that converts the most nervous person into the most enthusiastic airman.'

Carey learned to fly in 1916 after purchasing Maurice Guilleaux's Bleriot 60, the plane that had made aviation history by flying the first air mail between Melbourne and Sydney in 1914. Mastering the idiosyncracies of the Bleriot, Carey became the first private citizen in Australia to receive a pilot's licence and, by 1917, had flown the first air mail route in South Australia, between Adelaide and Gawler.

Determined to prove the scope and value of aviation, Carey became the first man in Australia to do aerial photography and aerial

R.G. Carey, pilot, with his son, Graham Melrose Carey, mechanic, and his wonderful flying machine, in 1928 at his Port Melbourne aerodrome where, with Australia's first Commercial Permit, he established Melbourne Air Service. Carey was quick to recognise the commercial possibilities of the aeroplane

advertising. He also established and operated Australia's first private flying school.

In the rough-and-ready days of barnstorming pilots and flimsy flying machines, Carey often flew 'by the seat of his pants'. Aerodromes were a rarity, so Carey would have to choose his landing fields with care — usually a big, flat paddock, a racecourse, or even a road. More than once Carey surprised local residents by putting his plane down outside a farmhouse or a general store.

In twenty years of flying, Carey took up more than 70 000 passengers without losing one of them. He made air travel seem ordinary and everyday — something in which anyone could be involved. And with his one hundred per cent safety record, he was certainly the infant industry's most convincing salesman.

Amram Lewis
c1880–1935
Miners' advocate
Written by: Billy Marshall-Stoneking
Nominated by: Allan 'Old Mick' Masson

There was a shudder, and then a grumbling noise from somewhere deep within the earth. Amram Lewis had heard these sounds before — the sounds of a mine explosion. He had heard them in Wales where he had worked as a trapper boy in a cooperative mine, he had heard them in Australia at Bellbird and Bulli, and he knew the wives and the children of many miners who had lived and died in the earth.

Amram Lewis was keenly aware of the miserable and dangerous conditions under which miners were forced to work, and he was determined to do something to change it. Self-educated, articulate and thoughtful, Lewis's intellectual prowess was nearly invisible behind his rugged, miner's exterior. But not many could stand up to him in an argument, especially when he was speaking on miners' rights.

Lewis was appalled by the conditions — no weekly wage, no holiday pay, no pay for loss of time, no sick pay, no pay to the 'dusted' men whose lungs gave out by the time they were forty, and very few safety conditions. Lewis had been dusted himself, and would suffer from lung complaints for most of his life, but this did not stop him from fighting the coal companies, and helping in 1915 to form the Miners' Federation, the first union in Australia concerned with the rights and needs of coal and shale workers.

As secretary, Amram, along with his many colleagues in the Federation, took on state and federal bodies and private industry to try to improve the miners' lot, and for the most part were successful. Opposed to direct action except in exceptional circumstances, Lewis counselled the miners to work to regulations as a weapon to improve their lot. But if direct action was necessary, Lewis was always at the forefront.

In the end, thanks to the efforts of men like Amram Lewis, many changes occurred. Dust-free mines, electric lamps, good holiday entitlements, and sickness benefits all came to be accepted as standard conditions for miners.

Speaking of Lewis, an old friend remembered: 'His heart was always filled with compassion for the worker. His sadness was always for the families of the miners.'

John Borland Brown
1874–1923
Sacrifice at Bellbird coalmine
Written by: Katie Lawley
Nominated by: Rodney J. Brown

John Borland Brown. His determination to rescue his trapped fellow miners led to his own death

John Borland Brown was a miner. An ex-Scots Guard, he rose from the ranks to become manager of one of the largest collieries in the world, the Aberdare mine in New South Wales.

On 1 September 1923, a gas explosion ripped through the Bellbird Colliery, trapping twenty miners hundreds of metres underground. As the thick, acrid smoke belched from the mine entrance, rescue teams were quickly formed. John Brown led these teams down the mine, discovering the bodies of workers as they went. They worked frantically, realising that other gas explosions were imminent. Brown and his mate George Marshall were working as far down the mine as possible when the second blast came. The poisonous gas hit them instantly and Brown was overcome. Marshall tried desperately to drag his friend up the shaft, but the latter insisted 'I am done for. I can go no further. Look after yourself.' Marshall, who left Brown and scrambled away to get more help, was found semiconscious near the shaft entrance.

The mine management soon realised that the only way to extinguish the fire and prevent more poisonous gas explosions was to lock off the four entrances and suffocate the blast area. Once the difficult decision was made, teams of men worked around the clock shovelling sand into the gaping pits. Twenty-one men had perished.

Twelve months later the mine was re-opened. They found the body of John Brown, stretched lengthwise across the tunnel, his head looking towards the pit mouth. His funeral was attended by over a thousand miners. His Edward Medal, posthumously awarded, was presented to his widow and five children.

Olivia Marquis Ferguson
1891–1954
Kindly mother of a dozen
Written by: Judith Elen
Nominated by: Sheila Van Emden

Born in Sydney in 1891, Olivia Marquis Charlotte twice began a new life. When her new husband returned from World War I, he was allotted land at Erigolia, 600 kilometres south-west of Sydney, under the Soldier Settlers Scheme. Olivia's daughter Sheila remembers their train journey to Naradhan Siding — her mother, six sisters and baby brother — while their father travelled with the buggy and horses.

For twenty months, home at Erigolia was a large marquee, while Olivia's husband built a house of logs and tin and carried out the back-breaking work of clearing and fencing the heavily wooded 570 hectares. To avoid forfeiture, this had to be substantially completed and crops planted within two years. To the children their father 'seemed to work all day and all night'; they would often see distant fires burning off the piles of mallee.

Sheila remembers the open fires on which her mother cooked until the house was completed, and the tree with a large barrel in its fork for the muddy water that their horse carted from the neighbour's dam. Olivia gave birth to her ninth child in the marquee with only her husband to help and the nearest doctor 130 kilometres away — a good day's travel over dirt roads. In the following years three more babies were born — a family of ten girls and two boys.

Times were hard, especially before the first harvest. Sheila remembers the kids trying to pick the weevils out of their porridge which was bought in bulk and had to be eaten to the last bit; and 'Mum made our sheets, petticoats, dresses and bloomers out of calico flour and porridge bags that rustled when we moved.' Nothing was wasted. The land was of poor quality and many pioneering families left. Sheila recalls: 'Mum helped us through red dust storms, mouse and grasshopper plagues, droughts, floods and bush fires, as well as nursing us through our illnesses and accidents.' Out of these hard years the Fergusons

Four of Olivia Ferguson's twelve children outside her Erigolia General Store and Petrol Agency, c.1930

Olivia Marquis Charlotte Ferguson in 1943. The community was an extension of her large, much-loved and well cared-for family

established a farm carrying wheat, sheep, pigs, poultry, goats, cows and horses.

One of the first women in the area, 'everyone looked to her' and Olivia refused help to no-one — settlement families, young Englishmen from the Big Brother Movement who came to work on the farm, passing swagmen. With her Red Cross and St John's Ambulance training, she did all the 'doctoring' in the district until the arrival of the bush nurse whom she helped to obtain.

Olivia also fostered a sense of community, establishing the local Country Women's Association; the Sunday School; organising camping, sports teams and district balls. She cooked for picnics and balls as well as for family, shearers and harvesters, visitors and often passing travellers. The Erigolia School, the Bush Nursing Hospital, the large hall and tennis courts in town, were all erected with the help of Olivia and her husband (a former Sydney 'brickie').

'Town', five kilometres away, consisted of three stores and a post office. When Olivia's husband opened a petrol agency there, she established the Erigolia General Store. Trading on the days the train came in from outlying areas, its stock ranged from clothing and separators to fruit and vegetables brought by truck from Griffith. The trucks also brought in large blocks of ice packed in wheat bags and sawdust, and Olivia's home-made ice cream was famous. At tables set up in the store, Olivia served hot meals for shoppers or people visiting town for a sporting fixture.

The store and petrol agency both offered liberal credit and when the long droughts came in the mid thirties, they suffered badly. Leaving the older girls in charge, Olivia went with her husband to the bank in Sydney to try to raise a loan. But these were the Depression years: while they were away the bailiffs moved in, taking possession of the farm, and depositing the kids and family possessions in the road, a couple of kilometres from the front gate.

The family returned to Sydney and began all over again. Adjustment was difficult, but Olivia did not despair and immediately began to involve herself in her new community. She joined the Housewives' Association, an early consumer organisation that worked to protect women's rights and interests.

When World War II broke out only three years later, Olivia's husband rejoined the forces along with three of the children. Olivia 'went straight into work with the VAD's, Red Cross and Air Raid Wardens and also knitted socks, and balaclavas in her spare time.' She did voluntary work in Army homes and hospitals, sometimes travelling to convalescent hospitals in Orange and Scone for weeks at a time, taking her two youngest children with her. Late one midwinter night she was called to help a desperate young neighbourhood girl who had gassed herself. She saved the girl's life by applying artifical respiration during the long wait for the ambulance, but in the process contracted pneumonia herself. All this was, however, overshadowed by the loss of one of her sons, who died of his war wounds.

Olivia Ferguson contracted meningitis in 1954 and died at the relatively early age of sixty-three.

'The mother's always at the top of the family I reckon. That's what my father used to say too,' recalls Myrtle, one of Olivia's older daughters. 'She's been dead more than thirty years but I still miss her; she is the one thing I miss in life.'

Angelo & Irene Palmos
1897–1976; 1903–
Marriage of cultures
Written by: Angelo Loukakis
Nominated by: Frank Palmos

Australia is a nation of immigrants. They have come at different times and in different ways, pushed by the exigencies of history, drawn by the possibility of a better world. The post World War II period has seen the most concentrated and most diverse group of new settlers — about four and a half million in all — and it is this group which has possibly had the most immediately felt impact on Australian society and culture. But in the colour and clamour of the postwar immigration years we have tended to forget the achievements of earlier arrivals. The story of Irene Fitzpatrick and Angelo Palmos is a vivid reminder of the contributions made by an older, pre-war generation to this most 'multicultural' of nations.

That Angelo Palmos arrived in Australia in 1922 at all had as much to do with the accuracy of his aim as anything else. In a time when honour meant somewhat more than it does today, Palmos, then a middle-ranking officer in the Royal Greek Navy, found himself forced into settling differences with a more senior officer in the old way — a duel with pistols. Although both amateurs, the younger man had the misfortune of shooting his opponent dead and finding himself —

because of recently enacted laws banning duelling — a wanted man.

Helped by fellow officers who had taken his side, Palmos boarded his ship bound for South Africa, Australia and Japan. Out of Durban however, there came a Marconi message demanding his return and he realised that saving himself would require a rather more drastic plan. So, when the ship arrived at Geelong, having secured the assistance of the other officers once again and left them with a letter of deepest apology to the dead man's family, Angelo Palmos jumped ashore for a new beginning. His tragic involvement in the death of another man was a turning point, the last time he would act according to the passing values of an older world. From then on, his life in Australia could only be described as one of affirmation and accomplishment.

While there was nothing typical about how he had come to land in Australia, Palmos was soon confronted with the usual problems faced by non-English-speaking new arrivals to this country. Speaking French and Greek, he found himself unable to communicate until he met an Indo-Chinese storekeeper who directed him to 'the only five Greeks' living in Melbourne. To them he explained his 'wanted in Athens' status, and soon had their help in taking out a lease on a fruit store in Sydney Road, Brunswick. He was twenty-eight years old at this time and the story of his life was about to take on a new, distinctly multicultural, turn.

Angelo Palmos's Saturday morning help was a young lady by the name of Irene May Fitzpatrick, one of eight children whose parents had both died about the same time. She had been working since the age of thirteen and by seventeen was supporting all her younger brothers and sisters with small help from local charities. Irene now took on the task of teaching Angelo English. Not much later, it was obvious that the communication problem had been well and truly mastered, for the two fell in love. They married in 1933, a Greek to a non-Greek, and a good Irish girl to a dark-complexioned foreigner.

Today we are used to intercultural marriages but then such unions were very often frowned upon. And this was exactly what happened to Angelo and Irene who were ostracised by such circles of family and friends as they had. Undaunted, they went on to open the first of the new style open-fronted and glassless shops in Sydney Road and to enjoy a brief period of prosperity. Brief because the Depression was soon having its inevitable effect — their shops were looted and three years' savings lost. With two children now, they struggled on. Not much later, it became obvious that a second world war was imminent and, despite being too old to fight, Angelo's insistence on doing his bit led to a Manpower job in the tiny Victorian bushtown of Noojee.

His job there was to ensure wood supplies for the army, and once installed — in a tin hut with an earthen floor, and open fire and hessian for windows — the Palmoses managed to keep going. Only now there was a third child on the way and they were living in a place where the earth was still charred from the devastating bushfires of Black Friday. These were hard times and Irene and Angelo shared in the general privation. Yet for this apparently oddly-aligned couple it was also a time for new directions.

It was while living in Noojee that Angelo understood how necessary it was that something be done to regenerate the ruined forests. Indeed,

Angelo Palmos and Irene Fitzpatrick on their wedding day in 1933, a League Of Nations affair in what was then an almost wholly Anglo-Celtic nation. Angelo, 34, one of a tiny enclave of Greeks then in Melbourne, married Irene, 20, with a neighbouring tobacconist's daughter, Sadie Sicree, as bridesmaid. The Sicrees themselves were rarities, one of the few Jewish families in Australia before the flood of the mid-thirties. The church was the Scots Presbyterian Church in Sydney Road, Brunswick

he felt so strongly about it that before long he came to see the renewal of the forests as his mission in life. He joined the Forestry Commission, his personal crusade initially finding expression in the growing of tens of thousands of tree seedlings each year. Mountain ash at first, then pines; in fifteen years Angelo Palmos was responsible for the planting of one million trees in southern parts of Victoria.

This physically demanding undertaking involved sometimes living in tents or huts, sometimes walking thirty kilometres to and from home. Whether heading a small team, or working on his own, his efforts were astounding and brought him to public attention. He became known as the Million Tree Man, prompting one of the incredulous who knew him to exclaim: 'Bugger me dead, but he was a Greek!' And another of his workmates who knew his capacity for both hard work and strong leadership to say: 'He's a Greek, but he's good-oh!'

Angelo's presence and activities eventually did much to break down resistance to newcomers in a small town. But at the same time, Irene herself was not exactly idle. A strong-minded person with ideas and ambitions of her own, she strove to educate herself to University level by correspondence and borrowing books from anyone passing through

— travelling salesmen, bus and lorry drivers, anyone who had access to the world outside. Irene also founded the Noojee and District Progress Committee, responsible for preventing the cutting of the few remaining old trees of the area, the banking of the river, the preservation of the great old trestle railway bridges, and numerous other public improvements which helped make this one of the prettiest towns in the state.

Irene was a conservationist in her own right, countering the old 'all trees are for chopping' argument with some reasoning of her own — 'some trees are for chopping, others for beauty, others to hold the soil, others for continuing the natural forest'. Against the odds she was able to convince the millers and loggers to look to their children and grandchildren's future. She certainly did her best towards the future of her *own* family. In often primitive surroundings she raised four children, all of whom have gone on to make successes of their lives. (The youngest son, Frank, was the first Western correspondent in Indonesia and reputedly the journalist on whom the character of Guy Hamilton in *The Year Of Living Dangerously* was based.)

Irene and Angelo Palmos: ordinary lives, but extraordinary also. Performing no heroic deeds in the romantic sense, they have been heroes just the same. If there are no monuments to their efforts, their testament lies instead in the way they each overcame difficult beginnings, joined one with the other against the cultural odds, and worked hard to realise some worthwhile beliefs and values. It is a story they share with vast numbers of their fellow Australians.

Angelo Palmos with future foreign correspondent Frank, 15 months, on his knee at a bush picnic

Sister Vianney Byrne
1894–

Angel of Charity
Written by: Lucinda Strauss
Nominated by: Sister Catherine O'Carrigan

Whizzing down the corridors of St Vincent's Convent, Potts Point, in her electric wheelchair, Sister Vianney Byrne, aged ninety-four, has little time to waste. For most of her seventy-four years with the Sisters of Charity she has nursed the sick and dying at St Vincent's Hospitals in Lismore, Cootamundra, Toowomba and Bathurst and in later years at the Sacred Heart Hospices in Melbourne and Sydney. As the longest-serving Sister of Charity in Sydney she says that she was 'only doing her job', but the hundreds of patients she cared for so skilfully think of her more as an angel.

The second daughter born to Mary Banko and John Kenrick Byrne, Irene inherited the best qualities of both her parents — the infinite gentleness of her mother and a natural ingenuity and practical inventiveness from her father, a designer and inventor of farm implements. As one of seven children growing up in the Victorian town of Tongala, Irene learned all the practical skills of housekeeping and running a farm that were to prove so useful in a life of bush nursing.

Convinced of her vocation from the age of eight, Irene had waited ten long years before she was old enough to join the order. At nineteen she was finally accepted for the novitiate but rejected for nursing because of a bad knee. Summoned by the Bishop, she approached him with trepidation, admitting that she had been 'praying to die' if she could not be a nursing sister. 'Would you bless my knee Your Grace?' Whereupon the Archbishop did so and the pain never came back. Irene had to wait a further eighteen months, however, to commence her three-year training.

Before graduating, Sister Vianney nursed many Gallipoli veterans, treated scores of victims of the Spanish Influenza epidemic of 1919 and earned the respect of renowned Sydney dermatologist, Dr Langloh Johnston, for her superb nursing of a case of pemphigus, where the patient had enormous blisters.

Her training complete, in 1924 Sister Vianney found herself pioneering in the lush, rolling hills of Lismore. In those days hospitals had few facilities and no government funding. Nursing sisters cleaned, scrubbed, washed, milked cows and served meals in addition to their primary duty of nursing. On call twenty-four hours a day with just one other, Sister Vianney recalls, 'It would be the middle of the night and you'd get an "urgent". One of us would fly down and light the copper, the other prepared the patient. We'd do the operation and then wash all the linen in the copper, hang it on the line and it would be dry by morning. There were no disposables in those days.'

In the mid-1920s Sister Vianney did more pioneer nursing at Cootamundra Hospital, where for two years, again with only one other sister, she operated, installed drainage systems, dug cesspits for typhoid wastes, carpentered and chopped the firewood needed daily to heat the cold, high-roofed wards. By 1927 she was suffering from physical exhaustion but after a brief convalescence set off for St Vincent's Lismore followed by a few years at Toowoomba.

Over the years she has worked as rectress at St Joseph's, Auburn, where she installed the X-ray and pathology departments, and at St Vincent's, Bathurst, where she helped to make the country hospital self-sufficient. It was thirty years before Sister Vianney returned to her home state of Victoria where she worked at St Vincent's Hospital Outdoor Department and then at Kew Hospice for six years.

Finally, in 1955, Sister Vianney came back to the place where her training first began. For the next twenty-seven years she endeared herself to the patients of the Sacred Heart Hospice in Darlinghurst. Sister Catherine O'Carrigan, historian for the Sisters of Charity, comments, 'She really made her mark at the hospice. She invented her own ways of preventing bedsores and making patients comfortable. All her energies went into alleviating their symptoms... Her experienced eye made her a great diagnostician, and anxious relatives relied on her guidance.'

Sister Vianney's nursing career ended prematurely when, at the age of eighty-one, she broke a leg which was eventually amputated. She's been in a wheelchair now for thirteen years. 'I'd still be nursing if I could,' she says. But though she can no longer be involved in active nursing, her talented hands are never idle. When she's not sorting the Convent mail, writing receipts or replying to correspondence, she's away in a corner running up an apron or a craft item for the Hospice stall. 'If your hands are busy, your mind is busy,' she says with a quiet smile as she whizzes down the hall and on to the next project.

Top. Irene Byrne, aged eighteen. She knew she had a vocation from the age of eight

Below. Sister Vianney Byrne today, dedicated and innovative nurse to the sick and dying for seventy years. Photograph by Lorrie Graham

Turo Downes
1856–1942
Ambassador of Hardy's Bay
Written by: Terri McCormack
Nominated by: Enid Deal

Turo Downes, local hero to a generation of children, at Hardy's Bay wharf in 1933

Much about Turo Downes is obscure, including the origin of his name, whether he was an Aborigine or a Torres Strait or Pacific Islander, and the date of his arrival at Hardy's Bay on the Central New South Wales coast. Certainly by the 1920s and 30s Turo had become a local landmark, greeting visitors at the wharf, caretaking holiday cottages, and minding the many children who adored him and his legendary tales. He was reputed to have crewed on local boats and was renowned for his swimming and running prowess and for his phenomenal memory for names and faces. Children loved the deep cave in which he lived with his ménage of stray animals, and everyone was charmed by his warm personality.

Turo delighted in taking visitors to the rusting boilers which were the only remains of the paddlesteamer *Maitland*, wrecked in a gale on a routine voyage from Sydney to Newcastle in 1898. Tales of heroism about this tragic event, which claimed some twenty-six lives, have passed into local folklore as have Turo's stories of his battles through pounding seas to rescue terrified passengers. He is not named in any contemporary accounts of the tragedy and there is now no way of judging how true this 'story' of Turo's might be.

However, to those who could not imagine their childhood at Hardy's Bay without this sincere and gentle man, Turo's participation in the *Maitland* rescue is irrelevant. In 1942, aged eighty-six, he took his secrets to his grave in St Paul's churchyard, Kincumber, the stone appropriately inscribed: 'Respected by all'.

Charles Frederick Maynard
1879–1944
Vision of justice for Aborigines
Written by: Billy Marshall-Stoneking
Nominated by: Mary Kondek

The boy waited until the superintendent had disappeared into the big white house, then took off. He knew the route by heart: down the bank, and along the river until it passed under the railroad bridge. He ran as if his life depended on it. He knew he would be in for a beating if the superintendent found out, or worse — he could be sent to a home for what the whites called 'incorrigible blackfellas'. No-one was allowed off the reserve without a reason, and prior permission from the white superintendent. Thinking of this made him scared, but it did not stop him.

The man with the round face and toothy grin was waiting for him by the bridge and waved his big hand in welcome as the boy approached. The youngster relaxed as soon as he saw him.

'You all right?' the man asked. The boy nodded. Then, after catching his breath, he passed on the messages he'd been given — a recital of various hardships and injustices, complaints about severe punishments and information from Aboriginal families living on the reserve to be passed on to relatives living elsewhere in the State — news that would never reach the outside world without the services of a 'runner' and this man with the long moustache who stood silently, listening intently.

When the boy was finished, the man praised him for his courage and sacrifice, and noted that he should not feel he had done anything wrong — he was simply helping his people fight injustice.

The man was Charles Fredrick 'Fred' Maynard. As far as the white authorities were concerned, he was *persona non grata* on Aboriginal reserves because it was believed his speeches and political views stirred up the tribes, making them dissatisfied with the conditions under which they lived and worked. But as long as there were 'runners' there was no way the whites could stop news passing in and out; and Fred Maynard knew that communication amongst his people, and the dissemination of information regarding the state of affairs on reserves, was essential in the struggle to change attitudes that had kept his people virtual prisoners in their own land for nearly 150 years.

Fred Maynard was born near Maitland, New South Wales, on 4 July 1879. His father was an English farmer and his mother an Aboriginal woman who died when Fred was only five. Shortly after his wife's death, Fred's father abandoned the children, and young Fred, along with his sister Emma, went to live with a Methodist minister who raised them with strict, Christian discipline.

But life with the minister also had its rewards. From the time he was eight, Fred read everything that was placed before him, and by the time he was twelve had educated himself on a wide variety of topics, from philosophy to biology. His most prized possession was a Scottish dictionary which is still in the family today.

But Fred's reading did not shield him from the harshness of life that awaited nearly everyone of Aboriginal descent, and before long he was experiencing at first-hand the prejudice and hostility his people had faced since the earliest days of white occupation. His reading and intelligence made him all the more sensitive to the injustice and brutality, and he resolved that one day he would do something about it.

Fred left home at sixteen and travelled the country, working for a time as a photographer, then as a drover, wharf labourer, and nurseryman. But work that merely put food in his mouth was not enough to satisfy him. Using whatever money he could save up from his labouring and other work, Fred began travelling up and down the north coast of New South Wales speaking out publicly for the rights of Aborigines.

Knowing injustice himself, and highly critical of government policies

Fred Maynard in 1924. Dignified, eloquent and charismatic founding president of the Aboriginal Progressive Association, he fought for the rights of 'our more ancient civilisation'

toward Aboriginal people, he addressed himself to the evils of the Aboriginal Protection Board — a government agency that had been established by an act of parliament to look after the interests of the Australian Aborigines, but which, as far as the Aborigines were concerned, was the main perpetrator of a monstrous and officially-sanctioned attack on the very heart of Aboriginal society and culture. Among its duties, the Protection Board operated the notorious Apprenticeship Scheme which involved taking children, mainly girls, from their families and relocating them in distant parts of the state as labourers for white farmers. It was a situation that could only happen within a society that saw Aborigines as less than human, and Fred, knowing the anguish and torment of so many Aboriginal families split up by the Board, used his abilities as a speaker to protest against, and inform people about, its work.

But even this did not seem enough. So, in February 1925, together with four other Aboriginal men and a white woman, Fred founded the Australian Aboriginal Progressive Association — a forerunner of the Aboriginal Progressive Association of the 1960s. Fred was the founding president, and by the end of its first year the AAPA claimed eleven branches with over 500 members.

Ordinarily, the Aboriginal Protection Board would have ignored the occasional public meeting and one or two petitions with a couple of hundred names, but Fred Maynard's organisation had them worried. Mainly because Fred Maynard was the president. Those who heard him speak still remember his great power to move and inspire his audience.

At the third annual meeting of the AAPA in 1927, several resolutions were passed regarding Aboriginal rights. The first and major demand was for enough good quality freehold land for each Aboriginal family to sustain itself by farming 'as an economic base and as compensation for dispossession,' the second was the request that Aboriginal children not be taken away from their families, and that the Protection Board be dismantled. The petition was sent to the Premier of New South Wales in June 1927.

When the Board learned of this petition its response was swift and predictable. It asserted that Aborigines were incompetent in handling their own affairs, and insisted that '[the Board] offered benefits to Aborigines which were not only adequate but which were far greater than those provided for poor white men.' The whole idea of Aborigines running their own lives was written off as 'impractical'.

Maynard's reply to this was as eloquent as anything he had ever said while travelling the back country. He wrote:

'I wish to make it perfectly clear, on behalf of our people, that we accept no condition of inferiority as compared with European people. Two distinct civilisations are represented by the respective races...That the European people by the arts of war destroyed our more ancient civilisation is freely admitted, and that by their vices and diseases our people have been decimated is also patent, but neither of these facts are evidence of superiority. Quite the contrary is the case.'

The Board tried its best to discredit Maynard, first by accusing him of not being an Aborigine at all, but a 'full-blood' American or a South African 'black'. Later, it even tried to implicate him in a sexual scandal by making public a letter he had written to an Aboriginal girl who had been raped by a white property owner, asking for details of the assault. Contrary to the Board's interpretation, however, the letter shows clearly the degree of personal commitment felt by Maynard to the girls whom the Board kept forcing into intolerable situations. In fact, Maynard's chief aim in seeking information from the girl was to build a case against the culprit so he could be brought to justice.

Economic hardships during the Great Depression diverted white attention away from Aboriginal issues, but Fred continued working for the betterment of his people until his death in 1944, and though he never saw the realisation of his dreams for justice, his ideals and the expression of his ideas helped immeasurably in forming a political model for Aboriginal people in their struggle for recognition and equality.

Friedrich Wilhelm Albrecht
1894–1984

Ingkata innura — the lame pastor
Written by: Niall Lucy
Nominated by: Barbara M. Henson

In 1926, barely able to speak a word of English and lame in one leg from a childhood accident in his native Poland, Pastor Friedrich Wilhelm Albrecht arrived with his young German wife, Minna Gevers, at the remote Aboriginal mission of Hermannsburg in Central Australia. He was thirty-two years old and no stranger to hardship.

Fritz, as he was known, had served on the Russian Front in World War I as a member of the German Medical Corps where his bravery under fire in tending the wounded of both sides had won him the Highest Order of the Iron Cross. But he would need even greater courage to endure the years of isolation, the severe climate, and the desperate struggle against apathy and the elements which lay ahead in the harsh Australian outback.

Fritz had chosen the missionary life as his vocation at an early age. After the war he had given up the chance to run the family farm and had illegally crossed the border to return to his studies in Germany where he had met and married Minna, whose history of tuberculosis had prevented her from going to a mission field as a nurse. When they received notice of their posting to faraway Hermannsburg, the Albrechts were overjoyed. 'We would have gone to the moon,' they said half a century later, and they could hardly have been further from the comforts of society had they done so.

The oldest mission in the Northern Territory, Hermannsburg had been established in 1877, a few years after the completion of the Overland Telegraph Line from Adelaide to Darwin. In 1926 it was a community of several hundred Aborigines, 130 kilometres — or three days by fast camel — west of Alice Springs, itself a tiny settlement in a vast and alien landscape. The nearest railhead, Oodnadatta, was 600 kilometres to the south and the only way for goods and mail to reach the mission was by camel. Carl Strehlow, the previous missionary, had died two years earlier because he was unable to reach medical help.

In addition to this physical isolation, Central Australia was in the grip of a severe drought that would last until 1930. During the seven years without rain, Aborigines starving in the outlying bush to the west converged on the mission for food, only to die in great numbers of a mysterious disease later diagnosed as scurvy. 'Death stared us in the face,' Albrecht wrote, 'and our prayers seemed hollow.' Eighty-five per cent of the babies born in the drought years died.

When the rains came and the desert bloomed, Pastor Albrecht did not forget the stark lessons of the drought or the inadequate diet which had caused the scurvy. He was determined to establish a water supply for the mission, although he was unable to convince either government or church to assist with its funding. With the help of Melbourne artists, Una and Violet Teague, and public appeals in Melbourne and Adelaide, a pipeline was built in 1935 to bring spring water from nearby hills to the mission. A large vegetable garden was planted and general health improved. At a time when it was considered inevitable that 'full-blood' Aborigines would die out, the birth rate at Hermannsburg began to exceed the death rate.

In the years following the drought, Fritz spread his goodwill and ministry across the length and breadth of Central Australia, trekking by camel across the desert to bring the gospel to the Aboriginal tribes in the area — Walbiri, Loritjas, Pintubi, and Pitjantjatjara. Trusted by all, he became known as *ingkata innura* ('Lame Pastor'). But the Lame Pastor was not only concerned for the spiritual well-being of

With painter Rex Battarbee on lead camel, F.W. Albrecht sets off from Hermannsburg on one of his many ministering trips to isolated Aboriginal tribes

the Aborigines: aware of the devastating impact of white settlement on traditional tribal life, he worked tirelessly with doctor and author Charles Duguid, and with Carl Strehlow's son, Ted, to establish secure reserves on tribal land, such as the large Haasts Bluff reserve, declared in 1941.

Aware that, to withstand the encroachment of white society, Aboriginal people needed economic security rather than charity, Fritz also helped to develop locally-based Aboriginal industries (a tannery, handcraft centres, a pastoral association) and played an important role in the early career of painter Albert Namatjira.

As demanding as these projects were, Pastor Albrecht still had to administer the daily affairs of a large-scale institution. With few staff, he had to attend to correspondence, accounts, building repairs and maintenance, as well as the endless stream of visitors and officials. Twice he suffered a complete breakdown in health.

But it was Minna's ill-health which forced the Albrechts to move to the now more urban Alice Springs in the early 1950s. From here the Lame Pastor would visit Aboriginal workers on outback cattle stations to the north and south, bringing supplies in a truck equipped as a mobile store. He believed that the cattle industry was an ideal means for the black community to establish its economic independence in the region, and lobbied vigorously for schools and training.

The longest-serving missionary in Central Australia, Pastor Albrecht kept up his fight against government apathy towards Aborigines by continuing to take part in the discussions and policy changes begun

F.W. Albrecht's daughter, now Helene Burns, with her best friend Sylvia McNorman and playmates, at Hermannsburg in the 1930s. Helene is still fluent in her first language, Aranda. Photograph by Rex Battarbee

in the early 1940s, and by writing passionately on Aboriginal affairs. His remarkable achievements in the field of Aboriginal welfare were officially recognised by many Australian and German awards.

Upon their retirement to Adelaide in 1961, again precipitated by Minna's ill health, Fritz continued to write prolifically on Aboriginal and mission issues. For over a decade he exchanged letters with the Aborigines of Central Australia and visited them in hospital when they came south for medical treatment. These were the cherished contacts of his final years.

Minna died in November 1983 at the age of eighty-five and was survived by her husband for only a few months. Fritz died at almost ninety and was buried in Adelaide by three Aboriginal pastors who had known him since the early days at Hermannsburg. Konrad Raberaba was a boy of ten when the Albrechts arrived in 1926, and later accompanied Fritz on some of his camel treks west; Traugott Malbunka was one of the sickly children Minna had fed in her kitchen during the drought years, and Eli Rubuntja grew up on the mission and became Fritz's truck driver on his visits to the cattle stations around Alice Springs. 'He is in the ground now,' they said, 'and we are the branches that come from him.'

In the detailed accounts of his camel treks that he published in mission newsletters, Pastor Albrecht never mentioned going as far west as Walunguwra in the Kintore Range near the West Australian border. But his name is included on a plaque erected there to commemorate those who brought the gospel to the area, and the Pintubi people will show the place where he camped: 'Old man Albrecht, he came on camels and camped there, and he shared us everything. Tea, sugar, flour, God's word. Everything.'

Pastor F.W. Albrecht, at Hermannsburg c. 1930. Barely able to speak English when he arrived in 1926, Pastor Albrecht preached his first sermon in Aranda within ten months

Mary Magdelene Bowers
1889–1973

Queanbeyan's earthy Nightingale
Written by: Lynette Ramsay Silver
Nominated by: Narelle O'Rourke

Mary Magdelene O'Rourke, the second of eight children, was born into of a close-knit, working-class Irish family in the New South Wales country town of Queanbeyan. It soon became obvious that Mary had inherited her father's fiery, dominant personality, a robust sense of humour and a zest for living which allowed her to tackle life head on. She also developed, probably as the result of being the eldest girl, an ability to delegate menial and boring tasks to others, a talent which she raised almost to an art form. Mary discovered quite early that the drudgery of washing and ironing could easily be avoided by appointing her younger sister to carry out these loathsome chores. Mary's word carried such authority that her sister obeyed without question.

During World War I, Mary trained at the Homeopathic School of Nursing in Sydney, then went to the Coast Hospital where she nursed soldiers with contagious illnesses. The proximity of the big city allowed Mary to indulge her passion for all things fashionable and she raised many an eyebrow among the staid Queanbeyan matrons when she blew into her hometown decked out in her city finery. With the raised eyebrows came the clacking tongues and the general consensus was that Mary O'Rourke was indeed a 'brazen hussy'. The criticism rolled off Mary like water off a duck's back.

In 1922 Nurse O'Rourke decided to add midwifery to her skills and spent a year qualifying at South Sydney Women's Hospital before returning home to Queanbeyan. Here she concentrated on midwifery, freelancing at the local hospital and the 'lying-in hospitals', which were gaining in popularity, as well as attending home confinements.

Mary's cheery face was also often seen behind the bar of Byrne's Hotel, dispensing beer as well as unsolicited and practical advice on all matters. The locals came to regard her as an extension of their own families, but her hotel employment was viewed with disfavour by some who felt the job was beneath the dignity of a 'professional person'. When this opinion was publicly aired one day, Mary leaned over the bar and announced in a voice for all to hear 'Ah, well, I never was far up the bloody social ladder, so I don't have far to fall.' With the same direct and fearless approach she continued to deliver her babies and attend to the sick and dying, walking for many kilometres to aid all those who needed her unless she could hitch a lift with anyone who happened to be passing by. Her requests for assistance were usually unsentimental. 'Hey Dooly,' she would shout, 'unscrew the shed door so I can lay poor ole Tom out!'

During a home confinement not only mother and baby benefited from Mary's attention. She took the whole family under her care, either bringing food from home to feed the household or 'volunteering' someone else to do the cooking. She never asked for payment and only expected it if the fee could be afforded. However, if well-heeled folk were tardy in paying up, Mary soon let all and sundry know that she was still waiting to see the colour of their money.

The menfolk, perceived by her to be the sole cause of all pregnancies, were constantly abused and berated while she attended to their wives with gentle understanding. Her attitude to unwanted pregnancies was simple. 'Why don't you do as I do?', the unmarried Mary asked an astounded female audience. 'Bloody well go without!' Yet under her down-to-earth exterior was a woman of immense compassion. Having just confined a young unmarried girl, and realising that the sight of a washing line filled with newly-laundered, specialised bedding would start tongues wagging, Mary took the soiled linen home with her.

The thirties brought both the Depression and marriage. At the age of forty-four, Mary married Alfred Bowers but marriage for Mary did not mean domesticity. Her work continued, made even more necessary by the poverty and unemployment of the time. She organised the townspeople into unpicking sacks and resewing them into blankets for the needy and applied herself with even more determination to the plight of the less fortunate. On one occasion she wriggled into a brick kiln to deliver the baby of a destitute woman, while on another she crossed the flooded Queanbeyan River, crawling over the railway bridge on her hands and knees to bring another baby safely into the world.

Mary's husband, a man of incredible patience, bore his wife's erratic

Nurse Mary Bowers, a woman of compassion and determination, photographed in a Queanbeyan street in the 1940s. Domesticity held no appeal for Mary. She regarded housework as a complete waste of her time and abandoned it very early in her life

working hours and even more erratic domestic arrangements with stoicism. It was not unusual for Alf to wake up and find that Mary was missing (along with his pants, taken to clothe some unfortunate soul), that his blankets had disappeared from his bed and been distributed to the needy and that last night's dessert was now on the breakfast menu. In Mary's eyes, household chores were an utter waste of time and were completely ignored. If someone could not be seconded to do the necessary tasks they were simply not done. Alf weathered this chaotic approach to household management by creating a garden of over a hectare, from which fruit and vegetables ended up on the plates of many a needy family.

Mary's calls were not always to the local workers. A summons once came to nurse a gentleman in his mansion at Yarralumla, another to the staff at Duntroon. Here Mary revealed her chameleon-like ability to shed the speech and the rough characteristics of the people she so often nursed. Out would come the silk gloves and hats and Mary would become a lady of refined sensibilities with speech and mannerisms to match.

As the need for home confinements decreased, Mary extended her horizons. In 1939 she became President of the local Red Cross, a post she held for sixteen years. She poured her energies into raising funds for the war effort and her organisational skills reached an all time zenith as anyone available was roped into sewing and knitting, cooking and preserving.

In the last two decades of her life Mary became a Justice of the Peace, a Life Member of the Red Cross and finally, in 1967, was awarded an MBE for her services to the community. When she died in 1973, Queanbeyan lost its most colourful character. Mary is remembered as much for her untiring work and devotion to duty as for her earthy turn of phrase but even today there are elderly women in Queanbeyan who cover their faces with their aprons and laugh in delighted embarrassment declaring, 'Oh, I couldn't possibly repeat what Mary said'.

This feisty woman of indomitable spirit, unfailing determination and deep compassion certainly deserves the title bestowed upon her by the people she served so faithfully for over fifty years — 'Mary Bowers, The Florence Nightingale of Queanbeyan'.

C.E.A. 'Mick' Cook
1897–1985
'Guiding hand' of Territory medicine
Written by: Elizabeth Riddell
Nominated by: Desmond Travers

In Australia, what would you call a man with the given names of Cecil Evelyn Aufrere? Inevitably, 'Mick'. So C.E.A. Cook, at school, through the army, university, and a high-powered career in tropical medicine in the field and the lecture hall, remained Mick. Except, that is, when he signed his frequently admonitory letters to the 'authorities' ticking them off in a scathingly dismissive way for what he saw as their ignorance, incompetence or pig-headedness.

Mick Cook was a formidable figure — very tall, very spare, grey-haired from the age of twenty-four and swiftly white after that, with a glass eye that was the result of a pea-rifle accident in childhood — whose enormous achievement was in the prevention and treatment of such obnoxious diseases as leprosy, cholera, hookworm, scrub typhus, scurvy and malaria. In 1927 he was appointed, at one stroke of the pen, Chief Protector of Aborigines, Chief Medical Officer, Chief Health Officer and Quarantine Officer in the Northern Territory. In twelve years of intensive work in health and education, of pushing and persuading various governments to take seriously the problems of the outback (and spend some money on them), of forcing himself and his colleagues and his notoriously overworked vehicles towards impossible goals, he changed the face of the North.

Mick Cook was already well known in the Territory before taking on his four jobs. After a year at the London School of Tropical medicine in 1923 he returned to Australia as a Wandsworth Scholar to research his subject. He reported on the incidence of leprosy among Aborigines in a study, *Epidemiology of Leprosy in Australia* (Commonwealth Govt, 1927), that remains a standard work, and conducted a health survey of indigenous people right across the north, during which time he contracted blackwater fever and malaria. From his efforts came the Northern Territory Medical Service; its nursing service; a leprosarium; the introduction of medical records and personal cards for Aborigines; vaccination of pearling crews and their on-shore workers; compulsory notification of disease; regulation of hygiene on mission stations; improved water supplies; control of food on sale and, eventually, new hospitals at Darwin, Katherine and Alice Springs; and at Darwin a maternity ward, TB, malaria and venereal disease clinics as well as maternal and infant welfare clinics.

Dr Mick Cook (right) whose lanky frame, overworked motor cars and mordant wit became familiar throughout the North during his twelve years as the Northern Territory's first Chief Medical Officer. Cook fought official apathy, incompetence and ignorance to give the people of the Territory a medical service that his friend Clyde Fenton, whom Cook shanghaied to help him in 1928, described as 'a monument to his wisdom, energy, and tenacity of purpose'. Darwin, c.1930

Dr Mick Cook, CBE, at the time of his survey of Aboriginal health in the Northern Territory, late 1920s

Mick Cook was born in Britain of English-Scottish parents. His father was a doctor who emigrated to Australia when he was two and settled in North Queensland. Cook would later recall an occurrence in childhood that shaped his life: 'The awe and dread inspired in me by the sight of a ship quarantined for plague outside Rockhampton...' He was to meet shipborne plague again as a young doctor in Brisbane General Hospital in 1921–22 — its last appearance in Australia.

From Southport High School Cook went to medical school at Sydney University, graduating in 1920 aged twenty-three. In all his long life — he died at Burleigh Heads in 1985, still active and interested in public medicine — Cook spent only a few months in private practice. His obsession was public health. It brought him underpaid jobs — much of the time in conditions that ranged from uncomfortable to appalling — and separated him for long periods from his wife and children. On his honeymoon in Sydney when summoned to his initial research post in 1924, Cook left his bride, caught the train with only a handful of silver in his pocket, and arrived in Perth a week later with 'three pence'. It was the first of many such separations. It is unlikely that Cook ever allowed such intensely personal feelings to show, but his private letters reveal a profound sense of loss at being separated from his wife whom he missed bitterly.

The essence of Cook's attitude to his profession is apparent in a letter written to the Western Australian Government when he was about to take up the post of Commissioner of Health in that State, following war service in Australia, Ceylon and New Guinea. He wrote, 'I feel I should be able to assist you in the postwar years to provide WA with a medical and health service which will be at once a model to the Commonwealth and an enduring monument to your administration.

'Such an opportunity has been my life's ambition and to secure it I am prepared to acquiesce in the separation from my family and the financial loss which acceptance will I fear involve.'

It turned out that the Western Australian administration did not quite live up to Cook's expectations. He stayed three years, however, bombarding the administration with ideas and rebukes until he resigned in frustration in 1949 in a letter that is classic Cook. The end reads, in part, 'I am unfortunately temperamentally unsuited to continuing in an office which demands tacit acquiescence in the maintenance of a mediocre service...'

Cook's firm belief was that medical affairs should be left to professionals. He did not want to make money, just to get things right. Once in the course of a speech farewelling a colleague he told the story of how, when he was very young in the north-west, a government functionary refused to allow him the bus fare to visit an aged man who was dying of leprosy. Cook added in his sardonic style, 'It was a dismaying indictment of lay control in a professional department and...has influenced my attitude to my lay colleagues throughout my working life.'

Cook's work with Aborigines should be seen in the context of the period, but he stands as the finest kind of product of his times. C.D Rowley, in *The Destruction of Aboriginal Society* (Penguin, 1972), suggests that Cook was the prime mover for a fixed cash wage for part-Aborigines in the pastoral industry and especially for those employed as drovers for whom cash would be essential to support their families. Despite enormous counter-pressure from pastoralists, he insisted on the responsibility of pastoral management to feed, clothe and house employees and their dependants and in 1935 was awarded the Cilento medal 'for Service to Native People'.

Clyde Fenton and Mick Cook were friends from the time Cook kidnapped Fenton in 1928 to be the other Northern Territory doctor. Together — Cook worked on the government while Fenton worked on raising a loan to buy a plane — these two remarkable men established the Northern Territory Aerial Medical Service with Fenton in his heavily-mortgaged Tiger Moths as Australia's first real flying doctor. In *Flying Doctor* (Georgian House, 1947), Fenton describes his 'chief':

'Over six feet tall, lean hardbitten, with a face burned fiery red by the tropic sun..., a snow-white thatch of untidy hair and a single vivid blue eye with which he could see far more than the average mortal could with two, he was known throughout the length and breadth of the Territory...he had travelled wherever it was possible to travel, mostly by car but quite a lot (according to report) on foot — he was an indifferent motor mechanic.

'A man of keen intellect with a fine command of language, he was a master of the mordant phrase and a hard man to get the better of in debate. On paper he was devastating, as many who crossed swords with him discovered to their cost.'

Cook was clearly not an easy man. Congenitally incapable of 'tacit acquiescence' in anything, he must at times have been uncomfortable to live with. 'Dad wouldn't tolerate being told,' recalls his daughter Robin with wry affection: 'He knew what was right.' It was, however, this same determination, energy and courage — the qualities of a tough visionary — that built up the medical service that Fenton describes as 'a monument to his wisdom, energy and tenacity of purpose'. Mick Cook was, writes Fenton, 'the moving spirit and guiding hand' of Northern Territory medicine.

Clyde Cornwall Fenton
1902–1982
Australia's first flying doctor
Written by: Suzy Baldwin
Nominated by: T.J. Meek; E.R. Mattingley

In 1928, the Rev John Flynn of the Australian Inland Mission (AIM) established an aerial medical base at Cloncurry in Queensland. Ever since, Flynn of the Inland and what became the Royal Flying Doctor Service are generally — though mistakenly — assumed to have been responsible for all aerial medicine in the outback. But Flynn's flying doctors were not, strictly speaking, flying doctors at all. They were flown. Flynn used commercial aircraft and pilots and, as a result, his service could extend only to those areas sufficiently well developed to have licensed aerodromes and the navigational aids demanded by the Civil Aviation Authority. The great problem area

— the vast, desolate outback of Central Australia — remained out of reach and its people inaccessible. Particularly during the six-month wet season, the ill and the injured were still faced with only two possibilities — they either recovered on their own or they died.

The man who came to their rescue combined compassion and extraordinary courage with devotion to medical duty, an irrepressible sense of humour and a robust disrespect for bureaucratic red tape. He broke every rule in the book and a few that were not. If the authorities cancelled his licence — which they did regularly — he flew without one.

Remarkable characters flourish in the Territory but few have become folk heroes so rapidly or have been as loved as Dr Clyde Fenton, Australia's first flying doctor. Fenton bought, flew and serviced his own planes. He maintained them at his own expense, and when he crashed one, as he did frequently, he either repaired it or plunged himself further into debt to replace it. In his book, *Flying Doctor*, first published in 1947, Fenton describes some of the adventures of those 'magic days' between 1934 and 1940 when he flew 3000 hours and 400 000 kilometres to provide medical aid to *all* people in the Territory.

Fenton's introduction to the Territory was a fine piece of comic swashbuckling, typical in scale, style and nerve of both men involved. Dr C.E.A. 'Mick' Cook had been in Darwin since 1927, the year he turned thirty. He was the first Chief Medical Officer of the Northern Territory Medical Service, Chief Protector of Aborigines, Quarantine Officer and responsible for the 'control and treatment of lepers in North Australia'. Single-handedly carrying out these duties, in his spare time he also ran the Darwin hospital and the town's medical practice. Cook had been trying for months to find another doctor to help him but, given Darwin's reputation, no one would take on the job. By June 1928, when the ship on which Fenton was travelling to Melbourne happened to call at Darwin, Cook was a desperate man.

He went down to the ship and tried to persuade the twenty-six-year-old Fenton to stay. Fenton was sympathetic but refused. 'Well,' said Cook, 'at least come to the house for a party.' Never one to pass up an opportunity for a little convivial imbibing, Fenton accepted, and woke the next day to find that 'I and my baggage were ashore and the ship had sailed'. Cook had successfully shanghaied himself a doctor.

In the five wet months before the arrival of the next ship, Fenton experienced the problems of providing emergency medical help to a sparse population scattered across the vast face of the Territory. He became convinced that a doctor flying his own small aeroplane was the only answer. He took his idea to Flynn at the newly-established Inland Mission base, but Flynn, a visionary in some areas, was shortsighted on this subject. 'One man, one job,' he insisted. Fenton left the Territory but he was hooked. He promised Cook that he'd be back, bringing an aircraft with him.

The Depression followed, however, and it was not until early March 1934, after many disappointments, that Fenton was able to fulfil his promise. Cook, 'master of the mordant phrase', had won another of his many battles with government departments and had persuaded Canberra to appoint Fenton as medical officer at Katherine and pay him a meagre allowance if he could find a plane.

A second-hand Gipsy Moth was available in Melbourne for £500.

Uneasy Peace 187

Refused a loan by Flynn, Fenton borrowed the money elsewhere. Not having flown for more than a year, he had a hasty dual check with the Aero Club at Essendon and set off for Darwin. He arrived four days later, tied the plane down in the open, and slept peacefully through most of the party in his honour. 'And so commenced the Northern Territory Aerial Medical Service.' It was a personal triumph for both Cook and Fenton, but for Fenton it was also the beginning of years of financial cliffhanging.

Clyde Fenton never turned down an appeal for help. As he explained in a speech to the Academy of Science in Canberra in 1971, 'There was one great advantage in a doctor doing his own flying — he did not have to argue with a pilot who might want to veto a flight because of the risks involved. In my dual capacity I had to argue only with myself, and I always won.' From his base in Katherine, Fenton flew anywhere and everywhere, landing on claypans, in paddocks alongside surprised livestock, and in clearings that a less sporting pilot would have left undisturbed. Take-off was also risky. On more than one occasion, the Moth's wings cleared the treetops only because, in Fenton's phrase, 'the trees ducked'.

Having no radio, night flying aids or navigation lights, Fenton practised night landings in Katherine by moonlight, 'to the wonder of the local populace' who echoed, more or less politely, the station owner who greeted Fenton's first attempt with: 'You bloody lunatic'.

A genius at improvisation, Fenton soon devised a simple flare path

'Pilot and ground staff, Katherine NT.' c.1935. Flying doctor Clyde Fenton and one of the second-hand Gypsy Moths that he flew to every corner of the Territory. Fenton paid for the planes, flew them, crashed them and replaced them

system but his many night landings were more commonly made by moonlight, car headlights, torchlight or, when all else failed, 'by guess and by God'.

A couple of months after his arrival in Katherine, Fenton was commissioned to fly the Commonwealth Geologist, Dr Woolnough, from Tennant Creek to Ord River. While he was there, he received an emergency call to a woman badly gored by a bull at Brock's Creek almost 1000 kilometres away. Fenton took off at moonrise, hoping to reach Brock's Creek by daybreak.

Flying along the Victoria River, his engine failed. Fenton successfully crash-landed in the bush, repaired the plane next morning, and took off again. Delighted to discover that he was not lost, as he had thought, he glided down to drop a note to Dr Woolnough who was waiting on the ground. While his attention was diverted, the aircraft stalled. 'The next moment the whole universe appeared to explode.' Fenton managed to free himself from the wreckage and, apart from numerous cuts and bruises was, miraculously, unhurt. 'But alas! my beautiful little machine was smashed to pieces. I could have wept with rage and grief. The irony of it!...In a moment, triumph had turned to disaster through a needless quixotic gesture.'

After enquiring throughout the Commonwealth, Fenton heard that Qantas had a second-hand Gipsy Moth for sale in Brisbane for £600. Despite the fact that the crashed Moth was uninsured and most of the loan still owing, Fenton, supported by Mick Cook, persuaded Qantas to send it up and proposed to Canberra that the Federal Government should advance him a loan, to be repaid by monthly deductions from his salary. 'How, they immediately asked, would they recover their money if, as seemed likely, I should predecease the instalments? I had a ready answer to that one; I assigned them my life insurance.' As an old Territory friend of Fenton's observed, 'The most remarkable thing about this is that he had any. He must have sneaked up on some unsuspecting company when they weren't looking.'

While one government department considered this offer, another threatened to cancel Fenton's pilot's licence on the strength of newspaper accounts of the night flight. A furious Fenton sent off a series of telegrams which Cook censored because they 'lacked tact'. The department, which Fenton re-christened the Uncivil Aviation Department, remained obdurate. 'Thus commenced a feud which was waged with some bitterness on both sides for the whole of my six years in the Territory' — and after.

Meanwhile, the Moth had arrived in Darwin. While one department hesitated and the other threatened, fate intervened. A horseman brought a message from an isolated station 650 kilometres away, requesting urgent help for a woman in childbirth. The Moth was the only aircraft in the Territory but Qantas refused to release it until cash or a guarantee was produced. Fenton went to the Administrator, who, of course, had no choice but to guarantee the money. In half an hour, Fenton was on his way to the maternity case, now paying off two aircraft out of a salary of around £8 a week. The new Moth's registration was VH-U0l — naturally, it was ever after referred to as *IOU*.

When this situation was repeated Fenton took on yet another plane and plunged himself even further into debt rather than turn down any emergency call. While *IOU* was in pieces on the Qantas hangar floor, undergoing a major overhaul, an urgent call came through from Roper River: an Aboriginal boy had been so badly burned that he was in danger of haemorrhaging to death.

Fenton sent an urgent message to the AIM base at Cloncurry. Would they handle the case? 'The reply came late that night. They regretted their inability to go to Roper River Mission as the insurance on their aircraft did not permit visits to unlicensed landing grounds. Luckily for my patients I had no such worries for no one would insure me whether the grounds were licensed or otherwise.'

As it happened, there was another second-hand Gipsy Moth for sale in Darwin for £450. Fenton hauled the Administrator out of bed and asked him to guarantee the money. Only when Fenton asked if he were prepared to be responsible for the boy's death did the reluctant Administrator cave in. Five hours later Fenton arrived at Roper River in the *Magic Carpet*. The boy lived, but it was two years before he was able to leave hospital.

To Fenton's disgust, the Government repudiated the Administrator's guarantee. Feeling morally if not legally responsible, the doctor arranged that *IOU* — like its predecesor, still unpaid for — should stand security for the *Magic Carpet*. His one amusement in all this was to see all concerned 'scared stiff that I might crash and be killed, leaving this fearful tangle behind as sole legacy to my creditors'.

Fenton performed extraordinary feats in these little Moths, not the least of them a solo flight to China and back in 1936 to be with his elderly mother after the sudden death of his sister. He installed an extra fuel tank in *IOU* and took off, evading the authorities with his usual flair.

Sadly, the engine of the valiant little *IOU* failed later that year and she crashed and burned during take-off. Fenton spent a week in hospital recovering from injuries, and brooding. The *Magic Carpet* had already bitten the dust and he could take on no further debts.

'Then suddenly two remarkable things occurred.' A public subscription in Darwin bought Fenton another Gipsy Moth, christened *Robin* in honour of Dr Cook's small daughter, and the Federal government, 'either shamed to action by this generous gesture or belatedly conscience-stricken after previous apathy,' finally provided the money for an ambulance plane.

When war broke out, Fenton joined the RAAF. After a spell as a flight instructor, Flight Lieutenant, later Squadron Leader, 'Doc' Fenton was given seven ancient aeroplanes and posted to the Northern Territory to form No. 6 Communications Unit. Known as Fenton's Flying Freighters, the unit carried mail, personnel and freight and evacuated the sick from outlying coastal and island radar stations from Broome to Groote Eylandte. When, in 1943, they acquired a couple of Walrus amphibians, Fenton's flyers ran an air-sea rescue service as well. Despite Airforce regulations that insisted, like Flynn, on 'one man, one job', Fenton never ceased to be 'the flying doctor'.

Displaying always what Cook described as 'resolute devotion to duty, compulsive acceptance of challenge and a wilful disregard of personal hazard', the tall, lean, mildly donnish-looking Fenton packed enough adventure for several lives into his years as flying doctor. A much-loved and irresistibly romantic hero, the irreverent 'Doc' Fenton could not have been less like the Reverend John Flynn if he had tried.

Squadron Leader 'Doc' Fenton, OBE, in the Northern Territory during World War II. At the outbreak of war, Fenton immediately offered his services to Air Board. 'The medical section was apathetic [and] the flying people said I was too old to fly and told me to get back in my bathchair.' But eventually the RAAF gave Fenton a handful of geriatric planes and sent him back up North to form a unit that quickly became know as 'Fenton's Flying Freighters'. It was, as one would expect, unique. Photograph courtesy Australian War Memorial

Ruth Heathcock
1901–

Pitjiri — the snake that will not sink
Written by: Lucinda Strauss
Nominated by: Karen Hughes

In 1936 nine naked Aboriginal elders swam across the Roper River and, in single file, silently approached a young white woman, Ruth Heathcock, a mission sister from Adelaide, who stood unafraid as they stared into her eyes and scrutinised her hands, feet and earlobes. Her terrified Aboriginal servant Kara, hiding in the saucepan cupboard, heard the men say that Ruth had belonged to their tribe 'before the Dreaming'. They bade her visit one of the region's most ancient, sacred and spectacular places, the legendary Burundju, the Ruined City. Then they disappeared across the river, their tracks never to be found.

At that time Ruth had spent seven years at Roper Bar, the Territory's most isolated police station, with her husband, the local constable. She had come to learn much about Aboriginal culture and spiritual beliefs. Her housegirls had taught her the language of the Alawar tribe and she had recorded their myths and creation stories. They passed on to her their herbal cures and knowledge of bush tucker.

The Aboriginal women sensed that there was something very special about Ruth and gave her the name 'Pitjiri, the snake that will not sink'. She was surprised that they should ascribe such a name to one who could not swim, so they took her to the river and pushed her down under the water — she always 'bobbed up and down like a bottle'.

From very early on Ruth was drawn to a life of healing and was fascinated by Aboriginal people. As a young girl in Wellington, South Australia, her family acknowledged that she had 'a healing power' and after school every day she could be found either playing with the Aboriginal children from the nearby Port Mcleay mission or listening to the stories of Louisa Karpenny, a formidable old tribal matriarch and one of her earliest teachers.

Born on 11 January 1901, Ruth Rayney was one of six children. Her father was a railway engineer and her mother, the daughter of an Irish baron. Ruth was an independent, confident young girl with dreams of mysticism and adventure. At the age of sixteen she enrolled as a trainee nurse at the Royal Adelaide Hospital with the aim of working as a nurse on John Flynn's Inland Mission.

Ruth then contracted a serious tuberculosis-related illness and lost a lung. After a year's convalescence, she finished her training and in 1928 set sail for Marranboy, a remote town in the Northern Territory, to run John Flynn's Hostel. It was here that she met and married the new mounted constable from Mataranka, an Englishman, twenty years her senior, named Ted Heathcock.

Although she had encountered leprosy at Marranboy, it was only when Ted took up his placement at Roper Bar that she began, illegally, treating the sufferers. Widespread among the Aboriginal people in Arnhem Land, leprosy was highly contagious and could be arrested but not cured. While a quarantine base had been established on Chanel Island in Darwin Harbour, the Aboriginal people refused to go there. Dying outside one's totemic birthplace without the correct funeral rites meant that the spirit would not have clear passage to the next world.

Ruth felt an empathy with the people's desire to live according to tribal lore. She also felt a certain amount of spiritual guidance in her work through the intervention of the 'golden hands' assisting her in amputations. While white people may dismiss the notion of psychic healing, the Aborigines had no trouble seeing the 'Two fella golden hands' that helped her.

Word spread quickly and people carried their sick for hundreds of kilometres to be treated by Ruth. Although the arrival of leprosy patients seemed to coincide with Ted's long absences on patrol, he was very much aware of what was happening. Concerned for the most part about the inhumane treatment of the Aborigines, as well as the illegality of the treatment, he successfully petitioned the League of Nations to have the law changed. As a result of his campaign mobile clinics were set up in the area to treat tribal Aborigines.

When the nine naked 'wild fella blackmen' swam across the Roper River in 1936 and bade Ruth come to Burundju, she was in no way surprised. She felt that she was destined to go there and gladly prepared to make the journey. Thought by the Aborigines to have housed a previous civilisation, the Ruined City is a vast eroded mountain with an infra-structure resembling the layout of a vacated city.

On arrival Ruth was met by the nine elders who took her to a cave. Here she found she was able to read the writings on the walls and chant old songs but as soon as she left the cave the gift of reading and chanting the Aboriginal language left her. After this initiation and what was supposedly an investment with new powers, Ruth was taken to treat a leper colony that had sought refuge in the caves.

Ruth Heathcock, the bush nurse who became a legend among the Aborigines, c.1920

Ruth's story has entered Aboriginal legend and today is told to Aboriginal boys of the Ngalikan tribe going through their three-month initiation ceremony. Dawson Daniels, Deputy President of Ngukurr Council says of Ruth, 'My people had a dream that someone would come and take our sick people to a better place. We believe that person was Sister Ruth.'

A few years later Ted was posted to Borroloola and Ruth took part in a heroic rescue. During the cyclone season of 1941, a call had gone out to the Flying Doctor to attend Horace Foster, a bushman, who had accidentally shot himself in the leg near the Wearyan River. Conditions were so poor that the plane could not land. Sister Ruth, guided by Roger Jose and his Aboriginal wife Maggie, paddled 145 kilometres in a dug-out canoe through flooded rivers and open seas to reach the wounded man. Awarded an MBE in 1951 for what the Northern Territory Chief Administrator called 'the bravest act in the Territory's history', Ruth is mindful of the debt she owes to the local people, 'There's not one thing I could have done without...[them]. Now is it I'm getting an MBE for me. And it's not me at all. I thought there's not one thing I could have done alone. I couldn't have existed up there.'

Today, at the age of eighty-six, Ruth lives a productive life in Adelaide. Widowed during the war she continued nursing up into her sixties. She rarely speaks of her experiences as a psychic healer among the Aborigines for she thinks people down south will say she has 'white ants' in her head. But one thing is certain, she has always loved the Aboriginal people with whom she lived: 'They were always terrific to me because I was one of them.'

Alyandabu
c1875–1961

'If you were white...'
Story and song written by: Ted Egan
Nominated by: Ted Egan

'Straight out of a Drysdale canvas you walked...' Alyandabu, Territory woman. Painting by Robert Ingpen. Courtesy Ted Egan

Probably my most vivid memory of my early years in Darwin is that of an old Aboriginal woman named Alyandabu who used to walk into town each day. She had the erect, graceful carriage achieved by many Aboriginal women as a result of being trained to carry things on the head, thus leaving their hands free to gather food. She was almost six feet tall, and, again like many other Aboriginal women of the period, smoked a pipe. Usually she wore a wide-brimmed hat, either felt or straw panama. She was often barefooted, wore simple cotton frocks, and carried a few items tied in a red handkerchief. She could have walked straight out of a Russell Drysdale canvas.

Alyandabu was called Alyan by other Aborigines, Wetji by members of her family, and Lucy McGinness by the non-Aboriginal people of Darwin. She was one of the few survivors of the Khungarakung tribe whose members had been given poisoned flour by early white intruders into their country. Yet Alyandabu was later to meet and marry a white man, an Irishman named Stephen McGinness, and raise a fine family of four sons and a daughter. The relationship between Alyandabu and Stephen McGinness was quite extraordinary for the times. Today, their many descendants throughout Australia are fiercely proud of their unique Aboriginal/Irish/Australian heritage, and especially fond of the memory of the matriarch who died in 1961 at the age of eighty-six.

Alyandabu and Stephen McGinness lived and worked in railway fettlers' camps on the old North Australia railway. Then they found the rich Lucy tin mine and worked it together, at the same time rearing their family and teaching their children all the things they would need to know if they were to retain their identity. The children were all thoroughly educated in both the Aboriginal and western sense. Two sons especially, Joe and Jack, were in the forefront of the national Aboriginal rights movement long before it was fashionable.

Following Stephen McGinness's untimely death Alyandabu was confronted by the realisation that in legal terms she was an alien in her own country. Her mine was forfeited, and she was instructed to go to Darwin where her younger children were to be taken into the Aboriginal compound. She had to engage in arduous physical jobs in Darwin in order to be near her children. When the children grew up the family was able to be reunited in Darwin, where Alyandabu lived until her death.

Alyandabu's grand-daughter says that Alyandabu inspired Xavier Herbert to write *Capricornia* and that the novel's O'Cannon family is based on the McGinnesses. When Herbert died in 1987, Ballantyne McGinness, Alyandabu's son, came down from Darwin to perform the funeral service in the language of the Khungarakung.

In standard Australian terms Alyandabu's was a straightforward pioneering life, tough in the living, admirable in retrospect. Most of her story remains to be told.

> And I wonder what you're thinking about
> As you walk on through your life
> Are you thinking about the Irishman
> Who took you as his wife?
> Or the kids you bore?
> The things you saw?
> The hard times you were made to endure?
> What's your story?
> Alyandabu.

Lucy Bryce
1897–1968

Blood transfusion pioneer
Written by: Judith Elen
Nominated by: Marjorie Pinder

Lucy Bryce's portrait by William Dargie hangs in the Lucy Bryce Hall at the Red Cross Blood Bank in Melbourne. Sir Dallas Brooks, opening the building in 1959, said, 'now so much a part of the life of the community..., blood banking was unheard of...twenty-five years ago.'

Lucy Bryce graduated from the University of Melbourne, BSc in 1918 and MB, BS in 1922. She took up a research post, spending some time at the Lister Institute in London, and in 1928 she began work at the Royal Melbourne Hospital. The following year she established Australia's first Blood Transfusion Service.

Inspired by reports of the service organised in London in 1926, Dr Bryce took a plan to the Victorian Red Cross and a panel of blood donors was established to attend hospitals when blood was required. Dr Bryce was honorary director and did the blood grouping (first discovered in 1900) and other testing.

In 1938, when Dr Bryce was in England during the Spanish Civil War, she heard of new methods developed by a Spanish doctor whereby blood donated by civilians was stored, refrigerated, transported and distributed to the wounded. Under Dr Bryce's supervision, these storage techniques were adopted by the Victorian Red Cross.

Lucy Bryce continued her work until two years before her death and was awarded a CBE for her twenty-five years of 'sustained devotion'.

Dr Lucy Bryce, CBE, who established Australia's first Blood Transfusion Service. Portrait by William Dargie. Courtesy Red Cross Blood Bank, Victoria

George Downton
1902–

Self-help for the unemployed
Written by: David Millar
Nominated by: Irene Morris

The Depression had not yet arrived when George Downton, his wife May and three small children moved from then scruffy Balmain to neat, tidy Gladesville. Life was simple but safe. George had a job with the Alston Soap Company, where he had lost the tops of a couple of fingers in an industrial accident.

On Sundays, the girls attended Sunday School, while on hot afternoons there was swimming in the salt water baths. For family picnics they walked down to the reserve on Sydney Harbour or across to Buffalo Creek. As a hobby, George earned five shillings on Saturdays umpiring local cricket games, and later would tell proudly of the times he umpired when Don Bradman played for Gladesville Hospital against the *Sydney Morning Herald*.

Then came the Depression and George Downton was sacked. He joined all the other men who had been stood down from the nearby Cockatoo Dockyard and two local brickworks. Like them, he was out of work, with a family to feed.

George earned a few shillings selling cheap cigarettes outside the local hotel. Like others, he took the tram to Circular Quay and filled his two chaff bags with the family ration for a week — seven loaves of bread, some tea, sugar, flour and a tin of treacle, plus a coupon for meat, usually sausages. If you wanted more, you had to scrounge for it — somewhere. When George's eldest daughter broke a pane of glass, she was forcibly reminded that the repair would cost all the extra money George had earned from a hot Saturday afternoon's umpiring. If you were unemployed, there was nothing in reserve for the unexpected.

George Downton, however, was a proud and determined man. He could not face defeat, so if he could not find a way, he would have to make one. He decided to establish a co-operative, in which the unemployed could pool their resources to improve their lot.

Determined and forceful, George approached local businessmen, telling them that if they supported the Co-op, the Co-op would support them. He persuaded the local paper to give him free advertising space and called a public meeting. The three hundred people who filled the old Ryde Fire Station voted for the inauguration of The Gladesville-Ryde Unemployment Relief Society and appointed George as its secretary.

The Co-op was a great success. It raised money by running a weekly carnival with Hoop-la, Housie, a Chocolate Wheel and a prize of a pork roast, and held a regular Sunday night variety concert (entrance by a silver coin) featuring songs, sketches, 'hilarious farces', and the singing and dancing 'Downton Daughters'. Because of the conservatism of the times, the committee had to send the programmes for each revue into the Chief Secretary's Department for prior approval and there was always a policeman at the show to make sure that the Australian Sunday was not defiled.

Trees culled from Gladesville Hospital gardens were cut up, bagged and delivered, providing over thirty tons of free fuel to the needy; bulk purchasing of sheep carcases provided meat for nearly 700 households, and coke from the AGL at Mortlake provided twenty bags of fuel a month. On Friday mornings, very early, members of the Co-op would board the first trams to the city, and make for Paddy's market, where they would haggle for bargains, before returning to Ryde with their sugar bags full of fruit and vegetables which were then evenly divided up amongst the unemployed. At the nearby public school, any child who came without lunch was given a sandwich, provided by a generous sweet shop proprietor, and milk and fruit provided by the Co-op.

The Co-operative Society continued until the Depression began to lift and members found employment. George Downton returned to the anonymity of a soap factory where he spent the rest of his working life. Now a widower, he lives near Nowra, on the south coast of New South Wales.

Irene Dorling
1909–1987
One woman's survival
Written by: Susan Hamilton
Nominated by: Frank Campbell

Irene Dorling was one of the many ancient crones laden with mysterious bags and trolleys who crisscross our city streets — women whose thinning hair, pinched features and shabby, eccentric clothes invite ridicule and neglect. But Irene's shopping trolley, to which she seemed almost welded, hid a treasure — the manuscript that tells her story, *Twentieth Century Family, an Autobiographical Trilogy*, published by her friends at the Social History Museum at Deakin University in Victoria.

Irene was born in North Wales in 1909, the unwanted child of an alcoholic merchant seaman and a miner's orphaned daughter. Mother and children were evacuated to the south of England during the Great War, where food was scarce and anti-Welsh feeling high, especially at school. The separation from her father was, nonetheless, a relief to Irene, who had been the victim of incest from the age of four. After Irene's father was killed in action, her mother remarried an Australian serviceman, with whom the little family emigrated to Adelaide in 1920. There, they lived with an ill-natured step-grandmother and were again the victims of prejudice, this time for being 'Poms'.

Her mother's terminal illness forced thirteen-year-old Irene to leave school and take over housekeeping for her stepfather who drank, gambled, womanised and beat her regularly. She stood up to him as best she could but, when her mother died, Irene was thrown out upon the world, fifteen and friendless.

At eighteen, Irene Dorling followed her mother's example and married an alcoholic. Part one of her story, entitled with a fine irony 'Shoe-string Stratum, a Journey through the Lucky Country', tells starkly and unsentimentally of life in a world where malnourished women with no control over their fertility bore child after sickly child. These children were 'lucky' to be born at all, since 'so many babies were lost because mothers were too weak to carry them to full term'. Irene was hungry all through her first pregnancy. She wrote later, 'Just before Christmas my baby girl arrived, a very weak child who could not keep any food down. It was a battle to keep her alive during those dreadful months ahead.' Despite her best efforts, it was a battle that Irene eventually lost: Dawn died on Melbourne Cup morning in 1935, just seven years old.

'We were,' Irene wrote, 'a low income family. A no income family during the Depression.' They were years of soup queues, charity and government hand-outs. Despite the 'remarkable...ideas one gets in order to fill the larder' (cadging suffocated chickens at the markets, stealing eggs, waiting by the railway line for coals to fall off passing trains) Irene was usually 'near starvation'. Her first son was born three months prematurely during this time. He died within minutes and she 'just about did not make it' herself. Then came World War II — 'The same old rationing again and so many shortages to be overcome, but as I knew nothing else, we managed.'

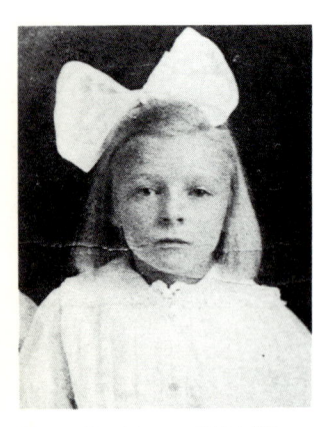

Irene Dorling, c.1914. Her life-long struggle against horrific odds began in her early childhood

Irene 'managed' by almost working herself to death. She sewed and cleaned, washed and ironed. Pregnant with her fifth child, she was badly injured by a patient in the nursing home in which she had been cooking, gardening and cleaning chicken coops. Moving to the country without her husband, she took live-in jobs involving manual labour, 'managing the thresher gang single-handed', and housekeeping for large families. She lived in a tent while peapicking, putting 'the two-year-old boy on a pram harness with a long lead and [driving] a peg into the ground so he could follow me down the rows of peas...'

Back in town, life deteriorated sharply. 'I got a job cleaning a theatre two days a week at a pound a day...At night I took a position frying fish and chips until three in the morning [when] I would take the children wrapped in blankets to a cafe where I scrubbed from six to nine, would drop the kids at [their] creche and go on to wash and iron at a few homes. Not much sleep for me and I started to feel run down.' At this stage, two of Irene's children were dead and another with her husband's people, 'where at least I knew she would be well cared for'. She put the remaining two into a home and spent two months in hospital.

When her husband was killed in action Irene married again. This marriage, though it allowed her to retrieve her children and was initially happier, repeated the old pattern. Dorling proved to be addicted to sedatives and 'very mean' with money. Two children were born before the marriage, prompting the Army to threaten withdrawal of her pension and the local Sunday School to expel her older children. Once more, Irene worked like a navvy and moved often.

Again and again she returned to the country. She loved it — 'Life is so good to one on the land' — but somehow she could never hang on to it. Despite years of hard work, raising chickens and growing vegetables, something always semed to force her 'back to the industrial zone'. In 1948 she and Dorling built a shack 'with second-grade timber' at Wallington in Victoria. It was 'the first place I had ever owned'. But 'when the older ones began attending high school I found I could not pay their fares and keep a good cupboard'. They moved to town, living in a 'huge airforce tent' while they struggled to build again. Unable to afford the first-grade materials necessary for a house in town, they went back to their 'cosy shack', only to find it so vandalised that they had to make do with a caravan for several months while they rebuilt it.

When her youngest child needed special medical care, Irene Dorling took a job in the Ford plant at Broadmeadows. She was forty-two. There, revelling in the security of her first regular wage, Irene was involved in an industrial accident which took the sight of one eye and damaged the other. The compensation from Ford enabled her to put a deposit on a small farm. By then separated from her husband, she and her youngest had some happy if demanding years raising dogs, poultry and calves. Finally, nearly sixty and unable to meet the repayments, she returned unwillingly to 'the concrete jungle'.

There she 'answered a call to take a new-born grandson whose Mum...had [had] a breakdown'. Dan, 'mate of my twilight years,' was hyperactive and a slow learner. Though he had special needs and tantrums which 'kept me on my toes', Irene loved Dan and was proud of him. He lived with her, sharing her dreams of 'hightailing it straight back to the bush', until her death in 1987, when he was eighteen and she seventy-eight.

Despite the terrible burden of her past, however, Irene's creative gifts blossomed in the last years of her life. She painted, read her own poetry in numerous Eisteddfods, and won a prize for an invention at a local show. She wrote on agricultural subjects for the *Weekly Times* and had articles published in her local paper about early life and old buildings in Geelong.

A week before her death, pushing her jeep on the street, Irene was discussing the publication of her book. 'It's really good to feel elated at the end of your life,' she said.

Irene Dorling on a Geelong street in 1987. Her shopping trolley held the record of her extraordinary life

Harry Ding
1907–1976
Mail along the Birdsville Track
Written by: Billy Marshall-Stoneking
Nominated by: J. Turner; K. Cummins

'I thought it the cruellest and most inhuman world...' an English journalist wrote after travelling up the Birdsville Track by mail car in the 1930s. 'When the wind blew hard, sand penetrated everywhere. It came in through the cracks below the doors, and formed miniature drifts under our feet. [It] was in the butter, in the sugar, in the cake and in the vegetables...and the nights were worse than the days...'

The Track, if you can call it that, between Yunta, South Australia, and Birdsville in Queensland, has always been something of a challenge to the adventurous in spirit. But it is also extremely treacherous, especially for the inexperienced and ill-equipped outback traveller.

Before the 1930s, transport of mail and essential supplies to remote stations in South Australia and southern Queensland was by camel, but even camels found it tough going at times.

No-one knew this better than Harry Ding; but he felt at home in this environment. He had been raised in it, and from an early age had carried supplies, by cart and horse, from his parents' store at Olary, South Australia, to the outlying stations in the district. Eventually he 'graduated' to motorised transport, and then, at the age of twenty-seven, bought the store at Yunta, along with a couple of mail runs.

While most Australians were going off to work in offices, shops, and factories, Harry Edgar Ding, and the men who worked for his transport company, were carting supplies and delivering mail to the isolated outposts along the Birdsville Track, and for hundreds of people in outback Australia in the 1930s and 1940s, the name Harry Ding meant service, courage, and reliability. He introduced motorised transport to the outback, and developed the first modern mail and freight cartage company to service the interior of Australia.

By 1940, Harry's freight business ranged over an area of nearly 500 000 square kilometres, stretching from the tributaries of the Diamantina River around Birdsville, across the gibber plains of Sturts Stony Desert, down to Yunta, South Australia.

More often than not, there was no road to follow, especially after rain, and sometimes it was necessary to obtain the services of an Aboriginal guide to help navigate around the quagmire of Goyder's Lagoon, a 3000-square-kilometre depression fed by the headwaters of the Diamantina, Cooper, and Georgina Rivers. 'When the rivers were in flood,' Harry explained, 'our drivers would often have to make a detour of 150 miles in an 800 mile trip.'

Flooding was not the only problem. On the track between Yunta and Birdsville, Harry's trucks had to cross the Ooroowillannie sandhill, a gigantic drift of sand, thirty metres high. Drivers would often have to make many tries before they could get over it, and it was not unusual to spend half a day or more overcoming that one obstacle. It was country that many people still believed was suited only to camels and Harry himself admitted many times that it was the 'world's worst country for wheeled vehicles.'

The country not only pushed men to their limits; it tested their machines as well. Mechanical breakdowns occurred regularly, and when repairs could not be made on the spot, it meant a long walk to the nearest property for assistance...if there was a property.

Harry was keenly aware that some form of communication between the trucks and the base at Yunta was essential to safeguard his men and vehicles and, after turning the idea over in his mind for some time, he contacted Alfred Traeger, the man who had designed radio equipment for John Flynn's Flying Doctor network. Traeger agreed to design and produce small, portable radio sets that could be carried onboard Harry's trucks, using the trucks' batteries for power.

Henry 'Harry' Edgar Ding, in 1974. His motor freight services replaced camels on the Birdsville Track

The radio sets, which were extremely compact, proved their worth time and again. Before long, thanks to Harry's initiatives, a network of radio communications was established between stations and trucks, and between Yunta and the outside world.

A letter to the editor of *Radio Call* (November 1939), reflects the feelings of a great number of outback residents whose lives and livelihoods were made more secure due to Harry's tireless service: 'As the mail contractor who gets through, as the carrier who delivers the goods, as the wireless operator taking a message from a country dweller to a city friend or an urgent call for medical aid, [Harry] has become a romantic personality.'

Harry's business reached its peak in the early forties. By then he had built up a fleet of twenty trucks, nine mail runs, depots in four towns in addition to the base at Yunta, a powerful radio network, and employment for a couple of dozen men. Then the war came along, and spare parts were difficult if not impossible to find; and in 1944, after nearly twenty-five years of service, Harry sold up and moved to Wilcannia, New South Wales, where he operated a smaller transport firm. In the 1950s he retired from the transport business for good and settled in Walcha, New South Wales where 'the soft, rolling countryside with ample vegetation and rivers every few miles is so different from the harsh, barren deserts of my youth.'

Harry Ding's truck bogged in heavy sand in the Corner Country. 'Some of these sandhills can be 100 feet high', wrote Harry Ding, 'and a truck may have to have three or four runs at it.' Even then, 'you had to be lucky to make it'. Driving mail and supplies through some of the loneliest, most inhospitable and dangerous country on earth was not for the faint-hearted

But, for all the hardships, Harry Ding would not have traded his life in the bush for anything. 'It is difficult to put into words,' he once remarked, '[but] in civilisation people seem to have a protective coating to cover their real feelings. Out in the sandhills when you camp the night or boil the billy it is somehow different.'

Fred Teague
1912–
Outback driver
Written by: Billy Marshall-Stoneking
Nominated by: Jane Kittel

Harry Ding's service to the outback would have been impossible without the assistance of men like Tom Kruse, Ken Crombie and Fred Teague, to name just a few. These were men, like Ding, who both loved and respected the country in which they worked.

Fred Teague's father had died of silicosis three months before Fred was born in Olary, South Australia, in 1912, and to make ends meet his mother took over management of one of two general stores in Olary, leaving Fred to be raised by his sister, Marjorie.

Fred had knocked about the outback for many years, droving sheep, trapping rabbits, and prospecting for gold. In 1936, Fred was carting wool around Yunta and stud stock interstate for Harry Ding's transport company. Then, in 1937, he was asked to drive up the Birdsville Track to assist Tommy Robinson, one of Ding's drivers, whose truck had come to grief in the Ooroowillannie sandhill.

Fred became a one-man relief party, carrying food and spare parts out to the stranded driver. But when he got to Ooroowillannie, he discovered that Tommy had had enough of the job.

'No more,' he shouted at Fred. 'This is the final bloody straw.'

And so Fred became the Birdsville mailman.

'You name it,' Fred says, 'we had it go wrong.' Overheating, flat tyres, broken axles — Fred had to deal with them all, and in the process set a number of outback transport records. 'One was driving non-stop for ninety-two hours. Another was taking sixteen days to drive twenty-five miles. In those days the roads were anywhere you drove your truck.'

In 1936, accompanied by Wally Blucher, he carted building materials, including seventy-three tonnes of cement from Maree and Lyndhurst to Birdsville for the new Australian Inland Mission hospital.

But Fred was not one for 'living out of a can', and after carrying mail around South Australia for more than twelve years, he bought a general store in Hawker, South Australia, and turned it into a garage and museum — now a well-known tourist attraction. Fred's knowledge and love of the Flinders Ranges has contributed greatly to the development of tourism in that area.

Fred still thinks about his days with Harry Ding and the Birdsville mail: 'At times, I wonder how we didn't die out there.'

Frederick 'Fred' Teague, one of Harry Ding's drivers, at Hawker, South Australia, where he and his outback museum now promote tourism in the Flinders Ranges

Percy Clyde Statton
1890–1959

Fearless firefighter
Written by: Billy Marshall-Stoneking
Nominated by: J.J. Cowburn

The bushfires that swept through Tasmania in 1934 were the worst anyone could remember. Months of below-average rainfall and above-average temperatures had turned the island state into a tinderbox. But when the first big blazes began, it was mostly up to volunteer firefighters to save the day. One of these volunteers, Percy Statton, was one of only ten Tasmanians at the time to have won the Victoria Cross.

Working in the dense undergrowth, clearing firebreaks and praying for a change in wind direction, Statton and the other firefighters were trying to turn the fire back from the homes of bush workers and their village. But as the fire raged on, it became apparent that the lives of the firefighters themselves were at risk. About 200 men, including Statton, sought refuge in a clearing beside the railway siding. All around them, the bush burned. As one of the men later said, 'It was a haven in raging hell'.

Then someone noticed that Jack Peterson was missing. The men exchanged glances — nobody could survive the inferno that surrounded them.

Tension mounted as everyone weighed up the odds, considering the options. Everyone, that is, but Percy Statton. Silently, and without fanfare, he made his way to the edge of the clearing.

Petersen and he lived in the same tiny bush village. They had worked together — they were mates. Statton was not going to leave his friend to perish in the bush if there was the slightest chance that he could be saved.

Statton disappeared into the smoke. Some of the others saw him go, and called for him to come back, but he either did not hear them or did not want to. 'To everyone who watched him stumble along the tramline it appeared a journey of no return.'

The men waited. Ten minutes. Thirty minutes. An hour. Still no sign of Statton. Certain that he had perished along with his mate, the men in the clearing fell silent.

Then there was a whoop, and looking up they saw a man walking out of the smoke towards them. It was Statton. They could hardly believe their eyes. But there he was, smiling and fit. 'Petersen's all right,' he announced. 'He's on the top of his hut with a bucket of water...but he's safe.'

The white teeth shining out of soot-stained faces could have been seen a mile off as the men laughed with relief. The thought of a man sitting calmly on top of his hut with a bucket in his hand to cope with a raging bushfire was certainly worth a laugh.

Percy Statton, VC, 1957. He fought the Tasmanian bushfires of 1934

Muriel Constance North
1901–
City woman drover
Written by: Suzy Baldwin
Nominated by: Elizabeth Fay Valentine

In 1934, Muriel North was living with her husband Max in Wingham, NSW. Although loans were impossible to find, someone had enough faith in Max's horse sense and integrity to lend him a thousand pounds. To the Norths, 'battling on the heels of the Depression', this was a 'bonanza' and they set off to make their fortune. They would buy horses 'dirt cheap' at horse sales in Queensland, overland the mob along the stock routes the 1600 kilometres back from Charleville to Wingham, then sell them at a healthy profit. While Max and the hired drover handled the horses, Muriel would drive the family's Essex utility and set up camp each night on the return journey. The only possible flaw that Muriel could see was that she did not know how to drive, but that, said Max, was easily solved — he would teach her along the way. On 24 September 1934, Muriel set off on this expedition with Max, their four year old son Phil, daughter Fay — then a baby of eighteen months — and the hired drover. Max packed the ute, known as the 'Gutless Wonder,' with bags of horseshoes, rolls of fence wire, rope, bells, hobbles and other droving necessities. On top went the old mattress that was to be their bed for the next two months. 'Now,' said Mac, 'you can add any extras, Muriel.'

To Max's horror, the city-bred Muriel's 'extras' included sheets and pillowcases and a 'best' outfit (crêpe de chine, 6/11d a yard) for herself and the two children for social occasions.

Max bought one hundred and fifty horses at sales and stations in Queensland. He did eventually teach Muriel to drive, only ten days before she took sole charge of the Gutless Wonder and drove, alone with the two children, the 1600 kilometres home.

The spirited and intrepid Muriel had many adventures. She was bogged innumerable times, fought off twenty centimetre centipedes and quickly learned the ways of the Australian bush. The hardest experience of all was the desperate loneliness so, while the men talked horses, Muriel wrote daily shorthand notes which she later gathered together into a lively account which she called *Horse Tails and Trails*.

Fifty years later, Muriel laughs as she recalls how utterly inexperienced she was. She remembers the hired drover as a 'real ordeal'. 'He was a decent fellow but I was a very green little city girl and I'd never come across these rough bushies. Looking back, I think too that I was jealous. They were two men together and I was one woman alone, so you can guess where the woman came in.'

Muriel's droving education began at Toowoomba, their first horse buying camp. Max had gone to look at horses, leaving Muriel alone with the drover.

'It was bitterly cold on Toowoomba's heights, with heavy rain sweeping over in gusts. The drover scrounged around searching for scarce timber and returned with a rusted, ancient sanitary pan. No lady could possibly warm herself by this fire. The drover's axe bit into the tin, slicing out a six inch square which was flattened onto the ground to form a little hearth. Then up on three bricks to create an upward draught and in a few minutes there was a roaring fire sending warmth and light to brighten this desolate spot.

'It was too much for me. I emerged from the ute and warmed my icy hands, the lowly origin of my new-found comfort forgotten. So commenced a city woman's initiation into make-do on the trail.

'The next day we moved camp to a shed at the saleyards. The Toowoomba saleyards were essentially a man's domain and our presence was unusual. However, no one took the slightest notice of us so, while caring for children and hanging nappies up everywhere in the shed, one could watch the activity of the sale ring.

'The sales were a mecca for horsemen and you caught a glimpse in the crowd of the mounted policeman followed by his black tracker, and of drovers' outfits with dozens of dogs exercising their lungs in the biggest spree in dog history. Wherever you roamed, the sole topic was horse flesh. Women did not enter this domain and I would wander about without drawing the slightest flicker of interest.'

Between Toowoomba and the next big horse sales at Charleville, Max taught Muriel to drive.

The driving lessons were not without drama. Fay 'screamed blue murder' every time Muriel took the steering wheel, Max had to yell instructions above the din ('You don't have to cross your legs to put your foot on the brake Muriel'), and the drover, a champion rough-rider who wasn't afraid of anything on four legs, 'looked quite peaky' after Muriel's first attempts at steering the heavy truck full of gear. To everyone's relief, on 13 September they arrived at Charleville.

'After days of endless bush, I couldn't wait to be in a town again so I bathed Fay and Phil, dressed them in their best clothes and, wearing my crêpe de chine frock and shady hat, drove into town. It was sizzling hot, windy and dusty, but we were at least back in civilisation and I was excited to see women and children and the few shops. I was so sure that my dark-eyed son and baby Fay would bring smiles. But not one noticed us. Not even a "Good morning".

'I bought the supplies that we needed from a frosty-faced man and, as he packed the tins, three pairs of eyes watched intently for the cone of paper, filled with boiled lollies, to be popped in as a friendly gift from the grocer. None appeared.

'As we drank tepid cool drinks from the Drip Safe, I made up for their disappointment by allowing the children to choose their own assortment of sticky sweets. Oh what bliss as they walked along the street with the sticky mess dripping on their clothes.

'The heat was overpowering as we slowly drove back to our camp in the bush; the sweets were gone and the children cross. I had this day experienced the cruel loneliness of women in the outback, not in an isolated camp, but in a town.'

Fresh laundry and fresh supplies were rare. Usually, Muriel did the washing whenever she saw a bit of water and would tie the nappies along the side of the ute to dry as she drove along. Soup or corned beef and vegetables were cooked in a kerosene tin over the fire or on a primus stove.

Although responsible for all food supplies, Muriel's lack of bush experience meant that she knew nothing of those great bush staples, damper and brownie. She eventually learned the art of the camp oven from an Aboriginal woman who looked after her at Brenda station at the end of the most gruelling ten days of the journey.

Supplies were running short, there was no feed for the mob and water was scarce. The horses were thirsty and difficult. Then it was discovered that six horses were missing.

'Those horses were our livelihood. We had to do everything we could to find them because they meant so much to us. We had so little, you see, so very little. So Max sent the drover back to find them. We thought he'd be gone for a day but it was ten days before we saw him again.

'That left Max with the rest of the mob — one hundred and fifty horses — to be kept together and yarded at night. What had taken two men all their time to accomplish now had to be managed by one man alone, day and night.

'We had been told that there was a good sheep camp on the Nebine River, with a yard to hold the horses overnight. Evening was fast closing in, so I went on ahead to try and find it. I came to the river but — will it ever be forgotten? — I missed the camp.

'It was now dark and no sign of the mob, so back I drove and found Max with the impossible job of keeping the horses together in the pitch dark. I got behind them and crawled along with the headlights on to throw some light ahead for Max. Somehow we got through that fearful place and the horses rushed the sweet Nebine water. Now a holding yard must be made.

'Max slowly edged the weary horses into a corner formed by the junction of two fences. I parked the Gutless Wonder on one side of the triangle with its headlights on to hold the horses in the improvised arena. Max heaved the coil of heavy rope from the ute, tied one end around the trunk of a nearby tree, then stretched it across the triangle and secured it to a fence post. This now formed the illusion of a horse yard — one single strand holding one hundred and fifty horses.

'But this on its own was not sufficient to hold them. With some surprise, I found that, even as my whole being longed for the safety of remote Tibet, my legs were actually walking up and down in front of the tightly-packed mass of horseflesh as I cuddled my sleeping daughter in my arms. The draught horses towered over us and the eyes of the brumbies were fiery in the moonlight. The stamping of hooves and squeals of rage as they fought amongst themselves, rearing and milling around in the tiny enclosure, petrified me. With every step, panic threatened to overwhelm me, terrified lest the horses rear up and those hooves pound us all into the dust.

'As Max worked, he kept up a steady patter of "Whoa there boy. Steady now". And then, remembering me, "Stick to it a minute longer Muriel. *Hang on.*"

'At last Max stretched a coil of fencing wire across the opening of the improvised holding yard and it was finished. He soon had a camp fire burning in front of the yard and all night he walked up and down, soothing and steadying the horses. I crept thankfully into the ute, settled Fay down beside Phil, and fell into an exhausted sleep.

'I woke at daybreak to see, within several hundred yards of our camp, the sheep yard which I had failed to locate.'

Fifty years later, Muriel says: 'I have never overcome my fear of horses. I was petrified of them then and I still am.'

Of all the features of the bush, the one that made the most profound impression on Muriel was the terrible loneliness of the women. The most physically isolated was a woman with three daughters whom Muriel met at a remote outstation. This woman had not seen another woman to speak to for eight months. Before that, she had lived even further 'off the track' and had not spoken to a woman for five years.

But the isolation of the bush is not only physical.
'As the men yarned over the campfire, I too shared the loneliness of outback women and saw the unconscious selfishness of the men. For the lore of the bush is handed down over camp fires, on droving runs. It goes on endlessly while wives and mothers plod through life in the isolated monotony of everyday living, cut off completely from mental affinity with their men.'

The Norths returned safely home with all their horses and sold them successfully. Back in Wingham, Muriel coped with the isolation of being a mother with two small children by continuing to make notes. 'I'd have my notebook beside me as I scrubbed the floor. I wanted to have something to show for my time.'

Several years ago, Muriel became totally blind. Showing that she has lost none of the spirit that was so apparent in 1934, she learned to read Braille when she was eighty.

With the same determination, Muriel North continues to write on a regular typewriter despite the enormous practical difficulties this

Muriel North, in her going-away outfit, making friends with husband Max's favourite horse, Roanie, just after her marriage in 1929. Although she has been married to a great horseman for almost sixty years, the city-bred Muriel says, 'I have never overcome my fear of horses. I was petrified of them then and I still am'

Muriel Constance North now eighty-seven, at home in Taree. On a droving trek with Max, two small children and 150 horses, Muriel wrote each night by the campfire. Her story provides an insight into the loneliness of bush women in a man's world. Photograph by Keith Barlow

presents for a blind person. She also knits and crochets, and is learning to play the concertina. 'When you're blind,' she says, 'you have to keep busy or you'd go mad.' But for Muriel writing is the most important: 'I do the other things as a diversion but I write to survive.'

For nine years before her marriage in 1929, Muriel worked as a secretary in a bank in the very centre of Sydney. 'I loved my work,' she says with pleasure. 'I loved everything about it — going to work, the excitement and the interest and the sparkle.' The common rules of the time were that any woman who married had to resign. Like many thousands of other women of her age, Muriel willingly gave up ideas of a career for marriage. 'Our heads were full of romance and sheikhs; you never imagined that you were going to be unhappy. And everyone did it. Now, I realise what a terrible thing it was for clever women.'

Although she regarded going to live in the country as 'a great adventure', the lively young Muriel used to become so homesick for the city that she would go down to the station in the morning to smell the smoke of the trains.

It is clear from seeing the Norths together that this marriage of sixty years is one of the very best. But the world of the city, of work and ideas and writing, still tantalises Muriel. On a visit to London, she spent most of her time in Fleet Street; on visits to Sydney a favourite pastime was to try to wangle an interview with a newspaper or magazine editor, 'just for the sport of it,' to talk books and writing. Given her vivacity and humour, it's not surprising that she often succeeded.

If Muriel were starting out again now, would she do it differently? Would she, like many modern women, juggle both work and children? Her response initially sounds traditional: 'I'm old fashioned. I think no one can raise your children like you can yourself. But,' she adds, 'I don't blame women for saying "I can't stand this home life anymore."'

Her daughter Fay, who has described her mother as a 'closet feminist', does not let this pass. 'I think if someone had offered you a job in a newspaper office you would have been very tempted.'

Muriel considers this for a minute or two, then nods thoughtfully. 'I think I might have been,' she says slowly. Then she smiles and her eyes sparkle. 'Yes,' she laughs, exhilarated even at the thought of another challenge, a new adventure; 'Yes, I think I might have been.'

John Riddoch Rymill
1905–1968
Polar explorer
Written by: Niall Lucy
Nominated by: Malcolm M. Carter

It was the eyes they remembered most, those who had worked with him — clear blue ice like mirrors of the sky. He was extraordinarily handsome.

John Rymill was no ordinary man. Even as a child he had shown remarkable skills in handling animals and mastery of practical crafts at his father's farm near Penola South Australia. But from a very early age, John knew that the farm could not hold him, and after reading every book on polar exploration that he could lay his hands on, John's fascination with exploring unknown regions could not be contained. In 1927, at the age of twenty-two, he went to England for the purpose of preparing himself to explore Antarctica, the great south land. At the Royal Geographical Society in London, he studied surveying and navigation, then took his pilot's qualifications from the De Havilland Aircraft Company at Hendon.

Rymill was the kind of man who attracted others to him, and he did not have long to wait for his first adventure. His break came in 1928 when he was sent to Canada as part of a research team from Cambridge's Scott Polar Research Institute. On that expedition he gained valuable experience in simulated polar conditions.

Then, in 1930–31, the renowned Arctic traveller, H. Gino Watkins, asked Rymill to accompany the British Arctic Air Route Expedition to Greenland. Appointed as a surveyor and pilot, Rymill acquitted himself with distinction by completing a notable 640 kilometre crossing of the island during which time he helped gather essential meteorological data for polar flights between Europe and North America.

But Antarctica was where the greatest challenges lay, and following his success in Greenland, Rymill set out to gain financial support for a major expedition to the icy continent at the bottom of the world. Inspiring others with his dream, he won government and private backing for the venture and secured a Murchison Grant from the Royal Geographical Society. Even so, the British Graham Land Expedition (BLGE), was the least expensive campaign of its type — a tribute to Rymill's foresight and organisational skills.

Described as 'the last great epic in the Heroic Age of Polar Exploration', the BGLE set sail under Rymill's leadership from St Katherine Dock, London, on 10 September 1934 in a three-masted schooner which Rymill christened *Penola*, after his birthplace. The ship carried thirteen men — only four of whom had previous sailing experience — and many tons of equipment and supplies, including seaplanes, sledges, a prefabricated hut, and a motor launch.

After nearly four months at sea, with only a brief stopover in the Falkland Islands, the *Penola* sailed into Port Lockroy in the Antarctic. At last, 'the full beauties of a polar land' that Rymill had read about in childhood came to life. Surrounded by a new world he was struck by the vast silence, 'broken only by the occasional roar of an avalanche, or a gull grumbling as an ice-cliff calved...'

After establishing a base in the Argentine Islands, fifty kilometres south of Port Lockroy, Rymill decided to confine exploration to the western side of Graham Land until the following summer. While some members of the party repaired the ship's engine, Rymill flew along the coast in search of a suitable point from which sledge teams could set off to explore the interior.

He found one, but bad weather held up the departure for several months. Eventually, on the morning of 18 August 1935, four teams set out through unexplored country to chart the coastline and establish a campsite eighty kilometres inland. Each team worked with a company of ten huskies and three men to a sledge, crossing up to thirty kilometres of barren ice a day, and pitching their tents at night in below-freezing

John Rymill in Greenland, c.1930. His expedition to the Antarctic, the British Graham Land Expedition of 1934–37, was the last great private expedition to the Antarctic. Described as the last of the expeditions of the 'heroic age' of polar exploration, Rymill's expedition made two major discoveries, established standards of safety and efficiency in the field and took a 'civilised approach to life both in the field and at base'

John Rymill (left) with fellow members of the British Arctic air Route Expedition to Greenland, 1930–31. Rymill became leader of this expedition when Gino Watkins drowned in 1932

temperatures.

Despite his awe of the land, Rymill never overlooked the scientific purpose of the expedition and scientifically, as in every other way, the BGLE was a remarkable success. The thirteen member party charted over 500 kilometres of previously unexplored and almost inaccessible coastline, and proved that Graham Land is in fact a peninsula rather than an archipelago as was previously thought.

They also discovered the vast channel between Alexander Island and Graham Land which Rymill named King George VI Sound. The channel was, in fact, a massive rift valley, comparable to the huge channel that separates Arctic Canada from Greenland.

During his almost three years in Antarctica, Rymill and his followers also pioneered polar survival techniques which became standard practice among succeeding expeditions. Everyone stationed in the Antarctic since has been indebted to Rymill and his men for the art of travelling safely with huskies, and the best means of setting up the warmest camp.

Like other great explorers of the past, Rymill underplayed his own achievements on returning to England and a hero's welcome in 1937. Ironically, however, the great success of the mission — while celebrated ever since in scientific circles — ultimately deprived the expeditioners of the popular acclaim they deserved. If Rymill's endeavour remains unsung by all but those who have followed in his footsteps, it is only because his was not an heroic failure but a triumph — and the press soon tired of a hero whose possibly greatest achievement had been to dispel the myth of inevitable death by misadventure in the frozen south.

But acclaim was unimportant to Rymill — he had accomplished his dream and he had done it without losing a man. And he had been to a world that few men had seen.

Majorie Dobson Silver
1910–
The Far West's flying sister
Written by: Lynette Ramsay Silver
Nominated by: Lynette Ramsay Silver

Although born into a conservative middle-class family in the New South Wales country town of Scone, on 16 June 1910, Marjorie Dobson Silver followed a career that was far from conventional.

'I always secretly wanted to be a doctor', Marjorie recalls, but on finding that was impossible, she opted for the next best thing — a triple-certificated nursing sister. On her eighteenth birthday she left home to begin her training and six hard years later, she was through. Discovering that regular nursing positions lacked the challenge and variety that she craved, in 1935 she accepted the offer of the Reverend Stanley Drummond, founder of the New South Wales Far West Children's Health Scheme, to become the outback's first Flying Sister.

Sister Silver found herself in Bourke where, as the Scheme's sole nursing sister for thousands of square kilometres, she was responsible for hundreds of patients, adults as well as children. Waiting at the Bourke airstrip was a single-engined Leopard Moth plane, converted for medical use. 'I couldn't wait to get going', she says, 'even though I had never flown before. From the moment the wheels left the ground I was well and truly hooked. I thought flying was sensational, which was just as well as the area I had to cover was enormous — Louth, Wanaaring, Urisino Station, Hungerford on the Queensland border, Brewarrina and Byrock.'

Sister Silver, now Mrs Margo Weiss

The Moth took her on regular trips to these far-flung centres sometimes returning with a patient who needed hospital treatment. At Urisino station, the plane was exchanged for a motor vehicle which transported Sister and her well-stocked medical bag across 320 dusty, bone-jarring kilometres of often desolate and isolated country to the remote huts of the bore keepers and struggling soldier-settlers. Her visits were a kind of salvation for the women, endeavouring to raise healthy children in a lonely, hostile environment which was short on water and fresh food but long on oppressive heat and choking dust storms. 'It was no picnic, I can tell you, travelling across outback tracks by car', she reflects. 'The temperatures often exceeded 60°C inside the vehicle and the dust was unbelievable. However, the welcome I received from the mothers, battling to make ends meet and well aware that the staple outback tucker of black tea and damper was no diet for growing children, made the trials of the trip worthwhile. They needed reassurance as much as anything else, though the fresh food I was often able to bring was always gratefully received. These women were truly heroic.'

At the larger centres the local ladies would congregate alongside the claypan landing strips anxiously awaiting the arrival of the plane. 'When I first met them and saw that they had worn their Sunday best, right down to hat and gloves, and with children who had been scrubbed until they glowed, I realised that the clinic rounds were to be a highlight in their lives. These people were in need of more than just routine medical care.'

Marjorie Silver was also responsible for the Aborigines at their camps by the rivers at Brewarrina and Bourke. 'They were wonderfully warm and gentle people who became very special patients,' says Marjorie, who developed a great affinity with the Aborigines over the subsequent years. 'I have this tremendous sadness when I realise that things have not changed since I was out at Bourke. Their three main problems are still poverty, poor health and lack of housing. Hardly a thing has altered in fifty years.'

'Of course, life was not always serious', she says with a smile, 'especially at Christmas, when, in full Father Christmas rig, beard and all, and with the temperature soaring to over 38°C, I would set off by plane and then by car to distribute a load of goodies to my "family". What a sensation we made, landing in those outback places, doling out sweets and toys to childen who had never before seen a toy, let alone a Flying Santa!'

Apart from the regular flying rounds, Sister Silver's duties included the Bourke Baby Clinic and stints at the local hospital. Soon her work began to pay dividends. 'It was wonderful to see those skinny, malnourished children fill out, and eyes that would have been blinded by trachoma slowly regain their sight. But perhaps my greatest thrill was the drop in the mortality rate among mothers and babies. With regular checkups I could make sure that all my mothers were safely in town, well before term, rather than giving birth alone in the middle of nowhere.'

After only nine months, the pilot Nancy Bird and the Far West parted company without warning, leaving Sister Silver without air transport. 'It was tough for a while', she says, the memory still vivid, 'for I was now forced to cover my territory by car, taking days to travel distances which I had previously covered in hours. The heat as summer wore on was almost unendurable, but as I was often the sole link

Sister Silver (second from left) in 1935 with pilot Nancy Bird (left) and some of the women and children for whom Marjorie provided more than just medical care and who greeted the flying sister's arrival out at the back of Bourke by wearing their Sunday best. The plane is a Leopard Moth. Photograph courtesy Mitchell Library

with the outside world, the lifeline had to be maintained.'

After a trip on which the driver made it patently obvious that he had things other than driving on his mind, Marjorie called a halt. 'I rang Mr Drummond to tell him it was just not on and when he heard the news he arranged for me to use charter aircraft. It was great to be airborne again!'

When this pioneering Flying Nightingale married a station manager in 1938, she reluctantly resigned from her post. Her contact with the outback and its need for medical assistance was not lost, however, for at every station property on which she lived over the next forty years, from New South Wales to Queensland and finally the Northern Territory, she set up a small hospital and cared for all those who had need of her skills.

When Marjorie Silver left Bourke in 1938, she was not replaced. However, the void created by the departure of this dedicated nursing sister, who had provided a unique and caring service for the people of the outback, was soon to be partially filled by an agency which also recognised the need for an efficient aerial medical service.

Once again the welcome drum of aircraft engines, bringing medical assistance to those in need, was to be heard above the lonely roofs of the homesteads around Bourke. At long last, the Flying Doctor had come to town.

Edmund Albert 'Ted' Colson
1885–1950
Man of the desert
Written by: Billy Marshall-Stoneking
Nominated by: Margery J. Plevin

On 11 June 1936, two men stepped out of the dust and heat into the Birdsville Hotel and, almost too casually to be believed, told the drinkers at the bar they had just crossed the Simpson Desert. No-one said anything at first, uncertain that the burly bushman doing the talking was not pulling their legs. It seemed as though the stocky little fellow with the scrub brush moustache and his lanky, Aboriginal companion had leaked through some hole in the landscape.

But this was no practical joke. It was Ted Colson and his offsider, Peter Aines, and they had, indeed, made the crossing — the first men in recorded history to beat the elements, and traverse one of the most forbidding places on the face of the earth.

Stuart, Lindsay and others had tried before them and all had failed. As recently as 1929, Cecil Madigan had made an aerial survey of the area and proclaimed the country 'impassable on the ground'. But Colson had not let this deter him, and now here he was, breasting the bar in the Birdsville pub and recounting his adventures in the desert to the enthralled residents of the tiny outback community.

Edmund 'Ted' Colson was no stranger to the bush. He was a man eminently suited to the task he had set himself. He had grown up

Bloods Creek, May 1936. Peter Aines (left), Ted and Alice Colson and camels pose for a farewell picture before Aines and Colson set off on their epic trip across the Simpson Desert. Alice was waiting for Ted when he returned, but Peter's wife, Mary, took a less stoic view

on the gold fields of Coolgardie, Western Australia, and in the early 1930s had travelled as a cameleer with explorer Michael Terry on two journeys through the centre of Australia. In addition to this, he spoke several Aboriginal dialects, and possessed an excellent knowledge of native plants, edible bush foods, and navigation.

While preparing for his trek into the unknown, a friend had asked him what he expected to find out there. Colson scratched his head and thought about it for a moment. 'Anything,' he replied.

'My object', he later wrote, 'was not altogether to be the first white man to cross the desert nor was it to prove wrong those who said it was impossible, but I desired, as an Australian, to let a little light in on one of the dark spots of our great continent.'

In Colson's view, the desert regions were not as desolate and unremitting as they had been described in the popular literature of the time. Certainly, such areas were bad during drought conditions — and the Territory in the mid-1930s had just come through one of the worst droughts ever recorded — but they were not always nor altogether the wastelands of popular legend.

Colson was an observer of the cycles of nature, and when the big rains came in 1936 he knew that the time had come and that a crossing of the vast desert to the east was possible. So, on 26 May 1936, Colson and Peter Aines set out from Blood's Creek station with five camels, 400 litres of water and enough food for three weeks. They left behind them the security of the homestead and two wives who could only wonder whether they would ever see them again. Colson's speculations concerning the condition of the country proved extremely accurate. The recent rains had created numerous temporary waterholes, and various types of native, water-bearing grasses were shooting up everywhere.

Passing Mt Etingambara, they entered unknown country, and Colson had to rely on his compass to get his bearings. His ultimate goal was Birdsville, the most remote outpost in all of Australia; but his immediate destination was Poeppel's Corner, located at the conjunction of the Northern Territory, Queensland and South Australian state borders.

The 220 kilometre trek between Mt Etingambara and the survey peg at Poeppel's Corner is extremely desolate country, striped by apparently endless sand ridges, some as high as twenty metres. Colson named several features along his route but there was little to describe apart from various salt lakes and the vegetation which, thanks to the rain, provided good feed for the camels.

Colson's compass work was so accurate that they missed the peg at Poeppel's Corner by a mere hundred metres. Secure in the thought that they had stayed on course, the remainder of the trip was relatively easy.

Two days after arriving in Birdsville, Colson looked at Peter and said, 'Well, we'd better make a move'. And once again the two men headed out into the wilderness, this time for the return journey to Blood's Creek.

Both men were concerned about their wives and were eager to get back. Colson was particularly aware of the sacrifice his wife had made. She had stayed behind, virtually on her own, looking after the homestead and the store they operated on the old telegraph line between Alice Springs and Oodnadatta.

Alice Colson was stoic about her husband's schemes and dreams. Heading off into the Simpson Desert in an attempt to accomplish something no white man had done before was completely in character, and she knew there was nothing she could do to stop him. But Mary, Peter's wife, was another story, and their relationship must surely go down as one of the unsung casualties of the exploration of Australia.

When Mary discovered Peter was going to trek into the desert she was furious. The idea of risking one's life in such a foolhardy enterprise seemed totally senseless, if not mad. She was not the kind of woman to sit around waiting for a man, and she could not forgive him for leaving her. Shortly after Peter returned, they separated, and did not see each other again for fifty years. Quite coincidentally, they ended up in the same pensioners' home in Port Augusta. By then, Mary had softened somewhat, and would actually speak to him again.

After his victory over the Simpson Desert, Colson quickly faded into an undeserved obscurity, an ironic footnote to the history of Australian exploration which notes down and remembers the great failures, and all but ignores the handful of those who were successful.

Ted Colson, an intrepid bushman who crossed the inhospitable Simpson Desert — twice

Joe Binstead
c1893–1973
Aircrash survivor
Written by: Terri McCormack
Nominated by: Russ Graham

On 19 February 1937 the Stinson airliner, *City of Brisbane*, vanished on a routine flight from Brisbane to Sydney. Sightings were reported from as far south as the Hawkesbury but Australia's largest aerial search was abandoned when it was assumed that cyclonic conditions had driven the plane out to sea. But Bernard O'Reilly, a pioneer of the rugged border country near the MacPherson Ranges, suspected a mountain crash. Using his superb bushcraft, he trekked for two days through jungle terrain before discovering the aircraft on the Lamington Plateau, nine days after its disappearance.

To O'Reilly's astonishment, there were two survivors — Joe Binstead, a Sydney wool broker, and John Proud, a mining engineer who appeared close to death. With traditional bush courtesy, a billy was boiled before O'Reilly, himself exhausted, returned down the mountain to organise the locals into one of the most spectacular rescue missions in Australia's history.

Three passengers on the port side had initially survived the crash. Despite an injured leg, Proud had helped Binstead escape from the blazing aircraft and together they dragged out the young Englishman James Westray before the fuselage exploded. A fit sportsman, Westray, although badly burned, insisted on going for help. His tracks and then his bruised body, bizarrely wedged in a seated position beside a thundering waterfall, were found by O'Reilly on his frantic return trip for assistance.

The two strangers, Binstead and Proud, waited for rescue beside the smouldering wreckage. Binstead bound Proud's fractured leg with broken wing fabric and found a metal coffee flask in which he carried water to the fevered man from a spring 300 metres down a vine-covered precipice. Overweight and then in his mid-forties, Binstead was a city man unused to such exertion. As the days passed without rescue, it seemed most likely that both men would perish from starvation, exposure and despair. But Binstead persisted, now crawling over the rocks for hours to bring water and berries to his younger companion who would surely have died without him. When O'Reilly made his almost miraculous discovery, Proud was virtually unconscious with a gangrenous leg and Binstead's hands and legs 'were like raw meat'.

Joe Binstead died in 1973 and the sole survivor, now Sir John Proud, acknowledges that he owes his life to this 'basically decent unassuming bloke', who demonstrated the courage that ordinary people can display under extraordinary circumstances.

Joe Binstead, exhausted after his nine day ordeal during which he kept his fellow survivor alive. Less fortunate were pilots Rex Boyden and Beverley Shepherd and passengers Roland Graham and Bill Fountain who died in the 1937 Stinson air crash

Doreen Flavel
1925–
'The Promise and the Challenge'
Written by: Lois Hunter
Nominated by: Donald Stuart McDonald

Until she was twelve, in 1937, Doreen Schiller, born and brought up on her father's property on Eyre Peninsula, near Cowell in South Australia, was a typical outback girl. She had a scanty education — five years in a one-teacher school, then patchy correspondence lessons — which her widowed German father thought ample for a country girl. But when she was twelve an operation for a brain tumour saved her life but left her totally blind.

The motherless Doreen had to teach herself anew how to run the house, clean and cook for her father and sometimes up to six men. Though she regained a small amount of vision in one eye it was insufficient to be of much use and any chance of further education was now stopped. The remote farm tied her to isolation. She sensed that Adelaide offered more opportunities to a blind girl than Eyre, but she stayed put and in the next fourteen years learned to do without sight what others managed with full vision.

At twenty-seven she decided to make a run for a new life in Adelaide. Despite reproaches and recriminations for leaving her brother in charge of the farm, and without any prospects, she lodged at the Adelaide YWCA and found a 'totally hideous' job making wire brushes.

Life improved when she worked for a year at the Royal Institute for the Blind where she began to feel that the challenge in life for her was to serve those who shared her blindness. But life intervened.

Doreen met and married Syd Flavel and went pioneering with him to Kangaroo Island. Five years and three children later the Flavels were still on the island but by this time they had established and were running a grocery store, a post office and a carrying business. By the time they moved back to the mainland they had five children and Doreen decided that it was time to resume what marriage and motherhood and pioneering had postponed — her need to work for the blind.

She worked as a member of the Blind Welfare Association but found herself handicapped, not so much by her lack of sight as by her lack of education. In her mid-fifties, Doreen joined the Adult Literacy Programme. Good luck, in the form of her tutor, a retired headmaster called Donald McDonald, was on her side. Between them, after five years' collaboration, they produced *The Promise and the Challenge*, Doreen Flavel's autobiography, which was published in 1986.

The Promise describes the early years of isolation on the Eyre Peninsula farm with its duststorms, floods, snakes, mouse plagues, heat and flies. And it includes the story she'd always wanted to tell of her German grandparents who had trekked from the Barossa Valley to

Doreen Flavel, for whom blindness was just one of the challenges

farm the virgin land that was to become the family home. *The Challenge* chronicles the pioneering life on Kangaroo Island and the outback.

To write the book, Doreen, as McDonald explains, faced enormous difficulties: 'she couldn't revise her own work and she had a very limited vocabulary'.

The death of Syd Flavel, in late 1985, was another loss. 'Yet alone,' says McDonald, 'she has developed tremendously.' Publishing her book at over sixty-three, says Doreen, has given her 'a personality I never felt I had'. Her next ambition is to write some fiction. It is unlikely, however, to make a better tale than her own life.

William Ashley Beet
1878–1957
Doctor of Beaudesert
Written by: Billy Marshall-Stoneking
Nominated by: Ailsa Rolley

Through the sound of the rain, he heard the bell ringing at the front door. Dr Beet rose from his chair and went to answer it. There was a man at the door, soaking wet. 'It's Willie Jacobs, Doc, he's taken ill. Elizabeth wants you to come straight away.'

The doctor did not need prodding. The Jacobs family were very close to him — he'd delivered all their children, and Willie, the youngest of six, was a particular favourite.

An hour later, Dr Beet pulled up outside the Jacobs' house. Elizabeth Jacobs stood on the front porch, watching as he dismounted and came up the front steps.

'I'm sorry doctor, but Willie's okay now.'

'Where is he?' Beet replied.

'Down the paddock, playing with his brothers.'

Another man might have been angry at being called out on a false alarm like this, but Beet took it in his stride. He was just happy the boy was not sick. But since he was here, he would have a look at him all the same.

To Dr Beet, the patient always came first, and the people who lived in farms all around Queensland's little rural community of Beaudesert knew it. Most of them, at one time or another, had had a sick child, and had watched the doctor sit up all night, tending his young patient as though the child were the single most important person in the world.

The hospital in Beaudesert in those early days was certainly a primitive affair, little more than a two-room cottage with accommodation for four patients. But it was all Dr Beet needed. More often than not, his patients would stay in their own homes and he'd visit them, day or night, rain or shine — he never complained about the hours or the demands made on his time and energy.

In the beginning, he rode a horse, sometimes riding 110 kilometres in one day to see a patient. Later, he went by buggy, then, when

Dr William Beet, country doctor for forty-four years. His patients always came first. 'Nothing was too much bother for him'

motorcycles appeared, he bought one and taught himself to ride it. Some old-time residents still remember Dr Beet as a bespectacled man with brown hair flying around the countryside on a motorbike. He always made it to his destination and back again.

Dr Beet retired at the age of sixty-nine. Ten years later, he returned to Beaudesert where he spent his last few months in the district to which he had given forty-four years of his life.

William John McBride
1887–1939

The miner's mate
Written by: Katie Lawley
Nominated by: A. Berry

William McBride, a Broken Hill miner for thirty years, poses for a studio portrait in his home town

Fifty-one-year-old William James 'Curly Top' McBride had worked in the Broken Hill mines for thirty years. On 3 February 1939, McBride and his partner, twenty-five-year-old Leonard Eaton, were lowered underground to the 300 foot (90 metre) level to begin their afternoon shift. Retimbering in the Number 3 main level drive, they were instructed at 5 pm to bore three holes in the footwall. After less than a metre, something struck them on the back. Within seconds they were buried under mounds of earth. After frantic struggling, McBride managed to free himself. He was horribly injured, but managed to crawl an agonising thirty metres, calling, 'Help, come quick. Len Eaton is buried.' A trucker heard his cries and immediately went for help. In reply to questions about himself, McBride called 'I was never better. Get my mate out.' When they were finally freed, both men were rushed to hospital.

William McBride died the next day. His mate, Leonard Eaton, also suffered severe injuries, but recovered to lead a normal life — a second chance granted to him by McBride's sacrifice.

Aileen Grice
1912–1985

'The Lord will provide'
Written by: Lucinda Strauss
Nominated by: Aileen Mary Crockford

For anyone growing up in Bundanoon over the past fifty years, Aileen Grice, wheeling down Railway Avenue on her ancient bicycle, was a familiar sight. A tiny sparrow of a women, she had a sixth sense when it came to detecting a person in need. With a ready smile and indomitable good humour, she 'collected' people as

Aileen Grice in 1930. Her life was devoted to mothering the needy and homeless

she rode along, adding to a house already brimming full of kids, friends, strays and passers-by.

From her large kitchen in the old weatherboard house next to the Rosnel Guest House, amid the smells of roast dinners and freshly baked scones, Aileen ministered to the needs of the town. 'I would like to gather all the hurt and starving people in my kitchen, and feed them and comfort them,' she once said in a letter to her niece. 'They wouldn't fit, of course, but they are in my heart.'

All sorts of people found their way to her kitchen. She helped drunks, girls who had run away from home, deserted wives with children. Mary Crockford, her adopted daughter, says 'I tried once to count how many people had been in our home, but it was impossible. It doesn't really matter. What does matter is that they were all helped and she did this on a very small income which wasn't nearly enough to feed a small family let alone all the extras. No-one ever went hungry, not one person was ever turned away.'

As a child, Aileen Grice knew well the meaning of suffering. The youngest of eight children she was afflicted from birth with a congenital hip disorder. Although this left her partially crippled, she was determined to enjoy the normal activities of other children even to the extent of learning to ride a bike.

She never married and when all her brothers and sisters left home, she stayed on, helping her mother run their guest house at Bundanoon. On the death of her mother, a deeply Christian woman whom she adored, Aileen inherited the old home. Unfortunately, she inherited the mortgage as well, and the responsibility for looking after her father, a very hard man, who had given them little support during his lifetime. Rosnel's Guest House next door, owned by her brother-in-law Charles Rose, was very much a part of her life in the early years. She worked there as a part-time cook and during the busy season earned extra money by letting rooms from her own house. Says Mary Crockford, 'God's plan for her life became obvious when a boy called Bill, who was working there, got into trouble with the law and was put in gaol'. Aileen had befriended him, and after visiting him regularly in gaol, took responsibility for him on release. Despite threats from her brother-in-law to cut off support, including her job, if Bill returned, she was adamant. 'This is Bill's home,' she insisted. Bill came home and the brother-in-law, fortunately, relented.

With her particular gift for understanding and nurturing children Aileen Grice found a succession of children entrusted to her care. In the late 1940s she was asked to have a little boy from a children's home; he was followed by another a year later. Around this time too, Bill befriended a prostitute who was pregnant and had nowhere to go. Says Mary, 'Bill found her crying in a park and took her home. When she had the baby [me], she gave me to mum [Aileen] to raise and later adopt.'

In time, Aileen's house became a refuge for the unwanted and homeless. If any strangers arrived in town, they were sent to Aileen's. One night when it was snowing a couple with six children arrived at the door asking for shelter. 'My husband has hepatitis and we are trying to get to Sydney but need somewhere to sleep,' said the wife. 'Come in,' said Aileen. 'The Lord will provide', was Aileen's answer when there was no food or money. 'And He usually did,' says Mary.

Although to many she embodied the best of Christian love and charity, Aileen was amusing company. At night, from her ministry round the kitchen table, she would entertain the assembled gathering with snippets of whatever book she happened to be reading. Betty Malone, who spent many hours there as a young girl, recalls 'She loved quoting from a Victorian manual advising the mistress of the house on the proper treatment of servants. She did this amidst gales of laughter.' Arthur Turrell, one of the many lodgers to experience her infectious good humour and sense of fun, captured her exploits in a series of poems and cartoons.

As a keen supporter of the Uniting Church, Aileen was also part of a formidable trio of ladies known as 'The Girls of Bundanoon'. Together with her friends Lil Calverly, the organist, and Madge Burrows, who kept the church and hall 'spotless', they would meet without fail every Saturday to arrange flowers for the following day's service. Aileen (the 'baby') taught Sunday School and also looked after young ministers during their placement on the South Coast.

The Rev Roger Bush, a lifelong friend, sent many people to her. 'It would be impossible to describe all the things she did for other people in her lifetime,' he says. 'She had a tremendous amount of courage and a profoundly simple faith in God.' Nothing illustrates this better than an incident Aileen once told Mary about Bill, desperately needing money, holding a gun to her head. 'She gave him all she had of course,' says Mary, 'but she wasn't afraid. She knew God wouldn't let him hurt her and she didn't fear death anyway.'

For Aileen Grice, disability provided a means of discovering the infinite possibilities of caring. Mary Crockford, a special recipient, knows best what that meant: 'Her whole life was based on love and material things were just not important. She valued people's lives and feelings above all. Somehow she helped people who came to her thinking their life was worthless to think it was worthwhile; those who came frightened not to be frightened...She never judged them, just loved them. She was a wonderful person and she was my mother — wasn't I lucky!'

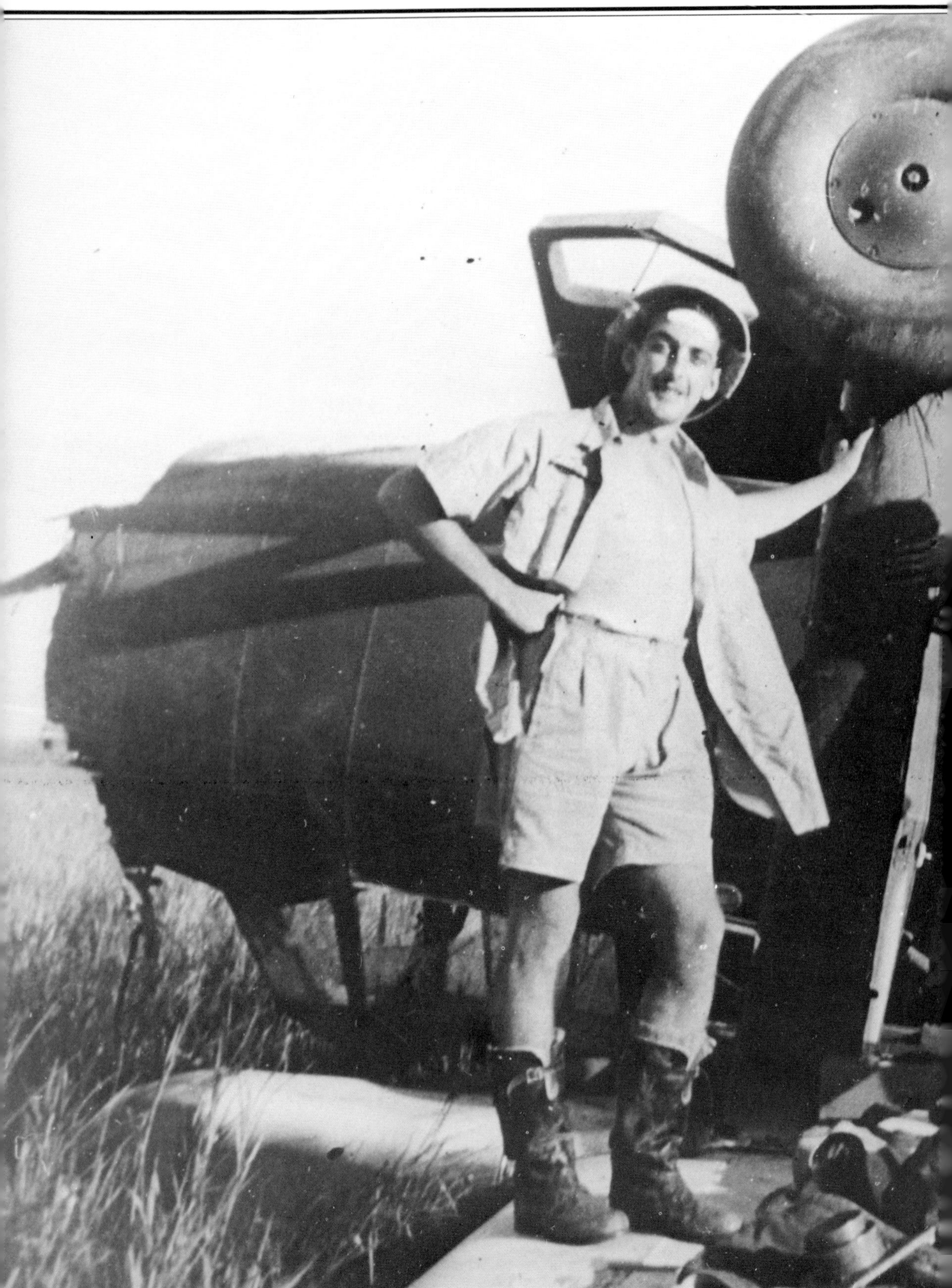

6
World War II
1939–1946

More than 70 years after Gallipoli, in a world changed utterly, the digger in the slouch hat — courageous, resourceful, endearingly larrikin and, above all, fiercely loyal to his mates — remains the popular archetype of the Australian at war. And these qualities are apparent in a number of the stories told here. But courage, resourcefulness, humour, and loyalty to comrades are not the special province of any one group. As these stories show, they are shared by Australians not represented by the image of the Anzac — women, sailors and airmen, Aborigines, immigrants other than Anglo-Celts, officers and non-combatants. Many post-war immigrants bring with them their experience of war in Europe and Asia: their stories are also Australian stories.

These stories tell, above all, of the fight to save lives. For, to those who are there, war is about death more often than glory. The wild heroism of the Anzacs is only one aspect of their story. The other, common to all wars at all times, is the tragedy of appalling waste. So it is not the wars that are honoured here, but the acts of bravery, endurance and affection by which the human spirit survives.

Berek Lewcowicz
1923–
Survival of the boy from Bedzyn
Written by: Lucinda Strauss
Nominated by: Leslie M. Lewis

Amid the rough and tumble of a busy Melbourne market, Berek Lewcowicz, a small wiry man, prepares for the day's trading. Quietly stacking the cardboard shoeboxes, his genial expression betrays nothing of a past filled with years of great privation and continuous terror. For Berek was one of only two Jewish male survivors from the notorious Small Fortress of Terezin, a Nazi prison camp from which no-one escaped.

The story of Berek Lewcowicz is remarkable in that it represents a triumph of the human spirit in extreme adversity. Years in labour and concentration camps pushed his body and soul to the limits of endurance. But his will to live, and confidence in his own ability to survive, enabled him always to find a way to beat a system whose logic was inhuman.

Reuben Berek Lewcowicz, was only sixteen when German forces poured across the border into Poland. On the night of 9 September 1939, in their town of Bedzyn, Berek stood by helplessly with his parents Moishe Aaron and Rivka, and sisters, Lola, Rusha and Paula, as the SS put a torch to the adjoining neighbourhood, killing all who tried to escape. Then the Nazis indiscriminately selected hostages and shot them before leaving the township ablaze.

This object lesson in terror was not wasted on Berek. Deeply sus-

Previous page. Pilot Frank Smallhorn (left) and medical orderly Philip Bronk on the wreckage of their Gannet in a swamp somewhere in Arnhem Land, May 1942

Moishe Aaron and Rivka Lewcowicz with their children before the war. Berek (right) and his sisters Lola (centre) and Rusha survived. The others are believed to have died at Auschwitz

picious of what was to come, he heeded a rumour that all Jewish boys were to be rounded up and sent to labour camps, and fled to the Soviet-occupied part of Poland.

As a fugitive, Berek escaped the bullets of German border guards while swimming the icy River San. On reaching Przemsyl, a border town in the Russian sector, Berek observed at once the inflated prices of bread. On hearing that prices were lower in the next town, he quickly established a small business trading bread between the two towns. Had he stayed, he may have been safe. But within six weeks, news of his mother's illness had drawn him back to Bedzyn.

Braving Russian bullets this time, the sole survivor of a group of fifteen, he swam the River San, and re-entered German-occupied Poland to find even heavier restrictions placed on Jews. In Cracow, fearing victimisation, he refused to wear the conspicuous Jewish armband and star. Impatient with waiting two days for a travel pass, he merely hopped on a train to Bedzyn. Then, placing himself in an empty carriage under the noses of two German soldiers, he pretended to read a German newspaper, his heart pounding so loudly he was sure they could hear it.

Berek seemed to get by with a mixture of bluff, luck and a great deal of chutzpah. 'I didn't know what fear was in those days,' says Berek Lewcowicz today. 'I was so young I just acted. I never told anyone what I was going to do. I just did it.'

His homecoming in Bedzyn was met with great joy, putting to an end rumours of his death at the hands of German guards. But freedom was shortlived and by 1940 it was apparent that the Gestapo was looking for him. Rather than endanger his family, he resigned himself

Berek Lewcowicz, survivor of the notorious Small Fortress of Terezin, now a retail businessman in Melbourne. Photograph by Ponch Hawkes

to the inevitable. It was not long before he was arrested.

For the next two years, Berek endured the rigours of Jelesia work camp. Formerly a resort for wealthy Poles, it was heavily bombed by the Luftwaffe and razed to the ground. With no tools, the prisoners set about the impossible task of reconstruction, subject to constant and vicious beatings. Men were murdered on the slightest pretext by brutal camp guards. Berek knew that his survival lay in not showing any sign of weakness and doing whatever work was required. To augment the meagre diet, Berek organised food parcels to be smuggled in from his family. Eventually, he had himself sent home in a detachment of sick men although this meant he had to deliberately cut his hand and expose himself to a severe beating.

But freedom lasted only as long as it took his hand to heal. Once again Berek was sent off to a labour camp, this time to Gliwice which eventually became part of the Auschwitz-Birkenau complex. On a diet just above starvation level, Berek knew that, this time, sickness would lead to the ovens of Auschwitz.

During the next few years he devised a variety of ways of bringing food into the camp, both for himself and for others. This was not as hard as it seemed for corruption was rife in the camp and Berek was both imaginative and quick to seize on an opportunity, especially if his survival was at stake. He used what was at hand to set up a complex trading chain. At the Gliwice camp there was a laundry which washed the clothes of Jews sent to the Auschwitz crematorium. The clothes were then shipped off to Germany. Berek arranged with the laundry workers to smuggle out some of the clothes which he then passed on to free workers who sold them outside. The free workers then smuggled food, cigars or whatever goods were required into the camp food. With this economy going, he was able to bring in great quantities of bread and even started to manufacture sweets.

All this came to end in January 1945 when the Germans, making their retreat, took the prisoners of Gliwice as hostages and put them on a forced march. When this proved too slow they were put into cattle trucks alongside 12 000 other evacuees — the sole survivors of hundreds of thousands of people from Auschwitz-Birkenau. Packed in these trucks for three and a half days with no food or water, people were trampled to death if they happened to fall. Berek knew that he had to escape, so he and his friend Youval leapt courageously from the moving train, dodging the telegraph poles placed every fifty metres and evading a spray of German bullets.

Freedom lasted a few short days before they were betrayed to the Gestapo by a Czechoslovakian peasant. Their last prison was the infamous Small Fortress of Terezin, a little known maximum security prison usually reserved for political offenders attached to the Garrison town of Terezin (or Theresenstadt) on the border of Czechoslovakia and Germany.

In a small suffocating cell designed for one, Berek was packed in with thirteen other prisoners. Here they stayed, virtually twenty-four hours a day, unable to move, slowly dying of starvation for just on four months. Every second night the cell door flew open and two Ukrainian SD guards would choose two prisoners for a brutal beating. Few survived such beatings and each morning the dead were turfed out, to be replaced with live prisoners.

The pressure of not knowing who would be taken pushed many men to the brink of insanity. Berek himself, at one stage of his imprisonment, went down on his knees and begged Adolf Eichmann, who was visiting the Fortress, to shoot him and end his misery. Eichmann kicked him aside and said that he would not waste a bullet as he would be dead soon anyway.

When Czech partisans liberated the town and entered the Small Fortress in May 1945, Berek, then weighing thirty-three kilograms, struggled to his feet to greet them, leaning against the wall for support and straining to see with eyes that had temporarily lost their sight. It was a day he had longed for since his capture five years before.

Within a few weeks Berek was re-united with his sister Rusha and later with his oldest sister Lola. But he had lost most of his family in the Holocaust. He believes that they were killed at Auschwitz although he can never verify this.

Although Berek can forgive his tormentors and those who wronged him, he cannot forget the past. His nights are crowded with waking dreams and nightmares. He passes the time by reading, history mostly, rarely sleeping more than an hour. Yet he survives and, at sixty-six, still puts in a full day's work. With good humour and resignation he describes himself as a fortunate man, but wants to tell his story so that succeeding generations will be reminded of what happened. That way, it may never happen again.

Rose Golding
1901–
'Rambling Rose'
Written by: Sophia Turkiewicz
Nominated by: Margaret C. O'Callaghan

In April 1939, Nurse Rose Golding sailed out of Port Melbourne on her way to England to begin a two-year working holiday. She was at last fulfilling her life long dream to travel.

There were already rumblings of impending world events but Rose was in her thirties and single, with a keen sense of adventure. She sailed out of Port Melbourne, alone, banking on her gregarious nature to help her through the lonely times of the solitary traveller. Less than a year later Rose was to find herself desperately fighting for survival in the middle of the Pacific ocean, her ship ablaze and sinking under German torpedo attack.

War had begun soon after her arrival in London and Rose's professional skills were in immediate and urgent demand. While she was nursing British soldiers who had been evacuated from the fighting in France, Rose heard of an appeal for trained nursing staff to escort a shipload of children who were being sent to safer areas in the Dominions.

Within forty-eight hours Rose was on board ship, along with eighty-two children aged between five and fifteen, sailing through treacherous waters on her way to South Africa, and then on to Australia.

The return trip to the UK was planned to proceed via New Zealand and northward to the Panama Canal to escape German ships known to be marauding on major European naval routes. But a few days out of Wellington, just before dawn, disaster struck. A German raiding ship torpedoed the *Rangitane*. Within minutes the bridge had been blown away and a fire had started below. The Captain recalls the bravery of Sister Rose and others of the nursing staff: 'The behaviour of everyone was magnificent. Never in my life have I seen women behave more valiantly. Some of them were helping to bind up the wounded, and others displayed no panic, though the ship was burning.'

In the heavy swell, the lifeboat survivors did their best to avoid capture by three prowling German ships, but they were soon rounded up and taken prisoner. Rose was the first to climb up the rope ladder. She was unceremoniously hauled aboard, clinging on to the few worldly possessions which she had managed to salvage.

The survivors were divided between three ships. They spent many days below deck, under armed guard, with very little food, and no fresh air. Rose refused to be intimidated by the circumstances. She recalls a German officer attempting to provoke herself and a friend into crying. The women resolutely refused to give the officer the satisfaction. 'We have no hankies,' was the cheeky response. The next day they were presented with a parcel of six handkerchiefs, along with the back-handed compliment, 'You British women never cry.'

The group had no idea where they were being taken, but they were eventually put ashore on the tiny Pacific island of Emirau, north of New Guinea, and left there to fend for themselves. There was three days' food for 500 survivors, many of whom were ill or wounded, and no shelter.

On Christmas Day, their food running out the group's luck turned when they were rescued by an Australian ship, the *Nellore*. The ship brought the survivors to Townsville, where they disembarked and travelled to Sydney by train.

Rose returned to Nathalia, her hometown in Victoria, to a totally unexpected heroine's welcome. She stepped off the train and was amazed to discover that the whole town had come out to greet her. Rose's response to her ordeal was typical: 'I wouldn't be afraid to go again.'

Which she promptly did. She returned to England to continue nursing throughout the war and was honoured by Queen Elizabeth for her courage.

After the war, Rose joined a contingent of Australian nurses escorting POWs from Singapore to Australia. She never followed the orthodox path of marriage and family, and continued to work abroad, mostly in India, thus acquiring her nickname, 'Rambling Rose'. Eventually, her father's illness brought her back to Australia, where she remained nursing until her retirement at the age of sixty-nine.

A small, unassuming woman who had no aspirations towards recognition or fame, Rose merely went where she thought she might be needed and in following her impulse she has revealed a character which is full of grit and spirit and courage. Now in her late eighties and living in country Victoria, she is probably astonished to find herself regarded as a heroine.

Sister Rose Golding, survivor of the sinking of the Rangitane *in 1940*

Ruby Boye-Jones
1891–

Courageous coastwatcher
Written by: Suzy Baldwin
Nominated by: Bonnie Davey; Alan Zammit

When World War II began, Ruby Boye was living with her husband, Skov, manager of the Kauri Timber Company, on the tiny South Pacific island of Vanikoro, last of the Santa Cruz group on the southernmost tip of the Solomon Islands. When the company radio operator decided to return to Australia to join the RAAF, Ruby volunteered to take over his job. In the twenty-four hours before the boat left, she learned to operate the powerful radio that connected Vanikoro with Australia and the other islands of the South Pacific and to gather and transmit weather reports in voice code. She later taught herself Morse code from a book. The Australian Navy, quick to appreciate Ruby's value, appointed her as a coastwatcher and asked her to broadcast detailed weather reports four times a day from which they compiled accurate forecasts for Allied warships and bombers.

When the Japanese swept into the South Pacific late in 1941, the authorities ordered the immediate evacuation of most European civilians and all women. But Ruby and Skov refused to leave. Few Europeans knew the Solomons and the Santa Cruz area as well as Skov, making him a valuable coastwatcher. Ruby, realising the importance of her reports, insisted on staying to operate the radio. When the ship sailed, they were two of only three Europeans left on the island.

It was a courageous decision. Neither of the Boyes was young — Ruby was fifty and her husband older — and their sons were both in Australia. Moreover, they knew that remaining on Vanikoro meant not only isolation, but very real danger. Should the Japanese invade the island they would be unable to defend themselves.

Ruby's decision was particularly heroic. Now ninety-six, she recalls that she spent a great deal of her time alone: 'My husband kept the timber works going for most of the war. They used to fell the trees high up in the hills and he'd spend days up there ... But I was active and the work was exciting so I was content.'

When the Americans arrived in 1942, Ruby's one-woman garrison became 'Third US Army Outpost'. Ruby was now under US Naval command.

Ruby was a vital radio link in the Allied Pacific communications system. She continued to send meteorological information and, able to get through when other stations could not, also transmitted coded intelligence messages from other coastwatchers to US Intelligence Headquarters on Vila in the New Hebrides (now Vanuatu).

'I'd been running the radio single-handed since 1939, so I was quite experienced by the time the Americans came. They seemed rather pleased to have me,' Ruby says with characteristic understatement.

That they were delighted to have her is apparent in the special attention Ruby received from the most senior US Pacific Naval Commanders. One morning, a large flying boat circled the island and landed on the lagoon. A small group of American officers came ashore. 'Name's Halsey,' said Admiral William 'Bull' Halsey, Commander South Pacific Force and South Pacific Area, as he shook Skov Boye's hand. 'I've come to meet that marvellous woman who runs the radio.'

In late 1943, after two gruelling gruelling years that Ruby describes as 'a bit nerve-racking', she developed shingles. When Halsey heard, he sent a US Naval Catalina Flying Boat to take Ruby back to Sydney for treatment.

While she was away, the Navy replaced her with no fewer than four men, two on duty and two off. Ruby, who for four years had been solely responsible for the radio, twenty-four hours a day, seven days a week, laughs as she remembers: 'They had a real beano, those young chaps. When I came back, the Navy sent an aircraft carrier to collect them but they were very loath to leave.'

By then, the Japanese had been defeated in the Solomons and the Allied offensive had moved northwards. However, from the beginning of 1942 to early 1943, the Solomons were at the very centre of the war in the Pacific. By early 1942, Japanese forces had captured Hong Kong, Malaya, Java, the Philippines, part of New Guinea and most islands to the north of the Solomons. They soon occupied the Solomons themselves, landing at Tulagi, the Islands' pre-war capital, on 3 May 1942. Vanikoro was now surrounded by Japanese forces.

In May 1942, the Battle of the Coral Sea took place only 1100 kilometres from Vanikoro, followed by the Battle of the Eastern Solomons in August. The Battle of the Santa Cruz was virtually on Ruby's doorstep and the famous Battle of Guadalcanal, fought in November of that year, was a mere 800 kilometres away. During this critical period, Ruby was a crucial link in the Allied Intelligence chain, continuing to transmit important coded meteorological data, acting as emergency relay station between other coastwatching stations and the US receiving station in the New Hebrides, and passing on information picked up by the islanders as they travelled by canoe from island to island. Admiral Halsey later paid tribute to the heroic work of Ruby and other coastwatchers when he said, 'The coastwatchers saved Guadalcanal and Guadalcanal saved the Pacific.'

The Japanese fought at Guadalcanal from the beginning of July 1942, to February 1943. During that time, Ruby was in easy range of Japanese aircraft which often flew low over Vanikoro. Surprisingly, the island was bombed only once.

There is no doubt that the Japanese knew about Ruby. Early in 1942, just after she had finished transmitting a weather report, a Japanese voice came on the air: 'Calling Mrs Boye. Calling Mrs Boye. Japanese commander say you get out or else...' At this point, the other coastwatchers jammed the airwaves, blotted out the rest of the message and told the Japanese operator, 'in language which they wouldn't repeat to a lady', exactly what the Japanese commander could do.

After a coastwatcher in New Guinea was tortured and murdered by Japanese, the Australian Navy immediately commissioned or enlisted all coastwatchers. In theory at least, combatants in uniform could not be executed as spies. Lieutenant-Commander Feldt, Supervising

Third Officer Ruby Boye, only honorary WRAN ever appointed, in the uniform dropped in to her on Vanikoro by parachute

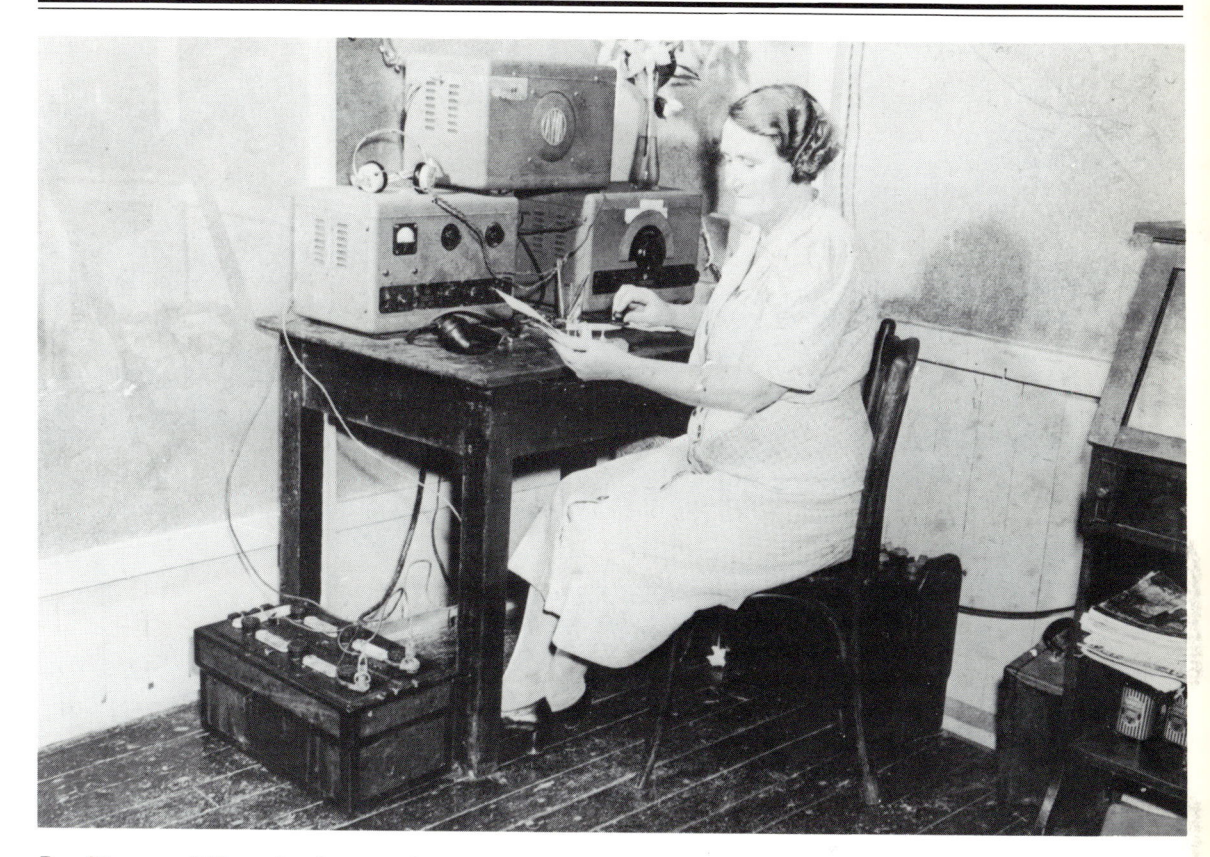

World War II

Ruby Boye, one-woman garrison, at the radio that was a vital communications link during the war in the Pacific. Vanikoro, Solomon Is, 1942

Intelligence Officer in charge of coastwatchers, visited Ruby, by then fifty-one, to commission her as an honorary lieutenant in the WRANS, the only honorary WRAN ever appointed. Her measurements were dispatched to Australia and her uniform dropped to her by parachute.

The Japanese were not the only danger: there were also the crocodiles. For safety reasons it was decided to relocate the tall radio mast and equipment across the river from the house. When the suspension bridge was destroyed in a cyclone, Ruby had to cross the crocodile-infested Lawrence River by punt four times a day, often in torrential tropical rain, then walk through ankle-deep mud to transmit her weather and intelligence information.

Was she ever afraid, of the crocodiles or the Japanese? 'Oh yes,' Ruby admits cheerfully. 'I was more scared than tame.'

After the war, Skov became very ill. Ruby brought him back to Australia where he died of leukaemia two weeks later. Ruby returned to Vanikoro to pack up and then, in 1948, left forever the islands that had been her home for twenty years.

Some years later, Ruby met and married Frank Jones and became known as Ruby Boye-Jones. Since Frank's death in 1962, she has lived alone.

Ruby is the only known female coastwatcher of World War II. In recognition of her invaluable work during the Japanese offensive in the Solomons, Ruby was awarded the British Empire Medal in 1944. She also received the 1939–45 Star and many letters of appreciation and commendation from England, the United States and Australia. The letter from Commander R.B.M. Long, OBE, Director of Australian

Ruby Boye-Jones, now 96, describes the crocodiles that lived around her home in the Solomons: 'The crocs would sit up on a rock with their jaws open while a particular bird cleaned their teeth'. Photograph by Keith Barlow

Naval Intelligence, thanks Ruby for 'your brilliant war work...Both Admiral Rushbrooke and myself...consider you cannot be adequately paid. You have written a page in the brilliant history of British women, showing in no uncertain manner of what they are capable.'

Whether Ruby could be adequately paid or not, the truth is that she wasn't paid at all. Her honorary rank gave her no financial entitlement, either during or after the war. Ruby did not apply for a service pension until she was eighty-seven and in fairly desperate straits, but was not granted her full Service Pension until 1984.

In recent years, Ruby has suffered from diabetes. Her left leg was amputated and, at the age of ninety, she learned to walk with an artifical leg.

Although now ninety-six and virtually blind, Ruby's dignified bearing and fiercely independent spirit are still impressive. 'I like my privacy; that's why I don't want to go into hospital. The doctor thought it would be nice for me to go into a private hospital for a few weeks for a bit of a rest. I hated every minute of it.'

In 1983, at the request of the Americans, Ruby donated most of her wartime papers to the Nimitz Museum of the Pacific War. She was invited to Texas for the opening of the museum and the Nimitz Memorial Park, named for Fleet Admiral Chester Nimitz, Commander-in-Chief of the US Pacific Fleet and Pacific Ocean Areas. As C-in-C of Allied Forces in the Pacific, Nimitz was naval signatory to the Japanese surrender, and, like Admiral Halsey, on whose flagship *Missouri* the document was signed, he was an admirer of Ruby.

Ruby was unable to attend the ceremony, but keeps the invitation in the front of the scrapbook her sons have put together for her. On the front of the invitation are five silver stars in a circle. 'There were very few five star admirals,' Ruby explains. There were even fewer Ruby Boyes.

John Margrave Lerew
1912–

'We who are about to die salute you'

Written by: Suzy Baldwin
Nominated by: Anonymous

There is about airmen of the two world wars a unique and irresistible romance. One cannot sail a battleship single-handed, nor are jungle or desert campaigns fought by battalions of one. But flying the small planes of the first half of the century is an intensely individual act. Driven by what Yeats calls 'a lonely impulse of delight,' the flyer is essentially a solitary. Like the mediaeval knight, he might set out on his quest with a small band of one or two, but he can, and often does, travel alone. And, like the knight of romance, the flyer can do something magical. For most of us, the longing to soar above the earth remains embedded in the powerful flying dreams of childhood; the dreams remain dreams and we remain earthbound. But the flyer turns the vision of freedom into reality. In machines whose absurd fragility is at once comical and touching, he conquers the element of the angels.

They once made films about flyers like this; flyers like Group Captain John Lerew. With his easy, gentlemanly charm and his dashing good looks — amused blue eyes, splendid moustache and one of the great chins — John Lerew is the David Niven and Errol Flynn characters rolled into one — the heroic leader of a gallant band who faces ridiculously overwhelming odds with cool courage, answers the pompous demands of safely desk-bound superiors with irreverent wit and defies unreasonable orders and apparently impossible conditions to lead his men to safety.

John Lerew began to fly in 1932, a twenty-year-old fresh out of university. 'I was very badly bitten by the flying bug. And I graduated during the Depression. So when I was offered a permanent commission in the RAAF, I grabbed it.'

Ten years later, Squadron Leader John Lerew led 24 Squadron's gallant defence of Rabaul — all the more moving for being utterly hopeless. Rabaul was the focal point of a crucial defence arc of islands radiating eastward from New Guinea: to defend it, Lerew had four Hudsons and six Wirraways. The Hudson was a light twin-engine bomber, the Wirraway a training aircraft, never meant as a fighter at all.

Flying the Wirraways up to Rabaul in early December 1941 was, as John Lerew explains, an adventure in itself. 'The Wirras were single-engined aircraft and we hadn't been allowed to get them any further than gliding distance from land. Now we had to fly them 300 miles or so across the sea to Port Moresby. We got there, but only just. We went through one aerodrome that was in such bad condition that we nearly wrote off several planes. The ground was so soft that the locals had to run under the wings and literally carry the aircraft to get them started.'

From the moment of its arrival in Rabaul a few days after Pearl Harbour, Lerew's squadron was chronically under-supplied and overworked, a fact that Area Headquarters appears not to have appreciated. Their specific directions for Lerew's handful of planes had, as the official history wryly observes, 'the quality of fiction'. The primary task of the Wirraways was to defend Rabaul, while the four Hudsons were to cover a wide area as reconnaissance craft, as bombers and as an air striking force. While Lerew directed all operations and flew both kinds of plane, he was also contending with two ill-equipped and under-manned airfields and a notoriously unreliable communications system.

Despite the squadron's valiant performance, late in December Air Board sent a scathing signal complaining about 'lack of information and bad reconnaissance reports'. After threatening Lerew with dire consequences, the signal concludes with the dramatic rhetorical flourish: 'Empire expects much of a few'. Lerew, unimpressed and irrepressible, responded by despatching the first of his famous signals. Asked to list his reasons for delay in communications, Lerew finishes with 'Disappointment in the lack of assistance rendered by the Almighty', and concludes his signal with an acerbic response to official rhetoric: 'The Empire expects much, repeat *much*, of a few.' There is no record of Air Board's reply.

From 4 January 1942, 24 Squadron was bombed heavily every day. Lerew had patrols of Wirraways in the air from first light attempting to intercept and stop the raids, but the courage and skill of the squadron leader and his men could not obscure the fact that they were outnumbered and outclassed. The only aircraft that the Wirraway could overtake was a flying boat and even then its ability to inflict serious damage was highly doubtful. In addition, despite repeated requests, Lerew had no proper shelter pens for his few precious aircraft. 'The only way we could protect them was to have them in the air. The Japanese would pattern bomb so your chances of being hit on the ground were very high. So as soon as we saw them coming, everyone would leap in and take off.' To ensure that all aircraft were warmed up and ready for take off at all times, the ground crew worked around the clock, doing all repairs at night.

Despite these efforts, a number of aircraft were damaged or destroyed during raids. Convinced that Rabaul was in for a major attack, Lerew sent an urgent request for labour and equipment, anti-aircraft guns and six 'modern' fighters. Six fighters! Even if the RAAF had had them to send, which they didn't, Lerew's squadron would still have been outrageously outnumbered on the day of the big raid on Rabaul.

On the morning of 20 January, the Japanese just kept coming. They had at least 120 fighters and bombers. To meet them, John Lerew had eight unsuitable aircraft. His tiny force put up a brave but hopeless fight. At the end of the day, Lerew was left with two Wirraways and a Hudson. '*Now* will you send some fighters?' he signalled Air Board. When Air Board replied that it had no more planes to send him, Lerew sent the two Wirraways off 'to survive things' and decided to act on the orders given him before he was sent to Rabaul. 'I'd been told that, if we were overwhelmed, I was to use my own discretion. So, after talking it over with the CO of the Army garrison, Colonel Scanlan, I sent a signal to say that I proposed to try to evacuate the Squadron — about 120 men. They were too valuable to the Air Force to be lost and were too untrained in ground fighting to be of any value to the army. 'I immediately got a signal back telling me to "Stay put", followed by another ordering me to hand over command to Squadron Leader Bill Brookes and then fly the last Hudson out. The Squadron was to be placed at the disposal of the army. Well, Scanlan nearly had a blue fit. The last thing he needed was my blokes.

'My own reaction was one of sheer outrage. I couldn't possibly take off and leave my men behind. I decided to disobey these orders completely.'

Lerew's first response was to send his badly wounded men off in the last Hudson. His second was to send one last message to Air Board. This was his now famous signal in Latin — the gladiators' farewell, *'Mourituri Vos Salutamus'* ('We who are about to die salute you.'). 'As they were throwing us to the lions, this seemed appropriate,' Lerew commented later. The signal also created a smokescreen: while Air Board in Australia was deciphering what it said — and then what it actually *meant* — Lerew was able to concentrate on getting his men out without further interference.

Lerew next sent a signal to Wing Commander Charles Pearce, Commanding Officer at Port Moresby, asking if he could send flying boats to pick them up at Put Put. Then, having destroyed as much of the installation as possible and blown up the petrol dumps, 'we commandeered every car and truck we could find and choofed off with the Japanese all around us'. The party had to dismantle and abandon

Squadron Leader John Lerew, 1942. After his squadron's gallant defence of Rabaul, he defied unjust orders and led his 120 men to safety

the vehicles at the Warangoi River, which they crossed by two native canoes, then waded along a jungle path in heavy rain. At one point, Lerew sent the thirty-three men who had wives and children off to Tol plantation to await rescue while he and the remaining hundred pushed on and eventually reached Sum Sum. 'We were further on from where we said we'd be and when we heard aircraft, we dived for cover. Then we saw it was two Empire flying boats so we all jumped about and waved like mad. They saw us and came in right under the noses of the Japanese. We packed fifty men into each of the boats, which were designed to carry twelve. The problem then was to take off. We had about four goes at it and finally unstuck just at dark.' Three hours later, they touched down at Samurai on the eastern tip of New Guinea. Here, Lerew discovered that Pearce had received orders from Headquarters not to attempt to pick the squadron up. A gladiator like Lerew, he too had promptly disobeyed.

When the men at Tol were collected the next evening, only four of Lerew's squadron had not been evacuated. One was listed as missing, two were captured, and the fourth, Sergeant Higgs, had voluntarily made his way to a plantation teleradio when the Rabaul transmitter failed. Two days after Lerew had led his 120 men to safety, the Japanese massacred many of the troops remaining on Rabaul.

Group Captain John Margrave Lerew, DFC, 1988. One of the last of the chivalric knights. Photograph by Neville Waller

John Lerew was flown back to Melbourne. 'I saw all the top brass and no-one ever said one word about disobeying orders,' he recalls with great amusement. 'In fact, they rather congratulated me and Charlie Pearce. Instead of being ticked off, I was immediately given command of another squadron — three flights of Hudsons that became 32 Squadron.'

Less than three weeks after leading 24 Squadron safely out of Rabaul, Wing Commander Lerew was back in New Guinea, leading three Hudsons in a low level attack on enemy shipping at Gasmata, when his plane was attacked and caught fire. Lerew instructed his crew to abandon the aircraft then he too baled out. He parachuted down in the jungle and struggled through eight days of privation and near capture before he was greeted by an Australian uttering the heavenly words: 'What about a cold one?'

Two months later, John Lerew was awarded the Distinguished Flying Cross for the Rabaul and the Gasmata action. It was one of the first DFCs awarded in the South West Pacific campaign.

He was a hero in anyone's terms. Yet, for John Lerew, honour does not depend on the heroics of battle. His most satisfying achievement has been the saving of flyers' lives — his goal in the evacuation from Rabaul and his job since 1943, first as founding Director of the RAAF's Directorate of Flying Safety, then as one of the chiefs of the International Civil Aviation Organisation based in Canada.

Courtly, energetic and extraordinarily charming, John Lerew at seventy-five is still handsome and sparkling company. He is delighted by beautiful women — including his tall, elegant wife — and cannot resist a party.

A discerning traveller and highly civilised man, John Margrave Lerew relishes the pleasures that the world has to offer. He suffers coffee at four o'clock but on the dot of five he rubs his hands together and his eyes light up: 'How about a little noggin?' In his Sydney apartment, under a fine seventeenth-century painting of his ancestors, one of the last of the chivalric knights pours champagne and chuckles.

Frederick Getty Higgs
1904–1973

'To Higgs. Good show... Lerew'
Written by: Billy Marshall-Stoneking
Nominated by: G. Higgs

Sergeant Frederick Higgs. Suffering from exposure and malnutrition after his epic voyage from New Britain, he was greeted with scepticism by the Cairns authorities

When Squadron Leader John Lerew evacuated his squadron from Rabaul, one of the only four men left behind was Sergeant Frederick Higgs, the squadron's radio operator. He had volunteered to make his way to a plantation teleradio 100 kilometres away when the Rabaul transmitter failed. It was Higgs who had sent the signal to Pearce then waited for three days to receive the all-clear from Lerew. Eventually the signal came through. It was short, and to the point: 'To Higgs. Good show. The job is done. All safe. Make a break for home. Good luck. Lerew.'

Higgs then commandeered a six metre sailing boat and, with only a compass and a page from a school atlas, set sail alone for Australia. Travelling mainly at night, and hiding in mangrove swamps during the day, he navigated his small craft over 3000 kilometres of ocean and, after three weeks of playing cat-and-mouse with the Japanese Navy and a few Japanese fighters, arrived in Cairns.

Higgs was awarded the British Empire Medal for his bravery and allegiance. As John Lerew says, 'He put up a tremendous show.'

Father Edward Harris
1905–1942
'Greater love hath no man than this'
Written by: Niall Lucy
Nominated by: David M. Selby

Edward Charles Harris was a boy of seven when he left England with his family in 1912 to live in Sydney. Like other children of his age, he raced billycarts and swapped marbles and was in trouble at school. Privately, however, he was set apart from his playmates, for young Edward believed that he was called to the priesthood. He entered the seminary shortly after graduating a Bachelor of Law from the University of Sydney in 1932 and seven years later was ordained into the Order of the Missionaries of the Sacred Heart. In 1941, Father Harris was appointed to Mal Mal Mission at Jaquinot Bay on the south coast of New Britain.

Life was tough at Mal Mal from the very start. Father Harris's arrival coincided with an outbreak of pneumonic influenza, and the Mission's medical supplies were inadequate to cope with the epidemic. But a starkly different set of problems arose when the township of Rabaul, 150 kilometres to the north, fell to the Japanese in January 1942.

Forced to retreat along the south coast, parties of dispirited troops from the defeated Australian garrison at Rabaul trod a weary path through swamps and dense jungle and high over rugged mountains in the hope of crossing to Port Moresby on the New Guinea mainland. Those who reached Mal Mal were exhausted, hungry, and stricken with malaria. Morale was dangerously low.

To the ragged troops who came to his Mission, Father Harris gave food and such medical treatment as he was able to provide. Vital as this aid was, the men's spirits were lifted even higher by the priest's cheerful and compassionate nature, and all were inspired by his implacable faith. By thus restoring their hope and renewing their strength, Father Harris revived the troops' precious morale.

After a number of troops had passed through Mal Mal, a small party arrived who believed that there could not be more than twenty men still to come. Father Harris gave this party his modest sailboat fitted out with an engine, together with food and medical supplies and enough petrol to get them to Moresby. A few days later, however, a large party of over 100 troops reached the Mission in the same miserable condition as those who had come before. Their spirits, too, were

Father Edward Harris, MSC, his unfailing cheerfulness so gratefully remembered by many Australian soldiers. Taken on the jetty at Mal Mal, New Britain, in April 1942, just before the departing rescue boat left the missionary to his inevitable fate

revived as despair gave way to hope under the influence of the priest's unfailing good cheer.

This latest party was too large to remain at the Mission, but Father Harris offered to care for the wounded and seriously ill while the others were moved to an abandoned plantation farther down the coast. There he visited the men from time to time, inspiring them with kindness and devotion.

Several weeks later, a rescue ship arrived and the troops tried in vain to persuade Father Harris to escape with them. The last to make a plea was D.M. Selby.

'You know the Japs will kill you when they hear you've helped Australian troops,' Selby argued bluntly, adding that if the priest were to come back to Australia until the war ended, he could then return to Mal Mal and carry on his work among the villagers. 'A dead missionary is no good to anyone.'

'I appreciate your point,' Father Harris replied, 'but this is mine: I came here to tell these people what Christianity means. If I deserted them now, could I ever return and preach Christianity again?'

Selby had no answer but to shake the priest's hand.

On their return to Sydney the troops began raising funds to buy a gold chalice for Father Harris in appreciation of his constancy and goodwill. They were not to know that he would never receive the gift. Within days of the rescue ship's departure from Mal Mal, the Japanese arrived and the priest was murdered.

Clive Roberts Bernard
1914–1942

'Come on my lot, we'll beat it'
Written by: Billy Marshall-Stoneking
Nominated by: David L. Bernard

Clive Bernard turned around as he heard someone yell that the Japanese were coming. Then twenty bombers filled the air, two explosions rocked the airfield at Wau, New Guinea, and people scattered.

Bernard, who'd been evacuating contract workers from the island, called out: 'Come on, my lot! We'll beat it!'

Out on the tarmac, exposed to the Japanese's 250 pound high explosive bombs, was a brand new Lockheed 14, one of two planes that Bernard and another pilot had been using to ferry people to mainland Australia. The young captain could not just let it sit there and be blown to bits.

Although he was a civilian pilot and had never had anyone shoot at him before, Bernard sprinted 365 metres across the airfield, dodging bomb blasts and machine-gun fire. On reaching the Lockheed, he unscrewed a loose cowling on the engine, started the plane, and taxied toward the small group of people huddled near the aerodrome. Hustling them into the aircraft, Bernard took off as soon as the door was closed.

In a hail of explosions and gun fire, Bernard, who had never flown

Clive Bernard, self-deprecating hero, and the Lockheed that perished with him in 1942 on one of his flights to evacuate civilians from New Guinea. He was one of three Bernard brothers to die in World War II

the Lockheed alone before, piloted the great machine down a long, yawning valley with three Japanese Zeros in close pursuit.

A passenger on board the plane recalled how 'Bernard flew so fast and straight. Then he soared over the mountains and dropped down until he almost skimmed their tops. [We] could see the Japanese turning and twisting above...evidently looking for the plane.'

But Bernard was too skilful for them, and although observers later discovered cartridges from the Japanese air cannons strewn over eight miles of the valley floor, the Lockheed escaped unscathed.

It was exploits such as this that caused people to think of him as heroic. But Bernard himself always seemed unconcerned about his adventures. 'As soon as I hear the sirens go,' he once admitted, 'I'm in a blue funk. I go like a hare for the nearest air raid shelter.'

Despite the stories he told against himself, Bernard was an able and reliable pilot. Older and more experienced flyers respected him for his piloting skills. 'His bravery and airmanship,' one pilot remarked, 'must be written among the historical and humane chapters of these times.' And, without any doubt, a large number of people in New Guinea owed their lives to his selflessness and his dedication to the job of rescuing those in peril.

But Clive Bernard was never able to finish all the tasks he had set himself. On yet another rescue flight to New Guinea, the Lockheed crashed in mangroves near Cairns, Queensland. Clive Bernard died as he had lived — in a plane.

Father John Corbett Glover
1909–1948
Flying priest
Written by: David Millar
Nominated by: Erin Patricia Carr

In the late 1930s, a young, good-looking priest returned to his father's hotel, The Royal, in Albury, New South Wales, to visit the family. Speaking to his younger sister, Carmel, he confided, 'I'm learning to fly up at Cootamundra. But don't tell mother yet, she won't be happy about it, I think, and it may only make her nervous.'

Someone else not happy to hear about the flying lessons was the Catholic Bishop of Wagga Wagga. An old Irishman, renowned for his authoritarianism when dealing with clergy, he was extremely angry to discover that one of his priests was learning to fly without permission. A peremptory order to 'please explain' arrived at the Cootamundra presbytery where Father Glover was a curate. Happily for the fledgling pilot, a timely change of bishops and the appointment of a more sympathetic Australian saw the interdict lifted and the flying curate was once again airborne.

Father Glover discovered a way to marry his new enthusiasm with his vocation - he applied to the Divine Word Mission in New Guinea to become one of their pilots. In 1938, the dashing young priest arrived in Alexishafen, and in a low-winged monoplane named *Petrus* was soon winging his way to and from the Highlands where the Mission Fathers had extended their work.

All this came to an end when Japan entered the war. By early 1942 The Japanese Imperial Army had captured Rabaul, and it now became imperative for Europeans in New Guinea to be withdrawn to Australia. This evacuation by air is a remarkable story. Despite Japanese fighters who could pounce out of the sky, heavy loads, inadequate landing strips and the awful vagaries of the local weather and terrain, evacuation flights that now seem incredible got under way.

In his little Spartan bi-plane which was really too small, too tired and too old, Father Glover helped ferry people to the main assembly points. From there, larger planes took them to Port Moresby or points southwards. When the war was over, a large number of the pilots involved in these escapes were awarded medals, but as the *Pacific Information Monthly* bluntly remarked 'there were extraordinary omissions from that list, and brave deeds known to hundreds of people have been ignored'. One of those ignored in this process was Father Glover.

There were several assembly points dotted around the country, and the one in which the young priest was to become so intimately involved was inland at Kainantu which had become a temporary home for an ever-increasing band of Europeans. To protect themselves from Japanese attack, the refugees settled down under the canopy of the plantation, dug air-raid trenches, and then strung a wire across the airfield in order to cripple the undercarriage of any unwanted airborne guest.

Because of large numbers of refugees turning up at the station, the fear that when the floods retreated the Japanese would arrive, and the increasing incidence of malaria, Glover was forced to reconsider the initial idea of flying the refugees out in handfuls of two or three. He decided to return to the coast, visit the Fathers at Alexishafen, and pick up an old *Tiger Moth* believed to be still there. With this plane and his seventy-five horsepower Spartan as a back-up, he would be able to fly more people to safety.

Rather than risk his little Spartan flying over enemy-held territory, Father Glover decided to walk the 250 kilometres down the slopes to the coast, living off the land, sneaking past enemy patrols and avoiding, wherever possible, the swamps that lay in his path as the result of recent heavy rains. As a companion he took Karl Nagy, an Hungarian mechanic with Guinea Airways, who would be able to check the Tiger Moth, and if necessary, make her airworthy. They eventually crept into Alexishafen, patched up the old Moth, and Father Glover took off. Nagy, who doubted the plane would make the trip if it was forced to carry two people without a thorough overhaul, returned to Kainantu by foot.

Time was now urgent. The two men worked long hours in the workshop fitting extra tanks, timing the engines, tightening wires and checking the airframes. Then came disaster. One day the Spartan was too heavy to take off clearly and had to return to the airstrip. Unfortunately, it collided with the trip wire, did a flip and the propellor was shattered. So were their hopes, for even an engineer of Nagy's capability could do nothing to replace such a vital part of the plane.

Father Glover, now reduced to one plane, decided that ferrying everyone to the main exodus point at Mount Hagan by shuttle service would only increase the risks tremendously. He would, therefore, do the seemingly impossible — he would take the Moth right over the Owen Stanley Ranges, make for Thursday Island, and from there radio for assistance. The attempt was foolhardy. The priest had never flown the route before, and his only map was one torn out of an old school atlas. The plane had a limited ceiling which made her vulnerable to mountain peaks and searching enemy planes. Moreover, a plane loaded up with extra fuel was a lumbering piece of sluggish machinery for which turbulence in the tropical conditions was a real threat. Nagy was very dubious. The refugees were fearful. Nevertheless, after one false attempt, the two took off, wobbled into the air, and began the erratic flight, southwards, flying over jungles and ravines that spelt death if anything happened to the frail craft.

While crossing the Owen Stanleys, Nagy continually fed petrol into the tank. Then as they approached the southern coast they ran into a particularly bad rainstorm. Petrol consumption rose rapidly and visibility dropped as quickly. Ditching their now useless craft on a lonely

Reverend Father John Glover, the fearless missionary whose audacious flight across the New Guinea mountains saved many Australian lives

beach, they hitched their way to Thursday Island by canoe.

Their reception was far from the rapturous one they were expecting. No-one believed that they had flown over the Owen Stanleys in a Moth, that Nagy was not a German spy, and that Father Glover was a man of the cloth. Despite their protestations and appeals for urgency, the suspicious Australians locked the two airmen in a cell. Then one of those remarkable coincidences occurred. When their captors radioed the mainland for instructions, the senior officer at the other end recognised Glover's name — they had been to school together back in Wangaratta.

Released from prison, Father Glover flew on to Australia, where Qantas agreed to fly in two DH 86s with Father Glover aboard, and to snatch the refugees from Kainantu. The planes flew in and out, undetected, and all the refugees were rescued.

Sadly, what the Japanese were unable to do, the flying conditions of New Guinea were able to achieve. In 1948, while landing a plane at the Catholic Mission at Mingende, Father Glover was killed. His memorial there reads:

'In everlasting memory of an heroic man of God who, in the dark days of 1942, organised and personally flew an airlift of nearly 100 people from the Highlands to safety in Australia.'

Arthur J. Bryant
1916–

Salvage at the bombing of Darwin
Written by: Billy Marshall-Stoneking
Nominated by: H. M. Walter

When the steamer *Niagara* struck a German mine off the coast of New Zealand in 1941, and sank with eight and a half tonnes of gold bullion on board, the Bank of England enlisted the services of Captain J.P. Williams to salvage it.

The treasure lay in seventy fathoms (130 metres) of water, and though the explosion of the *Niagara* itself had been shockingly spectacular, the job of actually salvaging gold from that depth would be even more amazing, for it called upon a select group of men to do something that had never been done before. If they were to be successful they would have to perform feats of courage, resourcefulness, endurance and seamanship of the first degree.

Williams did not need to be told how difficult it would be, and so he personally picked his team for the job. One of the first men he asked was Arthur Bryant.

Bryant had worked for Williams before as manager of a small plant treating mine tailings to win gold left behind from earlier workings, and Williams had found him to be both reliable and honourable. Bryant was only too happy to come along. He liked a challenge, and he liked Williams. Anyway, you didn't say 'no' to your mates.

As for the rest of the salvage team, they all looked upon Bryant as the most edifying member of the team. He did not swear, or smoke, and was 'never known to touch strong liquor'. Yet he was extremely popular with the men, 'probably because he refrained from "preaching", and relished a good joke'. He was also easy-going, as one of the crew remembers, 'One word from [Bryant] and we did as we liked.'

Bryant's valour and steadfastness in the face of danger, however, were not really put to the test until one morning in Darwin, in 1942. With the salvaging operation of the *Niagara* successfully completed, Williams and his crew were asked by the Australian authorities to salvage code papers from a Japanese submarine sunk between the Australian mainland and Melville Island. They were moored in Darwin Harbour when the Japanese attacked.

Williams was standing near the wharf, just before ten on the morning of the 19 February, talking to a Lieutenant Burke, as the first wave of planes approached from the north. Burke, distracted, glanced up: 'Americans, I suppose...' But even before the words were out of his mouth the first bombs were dropped.

It seemed as though the sky was falling in, and there was no place to hide. 'One moment the steamer, *Neptuna*, was at her berth and the next, a shower of sticks in the sky.' Williams and Burke hit the ground, then Williams looked up and surveyed the scene. What had, moments before, been a placid harbour, was now in turmoil. Oil tanks were on fire, and patches of burning oil covered the harbour. The big guns from the USS *Peary* boomed, and bits of flying debris filled the air.

Suddenly, two American ships were hit and started sinking, then an oil tanker went bottom up.

Williams' first reaction on seeing so many sailors jumping off sinking ships into the flaming waters was to run to his launch and pick up survivors. He waited for a lull in the attack, then made his dash. But on arriving, he discovered that the boat was gone. Arthur Bryant had had the same idea, and as the first wave of attacking aircraft had passed over, he had jumped into the launch and headed out on his own rescue mission, showing no concern at all for his personal safety.

Matters were made more difficult for Bryant by the fact that the gearbox on the launch malfunctioned and the only working gear was reverse. Bryant was, therefore, forced to manoeuvre the vessel backwards.

Williams called out, asking him to come back and pick him up, but the gearbox fault made it awkward, and with wounded men in the water every minute counted. So Bryant continued on, alone, towards the survivors while the attack went on around him.

It seemed as if bombs were exploding everywhere, and, once or twice, a Japanese plane swooped down and let go with a burst of machine-gun fire. But Bryant never flinched — he went about his business, picking up survivors, pulling them from the water, and taking them back to the relative safety of shore.

Williams watched in awe as Bryant defied the frightening military might of the Japanese Air Force that morning. He had never seen anything like it. But then again, you did not meet men like Arthur Bryant every day. 'Steady as a rock and as dependable,' was how Williams had once described him.

As sailor after sailor struggled onto dry land, they had little time to notice, let alone thank, the man who had risked his own life to

Arthur Bryant, to whose unassuming courage many American sailors owed their lives

save theirs. But then Bryant was not the kind of man who would have looked for any thanks. In a way, it was just part of the job, another salvage job of sorts; besides, as far as Arthur Bryant was concerned, he was just doing what anyone would have done in the same circumstances.

Before the war was over, Bryant would face enemy fire on at least four other occasions, but it is his actions on that day in Darwin that so many of those who served with him and knew him well will remember.

Archibald 'Snowy' Halls
1893–1942
Dutiful telegraphist
Written by: Billy Marshall-Stoneking
Nominated by: Christopher A. Halls

On the morning of 19 February 1942, Father John McGrath, a priest at the Bathurst Island mission, was just starting his day when a faint, but deep, droning sound caught his attention. He rose from his desk and strolled to the window. Still unable to ascertain the source of the disturbance, he turned and went to the door.

A bright, sunny day greeted him. As he stepped off his verandah, he looked off into the west. Then, just above the horizon, he saw something that made his heart crack. An armada of aircraft composed of maybe seventy or eighty planes, flying in strict formation, filled the sky. There had, of course, been many formations of aircraft over Bathurst Island in those early days of the war — American Kitty Hawks in transit to Java and the like. But these were not Kitty Hawks; they were Japanese Zeros, and they were headed straight for Darwin.

Father McGrath ran into the house and was on the radio at once. He radioed a message to the Amalgamated Wireless station in Darwin. Lou Curnock, officer-in-charge at the station, took the message and then relayed it to the RAAF operations room where it was received at just after 9.30 am. For reasons which are still unclear, even today, nothing was done. The minutes ticked away.

Archibald T.R. Halls had already been on duty in the Darwin Post Office since before nine that morning, testing the telegraph circuit. The traffic had been extremely heavy with priority military messages, and Halls was experiencing some technical difficulties getting through to Adelaide. Then, shortly before ten, he established contact.

Some weeks earlier, the postal authority in South Australia had called for a volunteer to travel to Darwin, remove the town's communications network and re-establish it in Adelaide River, a small community 180 kilometres to the south. 'Snowy' Halls promptly volunteered and, as he was a Signal Corps veteran and a communications expert with first-hand knowledge of the Northern Territory, was given the job.

He arrived in Darwin on the day Singapore fell to the Japanese and went straight to work. Of course, it would take time to transfer operations, and until this could be done Halls had to keep the telegraph station running, so he and another man alternated shifts.

Scores of people passed in and out of the Post Office that morning between nine and ten, among them the writer, Douglas Lockwood. Years later, he recalled that 'few lingered under the verandah protecting the private mail boxes; there was an air of tension, as though the men and the few women going about their business were subconsciously aware of the imminent tragedy.'

If Halls had any premonition of impending danger he did not express it. He continued his conversation with Adelaide.

Then the first explosions from the Japanese attack aircraft rocked the harbour area. The postmaster and his employees, knowing that an attack was possible, had drilled themselves for this possibility, and quietly but quickly headed for the air-raid shelter. A man ducked his head into the telegraphist's office and shouted to Halls that they were under attack. Halls didn't need telling — he could hear bombs exploding all around him. He glanced up at the time and told the man to hurry on.

The man disappeared, but Halls stayed at his post, operating the morse key: 'There's another air raid alarm on...' he tapped out. And the bombs rained down.

The police station exploded into flames. Government House shook and nearly collapsed. Machine-gun fire from the Japanese planes strafed the streets. People ran for cover.

In the air-raid shelter at the post office, the postmaster and others huddled in fear. Halls was still not there.

Adelaide was receiving news of the attack as it was happening. Transmission engineer Frank O'Grady, in Adelaide, could hardly believe what he was hearing. But Halls was not a man to exaggerate. Halls tapped his morse key again:

'Sec,' (meaning wait a second). O'Grady waited, then the tapping continued; 'The Japanese are attacking us... I cannot stay any longer... I'll see you shortly.'

It was Halls' last message. Suddenly, the line went dead.

O'Grady made several attempts to re-establish contact but without success. Within minutes, news of the Japanese attack on Darwin raced across the country.

Snowy Halls, who died at his post in Darwin in 1942

Darwin was in turmoil. Everyone now expected an invasion. The population, frightened and confused, poured out of the town, heading south along the only escape route. Within a matter of minutes, Darwin had been transformed from a pleasant, easy-going community into an inferno. Ships were alight in the harbour; rubble and dead bodies were everywhere.

An ambulance pulled up outside the shattered post office, or the place where the post office had been. Several men had run over there after it had been hit and were searching the wreckage for survivors. A doctor jumped from the ambulance and ran over to enquire about the injured. 'There's nothing you can do here, doctor,' one of the men said, 'they're all dead.'

Later, the superintendent responsible for staffing the Darwin telegraph office commended Halls for his bravery and sacrifice. 'If it had not been for the goodness of this man,' he said, 'to stay and pass the message along, we wouldn't have known about the attack for a long time.'

Charlie One Lampungmeiua
c1920–1980
Tiwi coastwatcher
Written by: Niall Lucy
Nominated by: Trevor LaBrooy

Charlie One Lampungmeiua (also known as Tippakalippa), Tiwi coastwatcher, in full ceremonial paint-up for the Kulama *ceremony in 1972. Photograph by Trevor LaBrooy*

A group of about thirty Aborigines who patrolled a 1600 kilometre stretch of coastline in the remote north of Australia during the World War II played a little known but vital role in the defence of Australia. Recruited for their tracking skills and keen knowledge of the local environment, men like Charlie One Lampungmeiua were given weapons training by the RAN and put in charge of coastwatch duties around Bathurst and Melville Islands.

Charlie sometimes travelled in US submarines on reconnaissance missions in enemy waters around Timor, accompanying a small party ashore at night to collect intelligence data on Japanese shipping and troop movements. On many occasions Japanese patrols spotted the party and fierce gun battles ensued along the beaches before Charlie and the others escaped in their inflatable dinghy to the relative safety of their rendezvous with an awaiting American submarine.

More commonly, however, the Aboriginal coastwatchers patrolled the desolate Arafura coast in dug-out canoes. Equipped with a two-way radio and heavily armed with rifles and grenades, they scoured the hazardous tidal creeks teeming with crocodiles and the shark-infested seas for Allied and enemy airmen shot down in the region. On one occasion they rescued the crew of a Mitchell bomber who were forced to flee the wreckage of their plane when it crash landed on the northeast coast of Melville Island. Tracking the survivors several kilometres inland to their make-shift campsite of a parachute slung over a tree, the coastwatchers carried the injured men on a bush stretcher back to the beach where an amphibious aircraft took them to a military hospital in Darwin.

The coastwatchers were also responsible for locating nineteen enemy mines washed up on the shores of Melville Island, and made several important sightings of Japanese submarines and planes. So desperate was the Navy's shortage of ships and men that, were it not for the surveillance of these Aboriginal coastal patrols, enemy activities along the entire coastline of the Northern Territory might otherwise have gone unnoticed.

Through an oversight that would not have been tolerated had the coastwatchers been white, however, the Navy neglected to pay the Aboriginal heroes during their three years of war service. It was not until 1962, at a ceremony on Melville Island, that the RAN honoured its debt. The survivors each received a £10 cheque, with the balance of up to £190 being paid into their bank accounts by the Government.

Charlie One Lampungmeiua was at the ceremony, finally receiving the recognition he deserved. He died in 1980 on Melville Island.

Colin Fleming Brien
1923–

He survived his own execution
Written by: Tim Bowden
Nominated by: Olga Leaver Steele

On 9 February 1942, Private Colin Brien of the 2/19th Battalion was blasted by an exploding Japanese grenade. Stunned and slashed with some thirty shrapnel fragments, he became separated from his unit as the Australian and British forces fought their last desperate actions before conceding the 'impregnable' island fortress of Singapore to General Yamashita's Imperial Japanese Army.

For eleven days, Brien existed on his own in the jungle. 'I was suffering badly from wounds in the face, wrist, body and legs — severed veins, nerves and an artery.' He used up all his own field dressings, and scrounged others from dead soldiers' packs. While taking food from an abandoned Chinese house, he was rushed and seized by a Japanese platoon.

Private Brien was taken to a divisional intelligence headquarters

Top. Colin Brien as an 18-year-old private in the AIF 2/19th Battalion in Malaya in 1941, the year before his execution

Below. Colin Brien, family historian and retired company director, in 1985. 'I will never forgive and I will never forget'

and questioned. He was given some food, but no medical attention for his stinking wounds. On the evening of Saturday 28 February, he was put on the tray of a truck to be taken to the Changi Peninsula where some 100 000 captured British, Australian and Indian troops were being assembled. But his driver became lost, and returned to the divisional intelligence headquarters.

At eight next morning, two soldiers and a Japanese officer with a pistol in one hand and some cord in the other escorted him behind a Roman Catholic Convent and through light jungle into a small clearing.

'There I saw about twelve to fifteen Japanese officers with their swords, a platoon of Japanese soldiers and a freshly dug grave about three and a half feet deep with a Samurai sword sticking in the mound of earth. I was aware that something was going to happen to me'.

The Japanese officer searched Brien and threw his pay book, wallet and other possessions on the ground, but the Australian picked them up and put them back in his pockets. The Japanese officer said, 'You are going to meet your God.'

Brien was directed to sit with his feet projecting into the grave. His hands were tied behind him, his shirt unbuttoned and pulled away from the back of his neck, and a small face towel tied round his eyes as a blindfold. The Japanese officer bent Brien's head forward.

'Well, I thought to myself, this is the end, but I just couldn't really come face to face with it — but there was nothing I could do about it. I prayed to my God. Then I felt a heavy dull blow on the back of my neck and I felt myself falling into the grave.'

Colin Brien regained consciousness some hours later, buried in his own grave. He could feel a terrible wound at the back of his neck, and another between the eyes where he had probably been hit with a rifle butt. But the grave had been carelessly filled in and by wriggling and twisting he managed to get out, and stumble across the clearing to collapse into some tall *lalang* grass where he lay till nightfall.

Using the serrated edge of an empty fish tin, he cut his bound hands free and managed to get some water from a Chinese squatter's well. 'That bucked me up a lot, and I tried to wash myself. But that wasn't much of a success.'

As he lay by the well, his neck wound became fly-blown. 'That was annoying, but doctors told me later it helped saved my life because the maggots help prevent gangrene and infection.' An old Chinese woman found him, and brought him some hot, sweet, milk coffee and biscuits. No words were exchanged.

'I'd been the subject of this execution attempt on Sunday the first of March, and by the evening of the second I realised that if I remained any longer there, I'd just die of exhaustion and weakness. So I had to do something.' Concealing his fearful neck wound with his execution blindfold, Brien staggered from light jungle into the streets of the Galang area of Singapore, and gave himself up to Malay police. Turned over again to the Japanese (fortunately, a different group), he was questioned again, but lost consciousness during the interrogation. A British POW ambulance was called, and he was taken to the Changi POW hospital.

There, Colin Brien's tough constitution (and, he believes, his Irish background) helped him pull through, and he began the long process of recovery. After surviving three and a half years of semi-starvation in Changi prison camp, he was selected to be one of the ex-POWs to give evidence at the Far East International War Crimes Tribunal in 1946, where he was the first Australian witness.

Colin Brien committed no crime; he faced no trial; his execution was the chance result of a driver taking a wrong turn. And he lived. An accountant and company director in Papua New Guinea in the postwar period, Brien now suffers from poor health. He does not complain about his physical disabilities but admits to looking back on his experiences with some bitterness.

'I am an average Australian male and I have my likes and dislikes. But as far as I'm concerned, what happened during the war I will never forgive and I will never forget.'

Marjorie Jean Lyon
1905–1975
Lion by name and by nature
Written by: Suzy Baldwin
Nominated by: John Lyon

'I abandoned my home on Wednesday, January 29th, 1942. The orders to evacuate Johore Bahru came on the evening of Monday the 27th whilst I was busy in the Blood Bank. They were not unexpected, as the Army Hospital...had been evacuated two days before and we had been handling both civil and military casualties. It was, however, a great shock to realise that we had to walk out and leave our homes.'

Dr Marjorie Lyon was one of the most highly qualified women doctors of her time. A surgeon specialising in obstetrics and gynaecology with additional qualifications in tropical medicine, she had been in Johore Baharu since she joined the Malayan Medical Service in 1937.

But by the early days of 1942, the Japanese were closing in. It was time to leave. As always, Dr Lyon's primary concern was for her patients. Only after the last one had been safely loaded and the lorries had driven away did she pack her car and follow. She was the last woman to cross the Causeway into Singapore, where her staff and patients were incorporated into the General Hospital.

On the morning of 13 February, all women members of the Malayan Medical Service were ordered to be on the quay at 2.30 pm with such luggage as they could carry. As there was now a surplus of underemployed male doctors at the hospital, Dr Lyon and her English friend and fellow-surgeon, Dr Elsie Crowe, decided to comply.

At the wharf there was chaos with bombs dropping almost continually. The two doctors had just been loaded onto a small, grossly overcrowded boat when twenty-seven Japanese bombers attacked the harbour, killing many passengers still on the wharf and causing two deaths and thirty casualties on board. While the two surgeons attended the wounded, their boat, still under fire, sailed out of Singapore Harbour.

The next day, near tiny Pom Pom Island, their boat was bombed.

With the vessel burning fiercely and sinking fast, Marjorie and Elsie jumped into the water 'with not a life belt between us'. As they swam for the island the bombers came back for another round. 'A terrific concussion and an almighty blow to my belly seemed to come instantaneously and I thought "Well, I'm done for." Then Elsie disappeared in a sort of whirlpool. I dived after her and grasped her dress and began to drag her up. Her dress tore at the shoulders and I lost her, but finally got her by the hair. She was unconscious for a few moments, and there were huge black bruises round both her eyes. Blood was trickling from her right nostril and I thought for a moment she was dead. The waves from the bomb were terrific and I had much difficulty in keeping our heads above water...at one stage I was sure we could not make it. However we managed somehow and finally grated on the shore.'

Although in great pain and bleeding from her stomach wound, Marjorie's attention was on Elsie Crowe who, it was now apparent, had suffered a fractured skull. Over the next few days, Elsie became desperately ill and 'looked like dying'. As Sir Albert Coates, who was to work with Marjorie some weeks later, wrote: 'But for the constant attention of Dr Lyon, she would never have survived.'

Pom Pom Island had no edible vegetation, virtually no water and no inhabitants apart from the 700 or so shipwrecked men, women and children who had managed to reach shore. Of these, about 100 were seriously wounded. With the help of some British nurses, Marjorie took charge of casualties, trudging painfully between the groups scattered around the island and always returning to Elsie Crowe.

Over the next few days, the survivors were rescued by an odd assortment of vessels. By the fourth night, all the women had gone except for Dr Lyon, the nurses, and sixty wounded, many of them, like Elsie Crowe, stretcher cases. On the fifth day, five British RNR appeared with a small captured Japanese fishing boat and picked them up. After 'a nightmare journey' of sixteen hours in which no one could move and most of the passengers were constantly seasick, the party reached the east coast of Sumatra.

Singapore had fallen on 15 February, the day after the bombing near the island. If the Pom Pom survivors could reach Padang on the west coast in time, they would be picked up by British ships sent to rescue the refugees who had escaped from Singapore. Those survivors who could travel on local buses made it in time and were safely conveyed to India. But stretcher cases could not be moved across Sumatra so quickly. Although warned that she was almost certain to be taken as a POW, Marjorie Lyon, refused to leave her patients.

The bedraggled group that landed on Sumatra was destitute, emaciated after five days of thirst and starvation, and scarcely clothed. Some of the women had torn up their dresses for bandages and now wore only their underwear. They had no medical supplies, no food, and no money, but in the two weeks in which they made their way across Sumatra with their casualties, only one person offered help — Mrs Hawthorne, an American missionary, who proved to be a practical Christian of extraordinary generosity and kindness.

Dr Lyon's party arrived in Padang two days after the British ships had left. When the Dutch refused to take the wounded into their hospital, the Canadian matron of the Salvation Army Hospital came to

Dr. Marjorie Lyon (centre) with a graduating midwifery class, Malaya 1947

the rescue. Dr Lyon and Dr Crowe were at this hospital with the female wounded when the Japanese arrived on 17 March.

For the next three and a half years, Marjorie Lyon was Camp Medical Officer. Assisted by Dr Crowe and seven British nurses, she was responsible for the health of about fifty British and 2500 Dutch interned women and children. The internees were moved from camp to camp, and finally to Bangkinang, 350 kilometres away in the middle of the jungle, where they slept fifty to a hut. The camps were all appallingly overcrowded and revoltingly insanitary, food was usually starvation rations (except for those with something to trade on the black market) and there was never enough water. Under these conditions, there were epidemics of diphtheria among the children, and tropical diseases — especially dysentery and malaria — flourished.

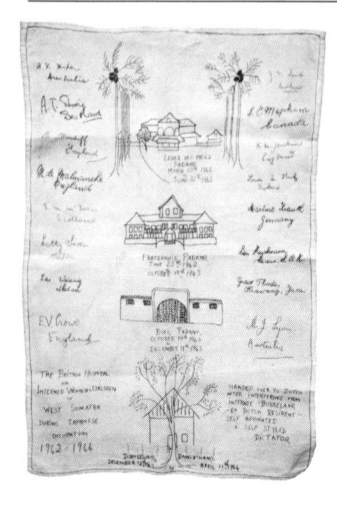

A cloth embroidered by Dr Lyon's medical team, showing their succession of internment camps and revealing old hostilities. Completed after release. Photograph by R. G. Hann

By the time they reached Bangkinang there were never fewer than 400 people at a time suffering malarial attacks.

Another feature of the camps, particularly in the first eighteen months, was the hostility between the British and the Dutch, some of whom objected to Dr Lyon's uncompromising attitude towards patient welfare. Marjorie organised the distribution of rations so that children and the sick were given priority, upsetting women who wanted to hoard precious milk powder; she insisted on quiet in the vicinity of diphtheria patients; and in an attempt to stop the spread of infection, she wrote sternly to the Director of one of the campsites — the Fraterhuis (monastery) — demanding the removal of the fraters and 'their attendant women and children, cats, dogs and parrots' from the hospital buildings. When one faction, claiming to represent the Dutch Camp Committee, complained about her and her British staff, Marjorie wrote an acerbic letter which she made public. The response to her offer to leave for the British Camp was an avalanche of letters from other Dutch women begging her to stay.

Marjorie wrote a daily diary — now transcribed onto 1000 typewritten pages — and kept all her correspondence from the camp. From this it seems, at times, as if she kept the Dutch alive in spite of themselves. But keep them alive she did. In the three and a half years in which she was responsible for their lives, there were only 160 deaths, mostly among the very young and the very old. This outstanding record was a tribute not only to Dr Lyon's great skill and her absolute dedication to her patients, but also to her extraordinary courage.

Although tiny and birdlike, Marjorie was a lion by nature as well as name. She stood up to the Japanese with the same unyielding toughness that she showed to anyone who attempted to impede her care of the sick. At great risk to her own safety, she would imperiously order her captors to provide medicine and dressings and, more often than not, the Japanese would eventually provide at least part of what she had asked for. One of the Dutch internees recalls: 'Dr Lyon was only small but she gave the Japanese hell. She was always demanding medicine and getting slapped for asking.' Dr Lyon, in an account written in 1945, describes these exchanges with characteristic matter-of-factness: 'I had a reputation for being able to handle the Japanese, but sometimes it didn't work and then I got knocked about a bit, though I never had a formal beating up.'

On 19 August 1945, the Japanese told the internees that the war was over. Marjorie immediately wrote to the Japanese commandant and demanded repatriation. On 1 September, Dr Lyon, Dr Crowe and the fifty British women left Sumatra for Padang. Although no-one had been tortured or executed in this camp, it was officially graded at the end of the war as the second worst in Sumatra.

Majorie Lyon's sense of responsibility towards her patients continued after her return to Australia. She wrote personal letters to the families of those who had died, and sent on last letters and personal possessions. One woman's watch and ring she had carried with her for three years, from camp to camp. It was, as the grateful recipient wrote to Marjorie, 'a labour of loving kindness'. It also revealed a kind of fierce honour that was characteristic of this uncompromising woman. In the last months, the British women were so desperate for food that they were trading their cherished wedding rings — their last possessions — on the black market. Marjorie, however, would have starved to death rather than betray a trust by trading the small treasures of the dead.

Marjorie was forced to abandon her surgical work after the war as the malnutrition of the camps had ruined her eyesight. However, she remained with the Malayan Medical Service until 1950, then worked with the Western Australia Health Department until her death in 1975.

Dr Elsie Crowe survived her fractured skull, dengue, and near-fatal dysentery. Now ninety-three, she has just moved into a nursing home in England. In a recent letter to Marjorie's family she speaks of the brave, brilliant and prickly Dr Lyon. 'She was a completely dedicated doctor. She pretended to dislike people en masse, but each and every patient was sacrosant. I have never met anyone of such integrity and I am proud to have been her friend.'

Joyce Tweddell
1916–

Forgotten prisoners of war
Written by: Suzy Baldwin
Nominated by: Margaret Taylor

Sister Joyce Tweddell was a nurse with 2/10th Australian General Hospital (AGH), sent to Malaya at the beginning of 1941. A year later, on 10 January 1942, the unit had to flee from its hospital in Malacca to a former boys' school three kilometres north of Singapore. Through at least four air raids a day, the operating theatres of this temporary hospital worked round the clock and patients flowed over into neighbouring houses.

On 31 January the causeway between Singapore Island and the mainland was blown up. On 10 February the order for the evacuation of all nurses was approved. Since none would volunteer to leave as requested, evacuation lists were drawn up and the nurses were sent off in two groups on 12 January. The first group left in the morning. The remaining sixty-five nurses, including Joyce Tweddell, continued to work until ordered onto the *Vyner Brooke* in the afternoon. Equipped to carry twelve passengers, the ship left Singapore Harbour carrying over 300, mostly civilian women and children.

The *Vyner Brooke* was sunk two days later. After making sure that every civilian was off the burning ship, the nurses swam for Banka Island — and capture by the Japanese. Joyce Tweddell and four other staff nurses were in the water for sixteen hours.

One group of twenty-three nurses, some of them injured, all of them in uniform with armbands, landed on the island during the night of 14 February. They put up a large red cross to show that they were non-combatants and began to take care of the wounded. However, the nurses discovered that Red Cross armbands had no effect on Japanese treatment of them when about twenty Japanese soldiers appeared, ordered the women into the sea and shot them. The sole suvivor, Vivian Bullwinkel, was left for dead. She eventually rejoined the other nurses and all were taken to the Chinese 'coolie' barracks, the first of the crowded, filthy and insanitary camps in which they were to spend the next three and a half years. Of the sixty-five Australian Army nurses who left Singapore harbour on the *Vyner Brooke*, only thirty-two were still alive. By the time they were rescued on 16 September 1945 from their last camp in the middle of a rubber plantation in Sumatra, their numbers had dwindled to twenty-four.

The nurses shared their camps with British and Dutch civilian women and children. There was the usual friction amongst some of the other internees, but from the very beginning the nurses were a strong, mutually supportive group. Humour and resilience prevailed.

Conditions in the camps were never less than appalling: food, water, clothing and medicine were always scarce, soap was non-existent and sanitation unspeakable. There was no privacy and the women were often harrassed by the Japanese. At one stage there was considerable pressure put on the nurses to become sexual partners for their captors and food was withdrawn as punishment for their refusal to cooperate. However, after two weeks of the nurses' implacability, the Japanese abandoned the idea and put their 'white coolies' to other kinds of enforced labour.

Sister Joyce Tweddell, Army nurse, in 1941 (top), and (below) in Brisbane in 1947, still recovering from her imprisonment after a year in hospital

As a result of malnutrition and conditions — bad enough in the beginning but progressively worse with each camp — the nurses' health deteriorated. One in four died. By the beginning of 1945, there were deaths daily. Joyce Tweddell, one of the youngest, suffered constantly from severe amoebic dysentery. By the time of liberation, she had lost seven stone.

At the end of the war, the Japanese did not admit to the existence of the nurses' camp. It was eventually found, largely through the efforts of Haydon Lennard — senior war correspondent for the ABC and the BBC — and a small flight crew, from information provided by other POWs. As they had hoped, the nurses had been sighted in their tattered uniforms which they wore every time they were moved from one camp to another. (They also wore full uniform for burials, on which occasions their Japanese guards were moved to take off their hats and bow their heads.)

After considerable detective work in monsoonal rain by the small band of rescuers, the camp was found and the women released. Flight Officer K. Brown reported that the smell alone was vivid indication of the conditions under which the nurses had been forced to live. He described the camp commandant as the most ruthless man he had ever set eyes on.

The nurses were taken to the local railway station where a train had been fitted out with bedding for them. Most were desperately ill, some could only shuffle because of the bloated knees that are a sure symptom of beriberi and some, including Joyce Tweddell, were 'little more than skeletons'. Yet the Australian Army nurses, as Catherine Kenny tells in *Captives*, her book on the nurses (UQP 1986), 'dressed in their rags of uniforms and, looking terrible and smelling worse... walked onto the train.' 'We wouldn't let anyone help us,' recalls Joyce Tweddell. 'It was a matter of pride.'

The nurses' re-entry into the world caused shock on both sides. Nurse Florence Trotter (now Mrs Syer) laughs: 'We thought we didn't look too bad, but from everyone else's reaction, we obviously looked pretty ghastly.' Flight Sister Chandler, who went into the camp with the rescue team, had trained with Joyce Tweddell at the Brisbane General Hospital. She did not recognise her friend. When the nurses arrived at the hospital in Singapore, Catherine Kenny writes, 'there was almost a riot...as male patients jumped out of bed and yelled abuse and threats at the Japanese for the condition of the women'. The story of the Banka Island massacre of the twenty-two nurses, kept secret during the war for fear of Japanese reprisals, was finally released to a horrified public. 'We all knew about it,' says Joyce Tweddell, 'but for three and a half years nobody mentioned it. We knew we were dead if we did.'

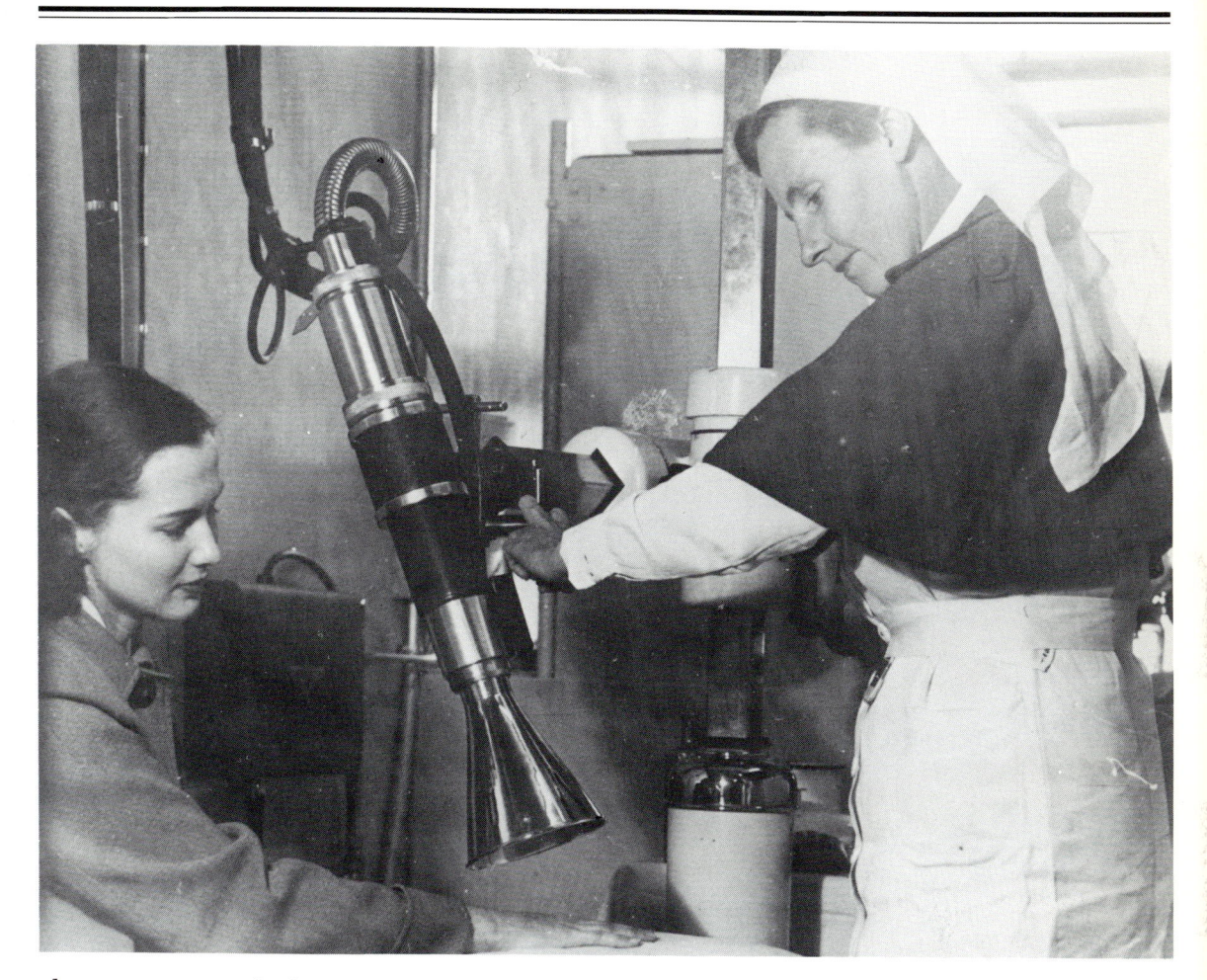

'One thing that particularly hurt us when we reached Singapore was that the army burnt everything — the things we had made in camp, notebooks, recipe books particularly. We thought they were going to fumigate them but they burned them. We were very upset: we'd treasured them for so long.'

Fed decently once again after four years of malnutrition, the nurses blew up 'as if we'd been pumped up with a bicycle pump'. The drama of this physical state was matched only by their sudden deflation some days later, 'as if we'd been pricked with a pin'.

Back in Australia, Joyce Tweddell had to learn to walk again and spent almost a year in hospital recovering from amoebic dysentery. She then joined the Queensland Radium Institute where she was Chief

Sister Tweddell (top), radiographer at the Queensland Radium Institute in 1949 and (below) at her 70th birthday party in 1986

Radiographer until her retirement in 1978.

After her release, Joyce Tweddell wrote: 'The comradeship and feeling for each other will remain and if possible we will always help each other.' For the twenty nurses who are still alive, this is as true today as it was in 1946.

Alfredo Jose Dos Santos
1899–1971
'The Great Rebel'
Written by: Billy Marshall-Stoneking
Nominated by: Antonio Dos Santos

Alfredo Dos Santos, 33-year-old plantation manager in Portuguese Timor, c.1933

The men smoked and played cards. They did not speak. Outside, they heard the truck pull up. Alfredo Jose Dos Santos threw down a card and looked at the other men around the table.

'Remember,' he said, 'don't get up; just keep playing.'

Suddenly, the door burst open and several Japanese soldiers entered. They glared at Dos Santos. He asked, casually, what the problem was, not expecting an answer.

The soldiers searched the house — the kitchen, the bedrooms, the attic. Dos Santos offered the Japanese officer a cigarette. he knew why they had come. At last, unable to find what they were looking for, the soldiers left.

Dos Santos pushed himself away from the table. A big smile formed on his face. Then he leaned forward and peered under the table. Strapped underneath were the guns the Japanese had been seeking — rifles and revolvers. The other men looked back at Dos Santos in amazement. Only Alfredo had that kind of cool courage — to sit in a room so calmly with the possibility of discovery and death so close.

But then Alfredo Jose Dos Santos had always been that kind of man. He had never tolerated injustice or bullying from anyone. In his native Portugal, he had been the major force behind the implementation of that country's first trade union. He had seen the need for improving the working conditions of his fellow countrymen, and he had done something about it. And because of his anti-fascism and opposition to the dictator Salazar, he had been deported. That was how he had ended up in Timor. The authorities in Portugal breathed easier knowing Dos Santos was not around.

When Japanese totalitarianism extended its power onto Rai Timor, Alfred's reaction was automatic. Fascism in whatever form, whether European or oriental, had to be resisted. To do this he helped form the famous 'International Brigade'.

During the Japanese occupation of Portuguese Timor in World War II, Dos Santos and 'The Brigade' fought an all-but-forgotten guerilla war against the invaders. The Japanese were triumphant everywhere and members of the Brigade had everything to lose in resisting them, but resist them they did — harrassing the Japanese camps, stealing their petrol, and throwing unguarded anti-aircraft guns into Dili harbour.

It just was not in Alfredo's nature to give up without a fight.

'One night [Alfredo and his men] lifted an entire wireless station — transmitter, receiver and generator — from under Japanese noses in Dili.' When asked how they had managed to get it past the sentries, Pedro — one of Alfredo's men — drew a bony finger across his throat and made a gurgling sound. 'It took thirty natives and ten horses to carry it back to Australian headquarters.'

In the end, the Japanese put a bounty on Dos Santos's head, and he became a hunted man. Eventually, with the assistance of the huge radio set they had stolen, a massive evacuation of the island was organised. Badly wounded, Dos Santos — along with a contingent of Australian soldiers from the 2/2nd Commandos — was able to escape what would otherwise have been certain death.

Several years later, Alfredo was filmed at the head of a parade in Sydney, bearing a banner which read 'Mussolini, Hitler, Salazar — All Cousins.' A print of this was one of Alfredo's prize possessions. 'Lesser men would have played it cool and quiet,' a friend of his wrote later. 'Though personally a quiet man, an intense spark burned in him. He not only believed in the Brotherhood of Man, but he was always prepared to bear witness to his belief.'

When the great rebel died in Sydney in 1971, his mourning comrades could only echo the priest's valediction in the language of the country that had expelled him so long ago: 'Vai com Deus, Alfredo.'

Alfredo Dos Santos in later life, an admired and respected Australian citizen

Ronald Taylor
1920–1942
Went down with his ship
Written by: David Millar
Nominated by: Dellarenza Pezzi

The war in the Pacific was going badly. Fleeing from the apparently unbeatable Japanese, a small convoy was making its way from Borneo to Perth, protected by the naval sloop HMAS *Yarra*.

As the tropical night gave way to the dawn of 4 March 1942, a number of silhouettes appeared on the horizon and the air above the convoy was pierced by the shriek of incoming shells, which threw huge plumes of water around the ships. The *Yarra* immediately began to lay down a protective smoke screen, while its clanging alarms summoned everyone to action stations. Running to number one gun was Leading Seaman Ronald 'Buck' Taylor. A Port Melbourne-born man, he had since a child been fascinated by the warships that docked near his home and had, at the age of seven, been appointed mascot to HMAS *Margaret*. It had surprised no-one when, at sixteen, Ronald Taylor had joined the RAN.

Now he watched while seven Japanese warships headed at thirty knots towards the slow moving *Yarra*, her six inch guns pathetically ineffectual against the larger, eight inch guns of the Japanese. The *Yarra* had but one option — to steer straight towards the enemy in

(Above) Leading Seaman Ronald Taylor

(Right) Ronald Taylor aged eight, mascot to HMAS 'Margaret', outside Melbourne's Parliament House

the hope both of closing the range and of giving the rest of the convoy time to scatter and make for Perth.

Half an hour later it was all over. The *Yarra* lay inert in the water, her decks splintered and blistering, her interior a twisted shambles. Only one of her three guns was operative and most of her crew lay dead.

When the order came to 'Abandon Ship,' the thirty-four survivors began to slip into the sea. All, that is, except 'Buck' Taylor. He refused to leave his gun, and single-handedly continued to fire it for another half hour in a futile but splendid show of defiance.

The end came soon enough. A bomb from a Japanese seaplane exploded close by. Her back broken, the *Yarra* slid under the surface of the water, carrying her stubborn gunner with her.

'Buck' Taylor's mother never forgot. On her death a year later, her ashes were scattered upon the Java Sea to join those of her son.

Frank Smallhorn
1922–1944

'Never a dull moment'
Written by: Suzy Baldwin
Nominated by: George Booth

Dawn 19 May 1942. Just south of Darwin, Air Ambulance No.2 takes off from Batchelor Hospital to pick up an Airforce casualty from Groote Island in the Gulf of Carpentaria. The pilot-navigator, barely twenty years old, is Sergeant Frank Smallhorn RAAF. He is accompanied by a nursing orderly, Corporal Philip Bronk, and an Air Force radio operator, ACI George Booth, at twenty-six the 'old man' of the crew.

Their plane, a Gannet, is probably the ugliest craft ever to fly. But its looks are not its only problem. The name of this ill-fated species of aircraft proves to be prophetic: the gannet is a seabird noted for its spectacular dives into the ocean.

At 11.00 am the coast below is barely visible. Through gaps in the low cloud, Frank, Phil and George see 'an absolute maze of creeks, swamps, islands, peninsulas and mangroves, none of which even remotely resembled our map. '"George!" yells Frank above the noise of the engines, "I haven't the faintest idea where we are."'

George attempts to make radio contact but all his efforts, including an SOS, meet with silence. Petrol is low. '"We'll go down for a look-see", announces Frank,' and heads the Gannet for what looks like a large flat area of grassland.

The plane touches down, lurches, then, at a ground speed of seventy kilometres per hour, 'puts her nose down and flips over onto her back'. The three men, bruised, scratched, but otherwise uninjured, scramble out onto the wing and survey the scene. They are in the middle of a vast swamp somewhere in Arnhem Land, lost in one of the wildest and most inhospitable regions on the face of the earth.

Thirty-two days later, 'much the worse for wear, but nevertheless intact', the three fall onto the beach at Milingimbi. They have travelled — travailed, as earlier epics in English are able to say, connoting a journey achieved by hard labour against great odds — 312 kilometres, most of it by sea.

Forty-five years later, George Booth writes their story. His book, *33 Days* (Greenhouse, 1988), recounts a truly epic journey.

At first, the three airmen assume that it is only a matter of time before they are rescued. They know that there will be a seven-day air search, so they spread a parachute on top of the swamp reeds, Frank makes a bonfire and they wait. For seven days, 'tormented by flies, mosquitoes and sandflies and harassed by mounting despair', they eke out their emergency rations as they look for the search planes that never come.

'We discovered that the easiest way to stay reasonably cheerful was to keep up a lively discussion about anything — the war...the Darwin shemozzle — and religion.' Religion becomes a subject of much affectionately irreverent joking between Frank, a Roman Catholic, and George, a Methodist. As they later explain to a rather shocked Rev Ellemor at Milingimbi, '"We have developed ecumenical banter to a fine art."'

However, attempts to remain cheerful do not obscure the obvious — things are looking grim. Phil and George make an agreement that, when food and water are gone, they will use the morphia in Phil's medical kit to 'soothe our last few hours. Phil and I both felt this made sense. Frank, however, thought otherwise. "Look here, you buggers! We're getting out of here if I have to kick you all the way home!" '

It is this refusal of Frank's 'to countenance defeat at any price' that saves them. Many times during the journey, George and Phil, utterly defeated, are kept going by the sheer strength of Frank's will and it is this indomitable spirit that is responsible for the first stage of this epic voyage — their escape from the swamp.

Twice during the first five days, Frank treks across almost a kilometre of squashy swamp to explore what they hope is a river but turns out to be a muddy creek, its banks forty metres of impassable mud. It is a ghastly journey, a three-hour struggle throught waist-deep mud that leaves Phil and George, each of whom goes once with Frank, utterly exhausted and demoralised.

By day 9, all hope of rescue has gone and there seems no possible escape. George and Phil are utterly wretched but Frank refuses to be beaten. He insists upon going back to the creek one more time to see if he can find some way across. George thinks it's so loony that he goes with him.

An hour later, the two stare ahead in disbelief. The muddy creek has become a fast-flowing tidal river.

'Simultaneously we saw daylight. "Build a bloody raft and go out with the river!" Frank shouts. "You bloody bewdy!" '

Frank's plan is simple but he is the only one capable of sustained physical effort. 'In the searing heat, Frank hacked the four petrol tanks from the Gannet and, using slender saplings for a framework, constructed a raft which he christened the "Santa Maria".'

The raft 'floats like a cork'. Frank and Phil position themselves on the front tanks, but George is less fortunate. 'To maintain balance, I had to sit on a slender sapling midway between the two rear tanks...with my backside barely four inches above the water.' The painful state of George's rear for many months afterwards turns out to be only one of the liabilities of this position.

'In the late morning, I half-turned, expecting to push the raft free from yet another threatening mud-flat. I had barely noticed an old dead tree trunk until it suddenly developed life — and legs — and appeared to come straight at me!' George sits frozen with fear while five long metres of Australian salt-water crocodile — 'the nastiest creature on earth' — dash past him, barely missing him in a lunge for the water.

'The great ugly brute — and some of his friends — trailed us downstream for a hundred metres...We saw forty or fifty but...they were either not hungry or not very bright.'

George is haunted by the first huge crocodile for the rest of the journey. Every night Frank comforts him as he screams in his sleep.

About midnight, the drone of mosquitoes and the barking of the

Matui, Chief of Elcho Island and 'an unforgettable leader'. 1942

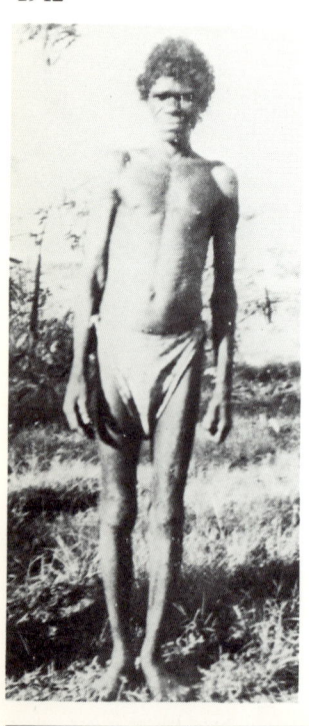

crocs gives way to deep silence. The raft has been swept into the sea. As it sits becalmed, free of the swamps at last, the dark stillness is broken only by Frank's gentle snoring. '"The sleep of the Just, or the just buggered?" George asks Phil.'

The next morning, undaunted by a huge white pointer shark that cruises beneath them (' "Never a dull moment" '), Frank rigs up a sail from the parachute and, as he compares passing islands and mainland coastline with his map, triumphantly announces that he knows where they are — ' "Arnhem Bay!" ' They now understand why no search planes found them — they were probably 160 kilometres off course. ' "Frank", I said with a grin, "what a great bloke you are — and what a bloody awful navigator!" '

Frank grins back and plots their route. They will head for Elcho Island where, according to the map, there is a mission station. But between them and Elcho is Flinders Peninsula.

Heavy surf and vicious rocks make the landing on Flinders a nightmare. As the only surfer, George is in charge. He decides that they will tie everything, including themselves, to the raft, catch a big wave, and ride it in. The plan is simple and effective, but George has underestimated the odds against them.

Tossed like twigs in the violent sea and hurled against rocks, they somehow reach the shallows, still attached by parachute cord to the raft, which is, amazingly, unharmed. Half drowned, they stagger ashore and, after thirty-six hours without food, 'thirty-six hours of crocodiles, sharks, gales and shipwreck', they collapse into an exhausted sleep. But, George recalls, 'as sleep claimed me I was vaguely aware that someone had lit a fire — a big, warm, comforting fire'. Having, like the others, crawled out of the sea more dead than alive, Frank has once again managed the impossible.

Next morning, having consumed the last of their food rations, they look for food and water. No water, but periwinkles are to become their staple diet for many days.

Although losing weight dramatically and steadily weakening, 'food seemed to be the least of our problems'. However, water is crucial and they have almost run out. On the raft they had sucked their shirt buttons to fight thirst. Now they ration themselves to five mouthfuls a day.

Apart from thirst, their biggest problem is how to sail the raft along the rocky Flinders Peninsula without damaging the buoyancy tanks. They can only leave their cove by waiting for the midnight tide out when there is no breeze to blow them back. Four nights in succession they try, pushing the raft and swimming in the dark, but each time they drift helplessly back to the rocks. On the fifth day (Day 15 of the journey), Frank has a better idea: ' "We'll row our way out." '

At 1:00 the next morning, with Frank-made oars, George and Frank row frantically through boiling surf in complete darkness and are at last out in the bay again. By dawn, 'wretched beyong belief', they row towards a beach for a much-needed rest. Seeing what they take to be 'large areas of flat rock just below surface', the three step overboard to wade ashore. Their mistake is agonisingly apparent — they find their legs grasped in 'the needle-like embrace' of jagged coral. 'We endured agony for only twenty minutes but it seemed like an eternity.'

Bleeding, despondent and barely able to walk, they set off again the next day. 'We were now not only much more listless...but our

'The famous Smallhorn grin'. Sergeant Frank Smallhorn. 1942

optimism had been severely blunted.'

Their spirits are suddenly lifted by a brief stay on Alger Island. Phil discovers a fresh water spring — a timely find as they have drunk the last of their existing water the night before — and Frank, whose marksmanship is not his strongest point, shoots a wild duck (' "unluckiest bird in Arnhem Land", comments George') which George makes into delicious soup. After their earlier experiences, 'it was almost...a holiday at the seaside'.

They eventually reach Elcho and set off to find the mission, wading now, and pushing the raft. But after two painful days they are forced to abandon the faithful 'Santa Maria' and all but the most vital survival gear.

On Day 24, 'the desire to lie down and sleep was almost overpowering. Phil was at times mildly incoherent. All I seem to remember was Frank's encouragement...Phil and I were just about finished. Perhaps one more day.'

Suddenly, they see a single set of fresh footprints. 'Like Robinson Crusoe, we stared in disbelief.'

By the middle of the next day — Day 25— 'we were completely exhausted. Only Frank had the strength to forage for food. Only he remembered that we had not really eaten for two days.'

Within three kilometres of the northern end of Elcho, they find more footprints. Following them, they come across a great new canoe carved from a huge tree. ' "This is it, chaps,' Frank announced... "George, break out the champagne!" '

George and Phil by now cannot stand unaided. At this point of collapse, 'we saw him: a lone Aborigine with a baby on his shoulders,

A miserable George Booth, radio operator and later teller of the tale, surveys the endless swamp, somewhere in Arnhem Land, May 1942. The three airmen and this film returned home after 33 days in the wilderness. The Gannet has never been recovered

striding purposefully in our direction.'

This saviour is Matui, Chief of Elcho Island. But his news is a shock for the three airmen: the mission has left Elcho and the nearest European is now at Milingimbi, 160 kilometres away.

Matui, however, agrees to help and has some of his tribe float the new canoe. After a false start, when the new boat capsizes, dumping the men and their few remaining possessions into the sea again, they eventually set off for Milingimbi. Six hot, uncomfortable, frustrating days later — days of Herculean effort by Matui — they see a light flickering on a beach.

'Five hundred metres — two hundred — fifty: our canoe grounded on the sands of Milingimbi. I was unable to move and felt wretchedly ill. Muttering, Frank climbed awkwardly to his feet. "Hail Mary, Mother of God, Blessed...Hail Mary, Mother... Hail Mary..."

'Frank was incoherent. Then, sobbing like a child, he collapsed in the arms of the missionary. As Matui's powerful arms lifted me from the canoe, everything went blank.'

The three men are flown back to Batchelor, where they are interviewed by fourteen war correspondents. Where the story is run at all, strict wartime censorship prevails and no names or places are mentioned. Phil spends a year in hospital in a successful attempt to save his leg from the effects of 'that horrendous wading at Flinders Point'.

George and his young wife spend his leave in a house in the middle of an orange grove and George's nightmares gradually fade. After the war he returns to teaching and he and his wife buy the house in which they still live. They name it 'Matui'.

Frank Smallhorn serves in No 2 Air Ambulance for another two years and survives two more forced landings. Late in 1944, to his great delight, he is promoted and sent on a conversion course at a Beaufighter Training Unit near Newcastle.

In the late afternoon of 7 November 1944, a Beaufighter returning from a cross-country training flight is hit by a vicious southerly. 'There were no survivors, no sign of wreckage. Frank's body was recovered from the ocean a fortnight later.' He was just twenty-three.

Geoffrey Hampden Vernon
1882–1946
Doctor of the Kokoda Trail
Written by: David Millar
Nominated by: H. E. (Lynn) Clark

At first, the newly-arrived medical officer with the 39th Battalion slept soundly on his sofa. Perhaps it was his deafness, a legacy from World War I, but it didn't take long for the sound of the attack to register in his consciousness and he was up and tending to the wounded.

A hand-held kerosene lamp gave him all the light he needed to

Captain Geoffrey Vernon, with his inevitable cigarette. Saved lives in two World Wars and cared for the Papuan carriers

operate and dress the wounds, but it also provided a target for the Japanese machinegunner. Suddenly, bullets began to scythe through the roof and to progress ominously down the walls. 'Damn those rats,' the doctor cursed under his breath, and continued his work.

Threading its way across the Owen Stanley Range, the Kokoda Trail runs for nearly one hundred kilometres northeast of Port Moresby in Papua New Guinea. Even today, tourists do not find it a casual stroll — one must be extremely fit and very well prepared. But during World War II, it was a virtual hell for thousands of Australian infantrymen and Papuan natives who had come to the aid of the Allies in their struggle against the Japanese.

Here, one of the bloodiest campaigns of the entire war was fought out in jungles, along razorback ridges, across slippery spurs and fierce river crossings. Nearly 6000 Australian men lost their lives, but they turned the Japanese back and, with great bravery, changed the course of the war in that part of the Pacific.

One of the most intriguing and, in some ways, unexpected heroes of the campaign was Captain Geoffrey Vernon, the deaf sixty-year-old doctor who had lied about his age so that he might again serve his country. In World War I, he had been awarded the Military Cross for bravery. Making his way behind the Turkish lines, with enemy bullets whizzing round him, he had rescued a wounded Australian soldier and virtually carried him back to a field hospital. Vernon was the kind of man who acted where others might have faltered.

At the end of World War I he had turned his back on a comfortable life and headed for New Guinea. There, he tried his hand at gold mining, then bought a plantation where he grew rubber, kapoc and coconuts. When war broke out again, Vernon immediately volunteered, and became the oldest man in the Australian forces in New Guinea.

Even men half his age found the Kokoda rough going, but Vernon never complained. He had a job to do, and he'd do it. Carrying his two triangular bandages — one containing drugs and dressings, the other his surgical instruments — he traversed the rugged wilderness, keeping up with his battalion, 'up on our hands and bellies, down on our backsides'.

As the campaign continued, the Kokoda Trail deteriorated as thousands of trudging troops turned it into a quagmire of squelching mud. They littered its edges with empty cans, filled its mountain streams with soap from the washing of thousands of sweaty bodies, and made latrines that swarmed with flies. No wonder Vernon contracted malaria. But, despite the headaches and listlessness, he struggled on, caring for the wounded soldiers — and their Papuan carriers.

Because the Australians were unable to truck supplies, Papuans were used as bearers. Hundreds of them formed ant-like columns, carrying upon their backs the supplies that sustained the infantrymen. The cost in physical terms was enormous. Blistered and bruised feet were common, as were chafed shoulders and exhaustion. Appalled by the plight of the carriers, Vernon cajoled, humoured and argued with his fellow Australians to give the bearers a fairer deal.

One evening Vernon sat down to have a smoke. In the jungles along the Kokoda there was a scarcity of cigarette papers, so it had become his usual practice to use anything that came to hand — from toilet paper to a piece torn out of an old newspaper. He had just rolled his cigarette when 'a decrepit old native collapsed on the ground. I was shocked when I tested the weight of his load. An officer standing by told me he was only shamming, but I could see that in a few more days of such overwork, he would have left his bones on the mountains.'

The conditions of the carriers caused him as much, if not more, concern than that of the Australian wounded, and he was furious when he observed some infantrymen dumping their packs and even their rifles on top of the carriers' own burdens. When he discovered that the carriers' food ration was little more than a meal of plain rice, and that their only protection against the shivering discomfort of the night was one blanket for every two men, he was incensed.

Pilfering his own medical supplies, defying witnesses to report him, he did everything he could to ease the carriers' burdens. Finally, with the support of a large number of Australian troops, Vernon was able to persuade the senior officers at Port Moresby headquarters that strict controls ought to be introduced. The new orders, he was pleased to note, 'called for greater consideration of the carriers', and emphasised 'what is now generally recognised — the valuable part they were playing in the campaign'.

The Kokoda Trail exacted a ferocious toll on 'Doc' Vernon. Months of dealing with Australian sick and wounded, and of protecting the rights of the Papuan carriers in an atmosphere of humidity, malaria and exhaustion, were responsible for his early death. A legend amongst Australian troops and a hero amongst the Papuans, he died at Samurai hospital in 1946 and was buried at Loge Island.

Edward Peachey
1917–1981
Escapee extraordinaire
Written by: Niall Lucy
Nominated by: Gloriana McKenzie

Edward Peachey was raised in Pascoe Vale, Victoria, and worked in a scrap metal yard before enlisting with the AIF in 1939. He escaped from a POW camp in Greece after being taken prisoner when the Nazis overran the islands, but was recaptured at Alamein in 1942 and interned in Italy. A notorious escapee, Peachey was among the most wanted POWs at large in Europe in the final years of World War II.

His greatest triumph was enacted shortly after being sent to the POW camp at the Duke of Aosta's farm in the Italian mountains. Word soon spread that Peachey was planning a breakout, and dozens of POWs were eager to be included. In great numbers the prisoners smashed through the front gates, whereupon the majority scattered and ran like hares — most of them being recaptured within twenty-four hours.

Peachey and two comrades, however, hid in the rice fields outside

Ted Peachey with the AIF at Tel Aviv. Twice a POW, Peachey became a captain with the Italian partisans

the camp entrance, breathing through reeds while submerged under water for the best part of two days, until the commotion died down and they were able to escape unnoticed. By chance, they met up with a group of thirty POWs who had managed to evade the German and Italian search parties, and together they tried to make their way across the Alps into neutral Switzerland.

After a few days, Peachey and his two comrades turned back, warning others that the treacherous snow and sub-zero temperatures made the trek too dangerous. But the other POWs went on to death from asphyxiation or frost bite due to their lack of preparation and the proper equipment.

Upon returning from the Alps, Peachey joined the partisans with whom he fought against the Axis troops until peace was declared in 1945. He often put his life at risk in defence of the Italian freedom fighters. Often, too, he came close to being recaptured. On one such hair-raising occasion an Italian farmer, who was under suspicion by the Nazis of harbouring partisans and escapees, hid Peachey behind a false wall in his kitchen while the Germans searched the house and its surrounds. Hardly daring to breathe, the Australian stayed motionless for several hours as the Germans conducted their violent search, smashing the farmer's furniture and threatening the life of his two-year-old daughter unless he confessed to the whereabouts of the wanted man. But the farmer could not be coerced into betraying the Australian, who frequently owed his life to such courage on the part of beleaguered civilians, so the Nazis posted a surveillance party and left. A few days later, the surveillance party was required for other duties and Peachey was able to escape.

Having taught himself to speak Italian, Peachey's military expertise and discipline were vital to the gallant but untrained partisans and it was not long before he was made a captain. From 1943 until war's end, he led the freedom fighters under his command in a succession of daring acts of sabotage against the Nazis, who proclaimed a huge bounty for his capture.

Weighing only seven stone, Edward Peachey returned to Australia after the war and, in 1957, was awarded the Italian Star, one of only one hundred such medals ever struck. He died in Victoria in 1981.

Bernard Hazelden Quin
1894–1943
Doctor to the Nauruans
Written by: David Millar
Nominated by: Peter B. Quin

On the island of Nauru, Dr Bernard Hazelden Quin is still remembered. A street and several Nauruans are named after him, and a monument dedicated to five Australians bears his name.

In the mid 1920s Bernard Quin, married with five children, was practising as a GP in Echuca, Victoria. Depression and drought had blighted the area, and doctor's bills could often not be paid. With a shrinking income, Bernard Quin was pleased to answer an advertisement to work in Nauru on a government salary.

Fond of his work, and increasingly fond of the Nauruans, the new doctor, with the assistance of two Australian nurses, trained several local people as orderlies and nurses. It was a pleasant life — a warm family circle, walks around the island, fishing for the next meal and games of cricket. But in 1940 German Raiders sank several ships off the island and then shelled the phosphate works. The idyllic world was now desecrated by shells and pom-pom guns. Thick, sluggish smoke rose from the oil dumps. It was no place for a family and the Quins sailed for Melbourne.

The Australian Government, however, decided that it needed a medical officer to look after its troops on Nauru, as well as the local population, and asked Dr Quin if he would return. He accepted, was appointed Captain, and sailed north.

At the end of 1941, when Japan entered the war, Australia decided that it could no longer give protecton to Nauru and withdrew its troops. 'My father and four other Australians were faced with the critical decision of leaving with the Army or staying behind', Dr Quin's son, Father Peter Quin SJ of Sydney, later wrote, 'They chose to remain. My father had come to love the Nauruans: they loved him and they needed him.'

The decision exacted a terrible price. The Japanese overran the island and summarily imprisoned the five Australians. Then, in March 1943, in retaliation for American bombing of Nauru, the men were led out and beheaded, Bernard Quin wearing his rosary around his neck as a public affirmation of his faith. He was forty-nine years old.

One of the last photographs of Doctor Bernard Quin whose dedication to the people of Nauru led to his execution by the Japanese in March 1943

Keith W. Mathieson
1908–1971
Padre in war and peace
Written by: David Millar
Nominated by: Robert H. Ridley

Rev J. K. W. Mathieson, wartime naval chaplain and padre on the Burma Railway, soon after his appointment as Superintendent of 'Orana' Methodist Peace Memorial Homes for Children in 1951

On a clear moonlit night in 1942, the USS *Houston* and RAN *Perth* were retreating before the victorious Japanese. As they sailed for Sunda Strait, the channel that separates Java from Sumatra, the two ships blundered into a Japanese invasion fleet. The enemy destroyers soon encircled the two cruisers and, illuminating them with searchlights, attacked their targets with ease. Defeat was inevitable. About midnight, after four torpedoes had slammed home, the *Perth* heeled to port and sank.

The survivors — about half the ship's complement — included the Rev Keith Mathieson, a Methodist chaplain. All covered in oil and smoke, they found themselves bobbing towards the Javanese coast on a raft. A badly wounded man, crying with pain and terror, attempted feebly to clamber aboard. Mathieson dragged him on. It was not the last time that Mathieson would go to the help of a fellow man when others would say that it was not worth the effort.

From Java, the Japanese moved the *Perth* survivors, with thousands of others, to the coolie life of the Burma - Siam railroad. Intended to bring supplies from Bangkok to the Japanese army in Burma, it forced its way through 120 kilometres of jungle, over ravines, across escarpments and through rocky outcrops. The work gangs were forever racing the clock. As one Japanese officer coldly said 'Railway must be completed. Nippon very sorry, many men must die'.

It was on this slave labour construction site, where men awoke every day with fear gripping their guts, that Padre Mathieson's reputation was made. As a former *Perth* stoker, Ron Walhouse, later said, 'Mathieson was a real man of compassion. I still takes my hat off to him.'

Besides the inhuman timetable, lack of food, brutal guards and rain that turned everything to mud and boots to cardboard, there was another element which made the men 'bitter, harsh and sour' — the favoured treatment that the Japanese handed out to Allied officers. The Japanese relieved them of any physical work, paid them a small sum each month, served them slightly better food and permitted them to run a canteen. To men for whom one egg might make the discrimination between death or life, the discrimination rankled.

There were, of course, many officers who used their position to pro-

Reverend Mathieson, here greeting new arrivals from England in 1951, provided a loving home for children orphaned by war

tect their men or alleviate their distress. Padre Keith Mathieson was one of them. As former Chief Petty Officer Vic Duncan of the *Perth* said, 'He was a little man with a big heart. He shone out in that place'.

A bearded figure in tattered enlisted man's clothes, Mathieson worked tirelessly in the hospital. Despite his own illnesses — the usual ration of tropical ulcers, dysentery, malaria — he made it his job to look after the hopeless and dying cases, holding the hands of young men as they died, urging others to 'hang on'. He scrounged spare boots or clothes, used all his monthly 'salary' on the prisoners, and stood up to guards with a fierce dignity when they attempted to empty hospital beds to make up the numbers for work parades.

Years later, when he became Director of the cottage homes at Orana, the Peace Memorial for Children in Burwood, Victoria, there was a constant trickle of ex-Burma Rail men to see him. After they had gone, he would sometimes turn to his secretary and say, seriously and self-deprecatingly, 'You must not believe everything they tell you. They exaggerate a lot, you know.' Those who knew him in the camps of the Burma railway would have found it reassuring to know that their Padre was the same as he had always been.

Bruce Hunt and Roy Mills
1899–1964; 1917–
Doctors on the Burma Railway
Written by: Niall Lucy
Nominated by: R. Kelsey & G. Beard; D. Smith

In April 1943, F Force, a working party of 7000 Australian and British prisoners of the Japanese left their Singapore goal for an undisclosed destination. The Japanese euphemistically described it as 'health camps': the Siamese called it 'The Valley of Death'. In that sodden, monsoon-swept hinterland in the northern reaches of the border between Thailand and Burma, thousands of Allied lives were lost in building the infamous Burma railway.

During their months of captivity in Singapore's Changi prison, the men had been forced to live under insanitary conditions and were fed on inadequate rations. Major Bruce Hunt, a forty-four-year-old veteran of the Great War who had practised as a gynaecologist in Perth before the outbreak of World War II, worked with other medical personnel to try to improve diet and sanitation at Changi, but many of the men who arrived at Bampong in Thailand in late April 1943 were unfit for the 300 kilometre march to the staging camps of Konkoita, Nieke, and Sonkurai in the Valley of Death. More than half of the 3600 Australian members of F Force died on the railway. Without the efforts of Hunt and Captain Roy Mills, a twenty-six-year-old doctor from Sydney, and the unfailing service of several other doctors and orderlies, it is certain that even more men would have perished.

Upon arrival at Bampong, the only amenities were a foul water supply and four filthy huts. Valuable food and medical stores were left unguarded by the Japanese, resulting in a serious loss of provisions to looting by the local villagers. Fatigued and undernourished, the men set out in groups a day and a half later, marching at night through steamy jungle trails turned to mud by the monsoons, for the northern end of the proposed railway line.

A trudge of twenty-four kilometres brought them to Tarsau on the Kwai River. Here there was a hospital among the several bamboo huts erected by the men of D Force, who had left Changi in March. In vain, Major Hunt tried to persuade the Japanese to allow those of his charges who were too weak for marching to remain at Tarsau for medical care. For his trouble, he was struck to the ground and kicked by a small circle of guards. The Australians immediately moved towards the helpless doctor who wore a rag painted with a Red Cross around his sleeve, but Hunt sensed the likely reprisals if the men became involved. 'Keep out of this, you bastards,' he growled in a voice that commanded immediate respect. 'This is a private fight.'

His arm broken, the Major fell into line with the rest of the men and followed the River Kwai for twenty-six kilometres beyond Tarsau, when permission was finally given to form a wayside infirmary of sorts — the rat-eaten lining of a marquee stretched across bamboo poles — for those falling sick en route. Hunt sought approval to go on ahead and arrange accommodation in advance for the disabled stragglers but this was refused.

Night after night the men were herded along the Kwai, over treacherous bridges and embankments and across the hazardous countryside of steep hills and deep ravines. Many were injured in falls and others developed sores on their feet and legs. Still more were suffering from dysentery.

Upon reaching the Valley of Death, almost two weeks after leaving Bampong, the Australians were sent to a series of jungle camps centred around the headquarters at Nieke. Three camps were located at Sonkurai to the north, and another at Konkoita sixteen kilometres south of the headquarters. On 9 May 1943, Major Hunt and his party arrived at Konkoita at the same time as a party of 700 men under the medical supervision of Captain Roy Mills was staggering into camp.

A pestilent death-trap, even by the unwholesome standards to which the POWs had become accustomed, at Konkoita cholera was rife among the civilian labour force of Tamils, Chinese, and Malays whose bivouac adjoined that of the Australians. The camp grounds were covered in human excrement and fly-blown corpses lay in pools of blood behind the bamboo walls of the coolie enclosure. In mid-May, the monsoons broke in earnest and the rains fell unabated until September. By June, an estimated ninety per cent of F Force was stricken with malaria and dysentery.

Major Hunt left Konkoita at the end of May to help those in need of medical attention in the camps farther north. Meanwhile, Captain Mills had alerted the Japanese to the danger of a cholera epidemic unless certain precautions were taken to prevent the disease spreading among the POWs. Swabs and innoculations were subsequently administered to the soldiers and their mess gear was sterilised; but

Major Bruce Atlee Hunt, 'The old doctor'

these measures were undermined by the failure to impose a similar regimen on the civilian labour force.

Powerless to contain the disease, Mills and the other AIF doctors were severely hampered by the inadequacy of their medical supplies which consisted almost entirely of quinine and a few bandages. The lack of hygiene claimed many more casualties from the rampant spread of dysentery and diptheria. The camps were often flooded with effluent because the men were too exhausted from working sixteen hours a day on the railway to repair the damage caused to latrines and drains by the ceaseless monsoonal deluge, and there seemed to be no way of controlling the compounding menace of disease-carrying flies which thrived in the pollution. In addition, sick men who should have been confined to camp were regularly made to work on the railway, further decreasing their already slim chances of survival, and those few whose illness did make them exempt from labour had their rations cut to a daily bowl of insipid gruel and a quantity of rice that was less than half a fit man's share.

Working against these overwhelming odds, Captain Mills did everything in his power to alleviate the suffering of those who were dying and to prevent as many deaths as he could. Often sick himself, he was frequently punished by the Japanese for his efforts to improve sanitation and to have men classified unfit for work.

Upon his arrival at Nieke and the northern camps at Sonkurai, Major Bruce Hunt imposed a rigid discipline in an effort to stem the cholera epidemic. He insisted that the camps be cleared of surface filth and that sterilising fires be kept alight in the huts for the purpose of disinfecting the men's eating utensils. Water had to be boiled for at least seven minutes before consumption, and it was forbidden to drink directly from the nearby creeks. In spite of these precautions, 650 Australian POWs died of cholera until the Japanese supplied a vaccine in early June of 1943 which finally brought the disease under control. Nevertheless, by July, in one camp at Sonkurai alone, only about 500 men out of almost 2000 were fit to work: staying the cholera epidemic had little impact on the overall sickness and mortality rates from other diseases, malnutrition, and complete exhaustion.

Typical of Major Hunt's disregard for the niceties of military protocol, he would frequently stride into the headquarters of the Japanese commander in charge of prisoners, Colonel Banno, and threaten to forward written complaints to the Red Cross in Switzerland unless he was given medicines. On one such occasion, Banno offered a jar of Marmite, saying he had nothing more to give, unaware that Hunt had already used the Colonel's name to cajole a supply of quinine from a Japanese orderly. With his haversack slung across his huge, hairy shoulders, and covered in mud from the waist down, the Major would then return to the labour camps to dispose of his spoils, afterwards reporting to the camp commandant for the inevitable beating.

Following a series of broken promises, the Japanese eventually agreed to the requests of Major Hunt and other senior officers to establish a hospital at Tanbaya in Burma, where 2000 of the most seriously infirm could be isolated from the labour camps. On August 3 1943, an advance party of Hunt and seven medical staff, together with a few administrative personnel, arrived at Tanbaya to find that only one hut and the cookhouse were roofed. With no tools except an axe brought

Captain Roy Mills. 'No praise is too high for him'

from Thailand, they built a hospital of nine wards out of bamboo and thatch and erected several storage huts; but medical supplies were no less scarce at Tanbaya than they had been in the Valley of Death. In the absence of proper facilities, one third of all patients at the hospital died within the first three months, chiefly from dysentery, malaria, beri-beri, and tropical ulcers.

The mortality rate at Tanbaya would have been even greater, however, but for the success of the wardmastering system. Hunt secured the services of many combatant officers to run the wards, putting them in charge of nursing procedures and domestic affairs. Each wardmaster was entrusted with such duties as sterilising the mess gear and water, attending to the fires, and enforcing standards of hygiene. This system raised morale and saved lives by relieving the medical staff of all but their direct responsibility to the patients, ensuring that each individual POW received the optimum medical care possible under the circumstances.

Bruce Hunt's stamina and the resolute tenacity of his dedication to the fight against disease won the admiration of the enlisted men who were otherwise often reproachful of the officers. The Major, who served in two wars, died in Perth in 1964.

Roy Mills returned to Sydney after the war. He took several years to recover from tuberculosis and regain his health, and lives now on the New South Wales coast at Nowra. In his official report, Lieutenant-Colonel Pond extolled the remarkable endeavour of the young doctor from the 2/10th Field Ambulance who 'never spared himself, though unwell for a considerable period, and earned the respect of every man in the party... No praise is too high for him.' But perhaps an even greater tribute was paid to Mills by survivors of the 2/29th Battalion, to whom he had given such honourable service in the Valley of Death, when they extended him a special invitation to attend their reunion on the Gold Coast in October, 1986. Such invitations are rarely issued to veterans of other units and the gesture clearly indicates the high regard in which the 2/29th holds Roy Mills.

Their dedication and their refusal, in the face of daunting odds, to give in to despair endeared Major Hunt and Captain Mills to the enlisted men. Their heroic defiance and stubborn optimism will never be forgotten by those whom they saved from the Valley of Death.

John Joseph Murphy
1914–

Courage rewarded with injustice
Written by: Tim Bowden
Nominated by: Tim Bowden

'I belonged to a Coast Watching organisation, known as M Special Unit, and I landed in New Britain on the night of September 29, 1943. Coming ashore from our submarine we were turned over in the surf and all our gear got wet, including our radio which was unserviceable from then on.'

World War II

It was not a good start for Captain John Joseph Murphy and his party and things quickly became worse. The Japanese were soon aware of the landing and the would-be coastwatchers were ambushed. The two other Australians with Murphy were shot and killed and he was wounded in the wrist, washed down a flooded river into the middle of the pursuing Japanese, and captured.

John Murphy, travelling to Rabaul in a Japanese submarine, was at first well treated by the crew, but after they took on board a dozen oil-covered Japanese sailors whose ship had been sunk, things changed: 'the Japanese sailors got hot tubs of water and washed and bathed themselves. But I was tied up in this blasted Japanese dunny all the way to Rabaul.'

In Rabaul, a blindfolded Murphy was led to an interrogation centre. He found himself in Ah Teck's tailoring shop, 'where I'd had my last pair of pants made'. Before the war Murphy had been a patrol officer in New Guinea, and he knew the area well. Now he was a prisoner where he had been a *masta*.

The Japanese had made it into a sort of prison camp and the headquarters of the *kempeitai* — the Japanese military police. 'They started to jeer at me and call me spy boy. One bloke told me I was for the big chop. "You know what we do with spies, eh?" That sort of approach. Well that was the wrong tack because it made me defiant. I thought, well if I am for the big chop there is no use trying to win friends

John Murphy (at right) with Japanese rifle, captured September 1942 near Salamanca. Photograph by Damien Parer

and influence people. I got a bit anti, and they were sort of frightened of me because they didn't want to lose face.' The *kempeitai* were not renowned for their kid-gloved treatment of captured Allied soldiers. But they thought they had an important catch in Murphy. He found out later that the Japanese had published a report that they had caught the great Australian spy, Captain John Joseph Murphy. Murphy's family and the Australian Government had made inquiries through the Swiss Government and the Red Cross. This caused the Japanese to think they had a great hostage whom they could trade.

Murphy maintained a belligerent attitude to his captors, and refused to answer unless he was called by his proper title. 'I was the only bloke they gave a title to in prison — Murphy-tai — "Captain Murphy" '.

Murphy-tai became the natural and acknowledged leader of the sixty-three Allied prisoners of war in Rabaul. He spoke the local languagge (he had once written a book on pidgin English, the *lingua franca* of New Guinea) and he took a firm line with his captors. He also started morale-raising camp concerts, religious ceremonies and other activities. Most of the other prisoners were American airmen who had been shot down over New Britain and many of them were extremely disoriented and demoralised in their alien surroundings. One of the American pilots later wrote about Murphy: 'There was a dynamism about him that commanded respect'. Another went further: 'he truly afforded a buffer between the POWs and the Japanese.'

Through 1944 and early 1945 the Allied prisoners were moved to various camp sites around Rabaul, and many of the Americans died. Murphy, at great personal risk, broke out of camp on moonless nights to steal food from Japanese kitchens. But of the sixty-three men gathered in the vicinity of Ah Teck's tailor's shop in late 1943, only seven survived. Murphy believed the Americans were particularly disadvantaged. Used to steaks, ice-cream and Coca Cola, they adapted badly to a rice diet barely sufficient to keep body and soul together. 'They just couldn't eat rice. For days and days they couldn't face it. I think malnutrition, as much as anything, killed them. There were one or two pneumonia cases, there was certainly dysentery and beri-beri. But their big setback at the beginning meant they never had anything to build on. I think that they didn't give themselves a chance by that abhorrence, that distaste, for the rice meals.'

A large group of prisoners died in a retaliatory massacre on a beach at Nordup after Allied aircraft strafed and bombed the Japanese party that was taking them to another location. But it was neglect — the deprivation of food and medical treatment — rather than physical brutality that caused so many deaths among the rest. On one occasion the prisoners suffered the added indignity of being guinea pigs for dubious medical experiments. Murphy was injected with serum from the blood of a Japanese soldier who had recovered from a bout of malaria.

At the end of the war Murphy was the only Australian survivor. Evacuated to Lae by the Americans, John Murphy was surprised — to put it mildly — to be arrested on his way to the officers' club for a few badly needed cold beers, and charged with treason and giving information to the enemy. His court martial did not take place until early 1946 and the Australian papers splashed headlines like 'AUSTRALIAN CAPTAIN AT LAE ACCUSED OF TREACHERY' and 'COURT TOLD A.I.F. MAN GAVE JAPS INFORMATION'.

Captain John Murphy whose courage was to be tested both during and after his incarceration by the Japanese

John and Marjorie Murphy after his clearance by the Court Martial in 1946. Murphy was the innocent victim of mistaken identity but groundless accusations against him persisted for many years

It was a case of mistaken identity. An elderly German missionary, under duress, had given information to the Japanese and his name — through a misinterpretation — had been confused with Murphy's. Murphy was finally honourably discharged — the army's way of saying that there was absolutely nothing at all in the original allegations.

The six surviving Americans from Rabaul were outraged that Murphy had been court martialled, and gave glowing testimony of his courage, leadership and defiance of the Japanese during the period of imprisonment. But in the eyes of many old New Guinea hands, the headlines had done their damage. Murphy's acquittal had been published, as he says, 'in a paragraph about an inch deep on an inside page of the Brisbane *Courier Mail*, and the southern papers didn't mention an honourable discharge'. Many long-time acquaintances in the New Guinea service regarded Murphy as a traitor, and were saying so. 'I was flabbergasted. I thought that I'd risked a hell of a lot, my own safety certainly, to jolly the prisoners along and keep them healthy and their morale up. I'd stood between them and the Japanese. Perhaps an encomium of some sort might have been due to me, maybe even a medal. But then to be slapped with this General Court Martial. Yes it was a blow'.

In many ways John Murphy's biggest challenge was still ahead. His greatest heroism lies in his survival as a balanced and decent human being despite the monstrous injustice of his court martial. There were years of considerable difficulty. 'My wife Marjorie will confirm I was irascible and difficult at home — inclined to be solitary and go my own way. But I slowly got over it. It took time.'

Today John and Majorie Murphy live in retirement in suburban Brisbane. Neighbourhood children drop in on their way home from school for a cold drink from the fridge and to score a few biscuits from the jar. If you were to meet this affable, charming man there would be no hint of momentous events, or the existence of an appalling injustice that would have permanently soured and embittered the soul of a lesser individual. That is the key to the real survival of John Joseph Murphy.

Owen Price
1912–1943

'An officer and a gentleman'
Written by: Billy Marshall-Stoneking
Nominated by: Roy G. Bettiens

Squadron Leader Owen Price, at Bundaberg Aerodrome in 1938. By 1943 he had exchanged this Gipsy Moth for the Beaufort in which he died

Everyone who knew Squadron Leader Price had a good word to say about him. He was a gentleman, quietly spoken, and a dedicated family man. And his friends knew they could count on him: he was dependable, and exceptionally loyal.

By 1943, the Japanese navy was playing havoc with Australian shipping lanes in the Pacific, and the possibility of invasion looked very real. The presence of a huge Japanese flotilla in Rabaul Harbour seemed an ominous prelude to a major offensive.

The powers-that-be reasoned that a strategic, lightning attack against the Japanese armada at Rabaul was better than waiting for them to move on Australia. But even more to the point, a successful strike by the Beaufort aircraft would justify the costly decision to outfit them with torpedoes, a decision which the Americans had advised against. Within days a plan was drawn up.

From the beginning, however, everything went wrong. Bad weather conditions on the night of the planned attack resulted in Wing Commander Geoff Nicholl cancelling the mission, an order which was rescinded by ACO J.E. Hewitt.

Nicholl and Hewitt clashed, but finally agreed that instead of the twelve Beauforts which had originally been assigned to the mission, they would send out only three — hardly enough to make even a dent in the Japanese forces.

Accompanying Nicholl on the night mission were his two senior flight commanders, Noel Quinn and Owen Price, both of whom volunteered for the task. The three planes left Kiriwina, New Guinea, on the night of 8–9 November 1943.

The attack was at deck level, and as the planes approached the Japanese fleet, the flak and anticraft fire became extremely heavy. Nicholl and Quinn released their torpedoes and veered to the left and right in an almost miraculous escape. But Price, in the middle, wasn't so lucky. He flew his Beaufort straight at a large ship, launching his torpedo only seconds before a massive explosion ripped the plane apart. Damage to the Japanese fleet was negligible, but four Australian airmen were dead.

Nicholl wrote a personal recommendation for a posthumous Victoria Cross for Price, but to no avail. The bestowal of such an award would have called unwanted attention to the misconceived mission, and neither the Air Force nor the politicians wanted any revelations concerning unsound judgements in high places. Price's VC was never awarded. Instead, he was Mentioned in Dispatches. An Australian hero became one of the great forgotten casualties of the war.

Squadron Leader Alan Bouch (standing), invalided out, is farewelled by his men, the 3rd Airfield Construction Squadron at Mindoro, Philippines, in May 1945

Alan Douglas Bouch
1903–

Ali Baba and his forty thieves
Written by: Niall Lucy
Nominated by: Barbara Cook

On 15 December 1944, US and Allied forces landed on the beachheads of Mindoro Island, south of Luzon in the Philippines. It was the most daring of General MacArthur's tactical manoeuvres to that date and the best-kept secret of any Pacific operation. As the island had only ever been referred to by its code name of 'Breau,' troops met with relatively little resistance on landing. Even so, during the landing, Allied air cover and anti-aircraft fire shot down twenty-four enemy planes.

Among the thousands of troops involved in the invasion was a group of 600 Australians led by Squadron Leader Alan Douglas Bouch. Officially, they were known as the Third Airfield Construction Squadron, RAAF, but everyone called them 'Ali Baba and His Forty Thieves' a nickname they had earned in Darwin in 1942 when Bouch and forty others were issued with half-a-dozen trucks and as many shovels and assigned to the maintenance of airfields and military bases in Australia's North-West. In order to carry out their repairs, often done while under attack from Japanese air raids, they were forced to beg, borrow or steal whatever building supplies and machinery they could find.

Bouch, a civil engineer with the Public Works Department in Sydney

A sprightly eighty-four, Alan Bouch, MBE, DSO, with his grand-daughter, Leanne Farnham, on Anzac Day 1987

before the War, was Mentioned in Dispatches for his services in Darwin and promoted to the rank of Squadron Leader. After almost two years of maintenance duties in the Northern Territory, the squadron was withdrawn to Melbourne in March 1944, for a month's leave prior to reforming at Ransford in Victoria. There, Ali Baba's crew was enlarged to a company of 600 men that sailed from Sydney on the 25 July for the island of Leyte in the Philippines. Despite being attacked en route by enemy torpedo bombers, Bouch and his men arrived safely at their destination without suffering a single casualty.

At Leyte, however, where they were awaiting orders to proceed with the Americans on the invasion of Mindoro, Bouch and many others contracted schistosomiasis, a debilitating tropical disease. Weakened and exhausted, they left Leyte on 10 December 1944, to join the invasion convoy, the only Australians — besides one wireless unit — to participate in the Pacific war zone north of Borneo.

Less than a week later, the No. 3 Airfield Construction Squadron (3ACS) landed with the first wave of American infantry on the Mindoro beachhead, losing one of their number to a Japanese air attack — the squadron's only fatality of the campaign. The following morning Ali Baba and his men began work on their immediate and near-impossible task. MacArthur's planned assault on Manila depended on an aerodrome being built in five days. The Australians, many of whom were still suffering from schistosomiasis, began to cut through the virgin jungle.

They finished the aerodrome on the night of 19 December — twenty-four hours ahead of schedule. By the following afternoon, ninety Allied bombers and fifty fighter planes had landed on the strip, immediately boosting the morale of the invasion force.

Mindoro was subjected to incessant air attacks and was the target for 336 raids in one hectic fortnight alone. But the most dangerous hours were those of the night of 26 December, when a Japanese naval force of two battleships, two cruisers, and seven destroyers bombarded the Allied installations ashore and attempted several troop landings. The fierce battle which ensued lit up the sky with searchlights, anti-aircraft fire, bursting star shells, and phosphorous bombs. Throughout this mayhem a contingent of 3ACS men continued to work on a second aerodrome while the rest of the squadron, armed with machine guns and .303 rifles, manned a 2000 metre perimeter around the camp base for four kilometres inland or transported bombs and ammunition from the beachhead to Allied planes on the main strip.

By dawn, the enemy attack had been repelled at great cost to the Japanese. Nevertheless, the intensity of enemy air raids did not lessen until after the American landings on Luzon in mid-January, by which time the men of the 3ACS had spent six almost sleepless weeks building and repairing MacArthur's vital airstrips on Mindoro.

In a letter to the Australian press, the US commander in charge of the engineering section of the Mindoro invasion, Lieutenant-Colonel William J. Ellison, Jr, wrote in praise of the 3ACS: 'It is with a feeling of gratitude that I submit the record of achievement of this outstanding unit ... Their efficiency, industry, and fortitude in the face of enemy attack was exemplary, and assured the successful completion of a key air-base on schedule.'

Ellison also officially recommended the squadron for the US Army's Meritorious Service Plaque. 'Despite repeated air attacks and extreme blackout conditions at night,' he submitted in his letter of citation to General Headquarters, 'this squadron continued its extremely high standard of performance and extraordinary devotion to duty. The men carried out their work during alerts until the last possible moment of comparative safety from air attacks [and] maintained a production record which would have done credit to a far larger and better equipped organisation.' Unfortunately, this particular award was reserved for American units only and the Australian squadron was not able to receive it.

Before departing from Mindoro on 19 June 1945, the 3ACS constructed two more airfields, maintained fifty kilometres of roadways, built hospitals and quartermaster stores, and planned and designed a sixty metre suspension bridge for which they cemented the foundations.

In need of medical attention for the tropical disease he had caught at Leyte and was was unable to shake off, Bouch left the squadron before its deparure from Mindoro. The plane which was to have taken him to Concord Hospital in Sydney was forced down in the sea off Manus Island in the South-West Pacific, where all hands were lucky to be rescued by an American destroyer. Squadron Leader Bouch was awarded a Distinguished Service Order after demobilisation, one of only a handful of non-flying RAAF personnel to receive this distinction.

Alan Bouch now lives in Adelaide and is visited still by ex-members of his squadron, the surviving Australian heroes of the Pacific war zone whom he led to renown as 'Ali Baba and His Forty Thieves.'

Conrad 'Connie' Larsen
1914–1944
Saves RAAF Rathmines
Written by: Terri McCormack
Nominated by: Rita Smith

On 18 December 1944, Leading Aircraftman Larsen was coxswain in charge of a fuel barge lying alongside the wharf at Rathmines RAAF Station on the shores of Lake Macquarie, New South Wales. An explosion in the engine cockpit of the barge caused a fire which threatened to ignite both the barge tanks and the adjacent main fuel storage tanks of the Station. Although suffering horrific burns, Larsen single-handedly fought the blaze with a small extinguisher until assistance arrived, thus saving Australia's largest flying boat base from a devastating explosion.

Larsen's sandshoe-shod feet were the only part of his body not burnt. He died six days later and was buried alongside his Danish-born parents in Brisbane's Nundah Cemetery. His story was buried with him until unearthed by the Cemetery Preservation Association and a Lake Macquarie historian almost forty years later.

The citation on a posthumous RAAF Commendation praised Larsen's 'gallantry of the highest order in the face of extreme danger without regard for his own safety.'

Reg
? –1945

The unknown soldier
Written by: Niall Lucy
Nominated by: Rev Josef Holman

It was 5 May 1945, and Prague was under siege. Thousands of Czech patriots, armed with a few weapons and their bare hands, stood behind barricades on the outskirts of the city as tanks and troops commanded by the notorious SS Obergruppenführer Karl Herman Frank tried to smash their way through to the inner sanctum of the capital. With the Allies surging across Europe towards the Bohemian borders, it would be only a matter of days before Prague were liberated. If only the Czech uprising could delay the Germans for long enough, the city was certain to be saved.

One of those who lent his courage and defiance to the uprising is Josef Holman, who lives now in the Sydney suburb of Edgecliff. In those crucial days in 1945 he manned a barricade on Benesovska Road in the Pankrac district of the Czech capital, alongside his father and dozens of his countrymen. But as Frank's panzer divisions were gaining ground, the patriots were losing hope: it seemed that the Allies would arrive too late to save the city from destruction.

Suddenly, however, when the struggle was at its most desperate pitch, a stranger appeared amidst the barricade on Benesovska Road as if he had been sent by fate to change the course of the revolution. He said his name was Reg and that he came from Sydney. After a brief interrogation, he was found to be an Australian soldier who had escaped from a POW camp in Sagan, Silesia, and fought his way into Czechoslovakia where he learned of the uprising in Prague. He had then rushed to offer his support and military expertise to the embattled partisans.

Reg was put in charge of the barricade and entrusted with the defence of the Pankrac district. On the fourth day of the revolution, after leading Holman and the other patriots in many bloody battles against the superior firepower of the SS, he immortalised himself in Czech history as the unknown soldier who gave his life to save Prague.

Like others whose heroic deeds have left a mark on history, he had no time to think: the huge panzer that was rumbling down Benesovska Road would wreak havoc in the city once it crashed through the makeshift barricade that stood in its path. It had to be stopped. Too many lives were at stake. Strapping a few grenades to the belt around his waist, Reg threw himself under the tank and blew it apart. The following day, the Allies entered Czechoslovakia and Prague was saved.

Outside a building on Benesovska Road today is a plaque with the inscription:

'Here bravely fought and gallantly sacrificed his life by throwing himself under a German tank during the 1945 revolution, so others could live in peace and freedom, an Australian soldier — a hero named Reg.'

Tom Hall
1933–

Lest we forget
Written by: Niall Lucy
Nominated by: Joy Craig

On 7 July 1945, ten Australian and British commandos were taken from their cell in Singapore's Outram gaol and escorted to a nearby field. They knew they were going to die. They shook hands with one another for the last time, smoked a final cigarette, perhaps, and cried or prayed or willed their minds to go blank in the awful moments before their cropped heads were lopped off by five Japanese swordsmen. One of their executioners was teased when he returned to barracks for being so unskilled that it took him several blows to cut through the necks of two commandos. Thirty-nine days later, the Japanese surrendered and the War was over.

Though they were all servicemen and undertaking a perfectly lawful operation of war, they had been put on trial for 'perfidy and espionage' at Raffles College. Yet the Japanese prosecutor praised the commandos for the 'sublime patriotism flaming in their breasts', and ended by declaring: 'The last moment of a hero must be historic and it must be dramatic ... As we respect them, so we feel our duty of glorifying their last moments as they deserve: and by our doing so the names of these heroes will remain in the hearts of the British and Australian people for evermore.'

But for a long time the men were no more than *forgotten* heroes, until the story of their courage and sacrifice was reconstructed over the course of twenty-eight years by someone who had nothing to gain but the satisfaction of learning the truth.

Tom Hall was a young Lieutenant in the Citizen's Military Force when his curiosity was first aroused concerning the fate of the twenty-three men who took part in Operation Rimau, ten of whom had been executed at Outram after three and a half months of torture and interrogation. None of their comrades had survived the mission either; but it would take Hall another quarter of a century to find out how and where they had died.

In 1958, Hall's unit, 1 Commando Company, advised author Ronald McKie in his research for a book on commando raids in Singapore Harbour during World War I, the most successful of which was an operation called Jaywick that sank seven enemy ships in September 1943. A year later, Operation Rimau was launched with six of the Jaywick raiders going back for more.

The men made a daring raid on Singapore Harbour in 1944 (a raid that Hall now believes was responsible for sinking at least three ships). It was known that a British submarine failed to keep its rendezvous with the raiding party at Merapas Island in the Indonesian archipelago, forcing the commandos to risk a desperate attempt to

(Right) Major Tom Hall of the CMF in 1967. His determined investigation of Operation Rimau met with implacable opposition. 'I wanted to know their names'

(Far right, top) Corporal A. G. P. Campbell, AIF

(Far right, below) Warrant Officer Jeffrey Willersdorf, AIF. One of two commandos to paddle 4000 kilometres to Romang Island

(Opposite page) (Left) Lieutenant A. L. 'Blondie' Sargent, AIF, was executed with other Rimau men at Outram Road Gaol, 7 July 1945. (Centre, top) Lieutenant Colonel Ivan Lyon, DSO, MBE, Gordon Highlanders. With Lieutenant H. R. 'Bobby' Ross, British Army (right), Lyon held the Japanese at bay on Soreh Island for several hours before being killed, enabling the rest of the Rimau men to withdraw towards the rendezvous at Merapas. Lyon and Lieutenant Commander Donald Davidson, DSC, RNVR, (centre, below) also took part in operation Jaywick. Davidson and Campbell were killed in combat with a Japanese patrol the day after Lyon died

paddle to Australia in their tiny canoes. Ten were captured and executed in Singapore; two died of starvation and torture in a Timor gaol; another was kicked to death (as Hall would learn in 1983) in a naval hospital on Java. The rest were killed by Japanese patrols. However, three Commandos were said to have paddled, against all odds, 2500 miles to Romang Island — only 650 kilometres away from the Australian mainland — before they were killed, more than two months after the raid.

In the course of his investigation, Hall met with resistance at the highest levels because it was the policy of the government not to pursue Japanese war criminals. His single-minded pursuit of the truth has cost him his military career.

In 1976, Hall set about the task of forming 1 Commando Association, a group dedicated to perpetuating the heroism of the Jaywick raiders and the men of Operation Rimau. By this time he had learned of the sacrifice made by Lieutenant-Colonel Ivan Lyon (Gordon Highlanders) and Lieutenant H. R. Ross (British Army) who held the Japanese at bay for several hours before being killed, enabling their comrades to withdraw towards the rendezvous at Merapas. The raiders were able to reach the rendezvous itself because of the further sacrifice of Lieutenant-Commander D. M. N. Davidson (Royal Navy) and Corporal A. G. P. Campbell (AIF) who lost their lives in combat with a Japanese patrol. Had a Major Walter Chapman of the Royal Engineers been there to meet them, as was prearranged, the others would have lived. In a bitter twist to the Rimau story, Chapman committed suicide in London in 1964 by swallowing the cyanide pill with which he had been issued in World War II.

Through 1 Commando Association, Hall endeavoured to convince the Australian Government to award the Cross of Valour to the dead men of Rimau and the Jaywick raiders. Of the fourteen commandos who took part in Operation Jaywick, five had simply been Mentioned in Dispatches in 1946 and only nine were cited for gallantry. Incredibly, the Rimau raiders had never received official recognition at all.

But the Australian Government declined to award the decoration to the thirty-one commandos. Refusing to accept defeat, however, 1 Commando Association struck its own medal — the Commando Cross of Valour — and presented it to relatives of the forgotten heroes at a ceremony in Sydney's Hyde Park on 8 July 1978.

At this time Hall still did not know the names of the commandos who had paddled the astonishing 4000 kilometres to Romang Island. In 1983, on a trip to Indonesia, Hall discovered that A.L.'Blondie' Sargent, thought to be one of them, had made it only to Maja Island, where he was captured, returned to Singapore and later executed as one of the ten found guilty of 'perfidy and espionage'. But two commandos did reach Romang, only to be taken prisoner there and killed on Timor. They were Lance Corporal H. J. Pace and Warrant Officer J. Willersdorf, both of the AIF. At last, Tom Hall knew their names.

Never a man to seek glory for himself, Hall was driven to learn the truth about Rimau out of a profound belief in the vital need to maintain our link with the 'traces of the past'. After a lifetime of ridicule and a ruined career, he would say that truth is its own reward.

THE FORGOTTEN HEROES OF OPERATION RIMAU

Lieutenant-Colonel
Ivan Lyon, DSO, MBE
(Gordon Highlanders)*

Lieutenant-Commander
D. M. N. Davidson, DSO
(RNVR)*

Captain
R.C. Page, DSO (AIF)*

Lieutenant
H. R. Ross (British Army)

Lieutenant
B. Reymond (RANR)

Lieutenant
A. L. Sargent (AIF)

Lieutenant
W. G. Carey (AIF)

Sub-Lieutenant
J. G. M. Riggs (RANR)

Major
R. M. Ingleton
(Royal Marines)

Warrant Officer
J. Willersdorf (AIF)

Warrant Officer
A. Warren (AIF)

Sergeant
D. P. Gooley (AIF)

Sergeant
C. B. Cameron (AIF)

Able Seaman
W. G. Falls, DSM
(RANR)*

Able Seaman
F. W. Marsh (RANR)*

Able Seaman
A. W. Huston, DSM
(RANR)*

Corporal
A. G. P. Campbell (AIF)

Corporal
C. M. Stewart (AIF)

Corporal
C. M. Craft (AIF)

Corporal
R. B. Fletcher (AIF)

Lance Corporal
J. T. Hardy (AIF)

Lance Corporal
H. J. Pace (AIF)

Private
D. R. Warne (AIF)

* also took part in Operation Jaywick

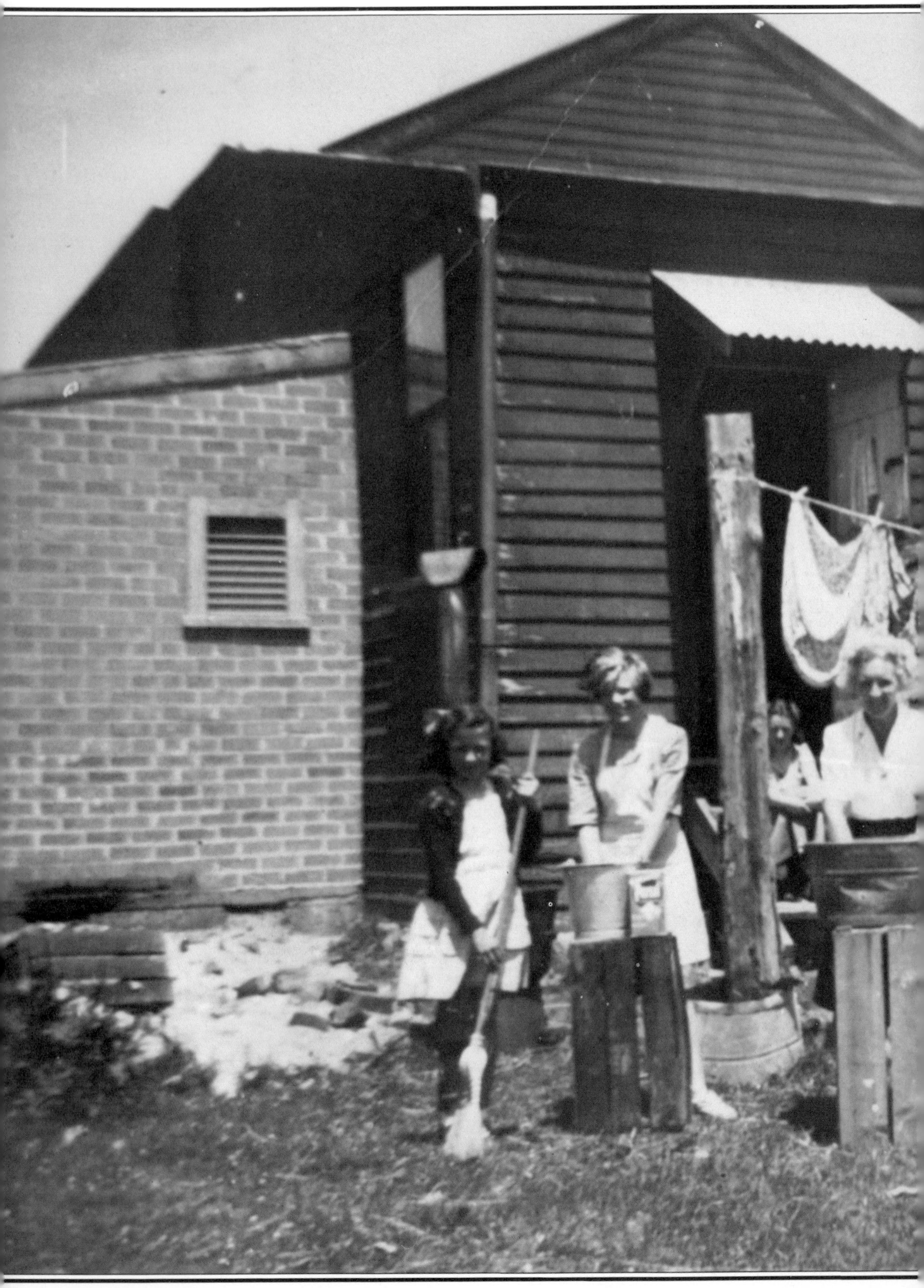

7
Recovery
1946–1968

Many of them came after the war with virtually nothing except their lives. Aware, like many of those born here who had also suffered cruelly, that to salvage a life is something — everything — they made of their own recovery a means to help others reconstruct a life: Leopold Siegellak, his wife and six children dead in Auschwitz, collecting Jewish refugees in his Willy's jeep; Albert Zinnbauer, interned on his arrival as an 'Enemy Alien', sleeping in his bathtub to give homeless refugees a bed, and Luigi Resciniti, a POW in Australia during the war, bringing out his family and many from his village to the place that he now saw as home and helped them to see as home too.

Some of these stories are about physical recovery — Harold Cochrane's work on penicillin, Totty Young's lifesaving and James Smith's Res-Q-Van all saved lives — while Malcolm Maloney's story is about the recovery of a past. Most, however, like the stories of the post-war immigrants and Elizabeth Rogers' girls at the Launceston Girls' Home, saved after having been abandoned and condemned as 'a festering sore' on the community, are about the recovery of a future.

Harold Cochrane
1910–
Penicillin pioneer
Written by: Jacqueline Kent
Nominated by: Valda A. Cochrane; Kate Bowyer

Previous page. Matron Elizabeth 'Matey' Rogers (hands in washtub) and some of the girls of the Launceston Girls' Home who flourished under her enlightened, affectionate care, on one of the annual beach holidays that she instituted for these previously mistreated girls. c.1950

Thousands of Australians owe their lives to the work of Harold Cochrane. An analytical chemist, Cochrane was working in the Commonwealth Serum Laboratories (CSL) in 1942 when Australian troops fighting the Japanese were falling victim to a variety of infections. Alarmed at the effect this was having on troop morale and efficiency, the Commonwealth Minister of Health decided that Australia should produce and refine quantities of penicillin to be despatched to the soldiers in the tropics.

Cochrane's boss, Major P.L. Bazeley, was sent to America to learn about the most efficient ways of producing the wonder drug. On his return, he appointed Harold Cochrane as officer-in-charge of the CSL's extractions department. He was to head a team to produce as much penicillin as possible.

From the start, this was an uncomfortable, even dangerous business. 'Penicillin culture is very unstable,' explains Harold Cochrane. 'The temperature has to be pretty low for it to work. At first we worked in a laboratory at an ordinary temperature and submerged the batches in a leaden bath full of iced water. We were working like mad, and one of the team had to scuttle back and forth and shove in blocks of ice every now and again to keep the temperature down.'

Not long afterwards, the Department of Works insulated a couple

Harold Cochrane with his wife, Val, and first son, Ian, in 1943 when he was working under hazardous conditions to provide wartime supplies of penicillin

of Army huts and installed refrigeration. In his new laboratory, the temperature was only 2° Celsius. 'We had to have fleecy lined flying suits, the sort the RAAF used,' recalls Cochrane. 'We also wore heavy flying boots and mittens; those of us who were married made our wives knit us balaclavas. It was so frustrating: here we were, trying to make as much penicillin as possible, and we could hardly move in all that gear!'

Inconveniences were one thing, hazards another. The ethylene dichloride used to extract the penicillin culture had devastating effects. 'It damaged the liver and the spleen and caused awful nausea,' says Harold Cochrane. 'In a way, the nausea was the worst. But we couldn't stop working.'

As the need for penicillin supplies in the war zones was growing every day, Cochrane's laboratory team often worked one-hundred-hour weeks. Cochrane collapsed several times; more than once doctors warned him to give up the work if he wanted to stay alive. But he kept going.

Production reached the level of 44 000 bottles of penicillin mould-yielding broth per day, giving more than 17 000 litres daily. And by the end of 1943, so great were the quantities made by Harold Cochrane and his team that Australia became the first country in the world to make penicillin commercially available to civilians.

By 1950, the technology of producing penicillin had been considerably refined. 'The extraction work was carried out in stainless steel tanks and pipelines jacketed with cold brine,' he explains.

Cochrane was appointed second in charge of the whole penicillin producing section of the CSL, with 250 employees, in 1950. He then became controller of the section and the manager of the whole CSL production division. This meant that he was supervising a staff of 600, producing all the vaccines, sera and other blood products made at the laboratories.

At about the same time, Cochrane developed a method for converting

Harold Cochrane, innovative chemist with the Commonwealth Serum Laboratories for more than thirty years, now retired. In another breakthrough, Harold Cochrane appointed the first female biochemists to the public service 'against a lot of opposition'. Photograph by Ponch Hawkes

amorphous penicillin into virtually pure crystalline penicillin — a breakthrough which made possible improved clinical use and the manufacture of new penicillin products. When pressed, Cochrane modestly admits that this was 'a personal achievement'. 'The Americans had developed a process, but they were keeping it top secret,' he says.

Harold Cochrane was also responsible for a pioneering breakthrough of another kind. In 1959, he appointed three women as cadet biochemists to CSL. 'I got a lot of opposition to that,' he says. 'But there was nothing in the rules to prevent it. They were the first female biochemists ever appointed in the public service... and I think they were the first women cadets in the public service ever.'

Harold Cochrane retired in 1970 and now lives in country Victoria. 'Our production methods were pretty primitive by today's standards,' he says, 'but they worked. And I'm proud to have made penicillin.'

Pearlie Watling
1905–

Shale miner and musician
Written by: Louise Egerton
Nominated by: Cindy Tiyce

Pearlie Watling was brought up with few of the advantages of life. When she was eight her mother died, leaving her and a younger brother to the care of a series of relatives. 'We soon wore our welcome out,' Pearlie recalls. Eventually she went to camp with her father in the Penrose pine forests, where he cleared land for tree planting. They were desperately poor. Pearlie would make damper and sometimes they would have honey or a bit of jam. When the odd tin of fruit came their way they would heat it up, add salt and pepper and call it soup. 'Christmas just came and went. Dad never talked about it because he didn't want to make us unhappy.'

The child barely saw the inside of a schoolroom. A misunderstanding with her Irish teacher in her first week of school quickly put an end to Pearlie's formal education.

In 1942 Pearlie's husband was killed in New Guinea and she was left a war widow with two children and a property to pay off. 'We ran a handful of sheep but at one shilling and three pence a pound for wool clippings, it wasn't enough to keep us going.' Her eldest son had been called up for the army. His health was delicate and Pearlie knew he would never survive New Guinea, so she set out to have him discharged. Opting for the direct approach, she travelled from Goulburn to the Army camp in Sydney where her son was training, and marched straight up to the gates.

It did not take her long to win the young guards over. They even pointed her in the direction of the lieutenant's office. 'I said to the lieutenant, my son would rather kill himself than kill another human being. Besides he's not strong enought to fight,' says Pearlie. She insisted that he be given a second medical examination to prove he was not 'A1' and, remarkably, the lieutenant agreed. Even more remarkably, the second examination revealed that he was indeed entirely unfit for active service and his release from the army was secured.

With characteristic determination, Pearlie now turned her attention to saving the property. She procured a loan from the bank and bought a truck. Her youngest son, Bill, was now fifteen and, in another round of negotiations with the authorities, she managed to obtain a special

Pearlie Watling in 1942, carting wood for the local brickworks. Today she is a popular accordion player at Goulburn dances

permit which allowed him to become the truck's driver.

Pearlie and Bill worked day and night collecting wood from local properties and delivering it to the brickworks in Goulburn. They would axe, saw, split and load six tonnes of wood a day.

Pearlie's next money-making venture was no easier and considerably more dangerous. She knew that she had plenty of shale, (an important constituent in the manufacture of earthenware) on her own property and it was not long before she had won a regular order from Fowlers of Marrickville, crockery makers. Pearlie blasted the decaying rocks out of her paddock with gelignite. 'I didn't know it was dangerous,' she says. After blasting, she would go in with the pick and shovel and load up the truck. Bill would drive it into Goulburn and then Pearlie would load the shale into a huge thirty tonne railway truck. For that, they received ten shillings a ton.

When Mr Fowler heard where his shale was coming from he came up from Sydney to visit Pearlie. He told her that he simply had not believed the stories that he had heard and had come to see for himself. He returned to Sydney full of admiration and the orders continued to roll in.

Pearlie kept the shale business going for eighteen years. When she was not working she was playing sports — tennis, football, cycling and cricket — or music. For twenty-seven years she was an enthusiastic cricketer, and was selected to play women's cricket for Australia. Today Pearlie lives in Goulburn and is still the life and soul of the party at the RSL: 'Now I've a little orchestra. We play old-time music and I seem to have quite a following.'

Ask Pearlie the clue to keeping on top and she will tell you, 'You must accept life and never look upon it as an ordeal'. Amazing words from one whose life could so easily be described as little else.

Albert Freund Zinnbauer
1911–1978
'Alien' pastor
Written by: Niall Lucy
Nominated by: Erna C. Mayer

In his native Austria, Pastor Albert Freund Zinnbauer had been a member of the anti-Nazi Social Democrat Party. It was, therefore, a bitter shock to find himself interned as an 'Enemy Alien' for four years when he arrived in South Australia in 1940 as a missionary for the Evangelical Lutheran Church. But Pastor Zinnbauer did not bear a grudge against his new country for the insensitivity shown to him in these early years and went on to help other new arrivals and needy Australians, regardless of their race or creed.

The egalitarianism of his approach to the ministry infuriated Church officials, who also objected to his hopeless bookkeeping and utter disregard of formalities. To Zinnbauer, however, petty officialdom and paper-pushing were simply impediments to his real work. So, too, was

Pastor A.F. Zinnbauer (right), more concerned with helping than converting, on the old bike on which he conducted his ecumenical pastoral rounds until he acquired a car which he drove in even more eccentric fashion. Passengers unidentified, but presumably confident that they are 'in the hands of one of God's own'

any concern for his appearance. He dressed out of the second-hand clothing bin and 'often looked like a tramp', a friend recalls affectionately.

Zinnbauer's driving was also famous. The police would stop traffic — whether out of reverence or fear is hard to tell — to let him pass. While many who knew him refused to get into his car, many others, like Mrs Mayer, 'felt that we were in the hands of one of God's own and would therefore be safe'.

For forty years, Pastor Zinnbauer worked ceaselessly to help new arrivals in hostels and those in need of care. He asked no payment of the poor for his celebration of weddings and christenings, and gave away most of the little money that he had. He and his wife, Dr Helga Zinnbauer, who between them spoke twelve languages, took in the homeless and showed them an exceptional charity, moving into the bathroom so that their guests could have the bedroom.

Pastor Zinnbauer was awarded an MBE in 1967 and was later decorated by the Austrian and German governments. He died in 1979.

Many of those who knew him believe that he was a saint.

Ned and Tabitha Tscharke
1918–   ; c1925–
Medical missionaries of Karkar
Written by: Jacqueline Kent
Nominated by: Allan Jones

In 1947 the Lutheran Church in New Guinea sent Ned Tscharke and his wife Tabitha to Karkar, to build and run a hospital. Karkar was a tropical island about fifty kilometres north of Madang known as the 'island of crooked people' because forty per cent of the 8000 inhabitants were crippled from malaria, leprosy, tropical sores, scabies or tuberculosis. Following war-time bombing, the villagers lived in makeshift camps where dysentery was rife.

Building a hospital on Karkar would have been difficult enough for a team of hospital administrators with a full medical backup staff. It was even harder for Ned and Tabitha Tscharke, who had no formal medical education.

Born in 1918 in Neales Flat, South Australia, Ned Tscharke had trained as a carpenter. At twenty-two he left his apprenticeship to help an uncle in the New Guinea Lutheran mission service and, in 1942, joined the New Guinea Volunteer Rifles. Recovering from malaria after the war, he became an army medical assistant, learning to diagnose and treat tropical diseases, administer anaesthetics and perform minor surgery. A devout Lutheran, he married the daughter of a Queensland pastor and rejoined the missionary service.

The Tscharkes, then, were medical missionaries. After a brief training period, they gathered up wood, roofing, iron nails and other building materials and on 2 September 1947 they arrived on Karkar.

The first task was to find a site for the hospital. Ned Tscharke knew exactly what they wanted: 'a place with plenty of good fresh water, a place to dispose of refuse, a level area so we wouldn't have to spend a lot of money on reconstruction before we even started building, and good road contact with the sea so we could communicate with the mainland,' he wrote in *A Quarter Century of Healing* (1972).

They found what they wanted in an area of dense bush, coconut palms and swamp land and 'hundreds of men, women and children arrived with axes and bush knives and lots of enthusiasm to clean up the area.' Eventually the first hospital was built, and was named Gaubin, after a local tree.

Gaubin was never intended to look like an ordinary hospital. 'I knew that the villagers wouldn't come if it did,' said Ned Tscharke. From the early days, patients have slept on woven palm leaf mats on the floor, not on mattresses between sheets. Their relatives, who visit them, bring their own food, clothing and cooking pots. Mothers are asked to hold their babies while anaesthetic is administered. All this is in the spirit of the Tscharkes' commitment to integrating the hospital with life on Karkar.

Soon after they arrived, about a dozen men were willing to train as *dokta bois* (medical orderlies). During the day, Ned taught the new orderlies basic skills: taking temperatures, measuring out medicine, making skin grafts. None of them could read or write Pidgin, the main form of communication on the island, so Tabitha taught them while Ned wrote the first medical text book in Pidgin.

Tabitha set up a weekly clinic for mothers and babies while Ned conducted open-air clinics in outlying parts of the island. He travelled on an old bicycle, later replaced by a small motorcycle, often pedalling along muddy jungle tracks in the pouring rain.

In 1957, the island suffered a TB epidemic. 'To the villagers TB seemed like just a cold...but they could see people slowly grew thin and tired,' said Ned Tscharke. 'I told them we had to expand our hospital by at least another eighty beds.'

The Lutheran mission supplied a brickmaking machine and a new wing was built, using the labour of the Karkar villagers. In 1959 an X-ray machine was donated and in 1967 the original wards and other buildings were reconstructed in brick. In the early 1970s, the government chose Gaubin as a training hospital and today, Gaubin's health record is one of the best in the Third World.

After establishing a medical scheme that became a Third World model, Ned and Tabitha Tscharke retired to Queensland early in 1988, Ned having been awarded the MBE in 1974 'for serving the people of Papua New Guinea in the fields of health and health education.' They admit that life on Karkar was often hard, but this is overshadowed by the joy of hearing the community say, 'This is our hospital!'

John Cade
1912–1980
'Mending the mind'
Written by: Niall Lucy
Nominated by: David Cade

Australian psychiatrist John Cade's discovery of the efficacy of lithium carbonate in the treatment of manic depression was estimated by the American National Institute of Mental Health in 1985 to have saved the world at least $17.5 billion in medical costs over the previous fifteen years. Dr Cade's discovery, a major breakthrough in psychiatric medicine, has been acclaimed in psychiatric circles around the globe.

A POW for three and a half years in Changi, Dr Cade resumed his medical career upon returning to Australia in 1945. The following year, at the age of thirty-four, he was appointed Psychiatry Superintendent at Bundoora Repatriation Hospital in Victoria. Believing that some mental illnesses were caused by an underlying metabolic disturbance, the identification of which could lead to rational and effective treatment, he set about investigating his theory in the disused kitchen of an old ward that served as his research laboratory.

Cade soon found that the urine of manic patients was more toxic than normal urine. With his subsequent discovery, by trial and error, that a lithium extract had a marked protective effect against this toxicity, he knew he was on the verge of a major breakthrough. In 1948, after testing its safety on himself, he experimented with the extract in the treatment of a greatly disturbed patient who had been confined to the high-dependency ward at Bundoora for the previous five years. Within a week, the patient became calm and was transferred to the open rehabilitation ward where his improved condition remained stable. A month after treatment began, the patient was able to return home to his family and former job. A further nine patients responded in a similar manner to the experimental treatment.

Cade published his findings in *The Medical Journal of Australia* in September, 1949. Immediately, his report on the curative effect of lithium carbonate in the treatment of acute manic psychosis aroused the interest of the international medical community. Recognition of his breakthrough came with the presentation of the Taylor Manor Hospital

Dr John Cade, a member of a distinguished medical family. His discovery enabled thousands of manic depressives to lead normal lives

Award in Maryland, USA, in 1970. Four years later, the Australian psychiatrist was named joint winner of the prestigious Kittay Scientific Foundation Award in New York.

In a distinguished career, Dr Cade served as President of the Royal Australian and New Zealand Colleges of Psychiatrists and was Dean of the Clinical School at Royal Park Psychiatric Hospital, Melbourne, for twenty-five years. He died in Melbourne in 1980 at the age of sixty-eight.

Elizabeth Rogers
1907–

'From the dust of ignominy...'
Written by: Suzanne Falkiner
Nominated by: Rhonda Matheson

Elizabeth Rogers in Launceston c.1950, when she was making radical changes as Matron of the Launceston Girls' Home

When Elizabeth Rogers disembarked from the aeroplane in Launceston, Tasmania, on 11 December 1948 to take up her voluntary position as temporary Matron of the Launceston Girls' Home, she was startled to find a journalist and photographer waiting in the air terminal to interview her. Separated from her husband, with few formal credentials, and accompanied by her two young children, she had agreed to help out for six weeks during the school holidays while she was not needed at the Uralla Hospital School, where she worked as assistant to the physiotherapist. She knew nothing about the new job. When the journalist pointedly probed her about her knowledge of the Home and her ideas about her position there, she began to suspect that it might be less straightforward than it had seemed.

At first sight, the institution on Wellington Street did little to allay her trepidation. Built of red brick, it was daunting and squalid. With grounds strewn with rubbish and brawling children climbing in and out of the windows, it was an affront to the well-kept suburban homes and gardens that surrounded it. Mrs Rogers' immediate reprimands were met with a stream of abuse.

The home, Mrs Rogers soon discovered, had been through seven matrons in the preceding eighteen months. Some of the local people had petitioned the government to close it down. The insitution that housed forty or so girls aged between three and seventeen had been described as a 'festering sore' on the community and had provoked ministers of religion to preach against it from the Sunday pulpit.

Established in 1876 as a Girls' Industrial School, the Launceston Girls' Home became, in 1885, a home for orphaned or neglected children. In 1948 administered by a Board of Governors consisting of prominent but elderly men of the city, and, in addition, a Ladies' Auxiliary, it had changed little in outlook since the nineteenth century.

Soon after her arrival, the governing bodies made clear to Matron Rogers that they were used to little opposition from staff. But Elizabeth Rogers 'was getting mad'. If the Governors and Ladies' Auxiliary had known a little more about the woman with whom they were dealing,

The girls of the Launceston Girls' Home decked in flowers at a spring picnic, one of the many pleasures instituted by Matron Rogers. c.1950. On her arrival two years earlier, these girls had been unruly, ill-treated and neglected

they might have been a little less highhanded in their treatment of her.

Born in Carlton, Melbourne, in 1907, and partially educated at a city school, Elizabeth's early life had been tough enough to prepare her for anything. Her mother had died when she was four. At the age of eight or nine her father left her at a boarding house for a holiday and, before he was able to come back to collect her, he also died of an illness. After some weeks she became the informal 'property' of the boarding-house keeper, a Mrs Fowler, who beat her and worked her hard but trained her to become a competent housekeeper. At thirteen, following years of ill-treatment, which through fear she had always denied to strangers, she was rescued by police after a complaint from a witness to a particularly severe beating. A young policeman, William Rapkins, who later became her guardian, placed her with other foster parents until he himself married, at which time she went to live with him and his wife.

When Elizabeth was old enough to work, she found a job with a nearby herbalist. Other jobs followed, in a dairy produce concern and in food preparation, all of which helped to give her a working knowledge of health and nutrition. In 1932, during the Depression, Elizabeth married Frank Rogers, the manager of a grocery and produce store, and later bore a son, Barrie, and a daughter, Fay. At the outbreak of war Elizabeth took over Frank's position as store manager while he went away to fight. Soon after his return, the couple separated. Elizabeth began work at the Uralla School Hospital after her daughter became a victim of the 1945 poliomyelitis epidemic, while taking on voluntary club work for the National Fitness Council in her spare time. It was through this connection that she was recruited to fill in at the Launceston Girls' Home.

Elizabeth Rogers had told the journalist at the air terminal to contact her after the weekend when she had had time to look at the home. After the initial shock of the smell, the filth, and the children running wild, she informed him and his paper that she considered it complete social irresponsibility on the part of the local community that they

Elizabeth Rogers Charlesworth, 1988. Until recently, she conducted a gym class for the over fifties. Photograph by Ponch Hawkes

had allowed such a situation to have arisen.

With other staff, consisting of two women who were old hands, and another newcomer, the cook, Matron Rogers set about making changes. By the end of the six-week period she had decided that she was, as she herself put it, 'in so deep' that she would have to stay, and she cancelled her plans to return to the mainland. At her first meeting with the Chief Secretary, Elizabeth Rogers told him that the Home was a disgrace to his administration and asked him, if it closed down, what he intended to do with its charges. Chastened, he asked her what she needed. With his initial grant of money she re-equipped the kitchen. Then she moved on to the beds and crockery.

The older men on the Board resigned and were replaced by younger, more influential men through whom Matron Rogers could reach the local community and ask for help to improve the Home. No contribution was too small: from a women's group Matron Rogers obtained a supply of new handkerchiefs; from the Masonic lodge, sporting equipment. There was nothing that was not needed. The local Service clubs were won over by the new Matron's no-nonsense approach, and funds began to multiply. But if the new committee was helpful, the Ladies' Auxiliary was soon intent on getting rid of her.

Some members of the Ladies' Auxiliary had been in the habit of regarding the home as a source of domestic labour for themselves and their society friends. During the four years of her reign, however, Matron Rogers removed the emphasis on placing girls in domestic service and instead began to train them for better-paid business and clerical positions. No child was considered irredeemable. She gained the trust of the children by approaching them as individuals and by demonstrating a fighting spirit.

Soon she had formed a drama group, a sports group and a choir, provided a well-equipped library and study, along with playhouses for the younger children, and made moves towards building tennis and basketball courts. Sports teams competed locally, and a vegetable garden meant a plentiful supply of fresh vegetables to keep the girls healthy. A more startling achievement in terms of organisation and discipline was that Mrs Rogers now took all forty girls on a three-week seaside camping holiday in January of each year.

This was part of her attempt to reproduce the features of a normal family life. As well, the older girls were expected to help with the younger ones and were taught the relationship of responsibility and privilege. This was so successful that when the girls reached working age, they were often unwilling to leave what had become home. In

Four of the girls from the Launceston Girls' Home who benefited from 'Matey' Rogers' approach to the care of orphaned, abandoned, or supposedly 'uncontrollable' girls. Her devotion, tenacity and fighting spirit gave them a new sense of their own worth

time, Matron Rogers, with her advanced ideas on education and physical fitness for girls, would have charges spread all over Australia, many of them crediting her with a start in life that they otherwise would have been denied.

By the end of four years, the Home was running well, and Matron Rogers felt she had done as much as she could. She was ready to leave. Her idea of buying the property at the back of the home and turning it into a hostel for the older girls — a halfway house from the institution to the rest of society — was blocked by the opposition of the women's committee which had now become a fundraising group with four members on the Board, so Matron Rogers resigned.

From Launceston Mrs Rogers went to the Quaker Friends' School in Hobart, and arranged for some of the girls from the home to come and work with her. She remained there while her children grew up, and subsequently worked with Legacy in Hobart. She then went on to the Melbourne Orphanage, which she transformed as she had Launceston. Meanwhile, a second marriage, to Harry Charlesworth, also ended in divorce. Later jobs included three years in Darwin as a Welfare Officer, five years with the Education Department, and volunteer work with the blind and mentally retarded until, in her seventies, 'Matey', as she was known at Launceston, retired.

In 1988, aged eighty-one, Elizabeth Charlesworth lives in a Waverley Council-sponsored unit in Melbourne, and restricts her activities to volunteer work. Her interests include bushwalking and teaching Sunday School. Until recently she worked for Meals on Wheels and conducted, through a church group, a gymnastic class for the over fifties. A great raconteur, she also has a deep concern for the children of today who live on the street because institutions are no longer adequate.

Mrs Rhonda Matheson, who grew up in the Home, has been so inspired by her mentor that she is working on a novel based on the story of Matron Rogers and the Launceston Girls' Home. She says of Elizabeth Rogers, 'Pulling forty children from the dust of ignominy... was achieved through a vision, tenacity and devotion to children perhaps unique in the field of child care. It won for these kids — and I was one — the interest and sympathy of a city that had once been divided against them.'

Arnold Cook
1922–1981
Stubborn visionary
Written by: Terri McCormack
Nominated by: Robert J. Daniel

Only those who cannot read these words can fully appreciate Dr Arnold Cook's contribution to sightless Australians.

Arnold Cook was a fifteen-year-old Western Australian clerk when, in 1937 he experienced peripheral eyesight problems. His condition was diagnosed as *retinitis pigmentosa*, a genetic disease in which the sight irrevocably degenerates. In his case the deterioration was rapid. By the time he was eighteen, this intelligent young man was totally blind and an inmate of the Perth Institute for the Blind, where he learned canework by day and Braille by night.

A chance encounter with a teacher who recognised his ability resulted in a group of her colleagues assisting him to matriculate and enter the University of Western Australia on a Commonwealth Scholarship in 1944. Being one of the few men on the wartime campus, Cook received ample reading help from his female fellow students, one of whom he married two years later. He graduated with honours in economics and, in July 1948, went to the London School of Economics on a Hackett Scholarship.

In England, Cook learned of the Guide Dogs for the Blind Centre at Leamington Spa and enrolled for training at a branch school in Exeter. Almost concurrently with the birth of the first of his four children, he returned to his London flat with Dreena, the black labrador who was to become Western Australia's most famous dog. Mrs Enid Cook recalls the amusing spectacle as man and dog negotiated the clutter generated by an increasingly active toddler.

In August 1950, Cook returned to the University of Western Australia as lecturer in Economics. In the first of many confrontations with intractable bureaucracies, Dreena was quarantined for six months at the end of which the Cooks had to retrain her themselves. None of those who paused to pat the working dog was aware of the complexities of training guide dogs but Arnold Cook soon changed that.

Cook was determined that others should share the increased mobility and independence that Dreena gave him. Through his persistence and publicity, the Guide Dog Association of Western Australia was incorporated in June 1951, and by November, Betty Bridge, his English trainer, had been employed. But they faced the problems of lack of finance, inadequate premises, unsuitable dogs, and official obstruction as well as opposition from established groups of what Mrs Cook terms 'sighted philanthropists'. By 1955, however, when Cook became President and the Association received a government grant, many of these and other unforeseen difficulties had been overcome. When the National Guide Dog Training Centre opened in the more climatically suitable Victorian suburb of Kew in November 1962, the initiative of Arnold Cook in inaugurating this valuable social service in Australia was acknowledged.

Underterred by his handicap, Cook pursued a distinguished career as an economist, gaining a doctorate from Harvard University in 1967 and spending time in Japan as a visiting scholar in 1970. Also in 1967, his alma mater provided him with a private secretary who assisted him with the research for which his Braille was useless. Enid Cook, equally capable of meeting a challenge, then resumed her interrupted career as a clinical psychologist.

In the early 1960s, Dr Cook formed the Western Australian branch of the Australian Guild of Business and Professional Blind, later becoming the Western Australian Guild of Blind Citizens. He also established the Western Australian Retinitis Pigmentosa Foundation, now part of an international organisation, which promoted and funded research into degenerative eye diseases.

Dreena, whom Cook had given to a young blind and partially deaf woman, died during his absence in America. The average working

Dr Arnold Cook in training with Dreena, the first guide dog for the blind in Australia

life for a dog is eight years and Dr Cook, on the eve of his retirement, was undergoing rigorous training with his fourth guide dog when he died from a heart attack in 1981.

According to his wife and no doubt the many whom he inspired, Arnold Cook's greatest achievement was his own example to young blind people that they can help themselves to a far richer life than that provided by a sheltered workshop.

Lloyd Stuchbery
1925–1984

'Happiness is helping'
Written by: Linda Whitford
Nominated by: Jennifer M. Tonkin

Lloyd Stuchbery at work on his farm. When polio rendered his legs useless, he applied his inventive brain to making life easier for others as well as himself

On Christmas Eve, 1947, Lloyd Stuchbery, twenty-two and married for just over a year, was struck down by polio. A racing cyclist who had won trophies throughout Victoria, he was never to walk again. After three years in hospital, ten weeks of it spent in an iron lung, Lloyd returned to his hometown of Portland, Victoria. Paralysed in both legs and one shoulder, with his left lung collapsed, Lloyd came home to his wife, Mary, and a one-bedroom house built by friends and locals while he was in hospital.

At school, Lloyd had had two ambitions — to be a sailor and a farmer. He had joined the navy at seventeen and served throughout the Pacific in World War II. Now, he set about becoming a farmer. With the loan of a tractor and a piggy-back from Mary up into its seat, he began to clear and plough his land. With one foot on the clutch and the other on the brake, he pressed down on his knees to operate the pedals.

With his brother's help, Lloyd soon designed and built a wheelchair which could travel over rough ground. The wheelchair took him everywhere, including the twelve kilometre trip into town.

During the 1950s, Lloyd worked from dawn to dusk on his own land, and for up to seven other farmers at once. He invented an automatic potato cutter, and an oiling mechanism for a potato planter manufacturer, in thanks for which he was given a new twin row planter. In this way, Lloyd Stuchbery became one of Portland's largest potato growers and contractors, and, with the help of Mary, his two sons and four daughters, established Hunt's Estate in South Portland and Cockatoo Valley Farm, a two-hectare showpiece of beautiful gardens containing an enormous vegetable garden.

Lloyd also taught himself to weld. He did his own car, tractor and machinery repairs, baled hay for himself and neighbours, fixed windmills and bores, cleaned dams and built sheds and fences. He cared for his sheep by training his dog to single out the one he wanted and bring it to his wheelchair or car door. He mowed the lawn by making a hand control lever for a rider-mower, and for many years mowed the lawns and oval at the North Portland School.

Lloyd's inventions extended beyond his own needs. Following his invention of an exercise machine for Erin Hardy, a neighbour's daughter who had suffered brain damage at birth, Lloyd was working on inventions to help a disabled Melbourne youth and a young Portland boy. Erin's exercise machine was featured in the Melbourne *Herald* of 7 April 1984. Lloyd Stuchbery, fifty-nine, died from a heart attack the following night.

Leopold Siegellak
1909–

'An anonymous righteous man'
Written by: Lucinda Strauss
Nominated by: Jack Frisch

'Siegellak is a man of absolute righteousness. He is known throughout the [Jewish] community and whenever he rings, nobody asks him for what or for whom. If Siegellak asks for something — it is needed. People trust his judgement. The key to his success is his absolute credibility.'
Alex Weinnberger, Talmudic scholar.

For hundreds of refugees fleeing from a war-torn Europe, docking in Sydney brought them face to face with the shining blue eyes and hearty laugh of Leopold Siegellak. As a stranger, he would help anyone who looked lost or had no-one to meet them. Gathering them up in his Willys jeep, he would take care of their most urgent needs, providing lodgings, if required, at his own expense for a week or so while he helped them find jobs. Sometimes only a phone call was needed but whatever it was, Siegellak was there.

'From the day he arrived in Australia, he was a one-man social welfare service to the post-war migrant Jewish community,' says Jack Frisch, whose family was one of many helped by Siegellak. He not only arranged the migration permits for hundreds of the Jewish refugees, but found sponsors and guarantors, helped locate the relatives of incoming migrants, and pressed the more affluent Jews of the day to employ the new arrivals.

'Siegellak's work did not finish when the needs of the post-Holocaust migrants fell away,' continues Jack. 'There were the Hungarians of 1956; the Russians of recent years; and those Jews who never struck it lucky on the new shores. There are always widows, orphans and the sick who need comforting. He never made a penny out of this work. He made just enough money to be able to support himself with the essentials of life and to this day he maintains that lifestyle. Siegellak has never received an award, taken a position on a committee, or even rated a mention in the Jewish press. It is not as if anybody would deny his work, it is simply a matter of being taken for granted. Few in the community would disagree about anybody more deserving.'

Of the hundreds of people helped by Siegellak, few know much about him. He was born on 27 April 1909 in Churst (once part of

Czechoslovakia, now part of the Soviet Union) and was the fourth of nine children to his parents, Herman and Ozsen. As a tinsmith, his father earned a meagre wage and everyone in the family did what they could to bring in money. While the women worked at home, all five boys were sent out at an early age to find jobs. Siegellak was only eight years old when he started his first job picking apples. As he grew older he took whatever jobs he could, eventually being apprenticed to a glazier, a trade which he practised for most of his working life.

With the Nazi invasion of Hungary, Siegellak lost his liberty as well as his family. For five years he was forced to work in a succession of labour camps throughout Czechoslovakia, Hungary and Poland. In May 1944, at a time when he was granted leave to visit home, he received word that his wife Esther and six children had been rounded up by the Nazis and taken to Auschwitz. By the end of the war there was no home to return to, for both his parents had been killed and those brothers and sisters still alive were scattered across Europe.

In 1946, from a United Nations Refugee camp near Munich, Siegellak applied to both Australia and the United States for immigration. Australia accepted him first and he arrived in Melbourne aboard the Yugoslavian SS *Radnik* on 2 April 1948. He was met by relatives and after a few days put on a plane to meet the Sydney cousins who had sponsored him.

Within a week he had not only found a job and a place to live but had set about sponsoring ten of his own friends who had also survived the war. He then started gathering the names and addresses of friends of friends. As his work became known, strangers would approach him in the street asking for him to sponsor a relative or friend so that eventually Siegellak was responsible for helping hundreds of people to find a new life in Australia.

Joseph Schwartz was only nineteen when he arrived in Sydney with his parents. He had known others in Vienna being sponsored by Siegellak and dreamed of meeting a short, fat man in a dark suit and Homburg, riding in a chauffeur-driven Cadillac. The reality was very different. In the chaos of arrival at Central Station a short, stout man in an ex-army jacket shouting 'Schwartz, Schwartz!' bundled them into his battered jeep and delivered them to their friend's flat in Rose Bay. He then raided the fridge, prepared them a meal and disappeared. It was not until the next day that they found out that this was indeed Mr Siegellak.

Jack Frisch, a small child at the time, remembers a kindly, gentle man who helped his bewildered parents find a place to stay on their arrival in 1951. Mrs Frisch's cousins, who had sponsored them, were not at the boat to meet them, and Siegellak took the family to a boarding house in Bondi while he made the necessary contact. It was the beginning of a long friendship.

'He came out of the blue,' say Shari Szatmari, who was helped by him shortly after her arrival in 1951. When Shari moved into a family hotel in Edgecliff with her husband and two babies she knew no-one there and felt unwelcome. The next morning she discovered a pram filled with baby clothes outside her door. Siegellak had found out about her. 'He was an angel to the newcomer,' she recalls, 'a selfless, helpful man who would never accept a thing for himself.'

These days, although retired from his glazing business, Siegellak actively pursues his charitable work from a flat provided by friends. When asked why he has devoted his life to helping others, Siegellak simply replies 'It's my nature'. Then he tells of his father, a generous man who, despite his own poverty, always gave food to hungry people who knocked at their door. He once asked his father why he did this, to which his father replied, 'I am giving these poor people something to save them from stealing. I am giving them Honour.' 'My father,' says Siegellak, 'only saw the good side of people. If someone threw him a stone, he would give back bread. I am very much like him. I see only the good side of people.'

Siegellak not only sees the good side but is able to bring out the best in other people so that they help each other. Jack Frisch explains: 'After my parents became well-to-do he would come and say there was a family that needed a couple of hundred dollars, and my parents knew that one hundred per cent of the money would go to the person in need. It was always done with discretion and dignity, and names were never mentioned. Recently, when my late mother was in hospital, he left a simple get-well note with a small bunch of flowers. I found out later that he had also arranged that a pious man pray three times a day for her health.'

'Always behind the scenes, he is there whenever needed,' says Rabbi Feldman from the Yeshiva Synagogue, 'a simple, humble man whose goodness is legendary.' Jack Frisch best expresses the admiration and debt of gratitude that many in the community feel to a man whose heart is always open. 'There is a Jewish tradition,' he says, 'that the world stands on the shoulders of thirty-six anonymous righteous men. I believe I am privileged to know one of them.'

Leopold Siegellak (right), wearing the uniform of a Hungarian soldier, in the Sianki Labour Camp, Poland, 1941. He came to Australia after losing his wife and six children in Auschwitz and has been, ever since, 'a one-man social welfare service' to post-war Jewish immigrants

Luigi Resciniti
1916–

The newcomers' friend
Written by: Judith Elen
Nominated by: Joseph Tucci

When Luigi Resciniti was conscripted into the Italian army and went to fight in Egypt, leaving behind his family and his young fiancé, Domenica, he believed that it was for the good of his country. The eldest son of a large peasant family in the small village of Bellosguardo, south of Naples, Luigi had seen the local peasants work the land, only to hand over three-quarters of their produce to the large landowners. He believed that Mussolini would right these wrongs. Captured in Tobruk and brought to Australia as a POW, Luigi felt that home was very far away. But as the years went by, he was to establish security for his own family, and for many other families besides, in the new home he had found in Australia.

After two years of war, Luigi was interned in a POW camp at Hay in New South Wales. Taken in 1944 to be billeted with a farming family at Korumburra in Victora, Luigi's life took a significant new direction. His honesty and hard work recommended him and Luigi came to regard these people as his own parents.

After the war he continued to work on the farm, earning the money for his fare home. When his Australian 'family' offered to sponsor his return to Australia as a migrant, Luigi accepted. In 1947 he returned to Bellosguardo and to Domenica, who for many years had not known if he were still alive. They married and had a daughter, Carmen. Then, in 1951, Luigi left the village where his family had lived for as many generations as anyone could remember and returned to Australia alone, to work and save.

For three years Luigi worked long hours on the farm at Korumburra, and later at GMH at Fisherman's Bend. When his wife, daughter and brother arrived on the boat from Italy in 1955, he was able to take them to their own house in Richmond. Luigi's nephew says that 'even today it makes my auntie cry' when she remembers her surprise.

Luigi was the first from his village to come to Australia but many followed him, all either sponsored or helped financially by Luigi and Domenica. Each of these relatives in their extended family was taken into the two-bedroom house in Richmond and given free board while they settled into the new environment. Often a family of five or six people would stay in the lounge-room of the small house.

Joe Tucci, Luigi's twenty-two-year-old nephew and one of 'over 120 people who owe their stability and livelihood in Australia to my uncle Luigi', tells the story of his own mother, Elisa, when she arrived in 1961. 'In her own words, it seemed that Australia at the time was offering only pain. Such thoughts caused her to cry continuously for months after her arrival. Luigi showed her that life was what you made

Luigi Resciniti, POW in Australia during World War II and hard-working immigrant after it, at his Melbourne home where he has welcomed and helped many bewildered migrants from his Italian village. Photograph by Ponch Hawkes

it — found her a job and took her to and from work every day. She earned enough money to sponsor her fiancé to Australia and after her marriage she became my mum and a happy one at that. Now she considers Australia her true home because of Luigi and never cries.'

Now seventy-two, Luigi Resciniti 'expects nothing...[other than] the occasional get-together to swap some old stories with the younger members of the family.' He has taken his ill fortune and turned it around. Out of the injustice and poverty in the village, the disruption of war, and imprisonment, he has steadily gathered his family around him to establish his own community in relative prosperity and happiness.

Marianne Mills
1919–1979
'Sister Pav'
Written by: Suzanne Falkiner
Nominated by: Moira Elsner

Marianne Perunov-Pawlovsky, a large woman, was a familiar sight in the early 1950s as she rode to work as a nurse at the Royal Perth Hospital perched on her Prima motor scooter. Not many women rode scooters to work in those days, but Marianne Pawlovsky — always known as 'Sister Pav' — was always a person who did and said what

Top. Marianne Schmoock (Sister Pav) at her graduation in Frankfurt in February 1940

Below. Sister Pav in May 1969, a leader in quadriplegia research and innovative care

she liked. Besides, her shift started at six, so she was up at four, and it was a three-kilometre walk from her housing commission home to the nearest bus stop and two changes of bus after that.

Nearly twenty years later, it was the same practicality and disregard for established procedure that most marked Sister Pav's distinctive administration of the Shenton Park Quadraplegic Centre, Western Australia—special beds, unlike the usual hospital design; gaily coloured blinds and floorcoverings to provide a non-clinical atmosphere; switches and taps placed at a suitable height for a person in a wheel chair and thought given to things that might psychologically help a paraplegic or quadraplegic patient, such as avoiding the routine taking of temperatures except in cases of actual illness.

Sister Pav was an example of the strength and determination that allowed some immigrants to come with nothing from the chaos and ruin of post-war Europe and not only rebuild their own lives, but make a significant contribution to their adopted country.

Sister Pav was born Marianne Schmoock in Zielenzig, Germany in 1919, and graduated as a nurse in 1940. She worked in various hospitals and clinics and as a voluntary Red Cross sister towards the end of World War II. In June 1942 she married Gunther Elsner, a mechanic in the German Navy. Her only child, Bernhard, was born in April 1943. Gunther Elsner was declared missing in action and later found to be a prisoner in the Middle East. Marianne, with her child and her parents, fled to Potsdam in the face of the Russian advance. After the war she separated from her husband and they eventually divorced.

She met her second husband, Sergei Perunov, a major in the Russian army, while working in a Russian 'Policlinic'. Marianne and Sergei defected from the eastern zone to the west and were evacuated during the Berlin Air Lift of 1948. At this time the couple were required to use an alias, 'Pawlovsky'.

After a period spent working in a displaced persons' camp, Marianne and her husband came to Australia aboard the *Anna Salen*, arriving in Fremantle on 19 January 1951. Sergei worked as a storeman, and in 1953 Marianne underwent a six-month trial period as a nursing aide at Royal Perth Hospital before graduating to nurse, Staff Nurse and later Ward Sister. In 1955 she began work at Shenton Park Annexe paraplegic centre.

Marianne Perunov-Pawlovsky was naturalised in 1965. In 1966, after four years incapacitated by a stroke, husband Sergei died.

In September 1969, Sister Pav, by then a Board Member of the Paraplegic Association of Western Australia became the first matron of the new Shenton Park Quadraplegic Centre, contributing to its design and formation. To keep up to date, she travelled overseas several times to visit quadraplegic centres in England and Germany.

Sister Pav was a determined woman who made enemies as well as friends, but if the nurses under her were a little frightened of her, they also respected her, and her patients loved her. They fondly remember her keen interest in horse racing and her habit of giving tips to people: she always bet on greys and usually won. 'She could mix in any company, talk to anyone,' her daughter-in-law, Moira Elsner, recalls. 'And she knew how to have a good time. I remember how, at the end of the day, she used to go out to the German club and drink champagne, let her hair down after the stress of the job.'

Marianne Mills, who had married Oswald Mills in 1972, died in 1979, a fortnight before her scheduled retirement date. With little public recognition, Sister Pav, Marianne Mills, had contributed twenty-eight years of service to Australia, a good proportion of it as a pioneer in paraplegic nursing.

Isabel McCorkindale
1887–1970
Far-sighted social reformer
Written by: Judith Elen
Nominated by: Isabel Hunt

At the 1951 Women's Christian Temperance Union Convention, Isabel McCorkindale spoke of future plans. 'The WCTU must work for Equality of the sexes;...for Road Safety, particularly in regard to the drinking driver;...[and for] Aborigines [to] have the same rights and privileges as white people.' Isabel McCorkindale was 'a charismatic leader' who 'set the Australian WCTU on a course that included not only temperance but a much wider social agenda.'

The caricature of the fierce temperance worker has always been a simplistic reduction of an important social force. Isabel McCorkindale's wide interests, range of service, progressive thinking and humour provide an excellent example of the broad perspective of many of these women. For Isabel, as for Marie Kirk, the WCTU provided a focus for a lifelong dedication to social reform. Like Frances Willard, they believed that 'Whatever touches humanity, touches us'.

In *Pioneer Pathways*, her short history of the WCTU (1948), Isabel explains the movement in its social context: 'To many women the Union...enabled [them] to do battle for the rights of those not able to help themselves'; others saw 'that women could do collectively what they were unable to do as individuals...it strengthened the spiritual, social and political consciousness of women.' In a period when women were effectively confined to the home and denied personal rights, drunkenness created a life of hardship and misery for many. 'The Home Protection Policy' of the WCTU fought the drunkenness that caused so much family poverty and domestic violence.

From 1911, when Isabel was twenty-four, until her death at eighty-three, she held numerous posts with the organisation: national director of education for nearly forty years, she was also Australia's first World President. She represented Australia at conferences and lecture tours in several countries, ran radio programmes, published books, edited the magazine, trained workers and organized campaigns. In 1950 she was an Australian delegate to the United Nations Status of Women Commission and in 1963 she was awarded an MBE.

Described as 'a rather elfin figure', 'slight, dark and bright-eyed' Isabel McCorkindale was appreciated by her colleagues for 'her charm, leadership capacity, sense of humour and eloquence'. She also 'raised

Isabel McCorkindale, a leading member of the Women's Christian Temperance Union, devoted her life to improving the status of women

her three step-sisters as her own family and was popular with them and their children'. One of these children says that Isabel 'made a pact with a fellow "WCTUer", Ada Bromham, never to marry'. According to this niece, Isabel used to say 'she couldn't stand to marry because she'd have to ask a man for 6s. 11d. every time she wanted a pair of stockings.' This apparently small, but telling, personal anecdote captures the relationship of women to men, money and power which Isabel and other women like her, fought to change.

For Isabel, financial justice was particularly vital for the poor woman, 'the degraded woman to whom financial independence, equal pay for equal work, has often proved the lifting lever to a rehabilitated life.'

Marjorie Stapleton
1915–

Emergency wage dropper
Written by: Lucinda Strauss
Nominated by: Gwenefa Greenfield

At dawn on a fresh January morning in 1952 an apprehensive Marjorie Stapleton strapped herself into the Auster as it taxied over the airstrip and took off over the Saracen domes and minarets of Kuala Lumpur to drop wages to isolated rubber plantations in the Malayan jungle. Born in New Zealand, Marjorie had come to Malaya in early 1947 with her two small children and her husband, a mining engineer in the British Colonial Service. Much had changed as a result of the war. In the turmoil of the postwar years, the balance of power was shifting and new, racially-based, political groups were emerging. With the Japanese gone, the Malayan Communist Party was now dedicated to ousting the British and de-stablising the country in what amounted to an undeclared state of civil war.

During 'The Emergency', as it was euphemistically called, the CT's (Communist terrorists) or bandits, attacked both military and civilian targets. In 1951 alone there were over 2000 terrorist casualties, half of them civilians. Even the most senior officials were not safe. Public confidence reached an all-time low in October 1951 when the British High Commissioner, Sir Henry Gurney, was brutally murdered by CTs during an ambush.

One of the main aims of the Communist offensive was to disrupt the country's economy, with the rubber estates and tin mines a primary focus of terrorist attack. The most vulnerable targets were the European plantation and mine managers in the outlying areas. Many were ambushed in their armoured cars on the lonely jungle roads and shot dead while carrying home enormous sums of money for the labourers' wages.

In an effort to keep the economy running and curb the loss of life, the Malayan Flying Clubs joined forces to provide a pay-dropping service to the thousands of Malay, Indian and Chinese rubber and tin-mine workers in bandit-infested areas. The drop team, consisting of ten regular and up to thirty volunteer pilots, were mainly English, Scottish and Australians. Setting off in their Tiger Moths or Austers, they flew day after day over humid jungle to drop wages to isolated mines and estates.

Leaving secretly in the early hours of the morning, they sometimes carried up to a quarter of a million dollars in their code-signed leather bags. The aim was to cross the mountains and return before the 'thermals' came up — the warm air currents which made flying difficult and uncomfortable. Indeed wartime flying experience proved invaluable for pilots in these conditions — aerobatic skills were crucial for planes flying low during a drop and there was always the possibility of being shot at by terrorists.

Marjorie's husband was one of the volunteer pilots and as Secretary of the Kuala Lumpur Flying Club she had an inside knowledge of its workings. Marjorie had been involved in the secret bookwork and knew of the millions of dollars in hard cash being dropped during the Emergency. Events in her personal life, however, prompted her to take a more active role in the operation. After Norah Stutchbury, the wife of a District Officer and a close friend of Marjorie's, was murdered in the jungle by bandits, Marjorie decided to become a 'dropper'.

When she applied for permission, the club committee warned Marjorie that her wrists should be strong: 'You might have to hold a heavy bag against a ninety-five-mile-an-hour gale.' As the time for her first drop drew near she felt a rising anxiety. Writing shortly after the experience, she recalls. 'My dreams on the last night of waiting were hectic. I was dropping bags all the night. Sometimes they fell into lakes, sometimes into the hands of bandits...In yet another dream the money bag pulled me out with it. I went to the air-strip next morning opening and shutting my hands.'

Marjorie was fortunate in having K.G. Hamnett OBE, president of the Kuala Lumpur Flying Club and commandant of the new training corps, as her pilot and trainer. Standing beside the Auster, on her first and only rehearsal, he handed her the bags and after a brief try-out issued the following instructions: 'When I say "Get ready," put the bag overboard, minding the wing and holding the bag in both hands. Grip it tightly. Then when I say "Drop", you drop, and you shout "Away".' 'Yes,' Marjorie thought, 'I'll probably drop dead'.

Handling the bags, however, did make her feel a little more confident. Her job was to untie the rope hung inside the aircraft, lift the money bag down without letting it touch the floor (as the weight of the coin could make it crash through the floor), re-tie the rope and sit with the bag securely on her knee until the word came.

After taking off that first morning, they flew for nearly an hour, past the gaping holes left by the mines and the long stretches of feathery rubber trees to the jungle. Suddenly the pilot spotted a small settlement with the white identification mark laid out on the manager's front lawn. After the Auster circled round twice with a great roar of engines, the manager, four armed guards and several assistants appeared. Further back stood the labourers. The women came to the doors of their houses, their children clinging to their skirts. All eyes were lifted to the tiny aircraft.

The pilot circled once more, coming in lower above the *kongsi* houses, shouting to Marjorie to get ready. Marjorie hauled the bag up and

Marjorie Stapleton in a Tiger Moth after dropping wage bags to isolated planters and mine managers during the Malayan 'Emergency' of the 1950s

over the side. 'Though I gripped it with both hands, and it was a heavy bag, it trailed horizontally beside the aircraft in the slipstream. We flew over the identification mark, and the next order came. "Drop". It dropped. "Away". [she signaled]... We circled... again and saw that the bag had been picked up and was being escorted along the ground by armed guards.'

By the third drop that day Marjorie was feeling like an old hand. Untying the rope and transferring the bag to her knees she prepared herself for a more difficult manoeuvre over a densely wooded dropping zone. 'I leaned out and felt the wind whipping at clothes, hair and even eyelashes. The world tilted sideways and we were gliding over the zone. There were the manager and the usual guards, and the expectant crowd of wage-earners gathered below, all tilted backwards and fore-shortened, so that they appeared to have stout chests and no legs. The children looked like midget adults in their sarongs and sarees.'

On the way home that first day, Marjorie reflected on the fact that $100 000 had 'dropped' through her hands. Now, relaxing, she looked down at the jungle below and imagined she could see 'fresh bandit tracks, newly broken-up camps and all sorts of sinister things'.

This was the first of over a hundred drops that Marjorie, the only woman to work regularly as a dropper, was to make from 1952 to the end of 1956. In 1952, she learned to fly in the dual-controlled planes that were used in case the pilot were shot.

Marjorie was given a seven-column banner headline in the London *Daily Mail* and hailed as one of the unsung heroines of the Malayan Emergency. Following the end of the Emergency, each member of the team was presented with a letter of commendation by the British Government for their valuable work in keeping the country running.

After her experiences in Malaya, Marjorie worked for many years as a journalist in Brisbane where she was Queensland editor of the *Woman's Weekly* from 1958 to 1966. Now retired, Marjorie is Public Relations Officer for the Tweed Shire RSPCA and rarely speaks about this exciting period in her life.

Maryanne 'May' McLelland
1902–1987
Plucky postmistress
Written by: Katie Lawley
Nominated by: Dorothy Gardiner

For over twenty-five years May McLelland was the postmistress of the Lurg Telephone Exchange and Post Office near Benalla in Victoria. Independently she sorted the mail three days a week and operated the switchboard every day.

On 6 February 1952, bushfire threatened the town. Miss McLelland, fifty-two at the time, was operating the switchboard as usual, monitoring the fire and relaying information to outlying farmhouses.

Not until her Post Office was actually on fire around her did May relinquish her post. Grabbing the cash box, she rushed to the dam and watched as her home and all its belongings were incinerated.

Although never officially rewarded for her bravery, May McLelland did not go unnoticed by the townsfolk, who held a party in her honour where the Superintendent of the Benalla Police Station praised her 'courage and strength in the face of adversity'.

Malcolm Maloney-Jakamarra
c1947–
Prodigal son
Written by: Billy Marshall-Stoneking
Nominated by: Lee Clayton

A dawn raid. Four of five policemen and a man from the Aboriginal Protection Board break down a door. Inside, kids scatter in all directions, running from their hiding places. The police grab the one or two they have come for, and throw them into the back of a waiting van. Driven off to foster homes, sometimes hundreds, if not thousands, of kilometres away, some of the children are too young to remember their mother's names, or where they have come from. The mothers, the fathers, the brothers and sisters, stand helplessly watching as the van disappears in the distance.

From the 1900s to the 1960s, events such as this were repeated over and over again, right around Australia. Under a government-approved programme known as 'the Apprenticeship Scheme', the Aboriginal Protection Board separated hundreds of Aboriginal boys and girls from their mothers and families, taking them away to be 'educated', usually as menials — maids, labourers, stationhands. It happened in Sydney, and it happened in the bush. Aboriginal families, particularly those with light-skinned children, lived in fear of 'the Board'.

Malcolm Jakamarra's story is the story of many Aboriginal people who were taken away from their homes and their families to become wards of the state, cut off from their people and their culture.

Jakamarra's mother was a Walpiri woman, and his father was of Irish descent. In the early 1950s, when he was about five years old, Jakamarra was playing in camp when he heard a curious rumbling noise. The noise grew louder and then he saw it — a strange-looking creature coming toward him. When it was still a little way off, it stopped and two men climbed out. But these were not ordinary men. Their skins were white as white clay and when they spoke Jakamarra could not understand what they said.

Next thing he knew, that they were coming toward him. His mother yelled, frightened, telling them to stop, but the men were not listening. They picked him up and placed him inside the strange-looking creature.

Jakamarra huddled in the back of the Land Rover, believing that he was inside a monster, or a beast. When the whitemen closed the back flaps, he was sure he must be inside the stomach. Smelling the fuel, Jakamarra imagined it was the odour of stomach juices. He curled up in a corner and kept very still.

Within a week, he was in another world populated almost entirely with men like those who had put him in the beast. But now he had learned that they were called 'whitefellas', or 'gubbs', and the horrible monsters were called 'automobiles'.

In Adelaide, he was sent to boarding school with other Aboriginal children, and as one year passed into the next the memory of the desert and of his mother faded. In the end, his head filled up with books, words of a new language, and reading and writing, and he made many friends from different parts of the country.

But Jakamarra retained the faint memory of another time and place and, after graduating from high school, went looking for his origins, his past. In the beginning, he spent a lot of time in Victoria visiting various Aboriginal communities in search of someone who might remember where he came from. But no one remembered. Months passed into years, and years into decades.

Then, one day, a man told him he should try the Northern Territory. A lot of the children in Adelaide foster homes had come down from the desert through Tennant Creek and Alice Springs. Jakamarra, keen to follow up every lead, headed north.

When he walked into the Aboriginal community after more than thirty years' absence he was immediately recognised by his family. All the time he had been gone, they had kept the memory of him alive by telling stories of little Jakamarra, and how he had been taken away. And as time had passed, little Jakamarra 'grew up' in the stories, from a young boy to a young man, to a man, so that his people carried this picture of what he was like in their minds. When they saw him walk into camp that day, they did not need to be told who he was. He was just as they pictured him.

Everyone was very happy. The boy whom they thought they had lost had come back. Jakamarra hugged his mother and shook hands with all the men. For thirty years he had lived pretty much like a white man. Now, back in his own country, among his own people, he had a lot of catching up to do.

Joyce Wilding
1903–1978
Compassionate mother to all
Written by: Sue Phillips
Nominated by: Muriel Langford

In the early 1960s a young Aboriginal man looking for a new life arrived in Brisbane. 'Brisbane was kind to me from the start,' Peter Hill says. 'I found a job — and straight off I heard about Mrs Wilding.'

And so, like hundreds of black people before him, Peter Hill made his way to the drab South Brisbane cottage which, for ten years, had been a haven for Brisbane's homeless Aborigines. 'In those days there were no hostels, there was nothing for Aborigines like there is today,' he says. 'There was just Mother Wilding's.'

Born in England in 1903, Joyce Wilding became a caring 'mother' to Queensland's dispossessed when, in the early 1950s, she offered her home and her care to an Aboriginal boy who was unable to attend high school in Brisbane because he lacked accommodation.

That was the beginning of her life's work, and thereafter the word spread — through Brisbane's parks, along the river banks and the railway stations, round the old South Brisbane pie-cart and out into the country towns. Those who found a home at Mother Wilding's might be from the country, unable to find accommodation. Or they might be the desperate — the deserted wife and children, the sick, the suicidal, the alcoholic. Sometimes there were as many as forty people sleeping on mattresses spread on the floor throughout the house.

The jobs Joyce Wilding was called upon to do were endless and harrowing: taking people to hospital, organising funerals, going out to pick up battered wives. And she helped white people too. Today, there are all sorts of helping agencies but back then there were only a few people like Joyce and Frank Wilding who seemed to care.

'They made you feel welcome from the start. On my birthday I got a cake, like all the regulars did. There were those little extra treats to make it more like home — which it was for so many of us.'

Putting a meal on the table, let alone providing 'little treats', was an uphill job. While regular lodgers in work paid board, and other lodgers contributed something when they had it, the wage of clerk Frank Wilding had to stretch to cover the costs of the ever-swelling 'family'. A fellow worker for Aboriginal rights remembers one occasion when the cupboard was absolutely bare. 'They prayed for help and soon afterwards there was a banging on the door. There were sacks of fruit, and vegetables, meat, all sorts of stuff from Police Commissioner Bischoff. I know what they say about him now, but he was a saviour to Joyce in those days, and a great friend to the Aborigines.'

While friends like this were few and far between, nevertheless support was gradually gathering for Joyce Wilding. In the early 1960s, when Wilding was again threatened with eviction, a group of concerned citizens made approaches to Dr Frank Noble, the Minister for Aboriginal Affairs. Out of these meetings was born OPAL (One People of Australia League). Funded by the government, it purchased a hostel in South Brisbane and paid an honorarium to Mrs Wilding so that, unharried at last, she could devote herself to her work.

While many of OPAL's functions have since been taken over by government and some Aborigines and others felt that the organisation became merely a mouthpiece for the Queensland government's assimilationist policies, its aims, says former Senator Neville Bonner, have not been diminished. Neither, a decade after her death in 1978, have people's memories of Joyce Wilding. 'She was,' says Heather Bonner, 'a loving mother for all those who so desperately needed mothering.'

Doris Taylor
1909–1968

Meals on Wheels founder
Written by: Rosemary Neill
Nominated by: Mick Young

At sixteen, Doris Taylor was declared incurable. She could not turn her head, feed or clothe herself or manipulate her tooth brush.

Doctors, believing that she would be forever a prisoner in her bed, recommended that she be sent to a home for incurables. But Doris's mother, a widow bringing up three children in Adelaide during the Great Depression, was adamant that home was the place for Doris, who had spent most of her childhood in a wheelchair following an accident that permanently damaged her spine when she was seven.

Doris, whose determination would take her where her body could not, later wrote: 'I had been in hospital almost continuously from the time of my accident and so, when I went home, I was shocked to find how bad things had become and how everyone was affected by the Depression. 'I thought...I must do something so I became secretary to the mothers' club of a kindergarten in which fathers of forty-six of the fifty-four children attending were unemployed [and] organised schemes to raise money.'

Doris, who had been a brilliant scholar and an accomplished pianist, proved a deft organiser and fund raiser. Still, she felt that she was not achieving enough. 'I decided that political action was what was needed,' she said. 'My reasoning was that good legislation could ensure security and protection for everybody.' Doris went on to become a successful Labor Party activist, an election campaign director for Don Dunstan, an office holder in the ALP's Norwood (South Australia) branch and a friend of Ben Chifley and Arthur Caldwell, but her ideological base remained humanitarian rather than partisan.

Politics brought Doris into wide contact with the community where she 'learned that old people were the ones most needing organised help'. From her own experience she knew the importance of independence and understood the need of the elderly to be looked after in their own homes. As she explained, 'To many of them, to go to an institution of any kind, to be torn away from their home, however small and poor it may be, to have to adjust to new surroundings and a totally new routine of living, is unbearable even to contemplate.' So in the early 1950s, armed with a $10 donation, an abhorrence of institutions, and research on English and Melbourne Meals on Wheels services, Doris began to evolve a service for Adelaide.

For months she bullied and cajoled both government and private companies to find a place from which the service could operate. News Limited, then a small Adelaide company, publicised her efforts but support was poor. Some people were hostile to Doris's plan, believing it would never work.

She was not dissuaded. She held the first meeting for South Australia's Meals On Wheels in her bedroom and on 9 August 1954, the service started up with eight patients and eleven helpers, who worked from a hut without sinks or drainage systems.

Today, South Australia's Meals on Wheels serves between 3800 and 3900 meals each day through its ninety-seven branches. It has 8600 helpers and includes home help, laundry, library, chiropody, frozen meal and hospital-based meal services.

Doris was awarded an MBE in 1959 and died in May 1968. Arthur Daly, who worked for her at Meals On Wheels, wrote in a tribute that she was one of the great Australians of this century. He added: 'The world is a better place because she lived in it. In the poet's words: "She has left footprints on the sands of time".'

Doris Taylor, MBE, whose own disability made her acutely aware of the need of the infirm for independence

Mother Giovanni Ackman
1886–1966
Founding spirit of Mt Olivet Hospital
Written by: Drusilla Modjeska
Nominated by: John Clarke Harman

The name of Mother Giovanni Ackman is an emblem of a life that gives a new perspective on the concept of 'ecumenical'. She was born Amy Vera Ackman into a Jewish family in Sydney's race course suburb of Randwick. Her father, Michael, was a businessman who also ran a racehorse. While Amy was still a baby, the Ackmans' Aborigi-

Above. Mother Giovanni, RSC, brought humour and an enthusiasm for life to her care for the dying

Below. Mother Giovanni with the first missionary group of Sisters of Charity at Bundi Airstrip in New Guinea, 1963

nal groom became seriously ill and was taken to St Vincent's hospital where he was nursed until his death. Michael and Annie Ackman were so impressed by the Sisters of Charity that they decided that, despite their own faith, Amy should be educated at a convent.

Before Amy was two, Michael Ackman died and his wife was left with a daughter to raise and support. Annie bought a fancy work business in Kyneton, Victoria, and Amy was sent to the local Mercy Convent school. At her mother's request she did not attend classes in religious education. But faith is not learnt solely in formal classes. In her final years of school, divided between her mother and her emerging faith, Amy faced a crisis of loyalty. She wanted to be baptised and to take steps towards becoming a nun, but she did not want to distress her mother or leave her without companionship and support. The Archbishop, turned to for advice, allowed a secret baptism but would not hear of Amy becoming a nun. She was not to leave her mother, he told her, but should have confidence in the future. Resolution of this conflict came eventually with her mother's death which left Amy free to follow her religious vocation.

In the years before her mother died, Amy had trained as an optometrist. She had a practice in Collins Street in Melbourne and frequently worked in the outpatients department of St Vincent's hospital. There she came to know the Sisters of Charity, whose novitiate she eventually entered in Sydney in 1914. As Sister Mary Giovanni she trained as a nurse at St Vincent's in Darlinghurst. One of her lifelong friends, Sister

Vianney Byrne, recalls: 'She was full of fun. She had a work basket which was useless as she had no idea of sewing, but which seemed to contain an unlimited supply of tricks.'

In the years after World War I, Mother Giovanni was put in charge of St Vincent's Private Hospital in Sydney, then St Vincent's Bathurst, and then Lismore before returning as administrator of St Vincent's Sydney. Sister Casimir Baptist, a young nun at Lismore in the early 1940s, recalls Mother Giovanni's self-deprecating funny stories and tells too of her kindness to the young nuns in her charge.

On 20 March 1953 Mother Giovanni set off for Brisbane and her biggest adventure with a heavy heart. She had never been to Brisbane before, she did not know what lay ahead, and she wanted to stay in Sydney for the first national Eucharistic Congress. 'I was ashamed of myself for being so tearful,' she wrote, 'but I felt that Our dear Lord understood.' She arrived in Brisbane to a warm welcome and the enormous task of raising funds to build and establish Mt Olivet, Brisbane's first hospital for the incurably sick and dying.

Here, two other remarkable women enter the story. Miss Mary Josephine Bedford had offered the Sisters of Charity the house in which she and her late companion, Dr Lilian Cooper, had lived for many years. Miss Bedford, by then nearly ninety years old, wanted to make a memorial to Lilian Cooper's work, and in particular she wanted her house and its adjoining land to be used for the bedridden and the dying. Although both Dr Cooper and Miss Bedford were Anglicans, it seemed to Miss Bedford that the Sisters of Charity could best achieve her vision. She had visited the hospice at St Vincent's in Sydney and was impressed by the sisters and their policy of welcoming patients of any creed or nationality.

Mary Bedford, an Australian, and Lilian Cooper, a tall Englishwoman, had met as young women in London in the 1860s. While Miss Cooper trained at the London School of Medicine, Miss Bedford studied art at the Slade School. Lilian Cooper graduated in medicine and surgery in 1891 and the two women moved to Brisbane. As Queensland's first woman doctor and one of the first women to work as a doctor anywhere in this country, Dr Cooper faced considerable prejudice but she persevered to become highly respected by both men and women. Meanwhile Miss Bedford became prominent in various areas of welfare work, particularly organisations benefitting small children. Not surprisingly, Lilian Cooper and Mary Bedford were both feminists. When the Queensland National Council of Women held its founding meeting in 1905, it was in their sitting room that the women gathered.

In 1926 the two women bought and settled in Old St Mary's, a spacious house on the Brisbane river. Dr Cooper died in 1947, and in 1952 Miss Bedford made over the property to the Sisters of Charity. The following year she met Mother Giovanni and the story of three remarkable women converges.

Mother Giovanni was charged with raising the money to build, fit and equip the hospital that was to stand on the land adjoining old St Mary's. When she arrived in Brisbane there was not even an office available for her, but St Vincent de Paul gave her a corner to work in so she borrowed an electric jug, bought a tea pot 'and a few other necessary items' and was in business.

The campaign was launched on several fronts. There was a door

Mt Olivet Hospice was built with funds raised by a Jewish woman who had become a Catholic nun on land given by an Anglican woman, Miss Mary Bedford (bottom), as a memorial to the life and work of her friend, Dr Lilian Cooper (top), Queensland's first woman doctor. Photograph Dr Cooper courtesy Queensland Women's Historical Association

to door appeal — 'begging', Mother Giovanni called it — committees set up to raise funds, and interviews with banks to find the best rates. As Sister Edna Skewes recounts in her book on Mt Olivet, *Life Comes to Newness* (Mt Olivet, 1982), Mother Giovanni persevered, walking to save fares, and recording donations of shillings with as much gratitude as larger bequests.

Within eighteen months of Mother Giovanni's arrival, the Mt Olivet scheme was known across Brisbane and sufficient funds had been raised to lay the foundation stone. Opposite the foundation stone another was laid:
'THE LAND ON WHICH THIS HOSPITAL WAS BUILT WAS GIVEN AS A MEMORIAL TO THE LIFE AND WORK OF LILIAN V. COOPER M.D., F.R.A.C.S., BY HER FRIEND M.J. BEDFORD.'

Mt. Olivet opened for patients on 8 September 1957. Missing from the opening ceremony were both Miss Bedford and her house. Miss Bedford had died at the end of 1955 and was buried with Doctor Cooper in Toowong Cemetry. The house, which had proved too expensive to modernise and restore, had been demolished and replaced.

Mother Giovanni was Mt Olivet's first administrator, establishing the tradition of care for which the hospice is known. True to form, she was a familiar figure in the wards, not an administrator behind closed doors. She visited the wards each day, knew all the staff, both nursing and domestic, and had time for everyone. She never left the hospice until the night shift was settled in.

Mother Giovanni's last position was in New Guinea. After an emotional farewell from Brisbane, she went to Bundi in 1963 where the Sisters were to take over the running of a school. But she was not away long. In July 1966 she returned to Mt Olivet, this time to receive its care. Her life was drawing to a close and she died at Mt Olivet on 23 August 1966. Only two weeks before, in true Mt Olivet tradition, the sisters had arranged an outing for her so that she could see the north coast one last time. At her requiem mass the Archbishop described her as someone who had become a public figure against her will. The congregation was overflowing.

Alice Briggs
1936–1984
Fierce fighter for justice
Written by: Jacqueline Kent
Nominated by: Bill Latona

From childhood, Alice Briggs refused to knuckle under to white authority. 'Us Aborigines were only allowed to sit in the five front rows of the cinema,' she said in a radio interview in 1984. 'I always sat up the back with the white kids and if the manager said "move" I wouldn't.'

She had many opportunites to rebel. Born in 1936 and brought up on reserves near Brewarrina, Kempsey and Taree in northern New

South Wales, Alice had to conform to the rules made by the State Protection Board, a government body responsible for Aboriginal welfare. Life was tough for blacks. 'We couldn't leave the reserve without permission, we couldn't associate with the white people,' said Alice. Aboriginal children were given very little education, on the grounds that the girls would become domestics and the boys handymen. 'I never finished primary school,' said Alice.

Alice took her first steps in becoming a public fighter for her people on the day her first child was born in 1954. When she was in labour in Kempsey hospital, the white nurses were horrified to find that they had let an Aboriginal woman into an all-white ward: nobody had registered her colour the previous evening when she was admitted. 'I had to get out of bed, bleeding, with the pains coming, and walk through public wards until I got to 'Darktown,' said Alice. 'Darktown' was the Aboriginal ward. All the items in it — bed linen, crockery, baby clothes, bedpans — were labelled ABO so they would not 'contaminate' white patients. 'In all the country hospitals,' said Alice, 'Aboriginal mothers and babies died because the white staff would leave them for hours without any medical attention.'

From this episode in her life stemmed Alice Briggs's determination to campaign for better medical treatment of Aborigines. In later years, she worked with the well-known doctor Archie Kalokarinos in treating the problems of glaucoma and deafness suffered by Aboriginal children in northern New South Wales.

When Alice's daughter left school the headmaster advised her 'Don't go to job interviews with your daughter. She's much lighter-skinned than you are. If they see she's got a mother who's as dark as you, she won't get the job.'

The memory of this and other injustices made Alice explode in frustration when she became a member of the New South Wales Aboriginal Education Committee. She attended a conference on Aboriginal education held in the Blue Mountains, west of Sydney, and listened as academics solemnly worried about it. 'I got sick of it,' said Alice. 'So I just stood up and said, "You people know it's a problem, you name me one person who doesn't. But you do bugger all about it. What are you going to do?" '

Alice Briggs was much more than a voice campaigning for her people's rights. One of her great strengths was her organising ability which she put to good use when the New South Wales Department of Main Roads announced its intention to extend the Pacific Highway through part of the Aboriginal reserve where Alice lived. 'It was bad,' says Alice. 'A few Aboriginal kids had already been injured or killed by speeding motorists.'

As president of the Biripi Aboriginal Co-operative, she mobilised the women on the reserve and told the road builders that they would all lie down in front of the bulldozers if necessary to prevent the builders taking the reserve land. Alarmed at the prospect, the builders capitulated. Though Alice and her supporters did not achieve total victory, they did succeed in modifying the original DMR plan.

Alice Briggs described herself as a feminist at a time when feminism was not fashionable. Unhappily married herself, she felt very strongly that Aboriginal men had been totally demoralised by white society. 'They can't be the breadwinners any more, they don't go hunting, so they drink and get violent,' she said. 'But at the same time, I reckon that men and women have equal responsibility to work for a just society.'

Alice Briggs died of lung cancer in 1984. A diminutive, fiercely intelligent woman who could express her opinions pungently and clearly, she had never stopped fighting for her people.

Eric James Stewart
1928–
Latter-day adventurer
Written by: Terri McCormack
Nominated by: Michelle Leigh Stewart

Born in South Australia in 1928, Eric Stewart grew up at Tatura in central Victoria. He regretted missing the action of World War II and did not find the adventure he sought working in Melbourne. Hungry for travel, he joined the Department of the Interior in 1954 and soon found himself involved in a most unusual adventure — making triangulation surveys of the vast unmapped tracts of central South Australia.

Parts of the Australian interior had been mapped by the explorers and some of the gaps filled in by Overland Telegraph Line surveys. However as recently as the 1950s, there remained great stretches of the continent that had bever been systematically mapped. Stewart's job was to assist the National Mapping Survey in compiling military maps. Living on tinned food made palatable with Keen's curry powder and the occasional rabbit or 'roo, he spent many months in remote areas and acquired an enduring knowledge of bush survival. He also, through his surveys north of the Flinders Ranges and east to the Great Victorian Desert, came into contact with the tribal and missionary Aborigines for whom he developed a lifelong admiration.

Stewart's next job was with the Atomic Energy Commission at Mary Kathleen where he assisted with the survey of the proposed township and treatment plant for Australia's first uranium mine. From this dry western Queensland country, he moved to the mangrove swamps of western Cape York Peninsula where, from 1957 to 1958, he was involved in a joint RAN and Queensland government hydrographic survey of coastal rivers for which the only charts were those made by Matthew Flinders 150 years previously. From Reverend Jimmy Wins' Weipa mission, Stewart and a team of thirty Aborigines were sent out by boat to survey the rivers, supplies being dropped in by helicopter. To alert the pilot to his ever-changing location, Stewart would stand on the beach waving an old white shirt hoisted on a stick. For months at a time, he remained in this inhospitable wilderness where green ants rather than crocodiles were the major problem but, he says, 'I rather enjoyed it'.

New Guinea was his next destination but, rather than wait twelve months in Melbourne for his public service application to be processed,

Stewart seized the opportunity to return to his beloved central Australia as a guide for Frome Broken Hill Exploration Company on an oil search. He spent isolated months in the unsurveyed corner bordered by South Australia, Western Australia and the Northern Territory, working through the McDonnell Ranges to Lake Amadeus and remembers with affection the people of Areyonga and Hermannsburg Missions.

In January 1959, Stewart made a dramatic change in both topography and career when he arrived in New Guinea, the 'incredible' country in which he spent the next fifteen years. He spent three years at Nonga Base Hospital near Rabaul being trained as a medical assistant for the Department of Public Health. His subsequent medical patrols took him to the remotest areas of New Britain, New Ireland, Bougainville and tiny offshore islands where his responsibilities were both curative and where possible, preventative. When the breakdown of medical services in western New Guinea following the Indonesian takeover in 1963 created a smallpox threat, Stewart's major task was the inoculation of some 100 000 island people. As quarantine officer, he was also responsible for protecting the vulnerable coastal population from contagious diseases spread by illegal visits from Formosan and Japanese boats.

After being transferred to mainland Wau, Stewart's patrols took him to the Western Highlands, the Ramu area north of Madang, and throughout the Morobe district. To thousands of people with little natural immunity and severe protein deficiencies, he brought Triple Antigen/CDt and smallpox vaccinations, and conducted village aid-posts and infant welfare clinics. With a hundred carriers for his patrol boxes, he spent months walking from village to village to bring medical assistance and education to sub-districts of 30 000 people. As with his island work, Stewart needed diverse skills to cope with the multiple diseases he encountered and had to contend with serious cases which could not always be sent long distances by stretcher or helicopter to hospital. Many times, Eric Stewart read the beautiful words of the twenty-third Psalm over the graves of children whom he could not save.

Stewart's memories of the wild Kuku Kuku people of the Papuan Gulf are still vivid. Aware of their reputation for hostility, he took such 'simple precautions' as keeping his patrol box under his camp bed ('to protect me from below') and keeping 'one eye open' at night to avert spear attacks. As recently as the 1960s, he carried tomahawks, ochres, mirrors, salt, and tobacco to trade with these Stone Age people and recalls one occasion when he arrived to find them eating human remains. The Kuku Kuku's memories of Stewart are probably equally vivid as he carried with him a record player which caused great astonishment as did his habit of removing his dentures.

In all his years of frontier medical work, Stewart met with little antagonism. This must have been at least partly due to his evident liking for the people — an affection which he shared with 'a little old woman' whom he encountered 'in the middle of the jungle' on Manus Island — Margaret Mead. His only 'minor problems' came from a few missionaries, one of whom prohibited vaccinations on the Sabbath and others who objected to his widespread family planning campaign — both problems which he managed to overcome. The indigenous people welcomed him.

As local training progressed, expatriates like Stewart made themselves redundant. In 1973, on 'the saddest day of my life', he left

Eric Stewart on reconnaissance for the National Mapping Survey in northern South Australia, 1955. As recently as this, vast tracts of the country remained unmapped

New Guinea with a reference acknowledging that 'the health services of Papua New Guinea have been built on the dedication and effort of health extension officers like Mr Stewart'.

After years of trying to adjust to city life in Melbourne, Stewart and his family moved to the more peaceful environment of Bribie Island in Moreton Bay. Despite permanent eye damage caused by the 1950s nuclear tests, which were carried out in ignorance of the mapping party's presence in central Australia, his love of travel and adventure is undiminished and, according to his daughter, 'given a chance he would do what he has done all over again'. It seems only a matter of time before Eric Stewart, with his New Zealand-born wife whom he met and married in Wau, is off again to the remote regions and peoples that he loves.

Sheila Stubbs
1925–
Jill of all trades
Written by: Susan Hamilton
Nominated by: John Stubbs

Sheila Stubbs is sixty-three. Her retirement appears to be a happy one: she owns a mobile home, has a garden, plays golf and bowls, and sees her son John as often as possible. She is a great raconteur, loves to reminisce and has a stack of photographs to remind her of days gone by. There seems to be nothing unusual about Sheila — until she begins to tell her story.

Sheila Goulding was born at Merriwagga, New South Wales, in 1925, one of ten children of a soldier settler and his wife struggling to survive on the usual tiny useless piece of land. Sheila was not quite thirteen when her mother died and her father, in despair, pulled down their scrap timber and iron shanty and went off to his second war. Sheila was sent, alone, to an aunt and uncle who lived and worked at Rookwood Cemetery but the arrangement did not work and she was packed off back to Merriwagga, where her two youngest sisters were in the same plight.

For about two years, Sheila looked after her sisters. She kept house, shot and cooked rabbits ('underground mutton'), ducks and goats, and helped them with their correspondence schooling. To keep them, she joined Frank Greyhurst, a father-figure who had boarded with the family when her mother was alive, at the sawmill and charcoal-burning camps where he worked. Here, she worked as a 'snigger', using a horse to drag felled trees to the edge of the charcoal pits. She loved the job, but she and her sisters were growing up, tongues began to wag, and the men's wives decided that the girls should return to town. Sheila persuaded a relative to take her sisters then, broke and homeless, took to the road in search of work.

For nine years she went droving with her brother, covering the regulation six miles a day with sheep, ten with cattle. Sheila took care of

Sheila Stubbs's mother (right) and her Aunty Mae, c.1920, outside the bag house in which Sheila's family lived on a soldier settlement at Merriwagga, New South Wales. 'My mother used to wash the dirt floor every day. She'd pour lots of water on it to make it all muddy, then smooth it and it would dry hard and shiny. I learned about keeping up standards from her — a fresh dress every day too, and look after your skin'

the dogs and horses, bought the stores, cooked the meals. 'We always had a scrupulous camp,' she declares proudly. 'We kept it raked, had wheat bag mats and our saucepans were cleaner than you'd find in town. We greased our saddles and polished our gear. The men shaved every day. I always wore make up and a lot of face cream at nights — if you didn't you'd end up looking like an old man. It was a great life. We used to say "The drover has pleasures the townsfolk never know."' In between the runs Sheila looked for work — often as cook, waitress or barmaid in different pubs — sleeping out often enough, or 'jumping the rattler' (goods train) in search of a bed with a relative.

In 1954 she married Robert Stubbs, a shearer whose job took them from Longreach, Queensland, down to Tasmania. Sheila was a shearer's cook. 'In those days you cooked,' she says, 'not like today when it's all processed stuff and they go home at weekends. I cut down all the meat and did all the cooking on open wood stoves twelve hours a day, seven days a week. We had John with us for about seven years too.'

Between shearing jobs the Stubbs went kangaroo shooting. It was rough work. They'd shoot all night, peg out the skins in the morning and take them into town to sell.

Sheila Stubbs, shearers' cook (below), with a team of shearers and her son John in Balranald in the fifties, and (above) today, finding it hard to stay in one place

Sheila was quite a shot. She was one of the few women to compete in the Queen's Prize in Melbourne, and was once runner up in Channel Seven's 'Sportswoman of the Week'. Her home is full of trophies, medals and clippings testifying to her skill with the 'big guns'.

After John was born, Sheila would have liked to have settled down. But Stubbs was a wanderer, and where he went, she followed. They made some attempts at suspending their itinerant lifestyle, but they didn't last long. There were periods in Melbourne, where Sheila worked as a sales assistant, and they had a milk bar in Corowa for twelve months. Sheila still remembers the hell of short-order cooking day after day in 37°C heat. They bought and worked a couple of farms, too. 'Toolebus (New South Wales) was lovely. We had a log cabin by the river. I thought that would have been it. But we went. You just go when you go.'

Nevertheless it was a good marriage. 'We had twenty-eight good years. We never went anywhere without each other, shared everything.' Sheila found the going hard when the marriage broke up six years ago. She spent the first three years travelling, 'wearing out my welcome with relatives', sometimes sleeping in the car with her little dog, before eventually settling into her mobile home.

Today, Sheila is restless again. She has been so active, and so often on the move, that life in a caravan park has become pale and predictable. She has not decided where she will go, but the story of Sheila Stubbs is not over yet.

Ronald Alfred Phillips
1908–1966
Founder of the MS Society
Written by: Lucinda Strauss
Nominated by: Beverley J. Cockburn

Ronnie Phillips had two overriding interests during his life: the Navy, which he joined at the age of thirteen, and the Multiple Sclerosis (MS) Society, which he helped form in 1956 and for which he worked strenuously until his death ten years later.

A quiet, unassuming man, Ronald Alfred Phillips was born in Grafton, New South Wales, the eldest son in a family of six. As a cadet with the Royal Australian Navy, he studied at Jervis Bay Naval College and later trained as an engineer at Keyham in Devon, England. He married there, returning to Australia soon afterwards to continue his naval career.

Ronnie Phillips first exhibited the symptoms of MS at a time when very little was known about the disease. In 1939, at the outbreak of the war, during a period of intense pressure, he suffered occasional bouts of double vision. Assuming that this and other passing conditions were due to overwork, he ignored them and applied himself to his duties in the engine rooms of many great warships. In 1940 he was promoted to Lieutenant-Commander aboard HMAS *Australia*, the Australian flagship at the Battle of the Coral Sea, and at the end of the war was promoted to the rank of Commander.

While the bouts of double vision increased, other alarming symptoms appeared, causing distress and misunderstanding. With the loss of balance and spasmodic muscle failure in his legs, rumours circulated about his lack of sobriety. But the officers serving closely with him showed enormous respect and solicitude as his youngest sister, Muriel Hayes, recalls: 'He hated being a nuisance and never wanted anyone to help him. Nevertheless, the younger officers were wonderful and always sensed the exact spot to position themselves to catch him if he suddenly lost balance.' Struggling with the debilitating disease, Commander Phillips continued to serve and set up the Navy's 'mothball fleet'. Eventually, in 1956, the disease was correctly diagnosed: shortly afterwards he was invalided out of the Service.

Approached before his retirement to form a society in Sydney, Ronnie Phillips lost no time. After convening a public meeting, he was elected Honorary Secretary of the Australian Multiple Sclerosis Society.

Beverly Cockburn, his daughter, remembers how 'grateful MS sufferers wrote to the society, or rang, and Ronnie spent hundreds of hours writing and talking to these people telling them as much as he could about new theories, treatments, helpful ideas to make life easier. But best of all, he gave the comfort that comes from knowing that there are others with the same problems and needs as themselves.'

Trying to establish a new centre, Ronnie was anxious to increase

Ronnie Phillips, midshipman who became Commander. His life was dedicated to the Navy and the Multiple Sclerosis Society

public awareness of the disease and saw this as a key to future funding. He worked long hours writing letters to the press and radio, sending out appeal letters and always working out new strategies for fund raising. Beverly has fond memories of the 2UE Awards contest when their house overflowed with rancid butter papers and Kinkara tea tops — tokens to be sorted out by an army of volunteers.

Over the next few years, through his efforts, MS centres were established in Cammeray and a physiotherapy unit was set up. Ronnie himself went regularly for treatment and continued as Secretary until his illness made it impossible. Eventually branches of the society were established in many country towns and cities, the correspondence became enormous and paid administration staff were employed.

Ronnie died in 1966. He is remembered with great affection by those he helped in the early days when MS was an even greater mystery than it is now. In his honour, a new centre in Chatswood, New South Wales, part of a complex serving MS sufferers, was named the R.A. Phillips Memorial Centre.

Christopher F.A. Cummins
1919–

First flying surgeon
Written by: Linda Whitford
Nominated by: Robert A. Cummins

Dr C.F.A. Cummins, who brought emergency surgical services to more than half a million square kilometres of outback Queensland

In 1959, Queensland Health Minister Dr. Henry Noble set up the Flying Surgeon Service (not connected with the Royal Flying Doctor Service), based in Longreach. Dr Christopher Cummins, who had emigrated from England the previous year, was appointed the inaugural Flying Surgeon and for the next eight years provided the people of outback Queensland with a service unique in the world. Previously, their only options when faced with the necessity of surgery had been to take their chances at the hands of the local general practitioner or to make the long, costly journey to a large coastal city for hospital treatment.

When the Flying Surgeon Service began, the surgeon and anaesthetist frequently performed complex operations in hospitals where surgical facilities were grossly inadequate, the equipment antiquated, and the staff undertrained. Often the pilot was called upon to assist in the operating room. At Dr Cummins's instigation, the equipment and facilities in regional hospitals were vastly improved.

As the main aim of the service was to avoid transporting patients, it was a rare event for the team to have one on board. In a 1961 article for the *Medical Journal of Australia*, Dr Cummins tells the story of their second patient-passenger who, once in the plane, was 'constantly trying to sit up on the stretcher, which, in the cramped space available and with a blood transfusion in progress, was very awkward. My anaesthetist was in turn constantly pushing him down and we both assumed that his condition was responsible for this. However, a few days later he told us that he had never been up in an aeroplane before and he wanted to look out of the window.'

Dr Christopher Cummins, Queensland's first Flying Surgeon, set the standard in a service which remains as important to people who live in remote parts of Queensland today as it was almost thirty years ago.

Frank R. Woodwell
1926–
A mission of justice
Written by: David Millar
Nominated by: Merle Woodwell

Anglican Archdeacon Frank Woodwell does not look for trouble. Yet his belief that the church has a mission of justice, and that faith means acting when ordinary people are manipulated or abused, has led him into some notable battles.

In 1960, young Frank Woodwell was the new rector of Cooma in the Snowy Mountains when Prime Minister R.G. Menzies, gearing up for an election, announced new contracts for the Snowy River Scheme. They would, he claimed, produce 4000 new jobs. He failed, however, to mention two important things: first, owing to deferral of other contracts, large numbers of migrant labourers would have to leave their Tumut camp in the Snowies and, second, the work force for the new contracts was already available and marking time from the completion of previous jobs. Misled by Menzies' selective announcement, men looking for work and dismissed labourers from Tumut flooded into Cooma. The spring weather was cold and wet, there was no accommodation, and to add to their misery a large proportion were recent migrants (mainly Italians and Yugoslavs) with little knowledge of English.

Woodwell's initial response was to open up the parish hall as a soup kitchen and doss house. His later response, however, was to expose the political expediency that played with the lives of innocent people, and then to force the Government to help provide some relief. Caught off balance by the large numbers flooding into the area in search of work, Canberra's politicians looked for a way out. They decided to deny the existence of the small army of unemployed, but failed to appreciate the damage being done to official credibility by the press, television and Woodwell's campaigning.

In an attempt to discredit both the unemployment figures and the rector, the Snowy Mountain Authority's security men began to visit the parish hall during the night and take head counts. Attempts by Frank Woodwell to obtain help for men sleeping out in culverts and under bridges were greeted with bureaucratic smiles of refusal and deprecation, 'Because, of course, Rector, the whole affair has really been blown out of all proportion'. Meanwhile, in Canberra, the heavy-weights set out to flatten any criticism. The Prime Minister and the Minister of Works met, with the result that Sir William Hudson, Chief Commissioner of the Snowy Mountain Authority (SMA), announced

Reverend Frank Woodwell. As rector of Cooma, then Bega, he took on federal and state governments to improve conditions for Snowy Mountains workers and dairy farmers, and stood his ground against local opposition to improve Aboriginal housing and health

Archdeacon Woodwell now rector of All Saints', Tumut, maintains his commitment to social justice. Photograph by Brian Wild

to both the mayor of Cooma and its Anglican rector that the local police inspector had denied the reports of large-scale unemployment. 'We have whitewashed the whole thing,' Hudson anounced triumphantly. 'The unemployment issue is dead. We've fixed it.'

Following this scornful statement came the threat. The mayor, Alderman Johnson, was given twelve hours to sign a statement supporting the official position of there being few unemployed or risk losing the special grant paid to council by the SMA in lieu of rates. Woodwell was, however, a harder rabbit to put back into the hat, for what no-one in Canberra knew was that he had been to the local police station, checked the records, and had already found out that the large numbers of men applying for 'track rations' totally discredited the public statement of the police inspector.

A letter by Woodwell and Johnson to that effect was then sent back to Sir William Hudson. The two men then called a public meeting. They stressed the seriousness of the situation, appealed for financial assistance, and asked for local people to offer work, even if only temporary, to the unemployed. The result of the letter of repudiation and the meeting was unexpected. A local SP bookie who declined to be named — 'just say I am a member of the sporting fraternity' — offered a free hot meal to every unemployed person for two weeks. And then, quietly, an official of the SMA called on the rector and offered whatever stores, blankets and equipment the parish needed to continue its work. The battle was won — the government's attempt to fudge the figures had failed, and official assistance was now to be given to those out of work.

Bega, the cheese-making centre on the New South Wales south coast was Frank Woodwell's next parish and once again he found himself fighting to help those in desperate straits. During the 1960s, the Bega Valley suffered an appalling drought. It lasted a long four years, until it broke on a memorable Christmas Eve in 1968. The effects of the drought were heightened by the recent Federal government's decision to end drought relief to all States. This left the distraught farmers of the area at the mercy of a State government which was cynically prepared to use the misery of the area to blackmail the Federal government. One result of this hard-line policy was that the local hospital eventually filled up with an increasing number of farmers and their wives whose physical and emotional lives were breaking up under the strain. Visiting these people in hospital, Woodwell became outraged. 'It is a crazy situation,' he told the *Bega District News*, 'that allows cattle to die of starvation while governments argue about who is responsible.'

With the permission of the Anglican Bishop of Canberra-Goulburn, Woodwell began to organise a diocesan appeal for donations of feed and agistment and, in the face of State and Federal government intransigence, persuaded his own parish to put $2000 into the fund. It was the spark that ignited the whole area. With the future mayor, Reg Clark, Woodwell went on a speaking tour — 'He was terrific', says Clark — to drum up support. Relief began to flow into the Valley. 'After 140 000 bales I stopped counting,' Woodwell later recalled. Over 10 000 head of stock were lifted out for agistment elsewhere. Then, together with aldermen, farmers and sympathetic politicians, Woodwell pushed a reluctant State government and a stubborn Minister of

Agriculture into helping with the trucking of feed and animals. This campaign, initiated by Woodwell and supported by the whole community, had long term results: it became the basis for the present-day State assistance to drought affected areas in New South Wales.

While still at Bega, the Rector became involved in a campaign that cut more deeply into the community than any other — Aboriginal housing. Dwelling in old dairies, humpies on the river bank, and in crude shacks erected by bean farmers on their properties to attract black labour to do the work that Europeans had long ago decided was too hot and dusty, the Aborigines were caught in a perpetual cycle of bad housing, low self-esteem, alcoholism, malnutrition and child mortality. Woodwell, deciding to do something not for, but *with* them, initiated the Bega Valley Aboriginal Advancement Association. It began to employ social workers who concentrated on housing and health and, working on the basis of self-help rather than hand-outs, bought caravans and chainsaws so that the first Aboriginal milling gangs could be established in the Eden area.

As government instrumentalities were indifferent and some of the locals hostile, land for housing in the town could not be found. Woodwell therefore had the local parish donate some of its land endowment — an action which raised a storm of protest within the community. At a public meeting to oppose the scheme, he moved a motion expressing support, in principle, for better housing for Aborigines. There was uproar as procedural matters were used in an attempt to filibuster the whole idea. But Woodwell stood firm, supported by those who agreed with him.

His stand was not without cost. There was talk of a public petition to have him run out of town and a walk down main street often meant passing a long line of critical newspaper billboards. At Rotary, he even suffered the ignominy of being fined — 'Its just a joke, Reverend' — for being seen talking to an Aboriginal man on the main street. But Frank Woodwell stood resolute. His reward, he says, was to stand at his eventual farewell from Bega, surrounded by Aboriginal children.

Now rector of All Saints' Tumut, Archdeacon Woodwell is still as determined a fighter against injustice as ever. To care about *all* people is, he says, 'our only real choice'.

Donald Norman Farquhar
1913–1984
Triumph over prejudice
Written by: Katie Lawley
Nominated by: A. Farquhar

'My father was a fiercely determined man, intent on encouraging greater international harmony,' says Donald Farquhar's son. 'Although blinded in World War II by a Japanese attack on the plane that he was navigating, he did not become bitter. In fact it seemed to make him more determined to pursue his belief in the necessity of building up goodwill between nations.'

In the late 1950s Donald Farquhar joined Rotary. To demonstrate his internationalist convictions, he turned first to Japan, the country at whose hands he had suffered the most. In 1961 his efforts were rewarded by an anonymous contribution enabling him to attend an International Rotary convention in Japan. The outstanding conclusion to this trip was his successful sponsorship of the first Japanese student to attend school in Australia — a young girl called Yoko Miyazaki who arrived in 1963. Given the post war climate of prejudice and hostility towards the Japanese, this was a major triumph.

Complementing this singular achievement, Farquhar was a dedicated worker in community services, providing a courageous example to the blind and giving counsel and assistance to many in his retirement years. He died having achieved a lifetime goal. His contribution to the Australia-Japan Student Exchange Programme helped it to blossom into a remarkable example of international cooperation.

James Edward Smith
1920–

Professional rescuer
Written by: Billy Marshall-Stoneking
Nominated by: Stephen Edward Smith

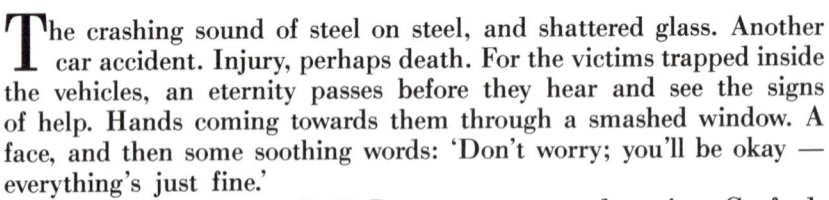

Jim Smith and his Res-Q-Van bring help to the victims of yet another bad accident

The crashing sound of steel on steel, and shattered glass. Another car accident. Injury, perhaps death. For the victims trapped inside the vehicles, an eternity passes before they hear and see the signs of help. Hands coming towards them through a smashed window. A face, and then some soothing words: 'Don't worry; you'll be okay — everything's just fine.'

A car over a cliff at Bulli Pass, an overturned semi at Gosford, a teenager stuck on a sandstone ledge at South Head: these were all part of the work-a-day life of James Edward Smith. For sixteen years, Jim Smith's world revolved around the traumatic scenes of roadside injury and accidents of every description. But it was no accident that he was involved in this line of work.

As co-organiser of the campaign to establish New South Wales's first rescue service, Jim had a profound interest in helping his fellow men and women. And he knew, from experience, where help was needed.

Up until 1961, the only rescue service in the state was the Police Rescue Squad. Jim, realising the need for a more efficient, comprehensive and wide-ranging organisation to look after victims of accidents and other disasters, started campaigning in earnest for a professional rescue service, and with the assistance of a Sydney radio station raised sufficent funds to purchase and equip a rescue unit, dubbed the Q-Van (Rescue Van).

The vehicle was stationed at the Rockdale Ambulance Station, and Jim became its first operator, never leaving the station for a holiday and making himself available on call twenty-four hours a day, every day of the week, for every week of the year.

But despite the pressures and pace of the job, Jim also found time to develop many types of rescue equipment and rescue procedures, a large number of which are regarded as standard today. Some of Jim's equipment is in current use around the world, and his lifting technique (Smith's Universal Lifting Ring) has revolutionised rescue procedures for people who have been injured in falls from cliffs.

Over the years, Jim was involved in rescues of all types — from car and cliff rescues to rescues from burning buildings and derailed trains and, of the thousands who owe their lives to him, there are many who remember him as a man who had a profound calming effect, a man who really did make them feel that everything would be all right.

Jim put his own life at risk many times in his attempts to save others, but he never lost his coolness of mind and his efforts continually won him him the praise of people everywhere. An American tourist, after witnessing an accident in Sydney and seeing Jim in action, wrote to the *Herald* newspaper, 'In Los Angeles we have a fire rescue squad... but it took Sydney Australia to show me the greatest unit I've ever seen'.

Colin Edward Johnston
1928–1974
Determined to teach
Written by: Katie Lawley
Nominated by: Denis Norman Johnston

Colin Johnston was a 'big man' in every sense of the word, a man whose motto was 'There is no failure in life except to give up trying'. Born into a family of six children, he grew into a big handsome youth. At the age of seventeen however, he began to grow very quickly and out of proportion. His jaw enlarged, his hands and feet became enormous and his legs and arms grew thin and brittle. At first the specialists suspected a brain tumour, but finally they diagnosed a malfunction of the pituitary gland. The prescribed treatment seemed to arrest his growth, but it also caused a permanent loss of hair on each side of his head. Colin now stood at 226 centimetres (7 foot 5 inches).

Normally a cheerful and exuberant man, Colin became very depressed. He suffered dreadful headaches which affected his concentration, his brittle limbs had to be encased in braces and eventually he had to give up working. He became reclusive and introspective and from the age of seventeen to twenty-nine he was an invalid pensioner.

'But no matter how bad things became', Colin's brother says, 'his unquenchable sense of humour rescued him from moments of complete despair.' Colin's sense of the ridiculous was matched only by his increasing determination to lead a normal life. He decided to become a teacher. Lacking all qualifications, he passed his Leaving Certificate in four months and went on to his Bachelor of Arts and Diploma of Education at New England University. He also acquired a Diploma of Religious

Colin Johnston at his graduation ceremony at Sydney University in May 1966. He overcame physical handicap to gain his Master of Arts

Education. Despite his qualifications, however, he was unable to obtain a teaching post anywhere because of his physical appearance. 'Even for such a positive person as Colin, this was a tremendous setback,' says his brother, 'and it was only his iron will to succeed that saw him through this period.'

A chance call from a charity collector led him into voluntary work for The House With No Steps, a name he coined for this progressive organisation for paraplegics and quadraplegics. He was their first Welfare Officer and went on to become the Director of Rehabilitation Services. He also established the magazine *Progress*, the official publication of the Wheelchair and Disabled Association of Australia.

Though devoted to this work, Colin still wanted to be a teacher. He continued to study, gaining a Master of Arts from Sydney University and a Diploma of Educational Administration from New England University. Finally, in 1967, after constant applications and much heartache, he scored a major success when he was offered a teaching post at Epping Boys High School in Sydney. Within three years he was appointed to the staff of Armidale High School. He went on to marry and further his academic career, adding a Research Fellowship and a Master of Education to his qualifications.

His unexpected death from a heart attack at forty-six came as a profound shock to his family, friends and colleagues. After all, this man who had fought the odds all his adult life was only just getting started.

Hazel McKellar

c1930–

Recording her people's history
Written by: Lois Hunter
Nominated by: John Stubbs

Hazel Wharton was born 'around 1930', the daughter of Dave and Annie Wharton, and grew up during the Depression years in the Aboriginal fringe camp in Cunnamulla, Queensland. A descendant of the Kooma tribe, Hazel was already acting for her people before she was ten, filling out Child Endowment forms and Police papers.

Before she was seventeen, Hazel married Bert McKellar. A few years later she joined him as a drover. As a drover, she earned a man's pay, taught her eight children on the trail while they were small and later sent them to boarding school with the money earned droving. In 1961, Hazel McKellar became a founding member of the Cunnamulla Native Welfare Association, a group which provided health, education and housing for Aborigines. Established with the help of three churches, it was 'the best incentive programme because Aborigines were helping themselves.'

Commitment and involvement in Aboriginal affairs made her a founding member of the South-West Queensland Aboriginal Co-op Society, which bought and sold housing for Aborigines. For two years, as a member of the National Aboriginal Education Committee, Hazel McKellar visited Aboriginal Community Councils all over Australia. And, because her peoples' story was 'a missing link in our history', she fought for Aboriginal studies to become part of the Education Curriculum.

In 1981 Hazel McKellar won the Scotties Achievement Award, given by Bowater-Scott to the Australian woman, 'who has done most to seize opportunities in her life; who has taken control of it despite the odds against her; who has dealt most triumphantly with adversity'. Hazel borrowed a dress and shoes to visit Melbourne to accept the award.

Hazel says that with the development of black bureaucrats 'nothing has really changed' for Aborigines in need of housing, education and health care; there's just somebody else with a 'whip over our heads'.

As Sites Recording Officer with the Aboriginal Institute, her job was to check on the existence and preservation of sacred and camp sites and when bulldozers moved in for a hundred kilometres she walked in front of them as she made last records of the locations.

Her book *Matya Mundu (Long Ago)*, is a history of the Aboriginal people of south-west Queensland. There is an urgency about recording the Aboriginal history of this area because so much has already been lost and there are only a few people left who still know something of the language, custom and beliefs.' Hazel McKellar's next project is 'a second book', to try to save a little more.

Hazel McKellar, author, drover, welfare worker, and conservator of Aboriginal culture. Photograph by David Bragg

Michel 'Mickey' Beaton
1914–1980
True friend of the Aborigines
Written by: Lois Hunter
Nominated by: Jill A. Beaton

In 1980 when Michel 'Mickey' Beaton died, 'too soon at sixty-six', her Perth funeral saw busloads of Aboriginal women arrive from as far as 600 kilometres away to pay her homage. The strength of feeling of the Aboriginal communities for Mrs Michel Beaton, 'the lady welfare officer', attested to more than just fifteen years' conscientious service to Aborigines.

The daughter of a Presbyterian minister whose work took him and his family (two boys and two girls) through the wheatbelt towns and to Boulder, she was raised, lived, worked and died in Western Australia. Mick 'the tomboy' was born in 1914, attended local convents and learnt violin, which she later taught. In her early twenties in the war years, Michel, 'the most beautiful young woman', met and married Donald Beaton, a tall young grazier's son, and had two children.

After the war, the Beatons moved to Northampton to farm and then on to the Pilbara region and station life. It was here that Mickey Beaton, the new manager's wife, came to learn and care deeply about Aborigines, and to want to change the long-entrenched and static system of white bosses and Aboriginal workers.

In 1964, after her marriage had broken up and she was fifty, Mickey

Mickey Beaton in 1963. She shared her 'unquenchable joy of life' with her many Aboriginal friends

joined the then Native Welfare Department as a field officer and was posted to isolated areas of Western Australia. It was the beginning of a fifteen year labour of love, often lonely, separated from family and friends.

Mickey's work took her to Mullewa, then Meekatharra, Moora and, eventually, Geraldton, living in dwellings that often ranged from corrugated iron rooms at the back of shops to caravans. But what made her different from many other conscientious welfare workers was not just that 'Beaton was available after hours, weekends, anytime anyone needed a shoulder...' or that she was 'a provider, and a good listener who served terrific curries along with the sympathy'. It was more than all that.

Aborigines were, to Mickey, 'a wise people' and, in the end, they were 'her people'. Holidays, brief respites from work, were spent with Aboriginal friends on their reserves where Mickey would just sit, eat, yarn and laugh.

Mickey 'sought to give Aborigines personal resources to build their self-esteem so they could tackle bureaucratic government systems'. She believed that one should not impose ideas on people but rather 'help them realise their goals as they see them'. According to Lee Peters of Western Australia's Department of Community Services, 'she worked mainly for attitudinal change, both in those who hold racist attitudes and in Aborigines to develop a pride in their own heritage. She could get the job done because she had a deep belief in herself and the community and, consequently, in peoples' ability to change for the better.'

When Mickey retired in 1979, many tears flowed. When she died a year later, her black and white friends came together to mourn their great loss.

Albert Edwin Young
1907–

Newcastle's life saver
Written by: Billy Marshall-Stoneking
Nominated by: Maureen O'Sullivan

There were shouts on the beach. People called out and pointed anxiously toward the horizon. A junior boat crew from the Newcastle Surf Club had been caught in a rip and a wave had capsized the boat. The beach inspector, Albert 'Totty' Young, watched the drama from the shore for a moment then, knowing that he was the only one on the spot who could help them, wasted no time. He ran into the surf, and started swimming toward the youngsters who clung to the sides of their overturned craft. Young swam almost a mile through the heavy surf to reach them, and with his capable assistance all were returned safely to shore.

They called him 'Totty' because he was only nine years old when he joined the Newcastle Surf Club and was small — 'just a tot'. But

Totty Young who spent more than fifty years saving lives and teaching children to swim

Albert Young, who weighed only three and a half pounds at birth, had a heart as a big as anyone's, and it did not take the Newcastle Surf Club very long to realise it.

The boy had pluck, courage, and was a top swimmer. In the aftermath of World War I, he was called upon to undertake compulsory training with the Royal Australian Navy, and did so from the time he was fourteen until he was twenty-one.

But it was as a swimming instructor and beach inspector that Totty gained the respect of thousands of people around the Newcastle area. By the time he reached the age of sixty-five, he had swum, by his own calculations, more than 18 000 miles and saved thousands from drowning. In 1948 alone, 'Tot' rescued more than 400 swimmers at Newcastle Beach and on one particularly windy day in that year, saved ninety-eight people from drowning.

The water was his second home, and although he realised its dangers, he was never afraid of it.

In 1961 Totty Young was awarded the MBE for services to the public. He also received the Award of Merit for his rescue of the junior boat crew, one of the most daring surf rescues ever recorded.

Anne Boyd
1936–

Mountain nurse
Written by: Judith Elen
Nominated by: Jeanette Marie Coleman

In 1964, twenty-eight-year-old nurse Anne Young, arrived in India. In Sydney she had met Leonard Cheshire and learned of the Foundations he had established with Lady Sue Ryder to alleviate suffering and to help contribute in this way to the promotion of world peace. He told Anne of the hospital for the treatment and care of the chronically ill that was being built in Dehra Dun in the foothills of the Himalayan mountains, a six-hour bus journey from Delhi. Anne decided to go.

At first Anne's lack of funds provoked some opposition from her father, but when Anne learned that her maternal grandfather had bequeathed her the exact amount needed for her return fare to India, 'I felt that I was meant to go'.

Anne arrived at the settlement in Dehra Dun to find that, although the hospital building was advanced only as far as its foundations, leprosy patients and destitute children were already being cared for. She spent six months — the period she had originally planned to stay in India — taking care of the administrative work while the hospital was being built. She recalls the long frustrating hours filling out forms to satisfy the Indian Government that she was competent to keep hospital records and record drug supplies.

When the hospital was completed, Anne became its first nurse, caring for patients with no other access to medical help. Later another nurse arrived and they extended the work to include patients suffering from TB — a widespread problem in the area. Anne explains: 'many of the people come from higher up the Himalayas near the Chinese border, 14 000 ft. above sea level. During the colder months they move to lower ground but have no established immunity and TB is rampant, even amongst the children.'

Many of the women needed hospitalisation for up to two years and Anne began to notice a serious secondary problem arising out of this situation. 'They came from communities where women do most of the work and men have more than one wife. The women often returned after long absences to find themselves displaced.' With no role in their community, they became destitute. Anne determined to find a solution for these women.

Meanwhile, with her first three years at an end, Anne went to England to undertake postgraduate work in thoracic nursing at London Hospital, to further her knowledge of tuberculosis. On her return to India, she spent six months working with Mother Theresa's nuns in Calcutta. She then returned to Dehra Dun determined to overcome the problem she had recognised earlier — the problem of the displaced village women: some other means had to be found of treating the women without disrupting the established patterns of village life.

Anne's answer was to take medical help out to the people. She envisaged a mobile clinic and began the scheme herself. With a local hill-woman as companion and guide she began taking her medical equipment to far-flung areas travelling on the mountain buses along narrow, poorly constructed roads, especially treacherous in heavy rains.

Anne learned Hindi and worked tirelessly to establish her scheme. Although her negotiations with the Indian Government were facilitated by the authority they attached to her London qualifications, she had to overcome official suspicions that she was really undertaking missionary work. This, she emphasises, was far from the truth, her primary concern being the *maintenance* of traditional village culture.

When she finally acquired a jeep, Anne drove it herself and for six months travelled the mountain roads accompanied by the same hill woman. She became skilled at such necessary tasks as siphoning petrol — since the round trip covered over 300 kilometres all fuel had to be carried with them. Despite the success with which Anne undertook this work and all its associated problems, she says that, in the eyes of the local population, it was 'better to have a man with them', a more 'appropriate' arrangement than two women travelling alone. So Anne finally trained a local man as driver and devoted herself to her medical work.

Anne's outreach scheme is still operating. It takes life-saving drugs to people in remote areas with no other access to medical help, has enabled many of the women to remain in their villages and, for those who need hospitalisation, the jeep is an ambulance service. The scheme has also established a programme of preventative care, a very positive result of which has been the vaccination of over 1000 children against TB, with an eighty per cent success rate.

The settlement at Dehra Dun is now in the charge of an Indian doctor, fitting in with Anne's ideal and the long-term ideals of the Ryder-Cheshire Foundations. Anne's vital gift — apart from her heroic determination in the face of difficulty, her bravery and her capacity for dedicated work — is her respect for cultures other than her own. Barbara Lewis, another volunteer worker at 'Raphael' (the Dehra Dun settlement), says: 'Anne has an ability to adapt to her surroundings and to other cultures that far surpasses that of any other volunteer I have encountered in ten years of working for Ryder-Cheshire overseas.' Barbara says that the few times Anne was away from India, everything she did was with her return to India in mind: 'If she wasn't over there, the chain was always pulling her back'.

Anne finally left India in the early seventies. She returned to Australia, married and settled in Singleton, New South Wales. She now has two sons, but remains dedicated to her work. On her own initiative and after several years of determined effort during which she raised twenty per cent of the necessary funds (government then providing the balance), she has established New South Wales's first Ryder-Cheshire home for the disabled. The home has two permanent residents at present and provides 'respite care' for young people who are mentally alert but physically handicapped. The centre, with its non-resident nurses, is a place where handicapped people can develop independence in an environment of their own. 'Respite care' allows disabled people normally living with their families to take up residence at the centre for one

Anne Boyd, who has put Ryder-Cheshire ideals into practice in India and New South Wales

or two months. While providing a break for the families, this also develops self-help skills that are vital for the establishment of identity and self-respect.

Everything that Anne has done reflects her commitment to Ryder-Cheshire ideals of self-help and the promotion of human dignity. Much help is needed for the world's ill and destitute. As the Indians of Dehra Dun ask: 'When will we have more volunteers like Anne?'

Brother Andrew
1928–
Missionary Brother of Charity
Written by: David Millar
Nominated by: Colin Deefholts

In the midst of teeming Calcutta stands Howrah Railway Station. For the station children, this world of hissing steam and jostling crowds is more than a transit centre — it is home. Moulded by orphanhood and destitution, they work as unlicensed porters, vendor's assistants and message runners.

Working amongst this devil's playground is a religious order which, until recently, had as its superior an Australian priest, Brother Andrew. Born in Melbourne's Hawthorn, this slim, bearded man was baptised as Ian and sent as a boy to Xavier College, Kew, for a solid, Jesuit education. Socially, Ian was a pleasant, quiet boy with a nice sense of humour, but he was also a closet gambler — not an occasional two bob sweepstake flutterer but a dedicated practitioner. The form guide hypnotised him; radio racing results were an obsession and he was well known to an SP bookie. He even failed his French Matriculation Examination as the thought of the tips in the evening paper completely derailed his concentration. On leaving school, he continued his 'racing studies', developed a 'system', and with it won half a year's salary in one afternoon. Lady Luck, however deserted him — one day his 'system' failed and he 'blew all his dough'.

It was while sitting in the midst of some perplexing and troubled introspection that Ian now felt a distinct calling: he would train for the priesthood and enter the Society of Jesus. Some years later, the schoolboy gambler had become Father Ian Travers-Ball SJ, a vocations director with the Jesuits in India.

If that was a dramatic change, there was more to follow. In 1965 Father Ian met the famous Mother Theresa and was granted by his order an 'experimental month' with her Missionary Sisters of Charity in Calcutta, working in their home for the dying and leprosy centre. It was here that, as Mother Theresa said, she 'kidnapped him from the Jesuits'. For some time, now, Father Ian had been attracted to the idea of serving the underprivileged, 'the poorest of the poor'. Mother Theresa meanwhile had been searching for a suitable male to look after twenty to thirty male novices whom she had inadvertently attracted after establishing her own order for women. Rome had insisted that without a male superior, Mother Theresa's 'hangers-on' could not be granted official status.

So, in 1966, Father Ian SJ became Brother Andrew of the Missionary Brothers of Charity and moved into their official dwelling in Calcutta as their first superior. As if waiting for his arrival, the order mushroomed — men came from everywhere, either to test their vocation with the new order or as temporary volunteers.

Unlike many religious orders, the Brothers of Charity do not own any conventional religious building. Rather, the members choose to live in the same slum conditions as the people they serve, believing, in the words of Mother Theresa, that 'our own poverty is both our strength and our freedom'. Hence all modern appliances are forbidden — even, where possible, the wrist watch. The brothers wear no conventional religious habit, only 'hand-me-downs' with a discreet crucifix over the heart. An individual's possessions can all fit into a shoulder bag and bedding is a roll-up mattress. They sleep wherever there is a space and, as for individual privacy, as one brother wryly commented, 'It's like being married to six wives when you join this order'.

Every day the brothers go out from their slum houses to love and care for the underprivileged. 'Anyone writhing on the pavements is seen as Christ' — the alcoholics of Los Angeles, the dying of Calcutta, the destitute of Seoul, the drifters of Paris or the children suffering from malnutrition in a Guatemalan village.

How is such relentless work sustained and such living conditions accepted? It is, the Brothers would say, 'by the practice of the presence of God'. Or, as Brother Andrew wrote in 1987, the revelation of the *something more* that lies hidden in the ordinary, the unlikely and the fearful'.

Lex Banning
1921–1965

'Poetry is not the wine but the cognac'
Written by: Sue Phillips
Nominated by: Brian J. Jenkins

'And Lex who cried *Poetry is not the wine but the cognac...*'
from 'Sidere Mens Eadem Mutato' by Les Murray

Lex Banning was born in Sydney in 1921, a victim of cerebral palsy. He never learned to speak without spluttering and grimacing, to write with a pen or to hold a knife and fork. Yet he overcame his handicap to produce poems which were often hauntingly beautiful and frequently ironic, and gave to other, younger poets a strong sense of the importance and value of their calling — whatever the world might seem to think of it.

'He ignored his disability, he snubbed it,' says Australia's most acclaimed poet, Les Murray, whose apprentice work was encouraged by

Banning. 'And a few minutes after meeting him, you forgot about it.'

Unable to complete high school because of the Depression, Banning narrowly escaped becoming an apprentice bootmaker, a career which the board looking after young cerebral palsy victims suggested as suitable. Fortunately, at least one board member recognised the boy's intelligence, and a job was found for him at Sydney Observatory where, during the two or three years he worked there, he learned to type. Details about the next few years are sketchy, but clearly he must have spent some of his time studying for, in 1944, he persuaded the University of Sydney Senate to admit him, as an unmatriculated student, to the Faculty of Arts.

Banning's years at Sydney University were brilliantly successful. He graduated in 1948 with honours in English and history, and began to write poems which were published in university journals. He also edited a number of university newspapers and magazines, both during his undergraduate years and later.

He was employed after graduation as a librarian at the Spastic Centre but, says his friend and biographer Richard Appleton, 'the twin axes of his world remained Sydney University and that group of "drinkers and thinkers" known subsequently as the Push. Paradoxically, despite

Lex Banning at the Assembly Hotel in the early 1950s; a fine poet and great company

his difficulties in speaking with clarity there was no better drinking companion than Lex.' Poetry remained dominant in his life, and throughout the fifties his poems, remarkable for their purity and compression as well as their irony and cynicism, appeared in magazines and newspapers as well as being collected in three slim volumes which quickly went out of print.

Despite this output, Banning was really only beginning to establish his reputation beyond his own immediate circle when, in the early 1960s, he took the fateful decision to leave Australia, 'exported' to England as a result of a series of fund-raising activities orchestrated by his friends and colleagues. In England he married Anne Ferry, the Australian doctor he had been courting by letter for two years.

Neither his marriage nor his writing career prospered, however, and Lex returned to Sydney in 1964, depressed and, says Appleton, 'obviously unwell'. After his death in 1965, his poetry remained largely out of print until the publication in 1987 of *There was a Crooked Man* (Angus & Robertson) edited by Richard Appleton and Alex Galloway. Through its biography, critical appraisal and collected poems, Lex Banning was rescued from threatened oblivion.

Amongst the poems re-published in this book is 'And to Be of Service', first published in 1952:

AND TO BE OF SERVICE

I have stood beside you
In the small hours of the night
on a deserted street corner,
with the rain falling,
waiting for buses that never came,
waiting for a tram that was late in arriving;
losing my loneliness in offering companionship,
losing my fear in offering you protection.

Often before had I stood
at the empty crossroads of the mind,
in the wind and the rain of time,
waiting for non-existent buses,
or for trams that were generally late in arriving;
lonely, and somewhat frightened.

But this time it was quite different, somehow,
although the buses did not come,
and the tram, when it arrived, was late, as usual;
for you were there,
both giving and taking from me,
so that on this corner I was not frightened,
nor was I lonely in these elements.

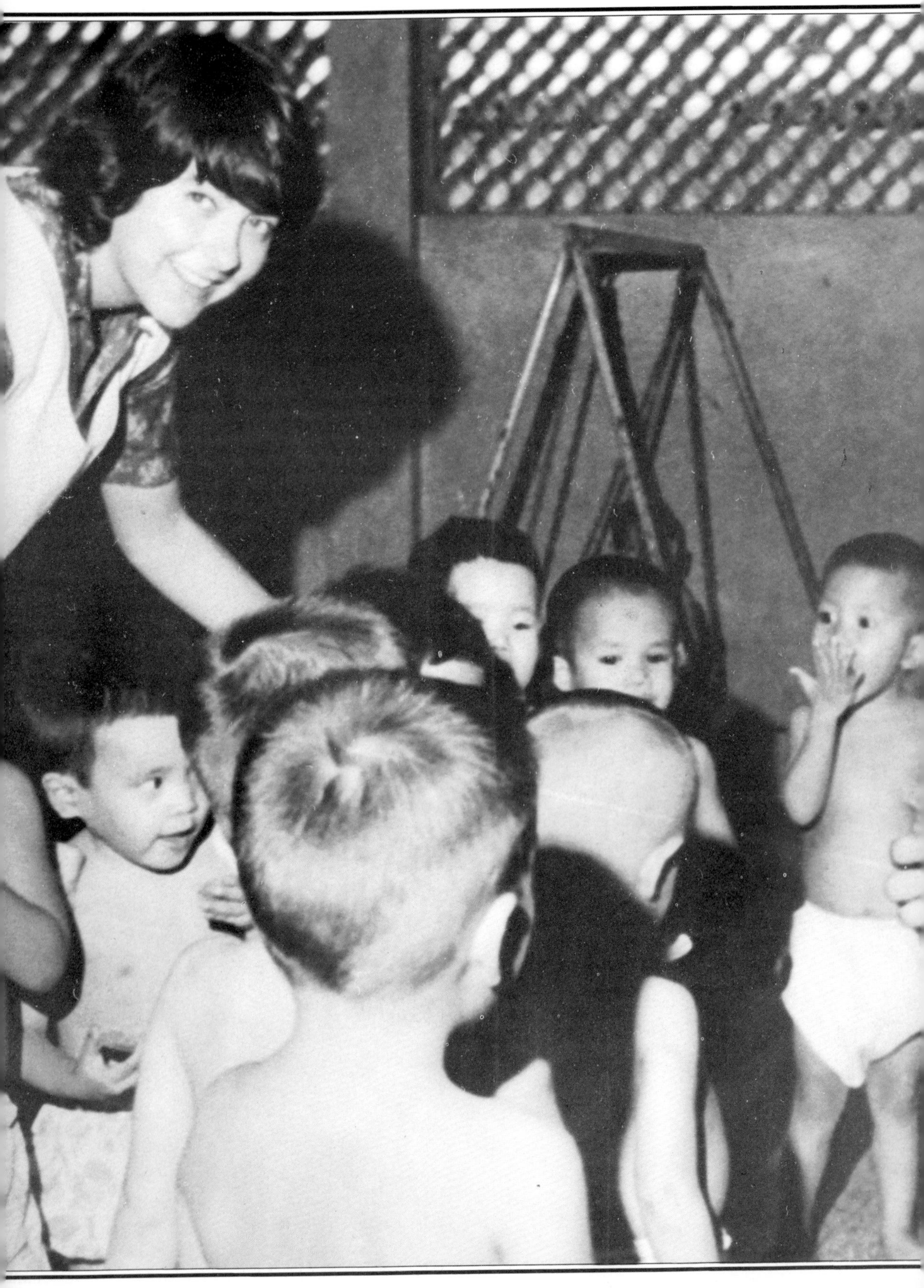

8
Survival
1968–1988

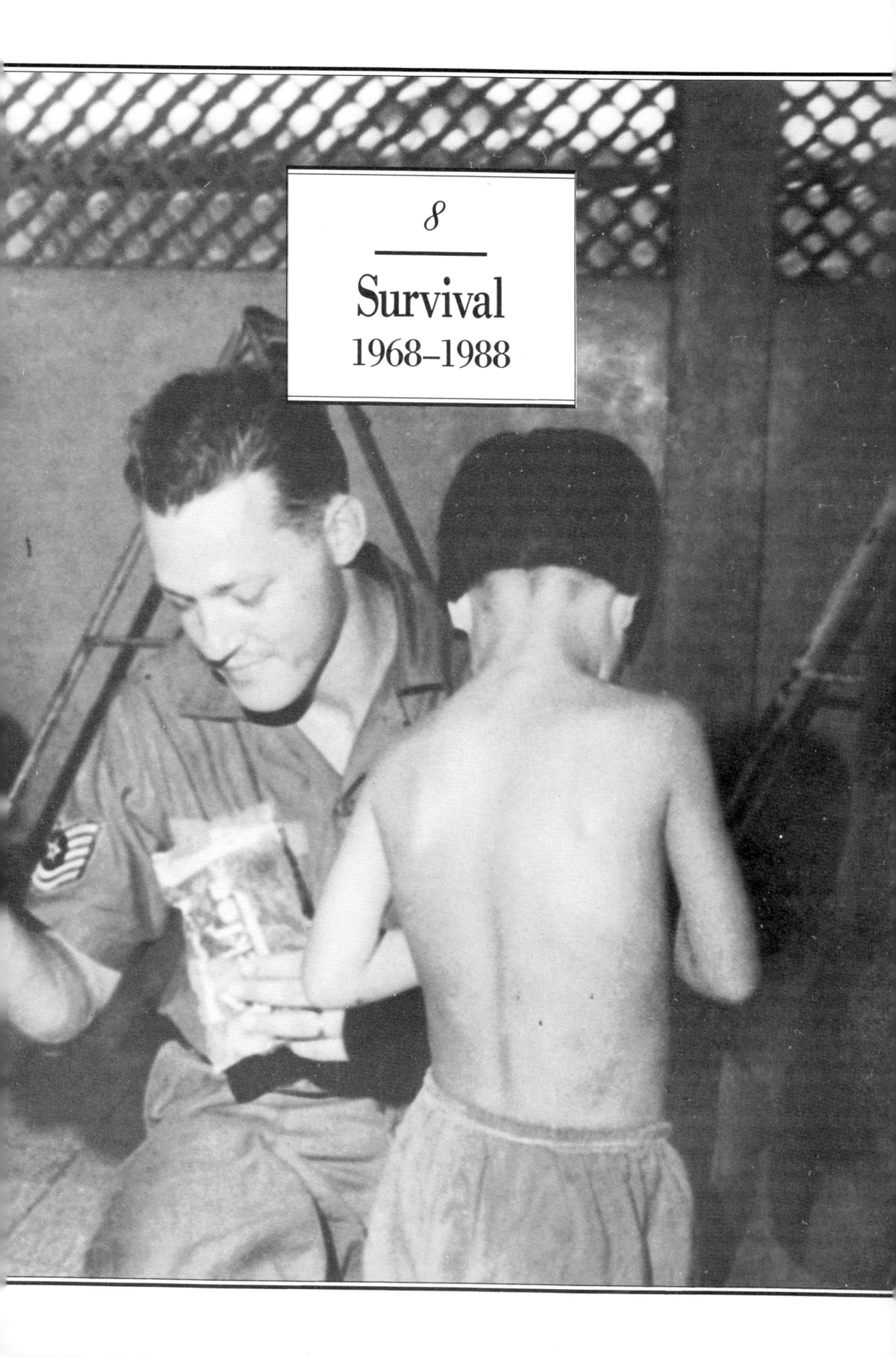

These stories all speak about the possibility of survival. Not everybody makes it.

Unlike the stories from the years of recovery, these stories reveal a shift from optimism about the future to, at best, uncertainty. We can launch humans into space, but cannot save them from suffering and despair. Yet we must persist. These are stories about acts of salvage and salvation; about preserving what we can before it is too late.

One man fights for the survival of a vanishing wilderness, another for a vanishing culture. The rest of the people whose stories are told here fight for the survival of the ill, the handicapped, the lost, the abandoned, the old and, most precious of all, the young.

Each story reminds us that, unless we treat the part of the world around us with honour, affection and compassion, it — and we — are lost. Wolves wearing the sheep's clothing of political expedience, profit, comfort and an easy life prowl outside the circle of fires that we must keep alight if we are to survive in any way that matters. In a very real sense, we are all behind the lines.

John Fraser
1945–1968

Vietnam. Killed in action
Written by: Billy Marshall-Stoneking
Nominated by: Frederick James Fraser

Vietnam. No victory. No glory. Even the pride of having done your duty lost in the hostility of political debate and the growing public perception that, far from being a righteous or necessary war, Vietnam is a shameful war, a needless waste of young Australian lives. A story of sacrifice.

John Fraser was always a leader. A brilliant student, Rugby player and cricketer, his business career was taking shape when his number came out of the barrel in the first Vietnam call-up. He did his boot training at Holdsworthy, and then went to Officer Training School where he impressed his superiors with his leadership qualities. Because he was able to get the best from his men, he was sent to Canungra Jungle Training Camp as an instructor. Real combat, however, still seemed a long way off. Then, with discharge only weeks away, he discovered that his battalion was being posted to Vietnam, so he re-enlisted.

24 March 1968. Hill 323, Phuoc Tuy Province. Pat Burgess, war correspondent, was on patrol with Lieutenant John Fraser and his platoon. He sent the story back to the *Sydney Morning Herald*.

'The gully between the two granite hills was a hundred yards wide. Both hills had the bleakness of a World War I landscape. The trees, shorn off by blast and shrapnel, were dead or dying. The grey granite boulders were weathered and covered by a grey-green dry moss...

Previous page. Saigon, 1967. Rosemary Taylor, Vietnamese orphans and one of the many servicemen who came to help. In eight years in Vietnam, Rosemary and her staff handled 4000 overseas adoptions. 'We were primarily a salvage operation in a time of war'

'With two platoons of Three Battalion we were edging our way along one ridge while the battalion's Charlie Company cleared the other. The hills have been seeded with land mines and booby traps by the Vietcong. For a platoon to move at all, riflemen give cover to two sappers with mine detectors who clear a narrow safe path. The path is marked with plastic tape and the whole platoon follows. Even then a mine can be detonated by remote control by Vietcong hiding in caves...

'Johnny Fraser's platoon was getting close to the dark cave entrances, no more than a triangular crevice and a small black oval.

'When the mine exploded everyone on the two hills and in the gully froze. This is now the established drill in the parched, slashed hills of Long Hai. As the dust of the exploding land began to settle, a voice echoed in the gully above the cries of the other wounded: "Don't come in for me, don't come in. There's more there." '

Fraser, leading his men, had put his foot down on a 'jump-up' mine — so-called because it could spring into the air, killing everyone around it. Hearing the device arm itself, Fraser put both feet together, directly on top of it.

The explosion knocked his men to the ground but they were safe. Fraser had stopped the mine from doing its real job.

The rescue helicopter arrived quickly and the winch came down with the basket. Fraser was lifted up and carried away. Shortly afterwards, the message came through on the radio handset: Johnny Fraser was dead.

They brought the former star athlete home to Surfers Paradise, gave him a big parade, and buried him with full military honours. There were better places for a young man of twenty-three to be.

Second Lieutenant John Fraser, talented and twenty-three, put both feet on a mine to save his platoon

James Gurriwiwi
1972–
The littlest hero
Written by: Billy Marshall-Stoneking
Nominated by: Maurie V. Burke

Five-year-old James Gurriwiwi, from northern Arnhem Land, was not sure exactly where he was. All he knew was that his mother, together with her two girlfriends, had taken him and his three-year-old brother, Peter, from Mada Mada outstation and set out for Yirrkala Settlement, 120 kilometres to the south east; and after walking for nearly two days, he and his brother were finding it difficult to keep up.

To make matters worse, their mother — Mari Mari — was completely unsympathetic. She had not really wanted to take the children with her anyway. Of course, everyone at Yirrkala knew she was 'mad', but no one had worried about her. The usual behaviour was simply to try and ignore her moods and emotional outbursts, and quietly hope that she did not hurt herself or anyone else.

Mari Mari also had a reputation for violence, and it was probably

James Gurriwiwi, five (left), and his three-year-old brother Peter, painted for the corroboree at Yirrkala that celebrated their survival for seven days alone in the bush. James is held by Margaret, wife of police tracker Muku Muku, who holds Peter. With them is clan leader Roy Marika and Sgt Maurie Burke of Nhulunbuy Police Station who coordinated the massive search party

this more than anything that kept her two companions from arguing with her when she suggested that they leave the two little boys behind and continue on their own. 'They be okay,' she whispered.

Mari Mari turned to James and told him to sit down and wait for her to come back. Then the women disappeared into the bush.

James and Peter waited patiently for several hours then, as the sun started to sink, the boys grew restless. James began to worry. Maybe his mother would not be coming back at all. He looked at his little brother, and watched with fear as Peter began to cry.

What could they do? They were alone, and eveyone knew that the bush and the swamps and mangroves were full of demons and devils, full of evil spirits just waiting to capture two little boys.

James took his brother by the hand and set off, following the tracks left by his mother and her two friends. Maybe he could catch up with them before it grew very dark.

But Mari Mari and her friends were miles away, and when the women arrived at Yirrkala the next afternoon, Mari Mari had already worked out her story. With tears streaming down her face, she explained how the two boys were taken by sharks and how the others had just managed to escape.

The police found the story credible. After all, stranger things had happened; but they wanted to be shown the spot where the boys had died.

Upon arriving at the location, one of the girls broke down. Fearful for herself and her own family if the truth were ever discovered, she admitted that the boys had been abandoned, explaining that she had been afraid to oppose Mari Mari.

The police and a few elders from the settlement exchanged glances for a moment. Somewhere out there in the wilderness were two frightened and defenceless small boys. A search party was formed immediately.

James and Peter, by this time, had now spent two frightful nights in the bush. 'Every rustle of grass, every flutter of a night bird, or snap of a twig seemed to announce the arrival of a spirit person in search of little children's kidney fat.'

But James, despite his youth, kept his head. He shielded his younger brother as best he could, covering the smaller boy with 'black boy' palms to create a shelter under which the toddler slept. He was frightened, but could not let the younger boy see it. As the older, he knew his obligations.

James remained awake most of the night, too terrified to sleep, and wondering all the time what would become of them. Now and then he would nod off, only to be woken by an unidentifiable sound. At last, the fatigue was too much for him, and next thing he knew it was morning.

Night after night, the routine was the same; and during the day, without knowing where they were or in what direction they were heading, James found various types of bush tucker — wild scrub apples and a native berry called 'raga' which is extremely high in vitamin C.

On the sixth day, James heard the cooees of the searchers, but was frightened that these were the sounds of some giant mythical frog, and ran away. By this stage, both boys had, as someone later said, 'become fugitives of their own imaginations'.

Finally, in one last dash to escape the evil spirits that were closing in on them, James ran headlong into the legs of a white policeman. He screamed loudly, sure that he was about to be killed. But then the clan leader from Yirrkala arrived. Speaking quietly, gently, he soothed the boy. A hundred metres away, other members of the search party found Peter, huddled under a bush.

For seven days and six nights, James and his brother had wandered alone through some of the most dangerous and inhospitable country in Australia. It was a miracle they were found at all, let alone found alive.

That night, the people at Yirrkala held a big corroboree. James and Peter were decorated for the occasion with feathers and body paint, and many adults, both black and white, celebrated and gave thanks for the safe return of the two tiny boys.

Ruth Frances Bishop
1933–
Research saves the children
Written by: Judith Elen
Nominated by: Leonard A. Hall

Dr Ruth Bishop, an Australian scientist with three children of her own now in their twenties, has devoted her working life to the good of the world's children. Twice chairperson of World Health Organisation scientific working committees, she is recognised overseas yet in Australia is unknown to all but family, friends and colleagues.

Unsung Heroes & Heroines

Since her graduation from Melbourne University with her first science degree in 1954, Ruth Bishop has worked persistently on the study of gastroenteritis from which five million people die every year. One of the world's biggest child-killers, the disease is particularly devastating in underdeveloped countries where access to hospitals is limited. It is not however, confined to poor countries and when an epidemic broke out in Melbourne in 1973, Dr Bishop was — providentially — on the spot.

One of a number of researchers world wide who had been attempting to isolate the cause of the disease, Ruth Bishop had an instinct that

Dr Ruth Bishop, DSc, PhD, MSc, MASM. Her discovery of the virus that causes gastroenteritis will save the lives of thousands of the world's children. Photograph by Ponch Hawkes

the culprit was a virus. Using an electron microscope on tissue samples taken from one of the affected children, she observed a single unknown virus. With her instinct confirmed, the search was over.

This, however, was only the first step. The next was to develop an oral vaccine for the severest forms of gastroenteritis in very young children. Such a vaccine could be used worldwide, becoming part of existing vaccination programmes so that distribution costs would be minimal. Several associated programmes have already been successfully completed and Ruth Bishop believes that the development of the oral vaccine is imminent. Her research team at The Royal Children's Hospital in Melbourne leads the world, but the search is hampered by a lack of funds — quite small amounts in research terms.

In 1978 Dr Bishop shared the University of Melbourne's Selwyn-Smith Prize for Clinical Research and is a nominee for the recent Bicentennial BHP Award for the Pursuit of Excellence in Science and Technology. A member of the politics and liaison committee of Women in Medical Science (WIMS), Ruth Bishop's work was directed and shaped by two older women doctors. She dreams of one day publishing a book that examines some of the work of her scientific sisters. 'In the books that have already been written the work of women in medicine and science has gone largely unrecorded.'

Winsome Mahoney
1930–

Triumph of day-to-day courage
Written by: Suzanne Falkiner
Nominated by: Barbara Dawn Lyford

It is the very ordinariness of this story, which could be the story of any number of Australian women, that makes it compelling. It reveals the day-to-day heroism of a woman who, despite a violent husband, poverty and the burden of numerous children, kept going, survived, and finally triumphed.

Winsome Longford was born in Sydney in 1930. While living at Tamworth, New South Wales, when she was about two, Winsome was left outside to play by a careless babysitter while her mother was at work. She wandered away and was lost in the snow. When found, she had severe frostbite which caused the loss of the fingers and toes of her left hand and foot.

Despite this handicap, Winsome grew up to complete her studies with a Diploma of Education from Sydney University and further training in teaching mentally handicapped and disadvantaged children. While teaching in Sydney she met Jim Lyford, an accountant, whom she married when she was twenty-six. Early in the following years, as she gave birth to and raised seven daughters and a son, she began to realise that Jim, an intelligent and complicated man with a volatile personality, was chronically violent. Although he loved her and the children, he would beat her in fits of uncontrollable temper.

Winsome Mahoney, kindergarten teacher, fought the government, misfortune and poverty to keep her family of eight children together

Throughout the eighteen-year marriage, as they moved from rented house to rented house in the Blue Mountains area, Winsome endured abuse, broken ribs, black eyes and sleepless nights. There were no women's refuges at the time and the police could not intervene without witnesses. Because Jim was a compulsive gambler who often lost his earnings on the horses, Winsome would wait until he went to work, then go out to work herself in a local delicatessen, or ironing clothes, or teaching swimming.

In January 1975 Jim Lyford was diagnosed as having cancer. He refused to stay in hospital so Winsome nursed him at home until his death. 'I chose to stay with him,' she says simply. 'I believe in loyalty.'

After Jim Lyford's death, Winsome was reported to the authorities as being destitute and unable to care for her eight children. She fought the government to keep her family and worked morning, afternoon and night at three jobs while a neighbouring pensioner cared for the children. During this time, she often found little gifts of food or clothes on the doorstep, and people who had heard of her plight sent anonymous donations of money. In this way, in March 1976 Winsome was able to buy a block of land at Winmalee for $4500, and a sympathetic local bank manager offered her a loan to build a house.

The years since then have been happy. In 1981 Winsome married Rex Mahoney, who bought her a childcare centre. That is now run by one of her daughters since Winsome has taken charge of the Winmalee kindergarten. With a loving husband and a family which, although grown up, remains remarkably close, Winsome Mahoney has been able to continue in the other love of her life — working with young children.

Terry Wu
1950–

Daring rescue by Cambodian refugee
Written by: Elizabeth Riddell
Nominated by: Rosemary J. Webster

On that night in 1979 there were nine people in the deserted farmhouse — four men, three women, two little children. It was quiet inside: not a whimper from the children, only the sound of breathing, water being poured into a cup, a whisper of movement as the family of Cambodian refugees shifted their tired bodies on the floor. And quiet outside. The ravaged landscape on the Thai-Kampuchea border slept.

Then one of the women began to gasp, holding a scarf to her mouth. She went into labour. In the dark a baby was being born while fifteen kilometres away in a truck hidden near the highway, a man waited to take his father, three brothers and their wives and children out of their ruined country.

The three who could not travel — brother, brother's wife and newborn baby — stayed behind in the farmhouse when the others left, silently crying and kissing, to walk to the truck, to a United Nations refugee camp and ultimately to freedom. Later, the other three were rescued by the Red Cross and are now in Switzerland.

The man in the truck was Terry Wu, from Melbourne. His is a remarkable story of family loyalty, ingenuity, and courage. No doubt there are others to match it known to the Cambodian community in Australia, which by and large keeps its own counsel. Terry Wu's genial but modest personality and his gutsy attitude to life in a new land, prompted an Australian friend to tell Terry's tale.

Terry Wu had another name in Cambodia/Kampuchea. His wife is now called Kelly, and that is not her real name either. In 1975, with the Pol Pot forces close on their heels, they walked with other refugees across country to the Thai border, and were put in a camp by the reluctant Thais. The Wus had a daughter in the camp, Kellent (that is her right name) and in 1976 they reached Australia in the first plane load of 300 refugees. Kellent was eleven months old. Terry, a watchmaker by trade, was twenty-six. They lived in the Eastbridge Hostel near Melbourne and Terry worked in restaurants. He was sponsored by Mr and Mrs Webster of Ringwood after Rosemary Webster had joined a women's auxiliary which aimed at helping Kampuchean refugees.

Before he left Thailand Terry had made some friends who promised to keep a lookout for members of the family. From them he heard that his father, Hay, and three of his brothers with their wives and children were in Camp Aranyaprathet in Thailand. That was good news, of a kind. Then in 1979, when Kelly was eight and a half months pregnant with their second child, Terry received a telephone call from his Thai friends that the camp was going to be emptied out — and the inmates sent back over the border into Kampuchea.

Terry acted with extraordinary speed. Having heard the news on a Sunday, he contacted the Websters; went to a bank and borrowed $5000 on Monday; was naturalised on Tuesday; obtained a passport on Wednesday and on Thursday was in Bangkok. The Department of Immigration and Ethnic Affairs certainly showed what it can do in an emergency.

Disguised as an electrician, Terry Wu went straight to the camp on the border and tracked down his father and the rest of the family, except for his mother, who had died, possibly of malnutrition while giving up any available food to the rest of the family. He arranged to borrow a truck, and organised the family into secretly leaving the camp that same night and going to a deserted farmhouse. From there they were to walk to a designated spot where he would be waiting. The big risk for him was in being apprehended by soldiers or police who would have taken his Australian passport and money and killed him without reporting his presence to the authorities. In fact the family reached the truck without mishap and Terry drove them to a United Nations camp near Bangkok. Next day most of those left in the original camp were loaded into trucks by the Thais and, unwittingly or not, dumped out into a minefield. Terry returned to Melbourne, where his wife had given birth to a son, Donny. Months later the Websters and the Wus assembled at Tullamarine airport to meet Hay, his two sons and their wives and children. Hay was fifty-six years old, very frail, weighing not much more than six stone. He wept when he met,

Terry Wu, refugee, returned to Thailand to smuggle his father, brothers, brothers' wives and children out of a refugee camp. They have now joined Terry and his wife and children in Melbourne

for the first time, his Australian grandchildren, now numbering three with the birth of another boy, Bobby.

The process of gathering the family together in Melbourne, where Terry now has a successful Chinese restaurant — Terry's antecedents are Chinese — goes on. Kelly Wu has six sisters and two brothers, some of whom are already in Melbourne, others waiting. In the extended families of Terry and Kelly, as of many other Kampucheans in Australia, as many are missing as have been saved from the bullets of the opposing forces and the degradation of the camps: some are dead, some have disappeared, perhaps only temporarily. One of the family walked from Kampuchea to Saigon.

Casey Antarctic Expeditioners
1979

Man against Nature
Written by: Niall Lucy
Nominated by: Graham J. Manning

1979 Casey Expedition. Mike Stone (back, third from right), Brian Clements (front right), Laurie Cole (centre row, second left), Leader Manning (far right), Geoffrey Reeve (front, second right)

On 3 August 1979 four men left their Antarctic base at Casey to conduct a field trip twelve kilometres away at Robinson's Ridge. Two days later, one of them went missing.

When Geoffrey Reeve left his hut on the afternoon of 5 August, the temperature was −12°C and the wind was gusting at an ominous five to ten knots. While Reeve's companions slept, the weather developed into a full-scale blizzard. Visibility was reduced to five metres as a gale-force wind of ninety-six knots howled over the ice and snow.

Upon waking, the three remaining expeditioners — Laurie Cole,

Brian Clements, and Michael Stone — realised that Reeve had not returned. Tying a life-line around their waists, they took four hours and many attempts to cross thirty metres to another building. Their companion was not there. In desperation, they radioed base for help — but blizzard conditions also prevailed at Casey and it would take several hours before a search and rescue party could be launched. Meanwhile, because of their depleted physical and mental state, they were forbidden to take any further risk on their own.

Ignoring this order, Cole, Clements and Stone continued to search throughout the night. At 8.45 am the following morning, they found Reeve alive but unconscious 750 metres upwind from camp. Soon afterwards, he stopped breathing and his companions began to apply external cardio-massage.

The search and rescue crew relieved the three men at 11.45 am, having taken almost four hours to negotiate their vehicles through the blizzard and across the twelve kilometres of heavily-crevassed ice. All forms of heat therapy were administered to Reeve, who was by now experiencing heart flutters, and he was put inside a sleeping bag and driven back to base. On the return journey, the expeditioners took turns in applying non-stop cardio-massage to their companion, but their rescue effort was in vain. Geoffrey Reeve was pronounced dead at 6.30 pm on the evening of 6 August 1979.

Jeannie Auld
1949–
Bush nurse
Written by: Jennifer Dabbs
Nominated by: R. Mate Mate; N. Sedwick

Jeannie Auld is one of hundreds of dedicated women who go about the business of health care in the most isolated and barren areas of Australia. They are the bush nurses. And they are all heroic, possessing extraordinary qualities and strengths which enable them to persevere in the face of harsh conditions and inadequate facilities.

The average stay in the outback is two years; Jeannie Auld worked in Central Australia for eight. Her territory covered fifty thousand square kilometres and she was responsible for the welfare of 1000 Aborigines scattered throughout the region in small, far-flung settlements.

Jeannie Auld developed a special relationship with the Aboriginal people, based on mutual respect and affection. 'We taught each other,' Jeannie says simply, and recalls their extreme tact and diplomacy in their dealings with her. 'They were very careful not to embarrass me when I'd go into a situation boots and all. Someone would take me aside and gently point me in the right direction; tell me which person I should be talking to, the tribal and family relationships I should be aware of, all that sort of thing.'

As a bush nurse, Jeannie's task was not simply to treat the endemic

Jeannie Auld plays patient to teach Josie, a trainee health worker at Titree Health Centre in the Northern Territory, to set a broken leg. Of her relationship with the Aborigines during her eight years as outback nurse, Jeannie says, 'We taught each other'

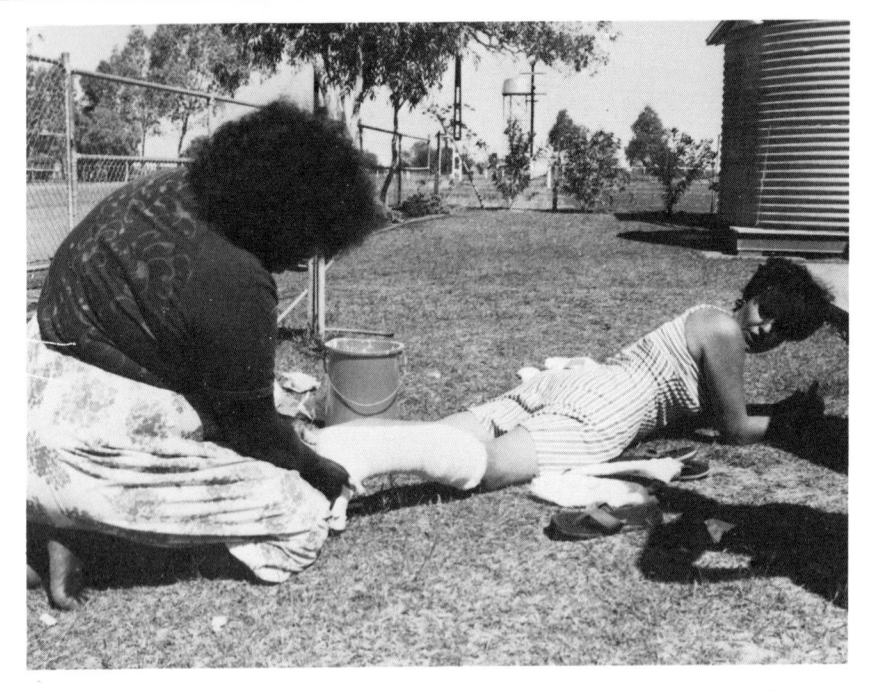

health problems like chronic infections, malnutrition and alcoholism that plague Aboriginal communities. The aim was, and still is, to train their own people as health workers in preventative medicine within each community. To do this, Jeannie found herself calling on many skills she was not sure she possessed: those of teacher, psychologist, social worker, go-between and friend.

'There's no such thing as a forty-hour week when you work in the bush,' she says cheerfully. 'Thirty hours or more overtime wasn't uncommon. It was more of the norm, actually.'

It is not surprising that this sort of deep commitment at a professional and personal level eventually leads to physical and emotional exhaustion. 'We burn out,' Jeannie says regretfully. 'It's an occupational hazard. It happens to all of us sooner or later. It happened to me after three years and I had to leave for a while.'

But she quickly found city life unrewarding and headed back to the bush as soon s she was declared fit enough. Another five years of dedicated, energetic involvement ensued until once again, she succumbed to exhaustion and realised that it was time 'to let go for a while'. She did this with some regret, as the Aboriginal children held a special place in her affections.

At present, Jeannie is nursing at The Gosford District and Community Hospital. 'It's necessary to update nursing skills every few years. I've been out of touch and I need to catch up with the latest drugs and technology,' she explains. But there is an undeniable wistfulness in her voice when she talks about her time as a bush nurse.

Will she go back? 'To visit, oh yes,' she says promptly. 'I don't know whether I'd work there again,' she hesitates. 'But there's so much to be done...' In the painful business of farewelling the many friends she had made in her eight years in Central Australia, an Aboriginal man paid her what she considers her highest and most valued compliment when he referred to her as 'Jeannie, one of my family'.

Edward 'Teddy' Burgess
1945–1986

Unexpected artist
Written by: Katie Lawley
Nominated by: Ruth Dillon

Teddy Burgess was born with Down's Syndrome. His mother, already responsible for a sick husband, four other children and a business, realised that she could not give Teddy the constant care he would need. So, at the age of three, he was placed in the Lorna Hodgkinson Home in Sydney.

Teddy soon became interested in the creative activities of the Home. 'He especially looked forward to concerts,' remembers his sisters. 'No matter how small or simple the task, he took great pride in whatever he did or any part he played.'

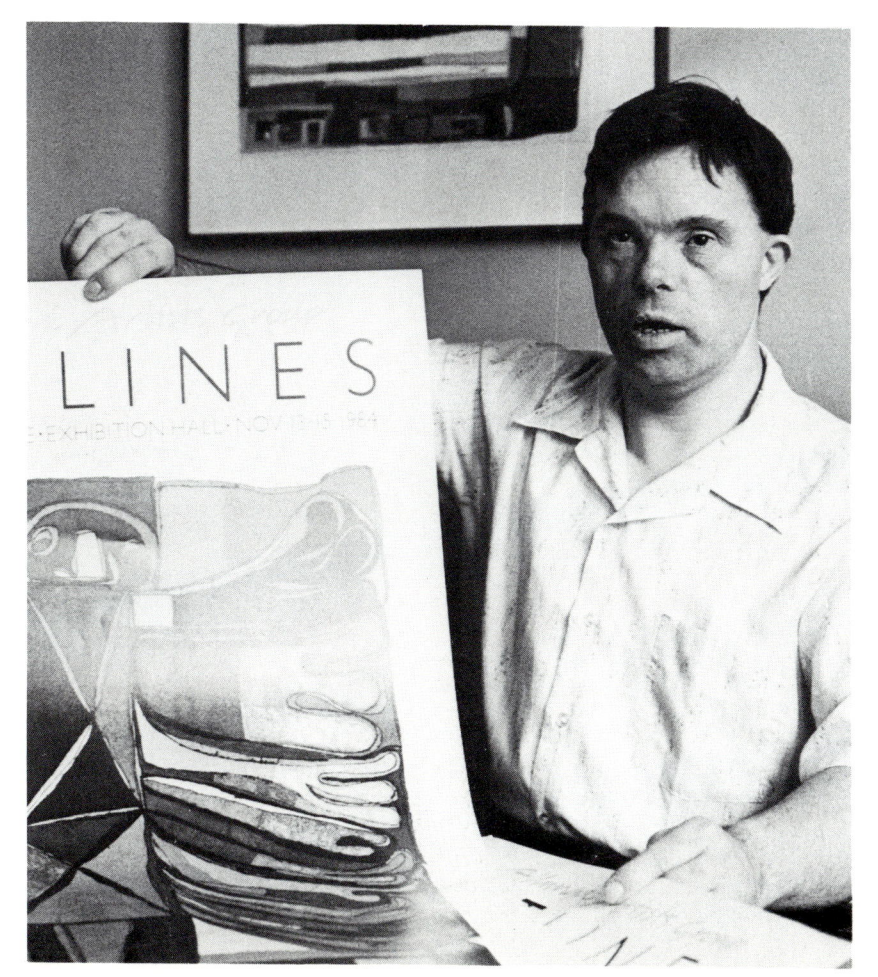

Teddy Burgess with the poster featuring one of his paintings that advertised the Allunga Artists Group Exhibition at the Sydney Opera House in November 1984

When Aldo Gennaro — artist, playwright, theatre director and therapist — came to the Sunshine Home, he inspired the people there with a new sense of self confidence. 'Teddy loved to dance,' says Gennaro. 'He always had such energy. He would use his hands as though he was creating a sculpture.'

Teddy's talents, along with those of other members of the Home, were soon recognised when Gennaro created a Theatre of the Handicapped, which culminated in a production at the Opera House called *Life, Images & Reflections*. This incorporated plays, an art exhibition and the film *Stepping Out* by Christopher Noonan. Teddy was a major contributor in each section but is most remembered for his role in *Stepping Out*.

'Teddy was also an excellent visual artist,' says Gennaro. He was a member of the Allunga Artist's Group and his paintings were widely exhibited and sold. A critic on the ABC's 'State of the Arts' program described Teddy's work as 'having brilliant colour, spirit and lack of selfconsciousness. What he achieved in a short time was something like Miro and Chagall spent decades trying to get onto canvas.' One of Teddy's works was made into a poster to advertise the production at the Opera House; another was chosen by the Bicentennial Authority for their 1985 Christmas Card.

Teddy travelled to the Allunga Artists Group by train three times a week to paint. On 24 March 1986, he caught the train as usual, but by mistake boarded an express, unaware that it would bypass his stop. When he saw his station approaching, he moved from his seat to the open doors and stepped from the speeding train. Teddy, then forty-one, was killed almost immediately.

Although handicapped, Teddy found immense personal fulfilment and expression through his art. Generous and warm he was an inspiration to those more fortunate than himself.

Clare Stevenson
1903–

Commonsense carer
Written by: Judith Elen
Nominated by: Rosemary Manchester

Clare Stevenson's note to well-wishers after her Australia Day Award reads: 'I have never carried out community work without the aid of others, I count the award as a tribute to those also.'

After completing a science degree at the university of Melbourne, Clare Stevenson became training and research officer at Berlei in 1932. One of Australia's few 'career women' at the time, Clare Stevenson went on to become Director of the WAAAF — the first female head of a war-time service. 'I learned a lot during the war — you can't have 28 000 women passing through your hands and not learn something.'

After the war, Clare put her experience to work for the community.

Clare Stevenson, MBE, early career woman and community worker. At almost 80, she led the Anzac Day March through Sydney. Photograph by Paul Wright, Sydney Morning Herald

During forty years' involvement with the Services Canteens Trust Fund, Clare says she 'spent millions' on education for children of Australian Defence Force members. 'I asked myself, if this is what *they* need, what happens to the children of civilian widowed pensioners? Out of this concern, Clare 'with a small group of friends', initiated the Scholarship Trust Fund for Civilian Widows' Children. Joan Clark, who has recently published *Just Us* (Hale & Iremonger, 1988), a history of the Association of Civilian Widows of Australia, says that Clare 'is one of the most remarkable women I have ever met...a woman of decided views'.

One of Clare's most significant contributions to the people of Sydney has been the establishment of the Kings Cross Community Aid Centre. 'The only thing of the kind in the area was church-operated,' she explains, 'and there were many people, either non-religious or of other denominations, who needed an organisation that was not church-based'. So Clare, an agnostic, together with 'a practising Jew, a Church of England member, and a couple of Catholics', started the Centre with a small government subsidy and money raised by Clare and her associates. 'We started in a terrible place,' Clare recalls. But they ran a voluntary information service for the council, and 'we impressed them so much that the council agreed to build lovely rooms for us, under the Kings Cross Library'. Learning that council had decided on 'The Clare Stevenson Community Room' as a title, she says, 'of course, that just made me mad', and she remains annoyed by the size of the 'great bronze plaque' bearing her name. More than a metre high, it is situated in the main room because, says a worker at the Centre, 'Miss Stevenson would not have it outside'.

The Centre is still going strong. Dealing with the aged in the area, it provides a wide variety of practical and cultural services, from a mending service to bus tours. In an area that has 'Sydney's highest

Clare Stevenson, first Director of the Women's Australian Air Force, 1941 to 1946, was the first woman head of any wartime service

number of aged persons per square mile', many of them living alone, the Centre is obviously a vital part of the local community.

The Carer's Association of NSW is another of Clare's notable achievements. Miss Stevenson tells the story: 'Averil Fink [then Executive Director of the NSW Council on the Ageing] became concerned about people leaving work before retiring age to look after an aged parent. She said, "we've got to find out why it's necessary for these people — always women — to leave." ' It was 1975 so, with a small grant from the International Women's Year Fund, 'a questionnaire was included with Social Security's cheques for domiciliary nursing care and so on. It asked people caring for an aged person at home to write about their problems.' Miss Stevenson says 'at least a thousand replies' were received, many of them long letters telling stories 'that would break your heart'. Out of this research, Clare's book, *Dedication*, was published in 1976. A voluntary sub-committee of the Council on the Ageing was set up dealing with 'carers', and later the Carers Association of NSW was established as a registered charity.

Now 'approaching 85', Miss Stevenson has to use a walking frame after breaking her hip but she is still President of the Carers Association which she runs by telephone with the help of an 'excellent administrator'. This takes much of her time, but for relaxation 'I read detective novels — I love them — and nature books, and I listen to classical music. Oh yes, there is always plenty to do — never a bored moment.' Until her accident, Clare frequently drove the forty minutes into town for meetings or the opera. Even now she does not confine herself to the retirement village where she lives.

'One of the tragic things', Clare says, 'is that so many people obviously do not know what is available in the community at the moment.' For much of what is available, the community has Clare Stevenson to thank.

David Henshaw
1946–

Open home, open heart
Written by: Robert Carter
Nominated by: Michael E. Humphries

At two o'clock in the morning a gang of drunken youths smash through the front door of David Henshaw's house. He is brutally attacked and beaten but does not retaliate. He is a pacifist; a man who lives by his own words.

On that morning in 1983, the housebreakers came to collect one of their own, a street kid given a home by David. Out of compassion for the homeless, David Henshaw created the Homesharers Club. The concept was simple: households in Melbourne would offer homeless young people shelter, meals and a chance to break away from drugs, street crime, prostitution and juvenile institutions. In return, homesharers would receive no financial assistance or support from Government or

David Henshaw with two of the many homeless adolescents to whom he gave a home and hope

private organisations; their homeless residents would be likely to depart at any time (perhaps with part of the furniture); and havoc would reign in a previously peaceful home for some time.

Amazingly, with David as inaugural president in 1980, the Homesharers Club grew to include twenty-five households throughout Victoria by 1984 and provided 4000 nights of shelter to seventy-two adolescents, alcoholics, arsonists, addicts, convicted robbers and glue sniffers.

Born in Glenhuntly, Victora on 28 March 1946, David Henshaw's early schooling was disrupted by asthma. Despite this, he went on to earn a PhD in education from Monash University. His doctorate, however, failed to insulate him from the frustration, injustice and humiliation suffered by other unemployed job seekers. His response was to begin a lifelong campaign in newspapers, journals and in action against a society that seemed to be turning its back on the poor, the unemployed and the homeless.

When his mother became ill with cancer of the brain and bladder, he nursed her himself for several years until her death. In 1980 he went to India with the Community Aid Abroad organisation and, on returning to Australia, committed himself to act on the words that others have merely mouthed. Homesharers was born.

'I have seen them plunge their clenched fists through windows, slash my armchair, stab my mattress, hack up my door post, singe my carpet, burn my sheets, uproot my garden, squander their money, abandon their valuables and smoke until they cough with bronchitis. And yet once these youths build confidence, their attitude is reversed and my house now is kept in fine trim by boys who were formerly arsonists and vandals.'

David now lives and teaches school at Mallacoota, where he continues to fight for his beliefs and for the inhabitants. The street kids and ex-street kids who continue to stay in touch with him understand and appreciate the gift that was offered so freely to them.

In a world not short of politicians, film stars, writers and artists willing to describe the suffering, poverty and misfortunes of others, it is inspiring to know of David Henshaw, a quiet hero, whose words became his deeds.

Luke Cuni
1911–1980
Man of peace
Written by: Lucinda Strauss
Nominated by: Mark Cuni

'Better death with honour than life without it'. These were the last words of Professor Luke Cuni broadcast on 3EA in May 1980. The topic of his program was law and order, yet a few hours later he lay dying in the corridors of the Family Court, shot by a man who had threatened to silence him.

On that particular day, Professor Cuni, a talented speaker of eight languages, was acting as replacement for a court translator who had stood down because of death threats. Despite pleas from his family and friends not to go, Luke, always a man of his word, felt compelled to offer his services to a fellow in need. The terrible irony is that Luke Cuni was, like his sister-in-law Mother Teresa, a pacifist who deplored violence.

Luke Cuni was born in the small Albanian village of Prizen on 31 August 1911. A talented linguist, he eventually gained a professorship at the University of Skopje in Yugoslavia. At the end of the war Luke, together with his wife Filomenia and two children, spent several years in refugee camps in Italy before migrating to Australia in 1950.

The first years were a struggle. To survive, the family had to split up, with Luke working at the Old Williamstown Migrant Hostel, Filomenia employed as a housemaid in Croydon and the two children, Rosa and Mark, boarding at separate schools. Eventually, in 1954, the family came together again at their new home in Yarraville, a suburb in Melbourne well-known for its mixture of ethnic groups.

Here Luke Cuni found ample opportunities to use his prodigious talents as a linguist, helping many migrants to settle into the new life in Australia. He came to be known as Uncle Luke or the Professor and as the *Mail* of 28 May 1980 wrote: 'People of Yarraville knocked frequently at the Cuni door. People in trouble, in search of guidance. And not only people of Albanian extraction: Greeks, Australians, Italians, Yugoslavs. They all knew they would get a hearing [and] usually get help.'

In the few decades after his arrival in Australia, Professor Cuni worked to achieve a peaceful co-existence of the many ethnic groups in the community, at the same time rising above the cultural and religious divisions of his fellow countrymen. As a devout Catholic, he sought, by virtue of his own example, to break down the barriers which separated Albanian Catholics and Moslems and he used his position as Chairman of the Legalite Movement (Albanian Loyalist movement) to serve the interests of all Albanians.

For fifteen years before his death Professor Luke Cuni was the acknowledged leader of the Albanian community in Australia. In assisting governments at state and federal levels with ethnic affairs as a

Professor Luke Cuni — 'Uncle Luke' — leader of Australia's Albanian community, not long before he was shot dead while translating at the Family Court

Luke Cuni (standing, second from right), his wife Philomena (left), children Rosa and Mark, and Albanian political refugees on Albanian National Day, 28 November 1951 at Independence Hall, Russell St, Melbourne. The Cunis had arrived early in 1950: for most of the other refugees this was their first National Day in a strange country. United by the common bond of exile, the Albanians at this stage were a strongly unified group

voluntary representative of the Albanian community his aim, always, was to promote a greater understanding between all people in the land.

Soon after Luke Cuni's death, Footscray's mayor, Councillor Paul Holmes summed up the feelings of the community elders: 'I feel that Uncle Luke should be compared with our pioneers at the birth of this great nation'. Luke's grand-daughter Michelle expresses the warmth that was felt by the children who knew Luke Cuni:

'My grandfather was every other
Child's grandfather as well.
With overflowing pockets of sweets,
And a generous heart
He put a smile on everyone's face.'

George & Maude Tongerie
1928–
Saviours of Oodnadatta
Written by: Judith Elen
Nominated by: Jimmy Aitken

George and Maude Tongerie arrived in Oodnadatta at the end of 1981 to find a town in its death throes. Formerly the northern terminus of the famous Ghan, the town lost its lifeline when the railway was diverted to Coober Pedy. The remaining inhabitants — 150 Aborigines and thirty whites — were trapped in a net of unemployment, lack of training, and widespread alcoholism. Oodnadatta looked like a lost cause. But in the face of official scepticism, George and Maude Tongerie offered themselves as community advisors and began the task of reclaiming the town.

The Transcontinental Hotel was both symptom and cause of the town's troubles. The general store also sold alcohol, shamelessly offering credit for $2 flagons of port. With an Aboriginal Development Commission loan (repayable, George stresses, and not a handout), the community bought the pub — *and* the general store, six houses and the historic railway station. The hotel, now run by an Aboriginal board, is still 'well patronised', but not abused now that the sale and consumption of alcohol is under responsible control. 'We got out the hard stuff,' George says, 'And now only beer or soft drinks are sold.'

Unemployment found a solution in the restoration projects where workers were trained on the job. Now completed, the houses are occupied and the restored station is operating as a tourist museum. The original programmes have also generated further work — 'It is wonderful,' Maude says, having revisited Oodnadatta, 'to see people just as busy. And the children have opportunities now: there are young people going on to high school, and others in TAFE courses at Port Augusta.'

An Aboriginal Health Office has been established, and a service that cooks for camp children and teaches women to read and various crafts. People swim and fish in the dam that was once polluted by cattle; there are dances and movies for the kids; and very little vandalism. The wrecked cars and broken glass that once littered the town have gone. Galvanised iron fences and sheds have been transformed by children's murals. The children also raised $3000 for the essential Flying Doctor Service when they walked 200 kilometres from Coober Pedy to Oodnadatta in the Tjitji (Children's) Walkabout. There is a new sense of pride in a community taking its affairs into its own hands.

Born in Oodnadatta, George is a graduate of the South Australian Institute of Technology's Aboriginal Task Force and Maude is a trained Welfare Worker. George emphasises the necessity of proper training for his people, then as Maude says: 'Governments have got to look at the people who have the skills in their own community rather than letting them be bossed around by whites as happened in the past'.

The Tongeries' success has inspired other towns to follow their lead and George and Maude have recently been awarded the Order of Australia for their work in Oodnadatta. Their leadership however, has been a two-way affair: 'In the end we feel that we were the privileged two — to be able to work with the people,' says Maude. 'I wouldn't have missed it for anything.'

Welfare workers George and Maude Tongerie who gave the Aboriginal people back their town and their pride. Maude was awarded the Aboriginal Community Centre Life membership medal in 1981.
Photographs by Don Price

Malen Rumbelow
1905–1985
'Last of his tribe'
Written by: Terri McCormack
Nominated by: G. Arch Grosvenor

Encounter Bay in South Australia was named for the historic meeting of Matthew Flinders and Nicolas Baudin in 1802 but is known to others as the scene of countless rescues in treacherous seas by Malen Rumbelow in his wooden rowboat.

The last of four generations of Rumbelow fishermen who had inhabited the Yilki area since whalers worked offshore, Malen knew the unpredictable weather which had claimed the lives of his father, brother, and cousins. Many ignored his warnings at their peril like the two panic-striken men who, after being rescued, still wanted to save their boat which was soon, as Malen knew, to be dashed against the rocks.

Having rescued so many, he was, towards the end of his eighty years, unable to save his nephew Geoffrey who insisted on going out to save his valuable fishing boat despite his uncle's warning: 'No man could survive under these conditions.' Unable to witness the inevitable, Malen drove over to Rosetta Head, the bluff where his ancestors had watched for whales and fish, returning only to help bring his nephew's drowned body ashore.

The fishermen have gone from Yilki now, as has Malen Rumbelow who is buried in the local churchyard. His aged widow treasures the mementoes of appreciation he received from a few of those who owe a debt to this unsung hero and his wooden dinghy.

Malen Rumbelow, Yilki fisherman

Terry Hill and Cliff Hills
?
Casual act of courage
Written by: Katie Lawley
Nominated by: Glen A. Morgan

Clifford Charles Hills, who dived into a sea full of sharks and sea-snakes to rescue a fellow worker off the Western Australian coast in 1982

It was changeover time at the end of a twelve-hour shift on the North Rankin Off-Shore Gas Platform, 132 kilometres off the north-west coast of Western Australia. The platform was approximately 200 metres from an old barge where the workers were housed. Each day they would go to and from the barge via a motorised rubber dinghy — 'the rubber duck'. 'On this occasion though, it all went horribly wrong', says Glen Morgan, one of the men on the platform.

The swell was running unusually high, with long rolling waves of at least two metres. The dinghy was 110 to 120 metres out from the platform when it flipped on its back as it went over a big wave, spilling the lone occupant, scaffolder Derick Oliver, into the ocean. Righting itself, it began to veer crazily in 360° circles; ever tightening, ever increasing in speed. On its third turn it ran over the hapless man.

'We watched in horror as Oliver lay stunned and motionless — in waters literally full of sharks and deadly sea snakes' says Morgan. Then rigger Terry Hill and fitter Cliff Hills, ignoring their own safety, threw off their overalls and boots and dived into the perilous waters. Hill swam to the still-veering dinghy and, after many attempts, managed to climb aboard and cut the motor. Hills meanwhile swam to the injured scaffolder and kept him afloat. Paddling the dinghy to his companions, Hill hauled them aboard and made it safely back to the rig, where Oliver was treated for burns and shock.

'The two men went back to work with no fanfare or commendation,' said Morgan. 'Yet it was an act of valour, the memory of which will remain with me for the rest of my life.'

Mt Macedon Volunteer Fire Brigade
Ash Wednesday, 1983

Anonymous heroes
Written by: Niall Lucy
Nominated by: Charles K. Taylor

No less than our ancestors, Australians in the late twentieth century are at the mercy of a brutal climate. Ours may well be the era of the silicon chip but on the 16 February 1983, we were powerless to prevent this country's worst-ever bushfires from destroying over 2000 homes and properties, untold livestock, and killing sixty-nine people.

The fire storms that blazed across the Victorian and South Australian bush on Ash Wednesday were fought by hundreds of volunteer firemen. Their courage was typified by the forty-five volunteers of the Mt Macedon brigade, who fought with heroic determination to quell the inferno. Two weeks earlier, these same men had battled another fire which was still smouldering on that day when nature conspired to turn the countryside into a tinderbox.

Nestled in sylvan landscape fifty kilometres north-west of Melbourne, Mt Macedon was one of many rural communities exposed to a hazardous combination of searing winds, low humidity, and a temperature above 40^0 C. At 1.30 in the afternoon, a small fire broke out twenty-two kilometres away in the township of East Trentham. Under the prevailing weather conditions, this fire spread at an alarming rate through the vast Wombat State Forest, gathering force and momentum and growing into the shape of a giant cigar. Unable to call on reinforcements because Victoria's emergency services were stretched to the limit in coping with major fires across the state, the Mt Macedon volunteers made their stand against the oncoming fire by trying to contain it to the far side of the regional highway that snaked around the outskirts of town.

But a sudden, cyclonic gust of wind put paid to their intentions. In an instant, the fire was driven at right angles towards Mt Macedon and its whole shape and character changed beyond recognition. Incredibly, the blaze was 'spotting' or leaping over distances of up to six kilometres at a time, driven by an energy far greater than that of the bomb which destroyed Hiroshima. Such was the intensity of heat that a trail of molten wire fences and machinery lay twisted in the inferno's wake, while the wind force was so severe that fully grown trees were uprooted and spun through the air. A brooding smoke cloud hung above thousands of hectares of flaming countryside. It seemed as if the whole continent were ablaze.

Nothing in the experience of the forty-five Mt Macedon volunteers had prepared them for the scale and magnitude of the fire which laid their town to waste on Ash Wednesday. But still they 'stuck to their guns' their captain says, preferring to combat the blaze as best they could rather than protect their own properties. Twenty-two of the men lost their homes in the fire which claimed the lives of eight people in the town and destroyed 450 houses. Virtually nothing was left of the Victorian houses and long-established gardens which were Mt Macedon's great charm.

Believing that they were just doing their job, none of the volunteers wishes to be named.

The main street of historic Mt Macedon the day after the Ash Wednesday fires of 16 February 1983 destroyed the town. Photograph courtesy The Age

Betty DeBono
1937–1984
Working Class heroine
Written by: Susan Hamilton
Nominated by: Ray Hogan

Betty DeBono died of cancer in 1984. She was forty-seven. There is a memorial plaque to her in the canteen of the factory in which she worked and four years after her death staff members chip in for Easter flowers for her grave. When Ron Hutchinson, an old workmate, speaks of her, his voice becomes husky and his eyes fill with tears.

'I'm not much of one for words,' he admits, 'but Betty was a shining person.'

Betty worked on the shop floor at the Taubmans Paint factory at Sunshine, Victoria, for twenty-three years. She spent eleven of these as union delegate for the members of the Federated Miscellaneous Workers' Union of Australia employed there. It was during this period that Taubmans Melbourne factory moved its architectural paints operation to Sydney and began to concentrate upon the manufacture of industrial paints: compounds which contained a far higher level of potentially injurious chemicals than its workers had been exposed to previously.

Today, occupational health and safety are recognised as important issues within the chemical industries. In Betty DeBono's time they were not: hers was pioneering work. She took courses in these and related subjects with the Trade Union Training Authority (TUTA) and read avidly. She constantly urged her workmates to inform themselves about the toxicity levels of the chemicals to which they were exposed, to take adequate care in handling them, and to press management for reforms.

Union meetings at Taubmans could become very heated. Betty would hear all sides, make her analysis, and then quietly state, 'I think this is what we should do...' When she spoke, the yelling stopped and people listened. They had an unshakeable faith that she would act in their best interests. They had seen her do it so often. Invariably, the course of action she proposed was adopted unanimously.

As union delegate, it was Betty's job to carry these claims to management. As well as the courage, wisdom and determination so admired by her fellows, Betty possessed considerable negotiating skills. Her initiatives resulted in the installation of new extraction systems at the factory, and the issue of safer masks. In fact, working conditions improved 'one hundred percent'. They continue to improve today. Ron Hutchinson, the current shop steward, reports, 'If I feel the members are getting slack, I remind them of all Betty did for us. I tell them we must stick together and carry on her work. I only have to mention her name and they're re-motivated — they push harder.'

In addition to the two sons for whom she was chief provider, Betty had an extended family at the factory. She helped everyone, even those who had been loudest in their opposition to her at union meetings. To some, like the young Malcolm Roy, whom she raised to co-delegate, she gave new purpose and direction. She was also a Justice of the Peace and spent hours of her time helping the underprivileged in the western suburbs of Melbourne. She found accommodation for homeless kids and investigated claims against the police, solving problems with compassion and dignity.

Betty DeBono did not smoke, drink or use caffeine, yet for years she suffered choking coughs and insomnia. When she complained to medical authorities she was prescribed Valium for 'stress'. Her work as a lab technician meant that for years she had been inhaling dangerous fumes, powders and dust. Her friends at the factory found it hard not to link her death with the hazards of her work: they believe that she sacrificed herself for them. When they stopped work to attend her funeral on 13 November 1984, the Taubmans management, in recognition of the depth of their grief and well represented at the funeral

Betty DeBono, committed Union Delegate who fought to improve occupational health conditions for her fellow workers. 'She was a shining person', says an old workmate

themselves, chose not to cut their wages for that day.

Betty DeBono was a great humanitarian. She believed that people should look after one another, and her life was theory made practice. 'She was a magic person', says Ron Hutchinson. 'Whatever you said you couldn't give her enough praise.'

Richard Willis
1936–1985
Champion of Youth Hostels
Written by: Lois Hunter
Nominated by: Sonja G.A. Willis

In 1959, when he was twenty-three, Dick Willis became a voluntary worker with the Youth Hostels' Association of NSW. In 1966, when he was thirty, he became the Assoication's first paid Executive Secretary. By the time of his death, in 1985, when he was forty-nine, he had transformed a local bushwalking club with a membership of 3500 and one part-time employee into a multi-million dollar organisation with almost 40 000 members, a staff of thirty-nine and thirty-two hostels of international standard.

In 1959, Dick Willis joined the YHA, intending to travel overseas to Canada. Instead, he became involved in committee work, first as Treasurer of the local regional group and soon as Vice Chairman. Within a year he was Honorary Secretary, his first project the establishment of the YHA of Queensland as an independent body.

Richard Willis had found his vocation as well as his job. For Youth Hostels meant more to Willis than the laudable idea of inexpensive accommodation for the young. His aim was 'to get young people to mix and understand each other on an international basis'.

There was of course a lot of plain hard work — the usual unpaid extras that ideals and dedication bring to a task. Willis aimed to be available twenty-four hours a day to staff and members but there was also his business acumen and his chartered accountancy skills, which he put to good use for the Association. Visits to Indonesia, Japan, and to Hostel Federation Meetings were at his own expense and undertaken to encourage exchange and to learn. Productive links with business and tourist interests and with government brought a high proportion of overseas visitors and substantial grants and concessions for the establishment of Youth Hostels at Forest Lodge (1975), Narrandera (1978) and Dulwich Hill (1980).

Dick Willis died in 1985 when he fell asleep at the wheel of his car while driving to Trial Bay in New South Wales. His final year had been devoted to lobbying the German Government to fund the Trial Bay Hostel as a Bicentennial Gift to Australia. (The old Trial Bay Jail had been used as an internment camp for German civilians in Australia during World War I.) When they heard the sad news of his death, the German Association and the International Federation pledged a contribution of £130 000 towards the project to be called

Dick Willis, who transformed a local bushwalking club into a major organisation with thirty-two hostels of international standard. His belief in building international understanding through young people became a vocation

the 'Richard Willis Memorial Youth Hostel'.

At the time of his death, Dick Willis had received the Richard Schirrmann Medal from the German Youth Hostel Association for his contributions to Youth Hostelling. But from Australia Richard Willis received no honours in any shape or form. Yet, according to two ex-YHA chairmen, Willis was the catalyst for the YHA's transformation; the man who gave 'work worth millions', whose innovations and efforts were absolutely seminal to the development of the Youth Hostel Association. Perhaps the cruellest irony is that the Trial Bay Youth Hostel, which should have been dedicated to him, is not now being built despite the required donations being available.

Sonja Willis, his widow, and seventeen year-old daughter, Kristina, continue to hope and battle for the Trial Bay Hostel and a memorial to Dick Willis.

Douglas Fong
1966–
Courage in Chinatown
Written by: Katie Lawley
Nominated by: Allan Fong

Douglas Fong, who helped twenty-four elderly men to safety in Sydney's Chinatown fire of 1985

Nineteen-year-old commercial art student, Douglas Fong, was woken at 5 am on 14 November 1985 by a fiery explosion ripping apart his Chinatown flat in Sydney. 'There was plaster and debris falling everywhere. My aunty and grandmother were trying to reach the phone when a second explosion shook the building. Furniture and paintings were upside down and our aquarium exploded, sending splinters of glass everywhere.'

Outside there was pandemonium. A gas regulator had been run over by a truck in the early hours of the morning causing explosions and fires all through the district.

Douglas's flat was in a block above the Green Jade Restaurant; one floor above a boarding home for elderly men. The restaurant was fully ablaze, its gas boiler being one of the first to explode. All that separated the Fong family and the boarding house from the inferno was a set of fire-proof stairs.

Douglas, his feet already cut by broken glass, saw his family to safety. He then returned to help the twenty-four elderly people in the boarding house. Quickly going to each room, he knocked on doors and assisted the old people out of the smoky building. They quietly watched as the firemen fought to control the flames, while their home crumbled before them.

The Chinatown fires received extensive media coverage. The *Sydney Morning Herald* recorded that 'The floors were caving in, the gas was sending up terrific heat, glass was exploding all over the place and the insulation in the ceiling was dripping down like hot tar.'

Douglas quietly faded into the huge crowd. His courage in risking his life to save the elderly men had gone unnoticed and unrecorded.

Sister Patrice Kennedy
1927–
River-bank dwellers' friend
Written by: Judith Elen
Nominated by: Anne Tannock; Zonta Club

Sister Patrice Kennedy of the Sisters of Mercy, a school teacher by profession, is now official welfare worker with the Christian Family Centre in Rockhampton. Unofficially, her work began on her arrival in Australia forty years ago.

At nineteen Sister Patrice left Ireland to join her older sister. For fourteen years she taught school in Central Queensland, becoming headmistress of several schools, and administrator and 'mother' at the St Joseph's Home for Children. But teaching was only a part of her day's work. When school ended, she would take materials and spiritual comfort to the town's poor and lonely. Now concentrating on the problems of adults and working largely with the homeless and the deaf, Sister Patrice adapts her help to fit the need.

For Sister Patrice, 1987 — International Year of Shelter for the Homeless — was a time for more action rather than just good intentions. She became aware of homeless people being turned away from established shelters, sometimes because of disruptive behaviour, and becoming 'river-bank dwellers'. Without financial backing, she established a drop-in centre that provides food and company, and where men and women, black and white, can find refuge knowing that they are safe from police surveillance.

Mercycare also runs a series of residential houses offering rehabilitation programmes for alcoholics. But as Sister Patrice recognises, 'there are some people who like sleeping out under the stars'. For them she began a river-bank 'soup kitchen'. Encouraging others to join her on cold winter mornings, she takes comfort of a practical kind to people who spend their nights in the open.

Recognising that unemployment and prohibitively high rentals can shatter families, her Mercycare team provides crisis accommodation, allowing families the breathing space to find more permanent solutions. But single people need help too. The man who had never known the shelter of a home since leaving an orphanage, died at fifty-one, but before he died he had 'spent time in a house where he was like a king, taking in all his friends'.

Sister Patrice's 'apostolate to the deaf' as she calls it, began when she 'had never met a deaf person'. Now she knows every deaf adult in the area. She learned to sign — 'I did a short course, but I became fluent only because of the help that the deaf people have given me' — and now acts as interpreter with Social Security, the CES, solicitors, police, landlords, and so on. She explains that, having had no special help as children, many of the adult deaf in Rockhampton are illiterate, which adds to their already isolated condition. Sister Patrice is seeking

Sister Mary Patrice, who provides Mercycare for Rockhampton's homeless and a voice for the deaf

an education grant for Rockhampton's adult deaf, but in the meantime, she is doing what she can on her own. Apart from everyday help, Sister Patrice also 'interprets the Liturgy and reception of Sacraments for churchgoers' who otherwise feel lost in services. At one special mass she signed the sermon and all of the hymns.

Outside her community Sister Patrice is unknown, but amongst the people who know her work, she commands devotion and respect.

Judith Louise Collins
1953–

Fostercare for foster parents
Written by: Lois Hunter
Nominated by: Paul Collins

When Judith Louise Vine was eight years old she announced that when she grew up she wanted to be a missionary or a writer. By 1963 she seemed to have decided there was a lot that needed to be done in the world and that action spoke louder than words. Accordingly, applying a missionary zeal to the task, she began to organise and run charity fetes in Bankstown, her home town. It was all her own idea and mostly all her own work. By then, she was ten.

Her career as Bankstown's child charity worker was brought to an abrupt halt when the family business, a grocery shop managed by her parents, failed. With her three brothers and parents she decamped to her aunt's double garage where the family lived for two months. Moving to Ingleburn, a pleasant country town in New South Wales, gave the Vine family space and a fresh start.

By the time she was twelve, the young High School student was concert manager and organiser of local plays and concerts. She designed the sets and costumes and rewrote plays for younger children and slow learners.

But the paragon was not all Pollyanna and perfection. By the time she was fifteen she was in revolt. An average student, she was more than averagely impatient with what she saw as the ineffectiveness of the school system. She quit, found a clerical job and at nights took herself to secretarial school.

A few months later she left home. She ran away, she insists, not as a protest against family but because she 'wanted to run her own race'. But these were hard years. Adolescence was 'sheer hell'. 'All I wanted to do was die. I was close to cutting my wrists...I had no direction.'

Escaping to Sydney, she worked for estate agents, hairdressers, lawyers, advertising agencies and publishers. Usually she wangled the job of systems organiser.

Lodging, not in Kings Cross but the Sydney suburbs of Strathfield, Burwood and Ashfield, she lived first in a girls' boarding house and then to a flat shared with some of the girls. 'One turned out to be a heroin addict and another a fourteen-year-old who was running a prostitution racket with elderly men as clients.' By nineteen, resolving that public service was to be her life's work, Judith Collins decided that she would never marry, would have no children and, to avoid emotional involvement, would never go out with the same man more than three times.

At twenty, however, she broke her own rules and married a twenty-year-old Roman Catholic civil engineering student. Just four months later, she woke up to find both of her legs had 'ceased to function' and left arm was almost immobilised. Bedridden for ten months, she was engulfed by shock. Tests finally revealed the immobility had been caused by spinal damage at birth. Through alternative medicine she had herself on her feet again, but she was left with a limp and a walking stick. These souvenirs and the several operations she has had to face were, her husband says, her reminders of what it is to be disadvantaged.

Clambering back into life, Judith Collins contacted a Catholic childrens' home and offered to take on a child over the Christmas holidays. The nine-year-old girl she took was emotionally disturbed and as Judith felt that she needed practical assistance and a permanent home, the Collinses asked to adopt her. The fostering agency, however, felt that the twenty-year-old couple were just too young to cope. To prove them wrong, Judith picked up the child each weekend for two years. Three years later the Collins family had six emotionally-disturbed foster children in residence. As well, they began emergency crisis fostering. And then Judith, the systems expert, put her methods to work. She was twenty-six years old and about to begin her most interesting work.

By 1979, from the garage in their backyard, Judith had founded and was running 'Witsend', a twenty-four hour, all-voluntary hotline for adoptive and foster parents in need of fast help. A successfully operated and worldwide advice service for the support and education of these parents, Witsend was unique. A battle for funding the service was, a year later, fought and won. Under the name of 'Fostercare Postal Libraries', Judith established emergency accommodation centres for children in crisis in New South Wales, courses for students of social and community welfare, a new design for the New South Wales Foster Care Association, lectures, a School of Fostercare for Sydney and a mobile school for out of town. All this and much more accounted for Judith's seventy-hour working week.

Ironically, Judith's worst disappointment came in 1983. 'I received the Advance Australia Award but funding was suddenly withdrawn and I was back to square one.' She went back to work as a do-it-yourself one-woman organisation. After another battle she was re-funded and, by the end of 1987, operating with a staff of nine from a 'totally converted' garage complex in Thirlmere, New South Wales.

'Of course you miss out on some of life but you get other bits...people think because I've moved bureaucratic mountains I'm perfect. What I think I am is more emotional...all I've done is get off my backside, roll up my sleeves and work.'

Apart from the office and the publication of over thirty books and pamphlets, Judith's other work has been as mother to the five children she has fostered: 'one from babyhood, one from a toddler, one from childhood and one from adolescence. I'm thirty-four years old and I have a twenty-two-year-old daughter, a thirty-year-old son-in-law and grandchildren who call me Nana.'

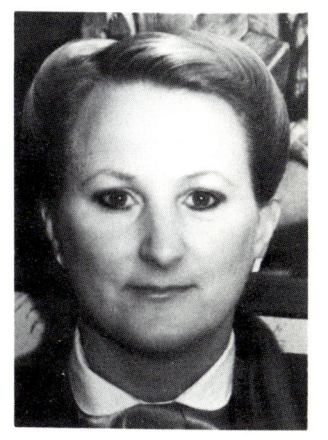

Judith Collins, foster mother of five and a born organiser, applied a missionary zeal to establishing 'Witsend', a twenty-four hour hotline for adoptive and foster parents in need of fast help

Peter Treseder
1957–
Runner in the wilderness
Written by: Lois Hunter
Nominated by: Elizabeth C. Treseder

Peter Treseder, cross-country runner, on the 'ultimate tiger walk'. 'I wanted to show that there is so little wilderness left in New South Wales and Victoria that one man can run through it in just ten days'

In 1986, Peter Treseder, a twenty-nine-year-old Sydney Bank Loans Officer, ran 1500 kilometres from Barrington Tops in New South Wales to Walhalla in Victoria. Deliberately choosing the wildest and most hazardous terrain, the mild-mannered, bespectacled bank clerk made it in just over ten days. The route he had chosen — inland between Newcastle and Melbourne — meant that he had run through dripping rain forests, sandstone escarpments, snow drifts, river gorges and atrocious scrub. It had taken him through some of the roughest country, not just in Australia, but in the world.

This unique solo marathon had been conceived, trained for and accomplished without sponsorship or back-up teams or special equipment. Treseder's aims were threefold: to experience and utilise what he calls 'the pioneering spirit'; to show people how little true wilderness is left in Australia, especially in New South Wales and Victoria, by running through what did exist in as few days as possible; and to help the Bush Rescue Service. As Assistant Director of Bushwalkers of the New South Wales Search and Rescue Unit, the more expert his knowledge of rough terrain and bad conditions, the better the information available to train rescuers.

The marathon — the 'ultimate tiger walk' as it was to be christened — was accomplished wearing only running shorts and a light jacket, and carrying a daypack with spare clothes, a few snacks, a headlamp and an initial twenty-two maps. Food, cooking gear, additional maps and protective clothes were left at sites along the way. Sleeping was a major problem because of the rain and because Treseder had decided against carrying a heavy sleeping bag.

Treseder set out from the Gloucester Tops and, ten and a half days later, came out at the end of Victoria's Alpine track. He ran the first two days non-stop and covered an incredible thirty-five kilometres. 'I knew I had to travel as far as possible while I was fresh.' Peter often ran at night because it was cooler and one night crossed Kosciusko in snow shoes because the coolness made the snow firmer.

Because he was travelling relatively fast — nine to ten kilometres an hour for the first two days — he saw a lot of animal life. 'You'll come screaming around a corner or over a rock to find baby possums, echidnas, kangaroos are still sitting there. I was bitten by a snake. I didn't see it till it hit me but I was about seventy per cent sure it was non-poisonous. It turned out to be a small bush python. So there I am with my pants around my ankles in the pouring rain, in thick scrub, with a stretch bandage out — but then I thought, this is ridiculous, so I just packed up and kept going.'

There were other injuries. Descending a gully, Peter slipped and hurt a leg; crossing the Colo River, which was waist-deep after the rains, he was washed 200 metres downstream. 'I was so tired it didn't seem to worry me that much. It's a strange, horrible feeling — as though everything inside you has been sapped out.'

At Kanangra Walls coal seam he met three friends then set off alone down the Ridge the next morning, along the Wollondilly River, and across the Shoalhaven into the Ettrema Wilderness, travelling by both day and night.

In Victoria the weather again deteriorated and a red-bellied black snake shot out from a rock and bit into his legging — 'It hung on while I kept running until I could find a stick to beat it off my leg.' He ran through snow for a third of the trip (unusual for November), was swept along by a flooded river and fell down steep escarpments. One night he shared his sleeping quarters with a pack of dingoes.

The ten and a half days' completion time was actually a day and a half ahead of his schedule. On finishing, he hitched a ride to Morwell, hired a car and drove himself home, suffering only from very sore knees.

Peter Treseder is probably the least orthodox of long distance runners, travelling so fast and so hard that one suspects he has no time to experience the much-celebrated loneliness that is supposed to be part of the run. His hobby is sculpture. With Henry Moore as his hero, he has three Moore-inspired Treseders standing in the back garden of his Wahroonga home.

Peter, who trains daily by running through the bush around his home in Wahroonga, holds informal records for unorthodox cross-country runs. He has run the length of the Blue Mountains and outpaced the cross-country skiing records between Kiandra and Perisher. His librarian wife, Beth, admires his courage and stamina but prefers to garden.

At thirty-one, Peter's 1988 project is to run from Wilson's Promontory to the Cape York Peninsula. 'I'd like to explore the country further north and maybe one day link all the parks together right up to Cape York. And I have always had it in the back of my mind to have a crack at getting across the Eastern Arthurs, the Western Arthurs and climbing Federation in a day. I don't know if it's possible.' You can bet that Peter Treseder will find out.

Elizabeth Johnson
1938–
Salvation for the young
Written by: Lucinda Strauss
Nominated by: Natalie Guy, NCW

Elizabeth Johnson has a special talent for getting to the heart of things. A tall, strong woman with snowy-white hair and a young face, she is well known for her disarming honesty and good humour. For, whether it's dealing with the policymakers of social welfare bureaucracies or with street kids from Kings Cross, Elizabeth brings to the encounter a calm directness that cuts through all the layers.

Born in Canberra in 1938, Elizabeth comes from a long line of Anglicans. 'Church was always a part of my life,' she explains with a smile. But her middle-class family of First Fleeters was not 'wildly excited' when, as a young woman of twenty-three, she was drawn to a practice of 'Christianity with its sleeves rolled up.' One night during a talk given by a duty nurse on the realities of caring, she felt that God had 'called her' and decided to join the Salvation Army.

Originally trained as a French teacher, Elizabeth attended the Salvation Army Training College for Officers and did her practical work in Papua New Guinea. Her first appointment as a Lieutenant was working with homeless women at Samaritan House in Surry Hills. Very soon she was 'typed' as being good with young people and worked at Canowindra Childrens Home, followed by concurrent appointments at Kalimna, a hostel for girls referred by the courts, and at Boothville, a home for unmarried mothers.

Elizabeth admits that the four years at Kalimna was one of her toughest postings. Dealing with victims of incest and broken homes, none of whom wanted to be in a closed institution, was a great challenge. Her technique for getting through to young people is to accept what they are, believe in them, and help them to believe in themselves.

The latter, she says, takes time and the results are sometimes not obvious for some years. Recently Elizabeth received a letter from an unmarried mother in Queensland telling her how important Elizabeth had been in helping the girl regain a belief in herself ten years before. Such feedback is rare in the helping professions and Elizabeth usually finds her satisfaction in the thought of a job well done.

Though the Salvation Army permits marriage and family, Elizabeth has preferred to remain single so that she is available to go wherever needed. In 1983 she was sent to Nîmes in France where she worked at La Villa Blanche Peyron, a home for 'difficult' girls. The violence of the French temperament frightened her a little at first and home visits in the back streets of Marseilles were never dull. 'More than once,' she says, 'I had a knife pulled under my chin.'

In more recent years, Elizabeth has been a familiar face on the streets of Kings Cross, Sydney. As a counsellor and Research and Development Officer with the Salvation Army Outreach Service, Elizabeth's job was to reach young kids within the first three days of arrival, before they are pulled into the web of drugs and prostitution. Working alongside the more 'hip' type of youth worker, she found that the kids had no trouble accepting her snowy-white hair and Sally's uniform.

With her considerable experience in the field, and solid academic background (Honours and Masters Degrees in Social Work and a Diploma of Psychology), the Major is a valued member of any policy-making team. Since 1983 she has acted as Convenor for the Social and Moral Welfare Standing Committee of the National Council of Women, regularly contributing to projects relating to the welfare of children and the family.

It has been twenty-five years since Elizabeth Johnson joined 'the Army. Approaching each task with an enormous amount of love, there is no doubt in her mind about her purpose in life. Now, as Assistant Territory Social Services Secretary, Elizabeth feels she is doing what she does best — helping the helpers.

Major Elizabeth Johnson of the Salvation Army practises 'Christianity with its sleeves rolled up' amongst addicts, prostitutes and other young people in crisis. Photograph by Neville Waller

Lily Jubilee Slattery
c1920–

Normanton's 'mother'
Written by: Suzanne Falkiner
Nominated by: Audrey Querruell

Lily Jubilee Slattery looked after children the way a good shepherd looks after stray lambs. Hungry, sometimes homeless, often caught in a cycle of violence, drunkenness and neglect in the fringe Aboriginal settlements of Northern Queensland, the children found shelter, warmth and love with Lily. Sometimes as few as three, sometimes as many as sixteen children lived with Lily, her husband Jubilee and their own son Teddy. Eventually, over thirty years, they took care of 105 children. For all of this time Lily worked as a kitchen hand and cook, laundress and, later, cleaner, in Normanton's hotels.

Lily, like many of the unsung heroes and heroines of Australia's history, is one of the quiet ones — one of those who, apparently in the background, hold things together. A strong and religious woman, her story gives clues to the strength and resourcefulness that she has revealed throughout her life.

In the 1920s, when Lily was eight or nine, her mother and younger sister were chained to a group of other Aboriginal women and children and forced to walk 400 kilometres from their own territory to the Mitchell River mission. Under the provisions of the government's notorious Apprenticeship Scheme, Lily was separated from her mother and sister and handed over to the owners of Miranda station as a domestic servant.

'They brought me a big sheet of paper and got my thumb print and that was my signature,' Lily says. The nine-year-old was told by the station manager's wife that this meant that she had 'signed on' and must not run away.

Heartbroken at the separation from her family, Lily was denied schooling with the other children of the station when the manager's wife called her away from correspondence lessons to work. 'I used to scrub the dining room, and polish the knife with a big piece of leather after every meal,' she recalls. 'The manager's wife used to stand over me and watch me do it.' In return, Lily was given board, clothing and a handful of sweets every Saturday.

Lily was still at Miranda station when she married Aboriginal ringer and drover Jubilee Slattery, also known as Ted, and bore their son Teddy. At the time Jubilee was driving the sulky that brought the mail man on his rounds from Normanton. Lily was sixteen or seventeen when she met him and they married around 1941. She remembers the bag dresses she wore and the scrubbing she had to do into the eighth month of her pregnancy. With her husband, she later turned her hand to looking after horses, timber-cutting with a cross-cut saw, and station cooking. Able to fell a killer (beast set aside for domestic slaughter) with a gun, Lily was also able to supplement the family's

Lily Slattery, forcibly separated from her own mother as a child and sent to work as a domestic, has since raised 105 children as if they were her own. Photograph by Peter Buchanan

provisions by catching birds and wildlife in the bush. From the colourful plumage of the birds, Lily would make feather flowers.

Lily started to look after other people's children when a family on Delta Downs station, where the couple worked for ten years, asked her to take in some of their children while they looked for work. Others followed. When Lily and Jubilee settled in Normanton and Ted was employed by the Commonwealth Public Service, he often came in contact with homeless, hungry and neglected children. Lily would find others.

'I would go down to the camp late at night and find that the mother was out drinking and the children were dirty and crying, so I would take them home and clean them up and give them a feed,' she explains. 'I'd wash their clothes so they'd be dry by morning and send them home after breakfast. Then they'd come back, and we couldn't send them away. I'd be in tears when I saw them.' Lily herself never drank and most of her children have avoided the traps of alcohol that ruined the lives of many of their parents.

Many of the children stayed from the ages of six or seven until they were old enough to leave school. During this thirty-year period, with no child endowment or other assistance available, Lily never stopped working. At home, the whole family helped with the housework.

Lily's husband Jubilee was awarded the Imperial Service Medal in 1979 when he retired after twenty-six years with the Department of Aboriginal and Islander Affairs. He died a year later. Lily's father, the late Dick Stirling, was famous throughout the Gulf as a stockman and has been commemorated in the Stockman's Hall of Fame at Longreach. Lily, like many women of the outback, remains unrecognised.

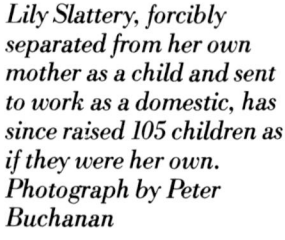

Her reward has been in the love of the children whom she nurtured.

Lily never left Normanton and its surrounding stations. Now in her late sixties and living on a pension, she still has four children of school age living with her in her bare, tree-shaded house on the banks of the Normanton River. Her son Teddy is a Department of Aboriginal and Islander Affairs field officer in the town.

Lily has no bitterness about the past, but one of her regrets is that, because she was never taught to read, she cannot read the citation given her beloved Ted with his Imperial Service Medal. 'I remember the good times,' she says. 'I couldn't wish for better than the happiness I had with him and with the children.'

Mert and Nell Thomas
1897–   ; 1898–
A couple of survivors
Written by: Niall Lucy
Nominated by: Margaret Gibbs

Henry Lamert 'Mert' Thomas and his wife Nell 1944–45. Having fought in the 'war to end all wars', Mert was 'terribly disillusioned' when World War II was declared

History is not only the version of events written down in books, but the way those events are lived through by ordinary people. Mert and Nell Thomas, both now in their nineties, have survived two World Wars and the Great Depression and have lived through every year of Australia's history in the twentieth century. They have been married for sixty-six of those years. The secret of their success? 'Give and take,' according to Nell. 'But I think the wife gives more.'

Nell Wedd first met her husband-to-be in 1920. Her brother, a keen sailor, had entered a sailing contest at Lake Macquarie near the New South Wales town of Toronto, a few kilometres from the family home in Newcastle. Because it was a windy day, Nell recalls that she had been 'brought along to act as ballast.' Soon after the race began, her brother's boat sailed too close to another yacht and caused it to capsize, tossing its hapless crew into the lake. The embarrassed skipper of the overturned craft was the Secretary of the Toronto Sailing Club, Henry Lamert Thomas. Mert and Nell were introduced to each other when they came ashore, and were married two years later.

By then, Nell was working as a tracer for BHP and Mert was a clerk in the New South Wales Railways. But steady jobs and idle weekends spent sailing on Lake Macquarie were a far cry from their experience of the war only a few year before.

When Mert Thomas enlisted for duty with the 30th Battalion of Infantry in 1915, he was not yet eighteen years of age. A boy barely out of school (like many others at the front), he was ineligible to vote in elections or drink at a pub. But his youth did not affect his usefulness to the Empire as a fighting man. This legal anomaly did not concern him at the time. 'Enthusiasm for the war effort was unanimous,' he says now. 'We were intensely patriotic.'

It's a wonder that his patriotism did not desert him, however, when this callow seventeen-year-old was thrown into the ill-fated Battle of

Fromelles, north of the Somme, a few months after enlisting. 'We in the ranks were given no information,' Mert recalls, 'other than at 6.00 pm on the 19th of July we were to go over the top, take two lines of trenches and consolidate.' The second so-called 'line of trenches' turned out to be nothing more than a drain filled with half a metre of water. But if Allied Command's planning for the offensive was characterised by blunders, the Germans, on the other hand, had planned their defence with meticulous care, positioning their machine-gunners at the best vantages along the battlefield. 'They simply mowed us down,' Mert laments with a note of astonishment still. 'The absolute waste of life...was like a mad and ridiculous crime.'

The Battle of Fromelles, scandalously ill-conceived, cost 5500 Australian lives in a single night of fighting — the highest loss sustained by any Australian division in any one night during the entire war. Mert's Battalion alone lost over one third of its strength, or 352 men. Under these circumstances, Mert was lucky to be captured by the

Mert Thomas (left), not yet eighteen, with two friends from the 30th Battalion, about to leave for the Front in 1915. Mert survived the Somme only to be taken prisoner. He dug his way out of the camp and escaped into Holland

Mert Thomas leaving Nell, his oldest son, Donald, and youngest son, Robert, to go to his Second World War. Casino Station, 28 November 1940. With her husband away and her two older sons in the RAAF, Nell, like thousands of other Australian women, raised her youngest children alone, worried, and worked for the war effort

Germans and taken to Dulmen in a desolate part of the Rhineland as a prisoner.

From Dulmen, Mert was transferred to POW camps at Dusseldorf and Munster before arriving as a member of a working party at the tar distillery at Duisburg-Meiderich in April 1917, nine months after Fromelles. He had been sent, at last, to a camp from which he felt he could escape. Wasting no time, Mert conspired with another Australian POW to procure maps, civilian clothes, and a compass in preparation for the hazardous trek towards the Dutch border. On the evening of 26 October, the two Australians, accompanied by a Russian soldier, dug their way under a barbed-wire fence on the camp perimeter and set out to cross the Rhine.

Heavy rains concealed their exit from the camp and lessened the chance of their being spotted in open terrain. Avoiding towns and farmhouses, they reached the Rhine four hours after breaking out of Duisburg-Meiderich but decided to travel farther north in the hope of crossing where the river traffic was less hectic. Two days later, they stole a ketch 'in the King's name' and three stout posts from a vegetable garden to use for oars and steerage. They rowed diagonally against the current to the opposite bank 'and set off for the frontier.'

Soaked to the skin and stricken with hunger, Mert and his companions were forced to proceed with extreme caution on the western side of the Rhine, 'as we found the whole country alive with groups of soldiers, and patrols.' On several occasions over the following two days they only narrowly escaped recapture, arriving at the barracks of the frontier guards late on the fourth night of their journey. Once again, the weather was in their favour: the near-freezing temperature made it impossible for the guard dogs to pick up their scent as the escapees crept soundlessly on their bellies through the steaming frost and slipped unnoticed into Holland.

Nell and Mert Thomas, now in their nineties and married for sixty-six years, have lived through every year of the twentieth century so far. 'I've done everything a person could do and I've still got me marbles,' says Mert. Says Nell, 'It's been a good life'. Photograph by Sandy Edwards

Having survived Fromelles and escaped from Germany, Mert Thomas might have been expected to return home once he and his companions had been flown to England. Instead, he went back to the Somme in 1918 as a gunner with the 1st Divisional Ammunition Column, and later with the 5th Battery, serving many more months of active duty at the front before the Armistice was signed on 11 November. 'There was still a war on in France,' he explains 'and I wanted to be in it. I still had a job to do.'

Mert was repatriated in mid-1919. He and Nell were married on 20 December 1922, and their first child—a son—was born a year later.

In her early married years, Nell took up community and charity work, giving important voluntary service to the Red Cross, Central Wesley Mission, Crippled Children's Association, and Dalmar Children's Home. She was also president for a number of years of the Eastwood Masonic Lodge Ladies Association, Mert having been a member of this lodge for over fifty years. It is only in latter years, as the result of operations for artificial hips which have restricted her mobility, that Nell has allowed her fund-raising and other community activites to lapse.

Despite their long and otherwise happy marriage, the Thomases endured severe economic hardship during the Great Depression. 'It was a pretty rough spin,' says Mert.

Even so, Mert and Nell struggled through with their dignity intact.

Resilient of spirit, and able to cook and sew and do their own repairs, they overcame the stark adversities of the period. 'I was a good manager,' Nell recalls with a degree of practical pride. 'I made the kids' trousers out of the bottoms of other people's trousers, and their shirts from other people's shirt tails. The people who didn't survive the Depression weren't good managers.'

When World War II broke out in 1939, the Thomases were shattered. 'That's why we fought in the first one,' Mert says, 'so that there'd never be another world war. It was terribly disillusioning.' Nevertheless, Mert signed on in 1940 with the 2nd/3rd Army Field Workshop Unit, maintaining and repairing guns and military vehicles in the field. 'If I go,' he told Nell, 'I might be able to keep the boys out of it.' But their two eldest sons, Donald and Kenneth, both enlisted for active duty with the RAAF when they turned eighteen, leaving Nell to care for the two youngest children, Margaret and Robert, on her own. She was later awarded a Next of Kin's Medal, with Two Stars and Bar, in honour of having two sons who served in the war.

Mert went first to Syria, then served with the 2nd/3rd for three years in New Guinea. 'We were under fire all the time, from bombs mostly,' he explains, 'but it wasn't as dangerous as being in a fighting unit.'

Returning from the war in 1946, Mert went back to his job with the Railways Department of New South Wales. His retirement in 1962 ended forty-seven years of service with the Department, the last five of which were spent as Superintendent of Staff in the Mechanical Division.

Although suffering a stroke in 1986, Mert has recovered to be in otherwise good health and fine spirits. 'I've done everything a person could do and I've still got me marbles,' he says. The Thomases continue to live in their own home in the Sydney suburb of Eastwood, where they have spent most of their married life. All but one of their four children are still alive. 'It's been a good life,' chuckles Nell. 'We've never had to ask anybody for anything. We've just always plodded through.'

Tim Rakuwurlma
c1900–

A man of his people
Written by: Billy Marshall-Stoneking
Nominated by: Richard Baker

Tim Rakuwurlma's grandfather always shook his head as he told the story of the young, pregnant Yanyuwa woman. She had run into the bush and climbed a tree in order to hide from white-skinned men who had raided the camp in which she was living. She watched her pursuers, silently, afraid, as they walked round and round under the tree talking in a language she could not understand. Then one of them looked up and saw her. He called to his companions. Seeing the woman six metres above them, they started to laugh. When the laughing stopped, one of the men pointed his rifle at the young woman and pulled the trigger. She fell to the ground dead.

'In the "wild times",' Tim explains "before we knew each other, white and black fought and there was plenty of killing on both sides.'

Tim Rakuwurlma had heard accounts of the 'wild times' ever since he was a little boy, from his father and his grandfather, and when he was older he had seen the violence himself.

Strange-looking men who could kill without even being close to you had been coming to Vanderlin Island in the Gulf of Carpentaria for years, but, unlike the Macassans who used to come every year to gather sea slugs, these white-skinned men had brought death, fear and suffering to the Yanyuwa tribe.

The violence and the hardships suffered under various raiding parties made Tim extremely aware that his people needed to keep together, to look after one another, to be strong. This had always been the case in the old times, but it was even more important now, especially as more and more Europeans moved into the Gulf area.

Not all of them were bad people, however, and by the time Tim had grown into young manhood, he had worked with a number of white men. There were some he liked, and some he did not trust, but he was not afraid of them.

For a number of years, Tim worked with his brother on a lugger in the Gulf of Carpentaria. The work was hard, and the long months away from family were difficult, but Tim did his job well and earned the respect of the men on board.

Then, hearing that their father was in trouble with the police at Borroloola, Tim and his brother asked for permission to return home to see him. When permission was refused, the two men 'sang up the wind', forcing the lugger to seek refuge at a nearby island. Under cover of darkness, Tim and his brother jumped ship.

They swam to the nearby island, then to another island and another until they had made their way back to the mainland. Each part of their journey was full of danger, especially from sharks which abound in that area, but Tim was not worried. His dreaming is the shark, and when the sharks came around him, he'd call to them, 'Hey, don't come here! I'm your countryman! I'm your boss; keep away!'

Over the years, Tim had many different jobs with Europeans. During the war he ran supplies out to an army observation post, then he worked for a company that was gathering salt from a coastal salt pan. After that, he worked for a while as a professional crocodile shooter, and then went droving in Queensland.

But his work and association with Europeans did nothing to subvert or undermine his understanding of his own culture and the values and beliefs taught through the ceremonial life of his people. If anything, his travels around the country strengthened his sense of self and the importance of his own cultural heritage.

When asked whether he wanted to be baptised as a Christian, Tim replied, 'You leave me here. I want to sing for young man [in initiation ceremonies]. I want to look after them corroboree...'

Tim has always taken a great interest in the history and culture of his people. Even as an eighty-year-old man, he continues to contribute to the life of his community, educating the young, teaching them the songs, the skills, the traditions and the wisdom of the tribe which

Tim Rakuwurlma, Yanyuwa elder from Vanderlin Island in the Gulf, keeps the traditional law of his people alive by telling stories and organising ceremonies. He remembers without bitterness 'the "wild times," before we knew each other'

were passed on to him from his parents and grandparents.

His knowledge of the natural world is such that he can still advise people on which week to go to which beach to find turtles nesting. Similarly, from knowing the connections between the time of the flowering of a wattle and the annual migration patterns of the dugong herds he is able to tell people both when and where to catch dugong.

In Yanyuwa culture, the emphasis is on the common good and the maintenance of a cultural system which is based almost entirely on a concept of individual equality. There are no 'stars' or 'famous people'. There is no word for 'hero'. People merely are what they are, and their stories speak for themselves.

Tim Rakuwurlma's life is not unlike the lives of thousands of Aboriginal men and women right around Australia whose lives have straddled two epochs of Australian history and two totally different worlds: the Aboriginal world and the white. And the fact that Tim, like others, has survived without bitterness and hatred is indicative of the strength and generosity of Aboriginal people.

Tim is philosophical and forgiving about the violent past, and he is full of compassion for both Europeans and Aborigines who died in the 'wild times'. But he is also aware of the great hardships that still lie ahead for his people, and it is clear to him that their struggle against injustice and prejudice will only be made more difficult if they turn their backs on their own culture and the laws that have been handed down over thousands of years from generation to generation.

Margaret Oats
1910–
Angel of Collingwood
Written by: Rodrick Faulkner
Nominated by: Richard Charles Evans

There is a strong sense of community in Collingwood, one of Melbourne's poorer inner suburbs. At its centre is a woman known as the Angel of Collingwood, Mrs Margaret Oats.

This part of Melbourne has always been a working-class area. There are narrow streets filled with cheaply made, tiny weatherboard terraces. High-rise Housing Commission flats stack poor and unemployed families one upon the other.

Poverty of environment is obvious in the dirty hollowness of the high-rise corridors, stairwells and lifts. It festers into another kind of poverty — that of the spirit. There are terrible struggles going on behind these corridors: aching loneliness, fear of the world outside and hopelessness for the future. Many people surrender under the great weight of desperation. Alcoholism and other drug abuses are common. Many struggle on until luck runs out and mental and physical fatigue take over. Families fall apart and children are removed from parents.

There are many people fighting against this desolation in Collingwood, but Mrs Oats is unique. Now seventy-eight, she has developed or worked with nearly every local community organisation as well as providing an extraordinary level of personal daily service to a great many Collingwood families. Her rapport with local people and credibility with charity organisations, police and local councils have been nurtured through years of advocacy on behalf of the community and by her honest concern for people's welfare.

Mrs Oats was born in Caulfield in 1910, one of five children. Her father was killed in 1919 and the family moved to the country where her grandmother owned a farm. An extended family network offered support with free milk, eggs, butter and meat. Margaret remembers her childhood fondly and the philosophy of communal sharing has become a cornerstone of her life.

Margaret married in 1933. Her husband, Daniel, was a member of the Society of St Vincent de Paul and Margaret made clothing and food for distribution by the Society.

By the late 1940s, Mrs Oats was a widow with four children. She worked full-time at Woolworths and saved to buy the small Collingwood cottage which is still her home. Her enormous dedication and courage as a community worker in the area began with simple daily sharing of her private time and her home.

'You wouldn't think we had spare money but we always had a bit left over to do something for someone. I was always bringing children home and putting them up for the night when either their mother was sick, or had died, or dad was having a bit too much to drink and there was a problem. My children were always bringing other children home and they used to double-up in their beds. After they grew up I still found that people needed a bed for a while.'

Since her retirement, Mrs Oats has devoted greater time to working with families. More than six people a day may call at her home, sometimes because they just need to chat, often for more specific help. In conjunction with a handful of other people from the Society and the Good Shepherd Order, Mrs Oats now works with around 500 Collingwood families each year. She visits them in their homes, offering mothers company or bringing food or clothing.

'We've had several cases where children are dying. That's dreadfully sad. One family where the little girl had leukaemia, I always went with a little doll or something and I'd sit and talk with the mother. Then we had a Greek family where the little boy died. I used to just pop over and see the mother. She didn't have a great deal of English but we could understand each other.

'Sometimes there are other problems. There might be a nice lady with some gorgeous children but she's married to an alcoholic. Or a young mum might hit the drug scene. If we think the children aren't being one hundred per cent cared for, we go more frequently. We pop back if we happen to be in the street just to try and build up the families a bit so they won't have any terribly traumatic problems. I just sit and talk to the girls if children are sick or if things have gone wrong. A lot of it is moral support.'

The greatest hope Mrs Oats has for the families of Collingwood is to be self-supportive or to help each other. She has worked hard to develop a spirit of neighbourliness.

'There's a marvellous sense of community in Collingwood because there just has to be. People are poor, they need the community. The council has been marvellous in all their services. There are all sorts of "supports" going on here. Well, the need is so great.'

One such support is Share Care, begun in 1984, with Mrs Oats as its founding Chairperson. Share Care enlists local families to care for children in emergency situations of any kind, whether their mother is ill or is overtired and just feels she cannot possibly cope. The idea is to prevent children going into long-term care outside Collingwood, which in the past often lead to loss of contact with their parents. It gives parents breathing-space to sort out their problems and minimises official intervention. The project has proved to be enormously successful. It has also helped develop Mrs Oats' goals of growing interdependence among the local underprivileged.

'In quite a few cases the host families become very friendly with the families of the children they help and they support them in other ways as well. We have some host families that are a little better off, but mostly they're just as poor as those they're helping. Some of the hosts are single mothers. They've been widowed or deserted and they're bringing up their own children, yet they're prepared to take home other children.'

A sense of individual self-worth among those she helps is another

Margaret Oats, who has brought comfort and care to families in inner-city Collingwood for over forty years. 'They call me "love". Practically all of Collingwood calls me "love".' Photograph by Ponch Hawkes

of Mrs Oats' goals. Cheryl, in her fifteenth floor high-rise flat is living, smiling proof of her achievements.

'Every Christmas Mrs Oats gives me a food hamper. Believe me, that really does help. I receive a lovely present for myself and my daughter. I've got a lot of praise for Mrs Oats and what she's done for me. She said to me, "Cheryl, are you pregnant?" I said , "Yeh." She said, "Well, I'll help you. Anything you need, I'll help you.' She's a marvellous lady, she really is. She said to me, "You can do it love, and I'll help you any way I can." And I have done it and I'm proud.'

Mrs Oats has been in the service of the Collingwood community for more than forty years and hasn't finished yet. She is adored by all locals, not just for her tireless work, but also for her refusal to pass judgement. Although children are especially important to her, all people are worthy of her attention. 'Even my dear old gentlemen up through the park who perhaps drink a little more than they should. I sit and chat with them from time to time. They call me "love". Practically all of Collingwood calls me "love".

It is hard to imagine anyone who deserves the name more.

Rosemary Taylor
1938–
Behind the lines
Written by: Suzy Baldwin
Nominated by: Diane Lewis

'We hold Earth's future in our hands. What shall we decide?' Teilhard de Chardin, *The Future Of Man*.

The images of Vietnam haunt us, those of us who were conscious then. Brought suddenly to mind, they compel us to remember. Hear 'napalm' and see a naked Vietnamese girl, her arms stretched wide, her face all pain and terror, running towards you. Think of the adoption of Vietnamese orphans and see a young European woman, her face a cry of such anguished grief and *anger* that heaven must surely turn its face away in shame. Her arms encircle a weeping Vietnamese woman and together they carry a tiny child and a baby, survivors from the wreck of the giant cargo aeroplane that was supposed to have carried hundreds of these children to a new life but instead plunged into a paddy field outside Saigon and burst into flames.

Seventy-eight of the dead children were from the nurseries and adoption agency founded and run by Rosemary Taylor. In the eight years that Rosemary had been organising overseas adoptions of Vietnamese orphans, her agency had grown from a one-woman project into Friends For All Children, the largest adoption organisation in the country, handling more adoptions than all the other agencies put together.

When it had become clear that Saigon would soon fall, Rosemary and the other agencies asked for passenger or Medivac planes to take

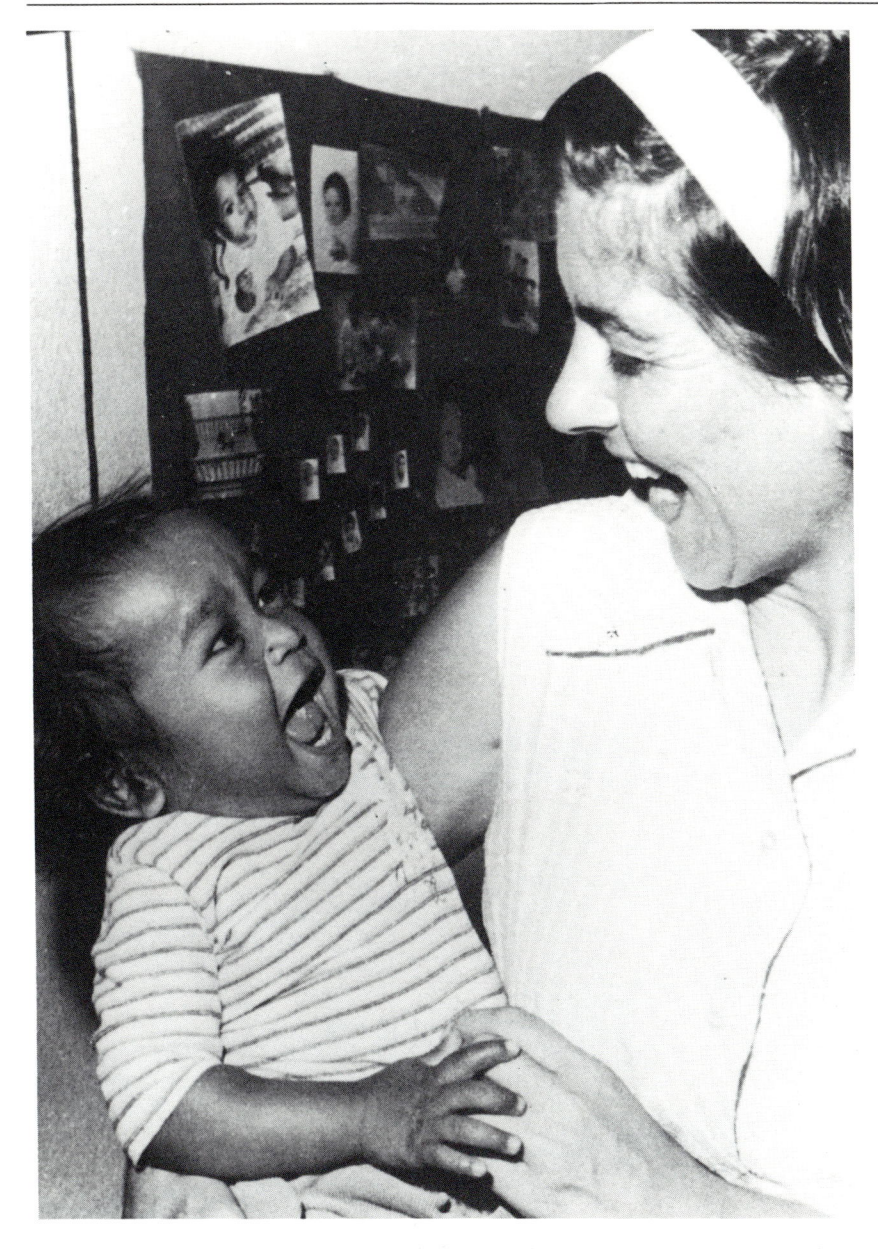

Rosemary Taylor in 1972 with one of the many mixed-race orphans at To Am ('Warm Nest'), the first of her four nurseries in Saigon

the children in their custody — 600 in Rosemary's case — to their adoptive homes. They were answered with prolonged dithering. Finally they were sent a plane designed to carry, not babies, but helicopters and lorries. Worst of all, it was unsafe and the fault responsible for the crash, the blowing out of the rear door, already officially reported. The terrible outcome was a final injustice to children who had already suffered to the limits of endurance.

Rosemary also lost six of her volunteer staff in the crash. Some had worked with her for many years; one — Margaret Moses — was her right hand administrator, greatest support, and close friend. In her book, *Turn My Eyes Away*, published the following year and dedicated to these women and children who died on 4 April 1975, Rosemary writes: 'We were numbed beyond emotion.'

Rosemary Taylor with a member of a US military civil action group at Phu My in 1967. At this orphanage, hospital and 'asylum for all that is pitiful in the human condition', Rosemary began the work that grew into Friends for All Children, the largest adoption agency in Vietnam

Later, there would be ten years of bitter legal dispute over the culpability of sending the Lockheed C5A Galaxy to transport the children. But in those last days before the fall of Saigon there was no time for anything except the most immediate crisis. Even grief had to be postponed.

Miraculously, 150 of Rosemary's children had survived the crash. Along with the rest of the children, they had still to be evacuated. In the emotional aftermath of the disaster, the passenger planes previously denied to the adoption agencies in Saigon suddenly became available. When the PanAm flight arrived in San Francisco, President Ford appeared on national television carrying one of the orphans in his arms. 'This is the least we can do,' he declared. 'And we will do much, much more.' Rosemary Taylor, who handled 4000 adoptions with virtually no official government help and who has little patience with fools, speaks witheringly of the cynical opportunism of politicians.

One of five children, Rosemary Taylor was born in Adelaide in 1938. After completing an arts degree at the University of Adelaide, she taught briefly in Sydney, then went to England. It was not however, the usual 'Big Trip' of the sixties. Rosemary had been a Sister of Mercy for five years but had left because she wanted to join a more contemplative, closed order — 'a very difficult thing to do'. After a year and a half in England, she was told that she would be accepted by a Carmelite order in Wales. 'Then it suddenly dawned on me: I could stay out. I could still live in a human way out in the world.'

'Out in the world' for Rosemary at the age of twenty-four was a remote mission amongst the Eskimoes in Alaska. After seven months, she was expelled because the FBI, discovering that she was working without pay or visa, suspected her of being a possible spy.

Rosemary's response to this early clash with government bureaucracy was characteristic: she refused to give in. She found a way to obtain a year's visa and returned to her work at the mission. When this permit ran out, Rosemary returned to Adelaide to wait for a permanent visa and there saw an advertisement for volunteers to go to Vietnam for two years. She applied and in February 1967 left for Vietnam to work in a refugee camp as an educational social worker with a team sponsored by the World Council of Churches. 'I had no idea what I was going to do,' says Rosemary, 'but I thought I would be able to respond.'

After two months in Saigon, frustrated by local mismanagement and the petty vanities of bureaucrats, the team was disintegrating and Rosemary, now twenty-seven, became an independent volunteer. She found herself a 'niche in the wall' at Phu My — orphanage, hospital and 'asylum for all that is pitiful in the human condition' — and worked in the nursery until the end of 1967 when a Swiss nurse asked her to take over the handling of overseas adoptions for the international organisation, Terre des Hommes.

Vietnam's orphanages were overflowing with babies. Some were identifiably war orphans; most were simply abandoned. Many were of mixed race — the unwanted children of American servicemen — and all were frail, malnourished and sick. But the orphanages were ill-equipped to care for them. With the mortality rate in some provincial orphanages as high as ninety per cent, the great problem was to keep the babies alive.

If Rosemary could bring some of these children to Saigon, she could at least 'save a few more of these tiny creatures'. When, in mid 1968, she was joined by a Spanish nurse, Rosemary opened the first of her four nurseries. They were primarily halfway houses where children were cared for while adoption was arranged, but one became a home for the severely handicapped where special programmes were developed for incurable and unadoptable children.

'We were primarily a salvage operation in a time of war,' Rosemary has written. 'Our very small war effort was to collect the human litter, too insignificant for the concern of the military strategists. We wanted to believe that every life is unique and has its contribution to make to the enlightenment of mankind.'

Most of the babies came from provincial orphanages, sometimes flown in by helicopter in condensed milk boxes — three babies to a box. For most of her time there, Rosemary received no official government assistance. 'But', she writes, 'this may have been to our advantage as the spontaneous help generated was sincere, competent and inexhaustible.' Mostly financed by personal friends around the world who sent money and supplies, Rosemary found that 'a lot of things just arrived at our door'.

Inside Vietnam, Rosemary's many military friends were skilled at the time-honoured practice of 'appropriating surplus commodities' which they would deliver to the nurseries. Other friends gave their services

— the opthalmologist draftee who went AWOL at every opportunity to treat Vietnam's poorest, including Rosemary's incurables; the sergeant major who spent every off-duty moment working in the nurseries; the British military attaché who emptied all the drawers in his house so that boxloads of babies could be bedded down, with airmail copies of *The Times* crumpled up as mattresses. And many others, among them the staff of the US and British embassies and the military chaplains who could be depended upon for practical miracles.

But money was always tight. By the end, there were sixteen foreign volunteers and 400 local staff. The volunteers drew no salaries at all, 'but every local person who worked for us received enough to support a family'.

By 1975, there were a million and a half orphans in South Vietnam and time was running out. Rosemary was angry and ashamed at Australia's official refusal to adopt these children and her response to critics of inter-country adoption was as articulate and passionate as her response to the Mother Superior who preferred to have children die in her large Catholic orphanage rather than send them abroad to families who may not be Catholic. 'Departure day is rebirth for every child,' Rosemary wrote in a plea to government departments. And every child was precious.

After the Galaxy disaster and the subsequent successful airlift, Rosemary closed the nurseries. But suddenly hundreds of children flooded in from the provinces and the nurseries were overflowing once more. Rosemary pressed authorities for permits and a plane and on Saturday 26 April, amidst utter pandemonium, Rosemary's last Vietnamese children — many of them in boxes — were loaded into a small US cargo plane and flown across the Pacific. Two days later, a US helicopter lifted Rosemary, the two remaining volunteers, Ilse and Doreen, and Ilse's four-year-old adopted Vietnamese daughter off the US Embassy roof and deposited them on the deck of USS *Blue Ridge*. The next day, the North Vietnamese marched into Saigon.

For two years, Rosemary travelled the world supervising the dispersal of the children. Then, confronted by 'expectations of me that I did not in any way feel like living up to,' she bought armloads of books ('theology and philosophy mainly') from a secondhand London bookshop and took them to a remote French farmhouse where she 'became a hermit, studied intensively and had a year and a half off'.

At the end of 1979, Rosemary went to work as a volunteer in a refugee camp in Thailand. She has been there ever since, working with Friends For All Children, helping with other people's projects, finishing her book *Orphans of War*, and continuing the intellectual work that is an essential part of her life. 'I am not directing anything,' Rosemary says firmly, 'and there is nothing remotely heroic about it.'

Rosemary Taylor has often been called 'the saint of Saigon'. If she is ever canonised, her presence will distinguish and animate the company. She is forthright, intolerant of idiocy, extraordinarily courageous and witty. Initially uncomfortable at being included in a book of 'heroes and heroines' — 'Vietnam was a team effort' — Rosemary finally accepts because it will help with her work amongst people who respect such honours. But she refuses to see herself as heroic. 'I do the things that give me satisfaction. I enjoy it. I don't need money for myself — I don't care about clothes and I'm happy with whatever food is there. The only thing that I'm ever interested in buying is books. Heroism is staying here, trying to do something for young people here. What I do is so easy by comparison.'

Like Teilhard de Chardin and Simone Weil — two earlier impassioned and unorthodox Catholics whose thought is evident in Rosemary's work — this outspoken, independent ex-nun with the dry sense of humour seems to belong to a party of one. It is impossible not to ask whether she is sustained by faith. 'Oh yes, but what do we mean by faith? Faith for me is a belief in human effort, in our responsibility to make the earth a better place.

'If you are a Christian, that's the meaning of Christ made man — God is in man so man is what counts. Each person is important; each person has dignity. It's quite explicit in the gospels. "Whatever you do for them, you do for me."'

Both passionate visionary and hard-headed realist, Rosemary's gift for outrage at injustice is tied to a profound conviction that 'We must continue to create the world; we *can* change things'.

Rosemary Taylor AM, 1988, on a brief visit home from Thailand where she is now working. 'I believe that we're all responsible for the little bit of world around us, and if we don't live up to that responsibility, that part of the world is lost.' Photograph by Milton Wordley

Index of Unsung Heroes & Heroines

Abbott, Gertrude	107
Abrahams, Esther	27
Ackman, Mother Giovanni	313
Albrecht, Friedrich Wilhelm	177
Alyandabu	192
Anderson, Maybanke Wolstenholme	93
Andrew, Brother	336
Armitage, Dora Robertson	89
Auld, Jeannie	351
Ballantyne, Esther Anne	52
Banning, Lex	337
Beadle, Jean	88
Beaton, Michel 'Mickey'	331
Beet, William Ashley	216
Benallack, Mary Ann	143
Bennett, Catherine Anne	124
Bent, Andrew	35
Bernard, Clive Roberts	236
Berry, Annie	110
Binstead, Joe	213
Bishop, Ruth Frances	345
Bouch, Alan Douglas	275
Bowers, Mary Magdelene	180
Boyd, Anne	334
Boye-Jones, Ruby	227
Brien, Colin	245
Briggs, Alice	316
Brown, John Borland	166
Bryant, Arthur	240
Bryce, Lucy	193
Buckley, Maurice (Gerald Sexton)	150
Burgess, Edward 'Teddy'	353
Byrne, Sister Vianney (Irene)	172
Cade, John	291
Carey, R. Graham	164
Carson, David	63
Casey Antarctic Expeditioners 1979	350
Chamberlain, William	31
Chisholm, Alice Maxwell	147
Cleary, Andrew	61
Cochrane, Harold	284
Cole, Margaret May 'Mabel'	115
Collins, Judith Louise	368
Colson, Edmund A. 'Ted'	211
Cook, Arnold	296
Cook, C.E.A. 'Mick'	182
Cosgrove, Cecilia	39
Collick, Edward M.	112
Cummins, Christopher	324
Cuni, Luke	258
Dadds, Charles Robert	163
De Bono, Betty	363
Degotardi, John	122
Deuffel, Carl	58
Devlin, Arthur Albert	99
Ding, H. E. 'Harry'	197
Dorling, Irene	195
Dos Santos, Alfredo Jose	254
Downes, Turo	174
Downton, George	194
Dowsett, Jesse	73
Fairey, Charles Frederick Bonfield	67
Farquhar, Donald W.	327
Farrar, Phoebe	97
Faunce, Alured Tasker	42
Fenton, Clyde Cornwall	185
Ferguson, Olivia Charlotte Marquis	167
Fiaschi, Tommaso Enrico	71
Flanagan, Ellen	85
Flavel, Doreen	85
Fong, Douglas	215
Fotheringhame, Pattie Lewis	82
Fraser, John	342
Glover, John Corbett	238
Golding, Rose	225
Gough, Evelyn	126
Grant, Douglas	148
Gribble, John Brown	69
Grice, Aileen	217
Grimaldi, Joseph	43
Gurruwiwi, James	343
Hall, Edward Smith	37
Hall, Tom	279
Halls, Archibald 'Snowy'	242
Hansen, Annie 'Topsy'	132
Harris, Edward	235
Harris, Rose	162
Heathcock, Ruth	190
Henshaw, David	356
Higgs, Frederick Getty	234
Hilder, Charles	153
Hill, Terry & Hills, Cliff	361
Hunt, Bruce	267

Ironside, Adelaide Eliza	59
Jacob, Eleanor	151
Jakamarra (Malcolm Maloney)	309
Jessop, Cecil P.	134
Johnson, Elizabeth	371
Johnston, Colin	329
Jörgensen, Simon Engelhardt	102
Kennedy, Sister Patrice	367
Kirk, Marie Elizabeth	86
Kneebone, Harry	113
Lakeland, William & Claudie	109
Lampungmeiua, Charlie One (also Tippakalippa)	244
Larson, Conrad	277
Latrobe, Herbert W.R.	146
Laycock, Thomas	30
Ledger, Charles	54
Lerew, John Margrave	230
Lewcowicz, Berek	220
Lewis, Amram	165
Lindsay, David	76
Lowe Kong Meng	57
Lyon, Marjorie Jean	247
Mahoney, Winsome	347
Maloney, Malcolm (Jakamarra)	309
Mathieson, Keith W.	265
Maynard, Charles Frederick	174
McBride, William	217
McCorkindale, Isabel	305
McCulloch, Robert	46
McKellar, Hazel	330
McLelland, Maryanne 'May'	309
McWilliam, Neville Gilbert	131
Merz, George Pinnock	144
Miller, Emma	96
Mills, Marianne 'Sister Pav'	303
Mills, Roy	267
Mt Macedon Volunteer Fire Brigade	362
Morris, William	135
Murphy, John Joseph	270
North, Muriel Constance	202
Oats, Margaret	381
O'Brien, Agnes Hyland	105
Oldham, Peter	41
Palmos, Angelo & Irene	169
Parry, John	66
Peachey, Edward	263
Pemulwuy	26
Phillips, Ronald A.	323
Price, Owen	274
Pym, Richard Elsworthy	44
Quin, Bernard Hazelden	265

Rakuwurlma, Tim	379
Reg	278
Resciniti, Luigi	302
Rogers, Elizabeth Charlesworth	292
Rumbelow, Malen	360
Rymill, John Riddoch	206
Schardt, Susannah K.	118
Shepherd, Arthur	125
Silver, Marjorie Dobson	209
Slattery, Lily Jubilee	373
Smallhorn, Frank	257
Smith, Henry John	155
Smith, James	121
Smith, James Edward	328
Smith, William Tipple	50
Solomon, Emanuel	34
Stapleton, Marjorie	306
Statton, Percy C.	201
Stevenson, Clare	354
Stewart, Eric James	318
Stubbs, Sheila	320
Stuchbery, Lloyd	298
Siegellak, Leopold	299
Taylor, Doris	312
Taylor, Ronald	255
Taylor, Rosemary	384
Teague, Frederick	200
Thomas, Mert & Nell	375
Thomson, Leslie James	136
Tippakalippa, Charlie One	244
Tongerie, George & Maude	359
Traill, Beattie	65
Treseder, Peter	370
Trestrail, Claire	140
Tscharke, Ned & Tabitha	289
Tweddell, Joyce	251
Vernon, Geoffrey Hampden	261
Vianney, Sister (Irene Byrne)	172
Wade, Mary	29
Ward, Lucy Ann	130
Warton, Joseph	33
Watling, Pearlie	286
Whitmore, Thomas	111
Wienholt, Arnold	119
Wilding, Joyce	311
Wilkinson, Amy Sanderson	160
Willis, Richard	365
Wollaston, Tullie Cornthwaite	100
Woodwell, Frank R.	325
Wu, Terry	348
Young, Albert 'Totty'	332
Zinnbauer, Albert Freund	288

Index

(c) = caption

Aberdare mine 166
Aboriginal Advancement
    Association 327
Aboriginal & Islander Affairs
    Dept. 374
Aboriginal Community Councils 331
Aboriginal Co-operative Society 330
Aboriginal Development
    Commission 360
Aboriginal Progressive
    Association 176
Aboriginal Protection Board 176, 309
Aboriginal Task Force, SA 360
Aborigines
    artists 179
    attacks by 26, 45, 64, 96, 98, 109, 116
    biographies of:
        men 26, 148, 174, 244, 309, 343, 359, 379
        women 132, 192, 316, 330, 359, 373
        children 343, 374; *see also* Apprenticeship Scheme
    coastwatchers 244
    culture 330, 380
    explorers 211
    health 178, 183, 190, 210, 317, 327, 330, 351, 360
    housing 311, 327, 330
    industries 179
    labour 70, 176, 185
    missions 69, 177, 271, 319
    murder of 46, 150
    pastors 180
    reserves 175, 373
    rights 150, 174, 192, 305, 312, 316, 330, 359, 373, 379
    servicemen 148
    trackers 62, 344(c)
    warriors 26
    welfare 69, 113, 180, 311, 327, 331, 359, 373
Abyssinia 72, 120
Acclimatisation Society of Victoria 55
Ackman, Amy Vera 313
Addis Adaba 121
Adelaide 34, 77, 102, 111, 164, 184, 191, 215, 242
Adelaide River 242
Admiral Berkeley 31
Adult Literacy Programme 215
adventurers 54, 102, 119, 136, 206, 318; *see also* explorers
aerial photography 164
Aines, Peter 211
Air Ambulance 257
air crashes 144, 213, 257, 383

air mail 164
aircraft, early 144, 164
aircraftmen 277; *see also* pilots
Airds 30
Airfield Construction Squadron 275
airmen *see* pilots
Alamein 263
Alawar tribe 190
Albanian migrants 358
Albany 111
Alexishafen 238
Algiers bombardment 32
Alice Springs 77, 118, 177, 179, 180, 183, 213
Allied Pacific Communication
    System 227
Allunga Artist's Group 354
alpacas 54
ambulancemen 146, 257, 270, 328
American Civil War 90
Anderson, *Professor* Francis 95
Anderson family 82(c)
Andes Mountains 54
Andromeche, HMS 32
Anglican clergy 37, 70, 112, 325
Angola 120
Anna Salen 304
Annandale 28
Antarctica 136, 207, 350
anthrax 99
Antwerp 140
Anzac Buffet 115
Anzac Day 153, 355
Appleton, Richard 338
Apprenticeship Scheme 176, 310, 373
Arabs 145
Aranbanoo 26
Aranda language 179(c), 180(c)
Aranyaprathet camp 349
Archibald, J.F. 83
Areyonga mission 319
Argentine 55
Argo 31
Armenian rebels 155
Armidale High School 330
Armitage, Charles 90
Arnhem Land 76, 191, 257, 343
Arthur, *Lieutenant-Governor*
    George 36
artists 59, 178, 179, 353
arts, the 59, 71, 82, 122, 337, 353
Assyrian rebels 155
athletes *see* sportsmen
Atomic Energy Commission 318
Aurora 136
Auschwitz 224, 300
Australasian Home Reading Union 94
Australia HMAS 323
Australian Army Medical Corps
    Reserve 72

Australian Comforts Fund 147
Australian Flying Corps 144
Australian General Hospital 251
Australian Guild of Business and
    Professional Blind 297
Australian Inland Mission, 185, 189, 190, 200; *see also* Flying Doctor, Royal Flying Doctor Service
Australian-Japan Student Exchange
    Programme 328
Australian Labor Party *see* Labor Party
Australian League 61
Australian Women's Service Corps 151
Australian Nursing Corps 143
Australian Workers Association 114
Austrian migrants 122, 288
aviators *see* pilots

Baccante, HMS 69
Baghdad 144, 155
Baker, Annie 64
Baku 157
Balmain 61, 93, 153, 160, 194
Balranald 322(c)
Ban Ban Springs 98
Bandjin tribe 149
Bangkinang camp 249
Banka Island 251
Banks, Mary 172
Banno, *Colonel* 269
Baptist, *Sister* Casimir 315
Barambah 154
Barkly Tablelands 77
barrister, blind 131
Basra 145
Bass Strait 66
Batchelor 257
Bathurst 38, 40, 50, 173, 315
Bathurst, *Earl* 32
Bathurst Island 242, 244
Battarbee, Rex 178(c)
Baudin, Nicholas 360
Bay of Biscay 104
Bazeley, *Major* P.L. 284
Bean, Willoughby 42
Beaudesert 216
Bedford, Mary Josephine 315
Bedzyn, Poland 222
Bega 326
Bellbird mine 165, 166
Bellosgurado, Italy 302
Benalla 54, 73, 309
Benallack, Mary 140
Bennelong 2
Bergman, George 28
Berlin Air Lift 304
Bicentennial Authority 354
Bidjigal sub-group 26
Bijah 155, 157
Biltara tribe 133

biochemists, women 286
Bird, Nancy 210
Birdsville 111, 112, 160(c), 197, 200, 211
Biripi Aboriginal Co-operative 317
Birmingham, Claire 142
Bischoff, Olive 130
Bischoff, *Police Commissioner* 312
Blackwood, *Captain* 45
Blanch, John 44
Bligh, *Governor* William 28, 31
Blindberry cow case 42
blindness 118, 131, 205, 215, 296, 327
Blood Transfusion Service 193
Blood's Creek station 212
Blucher, Wally 200
Blue Mountains 40, 50
Blue Ridge, USS 388
Boch, Thomas, artist 41(c)
Boer War 72, 113, 119, 121
Bolivia 55
Bolshevik Revolution 155
Bonner, *Senator* Neville & Heather 312
Booth, George 257
Booth, Lyall 85
Boothville Home 372
Borneo 45
Borodomaran station 53
Borroloola 191, 381
botanists 64(c), 101
Bougainville 319
Bourke 62, 209
Bourke, *Governor* Richard 42
Bowen 46
Boyden, Rex 214(c)
Boye, Skov 227
Braille 131, 205, 297; *see also* blindness
Bramble, HMS 45
Brewarrina 209, 310, 316
Bridge, Betty 297
Bridge, Joe & Deborah 115
Bringelley 31, 38
Brisbane 45, 59, 96, 273, 311, 315
Brisbane General Hospital 184, 253
Brisbane Water 42
British Graham Land Expedition 207
British Women's Temperance Association 86
Brock's Creek 98, 188
Broken Hill mines 217
Bromham, Ada 306
Bronk, *Corporal* Phillip 222(c), 257
Brooker, Jonathan 30
Brookes, *Squadron Leader* Bill 232
Broome 189
Brown, *Flight Officer* K. 252
Buchanan, Nat 116
Bullencourt 149
Bulletin 82, 86
bullock teams 59, 111; *see also* drovers
Bullwinkel, Vivian 251
Bulmer, Mary Ann Elizabeth 69
Bunbury 107
Bundanooon 217
Bunster, *Captain* 32
Burgess, Pat 342
Burke, *Lieutenant* 241
Burke, *Sergeant* Maurie 344(c)
Burma railway 266, 267
Burn, *Lieutenant* W.W.A. 145
Burns, Helene 179(c)

Burns Philp 153, 154
Burrows, Madge 219
Burrows *Surveyor* Charles A. 65
Bush, *Reverend* Roger 219
Bush Rescue Service 370
bushfires 170, 172(c), 201, 309, 362; *see also* fires
bushrangers 36, 40, 43, 61, 73
bushwalking clubs 365,370
Byrne, Joe 75(c)
Byrne, John Kenrick 172
Byrne, *Sister* Vianney 315
Bywong 125

Cairns 57, 71, 235, 238
Cairo 147
Calcutta 334,336
Calderwood, William 96
Caldwell, Arthur 313
Calverly, Lil 219
Cambodian refugees 348
camel transport 50(c), 77, 79, 101, 179, 198, 212; *see also* transport, outback
Cameron, *Sergeant* C.B. 281
Cameron, *Corporal* A.G.P. 280
Canning, A.W. 117
Canowindra Children's Home 372
Cape Wickham 66
Cape York Peninsula 109, 318
Carers Association of NSW 356
Carey, Graham Melrose 165(c)
Carey, *Lieutenant* W.G. 281
Catholic priests 108, 235, 238, 336; *see also* missionaries, nuns
Catterthun wreck 94
Cavenagh, George 43
Central Australia 78, 150, 177, 186, 318, 351
Central Wesley Mission 378
cerebral palsy 337
Ceylon 90
Champion, Janet Maxwell 148
Chandler, Flight Sister 252
Changi 246, 267, 291
chaplains 113, 265
Chapman, *Major* Walter 280
Chardin, Teilhard de 389
Charlesworth, Harry 296
Charleville 112, 202, 203
Chartists 96
chemist, analytical 284
Cheshire, Leonard 334
Chifley, Ben 313
child care 217, 265, 292, 348, 368, 373, 384; *see also* children's homes, foster care, orphanages, youth workers
children
 convicts 29
 courts 88
 homes 267, 292, 372, 378; *see also* foster care, orphanages
 magazines 85
 migrants 58
 stories about 58, 115, 125, 343
 walkabout 360
Chile 55
Chinatown, Sydney 366
Chinese migrants 57, 366
Chisholm, *Dame* Alice 140(c)

Churchill, *Sir* Winston 119, 121
Cinchona Calisya Ledgerianna 56
circus 105
Citizen's Military Force 279
Clark, Joan 355
Clark, Manning 38
Clark, Reg 326
Claudie River 110
Clements, Brian 351
Clermont 162
clinical researchers 284, 291, 345
Cloncurry 116, 185, 189
Clutha station 64
coastwatchers 227, 244, 270
coal miners 165, 166; *see also* miners
Coates, *Sir* Albert 248
Cochrane, *Admiral* 45
Cockburn, Beverly 323
Cocking, Mary & Tom 107
Coen 109
Colac 143, 144
Colbee 26
Cole, Mrs Ailsa 116
Cole, Laurie 350
Cole, Tom 117
Collingwood 381
Collins, David 27
commandos 255, 279
Commonwealth Labor Conference 97
Commonwealth Serum Laboratory 284
community workers 71, 88, 107, 118, 168, 194, 217, 292, 299, 311, 312, 330, 331, 334, 354, 356, 358, 359, 365, 367, 368, 371, 373, 378, 381, 384; *see also* child care, youth workers
confinements 181; *see also* maternity homes, midwives
Congregational ministers 68, 87
conscription 97, 115, 148
conscription of women 153
Connell, Mary 31
conservationists 172, 370
convicts 27, 29, 33, 34, 35, 39, 41, 42, 43
Cook, 'Mick' 186, 188
Cooke, *Captain* Walter White Wingrove 92
Cooktown 65, 109
Coolgardie 79, 111, 112, 114, 212
Cooma 325
Cooper, *Dr* Lilian 315
Cooper's Creek 112, 116, 198
Cootamundra 173, 238
copper mines 114
Cornish migrants 69, 113
Correspondence Schools 135
Cosh, Carl 111
cotton industry 79
Country Women's Association 168
Cracknell, Ruth 125
Cracow 222
Craft, *Corporal* C.M. 281
Crockford, Mary 218
crocodiles 229, 258, 318
Crombie, Ken 280
Crowe, *Dr* Elsie 247
Culton, Esther 109
Cumberland disease 99
Cunnamulla Native Welfare Association 330

Curnock, Lou 242
Curtin, *Prime Minister* John 89
Curtis, Ann 72
Czech patriots 225, 278
Czechoslovakia 224, 300

D'Albertis 44
Daley, Annie 133
Daniels, Dawson 191
Dante Alighieri Society 73
Dardanelles Campaign 146, 148
Dar es Salaam 120
Darling, *Governor* Ralph 37, 38
Darling Downs 119
Darlinghurst 63, 108; see also Kings Cross
Darlington Point 70
Darwin 77, 98, 183, 186, 191, 192, 257, 275, 296
Darwin, bombing of 240, 242
Davidson, *Commander* D.M.N. 280
Dayes, Edward, artist 26(c)
Daykin, Jane 111
deaf, interpreter for 367
Deepwater station 99
defamation 38, 43; see also libel
Defoe, Daniel 29
Dehra Dun 334
Delta Downs station 374
Deniehy, Dan 61
Depression, 1930s 162, 168, 170, 181, 194, 196, 202, 378
Devlin, James 99
De Wet, *General* 121
Diamantina River 111, 198
Dillon, Tom 62
Ding, Harry 160(c)
discoveries 99, 284, 291, 345; see also explorers, inventors
Divine Work Mission 238
doctors
  army 72, 185, 247, 261, 264, 267
  men 71, 144, 182, 185, 216, 291, 324
  women 193, 247, 315, 345; see also nurses
Domain, Sydney 54, 86, 150
Donaldson, *Captain* Alex 154
Donelly, Thomas 46
Donnison, Henry 42
Down's Syndrome 353
drovers
  men 115, 134, 175, 202, 320, 330, 373, 380
  women 97, 110, 115, 132, 202, 230, 330 see also overlanders
Drummond, *Reverend* Stanley 209
Duiguid, Charles 179
Duisberg-Meiderich 377
Duncan, *Chief Petty Officer* Vic 267
Dunstan, Don 313
Dunsterville, *Major-General* 155
Durack family 117
Dutch internees 249, 252
Dwyer, Kate 97

Early Closing Association 96
Eastern Goldfields 89
Eaton, Len 317
economist 297

editors 36, 38, 82, 114, 127, 309; see also journalists, Press
education see teachers
Edwards, Muriel 91
Egan, Catherine 124(c)
Egypt 147
Eichmann, Adolf 225
Elcho Island mission 259
Elder Scientific Exploring Expedition 50(c), 78
Ellemor, *Reverend* 259
Ellison, *Lieutenant-Colonel* W.J. 277
Elsner, Gunther 304
Embley, J.T. 109
emeralds 101
Emirau Island 226
Encounter Bay 360
engineers 134, 275, 323, 369
entrepreneurs 41, 55, 63
Eora tribe 26
Epping Boys High School 330
Equal Franchise Association 97
Erigolia 167
Essendon Aero Club 187
Eton 119
Eucla 112
Evangelical Lutheran Church 288
Exhibition of Women's Industries, 1888 91
explorers 30, 44, 63, 76, 109, 211, 318; see also adventurers, prospectors, surveyors
explosions 44, 277, 366
Eyre Peninsula 215

Fairfax, *Lady* 91
Fall, *Able Seaman* W.G. 281
Family Court, Melbourne 368
Far West Children's Health Scheme 209
Farnham, Leanne 276
Fassifern 120, 121
Federated Miscellaneous Workers Union 364
Feldman, *Rabbi* 301
Feldt, *Lieutenant Commander* 228
feminists 82, 86, 93, 96, 126, 142, 151, 206, 305, 312, 317; see also women, social reformers
Fenton, *Dr* Clyde 98
Ferry, Anne 339
Fiji 163
Fink, Averil 356
Finke River 77
fires 366; see also bushfires
First Fleet 26, 28, 59, 372
Fisher, Andrew 120
Fitzpatric, Irene 169
Fitzroy, *Sir* Charles A. 51, 52, 55, 56
Fitzroy Iron Works 51
Fletcher, *Corporal* R.B. 281
Flinders, Matthew 318, 360
Flinders country 64
Flinders Peninsula 259
Flinders Ranges 130, 200, 318
floods 111, 162, 198
Florence 71, 72, 73
Fly, HMS 45
Fly River 44
flyers see pilots
flying doctor 98

Flying Doctor 98, 186, 191, 198, 211; see also Australian Inland Mission, Royal Flying Doctor Service
flying priest 238
flying schools 144, 164
flying sister 209
flying surgeon 324
Flynn, *Rev* John 185, 186, 189, 190, 198
Foley, Magdalen 108
forests 160, 370
Forrest, Alexander 116
Forth, Tasmania 67
Foster, Horace 91
foster care 310, 369; see also child care
Fountain, Bill 214
Fowler's Pottery 288
Fox, Maude 82(c)
Frank, Karl Herman 278
Frankfurt 304(c)
Frederick 31
Fremantle 89, 106, 113
French's Forest Soldiers Settlement 153
Frisch, Jack 299

Galilee mission 70
Gallipoli 146, 147, 173
Galloway, Alex 339
Ganmain station 99
Garibaldi 61
Gascoyne River 70
Gasmata 234
gastroenteritis 346
Gaubin Hospital 290
Gawler 164
Geelong 53, 67, 68, 69, 197
General Hewitt 33
Gennaro, Aldo 354
geologists 50, 64(c), 188
George's River 28
Georgina River 133, 198
Geraldton 105, 332
German migrants 58, 118, 120, 177, 215, 303
German raiders 154, 265
German South-West Africa 120
Gevers, Minna 177
Gigealpa 111
Gilbert and Ellice Islands 154
Gipps, *Governor* George 42
Gladesville-Ryde Unemployment Relief Society 194
Glenelg River 47
Glenormiston 132
Glenrowan 74
Gliwice labour camp 224
gold discoveries 50, 79
gold escort 62
gold fields 57, 89, 106, 109, 110, 111, 112, 113, 114, 125, 212
Good Shepherd Order 382
Gooley, *Sgt.* D.P. 281
Goolwa 77
Goomburra station 119
Gordon, *Major* 120
Gosford District Hospital 362
Gough, Evelyn 87
Gough, Thomas Bunbury 127(c)
Goulburn 40, 70, 71, 148, 287
Goulding, Sheila 320

395

Governor brothers 124
Goyder's Lagoon 198
Grafton 100, 323
Graham, Roland 214
Graham Land 207
Grant, Robert 149
graziers *see* pastoralists
Great Central Exploring
 Expedition 77
Great Sandy Desert 117
Great Victorian Desert 50(c), 79, 318
Greek migrants 169
Greenland 207
Greenway, Francis 28, 33
Grey, *Earl*, 51, 52
Greyhurst, Frank 320
Gribble, *Rev* Ernest R. 71
Groote Eylandte 189, 257
Grylls, *Rev* 44
Guadalcanal 228
Guide Dog Association of WA 297
Guilleaux, Maurice 164
Gulf of Carpentaria 77, 97, 115, 257, 380
Gunn, Mrs Aeneas 98
Gunn, J.A. 100
Gurney, *Sir* Henry 306
Guy, *Constable* Joseph 47
Gympie 111

Haasts Bluff 179
Haines, Esther Anne 53
Halsey, *Admiral* William 228
Hamilton, Guy 172
Hamnett, K.G. 307
handicaps *see* physical handicaps
Hansen, Jack 134
Harbrow 125
Hardy, Erin 299
Hardy, *Lance Corporal* J.T. 281
Hardy's Bay 174
Hargraves, Edward Hammond 51, 52
Harrigan, Teague 30
Hart, Steve 75(c)
Hawker 130, 200
Hawkesbury 27, 30, 72
Hawthorne, Mrs 248
health, public 184; *see also* Aboriginal health, doctors, nurses
Heliopolis 147
Henty brothers 52
Herbert, Xavier 193
Herd, Eliza 44
Hermannsburg mission 177, 319
Higgs, *Sergeant* Frederick 233
Hill, Arthur 38
Hill, Peter 311
Hobart 31, 36, 41, 67, 296
Hodges, Percival 110
Hodgson Downs 98
Holman, Josef 278
Holman, W.A. 132
Holmes, Daniel 96
Holmes, *Major* Paul 359
Holocaust survivors 222, 299
Homesharers Club 356
Hopkins, Livingston 'Hop' 83
horse sales 202
horsewomen 99, 105, 110, 115, 163
hospices 172, 315
Housewives Association 169

Houston, USS 265
Howe, Michael 36
Hudson, *Sir* William 325
Huggins, W.J., artist 32(c)
Hughes, Susannah 99
Hungary 300
Hunter, James 44
Hunter, *Governor* John 28
Huon district 41
Huston, *Able Seaman* A.W. 281
Hutchinson, Ron 363

Ignatius, *Sister* 108
India 226, 334, 336
influenza epidemic 144, 173
Ingleton, *Major* R.M. 281
International Conference of Women, London, 1899 90(c), 92
International Women's Union 94
internees
 Austrian 288
 Dutch 249, 252
 German 365
inventors 102, 134, 298, 329
Ipswich 59
Irish convicts 30, 39
Irish migrants 61, 86, 110, 116, 169, 180, 192, 367
iron industry 51
Iron Range 109
Isaacs, Jacob 28
Italian army 302
Italian partisans 264
Italian migrants 71, 302
Italy 60, 263

Japanese Exchange Student 328
Jaquinot Bay 235
Java 56, 265, 280
Jelesie work camp 224
Jerilderie 69
Jerusalem 147
Jewish convicts 27, 34
Jewish migrants 171(c), 222, 299, 313
Joanna 33
Johore Bahru 247
Johnson, *Alderman* 326
Johnston, David 28
Johnston, *Lieutenant-Governor* George 28
Johnston, *Dr* Langloh 173
Johnston, Robert 28
Jondaryan 119
Jones, Ellen Mary 86
Jones, Frank 229
Jörgensen, Justus 105
Jose, Roger & Maggie 191
journalists 82, 113, 122, 126, 342; *see also* editors, Press
Julian, Mrs Esther 28
Jupiter 32

Kainantu 239
Kalgoorlie 110
Kalokarinos, *Dr* Archie 317
Kangaroo Island 215
Kantara 140(c), 147
Karkar 289
Karpenny, Louisa 190

Katherine 183, 186, 187
Keira station 64
Kelly, Dan 75(c)
Kelly, Ned 69, 74
Kenny, Catherine 252
Kew, Vic 173, 297, 336
Khungarakung tribe 192
Kimberleys 65, 116
Kincumber 174
kindergartens 88, 95, 348; *see also* child care, foster care
King, *Governor* Philip Gidley 27
King George VI Sound 208
King Island 66
Kings Cross 355, 371
Kiriwina 274
Kirk, Frank 86
Kirk, Marie 128(c), 305
Kirk, Mary 36
Kirk, William 64
Kirkpatrick, *Private* John 'Simpson' 146
Kokoda Trail 262
Konkoita 267
Kooma tribe 330
Korumburra 302
Kruse, Tom 200
Kuala Lumpur Flying Club 307
Kuku Kuku people 319
Kurdish tribesmen 156
Kwai River 269

Labor League 86
Labor Party 89, 96, 114, 313
Labor Women's Central Executive 89
Ladies' Typewriting Association 91
Lady Juliana 29
Lady Penrhyn 28
Lae 272
Lake Amadeus 319
Lake Eyre 65
Lake Macquarie 277, 375
Lake Nash station 133
Lakeland, Leo 110
Lambing Flat 61, 118
Lamington Plateau 214
Lang, *Dr* John Dunmore 60
Launceston, 31, 68
Launceston Girls' Home 282(c), 292
Lawson, Louisa 85, 93, 127
Laycock's Lake 31
Leander, HMS 32
Leichhardt, Ludwig 63, 77
Lennard, Haydon 252
Leo River 109
leprosy 183, 186, 190; *see also* tropical diseases
Lewin, John 33
Lewis, Barbara 335
Lewis Ponds Creek 50
Leyte 276
libel 36, 71; *see also* defamation
lifeboats 66, 102
lifesavers, surf 332; *see also* shipwrecks, swimmers
Light Horsemen 119, 147, 148, 151
Lightning Ridge 101
Lindsay, David 50(c)
linguists 289, 358
Lismore 100, 173, 315
Lister, J.H.A. 51

Lister Institute, London 193
livestock disease 99
llamas 54
Lloyd George, David 152
Lockwood, Douglas 243
Long, *Commander* R.B.M. 229
Longford, Winsome 347
Longreach 324, 374
Loritja tribe 178
Loughan, Edward 39
Love, Mary M 87
Lowe, Robert 62
Lurg Telephone Exchange 309
Lutheran missionaries 177, 288, 289
Luzon 275
Lyford, Jim 347
Lying-in Homes 130, 181; *see also* maternity homes, midwives
Lyndhurst 200
Lyon, *Lieutenant-Colonel* Ivan 280

Mabel Downs 117
Macarthur, *General* Douglas 275
Macarthur family 40, 55
Macassans 380
McCoy, *Professor* Frederick 64
McCredie, George 124
McDonald, Donald 215
McGinness family 192
McGrath, *Father* John 242
McIntosh, *Captain* 137
McIntyre, John 26
Mackay 64
MacKenzie, *Lieutenant-Colonel* John 43
McKie, Ronald 279
McKillop, *Sister* Mary 108
McNorman, Sylvia 179(c)
MacPherson Ranges 214
Macquarie, *Governor* Lachlan 28, 31, 32, 38
Mada Mada station 343
Madang 289, 319
Madigan, Cecil 211
magistrates, women 89
Maiana Island 154
mail services 164, 198, 200
Maitland 93, 175
Maitland, paddlesteamer 174
Maja Island 281
Makura 129
Mal Mal mission 235
Malaya 245(c), 247, 251, 306
Malbunka, Traugott 180
Malone, Betty 219
Manus Island 277, 319
Marathon station 64
Maree 101, 200
Margaret, HMAS 255
Marie Laure 33
Mari Mari 343
Marika, Roy 344(c)
Marranboy 190
Marsh, *Able seaman* F.W. 281
Marshall, Charles 40
Marshall, George 166
Marseilles 372
Mary Kathleen 318
Mataranka 190
maternity homes 108, 130; *see also* maternity homes, midwives

Matheson, Rhonda 296
Mathoura 135
Matui 261
Matunga, SS 153
Mayer, Mrs Erna 389
Mead, Margaret 319
Mayer, Mrs Erna 389
Mead, Margaret 319
Meals on Wheels 296, 313
Melba, Nellie 147
Melbourne 44, 57, 63, 89, 105, 144, 162, 165(c), 170, 222, 296
Melville, Henry 37
Melville Island 244
mental health 291
Menzies, R.G. 325
Merapas Island 279
Merbz 58
Merriwa 124
Merriwagga 320
Mesopotamia 144
Methodist ministers 69, 163, 175, 265
Midge 45
midwives 107, 124, 130, 181; *see also* confinements, maternity homes, nurses
migrants, non British *see* nationalities, e.g. Albanian migrants
Milingimbi 257
Miller, Andrew 97
Mills, Oswald 305
Millyn, Donald 125
Mindoro Island 275
mineralogists 50, 63, 77, 100; *see also* prospectors
miners 111, 114, 125, 165, 166, 217, 240; *see also* coal, gold, tin
Miners Federation 166
Mingende 240
Miranda station 373
missionaries 67, 69, 163, 177, 190, 235, 238, 242, 248, 258, 289, 318, 324, 336, 386
Missionaries of the Sacred Heart 235
Missionary Brothers of Charity 337
Missionary Sisters of Charity 336
Mitchell River mission 373
Mittagong 51
Miyazaki, Yoko 328
Monaro district 55, 56
Monitor, Sydney 37
Montsalvat 105
Moore, Henry 371
Moore, John 42
Moorhouse, *Surgeon* Matthew 47
Moreton Bay district 59, 120
Morgan, Glen 361
Morley, 31
Morrow, Marjorie 30
Moses, *Sir* Henry 119
Moses, Margaret 385
Mother Theresa 334, 336, 358
Mount Gambier Police Station 46
Mount Hagen 239
Mount Lofty Ranges 101
Mount Macedon 362
Mount Olivet Hospital 315
Mount Walker station 64
Mudgee 62, 72
Mueller, *Dr* Ferdinand 64
Muku Muku 344(c)
Multiple Sclerosis Society 323

Mungindi 160
Murchison, *Sir* Roderick 50
Murchison gold fields 107
Murray, Les 337
Murray, Robert Lathrop 36
Murrumbidgee River 70, 99
Mutabi 121

Nagy, Karl 239
Namatjira, Albert 179
Nasiriyeh 145
Nathalia 226
National Aboriginal Education Committee 331
National Council of Women 87, 92, 126, 128, 315, 372
National Fitness Council 293
National Guide Dog Training Centre 297
National Mapping Survey 318
Native Welfare Department, WA 332
Nauru 264
Nellarbor Plains station 112
Nellore 226
Neptuna 241
Netherby 66
New Britain 153, 235, 270, 272, 319
New Guinea 44, 231, 235, 236, 238, 247, 262, 271, 289, 316, 319, 372, 379
New Hebrides 227
New Ireland 319
New South Wales Corps 30
New South Wales Lancers 72
Newcastle 35, 261, 332, 375
newspapers *see* editors, journalists, Press
Ngalikan tribe 191
Nhulanunbuy Police Station 344(c)
Niagara 24]
Nicoll, *Wing Commander* Geoff 274
Nielsen, Johannes 102
Nimitz, *Fleet Admiral* Chester 230
Noble, *Dr* Frank 312
Noble, *Dr* Henry 324
Noojee 170
Noonan, Christopher 354
Normanton 97, 106, 115, 373
North Queensland 63, 71, 109, 132, 149, 184, 373
North Rankin Off-Shore Gas Platform 361
Northern Territory 76, 98, 177, 183, 186, 190, 241, 242, 343, 351
Norwegian migrants 102
Nundah 58, 277
nuns 108, 313, 367, 371, 386
nurses
  army 140, 143, 225, 251
  bush 190, 209, 351
  civilian 124, 172, 180, 190, 209, 225, 248, 303, 313, 334
  see also doctors, midwives

Oats, Daniel 382
Oberon 40
O'Brien, Mary Jane 108
O'Carrigan, *Sister* Catherine 173
O'Connor, Honorah 61
O'Grady, Frank 243

Olary 198, 200
Oliver, Derick 361
O'Neill, Frank Willestra 53
Oodnadatta 177, 213, 359
Ooroowillannie sandhills 198, 200
OPAL (One People of Australia League) 312
opal industry 101
Operation Jaywick 279
Operation Rimau 279
opium trade 58
optometrist 314
Orana Peace Memorial for Children 267
Ord River 116, 188
O'Reilly, Bernard 213
O'Rourke, Mary Magdalene 180
orphanages 267, 292, 296, 386; *see also* child care, children's homes
outback drivers 197, 200
outback women *see* women, outback
Outram gaol 279
Overland Telegraph Line 112, 116, 117, 213, 318
overlanders 64, 97, 110, 111, 115, 202; *see also* drovers, explorers, surveyors
Owen Stanley Ranges 239, 262

Pace, *Lance Corporal* H.J. 281
Padang 248
Paddington, NSW 123(c)
Paddykillan 112
Page, *Captain* R.C. 281
Pakington, *Sir* John 52
Palmer River 72, 109
Palmerston, Christie 109
Papua New Guinea *see* New Guinea
Papuan carriers 263
paralysis 298, 312, 337; *see also* physical handicaps
paraplegia 304, 330
Paris 60, 93, 141
Parkes, *Sir* Henry 39
Parry, *Bishop* 70
Pasteur, Louis 99
pastoralists 63 70, 99, 119, 185
patrol officers 271, 319
Pearce, *Wing Commander* Charles 232
Pearson, William Henry 63
Peary, USS 241
Pelly, *Major* Patrick 63
penicillin 284
Penola, SA 108, 207
Penola 207
Penrose 286
People's Advocate 61
Persia 155
Perth 63, 70, 89, 184, 297
Perth, HMAS 265
Peru 55
Perugia 60
Perunov, Sergei 304
Perunov-Pawlovsky, Marianne 303
Peters, Lee 332
Peterson, Jack 201
Petros, Agha 155, 157
Philippines 275
Phillip, *Governor* Arthur 26, 28
photo-engraving 82
photographers 84, 122, 164

physical handicaps 298, 312, 323, 329, 337, 353; *see also* blindness
Pie Creek 111
Pilbara 331
pilots
 civilian 164, 185, 206, 209, 306
 World War I 144
 World War II 185, 230, 236, 238, 257, 274
Pintubi tribe 178, 180
Pioneer Downs 109
Pitjantjatjara 178
plague 124, 184
Poeppel's Corner 212
poets 337
Point Cook Flying School 144, 146
Poland 222, 300
polar expeditions 136, 206, 350
police 46, 61, 62, 74, 190, 344
police magistrate 42
Police Rescue Squad 328
Polish migrants 177, 222
politicians 35, 115, 120, 313
Pom Pom Island 247
Pond, *Lieutenant Colonel* 270
Port Dalrymple 31
Port Essington 45
Port Jackson 26, 32
Port McLeay mission 190
Port Melbourne 165(c), 255
Port Moresby, 231, 235, 238, 262
Port Phillip 43, 63, 68
Port Said 147
Portland 298
Portuguese migrants 254
postmistress 309
POWs
 women 248, 251
 World War I 149, 154
 World War II 222, 225, 248, 252, 263, 267, 268, 270, 271, 278, 291, 302, 322, 376
Prague 278
Presbyterian ministers 60
Press, the 35, 37, 82, 113, 126; *see also* editors, journalists, printers
printers 35, 114, 122
Priscilla 41
prospectors 50, 100, 109, 126; *see also* explorers, mineralogists, miners
Proud, *Sir* John 214
Prussia, Mary Ann 57
psychiatrist 291

Qantas 188
quadraplegia 304, 330
Quakers 86, 296
Quarrier, *Surgeon* Daniel 32
Queanbeyan 43, 118, 180
Queensland Flying Surgeon Service 324
Queensland Imperial Bushmen 119, 121
quinine 56
Quinn, Noel 274
Quong Tart 58

Rabaul 153, 231, 234, 235, 238, 271, 274, 319
Raberaba, Konrad 180

radio operators 227, 234, 257
Radnik, SS 300
Rafa 147
Ragna, SS 102
Ramu area 319
Rangitane 226
Rapkins, William 293
Rathmines RAAF Station 277
Ravenet, Juan 27(c)
Rawson, *Sir* Harry 119
Rayney, Ruth 190
Raywood 101
Red Cross 72, 140, 142, 168, 169, 182, 269, 304, 349, 378
Red Cross Blood Bank, Melbourne 183
Red Rover 41
Redfern 63, 118
Redman, John 59
Reed, Richard, artist 28(c), 42(c)
Reedy 107
Reeve, Geoffrey 350
refugees
 Albanian 358
 Cambodian 348, 388
 German 304
 Jewish 222, 299
Reiby, Mary 93
Reid, *Sir* George 114, 119
religion *see* chaplains, missionaries, nuns, and names of denominations
Rembarunga tribe 76
rescue services 328, 370
rescuers, civilian 65, 66, 162, 174, 201, 213, 236, 238 240, 257, 328, 332, 350, 360, 361, 366; *see also* bushfires, self-sacrifice, and war stories
Reymond, *Lieutenant* B. 281
Reynolds, Catherine Anne 72
Richmond, Vic 88, 302
Ricketts, Beatrice 119
Rigg, Evelyn Anna Walker 127(c)
Riggs, *Sub-Lieutenant*, J.G.M. 281
Rivoli Bay 46
road contractors 160
Roberts, Agnes Emily 105
Roberts, John Thomas 105
Roberts, *Lord* 122
Roberts, Thomas 62
Robertson, John 55
Robinson, Tommy 200
Rockdale Ambulance Station 328
Rockhampton 64, 120, 163, 184, 366
Rocks area, Sydney 93
Rocky River 109
Rogers, *Matron* Elizabeth 284(c)
Rogers, Frank 293
Romang Island 280
Rome 60
Rockwood 52, 320
Roper River 189, 190
Rose, Charles 218
Ross, *Lieutenant* H.R. 280
Ross Sea 137
Rotary 328
Roy, Malcolm 364
Royal Adelaide Hospital 190
Royal Children's Hospital, Melbourne 347
Royal Commission on Shops, Factories and Workshops 96

Royal Flying Doctor Service 185, 324, 360; *see also* Australian Inland Mission, Flying Doctors
Royal Greek Navy 169
Royal Irish Constabulary 61, 62
Royal Park Psychiatric Hospital 292
Royal Perth Hospital 303
Royal Ryde Rehabiliation Hospital 119
Rowley, C.D. 185
Roxborough station 133
Rubuntja, Eli 180
Ruskin, John 60
Russian Army 155, 304
Russian migrants 111
Rutherford, Charles 62
Ryder-Cheshire Foundations 335

saddlers 111, 162
Sacred Heart Hospices 172
Sadleir, *Superintendent* 76
Saigon 360, 384
sailors *see* seamen
Sain Kala 155, 157
St James's Church, Sydney 37
St John's, Fremantle 113
St Joseph's, Auburn 173
St Joseph's Home for Children 367
St Leonard's Public School 131
St Margaret's Hospital for Women 108
St Vincent's Hospitals 72, 172, 173, 314, 315
salvage operations 41, 240
Salvation Army 248, 371, 372
Samurai 233, 263
Sans Souci 32
Sanderson, *Captain* Edward
Santa Cruz islands 227
Saphienbury 55
Sargent, *Lieutenant* A.L. 'Blondie' 281
Savage, Santiago 55
Savige, *Captain* Stan 155
Scanlan, *Colonel* 232
Schiller, Doreen 215
Schmoock, Marianne 304
Schwartz, Joseph 300
scientists 99, 284, 291, 345
Scone 169, 209
Scott, *Archdeacon* 37
Scott, Rose 93
seamen
  merchant 66, 102, 136, 153
  naval 44, 255, 323
  see also whalers
searches 343, 351
Second Fleet 29
Sefton, Robert 109
Selassie, *Emperor* Haile 120
Selby, D.M. 236
self sacrifices 217, 235, 242, 255, 264, 274, 277, 278, 280, 342, 358; *see also* bushfires, rescuers
Selfe, *Mrs* Bessie 82(c), 93
Sexton, Gerald 151
Shackleton, *Sir* Ernest 136
shale miners 166, 288
Sharecare 383
Shearer, William 62
shearer's cook 321

Shenton Park Quadraplegic Centre 304
shipwrecks 66, 94, 174
Shugg, Charles 85
Sicree, Sadie 171(c)
Silcock, Jabez 96
Silesia 278
Silver Plains station 109
Simpson Desert 77, 132, 211
Simpson's donkey 146
Singapore 245, 246, 247, 251, 267, 279
Singleton 335
Sir George Seymour 53
Sisters of Mercy 367, 386
Sisters of St Joseph 108
Skewes, *Sister* Edna 316
Slattery, Jubilee 373
Smallhorn, Frank 222(c)
smallpox vaccinations 319
Smith, John 62
Smith, John McGarvie 100
Smith, Thomas 51
Snowy Mountain Authority 325
social reformers *see* community workers, feminists, women — social reformers
Society of Jesus 336
Society of St Vincent de Paul 382
Soldier Settlers Scheme 167
soldiers 30, 42
  Boer War 119, 121
  World War I 146, 148, 150, 155, 375
  World War II 245, 263, 270, 274, 275, 278, 279, 302, 375
  Vietnam 342
  see also doctors, nurses, pilots, seamen
Solomon, Vaiben 34
Solomon Islands 227
Somme 378
Sonkurai 267
Sorell, *Lieutenant-Governor* William 36
South America 54
South Brisbane 311
Spanish Scientific Expedition 27(c)
Spastic Centre 338
Sphere 85, 88
Splashes weekly 85
Sportsmen 113, 164, 332, 343, 370
squatters *see* pastoralists
Starlight, Captain 62
Steele, *Sergeant* 76
Stenhouse, *First Officer* 137
Stenhouse, Nicol D. 61
Stephen, *Sir* Alfred 94
Stevens, Clare 163
Stewart, *Corporal* C.M. 281
Stirling, Dick 374
Stockman's Hall of Fame 374
stockmen 117, 134, 374 *see also* drovers, overlanders
Stone, Michael 351
Storm King 102
Strehlow, Carl & Ted 179
Stuchbury, Norah 307
Sturt's Stony Desert 198
Sudds, Joseph 39
suffragettes *see* women, social reformers
Sumatra 248, 252, 265
The Sun — a Journal for the Home... 127
Sunshine Home 354

Sunshine, Vic 364
surf lifesaver 332
surgeons 71, 324; *see also* doctors
Surry Hills 38, 107, 372
surveyors 76, 109, 207, 318; *see also* explorers, mineralogists, prospectors
Sutherland, James 64
Sutton, Maria Elizabeth 86
Suttor Creek 64
Suva 163
Sydney Gazette 42
Sydney Hospital 72, 73
Sydney-Jones, Enid Frances 120
Szatmari, Shari 300

Tamar River 65
Tanbaya 269
Tank Stream 30
Tanner, Les 83
Taree 206(c), 316
Tasmania 30, 35, 40, 65, 67, 155, 201
Taubman's Paint Factory 364
Taylor, Rosemary 342(c)
teachers 86, 93, 135, 151, 329, 347, 356, 367, 372
Teachers Association of NSW 94
Teague, Una & Violet 178
Tedbury 27
telegraphists 242, 309
Tench, *Captain* Watkin 27
Tennant Creek 188
Terezin Fortress 222
Terre des Hommes 386
Terry, Michael 117, 212
Thailand 267, 349, 388
theosophists 94
theatres 35, 354
Thirlmere 369
Thomas, *Bishop* 70
Thomas, Evan Henry 36
Thomas, Henry Lamert 375
Thompson, Herb 109
Thompson, Patrick 39
Thomson, *Miss* C.H. 127
Thomson, Edward Deas 51
Thursday Island 239
Tieryboo station 59
Tigris Valley 144
Timor 244, 254, 280
tin mines 65, 109, 192
Titanic 105
Titree Health Centre 362(c)
Tiwis 244
Tocumwal 53
Tom, James 51
Tongala 172
Toronto Sailing Club
Toolebus 322
Toowoomba 173, 202
Torres Strait 45
Torrigiani, *Marchesa* 73
Tracey, Cecilia 39
trade unionists 88, 96, 113, 165, 254, 363
Traeger, Alfred 198
Traill, *Miss* 91
Traill, W.H. 82
transport, outback 198. 200; *see also* camel transport
Travers-Ball, *Father* Ian 336
trees *see* conservationists, forests

Trial Bay Jail   365
tropical diseases   145, 183, 247, 249, 268, 277, 289
Trotter, Florence   252
tuberculosis   61, 177, 334
Tucci, Joe   302
Tuckanarra   107
Tumut   325, 327
Turkish troops   145, 146, 155, 156
Turner, *Mrs* Priscilla   74(c)
Turon river   50
Turrell, Arthur   219
Tweed district   100, 309
Tweedie, David Morton   101
typing school, Sydney   89

Ualah station   99
unemployment   194, 325, 359, 367
UN Status of Women Commission   305
Uniting Church   219
Uralla Hospital School   292
Urisino station   209

vaccination programmes   100, 319, 347
Valley of Death   267
Valparaiso   55
Van Diemen's Land Pocket Almanack   36
Vanderlin Island   380
Vanikoro   227
veterinary science   99
Victoria and Albert, Royal yacht   45
Victoria Cross   150, 201
Victoria River   188
Victorian Squatting Company   65
Victorian Women's Franchise League   87
Vietnam   342, 384
vintner   72
Voluntary Aid Detachments   142
Voluntary Workers Association   153
Vyner Brooke   251

Wadeley, photographer   75(c)
Walbiri tribe   150, 178, 310
Walcha   199
Walhouse, Ron   266
Walunguwra   180
war correspondents   115, 342
Warangesda mission   70
Warne, *Private* D.R.   281
Warren, *Warrant Officer* A.   281
Warrina   50(c)
Watkins, H. Gino   207
Watt, Agnes   132

Wau   236, 319
Webster, Rosemary   349
Wedd, Nell   375
Weemala   119
Weil, Simone   389
Weipa   318
Weir, John   111
welfare workers *see* community workers
Welsh migrants   119, 195
Wentworth, William Charles   60
Westray, James   214
whalers   31, 32, 41
Wharton family   330
wheelchairs   298, 330
White, *Captain* T.W.   146
White Cliffs   101
Wilcannia   199
Wilding, Frank   311
Willard, Frances   86, 305
Willersdorf, *Warrant Officer* J.   280
Williams, *Captain* J.P.   240
Wimereux   143
Windeyer family   93
windmills   134
Windsor, NSW   72
wine industry   72
Wingham   202, 205
Winmalee   348
Wins, *Rev* Jimmy   318
Witsend   369
Wolf, German raider   154
Wolstenholme, Edmund Kay   93
Woman's Equal Franchise Association   96
Woman's Voice   94
Womanhood Suffrage League of NSW   94
women
  Aboriginal   132, 192, 316, 330, 359, 373
  artists   59
  community workers   88, 107, 118, 172, 217, 292, 311, 312, 330, 331, 334, 354, 359, 367, 368, 371, 373, 378, 381, 384
  convicts   27, 29
  courageous deeds   65, 124, 163, 309
  early settlers   39, 52, 97
  entertainers   105
  outback   52, 97, 107, 109, 110, 115, 132, 160, 167, 202, 215, 286, 320, 330, 373
  professional   82, 85, 88, 89, 93, 126, 193, 247, 345, 354; *see also* doctors, editors, journalists, nurses, teachers
  religious   107, 172, 289, 313, 367, 371, 386

social reformers   85, 86, 88, 89, 93, 96, 126, 151, 305; *see also* feminists
trade unionists   97, 363
urban survivors   160, 195, 347, 375
war stories   140, 143, 147, 151, 225, 227, 247, 251, 306, 354, 384
Women in Medical Science (WIMS)   347
Women Workers Political Organisation   97
Women's Army Auxiliary Corps   152
Women's Auxiliary Australian Air Force   354
Women's Christian Temperance Union   86, 305
Women's Federal League of NSW   95
Women's Literacy Society   94
Women's Royal Australian Navy   229
Women's Service Corps   151
Wood's Lake   31
Woodman   31
Woods, *Father* Julian Tenison   108
Woolnough, *Dr*   188
Workers Educational Association   95
World Council of Churches   387
World Health Organisation   345
Wright, Phoebe   97
Wyndham   117

Xavier College, Kew   336

Yamashita, *General*,   245
Yanguwa tribe   379
Yarloop   107
Yarra, HMAS   255
Yarrabah mission   71
Yarraville   358
Yeshiva Synagogue   301
Yilki   361
Yirrkala   343
Yorkey's Corner   50, 51
Young, Anne   334
Young, *Sir* John   56
Young Australia   85
Youth Hostels Association of NSW   365
youth workers   356, 365, 372; *see also* child care, community workers
Ypres   143
Yugoslavia   358
Yunta   198, 200

Zinnbauer, *Dr* Helga   289